International African Library 31
General Editors: J. D. Y. Peel, Colin Murray and Suzette Heald

MEDICINE MURDER IN COLONIAL LESOTHO: THE ANATOMY OF A MORAL CRISIS

The *International African Library* is a major monograph series from the International African Institute and complements its quarterly periodical *Africa*, the premier journal in the field of African studies. Theoretically informed ethnographies, studies of social relations 'on the ground' which are sensitive to local cultural forms, have long been central to the Institute's publications programme. The *IAL* maintains this strength but extends it into new areas of contemporary concern, both practical and intellectual. It includes works focused on problems of development, especially on the linkages between the local and national levels of society; studies along the interface between the social and environmental sciences; and historical studies, especially those of a social, cultural or interdisciplinary character.

International African Library

General Editors

J. D. Y. Peel, Colin Murray *and* Suzette Heald

MEDICINE MURDER IN COLONIAL LESOTHO

THE ANATOMY OF A MORAL CRISIS

COLIN MURRAY and PETER SANDERS

EDINBURGH UNIVERSITY PRESS
for the International African Institute, London

© Colin Murray and Peter Sanders, 2005

Edinburgh University Press Ltd
22 George Square, Edinburgh

Typeset in Plantin
by Koinonia, Bury, and
printed and bound in Great Britain
by Antony Rowe Ltd, Chippenham, Wilts

A CIP record for this book is available
from the British Library

ISBN 0 7486 2284 5 (hardback)

The right of Colin Murray and Peter Sanders
to be identified as authors of this work has been
asserted in accordance with the Copyright,
Designs and Patents Act 1988.

For other publications of the International
African Institute, please visit their web site at
www.iaionthe.net

CONTENTS

LIST OF MAPS

LIST OF TABLES, FIGURES AND GRAPHS

NOTE ON PHOTOGRAPHS

The photographs which appear between pages 208 and 209 are attributed in section C of the Sources.

PREFACE

In Lesotho the subject of medicine murder is a difficult and controversial one, for reasons that unfold in this book. We had become interested in it independently, each of us having long experience in the country: Murray as an anthropologist and Sanders as a colonial officer and historian. We have been helped along the way by many different people in Lesotho, in Britain and elsewhere. Many of our debts, especially to the people we interviewed, are recorded in the list of Sources at the end. We would like to acknowledge the generosity with which they shared their experiences and opinions with us. We would also like to thank a number of individuals, likewise identified in the Sources, who assisted with the provision of photographs or other material. Other debts we wish to record here directly.

In 1996 we were prompted to join forces by Miriam Basner, whose husband H. M. Basner, as defence attorney for Chief Gabashane Masupha in his trial in 1948, had been convinced of his innocence, and who had herself contributed to the flourishing genre of fiction about medicine murder. We owe her much – for putting her 'young men' in touch with one another, and for her unfailing support and enthusiasm. She read and commented on an early draft of the manuscript, and it is a great sorrow to us that she died in 2003 and did not live to see this book in print.

We are also deeply indebted to David Ambrose of the National University of Lesotho. To many different questions from us, both esoteric and mundane, he responded most generously with his time and with his unrivalled knowledge of written and other sources on almost every aspect of life in Lesotho in the past and the present. He read through the first major draft of the manuscript with painstaking care and attention and made many valuable suggestions. Robert Edgar, whose deep interest in Lesotho crossed our own research paths on several occasions, especially in relation to the Lekhotla la Bafo, responded quickly to various requests. Stephen Gill, responsible for the Morija Museum and Archives, helped us with particular sources there, and also offered comments on and raised questions about Case Study 1 and Case Study 4.

We would like especially to thank Khalaki Sello, in Maseru, for his vital assistance to both of us on our fieldwork journeys in 1999 to different parts of the country in search of the testimony of key individuals who were caught up in medicine murder in one way or another: as relatives of victims or of perpetrators, as alleged murderers, as independent witnesses, or as observers with particular knowledge of local conflicts and circumstances. His diplomatic skills and his sensitivities of translation from Sesotho were invaluable to us in negotiating and carrying through a wide range of individual interviews. He introduced us to Nkherepe Molefe, a retired policeman who had his finger on the pulse of medicine murder investigations throughout the late colonial period, and indirectly to a number of other interviewees. We also thank Patrick Mohlalefi Bereng, Monaheng Maichu and Peete Mofoka for acting as occasional assistants and interpreters. For simplicity, in our accounts of individual interviews, we have often written 'we' in the main text. In practice, most interviews were conducted separately by Murray (CM) with Khalaki Sello (KS) or by Sanders (PS) with KS. This is made clear in section F of the Sources.

We are grateful to staff at many different institutions for their help in finding primary archival material: especially the Public Record Office (PRO, now the National Archives), London; the Records and Historical Department of the Foreign and Commonwealth Office at Hanslope Park, outside Milton Keynes; and Rhodes House, Oxford. Many other repositories of valuable information of one kind or another, in Lesotho, South Africa and Britain, are acknowledged in the Sources. It is appalling that the Lesotho National Archives, the most important single source of relevant primary material for our work, are now inaccessible to researchers, as described in the Introduction. Largely for this reason, we have included a substantial Appendix in this book that contains summary information on all the suspected cases of medicine murder in the colonial period that we were able to trace.

The Nuffield Foundation generously provided a grant which enabled us both to carry out fieldwork on oral sources in the course of 1999. We are very grateful for this financial support.

We have had the opportunity to make seminar presentations at the universities of Cambridge (1996 and 2001), Oxford (2001), London (2001), KwaZulu-Natal (2004) and Pretoria (2004); and at the biennial conference of the African Studies Association of the UK in September 1998. We would like to thank the participants for helpful comments and suggestions.

We thank Avril McIntyre for drawing our attention to press coverage of several '*muti* murders' in Johannesburg, and Tim Couzens for the same and for his great encouragement. Graham Taylor kindly lent us a rare copy of the souvenir booklet of the Royal Visit to Basutoland in March 1947. Michael Pollard, Derek Trillo and Nick Scarle at the University of Manchester were generous with their time and attention to fine detail in the preparation of photographs, maps, graphs and the genealogy. Megan Murray-Pepper helped her father grapple with the mysteries of Excel in preparing the first drafts of the three graphs, and through their late adolescence she and her sister Hannah accepted with good humour his preoccupation with the project.

Anita Jackson assisted with some of the first-hand work at the PRO; she read many drafts, took part in countless discussions with PS and offered comments and suggestions throughout the research. For this, and for her support in so many other ways, PS in particular is deeply indebted to her. CM would like to thank Jane Osgood for her love and support.

Finally, we would like to thank Elizabeth Dunstan, indefatigable chair of the Publications Committee of the International African Institute, for the grace and efficiency with which she 'opened the way' to publication. Three outside readers – Richard Rathbone, Jeff Guy and William Beinart – gave us positive and valuable comments on the manuscript.

Colin Murray
Peter Sanders
March 2004

NOTE ON NAMES, ORTHOGRAPHY AND PRONUNCIATION

Africans who live in Lesotho generally refer to themselves as Basotho. The singular is Mosotho. The language, culture and way of life are referred to as Sesotho. In the colonial period, the usages Basuto or Basutos were common, but are used here only in direct quotation.

The Sesotho language has two orthographies, one used in Lesotho, the other in South Africa. We use the Lesotho orthography in this book. It has several peculiarities. (1) A double consonant, as in *ho lla* (to cry), is invariably a prolongation of the single consonant. The double *Mm* in the prefix of a woman's name is written 'Ma-, as in 'Mantšebo. (2) When placed before another vowel *e* is often pronounced as *y*. (3) An *l* before an *i* or a *u* is pronounced as *d*. So *liretlo* is pronounced *diretlo* and Lerotholi is pronounced Lerothodi. (4) When placed before another vowel *o* is often pronounced as *w*. So Moshoeshoe is pronounced Moshweshwe. (5) *ph* represents an aspirated *p*; *th* an aspirated *t*; and š an aspirated *s*.

ABBREVIATIONS

BAC	Basutoland African Congress
BCP	Basutoland Congress Party
BNC	Basutoland National Council
BNP	Basutoland National Party
BPA	Basutoland Progressive Association
CAR	*Colonial Annual Report*
CRO	Commonwealth Relations Office
CP	Commissioner of Police
DC	District Commissioner
FCO	Foreign and Commonwealth Office, Hanslope Park (Records and Historical Department)
GS	Government Secretary
HC	[with no reference number] High Commissioner
HC	[with reference number] High Court
IHL	Imprisonment with Hard Labour
JC	Judicial Commissioner
JME	*Journal des Missions Evangéliques*
LNA	Lesotho National Archives
NUL	National University of Lesotho
PC	Paramount Chief
PE	Preparatory Examination
PEMS	Paris Evangelical Missionary Society
PRO	Public Record Office, Kew [now National Archives]
RC	Resident Commissioner
RCCR	Resident Commissioner's Court Records
RHL	Rhodes House Library, Oxford

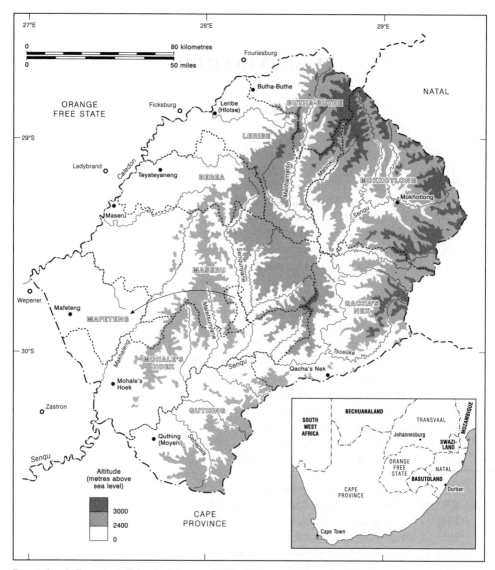

Basutoland (Lesotho): District Map, c. 1950s

INTRODUCTION

A DEFINING MOMENT

Two chiefs were hanged at dawn on Wednesday, 3 August 1949, in the gaol in Maseru, the capital of the British colony of Basutoland. One was Bereng Griffith Lerotholi, Principal Chief of the Phamong ward in the Mohale's Hoek District in the south of the country. Ten years before, he had expected to succeed his father, Griffith Lerotholi, as the Paramount Chief of the Basotho, but the Sons of Moshoeshoe, the ruling family, had chosen his half-brother Seeiso instead. Then, when Seeiso had died a year later, he had expected to become the regent for Seeiso's infant son, but again he was thwarted. The Sons of Moshoeshoe suspected that if he was given power he would cut out Seeiso's young son and arrange for the succession to pass to his own children. So instead, though she was not the boy's mother, they chose 'Mantšebo, Seeiso's senior widow. But Bereng was still generally regarded as the second most important chief in the country, and whereas he had accepted Seeiso's paramountcy he could never come to terms with 'Mantšebo's regency.

The other chief hanged was Gabashane Masupha, Principal Chief of 'Mamathe's ward in the Berea District to the north-east of Maseru. Gabashane was often described as the fourth most senior chief. He had supported both Seeiso and 'Mantšebo against Bereng, and for a few years, after Seeiso's death, he had been one of 'Mantšebo's closest advisers. By the mid-1940s, however, he had fallen out with her and switched his allegiance to Bereng. It was a move that was to cost him his life.

The crime for which Bereng and Gabashane were hanged was murder, but it was not murder of the ordinary kind. At first it was known as ritual murder; later, more appropriately, as medicine or *liretlo* murder. Parts of the victim's body, *liretlo*, were cut away, usually while he or she was still alive, for the purpose of making medicines which, it was believed, would strengthen those who made use of them. In this case, according to the prosecution, the two chiefs had enlisted the help of at least a dozen of their subjects to kill a man called 'Meleke Ntai. If they had been acquitted they would have had to stand trial for an earlier murder, committed in 1946. The victim then was a man called Paramente, who was caught at night as he came out of his lover's hut. Over sixty people were involved.

The cases of Chiefs Bereng and Gabashane drew the attention of the world to Basutoland, not only because the murders were so gruesome, but because they involved two of the highest chiefs in the land and because they seemed to be part of a rising tide of murder that was threatening to engulf the whole country. There had been occasional reports of medicine murders since 1895, but until recently they had been too few to disturb the colonial authorities. From two in 1941, however, the number of reported murders had risen to twenty in 1948, the year in which Bereng and Gabashane allegedly carried out the second of their murders, and the numbers of instigators and accomplices involved amounted to several hundred.

A climate of acute anxiety prevailed. Ordinary villagers were fearful of going about their daily business, and would rarely venture out at night. Chiefs who on one day spoke 'for the nation' in the Basutoland National Council were arrested for medicine murder on the next. Many, such as the regent 'Mantšebo herself, claimed to be worried about being framed. Witnesses who gave evidence about medicine murders, whether independently or as accomplices, experienced acute conflicts of loyalty and conscience. They were obliged to tell the truth before the court. But they were subject to the shifting winds of pressure from many different quarters: from the police, anxious to obtain convictions; from instigators, often their own immediate political superiors to whom they owed a duty of loyalty and obedience and who might have threatened them in order to keep them quiet; and from their own communities, often riven into factions by specific events and by the routine jostling of competing local interests.

The authorities at all three levels of colonial government – Forsyth-Thompson, the Resident Commissioner in Basutoland; Sir Evelyn Baring, the High Commissioner in South Africa, who was also the Governor of the three High Commission Territories of Basutoland, Bechuanaland and Swaziland; and Philip Noel-Baker, the Secretary of State for Commonwealth Relations in London – were confronted by a profound dilemma and were exasperated by the contradictions of diagnosis and policy that arose. They were determined to stamp out the virulent contagion of medicine murder, and this required vigorous investigation and prosecution of the crime in order to secure and sustain convictions. But these murders were largely instigated by the chiefs. In the face of pressing demands from the South African government for the transfer of responsibility for the three High Commission Territories – demands that became even more pressing after the National Party came to power in 1948 – and in the face of an incipient nationalist movement headed by the Lekhotla la Bafo, the Council of Commoners, the colonial authorities were explicitly committed to bolstering the chieftainship in order to nurture the integrity of the Basotho nation, to sustain the operation of indirect rule and to buttress their own authority.

More than any other case, the prosecution, conviction and hanging of

Bereng and Gabashane provoked a widespread belief amongst Basotho that the British were bent on destroying the chieftainship. In the first place, they were both very senior and respected chiefs. Few had imagined that the government would go so far as to hang them. Second, there were many allegations about the unlawful detention and ill-treatment of suspects in order to elicit confessions. Third, the first half of 1949, while the fate of Bereng and Gabashane hung in the balance, was characterised by particular confusion over the state of the law on accomplice evidence. The rejection of their appeal by the Privy Council in London was attributed by many Basotho to a plot on the part of the Basutoland administration. For all these reasons the concern felt by chiefs in Basutoland at the government's intense concentration on medicine murder turned to alarm and even terror. The lines of confrontation between chiefs and government were sharpened, and throughout the 1950s the alleged subversion of the chieftainship by the administration was pursued as a major theme in the articulation of nationalist politics.

OFFICIAL AND POPULAR REACTION

In 1949 G. I. Jones, a lecturer in anthropology at Cambridge University, was sent out to conduct a one-man enquiry into the causes of the apparent increase in medicine murders and to make recommendations for bringing them to an end. His report was published in 1951 and immediately became the authoritative text. He ascribed what he called the 'very startling increase' to four causes: the disputes arising from the unchecked use of the 'placing' system whereby a new chief was 'placed' over others; the conflict over the paramountcy between Seeiso and Bereng; the conflict over the regency between 'Mantšebo and Bereng, a 'battle of medicine horns', as he called it; and the series of reforms, beginning in 1938, which had introduced indirect rule into Basutoland and which, he believed, had led to widespread insecurity among the lesser chiefs in particular.[1]

By the time his report was published, however, it seemed that the worst was past. The main political and judicial reforms were now in place, the abuses of the placing system were now in check, and with the hangings of Bereng and Gabashane the battle of the medicine horns was over. 'The epidemic of *diretlo* killings appears to be coming to an end', Jones wrote, '... and the country can now settle down in peace ...'[2] Baring was even more emphatic: 'it is with sincere satisfaction', he wrote, 'that I can report the suppression of the outbreak and the comparative disappearance of murders of this nature'.[3] At first they seemed to be right. After the twenty reported cases in 1948 there were only five in 1949 and four in 1950. But then they rose again, reaching an average in the next decade, 1951–60, of just over ten each year – 101 cases in all. Again some of the most important chiefs were involved.

The British authorities struggled to find ways of putting an end to these murders. New laws were passed and old laws amended, more police posts were established, fresh methods of investigation were tried, conferences were convened and committees set up, propaganda campaigns conducted, days of national prayer observed. But all, it seemed, to no avail. Month after month the reports came in of mutilated bodies being found at the foot of precipitous cliffs or washed up on river-banks. Basutoland continued to attract extensive notoriety. When John Gunther, an American journalist, wrote his weighty and widely read work *Inside Africa*, he described these murders as the most repellent horror that he had found in the entire continent. Joy Packer, a South African writer, wrote in similar vein in her popular book *Apes and Ivory*, and several novelists followed suit, drawn by the macabre and the bizarre.[4]

Arguments about medicine murder intensified a long-running and broader debate about Sesotho culture and identity. For the churches, whatever their denomination, medicine murder was heathenism's mark of Cain. The tone had been set in 1896 by a missionary article in response to the first murder that came to the attention of the colonial authorities. This, it was said, was 'where paganism can finish up'.[5] The Roman Catholics in particular exacerbated the debate by claiming that medicine murders were closely connected with boys' initiation practices, since, or so they argued, the initiates were doctored with medicines compounded of human flesh and blood.

At first most Basotho were stunned and shocked by the murders and the apparent involvement of some of their most respected chiefs, and in the earliest debates in the Basutoland National Council the general reaction was one of shame and outrage. But over time a more defensive reaction set in. The belief gained ground that there was no such thing as medicine murder, or that, if there was, it was being committed by people of little importance and then exploited by the colonial authorities to undermine the power of the chiefs.

The response of the chiefs was not surprising, since they were the people most threatened by prosecution. But the Lekhotla la Bafo, the Council of Commoners, might have been expected to espouse the cause of the victims against the murderers. Instead it was driven more by its antagonism to colonial rule, and it spearheaded the argument that the prosecutions were a ploy by the British to destroy the natural leaders of the Basotho and so make it easier to transfer the country to South Africa. Lekhotla la Bafo's nationalist successors, the Basutoland African Congress (later the Basutoland Congress Party), followed much the same line of argument. Accusations of medicine murder came to be regarded and experienced as attacks on the Basotho people, and chiefs and commoners closed ranks. Cases were heard in crowded and excited courtrooms, judgements were listened to in rapt silence, and verdicts of not guilty were sometimes greeted with cheers and ululations. Those who were acquitted left the court in triumph and resumed their positions as respected members of the community. Accomplice witnesses were reviled as self-confessed murderers and traitors to their chiefs.

Yet by the late 1950s, although as many as forty-one cases were reported within three years, the sense of panic had largely subsided, and in the early 1960s, when the average fell to about five cases a year, no-one at senior government level was paying much attention to them. They were a matter only for the police and the judiciary. In 1962 there was a half-hearted debate on the subject in the Basutoland National Council, but chiefs, politicians and officials alike had more pressing issues to consider. The country was now belatedly caught up in the rapid political developments that were sweeping the British empire off the map of Africa.

Medicine murders continued after Basutoland became the independent state of Lesotho in 1966. In 1968 there were twenty reported cases, the highest number in any single year since the 'defining moment' of crisis twenty years earlier. After 1969, when there were nine more cases, the government of Lesotho did not keep any separate figures for medicine murders, subsuming and so losing them statistically under murders generally. Hardly any cases reached the courts. They continued to be committed, however, perhaps in substantial numbers, and mainly, it seems, not by the chiefs, but by traders anxious to improve their businesses. With about 500 ordinary murders a year in a population of approximately two million people in the mid-1990s, Lesotho had one of the highest murder rates in the world. The police were overwhelmed.

KEY QUESTIONS

In this book we look for answers to a series of key questions about medicine murder in late colonial Lesotho. We seek to understand the virulence of the phenomenon, and the intensity of the moral crisis induced by it, by exploring the many different and often conflicting perspectives that have been brought to bear upon it, at different times, both from 'inside' and 'outside' Basotho society itself.

The first question is whether medicine murder took place at all. Was it, like witchcraft in early modern England – a comparison sometimes made by Congress politicians and others – a perception without any grounding in reality? Did the 'heart of darkness' lie not in the beliefs and actions of Basotho, but in the fevered recesses of the colonial imagination? Worse still, were false charges of medicine murder, as many Basotho still believe, an elaborate official conspiracy against the chiefs? We have to raise these questions explicitly, not only because the 'counter-narrative' that was driven by Congress politicians and others became so widely accepted in Basutoland in the late 1950s, but because enough casual scepticism has been expressed, mainly by foreign academics,[6] at least to sustain some doubt on the issue. This book is committed in part to laying such doubt to rest.

The second question relates to the incidence of medicine murder in Basutoland in the 1940s and the 1950s. Was there indeed, as Jones and others believed, a 'very startling increase' in medicine murder in the 1940s, or was there merely an increase in *reported* cases, attributable in part to improved policing methods and in part to an increased readiness on the part of commoners to give evidence against the chiefs? We believe that there was a significant increase, though not as 'startling' as was believed at the time.

The third question relates to the causes of that increase. Many different diagnoses were made at the time, and of course each case differed in its particulars: the historical background, the immediate political circumstances, the principals involved, the motives. The weight of our analysis lies in our effort to understand the internal conflicts in the upper hierarchy of the chieftainship and the consequences of those conflicts, and the changing relationship between the colonial administration and the chiefs on the one hand and between the chieftainship and the people on the other.

Fourthly, what do we mean by 'moral crisis'? We use the phrase to refer to the convergence of a number of profound anxieties in the 1940s and early 1950s, within Basotho society and within the colonial administration. But there was no simple relationship between this sense of crisis and the incidence of medicine murder either in that period or afterwards. Medicine murder continued through the late 1950s and the 1960s and the period of independence. Yet it was no longer of any national political significance. The crisis went away. We need to understand why this was so.

A fifth question relates to the problems of reconstructing what happened from evidence given in court. Obviously, conflicting interpretations of events emerged from the adversarial character of the judicial process. The resolution of these conflicting interpretations turned very largely on the question of the acceptability or otherwise of accomplice evidence, that is, evidence given by persons who confessed to having taken part in the crime and whose primary motive for becoming Crown witnesses was to achieve immunity from prosecution and to escape the hangman's rope. For this reason, accomplice evidence was potentially tainted evidence, and required strong safeguards in judicial practice before it could be taken into consideration by the court. At the same time, accomplices had the advantage of first-hand involvement in the murder and therefore of intimate knowledge of the immediate circumstances. The question of the reliability of accomplice evidence was hugely sensitive and controversial. It recurs throughout our text, both in the detailed Case Studies in Part I and in our reconstruction in Part II of the process of medicine murder as a whole.

INVESTIGATING MEDICINE MURDER

We examined the records of all the cases of medicine murder which we were able to find. The strongest evidence relates to those in the colonial period, from the first recorded murder in 1895 to the last in 1966, just a month before independence. Tracking them down was not easy. When we began our investigation the High Court files were stored as part of the Lesotho National Archives (LNA) in a basement in the library of the National University of Lesotho at Roma. They were in very rough chronological order, but they were neither classified nor complete, and they were watched over not by a helpful archivist, but by a kindly cleaning woman whose only duty, apart from cleaning, was to open and close the room. In the absence of any catalogues we sat among the shelves and the stacks, pulling down one file after another, blowing off the dust, prising open knots that had not been undone for half a century, and then in each case, if the papers were all there, making our way through the District Commissioner's notes on the preparatory examination, the transcript of the High Court proceedings (sometimes more than 1,000 pages), and finally the judgement itself. In some cases these were supplemented by plans and photographs of the place of murder, photographs of the mutilated corpse, and black-edged documentation of hangings in the Maseru gaol.

In this way, through visits respectively by Sanders in November 1996 and Murray in April 1997, we went through about two-thirds of the potentially relevant case files stored on the shelving of the basement. When, however, Sanders returned in October 1997 to go through the final third, he was shocked to find that, in the week before his arrival, because the library needed more space, all the High Court files had been removed to a prison cell beneath the Magistrates' Court in Maseru. When Sanders gained access to the cell he found the High Court files randomly stacked from the floor to the ceiling. The floor of the cell was damp, which must have been bad for the prisoners who had been confined there but was even worse for the files, which were already beginning to rot away. It was impossible to unearth the papers which were at the bottom of the stacks against the walls, but in separate visits in October 1997 (Sanders) and January 1998 (Murray), by patiently dismantling the piles and building up new ones, we were able to find most, but not all, of the cases we were looking for. When Murray returned again in December 1998 he found that the High Court files had been moved to a basement in another building, the new High Court (the 'Palace of Justice'), where they were stacked on shelving in complete disarray. This time he found the records of two more cases on which we already had information from other sources. By November 2001, however, this shelving had collapsed and the files were strewn all over the floor.

Fortunately most cases of medicine murder were extensively reported in the press, most importantly in the *Basutoland News* (a paper mainly for the white community), *Leselinyana la Lesotho* (the French Protestant paper), *Moeletsi oa Basotho* (the Roman Catholic paper), and *Mochochonono* (mainly the mouthpiece of educated Basotho). The reports in *Moeletsi* were especially detailed, sometimes extending over many issues of the paper, with the verdict being made known to readers several months after it was actually delivered. Newspaper coverage was not fully comprehensive: because of the pressure of business the High Court was sometimes divided into two, and it was impossible for one correspondent to cover every case. So cases which appeared in the High Court records did not always appear in the press, and some cases which appeared in the press we were not able to find in the High Court records.

For the period up to 1949 we referred to the 'List of murders believed to be medicine murders' drawn up by G. I. Jones, who had had the benefit of assistance from the British authorities and other informants.[7] Even Jones, however, did not lay claim to comprehensiveness, at least for the period before 1930, and we identified several cases to which he made no reference. In many cases we found further evidence in other written records and, for murders in the Mokhotlong District, a detailed analysis prepared by the anthropologist Hugh Ashton in 1949.

Using all these and other sources we have recorded 210 individual cases of suspected medicine murder during the colonial period. They are sum-marised in the Appendix. For the cases that came before the High Court under colonial rule, we believe that the Appendix is either complete or nearly complete. There were many other cases, however, where preparatory examinations were held but the Attorney-General decided not to prosecute, or where mutilated bodies were found but no legal proceedings were brought, and for these the Appendix may be an incomplete record.[8]

The grimly detailed accounts of all these cases, whether in the High Court files or in the press, are a salutary corrective to many of the looser speculations about medicine murder, in particular to the views of those who have doubted whether such murders took place at all. In several respects, however, their explanatory power is limited. The lawyers were interested in only one question: was there sufficient evidence to prove beyond reasonable doubt that the accused were guilty of murder? No attempt was made to consider more generally the changing nature of Basotho chieftainship, the impact of the indirect rule reforms, or the rivalries over the paramountcy. Nor was it the lawyers' job to explore in depth the more parochial political and social conflicts which might help to explain the commission of such crimes. Despite their voluminous extent in many cases, the judicial records often did not satisfy our need to know about particular motives and social circumstances.

Accordingly, we were aware from the beginning that primary fieldwork would be a potentially valuable additional source of oral evidence, at least on the cases we selected for detailed analysis in this book. We carried out rapid fieldwork of this kind in the course of 1998, 1999 and 2000, amounting to about six weeks between us, on these cases and on certain others also. With the invaluable assistance of Khalaki Sello, a retired lawyer from Maseru, we were able to talk with elderly surviving participants in these local dramas, members of their families and independent observers. Somewhat to our surprise, we found them to be remarkably willing, on the whole, to reminisce about their experiences and perspectives, although their memories were often stretched to the limit. In many cases these events had scarred people's lives and moulded local antagonisms which have persisted for fifty years or more. Their recollections allowed us to make sense of, or to interpret more effectively than we had been able to from the bare details of the judicial record, some of the alleged motives, the particular circumstances, the social complexities and the aftermaths of particular cases.

As well as the evidence on individual cases, we read through the voluminous correspondence and debates about medicine murder in general. The files in the Public Record Office (PRO) in Kew (London), now the National Archives, are an absorbing record of the deliberations of the colonial authorities. They are drawn from two sources: the Commonwealth Relations Office in London, and the British High Commission in South Africa. To the extent that they include material from Maseru it was possible to follow the policy considerations of the Resident Commissioner and his officials in Basutoland. At first, however, we were unable to consult the files of the Basutoland government. Many of the surviving files were kept in the basement of the library of the National University but, like the files of the High Court cases, they were removed when we were on the point of consulting them. Sanders had the galling experience of watching them being thrown along a human chain of prisoners from the basement shelves in the library to a waiting truck in which they were then transported to a locked government house in Maseru. There they have languished in total confusion, in conditions entirely unsuitable either for the preservation of a precious historical legacy or for public access to it.

We eventually discovered, however, that many sensitive files had been removed from Basutoland by the Government Secretary in 1965, shortly before internal self-government, in order to protect them from scrutiny by the incoming government of Lesotho. In 2002 we traced them to a repository of the Foreign and Commonwealth Office (FCO) at Hanslope Park, in Buckinghamshire, where we were able to examine them in the early months of 2003. We gleaned fascinating additional detail from them, but they did not lead us to change our interpretation of events.

There is ample evidence of the views of the missionaries and of their followers in their journals and newspapers. The views of the chiefs and politicians are most powerfully reflected in the lengthy debates of the

Basutoland National Council and in *Mohlabani*, the organ of the Basutoland African Congress.

'RITUAL MURDER': THE POTENTIAL FOR BROADER STUDY

We concentrate rigorously in this book on understanding the phenomenon
of medicine murder in colonial Lesotho in the mid-twentieth century. But
medicine murder, or 'ritual murder', as it is still widely referred to, is not
confined to Lesotho, and the crisis of the late 1940s and early 1950s does
not stand alone. What frameworks of comparison might emerge through
more general study of such phenomena?

One possible framework might be defined as that of ethnographically
controlled intra-regional comparison. This would identify similar forms of
belief in the power of human medicine, and evidence of the practice of
medicine murder, in other parts of the region of southern Africa at different
periods of time. Another possible framework might be defined as that of
historically or chronologically controlled inter-regional comparison. This
would identify practices of murder in other parts of Africa – in the form of
single events or of statistical patterns – which carry striking resonance with
our study of medicine murder in Basutoland in the 1940s and 1950s not on
the grounds of ethnographic similarity but on the grounds of their
occurrence and investigation within comparable contexts of late colonial
rule in broadly the same period of time.

In the Addendum to this book we seek to suggest the potential for both
frameworks of comparative study. We illustrate the first approach through a
review of the Swazi crisis of the 1970s and the Venda crisis of the late 1980s.
We illustrate the second approach through reference, in approximate
chronological order, to the 'Kibi [Kyebi] murder' of 1944 in the southern
Gold Coast; the Bridge House murder of 1945, on the Atlantic littoral of the
Gold Coast; and the notorious 'man-leopard' murders in south-eastern
Nigeria in the mid-1940s. Whichever framework of comparison is adopted,
it is clear that medicine or 'ritual' murder or comparable phenomena cannot
be understood merely as recurrent atavistic spasms. Rather, their meaning
and significance should be reached for through detailed and sympathetic
exploration of the history and the culture of the region concerned and of its
contemporary socio-economic and political realities. Such intensive micro-
level studies are the proper foundation for a broader comparative analysis.

PART I

MEDICINE MURDER:
HISTORICAL BACKGROUND,
POLITICAL CONTEXT AND
CASE STUDIES

1

BASUTOLAND: 'A VERY PRICKLY HEDGEHOG'

> An unreformed Basuto Chieftainship will perish and the Chiefs must now be saved from themselves.
>> Sir Evelyn Baring, High Commissioner, to Lord Cranborne, Secretary of State for Dominion Affairs, 21 December 1944[1]

Throughout the period with which we are mainly concerned in this book, the arguments about medicine murder reflected political tensions between the British colonial administration and the Basotho chieftainship on the one hand, and the chiefs and their subjects on the other. In this chapter we analyse these political tensions as they developed through the first half of the twentieth century, in order to explain the context of socio-economic and political change in which the arguments of the 1940s (Chapter 3) and the 1950s (Chapter 4) took place. We identify the key elements of stress. We outline the administrative and judicial reforms introduced in the late 1930s and the 1940s. We then introduce the disputes over succession to the paramountcy which vitally influenced the internal conflicts of the 1940s and in our view gave rise, at least in part, to some of the most notorious cases of medicine murder.

A POLICY OF BENIGN NEGLECT

Lying in the shadow of the Union of South Africa, Basutoland and the other two High Commission Territories, Bechuanaland and Swaziland, were different from the rest of Britain's African possessions. They were integral parts of the larger economic region whose core was South Africa's gold-mining industry. The political threat of transfer to South African rule was very real.

In 1909, in the Schedule to South Africa's Act of Union, it was envisaged that at some unspecified time in the future – when, it was hoped, the liberalism of the Cape would have softened the intransigence of the old Afrikaner Republics – the three territories would be incorporated into the Union. Their peoples would be consulted, but there was no commitment that their wishes would be respected. In the meantime the British High Commissioner in South Africa would continue to act as their Governor – hence the term High Commission Territories – and would be represented in each of the territories by a Resident Commissioner. In 1925 this separation from the mainstream of colonial administration was reflected and confirmed in the transfer of responsibility for the territories from the Colonial Office to the Dominions Office. Though Basutoland's Resident Commissioners were invariably British, at least until 1946, many of their officers were recruited in the Union. For these reasons, as the High Commissioner reflected in June 1950, 'the Territory remained out of … the more vigorous currents which were influencing British colonial policy elsewhere'.[2]

Basutoland, entirely surrounded by South Africa, had already had experience of Cape colonial rule. It was only with the greatest reluctance, when the Basotho nation was threatened with dismemberment by the commandos of the Orange Free State, that the British government had stepped in to annex the country in 1868. Three years later, in 1871, it was handed over to the Cape Colony, which introduced magistrates and weakened the power of the chiefs, but then provoked a massive rebellion by its attempt to disarm the Basotho. From the Gun War of 1880–1 the Basotho emerged defiant and unsubdued. The Cape's authority was fatally undermined, and the British government resumed control in 1884.

Again, however, British intervention was hesitant. The first Resident Commissioner, Marshal Clarke, was instructed merely to protect property and to maintain order on the frontier, and to encourage the Basotho to establish a system of internal government sufficient to enable them to suppress crime and settle disputes among themselves. On no account was he to allow expenditure to exceed income. In 1889 the High Commissioner, Sir Hercules Robinson, spelling out the policy that was later to be enshrined in the Act of Union, declared that there was no place for 'direct Imperial rule on any large scale' in South Africa. The role of the imperial government in its colonies and protectorates was gradually to prepare the way for handing them over to the Cape and Natal 'as soon as such transfer can be made with justice to the natives and advantages to all concerned'. Because of this expectation of transfer to South Africa, the British tended to look upon their administration in Basutoland as a holding operation, a 'makeshift Government'.[3]

Unlike the Cape, the imperial government, so far from undermining the chieftainship, set out to build up the Paramount Chief. Its policy may be described as one of 'unite and rule'. The Basotho were divided among themselves, with several powerful chiefs setting themselves up against the Paramount and against each other, but after the defeat in 1898 of Masupha, the most fractious of the senior chiefs, the country at last began to enjoy the advantages of a settled peace. Once law and order were established, the Basotho were left very much to govern themselves. The British dealt with external affairs – mainly relations with South Africa and customs agreements – and internally their officials tried all cases of homicide, as well as all cases which involved whites. But outside the small Government Reserves the chiefs continued to allocate land and to administer justice through their courts. As long as they ensured that their followers were law-abiding and paid their tax they were left well alone. And provided that Basotho customs were not 'brutal or grossly repugnant to civilised thought', no move was made to change them.[4]

In the perception of most Basotho it was the chiefs who were their rulers, not the Resident Commissioner and his officers. The British, they believed, were only there to protect them from South Africa. They did not accept that Basutoland was a British colony, but saw it rather as a protectorate, and they did not accept that the British had any right to interfere in their domestic affairs.[5] According to Sir Alan Pim in 1935, they 'consider themselves to be not British subjects in the ordinary sense, but members of a nation in treaty relations with the British Government'. They are 'fanatically attached to their independence', he added, 'and deeply suspicious of anything which can be represented as an attack, direct or indirect, on that independence, more especially if it has any relation to their land'.[6]

The Basotho were confirmed in this view of their status by the government's own policy of non-interference, and also by the siting of the government's district headquarters, or 'Camps' as they were popularly known, which were strung out along the borders as if to give protection against the Free State and the Cape. In the words of one Mosotho, the British had come 'to guard the drifts so that enemies may not deprive us of our country'.[7] In spite of South African pressure, no white settlement was allowed. The country was not thrown open to white farmers, and missionaries, traders and labour recruiters could not own the land on which they carried out their work. There was no private ownership of land: in accordance with Sesotho custom, the country was held by the Paramount Chief in trust for the nation as a whole.

Although this policy of *laissez-faire* had been dictated by considerations that had little to do with good government and much to do with the need for economy, in the early years it was widely regarded by officials, philanthropists and popular commentators as one of the success stories of British administration in Africa. In 1898 James Bryce commended it as allowing 'the native … to develop in his own way, shielded from the rude pressure of the whites'.[8] In 1925 Godfrey Lagden, who had been Resident Commissioner in 1890, and again from 1893 to 1901, described what was happening in Basutoland as a unique opportunity to see how far 'these native people as a mass can rise on their own lines under paternal government and guidance, without being compelled by the presence of a European population to adopt a spurious form of civilization'.[9] This policy had been supported by his High Commissioner, Lord Milner, who found Basutoland '*perfectly delightful* and unspoilt', and was determined that 'colonial civilizers' should not make an end of it.[10] In 1926, the influential missionary writer Edwin Smith, while not pretending 'that everything is ideal in this highly favoured land', declared that here was 'an object lesson in the art of governing an African people'. 'Under this system', he wrote, 'an African tribe is given the opportunity of developing sanely and securely along the lines of its own ethos, while gradually absorbing the best elements of our European civilization.'[11]

This rosy view of the proper governance of an African people appeared to be confirmed in the early years by a flourishing economy. The population increased from 127,707 in 1875 through 348,848 in 1904 to 498,781 in 1921 (see Table 1.1). For many years from the late 1870s the country had been regarded as the granary of the Orange Free State and the northern Cape. The Basotho were productive farmers. 'No white population', wrote Lagden, 'would produce as much in the space available.'[12] Exports of grain, mainly wheat and maize, were supplemented, most importantly, by wool and mohair, and also by livestock, hides and skins. In 1919 these exports were valued at a record £1,380,000, and as late as 1928 they were holding up at £1,013,000.[13] Furthermore, by the 1920s, about half of the adult male population were normally absent working on the farms and in the industries of South Africa, many of them on the gold mines of the Rand.[14] On the one hand, their remittances and deferred wages significantly assisted their rural families to survive. On the other hand, the extent of dependence on the export of labour was itself a key index of the growing inability of Basutoland's economy to support a rapidly increasing population.

Already, in 1899, Lagden had noted the dual advantages of this dependence from a British imperialist perspective. Male labour from Basutoland supplied the 'sinews' of agriculture and industry in South Africa. It also 'fertilised' Basutoland with cash 'which is at once diffused for English goods'. Income from this source paid for Basutoland's imports, which consisted mainly of clothing and goods manufactured in Britain.[15] Further,

Table 1.1 Population, *de facto* and *de jure*, with (*de facto*) religious affiliations, 1894–1966

	1894	1904	1911	1921	1929	1936	1946	1956	1966
De facto population	219,082	348,848	404,507	498,781		562,311	563,854	641,674	852,361
De jure population			426,437	543,078		660,546	—	793,639	969,634
PEMS		40,000*			80,000*		118,833	140,003	206,340
Roman Catholic		5,700*			60,402*		151,312	215,921	328,793
Anglican							49,432	60,130	88,361
Other Christian							24,336	36,871	71,238

Sources: Basutoland (1894–1956) and Lesotho (1966) Government Census Reports; *Machobane (1990: 167).

there were no serious difficulties in collecting the so-called Native Tax, which, together with customs and excise, accounted for about three-quarters of government revenue.[16] Over the years this income was more than adequate to meet the very limited expenses of the very limited administration. The original instructions to Marshal Clarke had been observed. There was no burden of expenditure on the imperial government. Thus, as several commentators observed, there was a happy coincidence between the philanthropists' view that Africans should be allowed to develop along their own lines and the administrators' determination to balance the books.[17]

Edwin Smith, as we have seen, also favoured an African people developing 'along the lines of its own ethos', though at the same time 'gradually absorbing' desirable elements of European civilisation. Such 'absorption', in his view, was mainly to be measured by the progress of the missions. By the 1930s professing Christians made up nearly half of the population, a proportion which was to increase to about two-thirds by 1946.[18] The French Protestants of the Paris Evangelical Missionary Society (PEMS), who had been the first to arrive in 1833, still had the largest following, but they were rapidly being overtaken by their rivals, the Roman Catholics, who had begun their work in 1862. (Figures on religious affiliation at various dates are given in Table 1.1.) Whereas PEMS finances were devastated in the First World War, the Catholics, whose effort was led by the Oblates of Mary Immaculate, avoided that fate by transferring financial responsibility for their work to the French-Canadian segment of the Order.[19] Even more important, in 1912 the Catholics gained a great advantage when Griffith Lerotholi, who became Paramount Chief in the following year, was baptised into their faith. Many of the leading chiefs followed his example, and by the 1960s more than two-thirds of the Ward Chiefs were members of the Roman Catholic church.[20] There were smaller but significant numbers of Anglicans – 49,432 in 1946 – but very few adherents of Ethiopian, Zionist or other separatist churches.[21]

With support from the Native Education Fund, drawn from a levy of three shillings on every adult male, the missions provided nearly all of the education, and through their numerous schools the Basotho attained one of the highest literacy rates in Africa.[22] Until the establishment of Pius XII College at Roma in 1945, however, there was no provision for higher education in Basutoland, and those who wanted such education had to go to South Africa or even further afield. The emergence of a small educated élite, the *bahlalefi*, was one of the major developments of these early years of British rule.

Comparison was repeatedly drawn between the apparent prosperity and contentment of the Basotho and the wretched lot of their fellow Africans in the Union, whose lands had been thrown open for white settlement and whose chiefs had been undermined by magistrates. 'The Basuto ... have a spirit of freedom long crushed out of many of the tribes within South Africa', wrote

Margery Perham after her visit to the country in 1929.[23] And David Gamble, a visitor in 1935, commented on 'the general air of contentment and happiness everywhere'. 'In Basutoland', he wrote, 'there is a refreshing lack of sullenness and fear, qualities which are not at all uncommon in various parts of South Africa. Here the people stand up straight and fearless, without insolence but without apology.'[24] The contrast was reinforced, according to Godfrey Lagden, by Basotho memories of their own tribulations under the earlier rule of the Cape Colony. 'Their experience of ... rule by the Imperial Government ... left them contented and in a marked degree prosperous', he wrote: 'under the Colonial Government it had not been so.'[25] The British were gratified by repeated protestations of devotion and loyalty to the Crown.

No doubt much of this was heartfelt, but it sprang in the main from painful awareness on the part of the Basotho that the alternative to British rule was not a return to the 'good old days' of Moshoeshoe, but incorporation into the Union of South Africa. In the event Basutoland remained British. It was the narrow racism of the old Afrikaner Republics that triumphed in South Africa, not the liberalism of the Cape, and in spite of the damage to its relations with South Africa the British government was never persuaded that transfer would be consistent with its duties to the peoples concerned. Mindful of the country's turbulent past, it was also well aware of the danger of hostilities. 'Basutoland is a very prickly hedgehog', an official in London had written in 1908, just prior to the Act of Union. 'The Basutos are already asking questions, they are warlike and armed.'[26] Even so, the possibility of incorporation was the subject of repeated discussions between Britain and South Africa, and these discussions gave rise to constant alarms among the Basotho. The greater their fear of being taken over, of being 'killed' by the great 'snake' of the Union,[27] the fiercer their assertions of loyalty to the British.[28]

In the circumstances, it seemed, the British had reason to congratulate themselves. The Basotho were commonly described not only as loyal and contented, but as courteous, friendly, intelligent and hard-working. Dressed in colourful blankets and mounted on horseback, they made a powerful appeal to the imperial imagination. Add to this the magnificence of their mountainous country and the bracing highveld climate, and what emerged was an imperial idyll.[29] 'Basutoland', wrote Lord Milner in 1897, 'is a perfect marvel to me.' It is 'a modern Utopia', wrote Nellie Fincher, a visitor in 1918.[30]

ECONOMIC FAILURE AND CHIEFLY ABUSE

But the warning signs were there for all to see, and many people took a more critical view of British policy. In the final war with the Orange Free State the Basotho had lost much of their fertile land, the so-called Conquered

Territory, and from the very beginning of Cape and then imperial rule there were complaints and conflicts arising from the shortage of arable land and pasturage. Edwin Smith might have regarded the increase in population as a sign of 'African happiness' and prosperity,[31] but within Basutoland's constricted boundaries it led to increasing pressure on land and the devastating spread of soil erosion.[32]

Very little was done to develop the country, partly, perhaps, because the British saw no point in spending money in a colony that might soon be handed over to South Africa, but more because there were so few opportunities for profitable investment and because the Basotho could so easily find work in the Union.[33] So the downward slide continued. The increasing population placed increasing demands on the country's productive capacity, and as overstocking led to overgrazing the ravages of soil erosion spread unchecked. Disaster finally struck with the great depression and the drought of 1932–3, the worst in living memory. Basutoland's exports collapsed from an average of £811,057 in 1926–9 to £301,872 in 1930–3, and they never fully recovered. From being a net exporter of grain until the 1920s, the country became a net importer, dramatically so from the early 1930s onwards.[34] It became ever more dependent on migrant labour. It was no longer a granary, but a labour reserve, a backwater of the southern African regional economy. The growth in population stopped abruptly. In 1936 it was 562,311. Ten years later, in 1946, it was almost the same at 563,854 (see Table 1.1). In the intervening period many Basotho had migrated to settle permanently in the Union.

There had also been mounting criticisms of the system of administration. It was to be expected that South African politicians and officials should be disturbed by a 'native policy' that was so much at variance with their own. In 1909 John X. Merriman, the Prime Minister of the Cape, condemned the British government for ruling through the chiefs instead of breaking down their power.[35] In 1924 Edgar Brookes, in his influential study of the *History of Native Policy in South Africa*, while recognising that the imperial government had 'preserved order perfectly among the Basuto', commented that it had 'done little directly to civilise' and that the chiefs' courts were 'to-day a crying grievance'.[36] But there was also mounting concern among the British and the Basotho themselves.

The Basotho clearly preferred British rule to South African domination. But the concept of the Basotho 'developing along their own lines' had not been thought through, and it was now increasingly realised that the lines along which the chieftainship was developing were a long way removed from what the British wanted, or indeed from what many Basotho wanted. Lagden was right when he wrote of Basotho unhappiness under Cape colonial rule, but this arose mainly from the attempt at disarmament and less from the imposition of magisterial courts, which in fact were welcomed by many of the common people as an alternative to the arbirtrary administration of justice by the chiefs.[37] Now, under imperial rule, there were increasing complaints that the chiefs were becoming more oppressive and despotic. It was not just the new educated élite who were critical, though they were best able to catch the government's ear. The ordinary people also complained. Some demanded reform, but others wanted a return to the lost and much longed-for ideal of the chieftainship of pre-colonial days.[38]

This nostalgia was not wholly misplaced. There had been many complaints about the chiefs' oppression of commoners, even in the time of Moshoeshoe. But even so the old Sesotho proverb, *morena ke morena ka batho*, 'a chief is a chief through the people', reflected a profound truth. In a world of raids and counter-raids for cattle, a chief was only as strong as the number of his followers. If he wanted to retain their allegiance or to attract new followers, he had to provide them with sustenance and protection and he had to consult them and pay attention to their wishes. The *pitso*, the assembly of all adult men, was central to the workings of the chieftainship. People had the right to speak freely and critically, and any chief who ignored what they said would soon find himself in trouble. In the last resort his aggrieved followers might move away, either as individuals or as a group, or they might give their support to one of his rivals, some member, usually, of his own family. The British government's insistence on law and order and its support for the rule of the senior chiefs limited the possibilities of rebellion,[39] and after the imposition of Basutoland's narrow boundaries and the sharp increase in the country's population it was almost impossible for large groups to break away.[40] Even individuals found it more difficult: they could still, if they wanted to, drift across the border to South Africa, but if they went to join another chief there was no guarantee that he would be able to give them land. One of the most important sanctions against the abuse of power, or even against simple incompetence, had effectively disappeared.[41]

The chiefs did not need to consult their people as much as before. Throughout the country the *pitso* fell into disuse,[42] and at the national level the growth of population made it impracticable to hold a *pitso* on every issue of concern. In 1903 the British had established the National Council, which consisted of 100 members – the Paramount Chief and ninety-four persons, most of them chiefs, nominated by him, and five persons, all commoners, nominated by the Resident Commissioner, who normally chaired the Council. The Council had no legislative powers, and even its advisory function was limited to a consideration of the annual budget and any proposed laws 'of a domestic nature'. At first it met only once a year.[43]

In 1907 the Basutoland Progressive Association (BPA) was formed, consisting mainly of men educated in the schools of the Paris Evangelical Mission – interpreters, clergymen, clerks and school supervisors, traders, writers and journalists – and soon it became the practice for the Resident

Commissioner's nominees to be drawn from the BPA's members. In 1919 a rival organisation was formed, the Lekhotla la Bafo, the Council of Commoners. Its leader, Josiel Lefela, had been delegated by his chief to take his place on the Council,[44] but his new party represented peasants rather than the educated élite.

While the BPA has been characterised as moderate and reformist, accepting the good faith of the colonial administration, the Lekhotla la Bafo has been described as 'the more authentic progenitor of radical ideology and militant political organization in Basutoland'.[45] According to Robert Edgar, the most pronounced difference between them concerned the chieftainship. 'While both vented their ire against the excesses of chiefs, the Progressive Association supported reforms that would circumscribe their power and Lekhotla la Bafo advocated policies that would restore traditional authority and institutions to their original vigour.'[46] Lefela would later play an important part in the debates about medicine murder, and from the beginning his guns were trained on the British administration rather than on the chieftainship. By contrast the views of the BPA were much closer to those of the government.[47]

Many years later the National Council would be the main channel for constitutional advance, gradually being transformed into the legislative assembly of an independent nation. At first, though, compared with the pre-colonial *pitso*, its remit was limited and its membership restricted. It was a force of reaction, not of progress. The chiefs used it to oppose any attempt by the administration to cut back their powers, and the BPA condemned it as a council of chiefs.[48] Yet even in these early stages it provided an invaluable forum for commoners to air their grievances.

In the past the main form of wealth had been livestock, and one of the main differences between a chief and a commoner had been that a chief had more stock than a commoner and that he was expected to use these animals to support the community as a whole. Now, instead of lending out stock to his followers or helping them in other ways, a chief could spend his money on other commodities, such as a car, a large house, furniture, clothing and drink.[49] He still derived much of his income from the fees and fines levied in his court and from the sale of unclaimed stray stock, but he also took a cut of 5 per cent of all the tax collected from his followers. As well as looking to his court to support him he was now looking upwards to the British government. At the same time men and women earning money in South Africa to supplement their living from the land were no longer so dependent on the chiefs. Gaps were opening up between chiefs and people, and the old easy informality between them was replaced by more deference and formality.[50]

The chiefs were corrupted by their increased power. In the National Council and elsewhere there were repeated complaints about their abuses of office: their demands on their people for free labour on their lands over and above what had been accepted by Sesotho custom; their imposition of unreasonable orders on their followers and then their exaction of fines for disobedience; their improper appropriation of stray stock; their failure to share their wealth with their people; their delays in settling disputes informally, so that the parties had to take their cases to court where the fines and fees went into the chiefs' pockets; and the slow and arbitrary justice that was frequently meted out in their courts.[51]

The anthropologist Hugh Ashton, working mainly in the Mokhotlong sub-district in 1935–6, summed up the position as follows:

> Owing to the breakdown of the old sanctions, the chiefs have little inducement to win the support and popularity of their people by the exercise of justice, generosity and graciousness; and … many are more interested in satisfying their own desires than in serving their subjects; they abuse their authority and the privileges of their position for their own selfish ends. Many are drunkards, corrupt and immoral, and … oppose developments and innovations proposed or introduced for the benefit of the country.[52]

A further cause of contention was the excessive use of the placing system. Moshoeshoe had 'placed' his sons and brothers over other subordinate chiefs in order to bring them more firmly under his control. It was a practice that was much resented and on occasion resisted, but it was crucial in keeping the new nation together.[53] Since Moshoeshoe's time placings had had to be found for the descendants of his successors and for the descendants of the various Ward Chiefs throughout the country. By the 1930s, to quote a speaker in the National Council, there were as many chiefs in Basutoland as there were stars in the heavens.[54] In addition to the twenty or so Ward Chiefs,[55] there were about 1,200 other important chiefs, and about 2,000 more who were barely more than headmen, some of them with fewer than 100 followers. Such chiefs were often as poor as their subjects. Yet still the placings went on. Whenever a new chief was placed, of course, the chiefs over whom he was placed were demoted, and this led to constant friction and turmoil.[56]

These then were the lines on which the Basotho were developing. Yet in spite of the catalogue of chiefly abuses the chieftainship itself was still respected, even revered. In the 1860s Moshoeshoe's missionary, Eugène Casalis, had written that the Basotho had 'an almost superstitious respect' for their chiefs, and Hugh Ashton observed that the position was similar in the 1930s. 'The concept of the chieftainship', he wrote, 'is deeply rooted in the Basuto.'[57] Even when criticising the chiefs, one of the BPA leaders, Simon Phamotse, acknowledged that, 'like the English of old, the Basotho love their kings and will think twice before they declare against them', though he added that 'the love is only on one side'.[58] And in 1948 a speaker in the National Council declared that

The people of Basutoland are respected because they respect their Chiefs ... If their chieftainship breaks down and is ended, will they still continue as a Nation, will they not become as the Nation of the Hottentots, Bushmen? They had no chieftainship, and they wandered up and down the country.[59]

'If the Basotho ever lose their Chiefs', remarked Stimela Jingoes in 1975, 'they will cease to be the Basotho as I know them; they will become a faceless nation ...'[60]

Any action by the British administration to control the chiefs could therefore be seen as an attack on the natural leaders of the Basotho and on the very integrity of the Basotho nation. Since the chiefs had led the people's resistance to every outside threat, whether from the commandos of the Orange Free State, the troops of the Cape colonial administration or the would-be-incorporating politicians of the Union, it was suspected that any move to weaken the chieftainship was merely a prelude to handing over the country to South Africa and opening it up for European settlement.[61] In fact the British were fully committed to preserving the chieftainship: 'the administration', wrote one official in 1928, 'is concerned in upholding the existing hierarchy'.[62] Without it, they believed, Basotho society would disintegrate. But, like the BPA, they came to believe that it needed to be reformed in order to survive.

THE PIM REPORT

The first serious attempt to tackle chiefly abuses was made in 1922, after the Resident Commissioner, Sir Edward Garraway, was persuaded by the BPA to press for the establishment of a special Court of Appeal, headed by an Assistant Commissioner, to hear appeals from the chiefs' courts, instead of the Paramount Chief's court at Matsieng. But Griffith and his fellow chiefs rejected the idea out of hand when it was discussed in the National Council.[63]

Two years later the High Commissioner, the Earl of Athlone, expressed his frustration that the administration lacked effective authority over the Paramount Chief or, through him, over subordinate chiefs.[64] When Leopold Amery, Secretary of State for the Dominions, visited the High Commission Territories in 1927 he was shocked that the imperial government, 'instead of spending money and thought on developing their resources and, still more important, raising the general standard of their peoples', had been content merely 'to protect them from outside interference, leaving them to carry on under a very unprogressive form of indirect tribal rule as museum pieces ...'[65]

John Sturrock, who succeeded Garraway as Resident Commissioner in 1926, made the same judgement. Although the principle of indirect rule had been adopted in Basutoland, the manner of its adoption had been 'negative rather than positive – in other words we have not so much made a positive attempt to rule through the chiefs, as allowed conditions to stagnate under the chiefs'.[66] In 1928 he tried to change this situation by bringing forward two draft proclamations defining the powers of the chiefs and regulating their courts. These proposals ran into a storm of opposition. The chiefs resisted them, not just because they regarded them as an attack on their own position, but because they believed that the Resident Commissioner had no right to make laws affecting the way the Basotho governed themselves.[67] A committee appointed by the National Council rejected Sturrock's proposals, and they were shelved for another decade. One reform was enacted, however: in 1930 the court of the Resident Commissioner became the ultimate court of appeal from the Paramount Chief's court.[68]

The growing criticism – of the government for its failure to develop the country, either economically or politically, and of the chiefs for their corruption and their resistance to change[69] – was finally brought to a head by the collapse of the economy. In 1934 Sir Alan Pim was appointed as Commissioner to enquire into 'the financial and economic' position in Basutoland, as well as the other two High Commission Territories, but, as he said, he found it 'impossible to separate economic and political questions'. His report was damning. Basutoland's system of government, he said, had been described as indirect rule. But indirect rule implied much more than merely preserving the chieftainship. It also involved effective guidance, supervision and stimulus from the officers of the imperial government so as to ensure the administration of justice and fair treatment and the moral, material and social progress of the people. 'The history of Basutoland', wrote Pim, 'presents a very different picture and the Protectorate policy followed with reference to it has little in common with indirect rule. It has been a policy "of non-interference, of proffering alliance, of leaving two parallel Governments to work in a state of detachment unknown in tropical Africa ...".' Control from below had lost its effectiveness, and it had not been replaced by control from above. "The Nation is ruled by its Chiefs, and the Government can merely proffer advice".' The Basotho received 'protection without control' and they were 'obsessed by the idea of their absolute independence ...' A system which had been suitable for the transition from war and turbulence to peace and stability had proved to be wholly unsuitable for economic, social and political progress.

There were two alternative possibilities, he concluded. First, the introduction of indirect rule in the form in which it had been tried in the rest of Africa. The Basotho, with their strong, centralised chieftainship, were admirably suited to this. Second, the reduction of the powers of the chiefs so as to convert them into 'ornamental figures, the real work of the administration being taken over by official agencies'. Pim confidently recommended the first, and his recommendation was accepted. [70]

THE KHUBELU REFORMS OF 1938

Pim's report was a vindication of all the criticisms made by the Basutoland Progressive Association over the years. As soon as it was published, motions calling for the reform of the chieftainship, most of them inspired by the BPA, began to come in from every district for the consideration of the National Council.[71] When the matter was debated in 1937 the chiefs had to acknowledge the strength of feeling against them, and a BPA motion calling for reform was passed.[72]

In December 1938 the High Commissioner issued two proclamations, which were re-issued, together with an explanatory memorandum, in the following year. Since the Sesotho version of this publication was bound in red, the reforms became known as the *Khubelu*, or red, reforms.[73] The memorandum accepted Pim's criticisms without reserve, and the proclamations, while making some allowance for local circumstances, were based on the classic examples of indirect rule in Nigeria and Tanganyika.

Proclamation No. 61 of 1938, the Basutoland Native Administration Proclamation, changed the whole basis of the chieftainship. The Paramount Chief was now defined as the person 'recognised' as such by the High Commissioner, and chiefs, sub-chiefs and headmen had to be 'declared' as such by the High Commissioner in the Government Gazette. Their areas of authority would be specified, and they would be able to exercise only those powers delegated to them with the approval of the Paramount Chief. They would continue to be responsible for maintaining law and order in their areas. No new placings would be made except with the authority of the High Commissioner after consulting the Paramount Chief.

Under Proclamation No. 62 of 1938, the Basutoland Native Courts Proclamation, only those chiefs to whom warrants had been issued, spelling out their jurisdiction, would be entitled to hold Native Courts for the administration of Sesotho law and custom. These courts would be subject to the inspection and supervision of District Commissioners who would have the power to revise their judgements and whose approval would be needed for sentences of imprisonment. Appeals would lie to any Native Appeal Courts that might be established and from them to Subordinate Courts of the First Class, presided over by District Commissioners.

These reforms were a major revolution, for they smashed through the cherished doctrine of the independence of the Basotho under British protection. Although the government claimed that the High Commissioner was not 'appointing' chiefs but merely 'recognising' those chiefs with hereditary rights who had already been accepted by the people,[74] and although it protested that it was not creating anything 'new and strange' but 'merely giving recognition and legal sanction to the existing Native Judicial Institutions',[75] it was in effect bringing the chiefs and their courts firmly under its own control. Parallel rule was over. Ultimately the chiefs no longer held office by hereditary right, still less by grace of the people, but by the authority of the High Commissioner.

In order to draw up the list of chiefs, sub-chiefs and headmen to be gazetted, a senior officer of the administration, G. J. Armstrong, went round the districts with a representative of the Paramount Chief and, together with the local District Commissioner, consulted the leading chiefs and their advisers. After several months he produced his list which, after some amendments by the Paramount Chief, was duly published in the Gazette.[76] It contained 1,348 names,[77] classified as twenty-seven chiefs, 245 sub-chiefs and 1,076 headmen. Years later, when challenged by G. I. Jones, Armstrong acknowledged that some village heads had been excluded who might have been included, and some included who might have been excluded, but he maintained that 'by and large' the lists accorded recognition to 'the great majority of Chiefs, Sub-Chiefs and Headmen who were recognised by the people at that time'.[78] One of the main purposes of the reforms, however, had been to reduce the number of chiefs, and there is overwhelming evidence that the lists omitted about half of those who had some claim for recognition, among them men who commanded widespread respect and whose rights went back for several generations.[79]

The lists were also inaccurate and inconsistent. It was 'immediately clear', wrote Patrick Duncan in 1960, 'that no consistent criterion had been adopted of what was a chief or headman. In some districts village heads were gazetted as headmen, while in others headmen with large areas did not appear'.[80] Worse still, they were in some areas biased because the Ward Chiefs on whom Armstrong had relied so heavily had taken the opportunity to favour their friends and downgrade their enemies. In this way they had been able to use the reforms to fashion the chieftainship more to their own liking.[81] The government might have claimed that it was merely giving official recognition to the existing structure, but, as Jones was able to demonstrate, in many areas it had no clear idea of what that structure was at the lower levels. The result was widespread confusion and uncertainty.[82]

The people who suffered most from this were the many small headmen who were denied recognition. By not being gazetted they lost their offices, much of their prestige and authority, their courts and the income they derived from their courts, and their right to allocate land. They continued to administer their caretakings, and they were still expected to hold courts of arbitration, trying to sort out difficulties before the Native Court was 'opened',[83] but they could no longer exercise judicial powers themselves. There were others who were aggrieved because, although gazetted, they were given a lower grading than they thought they deserved.

The Basotho had previously resisted any interference with their domestic arrangements, and yet these reforms, so revolutionary in principle and in the end, as we shall see, so revolutionary in practice, aroused little opposition.

In the Berea District Josiel Lefela and his Lekhotla la Bafo put forward all their old arguments about Basotho independence, but when they went to present their case at Matsieng Paramount Chief Griffith treated them with contempt, threatening to have them 'blown out' of Basutoland.[84]

Unlike Sturrock in 1928, the Resident Commissioner, Sir Edmund Richards, did not even submit the draft proclamations to the National Council for discussion. It was only in 1941 that there was a full debate on the proclamations, and even then criticism was muted.[85] Most of the chiefs, including Griffith himself, now accepted that reform was inevitable: the pressure from the people was overwhelming, and the British administration would no longer be deflected. But Griffith also gained important concessions which helped to soften the blow. The administration had originally planned to make a much more drastic reduction in the number of chiefs and courts, but Griffith had insisted that, initially at least, every minor chief (though evidently not every headman) should be gazetted, and every gazetted chief and headman should retain his or her court.[86]

Another reason for the lack of opposition was that the reforms were not fully implemented at once. Because of the outbreak of war and the consequent shortage of staff, and because District Commissioners were transferred so often that some of them did not know what was going on in their districts, many headmen who had not been gazetted continued to hold their courts as before, while many new placings were made without check.[87] So most of the chiefs had no idea of what would be involved if the government were to implement the reforms in full, and when the proclamations were discussed in the National Council in 1940 and 1941 there was little awareness of the magnitude of the change.[88]

THE TREASURY REFORMS OF 1946

In his magisterial account of British administration in Basutoland, Lord Hailey expressed the view that the government had been over-cautious in introducing the reforms because it had underestimated the forces demanding change.[89] He was clearly right. But the same criticism could not be made of the next stage, which had an immediate and profound impact on relations between government, chiefs and people at every level.

Paramount Chief Griffith and the Resident Commissioner, Sir Edmund Richards, enjoyed a close and trusting relationship. They 'got on like a house on fire', said Rivers Thompson, a District Commissioner at the time, '... and during that period we had a very peaceful administration and a relatively happy one'.[90] Griffith, however, died in 1939 and was succeeded by his son Seeiso, and when Seeiso died in the following year his senior widow, 'Mantšebo, became regent for his infant son by another wife, 'Mabereng. Both the succession and the appointment of the regent were bitterly contested, as outlined in the following section, and left the Basotho seriously divided. 'Mantšebo never enjoyed the same authority as Griffith or Seeiso, and a series of British administrators found her sullen, suspicious and obstructive.

In 1942 Richards was replaced by the more dynamic and ambitious Charles Arden-Clarke, who had previously held office in Bechuanaland. Arden-Clarke was determined to complete the reforms started by Richards, and was not going to tolerate any opposition from 'Mantšebo.[91] There were still complaints of delays, incompetence and corruption in the administration of justice by the chiefs. Arden-Clarke believed that the 20,000 Basotho soldiers who were serving abroad in the Second World War would not put up with these abuses when they returned, and this view was shared by Sir Evelyn Baring, who became High Commissioner in 1944.[92]

Arden-Clarke's proposals had three inter-related aims. The first was to establish a National Treasury, based at Matsieng, which would be responsible for the collection of the Native Tax and which would draw its revenue from a proportion of that tax, the fines and fees of the Native Courts and the sale of stray stock. The second was to make the chiefs salaried officials of the government, paid by the National Treasury and no longer relying on their courts and stray stock. The third was to reduce the number of Native Courts and to have them run not by the chiefs as such or their nominees, but by officials – presidents, assessors and clerks – paid from the National Treasury.[93]

In 1944 a committee consisting of four nominees of the Resident Commissioner, eight of the Paramount Chief and four of the National Council reported in favour of Arden-Clarke's proposals.[94] 'Mantšebo herself was resistant,[95] and in the ensuing council debate several members spoke out against further reform. They were opposed to the increase in taxes that would be needed and the control that government would gain over the chiefs' incomes, and they were worried that the new changes would loosen still further the bonds between the chiefs and their followers. But in the country as a whole the common people wanted justice to be administered free from the whims and oppressions of the chiefs, and most members of the Council fell into line. Some of the leading chiefs were also attracted by the prospect of getting a fixed and certain salary, payable in cash, and no longer having to rely, at least in part, on an uncertain number of livestock paid as fees and fines; and the educated élite, the *bahlalefi*, foresaw the creation of jobs for themselves and their children in both the Treasury and the courts. Again, as in the initial stage of the reforms, the forces for change were much more powerful than the forces against it.[96]

The Treasury was eventually established in 1946, and the number of Native Courts was cut back from 1,348 to 121, a figure that was reduced further to 106 in 1949. The main people who lost out were those minor chiefs and headmen who were still gazetted, but who now lost the right to try cases in their courts and whose salaries were derisively small.[97] While the

Paramount Chief and the Ward Chiefs received fixed and generous salaries, the rest were paid from a block sum according to the number of their taxpayers. Their average income was only £50 a year, and headmen with fewer than 350 taxpayers were not 'normally' to receive any payment at all.[98] Like their ungazetted peers, however, they still held administrative courts and were expected to hold courts of arbitration.[99] For a few years there was great confusion while chiefs with no court warrants continued to exact fees and fines,[100] but gradually the new system was effectively imposed.

In 1946, and again in 1949, coinciding with the reductions in the number of courts, the list of gazetted chiefs and headmen was revised, though not substantially reduced. The overall figure of 1,152 in 1949 was only 196 lower than the 1,348 gazetted in 1939. There was also a change in classification. Some of the Ward Chiefs were designated as Principal Chiefs and the term Sub-Chief was dropped (although it continued in use). So now there were eleven Principal Chiefs, twelve Ward Chiefs, 270 Chiefs and 859 Headmen.[101] (For the sake of simplicity we refer to Principal and Ward Chiefs together as Ward Chiefs.)

The new 'Treasury Courts', as they came to be known, quickly gained popular support, and, although they were more formal and bureaucratic than the 'chiefs' courts' which they replaced, there was general agreement that they were quicker, more efficient and fairer.[102] But the chiefs were still heavily involved. It was the Ward Chiefs who had nominated the Court Presidents and Assessors for appointment, and many of the chiefs themselves had been appointed since they had the best working knowledge of Sesotho law and custom.[103] In 1954, however, the courts were reconstituted as Basuto Courts and their number was reduced to sixty-two. New staff were appointed and arrangements were made to ensure 'the complete removal from the judicial system of the influence and control of the chiefs'.[104]

The idea that a chief could only be a chief if recognised by the High Commissioner continued to offend many Basotho, especially the chiefs themselves, and well into the 1950s there were speeches and motions in the National Council calling for this reform to be repealed.[105] But when making a new placing it was the government's practice to ascertain the wishes of the local people and to consult the chiefs concerned.[106] While the High Commissioner's control might have been objectionable in principle, the outcome in terms of appointments made aroused very little opposition.

There were further reforms: the establishment in 1945 of District Councils; the increase in popular representation on the National Council, with the District Councils acting as electoral colleges; the empowerment of the National Council in 1948 to nominate the panel from which the Paramount Chief had to draw her advisers; and in 1950 the removal of the age-old right of the chiefs to call out work-parties, *matsema*, to work on their lands. At the centre, power was moving away from the Paramount Chief's court at Matsieng to the National Council in Maseru. In the villages the rights of commoners were being accorded more recognition.[107]

The British administration consistently recognised, however, that for most Basotho the main embodiment of authority continued to be their chief, that everyday government and the maintenance of law and order still rested in chiefly hands, and that the chieftainship was still central to the well-being of Basotho society. It did not like what it saw in South Africa and Southern Rhodesia, where the power of the chiefs had been deliberately broken and nothing done to fill the gap. 'That is not and could not be our aim today', wrote Baring in June 1950. 'We do not want to break the power of the chiefs and leave a vacuum, but to turn the chiefly institution into something more resembling a constitutional monarchy and to educate the mass of the people up to playing a full part in the conduct of their own affairs.'[108] It would be 'a bad fate' for the Basotho if the chieftainship was left unreformed, but 'a worse fate' would be for them to experience 'the collapse of tribal and family life which has been the portion of their fellow Africans in the Union'.[109]

DISPUTES OVER THE SUCCESSION

The Paramount Chief was the only 'Native Authority' who did not have to be gazetted under the Native Administration Proclamation. Under Section 1 he or she was defined as 'the Paramount Chief ... recognised as such by the High Commissioner'.[110] Within two years of the Proclamation's being issued the High Commissioner was called upon twice to confer such recognition, and on both occasions the succession was disputed.

The tortuous dispute that followed Griffith's death in 1939 was typical of the arguments that gave room for the Basotho to operate the law of succession so flexibly. When Letsie II died in 1913 he had only one son, a small boy named Tau. But Tau died soon after his father's burial, and Griffith, who was Letsie's brother, was asked, in accordance with Sesotho custom, to raise up seed by his brother's widows and in the meantime to act as regent. He had just been baptised as a Roman Catholic, and he refused either to raise up seed for his brother or to act as regent. In his own memorable phrase, he would sit on the throne 'with both buttocks' or not at all. The Sons of Moshoeshoe gave way, and Griffith became Paramount Chief in 1913.[111]

Seeiso, who was born in 1905, was the only son by Griffith's second wife. Since Griffith had no sons by his first wife, Seeiso would normally have had every expectation of becoming his father's heir and successor. In March 1926, however, Griffith announced to the British authorities that his most senior son was Bereng, the only child by his third wife. Seeiso protested, and later that year a family council was held at Matsieng. Although the decision there was in favour of Bereng by twenty-three votes to ten, most of the chiefs

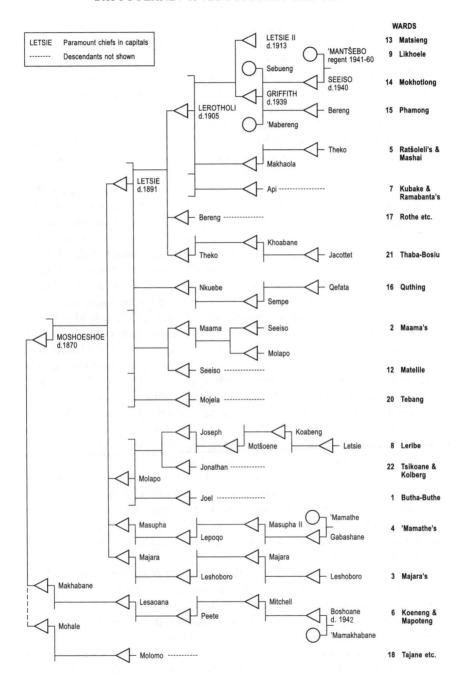

Figure 1.2 Selective genealogy of senior chiefs and their wards, 1940s

had abstained from voting and it was believed that they really supported Seeiso and had abstained for fear of offending Griffith. The government, taking soundings through its Assistant Commissioners, had evidence that throughout the country as a whole there was much more support for Seeiso than for Bereng.[112] When Griffith pressed the government to confirm the decision taken, he was told that a secret ballot would have to be held before the government would commit itself. He rejected this as contrary to Sesotho custom and the dispute was left unresolved. Griffith died in July 1939, and in the following month, at a meeting of the Sons of Moshoeshoe, Seeiso's claim was upheld by a large majority.

Griffith had objected to Seeiso as his heir because he did not believe that he was his natural son. He had been on bad terms with his second wife, Sebueng, and after many arguments and quarrels she had gone back to her father Nkuebe, Ward Chief of Quthing. When later she returned to her husband he claimed that she was pregnant by another man, and the child to whom she gave birth was Seeiso. This in itself would have been no obstacle to Seeiso's succession, because according to Sesotho custom any child born in wedlock is regarded as the legitimate offspring of the husband. *Ngoana ke oa likhomo*: 'the child belongs to the cattle', that is, the child is held to be the offspring of the person in whose name the marriage-cattle were transferred for the mother. But while Sebueng had been with her father, Griffith had married one of her sisters, and this woman had given birth to Bereng. He had transferred no marriage-cattle for her, and had declared that she was coming to take the place of Sebueng; and when Sebueng returned to him he did transfer cattle and declared that he was marrying her anew. After his death the Sons of Moshoeshoe rejected this interpretation of events. They took the view that Sebueng had never been divorced, since Griffith had not returned the original marriage-cattle to her father when she had gone back home; and they also took the view that the second payment of marriage-cattle was in respect of 'Mabereng, the mother of Bereng. So, according to Griffith, 'Mabereng had taken the place of Sebueng, whereas according to the Sons of Moshoeshoe this position was still held by Sebueng. It followed, according to the Sons of Moshoeshoe, that Sebueng's son, Seeiso, was Griffith's heir and successor.[113]

It has sometimes been alleged that the British conspired to exclude Bereng because they favoured Seeiso, who was more compliant and ready to co-operate with them.[114] The truth is simpler. The overwhelming majority of the chiefs and people supported Seeiso and his appointment was greeted with widespread rejoicing in the country as a whole. He might have been the government's favoured candidate, but in recognising him as Paramount Chief the High Commissioner was simply following the clear wishes expressed by the Sons of Moshoeshoe.[115]

Both Bereng and Seeiso were men of considerable ability, and both were well-disposed towards the government. Bereng, who had been born in 1902, had been placed by his father as the Ward Chief of Phamong in the Mohale's Hoek District in the south of Basutoland. It was said that, because Griffith could not be sure that Bereng would succeed him, he encouraged him to take as much land as possible, some of it at the expense of the Matsieng ward which was the personal caretaking of the paramount.[116] In 1940, he was described in an official report as

> well behaved and of temperate habits and a good chief but he is rather retiring and shy and it is not easy to gain his confidence ... His Court and Administrative work are good and he is very efficient in the collection of the tax in his Ward. He is a keen sportsman and is fond of games and takes a leading part in sport generally.[117]

Later he was noted for the full support which he gave to the government in its controlled grazing campaign,[118] and one British official who worked with him described him as 'a good, strong, forceful, intelligent, and progressive man. Physically too he had a commanding presence ...'[119] Rivers Thompson described him as 'a very powerful character' and 'one of the finest orators I have heard'.[120]

Seeiso, for his part, was outgoing and immensely popular both with his people and with the British authorities. According to Rivers Thompson, 'his chief virtue was that he was not a snob. He talked to anybody that he met on the road'.[121] He had been placed by his father in the remote mountain district of Mokhotlong, where he had to establish control over the Batlokoa of Chief Mosuoe.

> His main characteristics are his dignity, courtesy and personal courage. While at Mokhotlong he showed great tact in his treatment of the Chiefs and people over whom he had been placed and this was more especially so in the case of the Batlokoa tribe who at first showed great disinclination to accept him as their over-lord. He is progressive and takes a great interest in horsebreeding and owns several racehorses ...[122]

'He was a sport', said Rivers Thompson. While at Mokhotlong 'he used to chase the local equivalent of foxes which were jackals, and hyenas. He used to get all his staff out to do the same thing, even the very heavy ones, some of whom told me afterwards what a hard life they lived with Seeiso, having to rush along and gallop after these wretched jackals and hyenas with a non-descript pack of dogs'.[123] When the Second World War broke out he endeared himself to the British even more by offering to lead the Basotho troops abroad (an offer which had to be turned down), by encouraging his people to volunteer and by persuading the National Council to hand over £100,000 for the war effort out of the country's slender reserves.[124]

Seeiso had one major failing which he shared with many other Basotho chiefs, and that was his 'heavy drinking'. This was said afterwards to have been responsible for the illness in 1940 which led to his death during an operation by government doctors.[125] The inscription on his monument in the War Memorial Garden in Maseru refers to him as 'Paramount Chief Seeiso, than whom our King had no more loyal subject'.[126]

Seeiso's heir and successor was Constantine Bereng Seeiso, his infant son by his second wife 'Mabereng, and a regent had to be chosen to act as Paramount Chief until the child came of age. While Seeiso had been ill, because of his rivalry with Bereng he had nominated his principal counsellor, Chief Gabashane Masupha, to act for him, and when he died it was Gabashane who set in motion the procedures for choosing the regent. There were two contenders: Bereng, as the most senior chief in the country, and 'Mantšebo, Seeiso's senior widow, who was the daughter of Sempe Nkuebe, Ward Chief of Quthing. Bereng wanted the decision to be made by the more immediate family, the Sons of Lerotholi, who according to him numbered about ten. This would have excluded many of the most important chiefs in the country. Gabashane argued that it should be a wider gathering, the Sons of Moshoeshoe as a whole. The matter was referred to the British authorities, who in effect sided with Gabashane and convened a meeting of the Sons of Moshoeshoe presided over by the Government Secretary in January 1941. At this gathering forty-four chiefs spoke in favour of 'Mantšebo and twenty-three in favour of Bereng. Of the senior chiefs all except one, Theko Makhaola, supported 'Mantšebo. The vote went in her favour mainly, it seems, because it was widely believed that Bereng wanted not the regency but the paramountcy and that, following his father's example, he would cut out Seeiso's line and sit on the throne 'with both buttocks'. In accordance with their decision the High Commissioner recognised 'Mantšebo as Acting Paramount Chief.[127]

Again it has been argued that the British conspired to exclude Bereng, this time because they thought that with 'Mantšebo, a woman regent, they would be able to push through their reforms more easily.[128] No evidence is adduced to support this assertion, and again it is clear that in recognising 'Mantšebo the British administration was following the wishes of the Sons of Moshoeshoe. Although the Resident Commissioner, Edmund Richards, was aware of the widespread distrust of Bereng, he assured the High Commissioner that he had no intention of interfering with the wider ruling family's freedom of choice, and that if they chose Bereng that would be entirely acceptable to him.[129]

Bereng challenged the High Commissioner's decision in the High Court at Maseru. He disputed the procedures followed and argued that the appointment of a woman as regent was contrary to Sesotho custom. Under the levirate custom, he himself was now the husband of his brother's widows, including 'Mantšebo, and he should act as regent until the child came of age. The High Court rejected his arguments, and Bereng was again thrown back on his own bitterness and disappointment.[130] He never became reconciled to his exclusion from the succession, and he soon became embroiled with 'Mantšebo in a series of fierce disputes about Griffith's property and about the boundary between his own ward of Phamong and the Matsieng ward, the Paramount Chief's personal holding. He was constantly suspected of plotting to overthrow her, and at times she claimed to be in fear for her life.[131]

Confronted by such a powerful rival, it was difficult for 'Mantšebo to establish her authority, and perhaps it was especially difficult for her as a woman. At first there were good reports of her tact and ability, her conscientiousness and hard work, even her sense of humour. But she found the pressures of the job increasingly hard to sustain, especially after the arrival of the impatient and irascible Arden-Clarke with his determination to push through the Treasury reforms. She felt vulnerable and under threat and, lacking experience and training, she became heavily dependent on particular advisers, or favourites as they were commonly called, who alienated much of her support, especially among the chiefs. One was Matlere Lerotholi, her late husband's right-hand man in the mountain district of Mokhotlong, who was widely reputed to be her lover as well as her counsellor.[132] Though only thirty-seven when she was chosen as regent, she was badly overweight, had a weak heart, and from about 1945 was a diabetic as well.

Throughout her reign white observers made fun of her appearance and, as they saw it, her tantrums and unpredictability. Lord Harlech, Baring's predecessor as High Commissioner, referred to her as 'Her Amplitude'. Soon after Arden-Clarke arrived in the territory she was brought to him in tears because it was impossible to make a railway reservation at short notice. He took her to the Residency and soothed her with tea and chocolate cake. 'She is not a bad Chieftainess', he wrote to Harlech, 'but every inch a woman – and there are an awful lot of inches.'[133] When Baring visited Basutoland as High Commissioner in 1944, he was greeted, he said, 'by the striking figure of the Paramount Chieftainess, her remarkable bulk covered by a bright orange silk dress and a small brown hat perched insecurely on the back of her head'. At a party given by Arden-Clarke 'she spoke in conversation several times', but 'on other occasions her reply when spoken to was to thrust her thumb into her mouth and utter a treble giggle!' When called upon to speak at a meeting of the National Council she asked one of her advisers to read her speech.[134]

On matters of government, especially the Treasury reforms, she often took a strong and independent line and British administrators found her 'difficult' and 'unreasonable'. After a series of meetings in 1944, Arden-Clarke described her as 'stupid, inexperienced and incompetent' and 'maddeningly evasive', and he became so exasperated that even in front of her own advisers he accused her of 'rudeness, stupidity and obstructiveness'. 'It seems rather a pity after all', wrote an official in the High Commissioner's Office, 'that 'Mantšebo was chosen as Regent rather than Bereng ...' But, as Arden-Clarke himself acknowledged, her obstructiveness was essentially a reaction to the new relationship between the chieftainship and the administration. Instead of the old policy of non-interference, the Resident Commissioner was now intruding in many areas which 'Mantšebo and her advisers regarded as their own. 'She was silent, sulky and non-co-operative', wrote Baring in 1946, because she 'felt instinctively that the wings of Chieftainship were being clipped'. Whatever else might be said of her, the new regent was a consistent champion of the independence of the Basotho in the conduct of their own internal affairs.[135]

As early as 1944 Arden-Clarke was talking of the possibility of having 'Mantšebo removed from office.[136] Several years later, and much more firmly, G. I. Jones recommended her deposition, though he recognised that it would have to come from the Basotho themselves. It was not her opposition to government policies that concerned him. He was convinced, in spite of her pained protestations of innocence, that she was heavily implicated in medicine murder.[137] One murder in which she was allegedly involved is analysed in the following case study.

Case Study 1

THE CASE OF THE COBBLER'S HEAD: MORIJA, 1945

All of us took hold of the deceased and pressed him to the ground while his head was cut off.

Nkojoa Mokone, March 1946

He said that I had been asked to doctor this head to make a horn with it.

Ntjahali (Bernice Hlalele), March 1946[1]

'A MIGRATORY BODY'

On 16 May 1945, a dead body was found below the edge of a cliff, near to a rough bridle-path leading up from the village of Morija to Phahameng, a smaller village on a high terrace above.[2] According to Josiel Thoso, who saw it at dusk on that day, very soon after it had been discovered,

> The body was on a ledge; there were trousers on the body; there was a belt on the waist, from where the trousers and the belt ended there was no clothing on the body. The great coat and the jacket were under the body, he was kneeling on them. The great coat was not on the body ... He was on his face and the head was there, the hair could be seen on either side of the head but on the back of the head there was no hair, and also the flesh on the neck, from the back of the neck to the shoulders, there was no flesh there. Lesole reported to me as we went to the body that the crows had already devoured that body.[3]

By the following day, when the police arrived to investigate, the body was in a different position, on the steep slope below the ledge. The head was found eighteen metres lower down, having been with the torso – according to the account above – the previous evening. Captain Montagu Williams took photographs of the body, slumped awkwardly on its left side. Sergeant Thabiso Mohloboli observed that the corpse was dressed in trousers, belt and underpants; the breastbone and the right arm below the elbow were missing; the flesh of the left arm had been cut away; and both heels and one foot had been cut with a sharp instrument. As for the head, 'there was no skin on the skull bone. The lower jaw was missing, as also were ears, tongue and eyes'.[4] Who had moved the body overnight? This was evidently not the first time that it had been moved from one site to another. It was 'in fact a migratory body', the judge commented later.[5]

The head and body belonged to Stephen Thobeha. Known locally as Thulasizoe, he was described by the judge as 'an elderly, respectable, but perhaps slightly indigent bootmaker'.[6] He lived with his wife in a stone rondavel on a rocky hillside above the main village of Morija. He had attended a feast at Phahameng on Saturday, 5 May. Inebriated, he had been lured away from the party and, except by his murderers and a single witness, he was not seen alive again.

As a result of the initial investigation of this murder (case 1945/3) seven men were arrested: five from Phahameng and two from Morija. They appeared in late August 1945 at a preparatory examination held at Maseru, which was adjourned pending further investigation since it was thought that the ringleaders were still escaping detection. Seven more men were arrested in September. Five of these were much more influential in village affairs: the headman (often described as the chief) of Morija, Mahao Matete; his court chairman and acting headman, John Makume; and three of his councillors, Liau Lekhula, Maile Maepe and Josiel Thoso. The preparatory examination was resumed in November 1945. Of the fourteen accused men, seven were then discharged, including the headman, Mahao Matete, and seven were committed for trial at the High Court. One of these seven, Nkojoa Mokone, then turned King's evidence and became an accomplice witness for the Crown. On the basis of Nkojoa Mokone's evidence three of the men discharged were re-arrested, including Mahao Matete, and a fourth, Maile Maepe, one of the councillors, would have been re-arrested if he had not died in the meantime. Two other men were arrested in February 1946 for the first time. So eleven men appeared in the second preparatory examination held in March 1946. Three were discharged and eight were committed for trial at the High Court.[7] At the end of the trial, held in June–July 1946, seven of these men were acquitted and one man only – John Makume, the acting headman – was convicted. He was hanged on 14 August 1946.

These are the outlines of a complicated case. Who were all these men? Why should we now seek to track them down? There are several reasons for our interest in this case.

First, Morija was the headquarters of the Paris Evangelical Missionary Society (PEMS), popularly known as *Kereke ea Fora* ('The Church of France'), and had been so since 1833 when the first missionaries, Casalis and Arbousset, had been placed there by Moshoeshoe. Several generations of well-known families, who acknowledged the leadership of the church rooted in its soil, had been educated there over more than 100 years. The newspaper *Leselinyana* was printed there, as were many religious and educational books. A hospital was founded. A murder of this kind, apparently involving the most prominent members of the local community, and giving rise to what was described by the *Basutoland News* as 'one of the most gruesome witchcraft murder cases ever heard in the High Court of Basutoland', was particularly shocking to the sensibilities of Basotho who looked to Morija, 'the Jerusalem of Lesotho', for moral guidance in national affairs.[8]

Second, the suspicions arising from this case reached out from Morija to Matsieng, the home of the Paramount Chief regent 'Mantšebo, a mere five kilometres to the east. The headman, Mahao Matete, was acquitted of the crime partly because of alibi evidence connected with his duties as 'Mantšebo's private secretary. It was stated both in evidence at the time and in recollection long afterwards that 'Mantšebo needed human medicine for her horn, that on her instructions John Makume, the acting headman, had taken the victim's head to a certain doctor who would prepare this medicine, and that she had instructed the doctor in advance to carry out this work.[9] If there were any truth in this, it would have been surprising if Mahao Matete knew nothing about it.

Third, the outcome of the case was controversial and acrimonious. The congregation of the church and the Morija community as a whole were divided on the question of the guilt or innocence of the accused. Medicine murders were invariably carried out by more than one person, and it was unusual for only one of the accused to be convicted. The inference was reasonably drawn either that other guilty persons had got off scot-free or that John Makume had been unjustly condemned. The question arose whether Makume had 'taken the rap' for the chief.[10]

Fourth, our short but intensive fieldwork in this case was particularly rewarding. We were able to interview the policeman most closely involved in the investigation, Nkherepe Molefe. We recovered some of the lives and circumstances of the participants in the drama through several visits to Morija. Our efforts in 1998–9 to reconstruct the events alleged by the prosecution were greatly helped by the excellent sketch-map drawn by the police officer in charge of the case, Ken Shortt-Smith, and by photographs taken in January 1946 in the course of the investigation. These enabled us to follow the trail of Stephen Thobeha's last moments in life and the series of puzzling 'migrations' of his head and his trunk after death.

THE INVESTIGATION

The village of Morija lies due south of Maseru, at the base of the Ma-khoarane plateau. The headman of the village was Mahao Matete, who was about thirty years old at the time. He had been educated at Adams College in Natal, and was a direct descendant of Paulus Matete, Moshoeshoe's brother-in-law, who had been sent there in 1833 to protect the first missionaries and who had taken the name of Paulus on his conversion to Christianity. Mahao had taken over the headmanship in 1943 from his mother, who had been acting in the position for ten years following his father's death in 1933. For more than 100 years the Matetes had been chiefs at Morija and had been closely associated with the church.

Since Mahao, as 'Mantšebo's secretary, was often away at Matsieng, he had an acting headman, John Makume. Makume was a grandfather in a thoroughly respectable family and an elder in the Morija church, famed for the power and eloquence of his prayers: 'When he prayed it was something wonderful ... and people liked to hear him pray. He could move mountains'.[11] When Stephen Thobeha disappeared, it was to Makume that the initial report was made, and when the police began their enquiries it was Makume who was instructed to assist them.

On a terrace above the village was the smaller village of Phahameng ('On the Height'), where the acting headman was Sera Mokhajoa. Mahao Matete had no jurisdiction over Phahameng. There had been a quarrel over boundaries around 1942 and bad feeling persisted between Morija and Phahameng. The judge was to regard both these factors as significant.

Despite its long association with the church and a deeply-rooted tradition of education, the area was no stranger to medicine murder.[12] Eighteen years earlier, in 1927, a murder was committed at Phahameng (case 1927/2). The victim was a compositor at the mission's printing works in Morija, and two of the fourteen accused were his fellow-workers. All the accused were acquitted for want of sufficient evidence to convict. Three of them, all from Phahameng, were among those now to be charged with Stephen Thobeha's murder. The headman, Sera Mokhajoa, was one of them.

The first preparatory examination was adjourned in early September 1945 because it was clear that the seven accused men were lesser accomplices of instigators who had not yet been identified. A change was made in Ken Shortt-Smith's investigating team. Sergeant Thabiso Mohloboli, a Morija man himself who was friendly with the headman, Mahao Matete, was taken off the case and was replaced by Corporal Nkherepe Molefe, from the remote Mokhotlong District, whose methods were more robust. Shortt-Smith was satisfied: he had 'quite a good team, including ... Molefe', he remembered long after the case.[13] The chief's representative on the team, the acting headman, John Makume, was also removed and replaced by Knox Moshabesha, a former policeman.

Molefe picked up a rumour that two men had carried Stephen Thobeha's head on horseback to Raleqheka's, in the Makhalaneng valley to the east, where they had asked a doctor to make medicine with it. In following up this rumour he rode with Knox Moshabesha, the chief's representative, to the home of the doctor, 'Malipuo Bernice Hlalele, also known as Ntjahali. More than fifty years later, Nkherepe Molefe recalled what had happened. When he and Knox Moshabesha arrived at Raleqheka's they found that Ntjahali had gone to Matelile,

> where she had been called to doctor the area by the new black store manager of Frasers'. There was just the mother there, at Makhalaneng. We pretended we were from far: 'Now the new chiefs have

come to Mokhotlong, they are grabbing our land ... we need really strong medicine'.[14] The mother told me really everything. So I said, 'Let us go to Matelile'.

We put up at the village outside, and went to the store. My weight was heavy in those days ... in the store ... I see this princely woman coming, the *doek* [headscarf] really done in a way I had never seen, hands on hips, now in the store. Every store had a mirror in which you could see yourself. Just about getting near the mirror, she looked in my direction. I thought she must be a real doctor, she's going to detect me. We greeted each other.

'Where are you from?' 'Mokhotlong.' 'Oh. What do you want?' 'Cattle. You don't know me.' 'I am Ntjahali.'

Then she went off. Dammit, she gave me headache. She remained in the store for a while. She was far above me in her thinking. She was really dominating my mind. I didn't know what to do. I went to the premises of the manager. The curtains were broken [torn]. I thought, I'll come at night and see what is going on here. My intention was not to go through the gate. There was a stone wall, and pine trees. I got over the wall. When I was going to go to the window, there was a bulldog of this size [gesturing]. It just looked at me, it came slowly, I jumped back over the wall. I went round the house. There it was again. I got to the window ... It was wagging its tail, and so I knew I wouldn't be attacked. There was Doctor Ntjahali. Quite a number of chiefs of ... were in the dining room. The curtains were broken [torn], so I could see in. [With] something like a tortoise, she was scarifying ... a chief. About three chiefs were scarified. They washed and ate. I left, then told [Knox] Moshabesha.

Early in the morning at the store, she was going round pegging the place with medicine. I told her, because of the urgency of our case, we had to come out and wait for you here. The horse of her woman attendant was weak. Moshabesha's horse was a really sound one. I decided to remain behind [i.e. to ride behind] with the attendant, on our way [back] to Makhalaneng. I was questioning the attendant. When we got to Makhalaneng I introduced myself as a policeman ... I gave her straight questions. Ntjahali agreed. It was Makume and Liau ... one of them with a missing finger. 'They came with a head, somebody's head whom I know.'[15]

In his first interview with us Molefe stated that the two men who took the head to Ntjahali were John Makume and Liau Lekhula, that they went on the instructions of Mahao Matete, and that Mahao was 'Mantšebo's private secretary at Matsieng. In his second interview he added: '[Ntjahali] said that some time before the murder at Morija 'Mantšebo had called her to Matsieng and told her: "One of these days I shall ask you to help me by

making medicine from some human parts"'. He said he was 'quite sure' that
'Mantšebo was 'involved'. In the same interview Molefe emphasised that it
was because he already knew so much about Ntjahali – from questioning her
mother at Raleqheka's, watching her activities through the torn curtains at
Matelile, and questioning her assistant on the ride back – that she saw it was
useless to resist him and agreed to tell him everything she knew.[16]

Ntjahali picked out John Makume (No. 9) at an identification parade in
Maseru on 20 September 1945, and Liau Lekhula (No. 10) at a similar
parade in Morija on 24 September. Liau Lekhula had a distinctively
mutilated hand, and she recognised him by that feature. Thus were these
men drawn into the prosecution's net, alongside Mahao Matete (No. 8) and
Josiel Thoso (No. 13), another councillor. Morija was shocked by the arrest
of John Makume, and the whole country by the arrest of Mahao Matete.
Even the Catholic newspaper *Moeletsi* expressed its disbelief that a man of
Mahao's standing could be guilty of such a crime.[17]

THE PREPARATORY EXAMINATION AND THE TRIAL

With seven more men added to the list of accused the preparatory examination was resumed on 13 November 1945. It lasted for just over two weeks.
On 27 November seven men were committed for trial at the High Court:
Nos. 1–5, No. 9 (John Makume) and No. 10 (Liau Lekhula). The others
were discharged, including Mahao Matete, against whom there was still
insufficient evidence to establish a case.

At this point Nkojoa Mokone (No. 1) 'became panicky', as the judge
later expressed it. The hanging of five men from Qacha's Nek in the Maseru
gaol on 30 November 1945 for another medicine murder (case 1943/5)
induced him to reflect on his position and to seek urgently some way of
avoiding the noose himself.[18] He decided to turn King's evidence, and
emerged as an accomplice witness for the Crown. On the strength of his
evidence Mahao Matete was re-arrested, and among others he incriminated
was Mpharane Mokoetla (No. 15), his immediate neighbour at
Phahameng, who was arrested in February 1946. (In May 1999 villagers in
Phahameng recalled that there had been a violent quarrel between Nkojoa
and Mpharane at some time prior to the High Court trial.)

At the second preparatory examination, in March 1946, Nkojoa Mokone
gave evidence that about a week before the murder John Makume (No. 9)
convened a meeting at the chief's (Matete's) place at which it was agreed
that Stephen Thobeha should be killed. Although Mahao Matete was present,
the older man, Makume, took the lead. He explained that Mahao was planning to move to another village and therefore wanted to make a medicine
horn with Stephen's head. Mpharane Mokoetla (No. 15) would invite Stephen
to a feast that was to be held at Phahameng a week later, on a Saturday, and
arrangements were made to kill him on his way home. Each of the men from

Phahameng would be paid £100. Mahao Matete asked nervously if they would not all be arrested, but Makume assured him that the crime would be concealed. Mahao himself need not be present at the killing.

The feast was duly held at Khatla Molefe's (No. 14) place at Phahameng and went on all through the night. Stephen became drunk, and some time after dark he and Mpharane left and set off towards Morija. On the way Stephen was seized at 'Maselloane's rocks. Maile Maepe (No. 12) threw a strap around his neck, and Stephen was led and pushed to the place known as Rabele's forest. He cried out, 'Sera and Seleke! Why are you killing me?'

> When we reached the forest we seized deceased, threw him to the ground and killed him with a knife ... by cutting the deceased's throat and severing his head from his body. At that time only the head was cut off. No other parts of the body were removed. Deceased did not bleed a lot. The blood ran into a dish ... All of us took hold of the deceased and pressed him to the ground while his head was cut off.

As arranged at the meeting beforehand, Makume and five others then took the head to Mahao Matete, and when they returned, without the head, they said that Mahao had ordered that the body should be removed from where it lay as it was out in the open. 'We then removed the body from the forest at Rabele's to another forest, that is to a place beween the spot where the deceased was killed and the village of Morija. There we placed the dead body among the poplar trees underneath a bank.' The only other evidence that Nkojoa Mokone could give was that on the second day after the murder he saw people saddling up and was told that the head was being taken to the doctor.[19]

Twenty-three witnesses for the Crown were called, including the government doctor who had carried out the post-mortem (who said that the body was in such a state of putrefaction that it was impossible to ascertain the cause of death); the policemen who had carried out the investigation; and various villagers not themselves involved in the murder who gave circumstantial evidence relating to Stephen Thobeha's movements before his death, to the movements of the corpse after his death, to what they had heard near the track to 'Maselloane's rocks on the Saturday night, and to various encounters afterwards with some of the principal men involved.

Potentially the most important of these independent witnesses was a young man called Kuili Rammotseng, described later by the judge as a 'Bushman'. He had drunk so much beer at the party that he was vomiting it up when two of the accused, standing nearby, commented that 'the ox' (meaning the victim) was present and that they would see to it when the time arrived. When Stephen left the party with some of the accused, Kuili followed them, and was hiding behind a rock only five paces away when Stephen was attacked. There was no moon, he said, but it was not very dark.

When he went back to the party he reported what he had seen and one of the accused (No. 3) assaulted him, saying he had made it possible for them to be arrested. He then stayed at the party throughout the Sunday playing the banjo and drinking.[20] Another independent witness, a thirteen-year-old boy, Tšeliso Shata, gave evidence that he overheard John Makume say, 'This week will not end without us finding a *lenaka* [horn]'. He also explained how the chief's mother, 'Mamahao, had come to his mother's hut and prayed, apparently in a sinister manner, saying that her son had got into trouble on account of the house of Shata.[21]

The evidence of Ntjahali, who appeared in court as Bernice Hlalele, proved crucial:

> I remember two men who came to me last winter ... Accused No. 9 came to me with Accused No. 10. No. 9 called me. He said 'We are the messengers of the Paramount Chief'. He took out a head from his saddlebags and placed it on top of the saddlebags. He said that I had been asked to doctor this head in order to make a horn with it ... I said 'This looks like Stephen Tobeha [*sic*]'. He (i.e. accused No. 9) said 'Yes, it is on the order of the Paramount Chief'. I said 'I do not know how to medicine these things'. We argued. He called No. 10 accused Liau to take the head from the top of the saddlebags. I noticed that the hands of No. 10 accused were deformed when he removed the head from the saddlebags ... I told them I could do nothing with the head. No. 9 accused spoke. He said the Paramount Chief ordered me to treat the head. He said the Paramount Chief wished to make a horn. They did not explain what the horn was for. We argued, I refused to make the horn. The accused Nos. 9 and 10 then left.

Ntjahali said that she used only herbs in her doctoring. She never used anything else. 'It is my opinion that the presence of a dead body, or a part of the body, would upset the working of my herbs.'

The visit to Ntjahali by two men on horseback was corroborated by an independent witness for the Crown, Napo Khashole, who saw them outside her place. One of them muttered to the other in annoyance, 'She was impudent and refuses to work for us'.[22] When Napo asked Ntjahali who they were, she told him they were messengers from the Paramount Chief and had brought her Stephen Thobeha's head. Ntjahali reported their visit to her patients in order to explain why her medicine was not working. 'My medicinal powers had gone', she said, on account of the interference of the head that had been brought to her. In adherence to her medical ethics she did not report it to anyone in authority because 'as a doctor I have no right to speak of such things when I see them. It is not permissible for a doctor to give away such secrets'. She did, however, respond to Nkherepe Molefe when he came to see her and asked her specifically what had happened. Apart from Makume and Liau, she did not know any of the accused.[23]

At the trial itself, in June 1946, John Makume – elderly, tall and stooped – denied all knowledge of Stephen Thobeha's death and of any conspiracy beforehand. He had not raised the alarm about Stephen Thobeha's disappearance because, although it was reported to him, a man said that he would search for Stephen in two places where he was known to work as a cobbler. He and his councillors Liau Lekhula (No. 10) and Josiel Thoso (No. 13) regularly reported to Mahao Matete when Mahao came home to Morija at weekends from his duties at Matsieng, but he denied any meetings to discuss a murder plot or to take particular action in the immediate aftermath of Stephen Thobeha's death. He even denied any general knowledge of the sinister implication of the word *lenaka* (horn). He had instructed Josiel Thoso to see to it that the body was watched overnight, following its discovery on 16 May. But the body was interfered with and dragged about on the Wednesday night, and this, according to the Attorney-General, 'made it much more difficult to find out whether Stephen had fallen or had been killed'. He denied that he had gone to Raleqheka's and claimed that he could no longer ride a substantial distance on horseback.[24]

Josiel Thoso, the councillor instructed to watch the body, was also closely cross-examined. He described his observation of the position of the body on its first public discovery, cited in the opening paragraph of this case study. The men whom he told to keep watch at the site 'said they would not do it, they were cold, and … the man who gave the order was sitting next to his fire'. Why had he not then ordered certain individuals to watch the body? He had not been instructed to do so by John Makume. But on the following day Makume was annoyed, he said, when he learned that the body had been tampered with and that his orders to watch it had not been obeyed.[25]

Mahao Matete's defence relied on alibi evidence. Nkojoa Mokone had claimed that Mahao Matete had been present at a meeting of the conspirators in Morija on Friday, 4 May, the day before the murder. This was contradicted by Chief Kelebone Nkuebe, one of 'Mantšebo's advisers, who gave evidence that at the relevant time, dusk or thereabouts, Mahao was at Matsieng attending the Paramount Chief. And Ananias Mohasi, a veterinary assistant employed by the government, gave evidence that on the Saturday night, when the murderers were alleged to have taken the severed head to Mahao and consulted him about the disposal of the body, he had been in Mahao's presence from 5 to 11 pm and at no time had the two men been apart.[26] This evidence 'impressed the Court very favourably'.

THE JUDGEMENT

In his summing-up Judge de Beer, a South African, reviewed the Crown case. It relied mainly, but not exclusively, on the story of the one accomplice witness, Nkojoa Mokone. The judge rehearsed that story in detail, and then went on to explain the requirements of the law in respect of the reliability or otherwise of accomplice evidence. The relevant section of the Criminal Procedure and Evidence Proclamation in Basutoland allowed a court to convict on the uncorroborated evidence of an accomplice, provided that there was sufficient evidence of another kind to show that the crime had been committed. On account of the well-established principle, however, that accomplice evidence was actually or potentially tainted, a rule of practice had been laid down by which independent corroborating evidence was required which connected or tended to connect the accused with the crime.[27]

The medical evidence was inconclusive. Eleven days, from 5 to 16 May, had elapsed between death and the discovery of the body and by that time 'the torso of the body was in a most advanced state of decomposition'. 'But the condition of the skull was such as to lend strong support to the theory that that head had been denuded of all flesh and muscular tissue, cartilages like the ear and nose, by some artificial means.' Further, Stephen Thobeha could not have fallen over the cliff while drunk, since the body was not there between his disappearance on the evening of Saturday, 5 May and the discovery of the corpse there on Wednesday, 16 May. Otherwise it would have been noticed by shepherds grazing livestock in the vicinity. So a team of persons must have brought the body to the ledge and placed it there. 'There is also the fact that the shirt which the deceased had been wearing on the Saturday night had completely disappeared. I fail to visualise any fall which would enable a man to retain his coat and overcoat and yet lose his shirt in the process.'[28]

As well as the evidence of the 'Bushman', Kuili Rammotseng, the Attorney-General had relied on the following as evidence corroborative of Nkojoa's story:

1. A murder had in fact taken place, and during the following eleven days the body had been moved to at least five different spots. 'That could only have been accomplished had a team been engaged in so moving the body about.'
2. The boy Tšeliso Shata overheard John Makume remarking, 'This week will not pass without our obtaining that *lenaka*'.
3. Nihi, a young man employed by the chief's mother 'Mamahao, told the court that on the night of Saturday, 5 May he needed matches. He heard voices in another hut at the chief's place, and when he went to that hut he was angrily dismissed by Mahao Matete (No. 8). John Makume (No. 9), Maile Maepe (since dead) and Josiel Thoso (No. 13) were also there. This suggested that a meeting of a furtive and unusual kind was taking place late at night that involved several of the men now accused before the court.
4. A newcomer to the village, Ntemohi, gave evidence that a few weeks before the murder he had been tested by Mahao Matete as to 'whether he could or was prepared to kill a man'. He said no, he was afraid, and was given an alternative task of trapping an illicit beer-brewer. This was at a time when, according to the prosecution, Mahao Matete was seeking to recruit a team of conspirators for the murder.

5. Saul Tšehlana and his lover, 'Matefo, had heard a man cry out at 'Maselloane's rocks, 'Sera and Seleke, why are you killing me?' Nearly a week later Saul Tšehlana entered a spot in 'Mamahao's forest which was generally used as a latrine and 'smelt a bad odour there'. He reported this to Josiel Thoso (No. 13), suspecting it was one of his pigs that had died, and was surprised by 'a stony stare and a frigid silence' from Josiel Thoso, who then blurted out, 'You'll get hurt'. He was afterwards warned by Mahao Matete to say nothing of this matter, otherwise he would be killed.

6. Another woman, Ntsoaki, passed close by a rock cavity in the stream bed near 'Maselloane's, where she noticed a most offensive odour and 'in the dim light she made out what she took to be either a human foot or the foot of a human being with a dusty black shoe on it'. The inference was that the body had been moved from its place in 'Mamahao's forest to the place near 'Maselloane's rocks.

7. Lastly there was Bernice Hlalele's evidence of the visit to Raleqheka's and the corroboration of this by Napo Khashole.

Against this there were several doubts about Nkojoa Mokone's evidence.

1. There was no evidence to support his contention that Mahao Matete was planning to move his village, thus bringing into question the only alleged motive for the murder.

2. Although Nkojoa admitted that Stephen had called out, 'Sera and Seleke, why are you killing me?', he asserted that Sera Mokhajoa, his brother-in-law, was not there. This was contradicted by other witnesses.

3. There was evidence that, in the presence of at least half a dozen prisoners, Nkojoa had told a man in the Maseru gaol that, in order to save his own life, he was going to become a Crown witness and concoct a false story against the other accused. The judge, however, rejected this evidence as being highly improbable.

4. The judge agreed with defence counsel that, had Mahao Matete really wanted to enlist a group of conspirators, he could have done so from men of his own village, Morija, rather than, as alleged by Nkojoa, enlisting men from Phahameng, a village over which he had no authority and with which there had been a boundary dispute.

5. It was implausible that, knowing the conspirators' intention to kill him, Stephen Thobeha had walked along 'placidly and docilely'[29] from 'Maselloane's rocks to Rabele's forest, a distance of nearly 600 metres, passing close to several huts, without, apparently, struggling to escape or even calling out for help.

6. The judge accepted Mahao's alibi evidence. The veterinary assistant, Ananias Mohasi, 'impressed the Court very favourably', and since the judge accepted his evidence that Mahao never left his presence that night it followed that Nkojoa was not telling the truth.

The judge proceeded to deal with the evidence of the 'Bushman', Kuili Rammotseng, whom he described as 'a member of a lowly uncivilised race' and 'a poor specimen of a very poor race'. There were many inconsistencies between his evidence and Nkojoa's. For example, he said that Nkojoa struck the deceased whereas, not surprisingly, this was contradicted by Nkojoa. There were also inconsistencies between the statements he made at the preparatory examination and in the High Court trial, especially about the place where the attack on Stephen took place. The judge took into account the Attorney-General's argument that 'if you pressed an unintelligent person sufficiently long and sufficiently hard you were bound to get him to make statements which were inconsistent with each other', but even allowing for this he was not disposed to place any reliance on Kuili's evidence.

In the light of the inconsistencies and contradictions in Nkojoa's and Kuili's evidence the judge concluded that, although there was reason for grave suspicion against several of the accused, the requirements of the law were not sufficiently satisfied and they were accordingly acquitted. John Makume, however, was culpable as acting headman of the village for not having instituted a proper search for Stephen Thobeha, knowing that he had disappeared, and for having failed to ensure a proper guard over the body on the night of Wednesday, 16 May. The court accepted the evidence of Tšeliso Shata with regard to Makume's remark about the *lenaka*, and also Bernice Hlalele's evidence about Stephen Thobeha's head being brought to her in a saddle-bag. 'As a finding of evidence', the judge said, 'there is to my mind not the slightest doubt that this woman, Bernice, although inclined perhaps to be a little bit theatrical and inclined to focus the spotlight on herself, spoke the truth and nothing but the truth when she said she saw the head of Stephen on that Monday night.' Liau Lekhula, however, was given the benefit of the doubt that, not having been involved in the conspiracy or the murder itself, he might not have known the contents of the saddle-bag prior to his accompanying John Makume to Bernice's home.

Addressing John Makume directly, the judge summed up:

> Making allowance for every factor which I can make in your favour, the position nevertheless boils down to this: Stephen was murdered on Saturday night by having his head severed; murdered and the body concealed in a spot in the village of which you are the Chairman. On the Monday you are seen going about with that head in a saddle-bag, you wanted to have it turned into a 'Lenaka'. Coupled with this we have the evidence of Tšeliso who heard you prophesying that within a week a Lenaka would be obtained and the fact that you singularly failed to carry out your duty as a headman when this body identified as Stephen's was discovered, the very body whose head you had carted about on the Monday. When this body is discovered you adopt this lackadaisical attitude. Applying the requirements of the law in your

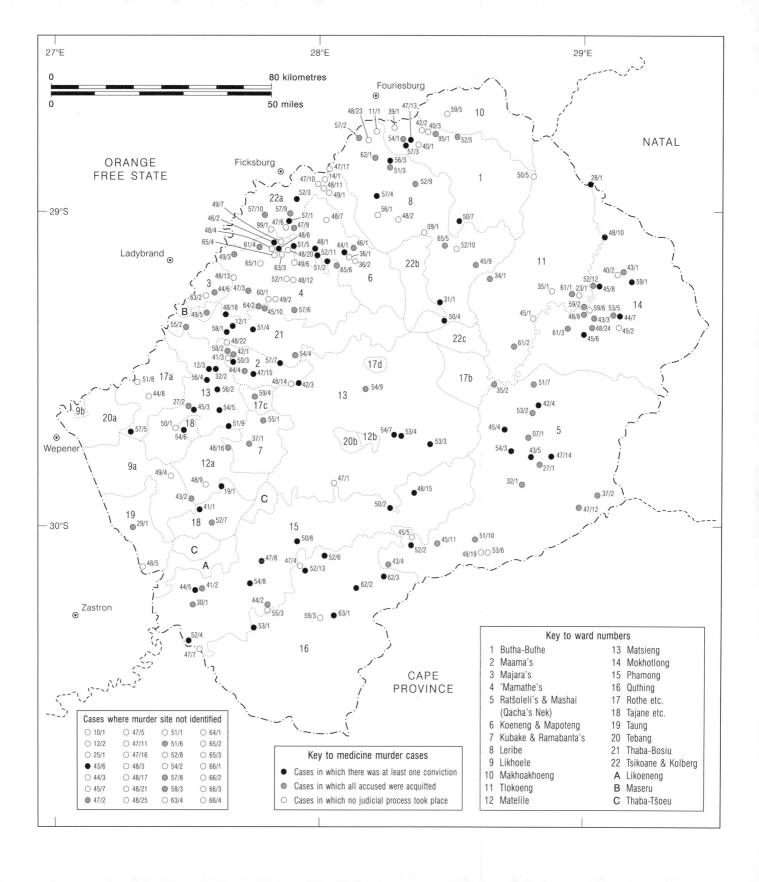

27°E   28°E   29°E

0 — 80 kilometres

0 — 50 miles

Fouriesburg ⊙

ORANGE
FREE STATE

NATAL

Ficksburg ⊙

48/23 11/1 39/1 47/13   59/5   10
57/2   42/2 40/3
         62/1   54/1   95/1 52/5
                   57/3 40/1
47/17   56/3   50/5   28/1
47/10 14/1   51/3
   48/11   52/9   1
48/7 49/1 57/4
22a 52/3   8   48/10
49/7 57/10 57/9 57/1 56/1 48/2
46/2 99/1 47/6 47/9   09/1   40/2 43/1
48/4   48/6   65/5 50/7 52/12 59/1
65/4 61/4 48/1 48/20 44/2 46/1 52/10 35/1 61/1 23/1 45/8
49/3 65/1 63/3 52/11 36/1   11 59/2 59/6 53/5 14
         49/6 51/2 65/6 36/2   45/9 48/8 43/3 44/7
29°S 48/13 52/1 48/12 6 34/1 45/1 61/3 48/24 45/2
3 63/2 44/6 47/3   22b   45/6
B 48/18 60/1 49/2   31/1 61/2
49/5 64/2 45/10 57/6   50/4 22c
55/2 12/1 51/4   17b 35/2 51/7
58/1   21   17d   42/4
58/2 48/22   54/4   53/2 45/4 07/1 5
42/1 50/3 57/7   54/3 43/5 47/14
41/3 44/4 47/15 48/14 13 54/9   27/1
12/3 56/4 32/2 42/3   32/1
51/8 17a 56/2 59/4   37/2
44/8 27/2 45/3 54/5 17c 55/1   47/12
9b 20a 50/1 54/6 51/9 37/1
57/5   18   7 54/7 53/4
9a 48/16   20b 12b 53/3
49/4 12a 19/1   47/1
43/2 48/9   48/15
41/1 52/7   50/2
19 29/1 18 50/6   45/5 45/11 51/10
30°S   52/2 48/19 53/6
C A 47/8 47/4 52/6 45/5
44/5 41/2 52/13 43/4
30/1 54/8 62/2 62/3
44/2 55/3 59/3 63/1
52/4 53/1 15
47/7   16

Wepener ⊙

Ladybrand ⊙

Zastron ⊙

CAPE
PROVINCE

Key to ward numbers

1	Butha-Buthe	13	Matsieng
2	Maama's	14	Mokhotlong
3	Majara's	15	Phamong
4	'Mamathe's	16	Quthing
5	Ratšoleli's & Mashai	17	Rothe etc.
	(Qacha's Nek)	18	Tajane etc.
6	Koeneng & Mapoteng	19	Taung
7	Kubake & Ramabanta's	20	Tebang
8	Leribe	21	Thaba-Bosiu
9	Likhoele	22	Tsikoane & Kolberg
10	Makhoakhoeng	A	Likoeneng
11	Tlokoeng	B	Maseru
12	Matelile	C	Thaba-Tšoeu

Cases where murder site not identified

○ 10/1	○ 47/5	○ 51/1	○ 64/1
○ 12/2	○ 47/11	◐ 51/6	◐ 65/2
○ 25/1	○ 47/16	◐ 52/8	○ 65/3
● 43/6	○ 48/3	◐ 54/2	○ 66/1
○ 44/3	○ 48/17	◐ 57/8	○ 66/2
○ 45/7	○ 48/21	◐ 58/3	○ 66/3
◐ 47/2	○ 48/25	○ 63/4	○ 66/4

Key to medicine murder cases

● Cases in which there was at least one conviction

◐ Cases in which all accused were acquitted

○ Cases in which no judicial process took place

favour in its most rigid form, the Court, the Assessors and myself have not the slightest hesitation in pronouncing you guilty. There is no reasonable doubt in our minds as to your guilt.[30]

DISCORDS

A report in the *Basutoland News* added to the court record:

> After sentence had been passed, the Judge addressed the Court and the Basuto Nation and said the Basuto people, who were the greatest Bantu race, were slowly destroying themselves by the practice of witchcraft. It had been demonstrated repeatedly, he said, that Basuto in responsible positions such as Chiefs and Headmen were practising witchcraft for their own benefit, and if this continued they would force the Imperial Government to take away the powers and authority of all chiefs and headmen. It now rested with the nation whether they would allow themselves to be destroyed.[31]

The Basutoland Progressive Association took up de Beer's call. The editor of its newspaper, *Mochochonono*, described it as a timely warning to the chiefs, sub-chiefs and headmen to refrain from these 'fiendish practices', otherwise their days would be numbered.[32] On the face of it de Beer's warning and *Mochochonono*'s threat were inappropriate in this case, since no chief or gazetted headman had been found guilty, merely an acting headman. Mahao Matete's alibi had been accepted. 'Mantšebo had not even been charged, no doubt because there was insufficient evidence against her. But they both lay under heavy suspicion.

Nkherepe Molefe had no doubt that 'Mantšebo was involved. The doctor, Ntjahali, told him that 'Mantšebo had warned her in advance that she would be asking her to prepare medicine from human *liretlo*. She also gave evidence in open court that Makume and Liau presented themselves as messengers from the Paramount Chief, and the wording of her evidence in the preparatory examination may possibly hint at orders previously given by 'Mantšebo – '[Makume] said that *I had been asked* to doctor this head ...' In the High Court she said she did not know why Makume and Liau had come to her, but acknowledged that she knew 'Mantšebo personally and was satisfied that the two men had been sent by her.[33] The judge was convinced she was telling the truth. It is possible that Makume and Liau were using 'Mantšebo's name without her authority in order to put pressure on Ntjahali, but this would have been a dangerous game to play if 'Mantšebo were not in fact involved. Makume was acting headman for Mahao Matete, and Matete was 'Mantšebo's private secretary. 'Mantšebo was involved in the battle of the medicine horns with Bereng. There were clearly grounds for suspicion against her. The regent resented such suspicion, of course, and – years later – vigorously protested her innocence in this and other cases.[34]

The alleged motive for Mahao Matete's involvement was his proposal to move to another village and his need for a medicine horn to protect and strengthen it. The fact that he was not planning to move his village was one of the factors which led to his acquittal, but if he was operating on behalf of 'Mantšebo he could well have put forward this motive as a smokescreen. It was not unknown for instigators of murder to mislead their accomplices about their motives.[35] Was it a coincidence that Chief Kelebone Nkuebe, who provided Mahao with an alibi for the conspiracy meeting, was one of 'Mantšebo's advisers? It was very unusual for judges to accept alibis. In this case de Beer was clearly impressed by an important chief and a veterinary assistant who were both articulate and presentable.

The case left bitter rifts at Morija between those who believed that the accused had been wrongly charged and those who felt that guilty men had escaped justice. Either way it seemed unjust that Makume only should have been convicted and hanged. There can be no doubt from the court record that Stephen Thobeha was the victim of medicine murder, and that the conviction of John Makume and the acquittal of the other accused were a matter of the balance of evidence one way or the other, some of it conflicting. Nkojoa Mokone and Kuili Rammotseng could not be relied on; Bernice Hlalele, Ntjahali, could. Because medicine murder was a crime committed by a number of conspirators, however, it was inconceivable that Makume alone was responsible for the murder. Was it possible, as Jones surmised, that he had acted for Mahao but without Mahao's knowledge and authority?[36] Again this seems unlikely in the light of the evidence.

There are indications, however, of discord within the Matete family itself. The Matetes belonged to the Bafokeng clan, and Mahao reported to the Bafokeng clan association that his mother and uncle had got him into this trouble. Although details never emerged of what they were supposed to have said or done, it was difficult for Mahao to throw off the taint of suspicion from his family.[37] He also claimed, in view of the long-running rivalry between the two villages, that witnesses from Phahameng had maliciously implicated men from Morija. How could he have overlooked his own people and entered into dirty work with people of Phahameng, over whom he had no authority? In response to his plight, his friend Jeremiah Mofokeng, the head of the Bafokeng clan association, organised a campaign on his behalf and acted as adviser to Basner and Steyn, the lawyers for the defence.[38]

Part of the aftermath of the case was a growing rift between the chieftainship and the church at Morija. Mahao's wife, 'Mampoi, was a Catholic, and in the view of some villagers she strove to use the murder case to drive a wedge between Mahao and the *Kereke ea Fora*. She was also able to stir resentment because the *Kereka ea Fora* had so much land at Morija that it was difficult for the youth to obtain residential and arable sites.[39]

Mahao Matete's career was not blighted, although his widow told us that the case 'used to grieve him a lot because it placed him in a bad light'.[40] He became a magistrate, a trusted government servant, and then superintendent of a leper settlement. In 1968 about 1,000 people attended his funeral at Morija, including the King and Prime Minister Leabua Jonathan. The long family tradition of the Matetes was invoked: just as Paulus Matete had looked after Casalis and Arbousset, the first PEMS missionaries, so Mahao had looked after the missionaries of Morija. The King declared that in his life Mahao had lived for Christ, and in his death he had died for Christ. He encouraged Mahao's son to be like his father: the right-hand man of the chief of Matsieng and the protector of the church.[41]

Some in the Makume family still blame Mahao Matete for John Makume's disgrace. We were told that he was a big and heavy man who could not ride a horse, a point that starkly conflicts with vital evidence given at the time by Ntjahali and another independent witness.[42] The accomplice witness, Nkojoa Mokone, left the area at the end of the case, changed his name and disappeared into the Orange Free State. Otherwise, people said, it was óbvious that vengeance would have been taken against him. His son in Phahameng likewise changed his surname to obscure his family connection. Mpharane Mokoetla (No. 15 accused), Nkojoa Mokone's old neighbour and adversary, acquitted because Nkojoa's was the only evidence against him, remained in Phahameng and died in 1992. The 'Bushman' witness, Kuili Rammotseng, was said to have confessed that he had been prompted by the police to change his evidence between the preparatory examination and the High Court case, but could not afterwards be found to commit this confession to paper.[43]

The doctor, Ntjahali, had claimed to be twenty-two years old at the time of the police investigation. When it was pointed out that she had a daughter of eighteen, she said that she did not know her age. After the case, she moved from her home-base at Raleqheka's in the remote Makhalaneng valley and established a successful career in Maseru. She built herself a fine house on a hill on the south-eastern side of the town. She was consulted by, among many others, a trail of supporters of the Basutoland Congress Party (BCP) who sought medicine to subvert Prime Minister Leabua Jonathan during the Emergency (*qomatsi*) of 1970.[44]

Nkherepe Molefe rose through the ranks and emerged as one of the most senior policemen in the country. He ran the Police Training School in Maseru but did not achieve the top job of Commissioner of Police because he ran foul of Leabua Jonathan. Many years later he looked back on this case as one of his greatest successes. He was particularly proud of the way in which he had prevailed on Ntjahali to talk. 'There was a woman, a *ngaka* by the name of Ntjahali', he told us, 'she was beautiful, I was a bit tempted …'[45]

2

MEDICINE MURDER:
BELIEF AND INCIDENCE

If you go to church and examine each Christian carefully, you will find that most of them hold on with both hands: with one hand they hold the medicine-horn ... and with the other they hold the Gospel of Peace ... You will find that many people, both educated and uneducated, both converted and unconverted, believe in their hearts that personal authority is built up with the medicine horn ...

J. K. Matšaba, 'Liretlo', *Leselinyana*, 22 March 1954
[translated from Sesotho]

This form of crime appears to be increasing alarmingly in Basutoland and there are numerous speculations as to the cause of it. Some are of the opinion that it has always been prevalent in the Territory on its present scale, attributing the fact that more cases of ritual murder are tried before the High Court to the increased efficiency of the police in investigating crime. This argument is most difficult to refute as it is impossible to say, if the crimes were never discovered, whether they actually took place or not.

Basutoland News, 17 August 1948

In the case of medicine murder analysed in Case Study 1 (1945/3), the doctor involved explained to the investigating magistrate that she only used herbs in her practice of medicine, and that she could not 'doctor' the bodily parts of a deceased human being in order to increase the power of a headman or chief. On the other hand, in an earlier case in the same area (1927/2), a different doctor claimed that she routinely used human flesh for medicine on behalf of clients involved in land disputes. The belief that medicine derived from human parts could be used to increase someone's social power is fundamental to an understanding of the conspiracies that we investigate in this book. In the first part of this chapter we explore the roots of this belief in so far as they can be recovered from the historical record. In the second part we seek to interpret the statistical evidence on the incidence of medicine murder, as it is derived from various sources, and ask to what extent the observation made in the late 1940s of 'a very startling increase' in the phenomenon in that decade was justified.

SESOTHO BELIEFS IN MEDICINE

In about 1804, shortly after his initiation, and ambitious to become a great chief, the young Moshoeshoe went to seek advice from Mohlomi, the most successful Mosotho chief of his time. As well as being a chief, Mohlomi was a celebrated doctor and rain-maker, and it was natural that Moshoeshoe should ascribe his success to his medicines and that he should ask the old chief what medicines he used. The reply which he received was unexpected, that a chief should acquire power by treating his subjects well and so attracting new followers.[1] But Moshoeshoe's question was deeply embedded in the Sesotho view of how the world worked.

In Hugh Ashton's formulation, the Basotho made no distinction between medicine and magic.[2] Medicines could be used not just to cure illness, but for many other purposes as well. They could bring rain or good luck; they could ward off hail and lightning, and give protection against witchcraft and evil spirits; they could make warriors brave, thieves invisible and women more attractive to men; they could help litigants in court, and they could strengthen a chief against his rivals and enemies. In short, medicines could be used to give support and reassurance in any situation in which the Basotho urgently needed success or in which they felt insecure or threatened and at the mercy of forces which they could not control. Without medicine a Mosotho felt at a disadvantage, exposed and vulnerable.

Individuals could own and make use of medicines, but the most important were those used for communal purposes, such as protecting the village and doctoring boys in the initiation school or men who were about to go out to fight. In the nineteenth century, according to Casalis, every chief had his own medicine horn and he was 'continually extolling' its virtues. The chief's medicines were smeared on pegs, *lithakhisa*, which were driven into the ground to protect the village against witchcraft and evil spirits, a formality, said Casalis, which was 'strictly observed' when people settled on a new site. During epidemics, or when public affairs were going badly, or when war was threatening, the people were gathered together and the medicine was rubbed into incisions made in their temples.[3] The medicine used for boys in the initiation school, *sehoere*, was given to them to eat with the flesh which they had torn from a living bull.

It was vital for the safety and well-being of any Basotho community that its chief should have powerful medicines, and a crucial role was played by the doctor who advised him on what medicines he should use and prepared them for him. Some doctors, like Mohlomi himself, travelled widely, picking up information about new medicines and impressing the local people with their knowledge. As in any society, there were doctors who enjoyed a high reputation and others who were dismissed as impostors, *lingakana-ntšonyana*, 'little black doctors'.[4]

In the later debates about medicine murder Europeans would often distinguish between herbalists and witchdoctors, a distinction which correlated very roughly with European ideas of medicine and magic. Herbalists were approved of: their knowledge might be limited, but they tried to cure illness through the use of herbs. Witchdoctors were condemned: they were dangerous quacks who claimed they could achieve ends which in fact were outside their control.[5] The Basotho themselves made no such distinction. There might be specialists in one area or another, and some might indeed be bo-ralitlama, herbalists, but they were all lingaka, doctors, working for the benefit of those who consulted them or the community at large. The distinction which was important to them was that between lingaka, doctors who used their medicines for good purposes, and baloi, witches who used their medicines to do harm. The European conflation, 'witchdoctor', had no corresponding Sesotho reference.[6]

It was believed that medicines imparted the qualities of the plants and animals from which they were prepared. Casalis noted that they might contain the thorns of the acacia, which presented an impenetrable barrier, or a few hairs from the mane of the lion, 'the most courageous of all animals', or tufts of hair from the base of a bull's horn.[7] For the chief's medicines these ingredients were burnt down and the ashes mixed with fat to form a black paste, mohlabelo.[8] Since human beings were the most powerful of creatures, medicines containing human flesh and blood were the most powerful of medicines. This, said Casalis, was 'the principal cause of the mutilations which the natives sometimes inflict on the corpses of their enemies', and he described them as bringing home bleeding pieces of human flesh from the battle-field.[9] The more powerful the enemy, it was believed, the more powerful the medicine.

This practice was no doubt of very long standing, and Dr Andrew Smith was told about it when he passed through the country in 1834.[10] The earliest recorded example is the use by Moshoeshoe's followers of the body of the Ngwane sub-chief, Madilika, who had been killed by his own people near Thaba-Bosiu in 1828.[11] It was alleged that some of the British soldiers killed in the Battle of the Berea in 1852 were mutilated, but this was disputed.[12] It is certain, though, that the corpses of several Free Staters were used for medicine in the Ntoa ea Senekane, the war of 1858, and their disfigured bodies, found at Morija, shocked their comrades and provoked them to atrocities of their own. According to one of those who witnessed the sight,

> portions of their skin were found in long regular strips about an inch wide, their scalps were taken off in small round pieces, and one man had the skin of his face torn off with the most barbarous nicety ... other parts of these unfortunate individuals, which need not be mentioned, have been found in a bag, with some traces of mutilation.[13]

There were further mutilations in the *Ntoa ea Seqiti*, the second war with the Free State in 1865–8,[14] and there is evidence that parts of the body of Commandant Louw Wepener, who was killed when he led the assault on Thaba-Bosiu, were cut out and used for medicine.[15] In the Gun War with the Cape Colony in 1880–1 mutilations were again carried out,[16] and the Batlokoa of Chief Lelingoana, former enemies of the Basotho, cut off the head of the magistrate at Quthing, John Austen, and sent it to Letsie, Moshoeshoe's successor, as a peace offering.[17]

Inevitably this practice gave rise to many misunderstandings. The Free Staters who found the corpses of their mutilated comrades at Morija believed that they had been subjected to torture and that their flesh had been cut up into strips of biltong. Fanny Barkly, the wife of a Cape Colonial magistrate, thought that she was confronting a form of cannibalism. 'After killing an enemy', she wrote,

> the Basutos have a barbarous custom, showing, it would seem, that they have by no means lost all traces of cannibalism, even in these enlightened days, as they actually cut out the hearts of their enemies and eat them. After a battle they do this, and eat all the hearts of their fallen foes.[18]

The French Catholic priest and ethnologist François Laydevant argued in 1951 that, because 'the Basotho warriors of old' believed that 'flesh taken from a living being is infinitely more powerful than that from a corpse', they were eager, when they overcame an enemy in battle, to take certain parts of his body before killing him.[19] He had made no mention of this practice in earlier articles, however,[20] and it seems likely that the unnamed informant on whom he relied was drawing inferences from the belief held later by many medicine murderers that flesh from a living being was more powerful than that from a corpse.[21] If the Basotho did try to mutilate their enemies before killing them, this practice would surely have been observed. All the evidence that we have suggests the contrary. The parts taken from the Ngwane sub-chief, Madilika, for example, would have been cut away after he had been killed, and on one occasion in the Gun War a Cape soldier actually witnessed the mutilations being carried out on the corpse of one of his comrades.[22]

In the debates about medicine murder it has not generally been disputed that in the past medicines prepared from fallen enemies were used for the chief's horn and for doctoring the warriors.[23] It has sometimes been denied, however, that the *sehoere* used in the boys' initiation schools contained human flesh, and this has been dismissed as a missionary-inspired slander designed to bring the schools into disrepute.[24] But one of the main purposes of initiation was to make the boys strong and courageous in battle. The man in charge of the school was always an outstanding fighter, the bull that was used should have been captured from another chiefdom, and the most powerful medicine for imparting strength and bravery was that prepared from the bodies of fallen enemies. The evidence for its use comes not just from missionaries and their informants. In the praises of Moshoeshoe's father, Mokhachane, which were probably composed towards the end of the eighteenth century, we are told that as a young man he was captured by his enemies, the Bafokeng of Chief Peo, and that he was held for so long that his people believed that he had been killed. When he returned to his village some jokers suggested that his head should have been cut off and used by his enemies as medicine for their initiates.[25] Many years later, in 1949, two senior chiefs, Matlere Lerotholi and the Batlokoa chief Mosuoe Lelingoana, told the anthropologist Hugh Ashton that 'a special "*lenaka*" [horn] was used for initiation schools', containing 'the flesh of an enemy killed in war'.[26] Our conclusion is that *sehoere* probably did contain human flesh, but whether or not the need for *sehoere* gave rise to medicine murder is a different matter and is considered in Chapter 4 below.

The missionaries conceded that some Sesotho medicines were genuinely effective, but for the most part they derided Basotho doctors as impostors trading on the credulity of simple and superstitious people. Their contempt was part of their rejection of Sesotho culture generally – of initiation, the payment of marriage-cattle, polygyny, the reverence shown to the ancestors, divination, rain-making and burial customs, dancing and the drinking of strong beer.[27]

Despite the rapid spread of Christianity and mission education, most Basotho remained deeply attached to their old way of life. As in many other societies confronted with Christianity – in Europe no less than in Africa over the last 200 years – the old beliefs retained their vigour alongside the new. Many people rejected the missionaries' teaching, and many converts, probably the great majority, saw no inconsistency between their new Christian beliefs and at least some of their old customs and practices. They might have ceased to be polygynists, but they continued to transfer their marriage-cattle in secret. They might worship the Christian God, but they continued to revere their ancestors. They might go to mission doctors and pray to God in time of need, but they continued to make use of Sesotho medicines. There were many different ways of responding to need, not just those prescribed by the missionaries.[28]

As early as the Gun War in 1880–1 Fanny Barkly noted that Christians as well as pagans would go to Thaba-Bosiu to be doctored before battle.[29] And in 1932, more than fifty years later, A. M. Sekese, writing in terms reminiscent of Casalis, said that every village head had a medicine horn, filled with *mohlabelo* and prepared by the doctor, to protect his village from danger.[30] In a National Council debate on medicine murder in 1946 speaker after speaker attested to the continuing and widespread belief in medicine.

'I think', said Joel Mataboe, 'when I look at all these Basuto before us, there is not one of them who has not his horn. Even though they may deny, if you look at them and look at their necks and the back of their heads, you will all find they have marks. There is not one Chief who has no medicine for purifying his village.' William Lethunya acknowledged that 'we may be found to hold in our possession certain medicine which may assist us ... If you go to my side-packs, you may find some medicine which I use against hailstones and the like ...' 'It is true', said Edwin Ntsasa, 'that all these Basutos in the Council believe that witchcraft can help them. Most of the Chiefs in this Council believe that.' And he accused 'Mantšebo herself, 'as well as her junior brothers', of having 'that same faith in medicine'. According to B. K. Taoana, several members of the Teachers' Conference had admitted 'that the Teachers themselves have the same beliefs, and that there was no way of stamping out this evil in Basutoland [i.e. medicine murder] because the people that are supposed to be educated still believe that they can get employment through this witchcraft ... I believe that amongst us, we Basutos', he went on, 'we still believe in witchcraft ... that is not only with the Chiefs, it still exists in the minds of Ministers of Religion and Teachers'.[31]

There were repeated acknowledgements in the pages of *Leselinyana*, the French Protestant newspaper, that practising Christians were still convinced of the power of medicine. In the campaign against medicine murder in 1954 the missionary Albert Brutsch spoke of Christians still placing medicine pegs around their houses, smearing them with *mohlabelo* (which Christians were forbidden to use), and having themselves scarified.[32] In the quotation at the head of this chapter J. K. Matšaba, a teacher at Morija, spoke of many Christians holding the medicine horn in one hand and the gospel in the other.[33] There are many other witnesses to this widespread belief in medicine, even among the converted and the educated. Bennett Khaketla, a teacher at the time, believed in the early 1950s that 'the majority of the people' were in 'this superstitious hold', including teachers who wanted to attract more pupils to their schools, businessmen who wanted to attract more customers to their shops, and even ministers of religion who wanted to attract more converts to their congregations.[34]

Hugh Ashton, writing in the late 1940s, but relying mainly on his fieldwork in the mid-1930s, estimated 'that almost everyone believes in and uses ordinary medicine; that fully half the people use *mohlabelo* and other protective medicines', though only 'a tiny minority' use human flesh; 'and that the vast majority believe in and fear sorcery and witchcraft'. Some people, he said, had become critical and selective, 'but, except for a few, even they share the general belief that medicine can do all that has been claimed for it'. 'Christianity', he concluded, 'has made little headway against belief in medicine in spite of a century of activity.'[35]

EARLY EVIDENCE OF MEDICINE MURDER

The first recorded medicine murder took place in 1895. There were three further suspected cases in 1899, 1907 and 1909, seven more in the 1910s, six more again in the 1920s, and twelve in the 1930s. These murders, it was said, were a new phenomenon. 'This terrible deed is absolutely exceptional in Lesotho', wrote the missionary Hermann Dieterlen, commenting on the case in 1895. When writing about a case in 1912 he described it as 'extraordinary, exceptional, almost an anachronism'.[36]

It seems most likely, as Jones and many others have observed, that medicine murders began towards the end of the nineteenth century when, because of the advent of peace, there were no longer any bodies of dead enemies which the Basotho could use, and those who still wanted to make medicine from human flesh and blood had to find alternative sources.[37] They could have made use of the bodies of people who had died of natural causes, or they could have cut the flesh from the living body and not gone on to kill the victim. For reasons which we can only surmise they turned to murder instead. Just as enemy warriors had been killed, so the victims of medicine murder were killed. Killing, it seems, was essential to the process.[38] It was also, of course, a precaution against being caught.[39]

There is a common assumption that, when the change was made from the use of enemies to the use of selected victims, there was also a change from mutilating dead bodies to taking the parts from the victims while still alive.[40] Later practice, however, was far from uniform. Most murderers preferred to take the parts from the victim while he or she was still alive, but many went on cutting after death as well, while others killed before cutting at all.[41]

According to Dieterlen, the murder in 1895 was generally condemned by Basotho, who said that it formed no part of their customs; many have since claimed that medicine murders were 'borrowed' from the Zulu or 'introduced by Zulu doctors',[42] while others have blamed the Cape Nguni, the Hlubi or the Ngwane.[43] But there is no need to postulate a Zulu origin. Certainly the Zulu believed in the power of human medicine, but, as we show in the Addendum below, so did many other African peoples in southern Africa, among them the Pedi, the Tswana, the Ndebele, the Swazi and the Venda. So too, of course, did the Basotho themselves, and we have already noted the grim logic whereby medicine murders began when the supply of enemy warriors came to an end. It is possible that Zulu doctors helped to establish the practice of murder: as strangers with access to strange medicines, they enjoyed a flourishing reputation among the Basotho,[44] and in two of the earliest cases (1895/1 and 1912/1) it was Zulu doctors, one of them especially summoned from Natal, who advised that murders should be carried out.[45] But Basotho doctors were also involved in some of these early cases.[46] We have already referred to one of them,

'Matumelo, who gave evidence in 1927 (1927/2) that she always used human flesh for preparing medicines in disputes that went to court.[47]

'Matumelo's statement is only one indication among several that during this period there were more medicine murders committed than those that came to official notice. Because many were not recorded we shall never know exactly how many there were, but it is important to explore this issue in order to establish, as far as we can, whether there was really an increase in medicine murder in the 1940s or merely an increase in reported murders.

THE INCIDENCE OF MEDICINE MURDER: 'A VERY STARTLING INCREASE'?

We have been able to identify 210 suspected cases of medicine murder in the colonial period, which ended in 1966.[48] They represent the statistical base for our analysis of investigations and outcomes in Part II of this book. Our sources in individual cases vary from brief and fragmentary press reports to several thick volumes of judicial record, and the confidence with which we can rely on them varies accordingly. Graph 2.1 shows the number

Graph 2.1 Suspected medicine murders per annum, 1895–1969

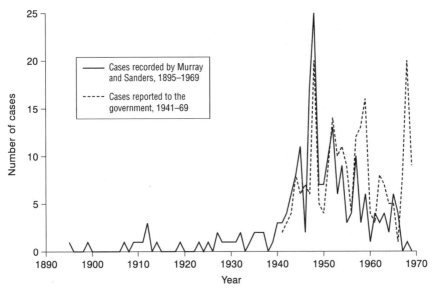

Sources. Suspected cases for 1895–1969 (continuous line) are derived from the Appendix, with one case (1968) outside the colonial period. Cases reported to the government (dotted line) are derived from Annual Reports of the Basutoland Government (CARs) and (after 1966) of the Lesotho Government, and apply only for the period 1941–69 (for 1941–7 they were published retrospectively in the 1948 Annual Report). The figures for 1968 and 1969 are drawn from the Annual Reports of the Commissioner of Police.

Graph 2.2 Bar-chart showing statistics on medicine murder cases by five-year cohorts, 1895–1969

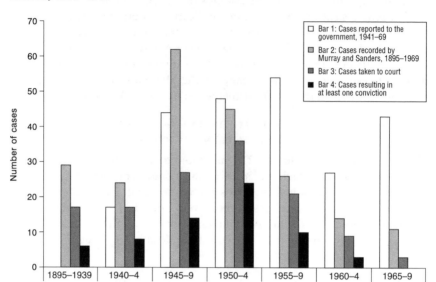

Sources. Bar 1 is the number of cases reported to the Basutoland Government (after 1966 the Lesotho Goverment) in the periods shown, drawn from Annual Reports. Bar 2 is the number of suspected murders committed in the periods shown that we have been able to identify. These figures are drawn from the Appendix, with one case (1968) outside the colonial period. Bar 3 (cases taken to court) and Bar 4 (cases resulting in at least one conviction) are sub-sets of Bar 2.

Note: the years 1895–1939 are aggregated here because of the relative paucity of cases in the early period.

of cases per year for the period 1895–1969.[49] Also shown on this graph is the number of cases of medicine murder reported to the government for the period 1941–1969, drawn from Annual Reports. Both sets of figures would appear to vindicate the observation, common at the time, of a dramatic increase in medicine murder in the mid- to late 1940s. The same sets of figures are reproduced by five-year cohorts in the bar-chart in Graph 2.2 (with the murders in the early period from 1895–1939 aggregated into one column because of their relative paucity in this period). Alongside these, however, are two other sets of figures: the number of cases taken to court; and the number of cases which resulted in at least one conviction. Both these additional sets of figures are drawn from the Appendix.

These four sets of figures in Graph 2.2 are by no means easy to interpret cleanly. For the first four decades of the twentieth century, the relatively thin record in the Appendix may reflect the numerous difficulties of identifying and investigating such crimes rather than the relative infrequency of their commission. The year 1948 was the single year with the most suspected cases in both our records (twenty-five) and official reports (twenty) (Graph 2.1). Otherwise, over the three decades from the early 1940s to the late 1960s, the differences between the number of cases reported to the government and the number of cases recorded in the Appendix vary significantly from one period to another. For cases reported to the government, aggregated in five-year cohorts, the peak was in the late 1950s. For cases in the Appendix, the peak was in the late 1940s (Graph 2.2).

For the 1940s, when we have the benefit of reports by Jones and Ashton, as well as judicial records and newspaper accounts, we have identified more cases than those reported to the government. This is probably because official figures were collected only retrospectively for the period 1941–7, and published for the first time in the 1948 Annual Report.

For 1950–4, when we do not have the benefit of Jones and Ashton, but still have judicial records and newspaper accounts, the discrepancy is small.

For 1955–69, a period embracing the last decade of colonial rule, the number of cases we have been able to identify is only two-fifths of the number of cases reported to the government. It is evident that from about 1955 onwards, although medicine murder continued, far fewer cases were investigated and prosecuted than during the height of the crisis in the late 1940s and early 1950s. In our view the striking discrepancies between the figures reported to the government and our figures from the Appendix for the late 1950s and the 1960s are largely explained by this loss of official enthusiasm for investigation and prosecution of the crime. We explore the reasons for this failure in Chapter 5.

When G. I. Jones was appointed in July 1949 he was asked to make enquiries into 'the proximate causes of and underlying reasons for the apparently increased incidence' of medicine murders. There is, however, no satisfactory discussion in his report of whether the increase which he was being asked to investigate was real as well as apparent. He established that there was an increase in the number of murders reported. He assumed that this reflected an increase in the number of murders committed. In drawing up his list of suspected cases he relied mainly on police and court records. Cases which did not appear in these records were included only if they were 'corroborated from a number of different sources'. He noted that for the early cases, by which he seems to have meant cases before 1930, the records were inadequate, and so it was impossible to draw any definite conclusions from them. For the later years, however, the records 'are fairly complete and show a very startling increase from 1940 onward'.[50]

The records do indeed show 'a very startling increase'. According to Jones' list, there were ten suspected cases in the 1930s and sixty-nine in the 1940s, and our own figures are twelve and eighty-six respectively. Jones' assumption that the increase in murders which came to the attention of the authorities reflected an increase in murders actually committed was shared by most Basotho and whites at the time.

The first newspaper reports of an increase in medicine murders began to appear in 1945,[51] and in July 1946 the editor of *Mochochonono* declared that they had 'occurred with alarming frequency' since 1943, when the discussions began on the proposals to establish a National Treasury and to reduce the judicial powers of the chiefs.[52] A few months later the regent 'Mantšebo issued a circular condemning 'this wave of replenishing medicine horns', a crime which was 'on the increase so much ... that this country is now overcast with a terrible cloud ...'[53] In the ensuing debate in the Basutoland National Council it was common ground that these murders, at least on their present scale, were of recent origin.[54]

In 1948 Chief Theko Makhaola, who had been acting as Paramount Chief in 'Mantšebo's absence, stated that the wave of medicine murders 'started about 1941 ... when the belief became widespread that human blood was necessary for the installation of a chief'.[55] Hugh Ashton was told much the same when he made enquiries in the Mokhotlong District in August 1949: he found a consensus of opinion, he wrote, that these murders 'were a new thing. Practically everyone when asked when they had started, instantly replied "after [Paramount Chief] Seeiso died"', that is, after 1940. When Ashton probed further, the two leading chiefs in the district, Matlere Lerotholi and Mosuoe Lelingoana, acknowledged that there had been earlier cases, but they and others like them nonetheless believed that these murders had 'latterly been occurring on a hitherto unprecedented scale'.[56] Bereng Griffith Lerotholi, writing from the condemned cell on the eve of his execution in August 1949, declared that it was 'seven or eight years today since murders and mutilating of bodies of the dead started',[57] and many of Jones' informants told him that the murders had begun after the Khubelu reforms of 1938.[58]

There was a similar unanimity, it seems, in the discussions of the Round Table Conference on Medicine Murder in 1953. Bennett Khaketla, in submitting his evidence, spoke of 'the present victim-hunting that is sweeping the face of Basutoland like a tornado', while M. B. Photane described it as 'a new "deluge"' which had brought misfortune upon the country. 'In the olden days', Photane wrote, 'doctors were satisfied with the use of fat from a black sheep, today it is not so, they are satisfied with fat from human beings.'[59]

For several years the whole country was in the grip of fear. In November 1945 a correspondent in *Mochochonono* complained that until a few years ago

> one would travel alone for many a mile in Basutoland without fear of being waylaid, and when overtaken by night one could go to the nearest village and ... be sure of kind treatment. But, alas! who can

dare do it today when our country is so infested with human hyenas, and be sure of leaving that village the following morning still alive?[60]

In her circular in 1946 'Mantšebo spoke of travellers being afraid to move around freely,[61] and in the debate in the National Council B. K. Taoana spoke of schoolchildren being afraid to go to school.[62] 'For the past two or three years', Hugh Ashton wrote in 1949, 'the Basuto have become acutely conscious of these murders ... Children's evening singing and dancing are now rarely heard, people hurry home from feasts and beer-drinks to be indoors by dark, and never before have the villages been so quiet. This atmosphere has even affected church attendance at early morning and evening services.'[63]

Even when so many murders were being reported, there were no doubt many more that escaped official notice or that could not be classified as medicine murders on the basis of the evidence available. As previously indicated, it was only in 1948 that the government began publishing the number of reported cases each year. The recording of cases before that time, going back to 1941, was therefore retrospective, and there are good reasons for believing that several were overlooked. In 1940–4, for example, there were seventeen reported cases, but we have been able to identify twenty-four murders that were actually committed during those years.

Bernice Hlalele, alias Ntjahali, the doctor in Case Study 1 (1945/3), told the court that it was common practice to make a horn with human flesh when a chief's son was placed, and she gave the names of two doctors who had told her that this was what they did.[64] In another murder committed in 1945 the doctor involved reassured the murderers by saying that 'this was a small matter, and that he had killed many other people without getting punished'; in 1958 a chief who was instigating a murder boasted of the number of cases he had won because his medicine horn was mixed with human flesh; and in 1961 a witness in another case admitted that he had taken part in eight medicine murders, only two of which we know about.[65]

The silences of the earlier period are as eloquent as the dire pronouncements of the later years. Some of the missionaries, in particular Hermann Dieterlen and Paul Ramseyer, drew attention to medicine murder, but even for them it was more a symbol of the evils of paganism than a serious problem in its own right. When Major Dutton wrote his account of the Basotho in 1923 he seems to have been unaware of the use of human medicine.[66] More significantly, when Hugh Ashton gave his account of 'Medicine, Magic, and Sorcery among the Southern Sotho' in 1943, at that stage he did not think it important enough to be mentioned, even though he knew about medicine murder from his fieldwork in the 1930s, and although he was later to write about it in detail.[67]

In the face of all this evidence it would seem that Jones had ample justification for believing that there had been 'a very startling increase' in the

1940s. Yet even at the time there were more cautious voices, including that of Ashton himself. In the earlier period it is highly probable that the number of murders committed was much greater than the number reported. We have already mentioned the evidence of 'Matumelo, the doctor in case 1927/2. She doctored, she said, whenever there were land disputes, and she had been a doctor long before this particular case. 'Whenever I doctor for a case in court, I want human flesh ... I must have human flesh for such medicines; any human flesh ... Any person would do ... I have previously doctored at Phamong for land disputes, and always with human flesh.' When cross-examined she said that she had used human flesh in three cases and had been successful in all of them.[68] Fifteen years earlier, in 1912, Hermann Dieterlen reported that in the Leribe District a year before people did not dare to travel around near the Pitseng plateau because, they said, an ambitious young chief had set out to make a medicine horn containing the flesh of persons from seven clans. He had already collected five and was now looking for the other two. This might have been a rumour, but, as Dieterlen observed, the mere fact that people were afraid showed that the story did not seem impossible or unlikely.[69] In 1926 his son Georges Dieterlen, reporting on another case, commented on how many people disappeared of whom there was never any further news.[70] Two cases in the 1930s (1936/1 and 1936/2) only came to light because the chiefs concerned carried out a further murder in 1944 and were caught. There were many other chiefs who told their followers that they wanted to 'replenish' or 'freshen' their horns: the wording suggests the possibility that they might have carried out murders before.

Bennett Khaketla, who was born in 1913 in the Qacha's Nek District, believed that there were many medicine murders before the first recorded in 1895, and many during his own boyhood, but that they went undetected because post-mortem examinations were not carried out.[71] According to Hugh Ashton, writing in 1949, his father, who was an Assistant Commissioner, mentioned several times between 1925 and 1933 'that a person had been found dead in suspicious circumstances of a now familiar pattern – i.e. under a kranz over which he was alleged to have fallen while returning home drunk from a beer-drink – but that the body was too decomposed for post-mortem examination to reveal positive evidence of mutilation'. Ashton went on to identify the underlying reason why the chiefs could, literally, get away with murder – the old system of parallel rule, of laissez-faire, of leaving the chiefs to run their own areas with little or no interference from the government. It was the chiefs, he noted, who wanted the medicines prepared with human flesh. It was the chiefs who had sufficient authority to have such murders carried out. And it was the chiefs who could suppress the evidence or prevent enquiries. 'A good deal of the investigation of crime was ... left to them', he wrote, 'and even when the police assisted with such investigations or undertook them on their own, they worked in close collaboration with the chiefs.' All deaths were reported to the Ward Chief, and if the Ward Chief said that he did not suspect foul play no further action was taken:

> furthermore, the power of the chiefs was considerable and they did not scruple to insist on blind obedience and to use their position to threaten possible witnesses into silence. The people were well aware that the government could not afford them material protection against the chiefs' reprisals and so had no option but to submit and hold their peace.[72]

When, in 1949, in advance of Jones' enquiry, Hugh Ashton was given permission by Forsyth-Thompson to examine all the relevant files,[73] he concluded that the recent increase was more apparent than real. It was not so much that the chiefs were committing more murders, as that they could no longer get away with them to the same extent. The first reason that he gave for this was people's greater readiness to report medicine murders to the authorities, because they had become increasingly critical of their chiefs and less awed by them and more prepared to risk their anger by giving evidence against them. Recent reforms, he believed, had encouraged this, notably the Khubelu reforms of 1938, the Treasury reforms of 1946, the creation of District Councils, and the increase in popular representation in the National Council. 'These reforms', he wrote, 'have both limited the arbitrary powers of the chiefs and have shewn that the government is not afraid of them.'[74]

The second, more important reason was the improvement in the efficiency of the police. The whole force had been reorganised following the Pim Report of 1935, since Pim's denunciation of the administration had embraced the work of the police as well. At that time there was no division between the two branches of government. In each of the seven district offices the full white complement was an Assistant Commissioner, a police officer and a clerk.[75] The clerks, who had no police training, could be promoted to police officers, though several police officers began their careers as stock inspectors or in 'other miscellaneous posts'; and the normal channel of promotion for police officers was into the administration. There was no separate head of police: this function was carried out by the Resident Commissioner.

Just as the administration was largely a border administration, so the police were still largely a border force, and there were very few police posts in the whole of the mountain area. At the time of Pim's report the strength of the force was thirteen white officers and 290 Basotho non-commissioned officers and men. The time they could spend on patrolling and investigating crime was restricted because they were expected to help out in other duties, such as tax collection, cattle inoculation and taking messages. Even when they did carry out investigations they could not act independently of the chiefs.[76]

One of the traders criticised the senior policemen for acquiring a 'love of their office chairs'. They 'seldom or never leave their camps, except to travel along the main road in their cars'. Even if a murder was reported the police were not always sent to the scene of crime: in some districts at least 'it devolves upon the chiefs to bring corpse, accused and witnesses into camp. I know of a case recently where the corpse was tied on to a horse and taken in hot weather a three days journey to the magistracy'.[77]

Pim's recommendation that there should be a separate police force under the control of a Commissioner of Police had been accepted. The detachments at the four police divisional headquarters were each placed under the command of a superintendent, and each of the remaining five detachments was placed under the command of an assistant superintendent.[78] During the war the force was allowed to run down, as many officers and men were away on active service – though there was also a marked reduction in crime since 20,000 young men were away on service as well – but after the war it was brought back to full strength. It was still, however, the same size as when Pim reported in 1935.[79]

Even after the shift from parallel to indirect rule the chiefs continued to be responsible for law and order. Indeed the principles of indirect rule required that their authority be respected, and where the police intervened they were instructed to approach chiefs, sub-chiefs and headmen through the proper channels.[80] In other words, the old system would continue: if a murder was reported the police would first have to approach the Ward Chief, and through him the chief of the area concerned, and those chiefs would allocate messengers to help the police in their investigations. These messengers, of course, could then obstruct or mislead investigations into medicine murder when the chiefs themselves or their friends or relations were responsible. In several cases in the 1940s it was found that the messengers allocated to help the police had themselves been accomplices in the murders.[81]

All this changed in June 1946, when 'Mantšebo was persuaded to allow the police to conduct enquiries without reporting first to the Ward Chief, and in November 1947 when they were given authority to conduct investigations by themselves, without any representative of the chieftainship being present. She also gave orders that, if it was necessary to avoid delay, reports of crime should be made direct to the police, not through the chiefs, and that if a body was found in suspicious circumstances it was not to be moved until the police had been called.[82] It was these changes that Ashton regarded as critical. 'This almost revolutionary innovation', he wrote, 'has vastly strengthened the position of the police and tremendously facilitated their investigations.'[83] At the time this appeared to be the case: according to the government's figures, the number of reported cases rose from six in 1947 to twenty in 1948.[84] A third reason, not mentioned by Ashton, might have been the government's enhanced awareness of medicine murder and its determination to stamp it out. The police now gave it a new priority: deaths that were previously ascribed to misadventure were now ascribed to medicine murder.[85]

Several others, notably Forsyth-Thompson, the Resident Commissioner, and the majority, it seems, of the District Officers, shared Ashton's view that the increase in medicine murders was less 'startling' than Jones supposed.[86] But it is difficult to assess the factors to which Ashton attached so much importance – the people's greater readiness to report murders, and the improved efficiency of the police – and the effect of the change in police procedures was less dramatic in the long run than it seemed at first. After the initial rise the number of reported cases fell from twenty in 1948 to five in 1949 and four in 1950 – fewer than the six in 1947 before the change was introduced. This might of course have been due to a decline in the number of murders actually committed, but we have no way of knowing.

Even Ashton, however, thought it probable that, though it was 'far less than is commonly supposed', there had been a real as well as an apparent increase in medicine murder. For the apparent increase he had given two reasons: the people's greater readiness to report murders to the authorities, and the police's greater efficiency. For the real increase he gave two further reasons that would later be emphasised by Jones: the impact of the recent reforms, and the disputes over the paramountcy.[87]

If it can be shown that a large number of murders arose from the causes adduced by Ashton and Jones, the case for a real and substantial increase will be strengthened. But there were other theories put forward about the causes of the increase, especially by the Basotho themselves, and they must all be considered. They arose, not only from the evidence thrown up by the cases, but from white views of Basotho culture and society and Basotho views of the British administration. They form part of the great debate about medicine murder, and indeed about Africa and colonialism as a whole. We turn to that debate in Chapter 3. Meanwhile, in Case Study 2, we analyse in detail the murder that Jones used in his report to illustrate the 'typical' case of medicine murder: that allegedly committed by Chieftainess 'Mamakhabane of Koeneng and Mapoteng.

Case Study 2

'THE CHIEFS OF TODAY HAVE TURNED AGAINST THE PEOPLE': KOMA-KOMA, 1948[1]

> Succession to the Chieftainship is a terrible thing in Lesotho: it causes hatred and violent disputes.
>
> Jingoes (1975: 139)

The village of Koma-Koma lies stretched on a narrow promontory of land above the valley of the Phuthiatsana river, to the north-east of Mapoteng. The track that leads down to it from the plateau above is steep, stony and rutted. On an afternoon in early December 1998, the huts and gardens of the village were sharply etched in summer sun and shadow. Following recent rains, its surrounding fields were green. Half a century before, Koma-Koma was the seat of the ward chieftainship of Koeneng and Mapoteng and the home of Chieftainess 'Mamakhabane Boshoane Peete. She was executed for medicine murder in June 1949. Her eldest son Chief Makhabane took the ward chieftainship to Bela-Bela, several miles north of Koma-Koma, on the other side of the Koeneng plateau. Left at the chief's place at Koma-Koma was a forlorn ruin, the substantial but uncompleted stone house of 'Mamakhabane's husband, Chief Boshoane.

On that December afternoon in 1998 their fourth son, Mohale Peete, the headman of Koma-Koma, emerged from his house nearby to greet his unexpected visitors (KS and CM). He looked dishevelled and bemused. We spoke about the murder that had taken place fifty years earlier. Did he think that his mother was guilty? He pointed to his chest and shook his head in implicit denial that such a thing was possible. Like others both today and at the time, he was convinced of his mother's innocence.

There are several reasons why we examine the 'Mamakhabane case (1948/1) at some length. First, G. I. Jones used it as the 'type' case with which he introduced his report on medicine murder. Second, we have, as well as the court record and the newspaper reports, a detailed account of the murder, published long after the event, drawn from the autobiography of Stimela Jason Jingoes, a man who was intimately acquainted with 'Mamakhabane herself, with some of the other key protagonists, and with the local political circumstances.[2] Third, Chieftainess 'Mamakhabane was the first woman to be hanged for medicine murder, and her case achieved a grisly notoriety for this reason. Fourth, and perhaps most important, the case starkly exhibits two polar positions relating to the interpretation of the evidence given, the conduct of the police investigation, and the corresponding inferences to be drawn about the guilt or innocence of the accused. On the one hand, the judge at the High Court trial noted that the prosecution case against 'Mamakhabane and her accomplices was 'one of the strongest' he had ever tried and 'bristled with corroboration'. On the other hand, Josiel Lefela, for the Lekhotla la Bafo, consistently alleged bribery and torture on the part of the police to extract incriminating evidence against 'Mamakhabane, who was his own chieftainess, and her fellow-accused. These allegations were taken upwards and outwards to London, where leave to appeal against the convictions was sought from the Judicial Committee of the Privy Council, and to New York, where representations were made to the United Nations on behalf of the condemned individuals.

'SOMETHING GOING ON IN THIS VILLAGE'

On the morning of Wednesday, 21 January 1948 a man's body was found at the foot of some low cliffs outside Moqhotsa's village in the Phuthiatsana valley near Koma-Koma. Stimela Jingoes, one of the search party, noticed that the man's teeth were 'grinning bare: he had no lips'.[3] Despite the face being so 'indescribably mutilated' that it was unrecognisable, the corpse was identified by a relative from the shape of the head and from a number of articles found nearby as that of Mocheseloa Khotso, from the village of Mapoteng.[4] Mocheseloa had last been seen alive at a marriage feast on the previous Saturday evening, four days earlier. Having been reported missing, he was found only thirty minutes after the search party was organised. 'We were amazed that he was so near', Jingoes remarked, 'and that he had not been found before. It was quite clear that his corpse had but recently been placed there …' The implication was that he could not possibly have fallen from the cliff on the night when he left the marriage feast.

Jingoes was working as a clerk for Chieftainess 'Mamakhabane. When Mocheseloa's disappearance had been reported to the office, his fellow clerk, Koenyama Cheba, said grimly, 'There is something going on in this village', and reminded him of 'the group that always holds meetings in secret with the Chieftainess'. Jingoes found it strange that, when they went to the spot and found the body, one of that group, Dane Rachakane, was there already, yet he lived at the village of Tsokung, some distance away on the plateau to the north.[5]

Jones' account begins with the wedding feast on the previous Saturday, 17 January:

> Mochesela Khoto sat in a hut drinking beer with Dane Rachakana and a number of other people who had come to a wedding feast in Moloi's village. While the party was proceeding the Chieftainess of his ward arrived with a number of her men, others were summoned from the

party and when they came were told: 'I want you to kill Mochesela for me, because I want to make a medicine horn (*lenaka*) which I will use in the placing of my son. Anyone of you who disobeys this order will be killed.' One of them was then sent to let Dane know that all was ready and when he saw him Dane got up and said to Mochesela 'Cousin, let us go outside for a while'. Mochesela followed him to where sixteen men were waiting for them with the Chieftainess and two of her women attendants. She greeted Dane, reminded him that he had already had her orders, and told the men to seize Mochesela. As one of them caught hold of him, Mochesela cried out: 'My father Pholo, are you going to kill me?' and when he did not reply, continued: 'Let me free and I will give you my black ox'. 'I am not your father and I want you not your ox', replied Pholo. He started to shout, but they gagged him and marched off away from the village, while Dane threw stones to drive off some boys who had been attracted by his shouting. When they reached a satisfactory spot they removed their blankets, stripped deceased of his clothes and held him naked on the ground. An oil lamp was produced and by its light they proceeded to cut small circular pieces of skin from his body with a knife. Pholo cut a piece from the calf of his left leg, another man a piece from his groin, a third from beneath his right breast, a fourth from the biceps of his right arm. The pieces as they were cut were laid on a white cloth in front of Mosala the native doctor who was going to make the medicine, and one of the men held a billy-can to collect the blood from these and later wounds. Then Dane took the knife and with it removed the entire face of Mochesela. He cut right down to the bone, beginning at the forehead and ending at the throat and he finished by taking out the throat, the tongue and the eyes. Mochesela died while his throat was cut. The Chieftainess, who had stood by watching, is then reported to have said: 'I thank you, my children, for having killed this man for me. I know the police will come here to investigate this matter and no-one must tell them about it. If they do, I will kill them in the same way as I have killed Mochesela. Take the body now to the house of Steve [Setene], where it will remain until Tuesday, when those of you who live near will take it to a place where people will see it.' After this she left for her home with two attendants followed by the doctor and another man carrying the billy-can and the pieces of flesh. The rest carried Mochesela's body to Steve's [Setene's] hut where it remained wrapped in his blanket and placed in a wool pack until Tuesday night. Then it was carried to some low cliffs near the village and after some of the clothing had been placed on the grass and on a tree nearby, it was thrown over and then dragged a little further downhill, to be found there the following morning.[6]

Jones' account, published in his official report in 1951, was drawn from notes he had taken from the judicial record of the High Court trial held in August 1948. Jingoes' account was published in 1975, many years after these events, as part of his autobiographical reminiscences. Although in January 1948 he was working as a clerk in Chieftainess 'Mamakhabane's administrative headquarters at Koma-Koma, 'a great rift' had opened up between the Chieftainess and himself on account of his long association with her son, Makhabane, as his tutor, and his alleged interference on Makhabane's behalf in a gathering dispute between mother and son over Makhabane's accession to the chieftainship. Later, however, after 'Mamakhabane had been hanged and Makhabane had become Ward Chief in her place, Makhabane came to believe that Jingoes was

> somehow responsible for his mother's death; either I had omitted to warn her about the consequences of such an act, or else I had informed on her to the police, or perhaps I was the one who encouraged her to kill Mocheseloa in the first place. I have never been sure exactly how he blamed me, but blame me he did.

It is perhaps not surprising that Makhabane's suspicions fastened on Jingoes. He was well known as a doctor, recognised the chiefs' need for powerful medicines, and as for the belief 'that human flesh makes *litlhare* [medicine] of uncommon power' he confessed that 'I, as a *ngaka* myself, although I abhor the practice, cannot say that this is not true'.[7] Jones was told that, according to local gossip, another murder (1948/7) was carried out to supply 'the antidote' to this murder. If this was true, then Makhabane himself, and perhaps Jingoes too, might well have fallen under suspicion. Makhabane was indeed arrested for a medicine murder in 1948, but this turned out to be a 'false alarm'.[8]

In 1952, because of this falling out with Makhabane, Jingoes removed himself to live at 'Mamathe's, the headquarters of the Masupha chieftainship. There, in 1969, Jingoes encountered the anthropologists John and Cassandra Perry, who undertook sixteen months' fieldwork at 'Mamathe's and employed him as their interpreter, adviser and companion. They recorded his reminiscences at length, including his detailed account of the murder of Mocheseloa Khotso.

> The story starts at Maqotsa's village near Koma-Koma on the day of a wedding feast for one of the headman's sons. In the evening Chieftainess Mamakhabane arrived in the village, where the feast was in full swing. She was with three women and three men ... The Chieftainess had her presence announced to Dane Rachakane and Pholo Rachakane, the headman, who summoned some other men. We later learned that when this group had gathered, the Chieftainess said to them, 'I am here. Now we must do what we all decided to do long ago'.

While they sat there, people from the feast came up to greet the Chieftainess. One of them was Mocheseloa. After he had greeted her, Chieftainess MaMakhabane said to him, 'I want you. I must make a *lenaka* out of you ...' When they grabbed him, he screamed to his uncle, Pholo, who was in the group, 'My uncle! Please leave me! I will pay with my big black ox ...'. 'We do not want your ox', Pholo told his nephew, 'we want you.'

All this took place near the cattle kraal of the village, and no one saw or heard except some herdboys. When the Chieftainess and her companions left the kraal with Mocheseloa, they did not go unobserved. When the little boys of the village heard that the Chieftainess had arrived, they rushed to see her, and their curiosity was aroused when they saw Mocheseloa caught and dragged off, struggling, into the dark. The party hurrying away with their victim noticed the boys following, and one called Mzimukulu picked up stones and flung them at the youngsters, telling them to get away. Most of the boys fell back, but Malefetsane Lebetsa still followed after them, stealthily keeping to the shadows, and always behind and to one side of them.

The Chieftainess and her group entered a shallow cave or overhang under some flat rocks. Growing above this cave was a *mosilabele* bush under which the boy Malefetsane crept, squirming right into it until he was quite hidden, and he spied on them by the light of the lantern they had lit. He could hear Mocheseloa still pleading, and he saw Mosala, the *ngaka*, approach him. Mosala's task at this point was to drug Mocheseloa so that his screams would not be heard from afar. The little boy said ... the *ngaka* lit some herbs and made Mocheseloa inhale the smoke.

After that they began cutting his flesh, while Mocheseloa was still alive and too drugged to struggle. The one to cut him first was Dane Rachakane, who cut away his lower lip ... The second to cut was Pholo, the victim's uncle. He wanted the tongue ... The boy lying in the bush watching all this said that while this cutting was taking place Chieftainess MaMakhabane was sitting on a rock nearby with Mosala next to her and a tin in front of her. The pieces of flesh were placed before them in the tin, and Raletsukana was pointing out where the pieces should be placed.

When her turn came, the Chieftainess asked Mzimukulu to cut for her. He did so. Mzimukulu was a butcher in the village, and when he was about to cut, he looked up and said he had never cut a man's joints before, and did not know how. 'Like a cow!' he was told. 'It's just like cutting a cow!' and so he cut.

While Mzimukulu was cutting for the Chieftainess, these were the words she spoke: 'Oh mercy, Mother Maria, for you know I am committing a sin, but I am doing this because I want to be known. I pray to Thy Holy name, that You do not count this as a sin, because I want to keep the Chieftainship of Matšekheng, and not to have it taken by Makhabane. Even after my death, Makhabane must not take the Chieftainship; it must fall on the shoulders of my younger son, Posholi' ...

The pieces of Mocheseloa's flesh in the tin were taken to Koma-Koma to the Chieftainess's place. The body – for Mocheseloa had died at last when his throat was cut away – was wrapped in an ox hide and taken to the house of Setene.

The other details of how Mocheseloa was cut I do not want to talk about. He was related to me, and beloved of everyone, especially of the Chieftainship and of his uncle, Pholo.[9]

Unsurprisingly, there are discrepancies of detail between these two accounts: the one drawn from the judicial record compiled seven months after the murder, but in a manner inevitably detached from the social and political context in which the murder took place; the other drawn – no doubt at the cost of some fallibility of memory after the lapse of more than twenty years – from the recorded reminiscences of a man who was closely caught up at the time in the local political circumstances which preceded the murder, and who heard at first hand the rumours, the embellishments and the conflicting accounts of what had taken place and of who had been involved.

Some of these discrepancies can be resolved by first-hand field investigation. The name of the victim, for example, is given as Mochesela Khoto by Jones and Mocheseloa Foso by Jingoes. We were told at Koma-Koma that his name was Mocheseloa Khotso.[10] The place of the wedding feast is given by Jones as Moloi's and by Jingoes as Maqotsa's [properly, Moqhotsa's]. On our visit to Tsokung in December 1998 we were told that Moloi's homestead was part of Moqhotsa's village – and by a remarkable coincidence the elderly woman who told us, 'Mamokhatsi Rachakane, turned out to have been the eighteen-year-old bride of January 1948, Ntsoaki Moloi, at whose father's homestead was held the wedding feast from which the victim, Mocheseloa Khotso, was seized.[11]

THE INVESTIGATION AND THE PREPARATORY EXAMINATION

Jones' account ends with the discovery of the body on the morning after its disposal. Jingoes takes the story further. Despite the warnings of the chieftainess and the efforts of those involved to hush the matter up,

the murder had been seen by a child [Malefetsane Lebetsa], and who can stop children talking? Rumours about the murder spread first from the school. One little boy, the son of Setene Sebajoa, told his friends, 'In my home, my father and some others came in with Chieftainess 'Mamakhabane. They placed something rolled in cowhide on the floor. They said it was Chieftainess 'Mamakhabane's parcel, and must not be touched by anyone. They told us not to enter the hut it was in. I cannot understand why they said it was a parcel, when Mocheseloa is missing ...'

This particular story spread fast, and it is said that when Setene heard it, he nearly killed his son. 'Do you want me hanged?' he shouted. With stories like this one going around, the murder could not be hushed up, and soon the police knew the whole story of that night.[12]

After the police investigation a preparatory examination took place in May 1948 before Gideon Pott, District Commissioner of the Berea District. Fifteen people appeared, and at the end of the examination, on 19 June, they were all committed for trial at the High Court on a charge of murder. They were listed in the indictment as follows:

1. 'Mamakhabane Boshoane Peete, chieftainess, aged fifty-one, of Koma-Koma.
2. Dane Rachakana, peasant, aged fifty-six, of Rachakana's [Tsokung]. (Jingoes, who was from Tsokung himself, identified him as a cousin (*motsoala*) of the victim.)
3. Raletsukana Posholi, peasant, aged fifty-eight, of Koma-Koma.
4. Mosala Kolotsane, native doctor, aged forty-three, of Rachakana's [Tsokung]. (It later emerged that he carried a certificate from the African Dingaka Association in Pretoria.)[13]
5. Pholo Tjotsi, native doctor, aged forty-nine, of Mapoteng. (Also known, according to Jingoes, as Pholo Rachakane, and described by him as the headman of Moqhotsa's.)
6. Mashapha Pokonyane, native doctor, aged fifty-seven, of Mapoteng.
7. Mohobosane Mohlokaqala, peasant, aged forty-eight, of Koma-Koma.
8. Lefu Sebajoa, peasant, aged forty-five, of Moqhotsa's.
9. Setene Sebajoa, peasant, aged forty-six, of Moqhotsa's. (Obviously the 'Steve' mistakenly transcribed in Jones' notes.)
10. Liphalana Mabote, peasant, aged thirty-nine, of Nthoba's.
11. Molefi Makhobalo, builder, aged forty-two, of Makhobalo's.
12. Molato Rachakana, peasant, aged thirty-five, of Rachakana's [Tsokung].
13. Kooe Mepha, peasant, aged fifty-two, of Rachakana's [Tsokung].
14. 'Malibuseng Ntho Weto, housewife, aged twenty-seven, of Koma-Koma.
15. 'Maseitebatso 'Malumise Posholi, housewife, aged thirty, of Koma-Koma.

According to Jingoes there was a man called Mzimukulu who threw stones at the boys to drive them away and who 'cut' Mocheseloa for

'Mamakhabane. No such name appears in the court record and, according to Jones, the man who threw the stones was Dane Rachakane. It is impossible to identify Mzimukulu with any certainty, but he clearly was not Dane Rachakane whom Jingoes knew well and who appears in his narrative as someone entirely different from Mzimukulu. The most plausible possibility is that he was Pholo Rachakane, also known as Pholo Tjotsi. In Jones' notes on the case Pholo Tjotsi (No. 5), referred to by Jingoes as Pholo Rachakane, is identified as Letebele and, specifically, 'Mtikulu' [Mtimkulu] by clan.

THE HIGH COURT TRIAL AND THE JUDGEMENT

The High Court trial was held in August 1948 before Sir Walter Harragin. According to the prosecution, nineteen persons in all were involved in the murder: the fifteen accused and four accomplice witnesses, the last of whom was not called at the trial either by the prosecution or by the defence, but was called by the court itself, and whose evidence was not taken into account by the judge because he was a simpleton with a speech impediment. The two women indicted, 'Malibuseng Ntho Weto (No. 14) and 'Maseitebatso 'Malumise Posholi (No. 15), were discharged at the end of the Crown case on the grounds that they had merely attended Chieftainess 'Mamakhabane as her 'ladies-in-waiting' and had taken no part in the murder.

In his judgement Harragin went over the case for the prosecution against the remaining thirteen accused. It relied mainly on three accomplice witnesses – Mahlomola Moloi, Mafikeng Lekeletsane and Motsemoholo Rachakane – supported by the evidence of eight independent witnesses who had not been involved in the commission of the crime. Harragin dealt very shortly with the law on accomplice evidence because he considered it to be so well established.

> In this country an accomplice's evidence can be corroborated by another accomplice, but the Crown says that even that is not of importance to them in this case, because they call eight other independent witnesses who corroborate some particular detail of the accomplice's evidence.[14]

The judge agreed with the prosecution on this point. Because of the strength of the evidence in this case the requirements of the law on accomplice evidence were more than adequately met.

There was some conflict of evidence over the degree of mutilation that had taken place. Dr Robert Ogg of Teyateyaneng, who conducted a postmortem on the day after the body was discovered, found it in an advanced state of decomposition, and maggots had infested the wounds.[15] Although the extent of decomposition made it impossible for Dr Ogg to be 'as helpful as doctors usually are in these cases', he was able to give his opinion that the deceased died of haemorrhage, and that a sharp knife had been used to skin the face, cut the throat and remove the tongue. 'This evidence', remarked the judge, 'disposes of the possibility of death from natural causes.' Whereas Ogg found no clear evidence of mutilation other than of the face and throat, a number of accomplice witnesses claimed that various circular pieces of flesh had been cut from an arm, the groin, a leg and the breast. Harragin was troubled by this discrepancy, but concluded that by the time the doctor was able to examine the body, four days after the murder, 'it was almost impossible to say whether there had been wounds or not'.

Harragin then summarised the evidence of the first accomplice witness, Mahlomola Moloi, 'who proved to be a very impressive witness'. This was along the lines spelt out by Jones in his report as quoted earlier. The two other accomplice witnesses, Mafikeng Lekeletsane and Motsemoholo Rachakane, gave similar evidence.

The independent witnesses gave the following important evidence:

1. A boy, Malefetsane Lebitsa, was outside the village near the spot where the victim was alleged to have been caught; he overheard someone calling out begging his father not to kill him and offering him an ox; as the group of people moved away, his presence was discovered and someone threw stones at him. He was with another boy, who could not now be found. (Malefetsane was evidently the same boy who, according to Jingoes, followed the perpetrators, hid above a cave and actually witnessed the mutilations. These were probably embellishments that flowered in the reconstruction of events by the boy himself, or by local people to whom he told his story, or by Jingoes.)

2. A woman, 'Mamona Moloi, saw Setene Sebajoa (No. 9) approach the hut and talk with Dane Rachakane (No. 2). Then she saw the victim being taken by Dane Rachakane towards a crowd a little way off. She heard someone scream out asking his father what he was doing and offering him his black ox, and she heard a voice which she recognised as that of Pholo Tjotsi (No. 5) saying, 'I do not want your black ox'.

3. Another woman, 'Mamorero, saw Dane Rachakane leaving the hut with the deceased.

4. Another woman, 'Mapontšo, 'who was rather a stupid, dull, but very definite witness', saw a group of people, recognised the voices of Setene Sebajoa and Molefi Makhobalo (No. 11), and heard someone screaming out and offering a black ox.

5. Then there was the evidence of two little boys, Ketseletso, the son of Setene Sebajoa, who was about eleven or twelve years old, and Likotsi, a little herdboy who was sleeping with him on the night of the murder. This related to what Harragin regarded as 'one of the most astounding facts of the case'. According to the accomplice witness, Mahlomola Moloi, when the perpetrators had taken the corpse to a hut belonging to Setene

Sebajoa, Sebajoa woke up the two boys and took them to see the dead body. The two boys confirmed this account. Harragin noted:

> Now I have given this matter deep thought, and it occurs to me that No. 9 Accused, if he did it, thought that it was better that these children should be shown the body and warned that they were not to tell anybody about it, than that they should, the next day, discover the body for themselves and go shouting the strange news all over the village. This of course is mere supposition. Whatever the explanation may be the fact remains that the children swear that they were shown the body.[16]

The judge then went through the cases for the defendants. Several of them put forward alibis which were supported by witnesses. Others said they were so drunk that they remembered very little of what happened and slept the night in the hut at the feast. Mashapha Pokonyane (No. 6) claimed that there was a police conspiracy against the accused and that the witnesses had all been 'coached'. In view of the strength of the prosecution's case all these defences were rejected. Harragin concluded:

> I can say without hesitation that it is one of the strongest cases for the Crown that I have ever tried ... One hesitates a long time before accepting accomplices' evidence at its face value, but this case bristles with corroboration. Take, for example, the case against No. 2 [Dane Rachakane] and No. 9 Accused [Setene Sebajoa]. Two perfectly independent witnesses tell the Court that after being called by No. 9 Accused, No. 2 Accused went out into the night with the deceased towards the crowd of people collected and the cries that took place, which is exactly what the accomplices said happened. With regard to No. 9 Accused, the Crown can hardly go further than call a man's own son to corroborate the all-important fact that on that night there was in fact a corpse in No. 9 Accused's rondavel. It is inconceivable to me that conspirators who, for some reason, wished to cause the death by hanging of those people, could have thought of procuring a man's young son to give evidence against him.[17]

The judge had no hesitation in finding all thirteen guilty. The statutory sentence was death by hanging, but in his confidential comments to the High Commissioner after the judgement he divided the accused into four groups, describing different degrees of guilt and recommending different sentences accordingly. Chieftainess 'Mamakhabane was 'the evil genius behind the murder'. Dane Rachakane was her 'principal executive officer', responsible for all the details of the plot, and the chief executioner. They should both be hanged. No. 3 Accused and all the others who 'took some part in the actual killing, either cutting or collecting the pieces of meat, holding the light, etc.' should be given life imprisonment, by which he meant fifteen years with hard labour. Finally, Nos. 10, 12 and 13, who though present were not proved to have played an active part in the murder, should serve seven years' imprisonment.[18] These recommendations were accepted by the High Commissioner.

STRUGGLES IN THE MAKHABANE CHIEFTAINSHIP

The judicial process 'screened out' the political contexts in which medicine murders took place. Accused persons and witnesses were stripped in court of their social and political identities, their individual histories and the broader circumstances of the commission of such crimes. The prosecution concentrated solely on the evidence relating to the involvement of the accused in a chain of linked events leading to the death of a person. In this case, therefore, it is very valuable to have Stimela Jingoes' detailed reminiscences relating to the history of the Makhabane chieftainship. They offer an unflattering portrait of Chieftainess 'Mamakhabane herself, and a lively account of her immediate preoccupations and resentments, that go a long way beyond the judicial record in their capacity to explain what actually happened. They show that medicine murder was one further method among other methods, albeit of a particularly brutal kind, for the prosecution of long-standing disputes familiar in the history of chieftainship in Lesotho.

Lesaoana, the son of Moshoeshoe's younger brother Makhabane, was allocated the area of Koeneng and Mapoteng as his chiefdom.[19] He was succeeded by his son Peete; Peete was succeeded by his son Mitchell; and Mitchell, in 1922, was succeeded by his son Boshoane. Boshoane succeeded only after a bitter dispute among the Sons of Makhabane which was eventually settled in the colonial courts. He was remembered by one District Commissioner as 'cheerful, fat and jolly'.[20] In 1940 the official report on the chiefs of Basutoland noted that his health was very poor, that at one time he had been a drunkard, but that he had recently improved in that respect. He was described as 'dilatory and unprogressive'. He could not be considered a good chief and his people did not respect him.[21]

Stimela Jingoes was of Swazi origin. At some time after 1868, when the boundaries of Basutoland were fixed, his grandfather Ngolozani came to settle at Tsokung, where he plied his trade as a blacksmith. He used to strengthen his spears with medicine, and grew wealthy as a result of his trade as a smith and his additional skills as a doctor. Jingoes himself was born on the same day as Chief Boshoane, and he was appointed as Boshoane's *letona* (adviser or right-hand man). For ten years, however, between 1927 and 1937, Jingoes worked for the ICU, the Industrial and Commercial Workers' Union, in South Africa. When he returned to Basutoland in 1937 he did not immediately work for the chieftainship but became a teacher at the African Methodist Episcopal Church, where one of his pupils was Boshoane's son,

Makhabane. In February 1940 he finally became a clerk to Chief Boshoane at Koma-Koma. Boshoane died at the end of 1942.[22]

Boshoane's principal widow, 'Mamakhabane, assumed the regency, and Jingoes continued working at Koma-Koma as one of her clerks. In the late 1940s discord set in when Makhabane wanted to return home from school to claim his father's position. 'Mamakhabane wanted him to finish his education, but Makhabane was determined to come home. 'I supported Makhabane in his quest for the Chieftainship', Jingoes observed, 'and so fell into disfavour with his mother.'[23] On his return Makhabane reported to Nkuebe Mitchell, his paternal uncle, who 'saw at once that his sister-in-law, the Chieftainess, had become fond of power and was not going to give up her position without a struggle'.

'Mamakhabane insisted that Makhabane could not be installed as chief until he was married, and then there were disputes about the woman he wanted to marry. The rift between 'Mamakhabane and Jingoes deepened. According to Jingoes,

> Whereas before she had included me in all her plans and taken my advice on every subject, she now hated me and saw me as Makhabane's man who had stabbed her in the back. In some ways this was very lucky for me … She allied herself with a *ngaka* to commit a tragic deed. We had noticed for some time that she had been holding secret meetings with a group of men who were not her regular advisers, but although we suspected her of some new ruse we could not guess at the depth of her desperation, nor at how ruthlessly ambition had seized her.[24]

At her trial the accomplice witnesses said she told them she needed medicine to assist with the placing of her son Makhabane, but it is clear both from the official correspondence that Jones was able to see[25] and from Jingoes' reconstruction of events that the opposite was the case. She needed medicine to assist her to prevent the installation of Makhabane as chief.

ALLEGATIONS OF POLICE MISCONDUCT

In his account of the case Jingoes made no mention of any allegations of police misconduct. On the contrary, he described Lieutenant Castle, the officer in charge of the case, as 'a fine man, and sensible of the gravity of his task'.[26] In the trial itself only one of the accused, Mashapha Pokonyane (No. 6), made a serious issue of such allegations. Pokonyane, alone of the accused it seems, belonged to Lekhotla la Bafo – he described himself as 'a very staunch member' – and in his determination to present his complaints before the court he dispensed with his legal adviser, du Preez, 'because he would not use this ill-treatment as a defence'. Two of the other accused, Raletsukana Posholi (No. 3) and Molato Rachakane (No. 12), also claimed later that they had been ill-treated, but Raletsukana's lawyers were said to have advised him it would be 'useless' to raise the issue in court.[27] Immediately following the case, however, these allegations dominated the official correspondence. We deal with the issue of police conduct generally in Chapter 8 below. Here we confine our discussion to the particular circumstances of the 'Mamakhabane case.

In the trial Mashapha Pokonyane alleged that one of the accomplice witnesses, Mahlomola Moloi, had been offered 'a large sum of money and possibly a pension for life' by Lieutenant Castle in order to induce him to incriminate Chieftainess 'Mamakhabane. The judge refused to believe this allegation. He pointed out that,

> whatever may have been said about the accomplices' detention by the Police before they made their confessions, there has been no suggestion by anyone as to why the other witnesses who came from Moloi's village should voluntarily give evidence which makes the accomplices' evidence so conclusive. They have nothing to fear, they were never going to be charged with any offence, they were not detained by the Police. I therefore reject the evidence for the defence without any hesitation ...[28]

These allegations about police bribery and coercion, and other similar allegations, were developed in the immediate aftermath of the trial by Josiel Lefela in a speech in the National Council on 20 September 1948, in which he asserted that 'the treatment made by the Police to the people is very terrible and tortuous'. In response to the Resident Commissioner's insistence that he be specific in his accusations, Lefela introduced a series of charges in respect of the 'Mamakhabane case, referring to the three accused persons above.

> A man called Mashapa Kokonyane [sic], he told me that at Teyateyaneng where he was kept ... in a very dark lock-up he never saw the light of day and he, Mashapa, was asked by the Police Officer Mr Castle that he must say that it was 'Mamakhabane who ordered him to commit the murder and that he would pay him £80. He said that Mr Castle said he would get a pension of £3 a month if he only said that 'Mamakhabane ... ordered him to do this. And the man called Raletsukana, he also was promised £20 if he said that 'Mamakhabane had committed the murder .... The other man is Molato Rachakana. He says that Lieutenant Castle showed him money, a red bag full of bank notes, and said, 'Here is your wealth if you will only say that the Chieftainess committed this crime' ... Mashapa and another complainant say they were locked up in a very cold house and where there was no food ... Now when a person, because of cold and starvation, when he wants to follow the Police's wishes, then the Police turn round and say that the man made a

voluntary statement. The voluntary statement is merely caused by the cold and the starvation that they have suffered.[29]

These allegations relating to the 'Mamakhabane case assumed a wider significance and reached a wider audience for two reasons. First, there was a significant overlap both in chronology and in the people involved between the 'Mamakhabane case, arising out of a murder in January 1948; a case of arson at Roma, arising out of an incident in August 1947; and the second case involving Chiefs Bereng and Gabashane, arising out of a murder committed in March 1948 (1948/6), which is analysed below in Case Study 3. Second, through persistent agitation by the Lekhotla la Bafo and the involvement of Michael Scott, an Anglican priest based in Johannesburg, questions rooted in the local arena of Mapoteng spread swiftly outwards into the national arena and thence into the international arena. Josiel Lefela and his colleagues played with needling perseverance upon the nerves of the British administration in Basutoland at every level.[30] Their campaign significantly raised the stakes in the administration's efforts to put an end to the scourge of medicine murder.

Mapoteng was Josiel Lefela's home, and he was a subject of Chieftainess 'Mamakhabane. Mapoteng was also the headquarters of the Lekhotla la Bafo, which despite its earlier criticisms had drawn the senior chieftainship into an alliance with itself over the issue of medicine murder. In the winter of 1948, having been arrested on a charge of arson, Lefela and other executive members of the Lekhotla la Bafo approached Michael Scott in Johannesburg for assistance with a message 'scrawled in pencil on a grubby piece of paper'.[31] Scott had a reputation for taking up unpopular causes on behalf of oppressed Africans. He had recently campaigned on behalf of squatters at the Tobruk camp on the edge of Johannesburg and on behalf of viciously abused farm labourers in the Bethal District of the Transvaal. He had also taken up the cause of the dispossessed Herero of South-West Africa.[32]

Despite the pressure of other commitments Scott travelled to Basutoland on 21 July 1948. He was accompanied by Solomon Burland, a Johannesburg attorney, and Jack Leviton, another Johannesburg attorney and a member of the Society for Peace and Friendship with the Soviet Union. During his visit he was in close association with Josiel Lefela; Thomas Mofolo, the well-known author, now a businessman and close adherent of Chief Gabashane; and Mr Matlosa, a staunch follower of Chief Bereng, who was also described by the police as a 'former insurance agent, butcher, and suspected trafficker in illicit liquor'.[33] Scott visited Mapoteng where, 'in a little mud hut, in an atmosphere of extreme nervousness and apprehension', he was 'told the version of the affair [the Roma arson case] which the relatives of the accused appeared to believe. They maintained that the Lekhotla la Bafo was very unpopular with the police, who were for the most part South Africans, on account of its determination to oppose any move by South Africa to incorporate the territory into the Union'.[34] Scott was sufficiently alarmed by what he heard at Mapoteng to pursue his own investigation into the possibility that the police had systematically intimidated witnesses or sought to suborn them, not just in the Roma arson case, but in medicine murder cases as well.

The Roma arson case arose out a fire on 30 August 1947 at Roma College, then both a boys' high school and a teacher training college, in which three students were killed. Suspicions centred on the Lekhotla la Bafo. One of its members, Harold Velaphe, was arrested on 22 May 1948 and signed a statement to the effect that Josiel Lefela had masterminded a plot to burn the college at Roma and had sent out two parties to do so. Velaphe escaped from police detention on 27 June 1948 and went back to Mapoteng to warn his comrades of what was happening. He claimed that he had been kept in solitary confinement in a cold and draughty cell, was so hungry and thirsty that he drank his own urine, and was told by the District Commissioner, Gideon Pott, that if he refused to sign a written statement drawn up for him by the police he would lose his life. Josiel Lefela's younger brother, Maphutseng Lefela, published these allegations, and similar accusations by other accused, in the *Inkululeko* newspaper, in which the Roma arson case was compared with the Reichstag fire. The aim of the British authorities, it was said, was 'to establish a fake "Communist menace" as an excuse for repressive measures'. The case was linked, it was said, with charges of medicine murder against those chiefs 'who are not prepared to adopt a servile attitude to the administration'.[35]

Josiel Lefela and his brother Maphutseng also sent cables alleging illtreatment to the High Commissioner in Pretoria, to the Foreign Office and the Dominions Secretary in London, and to the United Nations in New York. Velaphe was re-arrested on 2 July, whereupon he retracted these allegations and adhered to his original statement. Shortly afterwards Josiel Lefela and several others were arrested, at which point the frantic message was sent to Michael Scott.[36] Following his visit to Basutoland Scott returned to Johannesburg to secure the services of a lawyer to defend the men arrested.

As soon as he had done this, Scott drove back to Basutoland. During this second visit he interviewed several other prisoners in the gaols at Teyateyaneng and Maseru on 10 and 11 August 1948, a week before the 'Mamakhabane case was set down for hearing in the High Court. He also visited 'Mamakhabane herself. 'The chieftainess', he recorded, 'had a rosary in her lap and when I said that I hoped the whole truth would be told in court and that justice would be done, she replied enigmatically, "How will it help us to tell the truth in that court? Only if God helps us shall we have justice".'[37]

As a result of these interviews Scott summarised the specific allegations relating to four of the accused in connection with the 'Mamakhabane case.

1. With regard to Mashapha Pokonyane (No. 6 accused) he repeated what Josiel Lefela had alleged in the National Council (quoted above), that Pokonyane was offered £80 and a pension of £3 a month if he would incriminate Chieftainess 'Mamakhabane. Pokonyane refused to sign such a statement. Scott also recorded the allegation that Pokonyane was 'taken to the house where they are tortured where he was kept for over two months of sufferings'.

2. With regard to Raletsukana Posholi (No. 3) Scott repeated Lefela's allegation that Raletsukana was promised £20 if he incriminated 'Mamakhabane but added that when he refused he 'was put under torture for fifty-four days'.

3. With regard to Steyn [Setene] Sebajoa (No. 9) Scott recorded the allegation, not mentioned by Lefela, that he was tortured for over a month after he had refused to implicate Chieftainess 'Mamakhabane.

4. With regard to Mosala Kolotsane (No. 4) he recorded the allegation, again not mentioned by Lefela, that he was forced for a month and three days to implicate Chieftainess 'Mamakhabane and was threatened that he would otherwise be killed.[38]

From this point onwards the campaign broadened. Maphutseng Lefela wrote to Ernest Bevin, the British Foreign Secretary, and Trygve Lie, Secretary-General of the United Nations, describing the evidence of police coercion of witnesses, with specific reference to the three cases (the Roma arson case, the 'Mamakhabane case and the Bereng and Gabashane case).[39] The Basutoland Commissioner of Police, A. F. Apthorp, indignantly rejected these allegations of malpractice. He pointed out that the accused in all three cases had been together in Maseru gaol. They had 'concocted' the allegations, he claimed, and many were guilty of perjury. He defended the practice of detaining witnesses and suspects for long periods, and declared that in no circumstances would he tolerate 'third degree methods in the force'.

Meanwhile, in the Roma arson case, while all the other accused were acquitted, Velaphe was found guilty and given a four-year sentence, and in February 1949 Maphutseng Lefela was tried on a charge of contempt of court for his article in *Inkululeko*. In his defence he called not just Harold Velaphe and two of the other accused in the Roma arson case, but Moloi Ntai and Fusi Rakokoli, two of the accused in the second Bereng and Gabashane case, and Mashapha Pokonyane, Raletsukana Posholi and Molato Rachakane, the three accused in the 'Mamakhabane case to whom Josiel Lefela had referred in his speech in the National Council. The general tenor of their evidence was that before being formally charged they had been kept for long periods in small, dark, cold rooms either attached to or close to the police charge office at Teyateyaneng; that they had been poorly and irregularly fed, so that they became starved and thin; that they had not been given blankets to keep them warm; that latrine buckets were not provided; that they were let out only to go to the toilet; and that pressure was brought on them to incriminate either Lefela in the Roma arson case or the chiefs concerned in the medicine murder case. Against this the District Commissioner, Gideon Pott, the Medical Officer, Dr Ogg, and various members of the police force and prison service gave evidence that the accused made no complaints at the time; that they always seemed in good spirits and healthy; that ample food was regularly provided; that Velaphe's confession was freely and voluntarily made, and no bribes were offered to any of the accused. The District Commissioner trying the case described Velaphe's allegations as 'wild and scurrilous' and Maphutseng Lefela's article as 'scandalous'. He found Maphutseng guilty and sentenced him to a £50 fine or one year in prison.[40] (Maphutseng won his case on appeal, the judge finding that there was no proof that he had written the article, and that at the time when it was written Velaphe had not been charged with any crime.)[41]

The question of alleged malpractice on the part of the police is discussed at length in Chapter 8. Here it is sufficient to note that, despite Apthorp's impassioned arguments, the High Commissioner, Evelyn Baring, insisted that the prolonged detention of suspects should be stopped.[42] Moreover, although the District Commissioner trying Maphutseng Lefela had dismissed all the allegations about police misconduct, Judge F. E. T. Krause concluded that 'improper methods' had been used by the police in forcing a confession from Harold Velaphe in the Roma arson case.[43] For three hours he was questioned repeatedly, even though he had denied all knowledge of the crime. If such methods were used in the case against Velaphe, there is reason for believing they were used in medicine murder cases as well.

At the end of 1948 Michael Scott took his accumulated evidence to the House of Commons and to the Commonwealth Relations Office in London. On 24 December he sheltered in a doorway from the 'drizzling mist' of Parliament Square to re-read his covering letter to Philip Noel-Baker, the Secretary of State. 'The African tragedy being enacted in Basutoland seemed almost unbearable on that Christmas Eve', he wrote later, 'not knowing where the truth lay in all the conflicting allegations by chiefs and people and Government'. He urgently requested a Commission of Enquiry, 'since there are more than a score, perhaps several score of persons who have been sentenced or are awaiting trial on the charge of ritual murder …' He also asked, pending the establishment of such an enquiry and the emergence of its findings, for stays of execution.[44]

Scott's allegations were taken up by Colonel Frank Byers, MP, who made representations to Patrick Gordon Walker, Noel-Baker's Under-Secretary of State at the Commonwealth Relations Office. A meeting took place on 11 January 1949 between Gordon Walker, Byers, Scott and Mr Irvine of the Society of Friends. Officials found Scott 'a somewhat unbalanced person', and the allegations about the conduct of the trials were firmly rejected. There could be no question of stays of execution, but the idea of conducting an enquiry was already under consideration.[45]

THE FAILURE OF APPEAL

In November 1948 four of those convicted in the 'Mamakhabane case – the Chieftainess herself (No. 1 accused), Dane Rachakane (No. 2), Mashapha Pokonyane (No. 6) and Mohobosane Mohlokaqala (No. 7) – wrote to the Privy Council in London to seek leave to appeal against their convictions. In a letter couched in the distinctive style of Josiel Lefela, they alleged solitary confinement in cold and draughty cells where blankets and latrine buckets were denied them, where their food was just a little bread, and where they were pressed to accept slanderous allegations dictated to them by the police.[46] The grounds of the appeal, forwarded by Lefela himself in default of lawyers who were willing to pursue the case, were the conflict of evidence, already described, between Dr Ogg, who found no clear evidence of mutilation other than of the face and throat, and the accomplice witnesses who claimed that various circular pieces of flesh had been cut from other parts of the body. Lefela alleged that these additional mutilations comprised the 'dictated aspersive evidence rammed into the heads of witnesses' by police.[47]

Despite the absence of convincing grounds for appeal in the 'Mamakhabane case, the Commonwealth Relations Office was anxious to ensure that an application for leave to appeal to the Privy Council should not fail for lack of funds.[48] Eventually, the money was raised and the petition for leave to appeal was heard on 30 May 1949. Their Lordships decided, however, that there had been no miscarriage of justice. The trial judge, they said, had relied on the corroboration of independent witnesses and was fully aware of the danger of accepting the uncorroborated evidence of accomplices.[49]

Chieftainess 'Mamakhabane and Dane Rachakane were hanged at Maseru gaol on 8 June 1949. One of the other two appellants was still alive at Koma-Koma in December 1998: Mohobosane Mohlokaqala. At the age of about ninety-eight he had, however, lost his wits. As Nyalase Sebajoa – a cousin of Setene Sebajoa (No. 9 accused) and a brother of Lefu Sebajoa (No. 8) – expressed it to us, Mohobosane Mohlokaqala did not know whether his trousers were on or off. Those who were given life sentences, or fifteen years, had their sentences reduced to ten years, and so most of the accomplices returned home from gaol in the late 1950s. In December 1998 we met Nkapo Sebajoa, Setene Sebajoa's eldest son, at his house in Koma-Koma. In his slow, careful, deliberate way he denied all knowledge of the details of the case. On his return from prison his father simply remarked that he had been arrested on account of being trusted by the chieftainess. There was, it seems, an implicit conspiracy of silence. None of the accomplices had talked about the murder when they returned, Nyalase Sebajoa said, except to claim that they had been falsely implicated. But the prevailing belief at Koma-Koma was that they had committed the crime.[50]

3

MEDICINE MURDER: THE DEBATES OF THE LATE 1940s

We know there has been a plan that in the end Basutoland must go from the black people and that can only be achieved if all the chiefs are gone. We want to know if the investigations that are carried out are ... directed at people who have actually committed the crime, or whether they are so general as to do away with the chieftainship, and in the end we will find that we no longer have any chiefs ... many many innocent people have been hanged ... The way the Police are investigating their cases ... I am thinking that in about two weeks' time, the whole country will be gone.

Josiel Lefela, speech in the Basutoland National Council,
21 September 1948[1]

It is clear, therefore, that these ritual murders have their roots in the chieftainship, so are we going to object to the Government? If our chieftainship falls, shall we say that the Government did intend that our chieftainship falls? If a man throws himself over a precipice can anybody be blamed for that except himself? I don't think so. I really sympathise with the Resident Commissioner who rules this country. He is ruling this country during difficult times, at a time when the chieftainship is throwing itself over a precipice ... I say that the Territory of Basutoland is sick. It is in the throes of death.

Joel Molungoa, speech in the Basutoland National Council,
21 September 1948[2]

'THIS COUNTRY IS ... OVERCAST WITH A TERRIBLE CLOUD'

Before the mid-1940s there was little public concern about medicine murder. There had been the occasional report in the newspapers, but nothing to suggest that there had been any sharp upsurge in cases, and certainly no presentiment of the crisis that was soon to sweep through the country. When Sir Evelyn Baring reported back to London on his visits to Basutoland in November 1944 and December 1945 he made no mention of medicine murder,[3] and when a conference of District Commissioners was held in Maseru in July 1946 the subject was not considered important enough to be included on their agenda.[4] The Annual Report for 1948 was the first in which the government noted the existence of the crime.

But the first notes of alarm had already been sounded. In 1945 six murders were reported to the government: we now know of eleven that were committed in that year, and it is likely that there were several more. In response the local press denounced the chiefs and the doctors and called for swift and effective action. In January 1946, after consultations with the Resident Commissioner, Arden-Clarke, and probably at his instigation, the regent 'Mantšebo issued what seems to have been the first of several circulars on medicine murder. These cases, she wrote, 'are on the increase so much ... that this country is now overcast with a terrible cloud ...'[5] 'These ritual murders', 'Mantšebo went on, 'which are committed for the sole purpose of obtaining chieftainship medicine horns etc. I feel I cannot tolerate them and the Government will also not tolerate them.' This state-ment was a clear recognition that medicine murders were being committed and seemed to be a plain acknowledgement that responsibility lay with the chiefs. But the regent then weakened the statement's impact in two ways that were to figure repeatedly in the debate over the coming years.

First, while ordering full co-operation with the police, she warned both chiefs and commoners to 'be careful in the giving of information to the police that you may not give them false information based on hatred and because of which innocent people will be arrested', and she threatened to deal severely with anyone who gave false evidence of this kind. She herself was already under suspicion of involvement in medicine murder.[6] Of the thirty-five murders believed to have been committed since 1940, seven had been carried out in the ward of Mokhotlong, her own personal holding, where she had appointed her lover, Chief Matlere Lerotholi, to act as her representative.[7] Later, when accusations were made against her personally, she reacted by claiming that she was being framed. The fear, or the alleged fear, of false incrimination would be articulated time and time again not only by 'Mantšebo but by other chiefs as well.

Second, she declared her conviction that 'this wave of replenishing medicine horns is caused by these many witch doctors who are scattered all over villages and hamlets'. She ordered that no such doctor should enter any village without the chief's knowledge, otherwise he should be arrested. While acknowledging that the murders were carried out to replenish the medicine horns of the chiefs, she shifted the blame onto the *lingaka* who moved around without any form of control. It was because of them, she said, that murders had increased.

Seven months later, in July 1946, she issued another circular.[8] The chiefs were now under serious threat. Only a few weeks before, sitting in the High Court in the Morija case analysed in Case Study 1 (1945/3), Mr Justice de Beer had given an explicit warning that unless medicine murders came to an end 'the British Government may find it necessary to reduce the powers of the chiefs in Basutoland',[9] and *Mochochonono*, the mouthpiece of the

Basutoland Progressive Association, had warned that unless these 'fiendish practices' stopped, the days of the chiefs were numbered.[10] 'Mantšebo had particular cause to be worried. The case in which de Beer handed down his warning arose out of the murder of Stephen Thobeha in her own ward of Matsieng, only a few kilometres from her home. We have already noted that the headman who was charged, Mahao Matete, was a member of her staff and that, according to one key witness, the man who was condemned, John Makume, had claimed to be acting on her instructions.

Accordingly, 'Mantšebo had to be seen to be doing everything in her power to put an end to medicine murders. In spite of her earlier instructions, she said, 'matters still continue to be as bad as before'.[11] She threatened any chief found guilty with deposition, and she instructed any individual ordered by his chief to carry out a medicine murder to 'come direct to me to report so that I can take measures to punish such a chief'. Since she was so widely suspected herself, this circular was hardly likely to be obeyed, and for this reason the District Commissioner of Mokhotlong withheld publication pending further instructions. 'In this district', he wrote, 'not only are the names of all the Sons of Lerotholi (including Chief Matlere) connected with Witchcraft Murder, but also the name of the Regent Paramount Chief ...' It would have been far better, he said, if people had been told to report to the police and not to 'Mantšebo.[12]

CHIEFS, POLITICIANS AND POLICE

The regent then turned for advice to the Basutoland National Council, which discussed the matter at length in October 1946. This was the first of several debates which took place over the next sixteen years, and which provided the most striking demonstration of the changing positions taken by the leaders of the Basotho, both chiefs and politicians. It was held not only against the background of increasing concern about 'this wave of replenishing medicine horns' and of heavy press criticism of chiefs and doctors, but also in the immediate aftermath of the National Treasury reforms, which reduced the number of Native Courts from 1,340 to 121.

Nobody denied the fact of medicine murder, not even Josiel Lefela of the Lekhotla la Bafo. The horror was fully acknowledged. Medicine murder, one speaker said, was 'a terrible disease ... that might kill the whole of Basutoland'. It had brought shame and disgrace on the nation: it had 'bespattered the good name of Basutoland'. Nor was it denied that the chiefs were involved. But, just as in 'Mantšebo's first circular, and not surprisingly in a chamber dominated by chiefs, the main thrust of the debate was to put the blame on the *lingaka*. Chief Matlere Lerotholi even suggested that they should be abolished and 'we must only use European trained doctors', and a motion was passed, on similar lines to 'Mantšebo's circular, that *lingaka* should not be allowed to wander from village to village. Again as in 'Mantšebo's circular, some speakers were afraid of being falsely incriminated, and Chief Leloko Lerotholi, one of 'Mantšebo's leading advisers, claimed that in his experience 'a common person will kill a man in the country and carry the dead body and place it in front of the door of the Chief's son or of the Chief himself, because perhaps that person hates the Chieftainship or they hate the Chief ...'

But what were the causes of the recent increase? The very first speaker, Joel Molungoa, drew the connection between medicine murders and the recent Treasury reforms. The murderers, he said, were trying to build up their chieftainship: 'They think that by murdering others they would be allowed to keep Courts'. Another speaker, Goliath Malebanye, drew the connection with the Khubelu reforms of 1938. People were being deposed without any good reason, he said, and in response were turning to medicine murder. Attacking the very principles of the reforms, he argued that chieftainship was hereditary and that it should be returned to a firm hereditary footing. This, of course, was exactly what Josiel Lefela, the leader of the Lekhotla la Bafo, wanted to hear: 'when did these wholesale murders start?', he asked. Was it before the Khubelu reforms and Indirect Rule? The reason for all these murders, he argued, was the reduction in the number of courts. 'Now all these people who have been reduced begin to think, wrongly of course, if we use these medicines we will become Chiefs again. If all these people are allowed to return to their original positions all the medicine [murders] will be finished.' Other speakers rejected the connection between the reforms and the rise in murder. Talimo Joel said that he himself had not been gazetted, but he was perfectly satisfied with his position, and so were many others. He was at a loss, however, to explain what was happening. 'This is merely wickedness that has come upon the Nation for no reason at all.' His only remedy was 'that the nation should pray, they should wear rough blankets and return to God'.[13]

Nobody went to so far as to accuse 'Mantšebo of being involved in medicine murder herself. But one speaker, Edwin Ntsasa, criticised both her and the Sons of Moshoeshoe for their belief in medicine – 'the first thing they should do is to clear their house' – and Joel Molungoa hinted darkly that 'even very important people' were concerned with medicine murder. At this stage the involvement of 'very important people' was merely a matter of suspicion, and as long as it stayed that way it did not place any great strain on the relationship between the chieftainship and the government. When one speaker declared that it was the chiefs alone who were responsible for medicine murders, the Acting Resident Commissioner, who chaired the debate, rebuked him, pointing out that many commoners were involved as well.[14] And the government was pleased to support 'Mantšebo in her attempts to control the *lingaka*. In July 1947, perhaps as a result of the National Council's resolution, she issued another circular restricting their movements,[15] and in July 1948 the High Commissioner issued a proclamation forbidding anyone to practise for gain as a medicine man or herbalist unless they had been granted a licence by an administrative officer on the order of the Resident Commissioner after consultation with the Paramount Chief.[16]

Inevitably, as the involvement of the chiefs came more into the open, their relations with the government became more strained. They had a duty to keep law and order, but when they themselves were suspected of breaking the law it was impossible to co-operate with them in the same way as before. As far as medicine murder was concerned, the principles of indirect rule were unworkable. Already, in June 1946, 'Mantšebo had agreed to allow the police to report in the first instance to the nearest headman, rather than to the Ward Chief, in order to reduce delays. Now, in November 1947, after a long series of negotiations with the Resident Commissioner, she was persuaded, much to her later regret, to issue the circular directing that in cases of medicine murder the police should have the right, if they thought it necessary, to conduct investigations by themselves without the represent-ative of the local chieftainship; that people should report to the police direct, and then to their headman, if following the old procedure would lead to delay; and that if there was the slightest doubt about the cause of death the body should not be moved.[17] As we have noted already, in Chapter 2, it is possible that these new procedures led to more murders being reported to the police. What is beyond doubt is that they contributed to a worsening relationship between the police and government on the one hand and the chieftainship on the other. The chiefs were already scared of being framed. When the police turned up in their villages without warning and began questioning their followers in their absence, they became increasingly alarmed. Their fears of being incriminated, whether falsely or otherwise, were now focused on the agents of the colonial government as much as on disaffected commoners. Until about this time – late 1947 – the relationship between the police and the chiefs had been one of goodwill and co-operation.[18] Thereafter allegations of police malpractice became widespread.

The involvement of the senior chiefs was now being exposed in the courts, and there was no longer any need for dark hints. In 1947 six cases of medicine murder were reported, and in 1948 twenty; and we know of seventeen and twenty-five that were committed in those years respectively. Scores of people were accused, among them several of the leading chiefs, notably the Ward Chiefs 'Mamakhabane Boshoane Peete, Bereng Griffith Lerotholi and Gabashane Masupha (Case Studies 2 and 3).

Gradually the senior chiefs built up a dossier of cases in which, they alleged, false accusations had been made against them, and these were listed in a petition drawn up by 'Mantšebo on 16 September 1948. She acknow-ledged the existence of medicine murders but she protested about the official conduct of several cases, including that involving Chief Jacottet

Theko, the Ward Chief of Thaba-Bosiu, who had been arrested on a medicine murder charge without any reference to her (1945/10);[19] the case in which headman Seabatha Lerotholi of Mokhotlong, Matlere's half-brother, had been accused and found innocent (1943/3); and the case against Chief Lagden Majara, in which his own sons were due to give evidence against him but then said that they had been 'taught by the police to say that their father had murdered a person' (1944/6). Above all she complained that she personally had been accused of killing a man called Borane – a case that had collapsed dramatically when it transpired that Borane was still alive.[20] It was at this point that she asked for an enquiry to be held.

The chiefs were now finding new allies: Josiel Lefela's Lekhotla la Bafo. The colonial authorities found it surprising that a body devoted to the interests of commoners should be supporting the chiefs on an issue such as medicine murder.[21] But the Lekhotla la Bafo was not against the chieftainship as such: it wanted a return to the 'good old days' of Moshoeshoe, when the chiefs, it believed, paid more attention to the wishes and rights of their subjects. Above all it wanted a chieftainship free, as of old, from the control and interference of the colonial government. That was why it had resisted the Khubelu and the National Treasury reforms. Now Lefela argued that medicine murder was being used by the British government as a device for destroying the natural leaders of the Basotho and so paving the way for incorporation into the Union. The fears of a South African takeover were all the greater following the victory of the National Party in May 1948 and the renewed demands for incorporation.[22]

The Lekhotla la Bafo was itself under pressure at this time. In July 1948, as described in Case Study 2, Lefela and several of his colleagues were arrested in the Roma arson case and called in the Reverend Michael Scott to help them. Scott's arrival in Basutoland coincided with a mounting crescendo of concern about medicine murder. He interviewed Bereng and Gabashane, who told him precisely what Lefela was saying: that the action against them was 'an initial step to abolish or curtail the power of the chiefs and enhance the power of the administration as a possible preliminary to handing over Basutoland to the Union Government'.[23] He went on to see 'Mantšebo. 'She was very nervous', he wrote later, 'and told me that suspicions were now being directed against herself of charges of ritual murder. The police were spying on her and although she was the chief constable of Basutoland in name, she was not consulted about what they were doing.'[24] Scott later added his voice to hers in calling for an enquiry.

THE HIGH COMMISSIONER, THE CHIEFTAINSHIP AND THE QUESTION OF INCORPORATION

The British response was largely determined by Sir Evelyn Baring, the High Commissioner in South Africa. Those who worked with him described him as rather retiring and shy, but he was highly regarded in Whitehall and Westminster. He was only forty-one when he was appointed to South Africa in 1944, having previously served as Governor of Southern Rhodesia, and his term of office was twice extended. According to his biographer, Charles Douglas-Home, he performed his diplomatic functions in South Africa conscientiously, but 'his heart during all those years was always in the Territories'.[25] Like many other British officials, he became deeply attached to Basutoland, and confessed to feeling a catch in the throat and a surge of affection whenever, as he approached through the Orange Free State, he turned the corner and saw Maseru again and the wall of the Maloti behind it.[26] He was deeply committed to his Christian faith – in his papers, now kept by Durham University, there are several notebooks on his religious beliefs and biblical studies – and he brought to the issue of medicine murder not only a high intelligence, but a moral passion and intensity unmatched by any other colonial official.

Far from plotting the incorporation of the High Commission Territories into South Africa, Baring was implacably opposed to it,[27] and it is ironic that the danger of incorporation was receding just as Basotho fears of it were increasing. Jan Smuts, like many other South Africans, regarded Britain's refusal to hand over the Territories as a snub, an implied declaration that Britain had no confidence in South Africa's 'native policies'. It was, he said, 'the one remaining rock of offence between our two countries'.[28] It would have boosted his electoral chances in 1948 if Britain had transferred control to South Africa, and among some politicians and officials in London it was felt that, after his services to Britain in the two World Wars, he was entitled to some support and consideration.[29] But transfer would have been a betrayal of the Africans in all three Territories, it would have aroused powerful opposition in Britain, and it was no longer a realistic political possibility. After the Nationalists' election victory, although Dr Malan stepped up the pressure, the case for incorporation became weaker than ever before.[30]

Moreover, far from wanting to destroy the chieftainship, Baring was determined to preserve it as a strong and viable institution. This was why he was so concerned about medicine murder. He was profoundly shocked by it, and he was afraid that it would be seized upon by South African critics to disparage British methods of colonial rule,[31] but above all he believed that, if it continued unchecked, it would undermine public support for the chiefs. At first he ascribed the increase in the crime to two main factors: the unrest among the chiefs following the recent reforms, and the unsettling effects of the war. He also suggested that part of the increase was merely apparent, and due to some extent to improved policing.[32] Later, in a longer and more considered memorandum, he ascribed the increase to the chiefs' realisation that their powers were slipping away and to the greater readiness of the people to report crimes. Under the recent reforms many chiefs and headmen had lost prestige and income, and 'in a last desperate effort' to regain their former status and authority some of them resorted to medicine murder.[33]

This linkage of medicine murder with the recent reforms was not original. Several speakers in the National Council had made the same connection, and so had several officials and policemen and writers and correspondents in the local press.[34] But for Baring it was also a cause of some embarrassment, since it implied that it was a government initiative which had indirectly given rise to so many murders, and it underlined the need not to weaken the chiefs any more.

Throughout his term of office Baring hammered home the need to maintain a strong chieftainship. It was not just that the government depended on the chiefs for day-to-day administration. Baring also took the view that soil erosion was the greatest threat to Basutoland's economic survival, and that without the backing and commitment of the chiefs all efforts at soil conservation would fail.[35] In July 1948, following the arrest of Bereng and Gabashane, he reported that if they were convicted a severe blow might be struck at medicine murder, but there was no question of his welcoming this as a victory in a campaign to destroy the chieftainship. Instead he described it 'from a more general political point of view' as 'an exasperating development'. Although he regarded reform as necessary, he saw that it had struck at the powers of the chiefs and he wanted to 'attempt slightly to bolster up the chieftainship'. It was 'therefore most unfortunate that the most important Chief after the Regent, and one of the other four leading Chiefs in Basutoland should be involved in a scandal of this nature'. If Bereng and Gabashane were hanged, there might have to be 'drastic proposals' about the regency. 'This development shows that either the Regent has little control over her Ward Chiefs or – though this is as yet mere suspicion – she is herself involved in witchcraft practices.'[36]

Baring often returned to the same theme. Economic survival, he wrote in 1949, depended on soil conservation, and soil conservation could be achieved only through the chiefs. So getting rid of medicine murder must not involve getting rid of the chiefs.[37] If the chiefs, however, continued with medicine murder they would be putting an end to themselves. It was vital, therefore, to the survival and well-being of Basutoland that medicine murder should be stopped, and in September 1948 Baring took the unusual step of travelling to Maseru to deliver his opening address to the Basutoland National Council in person. He put on 'his smart blue uniform ...', he wrote to his wife, and 'made them a terrific speech praising the work of the chiefs in every other respect but speaking frankly about ritual murder'.[38] The chiefs, he said, should be the leaders of the people, but of the nineteen cases that had been taken to court since 1942 headmen or chiefs were involved in every case but one. If these crimes continued 'the chieftainship will be utterly discredited and undermined. People will cease to respect the Chiefs and the present system of indirect government through the Chiefs will break down entirely'. He threatened that, if necessary, the government would introduce legislation authorising 'hard, repressive measures such as the institution of collective fines and the quartering of police at the expense of the inhabitants in the area where the murder was committed'.[39]

After the speech he had a meeting with 'Mantšebo and twenty of the leading chiefs, who presented 'Mantšebo's petition complaining about the police and asking for an enquiry. Baring responded, according to his own account, 'by a very vigorous counter-attack'.[40] He told them that 'either the ward chiefs were implicated in ritual murder crimes or alternatively that they were ineffective administrators'. If ritual murder was not destroyed, the chieftainship might fall.[41] 'Their eyes really popped out of their heads', he told his wife. 'I thought the old girl ['Mantšebo] was going to cry.'[42] Afterwards he and the Resident Commissioner had a further meeting with 'Mantšebo and some of her advisers, and he told her plainly that if medicine murders continued 'she would not remain in her present power'.[43]

Baring wanted to support and strengthen the chieftainship, but his blunt warnings conveyed the opposite impression. Many Basotho were now convinced that the British were bent on destroying the chiefs and this coloured the subsequent debate in the National Council. 'I can see that there is much fright amongst the chiefs and the Members of Council', said N. M. Tlale, the President of the Basutoland Progressive Association. 'They speak and their minds are stampeded ...' 'The High Commissioner has become very angry', said one chief, 'and says that the chieftainship should be done away with because of these murders.'[44]

In this second major debate on medicine murder, in September 1948, there were again those who blamed the *lingaka*, and a motion from the Maseru District Council to this effect attracted some support. Several speakers clearly placed responsibility with the chiefs. Murders were rooted in the chieftainship, it was said, and they often coincided with the placings of chiefs' sons. Anticipating the arguments of Josiel Lefela, Joel Molungoa exonerated the government. In the words quoted at the head of this chapter, he told the chiefs that if they were throwing themselves over a precipice they had only themselves to blame. 'I direct my words to you, Paramount Chief. I ask you to meet your chiefs and take counsel together. This thing is committed by you.' Molungoa again pointed out the connection with the recent reforms: 'some of the people are trying to regain their power'.[45]

This was the argument that Joel Lefela had put forward in 1946.[46] But Lefela had now moved on. In one of the longest speeches in the debate he claimed that the government was using medicine murder as a pretext to destroy the chiefs so that it could hand the country over to South Africa. He acknowledged that murders were being committed but claimed that police were incriminating the chiefs by forcing or bribing their followers to give false evidence against them. No other speaker went so far as to accuse the administration of plotting to hand over the country to South Africa, but two speakers, Jacottet Theko, the Ward Chief of Thaba-Bosiu who had been arrested on a charge of medicine murder but subsequently acquitted (1945/10), and Leloko Lerotholi, 'Mantšebo's adviser, who had been present at the earlier meeting with Baring, supported Lefela in his allegations against the police.[47]

TOWARDS A CLIMAX OF DESPAIR

Whatever the causes, there was no abatement of the crisis. In November 1948 Chiefs Bereng and Gabashane were found guilty and sentenced to death for the murder of 'Meleke Ntai (Case Study 3). Five murders were reported in 1949 and seven are known to have been committed. These figures were much lower than in 1948, but again there were no doubt other murders which were never officially recorded. According to the Catholic newspaper, *Moeletsi oa Basotho*, dead bodies were 'being found everywhere, and constantly too: under cliffs, in rivers, in dongas, on mountains, in caves …'[48] Throughout the country subordinate courts held preparatory examinations into murders committed in previous years, and in Maseru the High Court was overwhelmed with cases. Because there were so many accused the proceedings often lasted for two or three weeks. Courtrooms were crowded, and in issue after issue the local newspapers carried gruesome reports on individual cases or impassioned articles and letters about why so many murders were being committed and what could be done to bring them to an end. Comparisons were made with the terrible times of the *lifaqane* in the 1820s and 1830s, when the small Basotho chiefdoms of the highveld were overwhelmed by invasions from below the Drakensberg and many in desperation turned to cannibalism.[49] Many people were afraid to go out after dark or to respond when summoned by their chiefs.

'Mantšebo continued to send out ineffective circulars. In December 1948 she ordered the formation of local vigilance committees, but by the end of March 1949 only three or four had been established.[50] In Mokhotlong people refused to take part: 'We are quite prepared to report secretly to the Police', they told the District Commissioner, 'but as for joining a Vigilance Committee, we will never do that because we will probably be killed ourselves'.[51] Soon they ceased to meet.[52] 'Mantšebo then toured the country holding *pitso*s about medicine murder. In view of her reputation it seems unlikely that they had any effect.[53]

In desperation 'Mantšebo turned to Josiel Lefela and the Lekhotla la Bafo, and at the end of January 1949 a meeting was held at Matsieng between Lefela and the leading chiefs.[54] Lefela had now developed his argument about medicine murder even further. In 1946 he had believed that the chiefs had turned to *liretlo* in reaction to what he saw as the iniquities

of the British government's reforms. In 1948 he had alleged that the government was falsely incriminating the chiefs in order to get rid of them. Now he
argued that there was no such thing as medicine murder. At Matsieng many
of the chiefs agreed with him, and the recently acquitted Chief Jacottet
Theko declared, at a public meeting in his own ward of Thaba-Bosiu, that
'there were no ritual murders in Basutoland. Only people bribed by Government said so'.[55]

Forsyth-Thompson, the Resident Commissioner, was shocked. He told
'Mantšebo:

> I had Lefela here the other day. I said 'It is an astonishing thing to me
> that you who are the self-appointed champion of the common people,
> the head of the Lekhotla la Bafo have never been heard in public to
> condemn ritual murder and say it ought to stop, although the common
> people are the victims of this crime.' He said: 'Ritual murder, why it
> does not happen!'

Forsyth-Thompson expressed his surprise that 'Mantšebo had taken this
'mischievous and wicked man' into her counsels, and warned her that Lefela
would draw the chiefs into trouble unless she resisted him. Although she had
agreed in 1947 to the conduct of independent enquiries by the police she
now wanted to go back to the old methods of investigation, with the chief's
messenger accompanying the police at every stage. Forsyth-Thompson
refused outright, thrusting before her a list of cases in which the messengers
appointed to help the police had turned out to be murderers themselves.
She also petitioned the High Commissioner to withdraw the proclamation
he had recently issued authorising collective punishment; again she was to
be disappointed, though in practice the proclamation was never invoked.[56]

The Lekhotla la Bafo continued to press for an enquiry in petitions to the
British Government and to the United Nations: 'under the pretext of suppressing murders', wrote Josiel's brother, Maphutseng Lefela, 'the British
Government is now at war with [a] peaceful nation'.[57] Michael Scott, also
asking for an enquiry, enlisted the support of several MPs, stirred up at least
one Parliamentary Question, and was granted an interview with the Under-
Secretary of State, Patrick Gordon Walker. He alleged police malpractice,
but the statements which he had taken in the gaols of Basutoland made no
impression on the officials of the Commonwealth Relations Office.[58]

But the correspondence threw up two serious causes for concern. First,
there was no proper system of appeal from the High Court of Basutoland.
The only course open was to appeal to the Privy Council in London. This
was a very long and costly procedure, and at the end of it the Privy Council
was limited in the range of issues it could address. The problem was
acknowledged,[59] but it was not until 1955 that the Court of Appeal for the
High Commission Territories was established. Second, in their determin-

ation to get evidence, the police were detaining potential witnesses for long periods – many months in some cases – away from their chiefs and others who would put pressure on them to remain silent. Baring told Forsyth-Thompson that this was indefensible, and although the Resident Commissioner and his Commissioner of Police protested, Baring insisted that the practice should be stopped. To soften the blow he authorised expenditure on the establishment of more police posts in the mountains.[60]

At about the same time, in April 1949, Baring initiated what he described as 'a new phase of Government activity'. He had a poor opinion of the Basutoland administration and he was determined to shake it up. He was convinced that the District Commissioners and officers spent too much time at their desks, and that as a result they had failed to explain how the reforms were needed to maintain 'the structure of the native society' and on this basis to win the support and co-operation of the chiefs. As well as setting up the new police posts, and insisting that the new Native Medicine Men and Herbalists Proclamation should be rigorously enforced, he gave instructions that administrative officers should be out on trek, away from their desks, for at least ten days a month. They 'must get down to it', he told Forsyth-Thompson, 'visit every village at regular intervals, preach against ritual murder daily, evangelise at the wayside whilst travelling, talk over the camp-fire at nights until every Mosuto has it straight from his District Commissioner that ritual murder must be wiped out ...'[61]

In June 1949 'Mamakhabane was hanged, the first Ward Chief and the first woman to be executed for medicine murder (Case Study 2). Then, towards the end of July, the Privy Council rejected the appeals of Bereng and Gabashane (Case Study 3). Forsyth-Thompson was on leave, and in his absence Armstrong, the Acting Resident Commissioner, was increasingly nervous. He received warnings that the executions of Bereng and Gabashane would lead to widespread disturbances or at the least 'a wave of anti-white feeling', and on 28 July there was a serious but unsuccessful attempt by the prisoners at the Maseru gaol to release the chiefs.[62] He demanded quick action, and on 2 August he received confirmation from the High Commissioner's office that Baring saw no reason to commute the sentences. Armstrong lost no time. At dawn on the following day the two chiefs were hanged.

It was the darkest day of Britain's rule in Basutoland. It marked the climax of public anxiety about the horror of medicine murder. In this chapter we have outlined the ebb and flow of often agonised debate about the causes of the apparently 'startling increase' in the late 1940s. In the following case study we trace the particular chain of events that brought Chiefs Bereng and Gabashane to the gallows.

Case Study 3

THE 'BATTLE OF THE MEDICINE HORNS': 'MAMATHE'S, LATE 1940s

What a case, what characters and what a climax! The upright chief, with a strong-medicine killing in his plans, standing beside the deposed chieftainess and rating [*sic*] against strong-medicine killings to the tribesmen. Masked or empty faces around: small wonder! The old witch-doctor, privy to the plan, jovially greeting my guide and myself as we drove from his house towards that of the chief, whom he had probably visited to discuss the matter. The huge woman on the mattress in the innermost palisade, who seemed to live with terror. The choice of the victim and the assent of his brother; the killing and the accusation by the killer's brother. Sentence of death and the mad old witch-doctor running amok in the court with a sjambok until he was overpowered and carried raving from the room. The appeal, and my Lords of the Privy Council in grave debate between breakfast in Kensington and lunch in St James's. The rejection of the appeal and the gallows in Maseru ...

Douglas Reed (1950: 234–5)

Douglas Reed's theatrical prose offers an approximate framework for the analysis of the most publicly dramatic of the medicine murder cases which we here investigate in detail. Who were the 'upright chief', the 'deposed chieftainess', the 'huge woman on the mattress', the two sets of brothers – the victim and his brother who gave assent, the killer and his brother who gave evidence against him – and the 'mad old witch-doctor'? Reed was an itinerant journalist whose eye for a racy phrase outpaced his reporting of sober fact. During an extensive journey in southern Africa in the early part of 1948, however, he met at first hand some of the key *dramatis personae* in the case that most directly fuelled the moral crisis over *liretlo*: the prosecution of Bereng Griffith Lerotholi and Gabashane Masupha.

TWO MURDERS

On 10 December 1946 Chief Gabashane Masupha, Ward Chief of 'Mamathe's in the Berea District, summoned a number of his men to come to him. There were four chiefs present: Gabashane himself; Chief Bereng Griffith Lerotholi, Ward Chief of the Phamong ward and second only to the regent 'Mantšebo in the hierarchy of senior chiefs in Basutoland; Jonathan

Masupha, a younger half-brother of Gabashane; and Ntoane, a lesser chief from Mohale's Hoek who had accompanied Bereng. Chief Gabashane gave instructions: under the leadership of Makione Mphiko, the local headman at 'Mamathe's, the men were to waylay Paramente Khothatso and take him to Letsatsi Piiti's hut in the nearby village of Chaba's. That night, however, they failed to catch him. The following night they lay in wait again and caught Paramente as he returned from his lover's hut in the early dawn. He screamed very loudly, and the men shouted and sang to drown his screaming. They took him to Letsatsi Piiti's hut and reported to the chiefs that they had been successful. They were told to meet at Piiti's hut on the following night, a Thursday.

When they went they found Paramente, a 'very fat man',[1] placed on an ox-hide in the middle of the hut. Mapeshoane Masupha, another younger half-brother of Chief Gabashane, described what happened:

> He was seated with his stretched legs before him. He was alive as I saw him. He appeared tired. His eyes were open. He did not speak. I saw Michael [Tseki] pass something before the nose of the deceased, and the deceased appeared to be sleepy. Michael took out yellow hand gloves ... He took a thin knife. I saw him starting to skin the deceased from the back of his head, from the bottom of the neck upwards ...

After parts of the face and throat were removed, the body was carried away and left at a place known as Malimong (Cannibals'), where it was found about six days later. According to the evidence of the medical officer at Teyateyaneng, Dr Ogg, who performed the post-mortem examination, the skull was attached to the trunk only by a piece of skin; the ears, eyes, nose, lips and scalp were all missing; and the cause of death was probably haemorrhage. Michael Tseki was the doctor's senior dispenser, and had learned how to dissect bodies from watching Dr Ogg. He was then about sixty years old, described by one observer at the trial as 'massive, ... with greying hair and thick-lensed glasses', the only one of the accused not wearing a blanket. In spite of his rheumatism and poor eyesight he had removed the neck vertebrae with clinical efficiency.[2]

In the subsequent trial it was alleged that over sixty people had been involved in this murder (1946/2). The Attorney-General thought it probable that 'everybody in the district was ordered to be present that night in order to get them implicated ... Possibly some of them were there unwillingly'.[3]

Nearly fifteen months later, on the evening of 3 March 1948, another meeting took place at Chief Gabashane's residence at 'Mamathe's. Chief Bereng was again present, as were many other men. Gabashane made an arrangement with Moloi Ntai that Moloi would 'sell' his relative 'Meleke Ntai to him for £100. On the following day a funeral took place at Ha Mahleke, nearly 10 kilometres to the south-east of 'Mamathe's. Four men of the Ntai family – 'Meleke, Moloi, Makhetha and Ntsane – went on horseback to the funeral. On their return home 'Meleke was left behind at the instigation of Moloi, who urged the others to race their horses, knowing that 'Meleke could not ride fast. 'Meleke, now on his own, was intercepted by a group of men and dragged from his horse. Two of them throttled and suffocated him. Chief Ntoane, accompanying Chief Bereng, then cut off portions of 'Meleke's upper and lower lips, which were handed to Bereng. Bereng remarked, 'This man of yours has no blood. He is no good'. 'Meleke was thought to be dead and Gabashane gave orders that his body should be disposed of in a donga. It was dumped in a ravine in a shallow pool of water, where it was found very early in the morning two days later. Dr Ogg's post-mortem report gave the cause of death as drowning and suggested crabs might have caused mutilation of the lips. A police officer who moved the body saw four small crabs where the body had been lying 'about the size of a half-a-crown apiece'. Later the body was exhumed and examined by Dr Whitworth. Neither Ogg nor Whitworth found any bruises that might have been caused by throttling.[4]

The account of the second murder (1948/6), like the account of the first, is based primarily on the evidence of Mapeshoane Masupha. In the months following the murder he and three other men who had taken part emerged as Crown witnesses. The others were Molemohi Mphiko, who was related to the headman Makione Mphiko; Sepalami Mathibe; and Sothi Chela. As a result of the police investigations thirteen men were arrested, mostly in mid-July 1948. They were:

Chiefs Bereng and Gabashane
Chief Ntoane
Mojauta Nonyana, Bereng's servant
Makione Mphiko, the headman at 'Mamathe's
Sankatane Masupha, Mosiuoa Masupha and Kemaketse Masupha,
    three relatives of Gabashane who lived in huts provided by the chief
Fusi Rakokoli, described as a 'native doctor'
Safere [Xavier] Ntsoso, a commoner under Gabashane
Ramabanta Mahleke, a messenger of Gabashane
Moloi Ntai, a cousin of the victim, 'Meleke Ntai
Titimus Ramashamole, who was later discharged.[5]

Chief Ntoane died in hospital while the case was pending. Before his death, the defence claimed, he made a 'dying declaration' which was not shown to the defence during the trial, and this became one of the grounds of subsequent appeal. This 'dying declaration', however, turned out to be 'delirious ravings' which were inadmissible as evidence.[6]

Information also began to emerge about the earlier murder of Paramente Khothatso. Three of the same accomplice witnesses – Mapeshoane Masupha,

Sepalami Mathibe and Sothi Chela – made statements about it in September 1948.[7] Five other accomplices were also persuaded by the police to testify for the Crown. Of the sixty or more persons said to be involved in Paramente's murder, thirty-seven were charged at the preparatory examination held in February 1949. Five of these thirty-seven were discharged at the end of that examination, and the Attorney-General withdrew charges against eleven others. Of the twenty-one who were indicted for trial in the High Court, five were removed from the list: Chiefs Bereng and Gabashane and the local headman, Makione Mphiko, who had been hanged for the murder of 'Meleke Ntai a week before the trial began, and Kemaketse Masupha and Sankatane Masupha, who had each been sentenced to ten years' imprisonment for the same murder. Thus only sixteen people were still in the dock when judgement came to be given in the Paramente case. Four of these were convicted of murder. Michael Tseki, the senior dispenser, was sentenced to death but had his sentence commuted to life imprisonment. Three others were convicted as accessories after the crime of murder and also of the crime of assault. (Two of them were already in gaol for their part in 'Meleke Ntai's murder.) Another was also convicted of assault and given two years' imprisonment.

There was thus a significant overlap of people who had taken part in both murders. While the Paramente Khothatso murder took place about fifteen months before the 'Meleke Ntai murder, evidence implicating Bereng and Gabashane and the other accused emerged in reverse chronological order, so that the investigation and outcome of the Paramente Khothatso case became secondary to those of the 'Meleke Ntai case. The preparatory examination in the 'Meleke Ntai case was held in July 1948 and the High Court trial in November 1948. Those convicted in the case pursued an appeal to the Privy Council during the first half of 1949. The preparatory examination in the Paramente Khothatso case took place in February 1949, and the High Court trial was adjourned, because of the overlap of participation, pending the outcome of the appeal in the 'Meleke Ntai case. It eventually took place in August 1949, a week after Chiefs Bereng and Gabashane, headman Makione Mphiko and Moloi Ntai were hanged. For this reason, although the murder took place first, the Paramente Khothatso case is treated as secondary for the purpose of the discussion below of the judicial and political arguments that arose. Analysis here concentrates on the 'Meleke Ntai case.

MOTIVES AND CONTEXT: TWO PRINCIPALS

While the details of the plots emerged clearly, the motives remained shadowy. We are left to infer them as best we can from analysis of the broader social and political context. The first question that arises is why Chiefs Bereng and Gabashane should have developed mutual friendship, trust and confidence to a degree sufficient for them to conspire together to instigate two medicine murders. Partial answers to this question may be sought in their characters and family backgrounds and the shifting political circumstances of the mid-1940s.

Bereng Griffith Lerotholi has already been introduced in Chapter 1 in the context of his dispute over succession to the paramountcy first with Seeiso and second with Seeiso's senior widow 'Mantšebo. Born in 1902, he was the only child in Paramount Chief Griffith's third house. His half-brother Seeiso, born in 1905, was the only son in Griffith's second house. There were no sons in the first house. Despite Seeiso's nominal pre-eminence, Griffith had favoured Bereng as his heir because of a dispute about the status of his second wife, the mother of Seeiso. Nevertheless Seeiso succeeded to the paramountcy in 1939. He ruled for barely more than a year, until his death in December 1940. His heir was Constantine Bereng Seeiso, who was still a young boy. In contention now with 'Mantšebo for the regency, Bereng lost out once again, a decision confirmed by Justice Lansdown in his judgement in 1943.

Bereng was in repeated conflict with 'Mantšebo. At first he refused to obey her orders, treating her in a way that was 'derogatory' to her 'dignity and position', and as a result, in 1942, he was threatened with imprisonment and deposition as a chief.[8] He also had a long-running dispute with 'Mantšebo over the boundary between the Phamong and Matsieng wards, which became a proxy for his persistent grievance over the succession and which at times seemed likely to lead to armed conflict. In 1946 he stormed out of the National Council in order to protect his territorial claims in person, and in the following year a Boundary Commission was established in an effort to settle the dispute. Its recommendations, which Bereng found unacceptable, were, it seems, being considered by the British authorities at the very time when 'Meleke Ntai was killed.[9] He also had a civil action over livestock against 'Mantšebo, which was heard in the High Court on 11 December 1946, the day after the night of the first attempt to catch Paramente Khothatso at 'Mamathe's. At the High Court trial for Paramente's murder, held in August 1949, Bereng's servant Mojauta Nonyana denied that Bereng wished to obtain medicine from human flesh to further his suit in this action.[10] At the time of his arrest, in July 1948, Bereng was described by one official as a 'stormy petrel' in view of his quarrels with 'Mantšebo and with the government.[11] Although there were very few medicine murders in Bereng's ward, one (1944/2) was committed in his own village of Phamong, and Jones was convinced that this could not have happened without his knowledge.[12]

Gabashane Masupha had succeeded as Ward Chief of 'Mamathe's in 1938 on the death of his father Masupha II. He had been educated at Roma, Lovedale and Fort Hare, but did not progress beyond his Junior

Certificate, mainly, it was thought, because of his lack of application. During Seeiso's brief reign he had been his senior counsellor and had acted for him as paramount while he was ill. After his death he had set in motion the procedures for choosing the regent, and after 'Mantšebo had been recognised by the colonial administration he continued to work closely with her at Matsieng.

At first the official reports were entirely favourable. In 1940 he was described as

> well educated and energetic ... He has reformed and reorganized his Courts and takes a great interest in his judicial work. He has also evinced a keen interest in the tax collection of his Ward which has resulted in an excellent collection. He is very temperate in his habits and is respected and liked by his people and he is both willing and anxious to co-operate with the Government in all progressive and development matters ... He has a pleasing personality and if he continues as he has started he should become a most excellent and capable Chief.[13]

He was particularly active in helping to recruit his followers as soldiers in the African Auxiliary Pioneer Corps in the war.[14]

Later assessments were more critical. While his personal ability and charm were acknowledged, the main points that were emphasised were that he regarded himself as 'a potentate with almost absolute rights' over land and *matsema* (work-parties); that he was selfish and short-tempered and had no consideration for his people's welfare; that he was hostile to the government, and (in 1943) 'decidedly inimical' to the proposed establishment of the National Treasury and the Treasury Courts; that he was President of the Catholic Federation for Basutoland (he was a 'very big Christian' according to one of his junior half-brothers),[15] and was strongly influenced by the Canadian Catholics (who at that time were in conflict with the government over its educational policy); and that he loved intrigue and power, trusted no-one and was trusted by no-one. There was some improvement in 1946: he could be a valuable administrator if he were more disinterested, he was taking more concern with his people's welfare, and the establishment of the Treasury Courts in his ward had on the whole been a success.[16] In other accounts he was noted for his 'beautifully tailored clothes' and for being 'most courteous in manner and speech'. He frequently went shopping to the Free State town of Ficksburg and, like several of the leading chiefs, drove a large American car variously referred to as a Buick or 'a thirty horsepower Mammalac'.[17]

In 1946 it was reported that he had fallen out with the Paramount Chief, against whom he was said to be intriguing.[18] The so-called Big Four – Chiefs Bereng, Gabashane, Letsie Motšoene and Theko Makhaola[19] – were holding meetings among themselves, and it was suspected that their object was either to make Bereng regent or at least to get rid of 'Mantšebo's advisers. Bereng in particular 'bitterly resented' junior chiefs such as Kelebone Nkuebe and commoners such as Molise Tsolo having more influence than him at Matsieng, and was described as being 'moody and depressed' at this time. In December 1946 he visited Gabashane at Teyateyaneng, leaving his ward without giving official notice, and in January 1947 Forsyth-Thompson, the newly-arrived Resident Commissioner, called him in for an interview about this and questioned him about the current rumours. Bereng was indignant, and explained that he and the other three senior chiefs were consulting each other about the dress they should wear on the occasion of the visit of King George VI which was due to take place in March 1947: lounge suits when they met the royal party at the border, they decided, and 'traditional' dress at the *pitso*. This may well have been true, but, as became clear later, it was also in December that Bereng and Gabashane, according to the prosecution, organised the murder of Paramente Khothatso.[20]

Gabashane was also on bad terms with his younger half-brothers, with whom he had fallen out after his succession to his father's position.[21] Rivers Thompson, who knew him well, described him as 'cruel to his own kith and kin',[22] and a notorious incident late in 1945 reflected a vindictive streak in his character. As Forsyth-Thompson described it, Gabashane had an ex-soldier 'handcuffed during the day and tied to a tree during the night for a period of six weeks'. He was found guilty of assault by the local magistrate but acquitted on appeal.[23] It was this case that one of Gabashane's half-brothers, Lebihan Masupha, identified as the crucial turning point in the relationship between Gabashane and 'Mantšebo on the one hand and Gabashane and Bereng on the other. More than fifty years afterwards, frail, hard of hearing and slow of speech, and scrupulous in distinguishing the things he remembered clearly from the things he did not, Lebihan Masupha expressed it in this way:

> It happened in about 1945 that Chief Gabashane arrested someone and treated him very badly before my eyes ... He beat him, and invited people to assault him. The government took it very seriously. I was a Crown witness against him over that charge. Gabashane wanted 'Mantšebo to help, but 'Mantšebo couldn't intervene on his behalf. That's where their quarrel started ... That's when he went to Bereng. Then the friendship between Bereng and Gabashane became very close. The Big Four – Bereng, Gabashane, Theko Makhaola and Letsie – turned against 'Mantšebo and started agitating that it was a mistake she was given the paramountcy.[24]

The incident caused 'big trouble' both in local politics, in that it exacerbated a rift between Gabashane and Lebihan and by extension his other half-brothers, and in national politics, in that it marked a dramatic shift in the political alignments of the senior chiefs.

Thus, whatever specific motives were imputed and denied at the trial, the presumption was strong that the context in which Bereng and Gabashane were drawn to commit medicine murder was the 'battle of the medicine horns' between 'Mantšebo and Bereng, with Gabashane being drawn in as Bereng's ally following his own fall-out with the regent over the assault described above. There is nothing in the evidence of the cases themselves to connect them with the Treasury reforms of 1946, outlined in Chapter 1. Gabashane himself was particularly affected by these reforms in that, almost more than any other Ward Chief, he stood to lose heavily in financial terms,[25] and in 1943 he was reported as being 'decidedly inimical' to them. Yet he himself was a member of the Committee that put forward these proposals, and on the whole, as noted above, the introduction of the new Treasury Courts into his ward was a success.

In an effort, then, to disentangle the various elements of resentment that may have come together to explain a plot on the part of Bereng and Gabashane, we may discern, first, the running sores of conflict between Bereng and 'Mantšebo over succession to the paramountcy, the boundary between Phamong and Matsieng, and the ownership of cattle; and, second, the assault case that is said to have alienated Gabashane from 'Mantšebo and thrown him into alliance with Bereng, as well as turning him further against his own junior half-brothers.

Gabashane's public face, of course, was set firmly against medicine murder. In January 1948 Chieftainess 'Mamakhabane, whose ward adjoined his, was charged with medicine murder (case 1948/1, Case Study 2) and suspended. At the end of that month the District Commissioner of Berea, Gideon Pott, held a public meeting at Mapoteng at which, while the displaced chieftainess looked on 'in mahogany impassivity, never moving a muscle or eyelid', he placed Gabashane in charge of her ward. Douglas Reed was there, and this was the meeting he described. Gabashane, he wrote, 'a great man in the land',

> faced the blanketed tribesmen in a white man's blue suit. He was an educated man and spoke English almost as fluently as his own tongue. If any face there showed expression it was his. It suggested deep concern, implied that he was on the side of the white angels, regretted this dark affair, and wished his hearers to mend their ways. He said as much.[26]

Hence Reed's description of him as the 'upright chief'. Barely more than a month later, according to the evidence presented at their trial, Gabashane joined Bereng in their own second medicine murder, the murder of 'Meleke Ntai.

MOTIVES AND CONTEXT: THE LESSER PLAYERS

The house of Masupha II

By contrast with the extravagance of Douglas Reed's writing style, Lebihan Masupha gave us the most sober and considered first-hand oral testimony on the circumstances of the case. We found him at home at Ha Bose, on the Mapoteng road, where he had been placed in 1958, with six villages under him, by Chieftainess 'Mamathe. A hailstorm battered furiously on the corrugated sheeting roof of his house. Conversation sputtered for half an hour until the storm wore itself out. Then he spoke slowly and deliberately about the relationships within the Masupha family and about the political context of the late 1940s. Gabashane Masupha, born in June 1908, was the son in the senior house of Chief Masupha II. Jonathan Masupha, born in 1910, was the son of the second wife, a daughter of Chief Majara. Lebihan himself, born in 1914, was a son of the third wife, who was a commoner and so ranked below Jonathan's mother despite having been married before her. Gabashane and Jonathan were educated together and got on with one another well enough. In 1938, when their father died, Gabashane married and took his father's seat and started to impose his authority on his brothers. 'That's when the friendship broke between Gabashane and Jonathan, although there was not open or intense conflict. The big trouble came later, between me and Gabashane ...' This was a reference to the assault on the ex-soldier, described above. Having worked closely with Gabashane at 'Mamathe's until this incident, Lebihan left for Johannesburg, probably in flight from Gabashane's anger.[27] When Bereng and Gabashane were arrested in July 1948 he was summoned back to Basutoland.

> I was placed as chief over the whole of 'Mamathe's. This led to bad blood between me and Gabashane's wife [Chieftainess 'Mamathe]. So the case went on, and defeated Bereng and Gabashane. I was very unpopular but I stuck it out. ... 'Mamathe came to govern after their death.[28]

Dissension was inevitable in the circumstances.[29]

Jonathan Masupha was charged as one of the accomplices in the Paramente Khothatso case. In the 'Meleke Ntai case he played no part, but four other relatives were involved. Mapeshoane Masupha, who became principal accomplice witness for the Crown, was a son in the fourth house of Chief Masupha II. He had been an assistant to Gabashane, but later had to be disciplined by his brother – a fact that was later adduced as a possible reason for his defection to the Crown.[30] The other three relatives, who were all, the judge said, 'acting under the powerful influence of Chief Gabashane',[31] were Sankatane Masupha, Mosiuoa Masupha and Kemaketse Masupha. Informants expressed haziness in respect of the precise genealogical connections of these lesser relatives. This arose out of the practice of chiefs by which illegitimate sons were incorporated into the family as *balisana* (literally 'herdboys') and assumed the chief's name; and out of the diffidence of informants by which it was not polite to refer explicitly to their formal illegitimacy. As Lebihan Masupha acknowledged, 'there wasn't a marriage there if you look at it closely'.[32]

The doctor

Fusi Rakokoli, the doctor, has a distinctive place in the various narratives from which we have sought to reconstruct these events. He was a practitioner of considerable standing and reputation. Lunatics from all over the country were entrusted to his care, and the colonial authorities, conscious of their own limitations in dealing with mental illness among the Basotho, also passed on these patients to him. 'I liked the old scoundrel', Gideon Pott recalled, 'as he was very good in curing mental cases.'[33] The assault on 'Meleke Ntai took place near his homestead, and Fusi pointed out to various visitors and passers-by 'Meleke's saddle, saddle-cloth, *sjambok* and handkerchief that were lying in the veld nearby. Fusi's assistant, Paulus Kahlolo, discovered 'Meleke's corpse very early in the morning of 6 March, 'just as the sun rose', when he took a group of patients down to wash in the stream in the donga.[34] Unusually, Fusi was standing at the top of the hill at the time, looking down. The inference was drawn by the prosecution that Fusi knew where the body was before it had been found.

Some time before the murder, Douglas Reed encountered Fusi on the road, presumably near 'Mamathe's, and with the lurid hyperbole that marks his style he described a 'grinning old herbalist-witch-doctor, showing the gaps in his teeth as he bent towards us in his saddle'.

> This jovial fellow, who looked like any other blanketed Basuto, reined in his horse and greeted my companion and myself with loud hallo. He was reputed to cure madness ... A few weeks later he was charged as the instigator of one of these murders and, on being sentenced to death, broke into a frenzy of rage (or madness). Seizing a sjambok, which was among the exhibits of the case and lay within his reach, he laid about him with such ferocity that a scene followed rare in the history of any High Court, even in a small Protectorate.[35]

In 1999 we were told that Fusi's widow 'Maluke was still alive, living with her daughter at Ha Molapo, a village in the valley below the ridge where Fusi's old homestead still stands. We learned from them that Fusi was the son of Jobo Motloang of Thaba-Bosiu. His mother had been 'gripped by the spirit (*moea*)', but the drumming that necessarily accompanied her own subsequent practice as a *lethuela* (a person possessed by the spirit) was embarrassing next to the church at Thaba-Bosiu, and so she was moved with her children to the place of her cross-cousin Rakokoli, near 'Mamathe's, where Fusi was brought up. It was his mother who taught him medicine (*bongaka*). He died in 1964, still a doctor. He used to cure mad people 'from all over' with his medicines. 'Maluke assured us that he was not mentally impaired. Explaining his sometimes extravagant behaviour, she remarked, 'It's medicines that give force of personality' (*ke litlhare tse etsang seriti*).[36]

The Ntai family

Who were the members of the Ntai family caught up in the case? The victim, 'Meleke Ntai, was not a strong man. He could ride a horse but was unable to gallop. He suffered from epilepsy and tuberculosis.[37] At the time of his death he was being trained as a catechumen in the *Kereke ea Fora*.[38] Moloi Ntai, who 'sold' 'Meleke to the chiefs, was his brother not in the close sense implied by the English word, but in the much looser sense implied by the common Sesotho phrase *ka malapa*, 'through families'. They were distant cousins with a collateral connection at least two generations back. The two other men who had ridden back from the funeral at Mahleke's, and who had ridden on ahead with Moloi Ntai, were Makhetha Ntai and Ntsane Ntai. Both spent periods in detention in the early phases of the investigation, and both became independent witnesses for the Crown. Makhetha Ntai was a first cousin of 'Meleke's, and Ntsane Ntai was a distant cousin.

We were given this genealogical account in May 1999 by Ntsane Ntai, who was the only survivor, as far as he knew, among the witnesses in the case.[39] We found him at his home at Ha Phirihlahe, on the western fringe of 'Mamathe's, dressed in a yellow oilskin against torrential winter rain. It was the first time, he said, in fifty years that anyone had asked him about the case. His manner was straightforward, his mind clear. The account he gave was much the same as that which he had given the court fifty years before. He stressed that Fusi, the doctor, when the body was found near his home, made an elaborate show of charging the men of the Ntai family with the murder. And he remembered that when he and others had raced up to report the murder, Gabashane had taken them to task for being in such a hurry: 'was this man the son of a chief?' Ntsane Ntai also gave an account of certain police methods. As far as he was aware there was no coercion, but he was detained for several months, and at one point he was taken behind a screen and told to listen carefully to what one of the accomplice witnesses was telling the police.

On the following day we went with him to the edge of the rocky escarpment near Fusi Rakokoli's old homestead, on the road leading out of 'Mamathe's to the south-east. He pointed out the donga, nearly 500 metres to the north-east, in which 'Meleke's body had been found. Imposing sandstone boulders jutted from the opposite hillside. Thickets of blue wattle sprawled along the valley. At the spot where we now stood he and Makhetha had stood during the course of the trial when the four accomplice witnesses were taken down to the intersection of two dongas and each in turn was asked to indicate by throwing a stone where the corpse had been found.

THE JUDGEMENT

The trial was held in the National Council chamber, and the editor of *South Africa*, J. A. Gray, was there on the day of sentence, 16 November 1948.

> The court was packed, and the door shut, before the Judge appeared. The eleven prisoners, heavily guarded, were already waiting. Only three, including the two Chiefs, could be squeezed into the dock. The others sat huddled together in front. Each wore a big number plate to distinguish him. It was stifling hot, and from time to time one of the prisoners fanned himself with his number plate. I watched them while the Judge summed up the evidence ... There was not the slightest sign of emotion on their faces ...[40]

Nevertheless there were 'wild scenes' in the court when the guilty verdict was announced and all eleven men were sentenced to be hanged. Women screamed and jumped through windows. 'No-one expected such judgement.'[41] One of the accused, Fusi, the doctor, 'seized a sjambok ... endeavoured to escape and assaulted the police, and struggled violently before being over-powered ...'[42]

The judge was G. G. Sutton, retired Judge-President of the Cape Supreme Court. Having briefly reviewed the Crown case, he explained that it relied mainly upon accomplice evidence. Of four accomplice witnesses, one, Molemohi, had been jettisoned by the Crown as unreliable. The other three were Mapeshoane Masupha, Sepalami Mathibe and Sothi Chela. The judge noted that, according to Dr Ogg and Dr Whitworth, there were no signs of an assault on the body, but he did not find this surprising since the victim had not made much resistance. With regard to the accused Moloi Ntai, there were two independent witnesses, Ntsane and Makhetha Ntai, both relatives of the victim, 'Meleke Ntai, who had been with 'Meleke and Moloi when Moloi had told them to ride ahead and to leave 'Meleke behind. With regard to Fusi, the doctor, there were two women who gave evidence that he was not at home on the night of the murder. With regard to Gabashane, the accomplice witnesses gave evidence that he had driven to the murder in his Buick car, an independent witness declared that he saw and heard the car, and a police officer found the tracks of a car in the area. But the defence produced evidence that Gabashane's car was under repair at Dare and Glynn's, a local firm, during the period in question. The judge was satisfied that there was a car near the scene of the attack on 'Meleke Ntai, but not that the car was Gabashane's.

The judge summed up the legal position on accomplice evidence as follows:

The law is that the evidence of an accomplice must be corroborated. One accomplice may corroborate another. The question to be considered in this case is whether these three accomplices corroborate one another, and if so whether this corroboration may be relied upon.

He found that the accomplice witnesses 'told a circumstantial and terrible story with a wealth of detail and I cannot believe that it was concocted'. Mapeshoane Masupha, in particular, 'gave his evidence well and conveyed the impression to me that he was speaking the truth'. He had not been shaken by vigorous cross-examination by the defence. For his part, Sothi was 'an unintelligent man of weak character, but in my opinion he tried to tell the truth to the best of his recollection and ability'. Sepalami's evidence was substantially the same as that of Mapeshoane. The accused put up alibis or simple denials, which Sutton found unconvincing. With the agreement of his four advisers (two Basotho assessors and two administrative officers) he reached verdicts of guilty against all the accused.

In cases of murder there was only one sentence available to the court, that of death by hanging. The judge could make recommendations afterwards to the High Commissioner, however, who had discretion, as colonial governor, over whether capital sentences should be carried out. In this case Sutton recommended that four men should hang: Bereng, Gabashane, Makione Mphiko (the headman of 'Mamathe's) and Moloi Ntai (who had 'sold' his relative for £100). The others should serve terms of imprisonment which reflected their lesser culpability. Most should be given ten years' imprisonment with hard labour. As for Fusi, the doctor, there was medical evidence that he was 'sub-normal', and this, together with his violent behaviour when the verdict was announced, influenced the judge to recommend that further enquiry be made into the 'state of his mentality' before the length of his sentence was determined. Baring, the High Commissioner, agreed.[43]

ALLEGATIONS AGAINST THE POLICE AND THE ACCOMPLICE WITNESSES

This impression of the accomplice witnesses' credibility was clouded by allegations of police abuse and coercion. In August 1948, between the preparatory examination and the High Court trial, and at the instigation of Lekhotla la Bafo, Michael Scott recorded complaints of solitary confinement over long periods, of being kept cold and hungry, of being forced to sleep on a concrete floor, and of police threats and attempted bribery. He submitted these at the end of the year to the Commonwealth Relations Office in London in the context of a plea for a commission of enquiry.[44]

Several of the accused also made allegations of police misconduct when asked by the judge at the end of the trial, according to convention, if they had anything to say why sentence of death should not be passed upon them. Fusi Rakokoli, the doctor, claimed that he and Mapeshoane Masupha, the principal accomplice witness in the case, were each offered £700 by the police at Teyateyaneng to incriminate Bereng and Gabashane. Safere Ntsoso, who had been arrested at the beginning of the investigation, was held for three months, he said, and threatened with being killed if he did not confess and also incriminate Bereng and Gabashane. Moloi Ntai told the court at great length that he was arrested on 7 March and had been away from his children for nine months, under arrest; that he had been asked to incriminate Gabashane; and that he had been taken to hear Mapeshoane Masupha's confession and then asked if he would turn King's evidence too.[45]

Some sense of the way in which testimony shifted according to the winds of the moment may be derived from conflicting statements made by Anacleta Masupha, the wife of Mapeshoane Masupha, the principal accomplice witness. Interviewed by Michael Scott in Maseru in August 1948, she said that Mapeshoane had told her he was compelled to make the statements he had made at the preparatory examination 'on account of the treatment he had received at TY and that he had been guilty of cowardice'.[46] Her tone was different, however, in response to a later police enquiry into the nature of the evidence she had given to Scott. She had been subject to pressure, she said, from three men closely associated with Chief Gabashane to persuade Mapeshoane to withdraw the incriminating evidence he had given at the preparatory examination. She had resisted this pressure. She had been taken to Maseru to meet Scott in Chief Gabashane's car. She told Scott, she said to the police, 'that Mapeshoane had told me that what he had said was nothing but the truth. Mapeshoane never said anything to me about ill-treatment by the Police ...'[47] These two statements are clearly incompatible, and help us to understand why conflicting retrospective narratives often emerged of the conduct of the judicial process.

Opinion among whites in Basutoland was also sharply polarised, both as to the guilt or innocence of the two chiefs and as to the balance of their respective responsibility. On the one hand, Gabashane's defence attorney, H. M. Basner, was convinced of Gabashane's innocence, although not necessarily of Bereng's,[48] while a prominent trader at Phamong, Lud Rust, who knew Bereng well, was equally convinced that Bereng had been wrongly implicated in a 'ritual murder perpetrated by Chief Gabashane'.[49] On the other hand, the District Commissioner at Teyateyaneng at the time had no doubt of the chiefs' guilt. Many years afterwards, Gideon Pott recalled an encounter with Bereng and Gabashane in Teyateyaneng on a day that must have been immediately before or immediately after the murder took place.

> I had gone to the local bus owner to collect a tyre he was repairing for me and I saw them there with two cars crammed with followers. The tension was terrific (as I mentioned to the police officer next day) but all were smiles when I asked for my tyre after greeting them and passing the time of day.[50]

Several whites outside Basutoland were involved in the campaign for clemency for the two chiefs, particularly for Gabashane, and the question arose as to whether the chiefs had been framed or, at the least, whether the accomplice witnesses had given false evidence against them for reasons of their own. A South African businessman, Henry Cooper, had been present at the public meeting so vividly described by Douglas Reed, a month before 'Meleke Ntai was killed. At a private meeting at 'Mamathe's afterwards Gabashane told him that he was especially 'apprehensive of the possibility of having a ritual murder fathered on him' by some enemy.[51]

Suspicion fell naturally on Mapeshoane Masupha, Gabashane's junior half-brother and the principal accomplice witness. In a petition drawn up at Pietermaritzburg by Bishop Ferguson-Davie and others it was pointed out that Mapeshoane admitted that Gabashane had once removed a knife from him that he might have used in a dispute with his wife, and that he had been 'given a whipping' at the chief's court, though he claimed to carry no resentment on that account.[52] Z. K. Matthews, a well-known and respected professor at Fort Hare, submitted an anthropological generalisation about the rivalry between half-brothers, and expressed his scepticism of the evidence of Mapeshoane for this reason.[53] Others pointed to another half-brother, Jonathan Masupha. Before being charged Gabashane himself blamed the murders of Paramente and 'Meleke on what he described as Jonathan's revolt against his chieftainship.[54] Jonathan, however, was one of those accused alongside Gabashane in the Paramente Khothatso case, though he escaped conviction.

THE APPEAL: ACCOMPLICE EVIDENCE

Between the High Court judgement in the 'Meleke Ntai case in November 1948 and the petition by Bereng, Gabashane and the other accused to the Privy Council in London in March 1949 for leave to appeal against conviction, the state of the law relating to accomplice evidence appeared to have changed. The reason for this was the Judicial Committee of the Privy Council's reversal on appeal, on 11 January 1949, of convictions at the Basutoland High Court in another medicine murder case, that of Tumahole Bereng and others (1945/11).

This background is set out in detail in Chapter 9 below, in our discussion of the law relating to accomplice evidence. It is important to an understanding of the judicial knife-edge upon which the fate of the two chiefs and their accomplices was ultimately resolved. The legal arguments are complex. Very briefly, from 1944 the law provided that a conviction could be secured on the basis of the 'single evidence of any accomplice' provided that there was satisfactory independent evidence of the offence having been committed. Until the Tumahole case it was held that this phrase meant the 'evidence of any single accomplice', and so independent corroborative evidence could be provided by another accomplice. In the Tumahole case, however, the Privy Council held that the 'single evidence of any accomplice' meant the 'evidence of accomplice(s) alone'. It followed that independent corroborative evidence had to be derived from a source other than accomplice evidence, such as medical evidence that the crime of murder had been committed. In the Tumahole case there was no such evidence.

This judgement threw the Basutoland administration into some confusion and dismay.[55] The implications for the Bereng and Gabashane case were obvious. The Attorney-General, A. C. Thompson, wrote a detailed memorandum on 'ritual murder'[56] and himself travelled to London in order to assist Crown counsel.

The appellants relied heavily on the Tumahole judgement. They argued that there was no evidence that the crime of murder had actually been committed, apart from that of accomplices, since the medical evidence was inconclusive on the point. The Crown argued that there was no other reasonable interpretation of the discovery of the body and of the circumstances in which he drowned than that 'Meleke Ntai had been violently attacked before he was placed unconscious in the donga.[57]

The Judicial Committee of the Privy Council rejected the appeal on 25 July 1949. Lord Reid delivered its reasons some months later, long after the executions of Bereng, Gabashane, Makione Mphiko and Moloi Ntai. It found that there was clear independent evidence that the crime of murder had been committed.

> It cannot be supposed that the deceased voluntarily dismounted, unsaddled his horse, walked in the direction of the donga and fell in ... The only conclusion which can reasonably be drawn from the facts is that the deceased was carried to the donga and was unconscious when he was put into it and left there.

The appeal failed on this ground alone. Their Lordships also found that one accomplice could corroborate another. So the appeal failed on that ground also.[58]

As Jones afterwards remarked, most people in Basutoland had difficulty in distinguishing the legal points at issue in the Bereng and Gabashane appeal from those in the Tumahole Bereng appeal,[59] and this added to the suspicions surrounding the case. There was no justification for the Basutoland African Congress' later implication of the Attorney-General's improper interference in the judicial process,[60] since Thompson, as senior law officer for the High Commission Territories, had himself conducted the prosecution in the High Court and was primarily responsible for briefing counsel for the Crown in London. But his vigorous intervention was interpreted politically – and rightly so – by significant numbers of Basotho at the time as a determined effort to sustain the conviction of senior chiefs for medicine murder. This impression was sharpened by the fact that both Forsyth-Thompson, the Resident Commissioner, and Apthorp, the Commissioner of Police, were on leave in England at the time.[61]

On Thursday, 28 July, three days after the rejection of the appeal, a riot took place in the Maseru gaol. About 130 male prisoners 'forcibly dragged the two chiefs towards the main gate of the prison which was open at the time. The two chiefs were stated to have resisted the prisoners who attempted to release them ... These prisoners were bunched together near the open door of the male yard. They were armed with sticks, stones and iron piping and were in a hostile mood'. The prison warders eventually managed to bring the situation under control.[62]

Warrants of execution were issued on 29 July. Jones visited Bereng and Gabashane in gaol on the morning of Saturday, 30 July.[63] The two chiefs protested their innocence to him, as they did to other visitors. As Bereng languished in his prison cell his mind went back to the High Commissioner's visit to Basutoland a year before:

> Sir, I still remember when you rebuked the Paramount Chief ... in the Board Room here in Maseru, saying that if [she] does not co-operate with the Resident Commissioner, Chieftainship in Basutoland will come to an end ... Therefore it is quite evident to me that the hanging of Chiefs and many other people is the result of that speech which you made. But as many have become aware that the Government has decided to destroy Chieftainship in Basutoland, the world will soon know these cruelties done by the Basutoland Government.[64]

The British authorities were besieged by petitions for mercy, especially on behalf of Gabashane. 'Mantšebo sent telegrams to the King, to the Pope and to chiefs in the other two High Commission Territories. But Baring, as High Commissioner, was 'unable to discover' any extenuating circumstances.[65]

The two chiefs were hanged at 6.30 am on Wednesday, 3 August, together with two accomplices in the 'Meleke Ntai case and three others convicted in another medicine murder case.[66] Many people were relieved that the government was taking such a determined stand against medicine murder, but few, it seems, had really expected it would go so far as to hang two such powerful and respected chiefs as Bereng and Gabashane. Throughout the country there was a sense of profound shock. Gabashane was buried in St David's churchyard near his home at 'Mamathe's, in accordance with his own wishes. Bereng was given a funeral at Matsieng. Over 5,000 people came in cars or lorries or on horseback or foot. The service was conducted by the Roman Catholic clergy, and in the speeches that followed the chiefs of Basutoland spoke of the terrible darkness and grief that had overcome the country.[67]

AFTERMATH

After the *pitso* at Mapoteng at which Gabashane was invested with authority over the area of the disgraced Chieftainess 'Mamakhabane, Douglas Reed visited Gabashane at 'Mamathe's. He described the chief's place as 'a natural fastness, standing on a high plateau between a steep abyss and a screen of trees', with a series of palisades and a maze of huts behind a stockade. He also visited Chieftainess 'Mamathe, Gabashane's formidable senior wife, in the innermost recess of the enclosure. 'She lay on a mattress, in impregnable isolation ... With difficulty she raised herself to a sitting position ...'

> Her face was fine in feature; she wore a red-and-white striped head covering, turban-like in shape, and a red blanket which were pictures-que and even beautiful. She received an incursive stranger with perfect composure and dignity, overlaid, however, with some impenetrable restraint. The atmosphere of the place seemed to me vibrant with unspoken things ... I felt this mountainous woman lived with fear.[68]

No doubt these words were written with the advantage of hindsight. Tragedy and fear continued to stalk 'Mamathe's. Following the murder for which Gabashane was convicted, the Appendix reveals eight more cases through the 1950s and early 1960s that took place within easy range of the village. Mapeshoane Masupha, the principal accomplice witness, boldly returned home after the case, but not long afterwards he collapsed on his way home from the fields. He said he was thirsty, someone rushed to get water, but he died. This gave rise to suspicion, but since he was with his friends it was concluded that there had been no foul play.

The motif of fear recurs in descriptions of 'Mamathe herself in later years. In 1969, John and Cassandra Perry were living at 'Mamathe's, pursuing anthropological fieldwork on the workings of the Sesotho judicial system. In a letter written almost thirty years later John Perry recalled the atmosphere at the time:

> People were dead scared of the chieftainess. She was imposing and more than a match for most of the men she had to deal with. People also used to talk about poison and the arts of 'women at court' and some of them were hated because of supposed witchcraft powers. I never heard it denied that ritual murder had happened at 'Mamathe's.[69]

Perry's own relations with 'Mamathe were good, although 'she would only speak from her bedroom through a system of relayed messages and toings and froings from what I suppose we would call ladies-in-waiting'.

In June 1999, we visited Chieftainess 'Mamathe at her home. We were ushered into a dark room with a high ceiling, lit only by a hurricane lamp in one corner. High on one wall was a stag's head, and at eye-level a large photograph of the Pope and two representations of da Vinci's Last Supper. A blanketed figure appeared. We were asked to sit down. 'Mamathe sat still, completely silent. PS explained why we had come. 'I had read all the papers, and now wanted to hear what she had to say. Silence. I went on: there were so many conflicting stories. Some said one thing, some said another. It was very important to hear her account. Again silence. I went on again. The papers told me many things, but history was much more than papers. It had to do with people, and in this case she was the most important person still living. It would be very helpful if she could tell me what she knew.' Again silence, but eventually she spoke, in a voice shaky with age:

> It is very difficult to talk about this thing. It is always in my thoughts, never out of my mind … When you have been with a person the same night, and then you are told he was elsewhere – it's a pure trick. The English had lived for a long time with chiefs who were uneducated, and it was clear that when they had somebody who was enlightened they didn't like it. It was very suspicious. It was clear that the police had been instructed to find people who would claim they were present when in fact they were telling lies. There were people who claimed they were forced to give evidence by the police. They wanted to disown the evidence they had given. It was heartbreaking. It was such a heartbreaking lie. I don't think I can tell you much, the way I feel about it. The British didn't seem to like my husband.

What about the accomplice witnesses from Gabashane's own family?

> Some were fighting about the inheritance. That was their motive, and that was why they co-operated so easily with the police. After the case I was scared of them. I could not even look at them. And they were scared to come to the house … Those people who gave evidence against my husband all died quickly after the case. Mapeshoane was found dead in a donga … None of those people lived long. I think they were unhappy in their hearts.[70]

4

NARRATIVE AND COUNTER-NARRATIVE: EXPLAINING MEDICINE MURDER

'The Undying Barbarian'

Cape Argus, 28 April 1951,
headline on publication of the Jones report

I feel I am unable to be silent but have to say that it is untrue that these cruel murders are committed by the chiefs. The Government has found a trick by which the Chiefs can be taken by surprise and killed under the pretext of law, and do away with Chieftainship.

Chief Bereng Griffith Lerotholi
to Sir Evelyn Baring, 2 August 1949[1]

COMMISSION OF ENQUIRY, 1949

A few days before their execution Chiefs Bereng and Gabashane were visited by G. I. Jones, the Cambridge anthropologist who had been sent out by the Commonwealth Relations Office to enquire into the causes of medicine murder and to recommend how it might be ended. Together with a fellow anthropologist, Hugh Ashton, Jones recommended a commutation of sentence in order to avoid an upsurge of anti-white feeling. His advice was resisted, and on reflection he withdrew it.[2]

Jones' appointment was the outcome of a tortuous correspondence over a period of six months between Forsyth-Thompson, the Resident Commissioner in Basutoland; Sir Evelyn Baring, the High Commissioner in South Africa; Philip Noel-Baker, the Secretary of State for Commonwealth Relations in London; and the Colonial Social Science Research Council (CSSRC), also in London, represented in this matter by the social anthropologist Raymond Firth. Other names had also been considered. The first was that of Vernon Sheddick, who was then doing research into land tenure in Basutoland under the supervision of Isaac Schapera, but it was thought that conducting an enquiry into medicine murder would jeopardise this work. Schapera's name was also canvassed. He was Professor of Social Anthropology at the University of Cape Town and had worked extensively in the Bechuanaland Protectorate, but Baring and Forsyth-Thompson believed that the Basotho would have more confidence in someone who came from outside South Africa. Hugh Ashton's name was put forward, with strong support from Margery Perham. It was agreed that he knew more about the Basotho than any other anthropologist, but as the son of a former Assistant Commissioner he had too many local connections. Evans-Pritchard, Professor of Social Anthropology at Oxford, already well known for his work in the Sudan, was ultimately the favoured choice, but he had to turn down the invitation because he was unable to spare the time. Gwilym Jones, the second choice, was then approached and accepted. The son of a Welsh minister, Jones had been for twenty years a district official in Eastern Nigeria, where he had encountered at first hand the wave of 'leopard murders' in Calabar Province in the 1940s.[3] He was now a lecturer in social anthropology in Cambridge, where he had taught several officers of the Basutoland administration in the course of their colonial service training. It was hoped that Ashton would help him as an adviser, but Ashton had been offered an appointment as Director of Native Administration in Bulawayo and could assist for only ten days before he had to leave.

When putting forward their recommendations the CSSRC had insisted that what was needed was 'a thorough analysis of Basuto social structure'. There was no argument with that. But it also maintained that the enquiry would have to be conducted in secret on the ground that it would be 'entirely prejudiced if its object were known to the Basuto people'. This brought down the scorn of the men on the spot. Baring pointed out that in a small country such as Basutoland it would be impossible for anyone to carry out an enquiry into medicine murder on a confidential basis, and when Forsyth-Thompson went to Britain on leave, one of Baring's officials asked him to impress on the CSSRC 'that no anthropologist would get away today in Basutoland with an impersonation of a travelling bagman'. In any case the administration had no real choice. In January 1949, soon after these consultations had begun, the regent 'Mantšebo had asked for an enquiry and she had to be told that an enquiry would be held.[4]

Jones' appointment was announced on 14 July. His terms of reference were 'to inquire into and report on: I. The nature and significance of the large number of murders recently occurring in Basutoland; II. The proximate causes of and underlying reasons for the apparently increased incidence of the crime; III. The steps which the Basutoland Administration might take to remedy the position'.[5] The press was predictably drawn to the more bizarre aspects of Jones' mission. 'He's paying the Ju-Ju men a call', wrote the *Daily Mirror*. 'Mr Jones walks into a wave of terror', said the *Daily Herald*. 'Sherlock Jones Fights Voodoo', said the *Daily Mail*.[6] In response to all this publicity several people offered their services as interpreters, photographers and consultants, among them Z. K. Matthews, the veteran ANC leader.[7] None of these offers was accepted.

Jones arrived in Basutoland at the end of July 1949. He spent four and a half months in the country, a period, he said, which was much too short to

allow 'any normal anthropological field study'. His method was to carry out
a broad general survey of Basotho public opinion and to check this against a
more intensive study of three particular areas: Butha-Buthe, Mafeteng and
Mokhotlong; to study the criminal records of each murder or suspected
murder; and, since 'this disclosed that in the majority of cases the underlying motive was political', to study Basutoland's recent constitutional
reforms. He did not conduct interviews with individuals, except with
government officers, but used the technique of 'multiple interviews', mainly
with 'the common people and the "intelligentsia"' rather than with the
chiefs or with whites living in Basutoland.[8]

For the first three months of his mission Jones was helped by the Reverend
J. P. Ramseyer of Adams College in Natal. Ramseyer, the son of a missionary, acted as interpreter and guide and, through his friendship with the local
chiefs and people, helped Jones 'to understand and to be accepted' by the
people in two of the areas where he carried out his more intensive studies,
Mafeteng and Butha-Buthe. He also had a Mosotho interpreter from
outside the territory.[9] He drew on the manuscript of Hugh Ashton's
invaluable book on the Basotho (finally published in 1952), now largely
incorporating the paper on 'Ritual Murder in Basutoland' written for the
Basutoland administration a few months earlier. Ashton also made available
a paper entitled 'Mokhotlong District', which gave a detailed account of the
chieftainship disputes as a background to the murders committed there, and
an 'Analysis of ritual murders and their relation to various administrative
events', which firmly linked the increase in murders, such as it was, to the
paramountcy dispute and the role of 'Mantšebo, and to a lesser extent to the
Treasury reforms and 'the continued system of placing'.

Although his first paper was entitled 'Ritual Murder in Basutoland',
Ashton made it clear that the term 'ritual murder' was a misnomer, since no
rites, religious or otherwise, were involved.[10] In September 1949 Leloko
Lerotholi, 'Mantšebo's adviser, made a similar point in the Basutoland
National Council. Baring had referred to 'ritual murder' in his speech at the
Council's opening, and Leloko wanted it expunged from the record. Such
murders were not a custom of the people, he protested, and the term was 'an
insult to the nation'.[11] Josiel Lefela and others supported him. The Secretary
of State, Patrick Gordon Walker, was sensitive to this argument, and he
eventually insisted that the term 'Ritual Murder' should be dropped from
the title of Jones' report and replaced by the term 'Medicine Murder'.[12]

The report which Jones produced reflected his conviction, widely shared
by anthropologists, that the explanation of social phenomena was to be
found not so much through the examination of individual cases as through
the analysis of changes in society. He went through all the court records that
could be found for him, but nowhere in his report is there any detailed
discussion of the motives that were expressly given for the murders – to win a

court case, for example, or to resist the placing of a senior chief. He was much more concerned with the recent changes in the 'Native Administration'.

After chapters on 'Background' and 'Medicine Murder', Jones set out what he described as eight schools of thought on the causes of the outbreak. The first placed the blame on the doctors, the *lingaka*. This was the thinking that lay behind the Native Medicine Men and Herbalists Proclamation, which made it an offence to practise as a doctor without a licence issued by the government. 'Control the doctor', it was said, 'and you will control [*liretlo*] killings.' Jones was unimpressed. No doubt the *lingaka* encouraged the belief in protective medicine made from *liretlo*, but this belief was already widespread among the chiefs and the people at large.

The second school of thought, prevalent amongst the missionaries and their followers, particularly the Catholics, blamed the 'heathen institutions' of the Basotho, above all the initiation schools. Again Jones was unpersuaded. It was merely speculation that the use of human medicine for the purpose of initiation still continued, and there was no suggestion in any murder case that the *liretlo* were needed for initiation.[13]

The third school of thought listed by Jones placed the blame on the missions, especially the Roman Catholics. They had undermined Sesotho institutions without understanding their value, and it was thought to be no coincidence that several of the chiefs convicted of medicine murder were members of the Roman Catholic Church.[14] Jones rejected these arguments as well. He acknowledged that some of the chiefs involved in medicine murder were Catholics, but since most of the chiefs were Catholics this was only to be expected; and he saw nothing in common between the Catholics' veneration of relics and the use of medicine by Basotho.

The fourth school of thought blamed 'the contaminating influences of European civilisation', believing that the origin of these murders lay in the Johannesburg underworld or in the activities of white criminals in the Union. Jones responded that there was no evidence of *liretlo* murders in the townships of Johannesburg, and that the murderers in Basutoland were not returned city thugs but 'peasants, their native doctors and their chiefs and headmen'. It was possible that a few exceptional murders were committed to obtain *liretlo* for commercial ends, but most were 'a local product in answer to local needs'.

It was the next three schools of thought which carried the most weight with Jones. The fifth ascribed the murders to the chiefs and their personal ambitions; the sixth to 'the lesser chiefs and headmen', since they and their followers made up the majority of those who had been hanged for medicine murder; and the seventh again to the lesser chiefs and headmen, but on the ground that they would never have resorted to *liretlo* if they had not been deprived of their authority by the reforms of 1938 and 1946.

These arguments had already been widely canvassed, and Baring himself had ascribed the increase in medicine murder to the chiefs' perception that their powers were slipping away. Hugh Ashton had been more cautious. The 1938 Khubelu reforms he discounted, since in his view they made no real difference on the ground. In the period preceding the 1946 Treasury reforms, when it was known that the number of Native Courts was going to be reduced, many chiefs had felt threatened and insecure, but having analysed every case up to April 1949 Ashton could find no more than four which arose from this insecurity, only two of which were 'possibly directly attributable'.[15] He attached more importance to the dispute over the paramountcy. He believed that the rivalry between 'Mantšebo and Bereng had given rise to four murders directly and two indirectly. He also pointed out that the districts with the greatest number of murders, eleven each by his calculation, were Mokhotlong, where 'Mantšebo had her personal holding, and Berea, where Gabashane Masupha was the leading chief; and nine of the eleven Berea murders had been committed since the end of 1946, by which time Gabashane was said to have turned against 'Mantšebo and joined forces with Bereng. There had only been four murders in Bereng's ward of Phamong, but Ashton had been told that it was only recently that Bereng had believed in medicine murder. Alternatively, he suggested, Bereng's rule was so strict that he had been able to suppress the evidence. The effect of the paramountcy dispute, however, went far beyond the murders committed by the parties concerned. The involvement of the great chiefs had 'almost certainly' encouraged some of the lesser chiefs to follow their example.[16]

To evaluate these theories Jones analysed the nature of the Basotho chieftainship. At higher levels he considered the troubles that had arisen from the disputes over the paramountcy and from the weakness of a female regent. Many people believed, he said, that the murders which Bereng and Gabashane had allegedly instigated were part of a 'battle of medicine horns' between 'Mantšebo and Bereng. At lower levels he considered the troubles arising from the abuse of the placing system. This had reached a peak about 1938, when the government had intervened with the Khubelu reforms, but 'only now' were these beginning to have some effect. Many people believed that it was the uncertainty arising from the placing system that had led lesser chiefs and headmen to resort to medicine murders.

Then, in a chapter making up almost a quarter of his report, he analysed in great detail the process of reform that had begun in 1938 and was still in progress. While broadly agreeing with the need for change, he was critical of the Basutoland administration, not just for gazetting a political structure when it did not know what was happening at the lower levels, but for applying the reforms 'from the top downwards'. The greater chiefs had been consulted, but not the lesser chiefs and their people. The overall result had been 'to give the greater chiefs more security, but to depress the lesser chiefs and headmen still further at their expense and to make them more than ever dependent on the greater chiefs'.

Before drawing any inferences from this analysis Jones went on to consider the eighth school of thought, which, he said, was 'the one most frequently met with'. This alleged that the government could easily have put an end to medicine murder, but instead was using it to destroy the chieftainship so that it could hand the country over to the Union of South Africa. To achieve this the police were detaining witnesses for long periods and extorting false evidence against the chiefs. Jones dismissed the allegation of betrayal to South Africa as a 'legend', and argued that, because ordinary 'peasants' were loyal to their chiefs and afraid of them, it had been necessary to detain witnesses for longer periods than was normal. There was, however, nothing to support the assertion that the police had fabricated evidence against the leading chiefs or forced witnesses to do so.

Jones then moved on to his conclusions. The 'primary cause' of medicine murders was the belief in the efficacy of medicines prepared from human flesh. The 'secondary causes', and 'the reasons why they suddenly became so frequent and fashionable', were almost entirely political. They were: (1) the unchecked development of certain parts of the Basotho political system, in particular the undue multiplication of minor chiefs and headmen, and the placing system which gave them no real security; (2) the friction over the paramountcy between Bereng and Seeiso, the appointment of a female regent, and the consequent shift in the balance of power, with the greater chiefs gaining at the expense of the paramount; (3) the dispute over the regency, which became linked in many people's minds with the prosecution of Bereng and Gabashane, and which encouraged the belief that these medicines must be effective as they were being used by the most powerful chiefs in the country; and (4) the political reforms introduced by the government, which 'instead of remedying this situation' had 'intensified it'. For these reasons, he wrote, the lesser chiefs and headmen, the people most adversely affected by the changes, had turned to medicine murder, a course they were all the more ready to take because they believed that the greater chiefs were doing the same. Instead of stamping out medicine murders, the chiefs had left this job to the police, and had then criticised the police when they or their relatives had been threatened.[17]

Jones then turned to the question of remedies, which he dealt with under two heads: first, punitive and protective action; and, second, political remedies. Propaganda against medicine murder, he argued, would never be effective as long as people were sceptical of the chiefs' declarations against medicine murder, and they would go on being sceptical as long as the regent and her advisers took no action against chiefs who were thought to be involved in medicine murders or were failing to put a stop to them. As for the police, they were now hampered by the widespread antagonism whipped up against them, by their not being allowed to detain witnesses for long periods, and by their inability to protect Crown witnesses. Finally there were 'the hazards of the British judicial system'. By Jones' reckoning 43 per cent of the murderers escaped prosecution, and if they were brought to trial they had a 50/50 chance of acquittal. Jones recommended that the regent and her advisers should take strong action against chiefs who were ineffective in tackling medicine murder, and that extra police should be recruited, at the expense of the local people, to protect witnesses who had given evidence in medicine murder cases.

In his political remedies Jones addressed the structural difficulties which he had analysed before. To satisfy the ambitions of the greater chiefs they should be given increased responsibility in the councils of the nation – on committees of the Basutoland Council, for example, and on District Councils – and by replacing the Paramount Chief as the Native Authority by the Paramount Chief-in-Council. A hierarchy of local councils should be established, where the ordinary people could express their views, where certain powers could be decentralised and exercised, and where there could be much more contact between the British administration and the greater chiefs on the one hand and the ordinary people on the other. In this way government would work from the bottom up and not the other way around, and the gulf between the rulers and the ruled would be narrowed. The goal should be the greatest measure of self-government that was possible in Basutoland's situation, bearing in mind the country's dependence on South Africa.

REACTION TO THE JONES REPORT, 1951

Jones' report made little impact on Basotho opinion, partly because it was never translated into Sesotho. 'Mantšebo was dissatisfied and resentful, no doubt because it dismissed her allegations and anxieties as groundless and only just stopped short of accusing her of murder, but she does not seem to have protested very loudly.[18] It was not debated in the Basutoland National Council, and when medicine murder was discussed its analysis was virtually ignored. The councillors were much more concerned with what they regarded as police malpractice and false allegations against themselves. In later debates the discrediting of the whole idea of medicine murder necessarily entailed the discrediting of Jones. In the meantime the debate in the Sesotho newspapers went on almost as if the report had never been published. Among the missions the main criticism of the report appears to have come from the Roman Catholics, who believed that Jones was mistaken in rejecting initiation as one of the main causes of medicine murder.[19]

In government circles the report was generally well received, which was not surprising since it coincided so closely with the views already expressed by Baring, Forsyth-Thompson and others. Gordon Walker referred to Jones' 'able, careful and thorough investigation' and accepted the report as 'eminently fair'; Baring described it as 'a well-balanced report' which confirmed his own analysis.[20] Forsyth-Thompson was more guarded:

> Mr Jones is to be congratulated on the report he has produced. Though it contains mistakes and inaccuracies ... and though some of the solutions he suggests are either impractical or out-of-date, he has analysed with skill the history and causes of medicine murder and his conclusions I believe broadly to be correct.[21]

In fact, as Forsyth-Thompson realised only too well, the report was a damning indictment of the Basutoland administration. 'Well, you've seen the report', Rivers Thompson remarked much later. 'He blamed the local officials for everything.'[22] G. J. Armstrong, the official who had been centrally involved in the Khubelu reforms, was particularly offended.[23] In this respect, however, the report merely confirmed Baring and his colleagues in their poor opinion of the administration. In 1951 Arthur Clark, the former Chief Secretary, now in the Commonwealth Relations Office, asked why the chiefs had turned 'en masse' to medicine murder. He squarely blamed the local administrative staff, for having 'made a mess' of the regency affair, for having failed to explain and implement efficiently the 1946 reforms, and generally for being out of touch with and aloof from the people.[24]

At first Jones' analysis of the causes of medicine murder was broadly accepted.[25] On the official files the only serious voice of dissent was that of the anthropologist Vernon Sheddick. In a brief but blistering attack he criticised Jones for setting about his task not as a social anthropologist, but as a former administrative officer in the Nigerian service; for failing to subject medicine murder to any sociological analysis, but regarding it as being solely a political problem, which might or might not be correct, but there was nothing in the report to justify this assumption. As for the causes of 'Ritual Murder',

> it is important to note that the suggested causes are not in fact scientifically determined causes. In the absence of empirical evidence they can be regarded as little more than a set of assumed causes. ... They are, in fact, the possible factors that have always been suggested by the Administration as being responsible for Ritual Murder. They acquire no extra validity by being reiterated in this Report in the absence of conclusive proof or searching examination.[26]

Sheddick's analysis did not influence official thinking. Shortly afterwards, however, Lord Hailey argued that Jones had overestimated the part played by the Khubelu and Treasury reforms[27] – an argument which won acceptance in the High Commission and to which we shall return in Chapter 5 below. And later still, in January 1953, a High Commission official suggested that Jones had underestimated the part played by 'Mantšebo, 'whose succession coincided more or less with the developments ... just described'.[28]

In fact Jones had been more critical of 'Mantšebo in his draft report than in the report which was finally published. In paragraph 106 of the published

report he referred to the popular belief that the murders in the wards of
Mokhotlong, Phamong and 'Mamathe's were part of 'a kind of battle of
medicine horns between the Regent and Chief Bereng', and that the lesser
chiefs or headmen charged with most of these murders had been acting on
the orders of their superiors.[29] In a paragraph that he had eventually left out
he had gone on to say that 'not all' of this could be 'dismissed as fantasy'.
Some murders had been committed in the chiefs' own villages – in
Gabashane Masupha's village of 'Mamathe's, Bereng's village of Phamong,
and Matlere Lerotholi's village of Masaleng – and, no longer quoting public
opinion, he expressed his own view that it was very improbable that this
could have happened without their knowledge. Following the same argument as Hugh Ashton, he drew the connection between several of the
murders in the ward of Mokhotlong and Matlere Lerotholi and his relatives.

> Until the mystery and suspicion which surrounds these Mokhotlong
> murders is dissipated, the Mokhotlong people will continue to think
> that the Regent, and Matlere Lerotholi who acts for her, are involved
> in them, and people in other parts of Basutoland will consider that as
> long as the Regent and her favourite councillor remain under suspicion
> of using Diretlo medicines, lesser chiefs and headmen will be en-
> couraged to do the same.[30]

Jones had even recommended to Baring, though not in his report, that
'Mantšebo's removal should now be one of the government's main objectives.
'This should not be done by direct government action, but if the Basutos
themselves would do it then the cessation of ritual murders is possible.'[31]

When commenting on the draft report Forsyth-Thompson had voiced
his concern that, if the paragraph quoted above was published as it stood,
Matlere Lerotholi might have grounds for a libel action, and he had
suggested that it should be amended to make it clear that Jones was merely
reporting popular opinion.[32] Baring too had raised the question of a possible
libel action, and he had also felt that unless the paragraph was amended 'we
could hardly continue with the present Regent in her office. Yet it might in
present conditions be unwise for us to depose her'.[33] At a meeting in
London at which both Jones and Baring were present it was agreed that the
paragraph should be removed, rather than amended,[34] though Jones noted
tartly in his private papers that it was the Resident Commissioner who had
first asked him to put it in.[35] These records make it clear that officials were
seeking to avoid the destructive political consequences of the administration's appearing to inculpate 'Mantšebo without judicial authority.

Jones' political remedies attracted less support. Baring feared these
would expose the High Commission's policies to hostile comment from
South Africa, and in any case thought it unwise to endorse Jones' proposals
until Lord Hailey, who was due to visit Basutoland at the end of 1950, had

made his recommendations. Hailey himself declared that the report contained much that was open to criticism and much that it would be inadvisable to publish.[36] Publication of the report was in fact held up, and there were suggestions that it should not be published at all. It was Gordon Walker himself who insisted on publication, and the report was eventually presented to Parliament in April 1951.[37] Although Jones' recommendations were formally accepted, very little was done to implement them. Efforts to improve the administration continued, but no attempt was made to set up the hierarchy of local councils that Jones had proposed. Instead the government embarked on the abortive reforms that are described in Chapter 5.

Gordon Walker also accepted Jones' recommendations for punitive and other action to suppress medicine murders, but he thought it unnecessary to appoint extra police. This was because, as he believed, medicine murders had almost come to an end. In November 1950 Baring had reported 'with sincere satisfaction ... the suppression of the outbreak and the comparative disappearance of murders of this nature'.[38] Only one murder was known to have been committed in that year, and that had been successfully investigated with 'Mantšebo's full support.[39] Jones himself agreed. In the Introduction to his report, written in July 1950, he noted that since he had left the country medicine murders, though not ended completely, were 'certainly on the decline'. The 'abuses of the placing system' were now 'a thing of the past', and, although he did not say so in the report, Bereng and Gabashane had been hanged and so 'the war of the medicine horns' was over. 'The epidemic of *diretlo* killings appears to be coming to an end ...', he wrote, 'and the country can now settle down in peace to consolidate and extend the constitutional reforms made during the last twelve years.'[40]

'Mantšebo even began to come back into official favour. After visiting Basutoland in August 1950 Baring reported that her relations with the government had improved, that she had co-operated well in grazing control, and that she was on better terms with the police, to whom she had given every assistance in the single case of medicine murder that year. Her health too had improved: she had been diagnosed as suffering from diabetes and was now using insulin.[41] When Gordon Walker visited Basutoland in February 1951, she expressed the hope that he had heard that she was doing everything she could to put an end to medicine murder, and in return he acknowledged her offer of co-operation.[42] Later that year she visited Britain, where she was received by the Queen, the King being ill.[43]

It was all an illusion, and it did not last long. There were seven murders committed in 1950 that eventually came to light, and in 1951 ten more. Although the great crisis has always been located in the spate of murders in 1948 and the hangings of Bereng and Gabashane in 1949, in fact, as Graph 2.2 shows, there were many more cases reported to government in the 1950s than in the 1940s: 102 compared with sixty-one. Even if we compare two shorter periods, 1945–9 and 1950–4, the figures are forty-four and forty-eight respectively. These figures may not be very reliable as indicators of the actual incidence of murders, but they certainly do not suggest a decline. Moreover, although none of them was hanged, the senior chiefs continued to be involved. Most crucially of all, in 1953 'Mantšebo's favourites and counsellors, Matlere Lerotholi and his half-brother Mabina, were charged with the murder of a man in Mokhotlong, and there was evidence which strongly suggested that Mabina had taken some of the *liretlo* to 'Mantšebo at Matsieng.[44] Although all the accused were acquitted, 'Mantšebo and her close associates were mired in suspicion again.

THE OFFICIAL NARRATIVE: 'HEART OF DARKNESS'[45]

By the time that Jones' report was published two broad narratives of medicine murder had been established. In the first, the official narrative, murders were being committed by chiefs and headmen, among them the most powerful people in the land. The police were conducting their investigations fairly and to the best of their abilities, and the judges were conducting their trials in the best traditions of British justice. In the second, a counter-narrative to the first, there was no such thing as medicine murder, or else such murders were being committed by persons of no importance: in either case the British authorities, by abusing the powers of the police, were exploiting them in order to destroy the chieftainship, and some Basotho believed that their ultimate aim was to hand the country over to South Africa. Many who began as supporters of the official narrative shifted over time, either through conviction or under pressure, to a position more supportive of the counter-narrative. In the early debates in the Basutoland National Council medicine murder was condemned as a Basotho crime, in the later debates as a colonial slander. There were many, like 'Mantšebo herself, who would subscribe to one narrative when dealing with the British authorities and to the other in situations where the Basotho were dominant.

Both narratives carried with them – usually implicitly but sometimes explicitly – powerful constructions of culture and identity. Chieftainship was one of the defining institutions of Sesotho culture, and belief in the power of medicine was widespread. The assertion that Basotho chiefs were guilty of medicine murder and that they were being assisted by hundreds of their followers was bound to have profound implications for views and evaluations of Sesotho culture as a whole, and indeed of the Basotho people.

Some observers, notably Ashton, were careful to point out that, while most Basotho believed in the power of medicine, only 'a tiny minority' were actually making use of human flesh.[46] These observers condemned medicine murder while expressing at the same time a deep-felt admiration of many other aspects of Sesotho culture. And some people drew a distinction between those elements that, as they saw it, were presided over by the 'witch-doctor' and that included medicine and initiation, and the rest of Sesotho culture, which had many strengths and virtues.[47] But others, in varying degrees, believed that medicine murder was integral to the culture, the natural outgrowth of a pagan and primitive way of life and of a system of crude and irrational beliefs unenlightened by Christianity and civilisation.

By building on the horrors of medicine murder the official narrative gave added legitimacy and justification to the work of the missions and the British administration,[48] and inevitably missionaries and officials were prominent among those who broadened the attack. We have already quoted Hermann Dieterlen, writing in 1896 after the first recorded medicine murder: 'this is where paganism can finish up'.[49] More than half a century later, in 1951, his son, Georges Dieterlen, described the latest murders as 'Manifestations of Modern Heathenism'.[50] The Catholic paper *Moeletsi* declared that medicine murders were 'prompted by the most deeply-rooted superstitious instincts ingrained in the soul of our nation',[51] and Catholic missionaries, especially Father Laydevant, took the lead in connecting medicine murder with male initiation.[52] The Anglican Archdeacon Arthur Amor described the Basotho as 'utterly barbarous, unfit to receive benefits from outside ... unworthy of acceptance into the brotherhood of free nations'.[53] Cyprian Thorpe, another Anglican, perceived the recent outbreak of medicine murders as part of 'a wave of aggressive paganism', a new form of resistance to European pressure and influence.[54]

Some government officials took similar views. In 1949 one of the policemen most directly involved with investigating medicine murders, Lieutenant M. C. van Straaten, described them as a reversion to barbarism that revealed 'the undercurrents of strong primitive feelings that still exist despite the Africans' development under European guidance'.[55] Baring's Chief Secretary, Arthur Clark, wrote in a draft memorandum for the High Commissioner that the Basotho had 'disclosed by their reversion to this savage practice how thin was their veneer of apparent progress', and that they had 'to be encouraged as fast as lies within our power into ways of life more consonant with civilized ideals'.[56] J. A. Steward, a High Commission official, added a new explanation of his own, that Africans were more cruel than Europeans and had less respect for human life, adducing as (supposed) evidence for this statement 'Chaka's decimation of his regiments before battle' at the beginning of the nineteenth century.[57]

The missions' Basotho adherents and the *bahlalefi*, the educated élite, followed the same narrative, though not always to the same extent as the missionaries and the officials. Many people rejected the link between medicine murder and initiation, and *Mochochonono*, the mouthpiece of the Basutoland Progressives, took van Straaten to task for his allegation that 'a number of influential chiefs' were still drawn to pagan rites, arguing that only two such chiefs had actually been found guilty of murder.[58] Many others, however, used the missionaries' vocabulary of 'darkness' (*lefifi*) and 'heathenism' (*bohetene*) to argue that only when the nation genuinely embraced Christianity would medicine murder come to an end.[59]

In South Africa the murders strengthened the conviction that African culture was hopelessly benighted. 'The Undying Barbarian', the quotation at the head of this chapter, was the headline in the *Cape Argus* in April 1951 when Jones' findings were presented to Parliament. 'Although drawn up in the sober dispassionate style of the trained anthropologist, the Jones report must be one of the most blood-curdling documents ever laid on the table of the House.'[60] Later in the same year the South African writer Joy Packer visited Basutoland. She arrived on the eve of Forsyth-Thompson's departure, and stayed with G. J. Armstrong, the Government Secretary. Her only interest was in medicine murder, the 'skeleton in Basutoland's cupboard'. She attributed the 'mutilated horrors' to 'ancient African beliefs, super-stitions and sorceries that come to the surface in time of stress'. The stress, she said, taking her cue from Jones, had its origin in the recent political reforms. She wished that some of the critics of 'native policy' in South Africa could understand a 'wider difference' between Africans and whites than colour alone. She was taken to meet 'Mantšebo at Matsieng, and her disparaging description of the regent was entirely of a piece with her discussion of medicine murder: 'a ponderous silhouette appeared in the doorway, and 'Mantšebo Seeiso lumbered in with a nautical roll', her 'broad face about as expressive as a damp sponge'.[61]

Packer's narrative may have been the most racist and offensive to be printed, but at least she had stopped short of accusing 'Mantšebo of medicine murder. John Gunther, the American commentator, was less guarded, and the publication that caused the greatest outrage in Basutoland was his *Inside Africa*, first published in 1955.[62] He too was concerned only with medicine murder – it was that alone, he said, that made Basutoland 'interesting' – and in substance, though not in style, his interpretation was also very largely based on Jones. Medicine murders, he said, arose 'out of the most ancient and entrenched superstitions of the Basuto nation', and involved 'people of the highest rank'. Every chief had his own medicine horn, 'whether it is filled with human flesh or not', and these horns had been passed down 'from father to son since the founding of the nation', '*but no murder horn has ever been found*'. After this invocation of the mysteries of darkest Africa, Gunther repeated Jones' account of 'Mantšebo's apparent victory in the battle of the medicine horns and suggested that things would be better when she was no longer regent. To avoid any possibility of a libel action, he 'pointed out carefully that she has never been accused of any crime, although her name was mentioned in at least one trial', but the implications were unmistakeable.[63]

THE COUNTER-NARRATIVE: COLONIAL CONSPIRACY

At the beginning of the discussions and debates about medicine murder the official narrative, with its several variants, was almost the only one to be heard. There was merely a faint prefiguring of the counter-narrative in the worries of 'Mantšebo and other chiefs about their being falsely incriminated for murders they had not committed. But within a few years the full counter-narrative was being vigorously expounded by Josiel Lefela and his Lekhotla la Bafo, and as more and more of their number were accused of murder it was taken up increasingly by the chiefs. Perhaps the most decisive event was the hanging of Bereng and Gabashane, for this showed that the British would stop at nothing in their determination to put an end to medicine murder. When Jones conducted his enquiry he found that this 'school of thought', as he called it, was 'the one most frequently met with'.[64]

As in the first narrative, statements about medicine murder were caught up in accounts of Sesotho culture as a whole, and also of British imperialism. For Lefela the times of Moshoeshoe were a 'golden age' when the Basotho enjoyed their independence and a chief was a chief through the people. The British, he believed, had corrupted the chiefs, and their recent reforms had hastened their transition from fathers of their people into salaried officials. He was deeply disturbed by the increasing dependence of the Basotho on the South African labour market, and he was critical of the missions for their attacks on Sesotho custom. For Lefela whites were destroyers of a rich and valued way of life, not civilisers and educators, and the British administration was not a benevolent protector, but a potential betrayer. The prosecution of the chiefs for medicine murder was just a part of this larger scheme. Even if not inventing the murders the British were exaggerating and exploiting them, and in a final twist to the argument he accused the government of employing thugs to commit the murders themselves and then getting the police to incriminate the chiefs.[65]

At first Lefela was distrusted by the chiefs. They resented his criticism of their abuses of power, and when he demanded more popular representation in the National Council they saw him as a potential rival. As the allegations of medicine murder swirled around them, however, they began to clamber onto common ground. Lefela's own chief, 'Mamakhabane, turned to him for help when she was accused of murder, and 'Mantšebo, as we have seen in Chapter 3, sought his advice at a meeting of the Sons of Moshoeshoe at Matsieng. The chiefs not only complained that they were being falsely accused, but took on Lefela's conspiracy theory as well. Two of the most important converts were Bereng and Gabashane. Another was 'Mantšebo herself.[66]

In 1952 the attack on the government was given a new impetus by the founding of the Basutoland African Congress (BAC) under the leadership of Ntsu Mokhehle. Almost at once the BAC took over the mantle of Josiel Lefela's Lekhotla la Bafo and established itself as the leading nationalist organisation in the country, while the old Basutoland Progressive Association, which had never struck deep roots outside the educated élite, rapidly lost all serious influence. Recognising the incipient threat to its authority, the British administration was both hostile and alarmed.[67]

A graduate of Fort Hare and now a schoolteacher, Mokhehle had been a member of the Lekhotla la Bafo, and he admired in particular the movement's aim to preserve and perpetuate 'the Basotho culture in its indigenous and purer form, unadultrated [sic] by any foreign culture'.[68] He acknowledged and paid tribute to the part played by Lefela in arousing national consciousness, shared his unwavering hostility to the British government and agreed with his account of medicine murder. It was, he said, a 'trick intended to discredit the Chiefs and pave the way for the eventual incorporation of Lesotho into the Union of South Africa'.[69] He was also acutely conscious of the shame which the accounts of medicine murder brought on the Basotho people. The BAC's Manifesto, published in October 1952, set out three main objectives: to prevent incorporation into South Africa, to put an end to racial discrimination, and to achieve immediate self-government.[70] Since Mokhehle, like Lefela, believed that the British were using medicine murder to prepare the way for incorporation, part of his campaign was to get rid of this 'stigma'. A year after its foundation the BAC identified this as one of the three most important problems it had to face. Jones, it said, had offered nothing new. What was needed was a new Commission 'to enquire into this unfortunate position to rid our nation of this stigma'.[71] Bennett Khaketla, who became Deputy Leader of the BAC, later recalled that 'in all his political meetings [Mokhehle] never failed to say something about the murders. The whole thing had become such a threat that all the Chiefs were dead scared, and none felt himself immune from its vile, all-embracing tentacles'.[72]

Mokhehle developed his case most fully in his Presidential Address to the BAC's Annual Conference in December 1956.[73] It was a remarkable *tour de force*. Piling quotation on quotation about medicine murder, he accused government officials, judges, the press, ministers of religion and white traders of conducting a propaganda campaign to spread the idea that the mutilated bodies being found throughout the country were the result of 'murders perpetrated by the Chiefs and their followers'. 'I believe it was Herr Hitler, the great Nazi', he said, 'who once wrote that if a false assumption or a lie is repeated often enough and by a sufficient number of persons, especially those in high places, it soon becomes a matter of belief.' And once the belief had become accepted, it became impossible for believers to consider evidence objectively. Whenever, therefore, a mutilated body was found, the police already believed that a medicine murder had been committed and were incapable of conducting unprejudiced inquiries. Mokhehle gave instances where these assumptions had proved to be false.

He then quoted extensively from the counter-narrative, from statements by the Lekhotla la Bafo in particular, alleging that medicine murders were 'a fiction of the imagination', a plot to do away with the chieftainship.

What, after all, were the sources of information about medicine murder? The answer was accomplice evidence. Witnesses were kept in police custody 'for weeks, months, nay even for years', and they were bribed, or threatened with prosecution and hanging, if they did not confess and become Crown witnesses. It was on the basis of the evidence of these accomplice witnesses that chiefs were prosecuted and hanged. Several people had made statements testifying to such treatment at the hands of the police, and Mokhehle quoted them at length.

He then turned to an analysis of the law on accomplice evidence. At first, he said, it followed the English rule of practice. Under this a person could not be found guilty of murder on the basis of accomplice evidence unless it had been corroborated by 'any material, independent evidence proving the crime to have been committed, and linking the accused with the crime'. That was why Tumahole Bereng and others won their appeal to the Privy Council in 1949. 'Then', said Mokhehle, 'a queer thing happened.' The law was amended, and the English rule was replaced by the South African rule, under which a person could be convicted 'on the single evidence of any accomplice; provided that the offence has, by competent evidence other than the single and unconfirmed evidence of the accomplice, been proved to the satisfaction of such court to have been actually committed'. It was on this basis, Mokhehle alleged, that Bereng and Gabashane were convicted. He also alleged that the change to the South African practice was made because 'Britain is committed to a policy of approximating the administration of the Protectorates with that of the Union of South Africa with a view to making incorporation smooth, easy and unobtrusive'.[74]

The English, he said, were well aware of false trials in other countries: Nero's prosecutions of the Christians, Hitler's prosecutions of the Communists, and the show trials of Stalinist Russia. Above all they knew of the witchcraft trials that had taken place in their own country in the seventeenth century, and Mokhehle pointed out several parallels between these witchcraft trials and the medicine murder trials. The English, like the Basotho, believed in witchcraft; the prosecutions were based on the admissions and confessions of accomplices; these admissions and confessions were said to be made voluntarily; and the courts accepted the existence of witchcraft and were ready to believe everything that was confessed. With this experience the English in their own country were no longer prepared to base convictions on uncorroborated accomplice evidence; yet they were willing to hang the Basotho on just such evidence.

It was because of the public's loss of faith in the British administration of justice that the government had called in G. I. Jones, or 'Professor Jones' as

Mokhehle called him at this stage. But Mokhehle was contemptuous of 'the honourable Professor'. Jones admitted that the police had sometimes obtained statements by means of questionable methods, but it did not follow, he said, that the statements were false. Lawyers, Mokhehle pointed out sternly, took a much more serious view. Worse still, Jones had come to his enquiry with his mind already made up, for he already believed in the fact of medicine murder. It was small wonder that the report was so highly regarded by the government. It was like a tortoise shell into which officials and police could retreat when attacked.

Mokhehle argued that in not a single case had it been proved that any medicine contained human flesh or blood, and that the confusion over the name – witchcraft murders at first, then ritual murders, then medicine murders, now *liretlo* murders – reflected a hopeless confusion of mind. He dismissed Jones' 'battle of medicine horns' between 'Mantšebo and her rivals as 'a phantasy – a wishful creation of the honourable Professor's own misguided imagination … The Paramount Chieftainess has never committed any type of crime – to say nothing about her committing murder'. He reminded his readers about the case in which 'Mantšebo's alleged victim, Borane, had reappeared alive and well. He rehearsed again those cases in which accomplice witnesses had been unmasked as liars or had claimed to have given their evidence under compulsion, and he found it remarkable that not a single convicted murderer had ever made a pre-execution confession, if not to save their skins, at least to save their souls.[75]

In response to this speech the BAC conference passed a resolution that there were no Sesotho medicines made out of human parts; that Jones' report was 'false and misleading'; that because there were no medicines made out of human parts 'the idea that the mutilated bodies found in our land are by the chiefs who kill humans to make medicines out of their parts is false'; and that the United Nations should send a commission of enquiry into the matter.[76]

The BAC's stand attracted the support of several chiefs, who, according to Khaketla, 'believed that the BAC was their only salvation'.[77] But this unity of interest on medicine murder was more than offset by the inevitable struggle for leadership between chiefs and politicians. The BAC was critical of the chiefs' abuses of their powers, and warned that the chieftainship could survive only if it was responsive to the needs of the people. More important, it wanted more popular representation on the National Council, with the chiefs being reduced to a minority. Soon the allegation was being made that the BAC was resolved to destroy the chieftainship.[78]

The counter-narrative on medicine murder made no impact on British officials, except to confirm them in their view that Lefela was crazy and the BAC leadership dangerously irresponsible.[79] At times they found it hard to accept that Mokhehle and his colleagues were sincere in their allegations, and suspected that they were using medicine murder as a way of gaining support and whipping up hostility against the government. It was all part of the BAC's nationalist programme.[80]

Nor did the BAC's denial of medicine murder make any impact on the leadership of the churches, and the editors, contributors and correspondents of their newspapers, *Leselinyana* and *Moeletsi*, referred to it only in order to dismiss it. Writing in *Leselinyana*, Edwin Leanya of the Basutoland Progressive Association accused the BAC of trying to flatter the chiefs when it denied that there was any such thing as medicine murder, and he condemned it for teaching children to hate Europeans. The editor of *Leselinyana* was at a loss to understand how anyone could deny the existence of medicine murder and could only suggest that those whom the gods wanted to destroy they first made mad. How could the Basotho fight medicine murder, asked one correspondent, when so many were denying that it even existed? Another put the question that the BAC could never satisfactorily answer: why were so many mutilated bodies being found if there were no medicine murders?[81] According to the editor of *Moeletsi*, everyone who read his newspaper knew of the existence of medicine murder, and he made a point of publishing long and detailed reports on murder cases to make sure that his readers got the message.[82]

But there is no doubt that the second narrative commanded widespread support. In 1949 Jones had found it to be the school of thought 'most frequently met with'.[83] Government officials acknowledged its growing strength, especially among the chiefs,[84] and in 1955 a contributor to *Leselinyana* expressed his shock that so many people, even a majority (*bongata ba batho*), said that there was no such thing as medicine murder.[85]

Opinion in the early and mid-1950s, then, was sharply polarised. On the one hand, the repeated discovery of mutilated bodies and the gruesome details adduced in court cases were incontrovertible evidence, for very many people, that medicine murders were being routinely committed. On the other, accomplice witnesses were allegedly coerced by the police into falsely incriminating chiefs and headmen, as part of a colonial conspiracy to discredit the chieftainship and undermine Sesotho culture. These narratives formed part of the battle for the hearts and minds of ordinary Basotho which engaged colonial officials, missionaries, chiefs and nationalist politicians. Analysis of this battle follows in Chapter 5. Meanwhile, in Case Study 4, the spotlight shifts to the remote Mokhotlong District, where much of the drama was played out through the robustly ambiguous person of Matlere Lerotholi, 'Mantšebo's lover, favourite counsellor and deputy in her own ward.

Case Study 4

'A MOST UNSAVOURY STATE OF AFFAIRS': MOKHOTLONG, 1940s–50s

Chief Matlere Lerotholi ... was a very impressive figure of a man, and quite incongruous in this wild setting of a cluster of thatched mud huts with the small courthouse in the centre. He was dressed in an immaculately cut Savile Row suit, and over his highly polished shoes he boasted spats ... There was an aura of power and authority, and something of mysticism.

David Alexander[1]

Although Matlere was undoubtedly a murderer, we soon formed a close and happy relationship. It was clear that he had the interests of his people at heart ...

Ray Cordery[2]

If I were to tell you about all Sesemane's murders we would be speaking until sunset. There were many murders, and they were all for Chief Matlere.

Molosi Kao[3]

Mokhotlong was a remote and windswept place, sometimes described as 'the most isolated outpost of the British Empire'.[4] From the Natal side to the east, it could be reached only by the very steep Sani Pass, initially a rough donkey track and later a jeep track, that scaled the forbidding heights of the Drakensberg escarpment. From the north-west the dirt road from the Lesotho lowlands was often impassable in the summer months when heavy rain fell, and in the winter months when snow blocked the upper passes at heights of 3,000 metres. Otherwise there was a small airstrip. Administrative officers sometimes found it convenient to be cut off from the busy routines of the much more populous lowland districts. But sometimes they found the isolation monotonous and oppressive, and postings there were seldom longer than two years. At the end of the Second World War the administrative district of Mokhotlong, which until then had been a sub-district of Qacha's Nek, became a separate district in itself.

In the 1940s and 1950s the district of Mokhotlong contained three senior chieftainships: Mokhotlong, under the Ward Chief of Mokhotlong, who was also the Paramount Chief (we refer to this as 'Mantšebo's); Molumong and Nkokamele, subordinate to the Ward Chief of Mokhotlong (we refer to this as Rafolatsane's); and Malingoaneng, under the chief of Malingoaneng (we refer to this as Tlokoeng). Officially the chief of Tlokoeng was also subordinate to the Ward Chief of Mokhotlong, whose fiefdom thus embraced the whole district.[5] The relationship of the chief of Tlokoeng to the Ward Chief of Mokhotlong was, however, sensitive and controversial. How it came to be so is outlined in the political history of Mokhotlong District which follows.

A SIGNIFICANT CLUSTER?

The Appendix reveals twenty-four cases of confirmed or suspected medicine murder in the Mokhotlong District in the colonial period: two in the 1920s, two in the 1930s, twelve in the 1940s, five in the 1950s, and three in the 1960s. In Table CS4.1 these twenty-four cases are listed by the area in which the murder or suspected murder was committed. We have been unable to identify the site of one murder (1945/7) with any precision. Otherwise, six murders were committed in Tlokoeng, three in Rafolatsane's area, and thirteen, all in the 1940s and 1950s, in 'Mantšebo's area. 'Mantšebo's area (Mokhotlong) was originally carved out of the Rafolatsane area in the early 1930s. The second case in the series (1928/1) occurred before this division and is not listed for that reason either under 'Mantšebo's area or under Rafolatsane's.[6]

The Appendix does not purport to be definitive. But two observations are striking. First, thirteen out of the total of twenty-four – more than half – were committed in 'Mantšebo's area, which in the late 1940s had about a quarter of the district's population.[7] Second, these thirteen all took place within the two decades (1941–60) of 'Mantšebo's rule as regent at Matsieng, and of Chief Matlere Lerotholi's rule as her representative in the Mokhotlong ward. These observations imply significance in the identification of an 'inner' cluster of medicine murders in the district: those shown under the heading of 'Mantšebo's area in Table CS4.1, ranging from case 1940/2 to case 1959/2. The question is: what significance?

Our starting point is the repeated suspicions of instigation and complicity that hung around the family of Matlere Lerotholi throughout this period, in its relationship to the political intrigues in the Mokhotlong District and to the person of the regent herself. The root of the enduring connection between the two was the placing in 1925 by Paramount Chief Griffith of his son Seeiso as Chief of Mokhotlong, followed by 'Mantšebo's succession as Chief of Mokhotlong after Seeiso's death in 1940. This had the consequence that local political conflicts in the district were affected by the dispute over the regency at national level between 'Mantšebo and Bereng. Meanwhile Matlere Lerotholi and his relatives, who were initially humble clients of Seeiso, were able through his patronage to insert themselves into,

Table CS4.1 The distribution of medicine murder cases by area within the Mokhotlong District, 1920s–60s.

Tlokoeng	'Mantšebo's	Rafolatsane's	Unidentified
1923/1			
	1928/1		
1934/1			
1935/1			
	1940/2		
	1943/1		
	1943/3		
	1944/7		
1945/1			
	1945/2		
	1945/6		
			1945/7
	1945/8		
		1948/8	
	1948/10		
	1948/24		
	1952/12		
	1953/5		
	1959/1		
	1959/2		
		1959/6	
1961/1			
1961/2			
		1961/3	

and partially displace, existing hierarchies of authority in Mokhotlong. They were bitterly resented for this reason, both as outsiders to the district and as unscrupulous opportunists committed to their own aggrandisement. Matlere himself was long reputed to be 'Mantšebo's lover, and in later years he often acted for her as Paramount Chief at Matsieng. Inevitably, as her administrative representative in the Mokhotlong District, he found himself at odds both with the Ward Chief of the Batlokoa and with many representatives of the Rafolatsane chieftainship who were displaced from power. It is Matlere's position, as the 'strongman' of local politics for two decades, who was also directly and personally accountable to the regent, that comes under particular scrutiny in our effort to explain the pattern of medicine murders recorded in the district.

Through repeated rumour and circumstantial evidence, despite his acquittal in the two cases in which he was himself indicted, a series of district officers thought him deeply implicated in the practice of medicine murder, probably on behalf of his patron and lover 'Mantšebo.[8] Otherwise, as a strong and capable chief, Matlere was respected and admired by the colonial administration, not least for his consistently vigorous support of measures for the conservation of grazing land in the mountain areas. A report in 1948 found him 'intelligent, practical, resourceful, ruthless, cunning, anxious for the general progress of his people, energetic, trustworthy on indifferent matters but not perhaps where his personal interests are touched nor re ritual murders in which he is widely believed to indulge'.[9]

As a bizarre counterpoint to these suspicions, he was one of Ashton's key informants on the murders in Mokhotlong in the 1940s. His response to detailed questioning in August 1949 was to acknowledge the fact of the murders but to suggest that, for some reason, ordinary people wished falsely to incriminate their chiefs.

> He says he can't think what is causing them, and that he is really uneasy and baffled by them. He cannot believe that flesh and blood placed in the medicine horn can produce any results whatsoever.[10]

There are two key reasons for a detailed investigation of the Mokhotlong cluster of medicine murders. The first we have already touched on: its alleged connection with the notorious 'battle of the medicine horns' between 'Mantšebo and Bereng. The second is the density of analysis of the political conflicts and administrative changes in the district between the 1920s and the late 1940s that is available in the 'Mokhotlong files' passed by Rivers Thompson to David Ambrose, in the published and unpublished work of Hugh Ashton, and in certain files in the Public Record Office in London.[11] Two documents, which Ashton wrote after his brief visit to Mokhotlong in August 1949, are particularly important in respect of the links they suggest, albeit often speculatively, between individual motives and shifting political circumstances.[12]

MOKHOTLONG DISTRICT: A POLITICAL HISTORY

In 1925 Paramount Chief Griffith placed his son Seeiso in the Mokhotlong District over the two long-established chiefs in the area, Lelingoana and Rafolatsane. Lelingoana was chief of the Batlokoa. In return for his assistance to the Basotho in the Gun War of 1880–1 he had been given a large area between the Senqu and the Malibamatšo rivers, from the confluence of those rivers to the escarpment at Phofung (Mont-aux-Sources). In the early 1890s Rafolatsane Letsie was sent up to supervise a 'mixed collection of Basotho' who had occupied the area between the Senqu and the Drakensberg escarpment along the eastern boundary of Basutoland. Both chiefs were directly accountable to the Paramount Chief. In placing Seeiso over them Griffith required that each of them give up an area of land for Seeiso's personal caretaking. Very different outcomes emerged, however, in respect of these two claims. The Batlokoa ultimately succeeded in their resistance to the excision of a substantial portion of their territory, and Seeiso's caretaking was carved out exclusively, as it turned out, from the Rafolatsane area.

Tlokoeng

Chief Lelingoana strongly resisted the super-imposition of Seeiso. He claimed to be in a position similar to that of Moshoeshoe's sons Molapo, Masupha and Majara, over whose areas the Paramount Chief was not entitled to place anyone.[13] In 1928 the Resident Commissioner and the Paramount Chief appear to have agreed that the chieftainship of the Batlokoa should be relegated to a sub-chieftainship, but that on account of his age and seniority Chief Lelingoana should retain the title 'Chief' until his death. He died in 1933, reputedly at the age of eighty-eight, a 'thin stick of a man' who had been chief of the Batlokoa for well over fifty years.[14] He was succeeded by his son Mosuoe, who was described by officials as shy and retiring in personality. Seeiso tried to enforce his rights over Mosuoe but the results were inconclusive and a stalemate ensued.[15]

The struggle with the Batlokoa was resumed by 'Mantšebo in 1944 when she asked Mosuoe for a *bokhinapere* area in which, figuratively, to 'knee-halter her horse'. Mosuoe resisted, and after a series of see-sawing judgements was able to maintain his position. In practice the *bokhinapere* area reverted to the Batlokoa but, according to Ashton, writing in 1949, 'Matlere [as 'Mantšebo's representative] quietly continues his intrigues'.[16]

Rafolatsane's

When he was placed in 1925 Seeiso established a village site close to Mokhotlong camp, in a small part of Rafolatsane's area set aside for his personal occupation. Initially he had no room to accommodate his followers. A considerable dilemma became apparent. Having 'little income, expensive tastes and an important position to keep up', Seeiso quickly fell heavily into debt.[17] It was not until 1933, after Rafolatsane's death in 1930, that a peaceful division of the area was effected, with about three-fifths of it passing to Seeiso and about two-fifths remaining to Rafolatsane's heir, his daughter-in-law 'Mankata. Seeiso's area comprised the northern and eastern sections of the 'original' Rafolatsane area, to the Drakensberg escarpment, and embraced Mokhotlong camp. The Rafolatsane chieftainship was left with a greatly reduced area, with its headquarters at Molumong, between the Senqu and Sehonghong rivers.

'Mankata's succession to the chieftainship was disputed by Rafolatsane's senior widow, 'Makori, and others. Hostilities broke out. In one battle 'Mankata, who was described as 'flamboyant' by Ashton, led her men at a gallop with a revolver in each hand.[18] Eight people were killed and in 1933 she was sentenced to six years' imprisonment. She became insane in 1936 and was released from gaol, but never recovered her position.[19] The disputes over the succession became more complex and confusing. In 1938 Taelo Letsie was appointed to act as chief for 'Mankata, but in 1947 he was replaced by Lerato Rafolatsane. 'Mankata died in 1953, the dispute flared up yet again and was still outstanding in the late 1950s.[20]

Seeiso's/'Mantšebo's area

After he had carved out his own caretaking in 1933 from the 'original' Rafolatsane area, Seeiso established his new headquarters at Thabang, close to Mokhotlong camp. By 1939 he had placed fourteen followers over existing headmen. The most important of these was Matlere Lerotholi, who was listed in the 1939 official gazette as sub-chief of Masaleng, a village overlooking the Mokhotlong river. He had come up to the Mokhotlong District with Seeiso, and those who resented his new importance described him as Seeiso's herd-boy. His mother was a junior wife of Paramount Chief Lerotholi, the father of Paramount Chief Griffith, 'her position being somewhere in the tens'.[21] He was therefore heavily dependent on Seeiso's patronage. His position was strengthened in 1939 when Seeiso became Paramount Chief and moved to Matsieng and left him as his local representative at Thabang. He continued in this position when Seeiso died in 1940 and 'Mantšebo became Paramount Chief regent. Unsurprisingly, in the hostile terrain of Mokhotlong, his loyalty first to Seeiso and then to 'Mantšebo was unquestioned.

Matlere in turn placed his own half-brothers. He had much more scope to do this after he moved his own chieftainship from Masaleng to Motsitseng, on the Moremoholo river, in the early 1940s, when he became chief over thirteen headmen instead of sub-chief over four.[22] The most prominent of Matlere's half-brothers were Mahlomola, Makhahlela, Mabina, Mosiuoa and Seabatha. Mahlomola was appointed a 'small headman' at Linotšing, a village ten kilometres south-east of Mokhotlong. Makhahlela took Matlere's place as headman of Masaleng.[23] Mabina was appointed headman at Maphiring, in the Sehonghong valley. Like Matlere, he was one of 'Mantšebo's favourites, and in the early 1950s sometimes acted as Paramount Chief when she was absent or indisposed. He was also a devout Catholic, and took the name of Joseph. Mosiuoa was placed in the Senqu valley, over 'an excellent man', headman Nkau, to which appointment there was much local opposition. Another half-brother, Seabatha, was appointed as headman of Mojakisane's village, south of Mokhotlong camp, early in 1942, an appointment resisted by the established headman, Maraene Tšita.[24]

When 'Mantšebo became regent she wanted formally to appoint Matlere as Acting Chief at Thabang but this was opposed by the Assistant District Commissioner 'on the grounds of his being too strong-willed; his hatred of the Batlokoa, which would stir up the trouble with Mosuoe which was dying down; and popular resentment at the growing power of Matlere and his family'.[25] Gideon Pott, newly-appointed Assistant District Commissioner for Mokhotlong, reported on them in disparaging terms in August 1941, although he had not yet met Matlere himself:

On looking into this branch of the Lerotholi family I think I find the reason for their unpopularity. They come from a very junior house of Late Paramount Chief Lerotholi and as my interpreter and servant state 'would be nobodys' in the lowlands. Matlere was Seeiso's herd-boy and everyone knows that. His brothers, Mahlomola, Mabina and Mosiuoa are mere usurpers who have suddenly been thrust into power here through influence and not by ability or by right. The people resent this very much and will continue to do so. All of this family (bar Matlere whom I have not seen) have that unpleasant, crotchety look far too often which shows that they do not get orders carried out as they wish and are not shown the respect they would like.

The following year Pott wrote in his characteristically forthright manner:

> These four brothers of the Lerotholi family, i.e. Matlere, Mabina, Mahlomola and Mosiuoa are thoroughly disliked, are self-seeking individuals and are only tolerated because Chief Seeiso placed them here. They will stop at nothing to enrich themselves in spite of an apparent social charm. [26]

In the late 1940s Ashton thought that the 'Rafolatsane people ... are probably still sore, besides being resentful about the progressive ascendancy of some of Seeiso's followers, notably Matlere and his kin', and that the authorities in Tlokoeng were still 'not reconciled to their subordinate position under the chief of Mokhotlong'. He speculated that the Rafolatsane 'group' carried out a murder (1948/8) in order to improve their position, and was told both by Chief Mosuoe and by Gray, the local official, that when Matlere rebuked them for this murder he was angrily asked who he was to rebuke others for doing what he was doing himself.[27]

Ashton noted that there were now thirty-two recognised 'native authorities' in 'Mantšebo's personal area; thirteen in Rafolatsane's area; and twenty-seven in Tlokoeng under Chief Mosuoe. Under the 1938 reforms the number of native authorities in Tlokoeng had been reduced from ninety to twenty-seven – a disproportionate cut, with the result that 'each authority in Mosuoe's area has almost three times as many taxpayers under him as each authority has in Seeiso's personal area'. 'This point', Ashton went on to emphasise, 'is relevant to the present enquiry as it shows that the apparent change has been greater in Mosuoe's area (where only one ritual murder has been suspected since 1939), than in the rest of Mokhotlong, where nine ritual murders have been discovered or suspected in the same period.'[28] In other words, the significance of the cluster of medicine murders in 'Mantšebo's area did not plausibly lie in the impact of the 1938 reforms.

Even greater changes were introduced in 1946, on the establishment of the Native Treasury. In the Mokhotlong District as a whole the number of recognised courts was reduced from seventy-two to ten, with a corresponding loss of prestige and income for the sixty-two chiefs and headmen who lost out. They were reduced, they complained, to being 'nothing more than scarecrows'. In commenting on the changes to Ashton, Matlere indicated that there was now (in 1949) more rivalry and jealousy than before, with so few recognised courts and paid posts attached. But, he said, he did not think the murders could be attributed to the government's reforms. 'From my own observations', Ashton wrote, 'I am inclined to support this.'[29]

MEDICINE MURDER IN 'MANTŠEBO'S AREA

To explain the repeated suspicions that hung around Matlere and his brothers, we here briefly summarise the series of thirteen medicine murder cases in 'Mantšebo's area identified within the twenty-year period, from 1941 to 1960, of 'Mantšebo's rule at Matsieng and of Matlere's rule at Mokhotlong on her behalf (see Table CS4.1). In the following sections we concentrate in more detail on the two cases in which Matlere himself was directly indicted, with brief reference to a third, closely related, case.

The first of the murders recorded in 'Mantšebo's area (1940/2) apparently took place in Matlere Lerotholi's own village of Masaleng, but no criminal proceedings were brought.

Matlere was principal suspect, although he was not indicted, in respect of another murder in his own village (1943/1). No prosecution took place because the Attorney-General thought the accomplice witness was shielding the real instigator.

One of Matlere's half-brothers, Seabatha Lerotholi, was arrested and charged for a murder in July 1943 (1943/3), but acquitted in November 1946. Ashton speculated, presumably in view of the coincidence of timing, that this murder might be attributed to fear of Bereng Griffith's taking an appeal to the Privy Council against the judgement in the Regency case.[30]

Matlere's half-brother Mahlomola Lerotholi, a headman at Linotšing, was arrested in March 1945 for a murder committed in November 1944 (1944/7). He was convicted and hanged with eight other men in 1947. The motive suggested here was Mahlomola's fear of being demoted or deposed from his headmanship.[31]

In February 1945 'Mantšebo and Matlere were allegedly both present at Masaleng where a man kidnapped at Absalom Letsie's village of Liphakoeng was taken and killed (1945/2). 'Mantšebo needed medicine, it was said, in connection with the proposed placing of her daughter, Ntšebo, at Makhaleng. The case was closed for lack of sufficient evidence.

Another case (1945/6), relating to a murder at Ha Koeneho, was described by Ashton as 'self-contained' in the sense that it seemed to involve conflict over minor headmanships and not the main protagonists above.[32]

In November 1945 Tsotang Griffith, an ungazetted headman at Motsitseng, allegedly committed a murder (1945/8) to resolve various grievances over his position. Tsotang Griffith was a half-brother of Seeiso Griffith and a nephew of Matlere Lerotholi. Four of the accused were acquitted, including Tsotang Griffith, while the doctor involved made a full confession and was convicted and hanged. Tsotang Griffith was later sentenced to seven years' hard labour for conspiring to murder a Crown witness in this case.

In April 1948, headman Khethisa Molapo allegedly committed a murder (1948/10) for his chief, Matlere Lerotholi, inducing speculation by Ashton that 'Mantšebo needed medicine to counter the second murder initiated by Chiefs Bereng and Gabashane in March 1948 (1948/6, Case Study 3).[33] Khethisa Molapo was Matlere's brother-in-law.

Another half-brother of Matlere, Mabina Lerotholi, who was one of 'Mantšebo's advisers and a 'great favourite' with her, was indicted for a murder at Maphiring on Christmas Day 1948 (1948/24). It was rumoured that medicine was needed to protect the regent's daughter, Ntšebo, who was facing a criminal prosecution in January 1949. The accused were acquitted, contrary to expectations.

Matlere himself was identified as the instigator in case 1952/12, in which it was alleged that the *liretlo* were taken to Maseru by air by Mabina Lerotholi on his behalf. Matlere was acquitted on account of discrepancies in the evidence given by witnesses for the prosecution. This case is discussed in detail below.

A baby was found mutilated in November 1953 (1953/5) at Linotšing, a village which had been under the executed headman Mahlomola Lerotholi, but this case was apparently unrelated to the sequence involving Matlere or his relatives.

Matlere was indicted again in 1960, but escaped conviction on account of an alibi at Maseru on the date of the murder alleged by the prosecution (1959/1). Again, this case is discussed below.

Several of the conspirators in that case, including a notoriously unreliable accomplice witness, Sesemane Kao, were involved in another murder immediately following it (1959/2), in which the alleged instigator was a close friend of Matlere. This case is the last of the sequence of thirteen recorded above in 'Mantšebo's area.

In addition to these cases there were rumours of attempted murders, as for example at Matlere's old village of Masaleng in February 1950, and of many plots to commit murders. In November 1952 the District Commissioner, Rivers Thompson, reported that there had been eight 'scares' since he came to Mokhotlong and all had been 'scotched by someone talking beforehand'.[34]

Following the accession of Constantine Bereng Seeiso to the paramountcy early in 1960, Matlere Lerotholi was removed from his position as representative of the Ward Chief of Mokhotlong.

MATLERE ACQUITTED (1):
THE MURDER OF TŠOEUNYANE RABOLAI, 1952

On 8 November 1952 Chief Matlere Lerotholi reported to the District Commissioner's office that Tšoeunyane Rabolai was missing. On the same day his body was found in the Senqu river. The upper and lower lips were missing. The skin and flesh had been cut out with a sharp instrument from chest to pelvis. The right lung, heart and one kidney were missing. The left arm and the penis had been amputated. The police photographs are gruesome testimony as to the nature of these wounds, which the doctor who carried out the post-mortem certified had been caused by human agency (case 1952/12).[35]

Tšoeunyane Rabolai was from Mohlaoli's, a small village to the west of Matlere's own village of Motsitseng. He had recently clashed with Matlere, when he had twice interrupted him at a meeting to protest against the treatment of an elderly female relative in a land matter. Matlere said to Tšoeunyane, according to one of the accomplice witnesses, 'As you appear to have come to run the *pitso* I'll take you through the Nek and you will not be seen again'.[36]

Chief Matlere and seven others, including his half-brother Mabina Lerotholi, appeared at a preparatory examination before W. G. S. Driver in Maseru in January 1953, and then in the High Court trial before Judge Harold Willan in Maseru in the following month. Evidence was heard that the murder had taken place on 29 or 30 October 1952, over a week before the body was found. The prosecution case was based primarily on the evidence of four accomplices, two of whom, Matjoa Tšita and Seane Klaas, had played a central part in the murder. There was also an independent witness, 'Mahalieo Makoto, a maidservant of Matlere.

It was alleged that Matlere instructed Matjoa Tšita to kill a person because he, Matlere, required the flesh for medicine. Matjoa was left to recruit his own assistants. Seane Klaas, who was trusted by Matlere, was then brought into the plot, and six other persons were also recruited. According to Seane Klaas,

Matlere handed him some powder and told him that when they were ready to carry out their plan of getting a person for him for medicine he should burn the powder on a fire made from cow-dung. He should call the name of Tsoe[u]nyane, and he would come. The Chief also gave him a canvas bag and told him to bring the excised parts to him. The Chief said he would require the lip, the heart, a lung, a kidney and an arm for medicine ... On the Thursday night [Seane Klaas] made a fire near the house of Tsoe[u]nyane. He put the powder on the fire, spoke into the smoke, saying 'Tsoe[u]nyane, we want you here'. Shortly after, Tsoe[u]nyane arrived dressed only in an overcoat. He was caught and taken to a shallow stream where the parts which the Chief had required were excised with an axe and knife. The body was then removed to a hut and the following night it was thrown into the Orange River. [Seane Klaas] took the excised parts to the village of Chief Matlere and handed them over to the chief personally.[37]

The maidservant, 'Mahalieo Makoto, gave evidence that she saw a man hand over a canvas bag to the chief. Later the same day she saw the bag in a wardrobe in his room, containing the heart, a lung and the liver of a human being. The canvas bag was then wrapped in the blanket roll of Chief Mabina and taken to Chief Matlere's tractor which conveyed it to the airfield at Mokhotlong. Chief Mabina carried the bag to Maseru by air.[38]

The evidence of 'Mahalieo, the maidservant, was disregarded by the court because she reported both that Matlere had warned her against looking in the wardrobe where she saw the pieces of human flesh and that he had instructed her to place two boxes of matches in the wardrobe. The judge regarded this as unlikely. 'Mahalieo also gave conflicting evidence as to the day of the week on which this incident had taken place. The Crown case therefore came to depend on the evidence of the accomplices only. Here a critical discrepancy arose between the evidence of Seane Klaas and Matjoa Tšita as to the colour of the canvas bag in which, on instruction from Chief Matlere, the pieces of flesh had allegedly been placed. At the preparatory examination both agreed that the colour of the bag was yellow. At the High Court Seane reported that the bag was light blue in colour, Matjoa that it was dark blue. There were other discrepancies between evidence given at the preparatory examination and evidence given at the High Court trial, and between evidence given by different accomplice witnesses, relating, for example, to the points at which the identity of the victim was revealed and the date of the murder was fixed and which parts of flesh were cut by which conspirators.

The evidence against Mabina Lerotholi, even as an accessory after the fact, was so weak that he was discharged at the end of the Crown case. The other accused were all found not guilty. Judge Willan was satisfied that Tšoeunyane Rabolai had been cruelly murdered, but because of the incon-

sistencies in the accomplice evidence and the insufficiency of the corroboration he was unable to convict. The acquittal was greeted with loud clapping
and cheering in the crowded courtroom. Even the police joined in.[39] More
generally, it was reported, the chiefs were pleased, but the public was
divided in its opinion, since a significant section of the population which
supported Chief Bereng had been gratified by the arrest of Chief Matlere.[40]

In commenting on the case, Resident Commissioner Arrowsmith remarked
that Mokhotlong had the worst reputation for medicine murders, and they
were all linked with political affairs. 'They also coincided with some prominent person travelling from Mokhotlong to Maseru a week or so afterwards.' He observed that it seemed 'most likely' that 'Mantšebo instructed
Matlere to arrange this murder, and noted various rumours about her
anxieties. One of them was the possibility of the early succession of the heir
to the paramountcy, Constantine Bereng Seeiso, a possibility urged by his
mother 'Mabereng.[41]

The acquittal of Matlere and his co-accused raised doubts yet again
about the validity of accomplice evidence. The judge had rejected it as
unreliable, and after the case, whether or not they had told the truth in
court, the accomplice witnesses had a strong interest, especially when the
accused were acquitted, in disclaiming what they had said and in alleging
that it had been forced on them by the police. A year later, following
acquittals in another important case (1953/2) as a result of discrepancies in
the accomplice evidence, the police in Basutoland were beginning to
suspect that a new technique was being developed whereby accomplice
witnesses secured acquittals not by retracting their statements and so losing
their immunity, but by changing them between the preparatory examination and the High Court trial.[42] Both these considerations have to be borne
in mind when considering the testimony of Seane Klaas, the only accomplice witness in this case who was still alive in the late 1990s.

In May 1999 KS and PS found Seane Klaas at his village in the Senqu
valley. He took us inside the rondavel that served as his living room. We sat
at a table on which several religious books, including a bible, were piled up.
On the wall was a picture of the crucifixion, with the angels collecting
Christ's blood in sacred vessels. There were also photographs of the Pope
and Father Gérard, the first Catholic missionary in Lesotho. Seane claimed
that he and others had been subject to strong police pressure to learn a
consistent story and to repeat it in court.

> We were told to say these things by a European officer who came from
> the Republic [i.e. South Africa].[43] He was helped by two Basotho,
> perhaps policemen. They were not from Lesotho. Their job was to
> teach us what to say. When they were sure one day we remembered
> what we had to learn, the next day they would teach us some more. We
> were so indoctrinated that we ended up believing what we were taught

and could repeat it with enthusiasm. You would be isolated and interrogated alone ... They would take turns with you. During the day each one of us had a policeman to look after us, to make sure we didn't speak with anyone else. You had a policeman with you even when you were asleep. It deprived you of your humanity ... If you resisted, then these people, who seemed to be superior to police, made you wear something like a jersey which came right down and had metal things attached to it. They would switch something on and give you a shock.

Asked about the discrepancy in evidence over the colour of the canvas bag, Seane said:

You must realise that that conflict was deliberate. The interrogation was being held in a group of tents, and we walked away together. I said to Matjoa: 'These people are going to be killed. There are many people from my area. How can we save them?' I then suggested that those of us who testified in connection with the bag should attribute different colours to it. I said, 'We must stick to our evidence in other respects, but we must disagree over the colour'. I said this to Tjokoteni [the third accomplice witness] and to Matjoa ... This was all my idea.

After the case, Seane Klaas reported, 'people hated and feared us at first'. So too did Matlere, 'saying that we and the whites had nearly killed him'. So Seane told Matlere his story, which astonished him, and after that, he said, 'the accused helped us to regain the confidence of the people, because they corroborated our story'. He also regained his standing in the church.

We were Catholics. Those of us who testified as accomplice witnesses were regarded as killers. Our standing in the church had suffered. The priest took down my statement and after that appealed to the congregation not to regard us as killers. The services used to be held in my house, but because of the case they had been removed. The priest ordered that this arrangement should be reinstated.[44]

Seane claimed that Tšoeunyane Rabolai had been suffering from an evil spirit, a *thokolosi*, that he had met his death because the *thokolosi* had taken him from his home, that this was well known to Tšoeunyane's family, and that for this reason they did not believe he had been murdered. They were 'surprised to hear us say that we had killed him'. He also claimed that the corpse had been eaten by dogs, but not mutilated.[45] KS and PS, however, found the victim's son, Motleri Rabolai, who said that after the case his mother had left the area and gone to live in South Africa, unable to bear living with the people who had killed her husband. He brought her back in 1957, but they never discussed the murder. He was sure that Matlere killed his father. In response to Seane's claim that Tšoeunyane had suffered from a *thokolosi*, Motleri said:

No, he did not. There is no truth in the statement that he was ill in any way. We never believed that he was taken by a *thokolosi*, and when the body was found it was mutilated. The right hand and right eye were missing, and so were the genitals. The dog merely pulled him out of the river. It did not touch him in any other way. A sharp instrument had been used.[46]

The police photographs also starkly refute Seane's statement that the body was not mutilated. There is also contemporary evidence that the Rabolai family wanted to sue Matlere and the alleged accomplices but for some reason did not bring a case.[47]

Seane still took a certain pride in his role. 'To be chosen as an accomplice witness you had to be very sharp. The first accomplice would always be an outstanding man ... The teachers told us afterwards ... I had given my evidence very well, I had been the best of all ...'[48] Independently of his own claims, he had a reputation for eloquence. When some of the accused, sitting in the Mokhotlong gaol, saw him in the company of the police they 'got such a fright' and they said to each other, 'We're finished!' (*re felile*). After the trial they reported this to a local teacher, Elliot Teboho Morojele, who in 1999 was eighty years old and owned a hotel in Mokhotlong. Their sense of being threatened by Seane's evidence strongly suggested to Morojele an earlier conspiracy between them and Seane Klaas. Otherwise what would they have to fear?[49]

MATLERE ACQUITTED (2):
THE MURDER OF KAISER MOFANA, 1959

A headless body was discovered on 22 September 1959 in the snow near a cattle-post known as Nkuebe's. It was identified as that of Kaiser Mofana, a young herdboy who lived at Motsitseng, Chief Matlere's village, with a school-teacher whose cattle he herded. The alleged date of the murder was 29 May 1959, almost four months earlier.[50] Matlere Lerotholi was arrested in July 1960, shortly after he had been displaced from his position as representative of the Paramount Chief in Mokhotlong. The preparatory examination took place in August, and the High Court trial in November (case 1959/1).

There were six accused: Matlere Lerotholi, chief of Motsitseng; Makhahlela Lerotholi, his younger half-brother, the headman of Masaleng, who had figured in previous cases; Morabaraba Nyeoe Matjama; and three others. This case was closely connected with the Mathaba case (1959/2, see below) in which the murder was committed about a week later. Mathaba was a close friend of Matlere, and both Makhahlela Lerotholi and Morabaraba Nyeoe Matjama, who were accused with Matlere of the murder of Kaiser Mofana, were charged in the Mathaba case as well. Others were also connected with both cases. Sesemane Kao was an accomplice witness in both cases, and achieved a distinctive notoriety for this reason. Khoaele Lekhoba, an accomplice witness in the Mathaba case, was one of the accused in the Matlere case. Accomplice witness Nyakallo Khare in the Matlere case had been asked to take part in the Mathaba case, but did not do so.[51]

The case for the Crown rested mainly on the evidence of three accomplice witnesses: Sesemane Kao, Nyakallo Khare and Moqabang Damane. Sesemane had approached Chief Matlere in the spring of 1958 to ask him if he could become his subject.

> The witness said that the first accused [Matlere] told him that he wanted his assistance in the killing of somebody, and gave as a reason that there were differences between members of the Paramount Chief's family at Matsieng; that some chiefs wanted the new Paramount Chief installed, but that he and Chieftainess 'Mantšebo ... were against it because the new Paramount Chief was too young and his education should be completed before he was installed. He said that he was told that certain portions of a human body were required, so that 'Mantšebo should not be deposed and the new Paramount Chief installed; also that very important work had to be done in connection with the villages of the first accused and that human blood was required for medicine for the purpose of strengthening the villages ...[52]

In return for Sesemane's help, Matlere would try to assist Sesemane to obtain some land under a neighbouring headman, Lebopo Nkherepe.

Further conversations took place. Rumours leaked out that a murder was being planned, and a *pitso* was held at the village of a local chief, Rapase Phakisi, at which warnings were issued against taking part. Rapase in fact gave specific warnings both to Sesemane and to Khoaele Lekhoba (No. 6 accused). Sesemane became nervous and reported this conversation to Matlere, who apparently reassured him. There was also a reference to 'other work' involving Mathaba, with Sesemane suggesting that one victim would meet both needs. Matlere refused to agree to this. The putative victim was then identified as Kaiser Mofana, and the schoolteacher who employed him apparently said 'he did not have any objection to this'. Several other accomplices were involved in these discussions, but Makhahlela Lerotholi, Matlere's half-brother, who had been central to all the arrangements, now excused himself from direct participation on grounds of illness. Two other men stood in for him.

The conspirators induced Kaiser Mofana to join them at a disused cattle-post on a ridge between the Moremoholo and the Bafali streams. Sesemane gave a graphic account of the killing itself.

The boy was first taken into the hut and made to kneel on an ox-hide, and his hair was cut. The boy then appeared to be frightened and asked to be allowed out the hut to pass water; he was taken out with his hands tied and brought back again ... After he had been brought back into the hut his feet were tied, he was thrown or put down on to the ox-hide, the third accused then proceeded to cut his throat, while the fifth accused held a dish and caught the blood, which was poured into a billycan by the sixth accused. The head was then cut off and flesh was cut by the third accused from under the right armpit and from inside the cut where the head had been severed ...

After this the body was taken off on horseback and deposited beneath the cliffs near Nkuebe's cattle-post, where it was found four months later. Sesemane and Morabaraba Matjama (No. 3 accused) took the *liretlo* to Matlere's home in Motsitseng, where they found Matlere in bed. He got up, took them to one of his rondavels, and put a sack on the floor on which the *liretlo* were placed. He also brought in the doctor, Maqhomisa. Some time later Sesemane saw Morabaraba Matjama 'with pieces of flesh, which had either been cooked or burnt, and he was grinding them up for medicine'.[53]

The other two accomplices, Nyakallo and Moqabang, gave evidence similar to Sesemane's. There were differences of detail, but Judge Roper attached no great importance to these. They were giving evidence about what had happened eighteen months earlier, and, with regard to the murder itself, at night in a small hut about three metres by four metres, with seven people clustering around the victim by the light of only two electric torches.

There was a fourth accomplice witness – though Roper had doubts as to whether he was properly an accomplice – the Zulu doctor, Maqhomisa George Ndaba. His testimony was summarised by Judge Roper as follows:

He testified that he had been employed in 'pegging' Matlere's village. One night he was woken up by Matlere and taken to a hut where he saw Sesemane, the accomplice witness, and Morabaraba Motjama [*sic*] (No. 3 accused). On the floor he saw a human head from which the hair had been cut off, a forearm, some pieces of flesh on a whitish cloth, and a billycan. Sesemane and Morabaraba then left.

The first accused [Matlere] said that the parcel which he needed was now there and the witness was now to strengthen him. The witness told him that for that purpose he would need the blood of an elephant and of a lion and of some other animal ... and the first accused told him that he could supplement that with human blood, and gave him a small bottle of blood which the witness recognised as human blood. The witness took this and mixed it with some of his own medicine, and thereafter scarified the first accused with this mixture, on the top of the head, the front of the neck on the collarbone, at the back of the neck and on the knees, ribs and both knees. He said that the first accused told him that the head and the blood were leaving for the big chief, and told him that he was about to leave for Matsieng and was going to stay there; and that, in fact, he left a week later.[54]

All this suggested that Matlere, though a practising Catholic, was still deeply immersed in Sesotho beliefs and practices – an impression that Matlere tried vigorously to dispel. He protested that he had asked Maqhomisa to treat his wife for sore eyes, but only after white doctors had failed to help her; that he had never asked him to peg his village; that he had believed in pegging before he became a Christian, but not now; that all the marks on his body were from 'old scarifications' and that he now thought that scarifying was 'useless'; that, although he had three wives, he had married them before becoming a Catholic and only one of them now was recognised as his wife.[55]

At one point in preparing for the trial the High Commissioner's office had asked for the help of a pathologist from South Africa to examine Matlere's scarifications, but the South African authorities were afraid that if Matlere was convicted on the basis of this evidence it would give rise to bad feeling against the Union.[56]

Judge Roper reflected on the credibility of the accomplice witnesses. Sesemane Kao was a bad character with other convictions, and shifty and unreliable on points of detail. 'At the same time he did not give me the impression of having fabricated the whole of his evidence ...' The second accomplice witness, Nyakallo Khare, was intelligent and substantially truthful. The third accomplice, Moqabang Damane, was an old man, between sixty-five and seventy years of age, 'a good stamp of Basuto tribesman, loyal to his Chief. I was favourably impressed by his demeanour and he appeared to me to be a truthful witness'. Roper concluded that 'Sesemane's evidence, bad though it is, is corroborated on a number of essential details by that of the two other accomplices'.[57] The fourth accomplice witness, the Zulu doctor, was not very intelligent, his Sesotho was poor, and there were difficulties in understanding what he was saying. He did not seem to be untruthful, but because of these difficulties it would be impossible to convict on his evidence alone.

Apart from Maqhomisa's testimony, however, there was other corroborating evidence. The nature of the injuries found on the body was consistent with the story told by the accomplices. Matlere had indeed written a letter to headman Nkherepe asking him to accommodate Sesemane. There was known to be dissent over the succession of Constantine Bereng Seeiso.

The defence relied mainly on alibis. As far as Nos. 2–6 accused were concerned, the judge was unimpressed and found them all guilty. Matlere, however, was a different case. Relying on the accomplice witness, Nyakallo, the Crown had fixed 29 May 1959 as the date of the murder. Matlere claimed that from 24 April to 16 July 1959 he was in the lowlands, and for the period from 22 May to 31 May he was able to support this with irrefutable evidence. There was even a white woman working at Lancers' Inn, in Maseru, who produced her off-sales register to prove that she had sold him liquor on 29 May.[58] The Crown argued that it was open to the court to convict Matlere if it was satisfied that he had taken part in the murder, even if there had been a mistake over the date, but Roper rejected this argument. In his view

> it is clearly proved that he [Matlere] could not have been present on the 29th May or within about a week thereafter ... I have come to the conclusion that the case which the Crown set out to make against this accused has not been proved, and therefore he must be found not guilty and he is discharged.[59]

Matlere had escaped by a hair's breadth. Roper in fact was convinced that he was 'the instigator of the crime and therefore the principal criminal', but felt that he had to acquit because of the error over the date.[60]

The other five accused appealed against their convictions. The appeal judges found that Roper had given too much credence to the evidence of Sesemane Kao, since parts of his testimony were demonstrably false and he could therefore have concocted other elements of his story. Since the case against Makhahlela Lerotholi (No. 2) rested almost entirely on Sesemane's evidence, Makhahlela's appeal was allowed. Morabaraba Matjama (No. 3) had died pending appeal. The remaining three convictions stood.[61] Since, however, both Matlere Lerotholi and Makhahlela Lerotholi, the two 'ringleaders', had now escaped conviction, it was decided that the other three men's sentences should be commuted to imprisonment for twelve years.[62]

Reflecting on the outcome of this case, Chief Justice Herbert Cox, who heard the appeal of Makhahlela Lerotholi and others, alongside Sir Walter Harragin and Mr Justice Schreiner, noted:

> We considered it most unfortunate that the person whom the trial Judge, in our opinion, rightly, considered to be the chief instigator of the crime [Matlere Lerotholi], should have been acquitted, and that we should have been forced to allow the appeal of the next most reprehensible offender [Makhahlela Lerotholi], but we feel obliged to do so for the reasons set out in our judgment.[63]

THE NOTORIETY OF SESEMANE KAO

In a closely related case (1959/2), a three-year-old boy, Motheea Ntjanyana, of Ha Chopho, in the Bafali valley, was murdered on 5 June 1959. Three people were accused at the preparatory examination in February 1960: Edwin Hantsi Mathaba, a fairly well-educated senior assistant at Storm's store in Mokhotlong, a man of considerable standing in the community, and a close personal friend of Matlere Lerotholi; Ntau Kali; and Morabaraba Matjama, a man of Chief Letsie Theko's area in the Maseru district, who had removed himself from his home in the lowlands to live at Bafali.

The High Court trial took place in January 1961. By that time the names of the second and third accused, Ntau Kali and Morabaraba Matjama, had been withdrawn since they had already been convicted in the Matlere case discussed above. So Edwin Mathaba remained as the sole accused. Sesemane Kao was once again an accomplice witness. In this case he was the victim's uncle. Khoaele Lekhoba was also an accomplice witness but he defected because he had been condemned to death in the Matlere case. So only Sesemane was left, a man of known bad character, and Judge Elyan was not prepared to convict on this basis. After these two cases Sesemane's name became synonymous with the taint of unreliability and ulterior motive that was attached in principle to the evidence of accomplice witnesses.

In commenting on this case (1959/2) and on one that followed it (1961/1), in which sixteen persons accused had to be discharged because all five accomplice witnesses defected, the prosecutor, E. K. W. Lichtenberg, who had also prosecuted in the Matlere case, remarked:

> This type of thing goes on all the time in Mokhotlong, the district with, I think, the highest frequency of ritual murders in Basutoland. I have very little doubt that Mathaba and Matlere (who are very great friends) are the persons who prevent justice being done in respect of ritual murders in that district.[64]

The Chief Justice, Herbert Cox, was of the same mind: 'These two cases taken together [the Matlere case and the Mathaba case] clearly indicate a most unsavoury state of affairs existing amongst the so-called intelligentzia and leaders of the country'.[65]

In our field visit to Mokhotlong we sought to trace surviving relatives of Sesemane Kao who might be able to comment on his involvement. In May 1999 KS and PS encountered Molosi Kao in a work-party for winnowing grain in the Moremoholo valley. Aged seventy-four, he was a half-brother of Sesemane, he told us. They were the same age. Sesemane was 'very, very, very, very clever (*bohlale-hlale-hlale-hlale-hlale*) ... very sweet-tongued ... he was intimate with Chief Matlere, and Matlere trusted him very much'.

> There were many murders ... I can't say how many. First he abducted a child from Bafali, where we were living, and the corpse was found between the Tololi and Tolotsana rivers. Sesemane said that this murder was for himself and Hantsi Mathaba. This murder was not for Matlere. Then there was the murder of Kaiser Mofana. He was found right up in the mountains without a head ... Matlere was accused of his murder, and Sesemane became an accomplice witness. I don't know why he went against his friend, and he never told me why, but he

said in court that Matlere had ordered him to carry out a murder ... Matlere was very angry with him. Other murders were carried out from beyond our village to Mokhotlong. I don't know the names of the victims.[66]

As Molosi Kao remembered them, the relative chronology of the two murders was reversed. But there was no doubt in his mind of Sesemane's involvement in both and of the part played by Matlere. His statement that Sesemane was involved in many murders was borne out by Sesemane himself in court, when he said he had been involved in eight murders in all.[67] Sesemane's widow was in the same work-party, and although Molosi warned us that she would not talk to us he nevertheless asked her if she would. She became very agitated and ran away: 'They already know all these things', she said. 'They already know all these things.'

5

DIAGNOSES AND RESOLUTIONS:
FROM FAILURE TO RECRIMINATION
TO SILENCE

My dear Mum and Dad,
I have had a most interesting week as Chairman of a Conference on
Medicine Murder! It has been very revealing to me … It is a queer
business. Many Basuto genuinely believe there is no such thing, but
that it is all a vast plot of Machiavellian character on part of
Government to discredit their Chiefs, and perhaps their Paramount
Chief … They feel they are branded before the world as primitive
savages, and want desperately to disprove it, even by denying the
existence of medicine murder. Great play is made of the fact that while
mutilated bodies are found, no flesh from said bodies has ever been
found in a chief's medicine horn, because no such medicine horn has
itself ever been found. Nor are they likely to be, for they are guarded
like the crown jewels, but unlike the latter, never displayed.
Meanwhile the Police are thoroughly unpopular for doing their simple
duty in trying to stop the nasty business. It certainly is very queer and
quite baffling.

> Gordon Hector (Government Secretary) to his parents,
> 2 September 1956[1]

PROPOSALS FOR CHANGE

Sir Evelyn Baring left South Africa in 1951, to enjoy a year's break and then
to take up his next appointment as Governor of Kenya, where within a
month he declared a state of emergency in order to deal with the Mau Mau
rebellion. He was replaced as High Commissioner by Sir John Helier le
Rougetel, a career diplomat with no colonial background, whose most
recent appointments had been in Persia and Belgium. Baring had regarded
medicine murder as a terrible and dangerous phenomenon that was
threatening to destroy the chiefs and so to ruin the country. He had thought
deeply and written about it at length, and his voice had been the clearest and
most influential in the British administration. The ferocity of his response,
as we shall argue in the Conclusion, had intensified the sense of moral crisis.
Le Rougetel was much less involved. He told the Basutoland National
Council that no matter caused him more concern than medicine murder,[2]
but for the most part he relied heavily on his officials. In the absence of any

strong lead from the High Commission the initiative in combating medicine murder fell largely to the new Resident Commissioner in Basutoland, Edwin Arrowsmith.

Forsyth-Thompson, Arrowsmith's predecessor, had a reputation for standing on his dignity. Arrowsmith was more relaxed and, it was said, more able.[3] It was also alleged that towards the end of his term of office Forsyth-Thompson had been unable to stand up to 'Mantšebo's 'histrionics' – her throwing of 'fits' and 'hysterics' – and had been prepared to obtain peace at any price. The High Commissioner's office expressed the hope that Arrowsmith would be able to bring her back under control.[4] Yet two of the most important initatives undertaken while Arrowsmith was in office ended in failure and acrimonious debate. The first related to constitutional reform, the second to medicine murder.

It was time to review how the Khubelu and Treasury reforms were working. The Basuto Courts had now been largely divorced from the chieftainship, and although there were various proposals for improvement there was no demand and no need for any further radical change. But there were still major difficulties over the 'Native Administration'. Lord Hailey, who visited the country in 1950, found that in spite of the Pim reforms there was still too much 'dualism', with the Native Authority at Matsieng seeing and conducting itself as a rival organisation to the government at Maseru. He recommended more integration between the two and also, like Jones, more decentralisation of authority. There were also difficulties in the relationship between the Native Authority and the people. The problem, as le Rougetel defined it in 1951, was 'how best to balance the need for increased popular representation and participation in the conduct of affairs with the unquestioned need to maintain the authority of the Chieftainship'.[5] Hailey argued for increasing the powers of the District Councils. He also pointed out that the normal consequence of more popular representation in the National Council was the grant of legislative powers, and yet, at the time when he wrote, the government had no intention of granting such powers.[6] Hailey's findings were published in 1953, a year after the Basutoland African Congress (BAC) had been founded and had put forward its demand for immediate self-government.

In 1954 an Administrative Reforms Committee was set up under the chairmanship of Sir Henry Moore, a former Governor of Kenya, 'to examine the structure of Native Administration in Basutoland and to make recommendations regarding the lines of its future development ...' Mindful of the supposed consequences of the Khubelu and Treasury reforms, the High Commission was concerned that any new reforms should not provoke a new wave of medicine murder.[7] Moore, however, recommended a drastic reduction in the number of chiefs carrying out administrative duties, improvements in pay based on responsibility and performance, and a tightening-up of discipline. In order to overcome the 'dualism' which Hailey had criticised so cogently, Moore recommended more integration between the Native Administration and the government. The form of this proposed integration, which involved the removal of the Native Administration from Matsieng to Maseru, was widely regarded as a way of bringing the chiefs under closer control.

What gave rise to the greatest outcry against Moore's report was not what it contained, but what it did not contain. The BAC had mounted its first effective campaign, both with the people throughout the country and with members of the National Council. As Moore's committee had gone round the territory it had been told repeatedly at public meetings that what the people wanted was self-government: the National Council should cease to be merely advisory, and it should be given legislative powers over the internal affairs of the Basotho. Moore had ruled these representations out of order on the ground that his terms of reference did not include any consideration of self-government. When, therefore, the report was discussed at a special session of the National Council in March 1955 it was overwhelmingly rejected, an outcome that was seen as a triumph for the BAC. Arrowsmith then made matters worse by saying that the Council had not done its duty, but had debated the report unintelligently and irresponsibly.[8]

The second initiative that ran into trouble was the campaign to put an end to medicine murder. After the apparent lull following the hangings of Bereng and Gabashane, more murders were being reported. The Commonwealth Relations Office looked to the High Commission for a plan of action, and the High Commission looked to Arrowsmith. He had no shortage of advice – from the chiefs, the missions, Lord Hailey, the staff of the High Commission and his own District Commissioners – but it did not all point in the same direction, and while much of it was helpful and carefully considered, some of it revealed more about the interests of the advisers than about the problems to which it was meant to be addressed.

In April 1952 'Mantšebo summoned the senior chiefs and district representatives on the National Council to a conference at Matsieng to give their advice on how medicine murder could be ended. The chair was taken by her close adviser, Chief Mabina Lerotholi, who had been acquitted of medicine murder in 1949 and was soon to stand trial again. Many conflicting opinions were reported, but the main thrust of the conference was that the chiefs' messengers should once again work closely with the police in their investigations; that accomplice witnesses should be prosecuted, convicted and hanged like other murderers; and that the activities of disreputable doctors (bo-ngakana-ntšonyana) should be brought to an end.[9] The conference's main concern was clearly to protect the chiefs rather than to put an end to medicine murder.

The missions pointed to the iniquities of paganism. Though recognising that the chiefs were the instigators of medicine murder, they were much more vociferous in their condemnation of *lingaka*, the doctors. Their emphases were not always the same. While the Catholics continued to stress what they saw as the pernicious influence of the initiation schools, the Protestants were more concerned about the evils of *joala*, the strong beer which the Basotho prepared from millet, since many murders were carried out after beer-parties at which the victims were rendered helplessly drunk and the murderers themselves drank heavily. But all agreed that what was needed was a change of heart. Medicine murders would come to an end only when the Basotho gave up their superstitious belief in medicine and were converted to Christianity. If it was argued that many of the murderers were Christians, the response was that their Christianity was merely superficial.[10]

Lord Hailey was profoundly critical of Jones. He was not persuaded that there had been a surge in medicine murder in the late 1940s, he believed that Jones had exaggerated the Khubelu and Treasury reforms as a cause of medicine murder, and he was therefore sure that the remedy was not going to be found in political or constitutional changes. From the suppression of *sati* [suttee] in British India to the present time, he asserted confidently, history had provided 'only one lesson for the successful treatment of such disorders': in the short term the firm maintenance of law and order, and in the long term 'the improvement of the economic and social standards of the people'.[11]

Hailey's views were highly influential with le Rougetel and his staff. They were already committed to social and economic improvement, and in the belief that the hangings of Bereng, Gabashane and 'Mamakhabane had had a 'stunning effect' on the chiefs, resulting in a temporary decline in medicine murder, they cast around for similar deterrents. They contemplated deposing or suspending chiefs who were suspected of murder or who failed to prevent it, but they knew they could not count on 'Mantšebo's support. 'The seat of the difficulty is in the Native Authority itself and to proceed against it would be of such importance locally that there would need to be strong and clear grounds for action.' In the meantime they waited for the outcome of Arrowsmith's deliberations with his District Commissioners and other officers.[12]

At a conference held in January 1953 the District Commissioners also emphasised the need for strong measures. They agreed that it would cause 'big trouble' to take action against 'Mantšebo unless there were clear grounds for doing so, and they did not want the collective punishment favoured by Evelyn Baring, since that would antagonise those Basotho who were co-operative. But they applauded the hangings of Bereng and Gabashane and deplored the commutation of the death sentence in other cases. They wanted more police patrols and better intelligence, and also a campaign to stir up public opinion. At the same time they had taken on Lord Hailey's advice, for by way of 'indirect action' they thought it essential to improve the social and economic condition of the people.[13]

The District Commissioners were sceptical about the value of any efforts made by 'Mantšebo, since she was under such heavy suspicion herself. A few months earlier Arrowsmith had assured the High Commission that,

> Whatever the Paramount Chief's attitude may have been in the past, we believe that she is genuinely anxious to put a stop to these murders. This is not because she has ceased to believe in the efficacy of the medicine, but because she fears the continuance of these murders may result ultimately in the overthrow of the Chieftainship either by direct action of Her Majesty's Government or by the Basuto themselves.

Then, in November 1952, came the murder of Tšoeunyane Rabolai, in which 'Mantšebo and Matlere Lerotholi were thought to be closely involved (1952/12, Case Study 4). Arrowsmith had to acknowledge that, if his suspicions were correct, then his earlier statement had been wrong. 'Mantšebo's denunciations of medicine murder had been mere 'window-dressing' and most Basotho would now believe that her warnings were insincere.[14] Yet in spite of these misgivings he continued to work with her. Like his predecessors, he found her difficult and unpredictable, still liable to burst into tears under pressure. But she did at least co-operate with him and, as he wrote a year later, 'we would get nowhere if we sat glowering at each other across a table, and if she believed that my main aim in life was to have her convicted of medicine murder'.[15]

Acting with the Paramount Chief, Arrowsmith undertook two initiatives. First, in May 1953, in an effort to counter the allegations that the police were framing innocent people, he set up a two-man Administrative Team to be present when statements were taken from accomplices. His own representative was Major A. R. Donald, a senior officer, while 'Mantšebo was represented by one of her Ward Chiefs, Leshoboro Majara, 'a man whom we trust', said Arrowsmith.[16] Leshoboro had a reputation for being bluff and outspoken: the government would find that this was not always to its advantage.

Later in the year this Administrative Team added a twenty-one-page report to the mountain of advice that was piling up on Arrowsmith's desk. The report drew the now familiar distinction between the long-term 'sociological problem of weaning the Basuto away from ancient and barbarous beliefs and practices' and the more immediate problem of 'preventing people from committing medicine murders irrespective of sociological progress'. Much of what its authors said was sensible and straightforward, though hardly original: they pointed out the strong link, for example, between medicine murders and placings. But some of their recommendations verged on the bizarre, such as their proposals for the establishment of a new kind of initiation school run by former NCOs, the use of Boy Scouts for gathering information, and the encouragement of organised games and competitions, agricultural shows and eisteddfods. Although the report was located firmly within the official narrative on medicine murder, they acknowledged at least some of the concerns of the government's critics. They recognised the undesirability of relying so heavily on accomplice witnesses, and they recommended 'most strongly' that urgent action should be taken to improve relations between the public and the police.[17]

Although this report was sent to the High Commission it had little impact on the subsequent debate and there was no further reference to it on the High Commission files. Far more important was Arrowsmith's second joint initiative with 'Mantšebo. Following up the suggestion made by his District Commissioners, he decided to embark on a campaign that would stir up the entire Basotho nation in the struggle against medicine murder. This would now be the main thrust of official policy and action. Le Rougetel and his officials were unconvinced. They suspected that Arrowsmith was making a fool of himself by working with 'Mantšebo, and they had no faith in campaigns of this sort. But for the time being they set aside their enthusiasm for stronger action and waited to see how the campaign fared.

THE ROUND TABLE CONFERENCE OF 1953 AND THE ANTI-*LIRETLO* CAMPAIGN

In the winter of 1953 the Resident Commissioner and the Paramount Chief summoned a Round Table Conference to consider what could be done to put an end to the blight of medicine murder. They invited representatives of government and the police, the Basotho administration and chieftainship, the District Councils, the three principal missions and the Chamber of Commerce, together with certain private individuals who were held to have particular knowledge of the subject. At the same time they invited members of the public to send in written comments and suggestions. Arrowsmith was determined to keep the Conference on what he regarded as constructive lines. He did not invite the BAC, and when the Berea District Council appointed Josiel Lefela as its representative he seriously considered whether he should allow him to come.

The Conference went better than Arrowsmith had expected. With the Resident Commissioner himself in the chair, and with 'Mantšebo's personal representative, Nkuebe Mitchell, in attendance, it met for four days in September 1953. On the first two days it drew up a list of seventy-three possible causes of medicine murder, and on the third a list of 134 possible remedies. The whole tone of the discussion was encouraging, and even

Lefela was subdued. He admitted – for the first time, Arrowsmith thought – that medicine murders were being committed, but believed that police operations were being directed by Scotland Yard, an organisation which was expert in framing innocent people.[18]

Seven hundred pages of written evidence had been submitted and,[19] if we can judge by the summary made of their recommendations, they too were within the framework of the official narrative. There were criticisms of the police and worries about the reliance on accomplice witnesses, but no mention, it seems, was made of any government conspiracy against the chiefs or any intention to hand over the country to South Africa.[20] The BAC itself made no submission,[21] but Bennett Khaketla, who was later to become the party's Deputy Leader and the editor of its newspaper, *Mohlabani*, submitted a paper thirty pages long in which, contrary to the views which he later expressed, he stated explicitly that murders were being committed for the purpose of making medicine. He was also silent on any government conspiracy.[22]

At the end of its deliberations the Conference appointed a committee, to be known as the Liretlo Committee, to draw up a report and make recommendations. There was little danger of its straying far along paths that the government would not want to follow. It was chaired by a senior District Commissioner, its secretary was Major Donald, and of its five members two were missionaries, one was a Mosotho civil servant and two were chiefs whom the government trusted: Leshoboro Majara and Kelebone Nkuebe. The first outcome of the Committee's work was the anti-*liretlo* campaign which was held during the coming year. Public meetings, *pitsos*, were held throughout the country by the Resident Commissioner and the Paramount Chief, followed by *pitsos* summoned jointly by District Commissioners and Ward Chiefs. In addition, 100,000 copies of a leaflet, with a foreword by 'Mantšebo, were printed and distributed; 1,500 badges were made and slogans were devised: 'Tear out medicine murder!' 'Lesotho is going to perdition: wake up!' February 1954 was designated anti-*liretlo* month. An anti-*liretlo* prayer was formulated by the churches, acting together for once, the Sundays at the beginning and end of the month were set aside as national days of prayer, and talks on medicine murder were given to school-children. The debate in the mission newspapers reached a new pitch of intensity.[23]

There were also moves to strengthen the police. The Administrative Team of Major Donald and Chief Leshoboro Majara was said to be working well, and the temporary increase in the number of police posts approved in 1949 was made permanent. A new intelligence unit was set up: at first it concentrated on the BAC, but there were plans to shift its attention to medicine murder.[24]

By October the Committee's report was ready. There were familiar references to the proliferation of placing disputes, the effect of the Khubelu and Treasury reforms, the instabilities arising from the appointment of women as chiefs, and the profound changes in the relations between chiefs and their followers. The criticisms relating to accomplice witnesses were met to the extent of making a recommendation that accomplices should lose all their civil rights, regardless of the outcome of the case, but criticisms of the police were firmly rejected. There was no mention of the role played by 'Mantšebo, though at least one of the written submissions to the Conference had suggested that she was heavily implicated.[25] In the long term the only 'antidote to the belief in magic' was said to be Christian education and civilisation. For the short term more than fifty recommendations were made, ranging from the detailed and particular – such as the suggestion that 'a European Police Officer and an intelligent Mosuto NCO' should be sent on a training course in England – to the general and far-reaching, such as the proposal that 'every Chief and Headman performing the duties of Chief or Headman should be recognised in the Gazette, irrespective of the size of his holding'.

The report reflected its origins. It was an attempt to enrol the whole nation behind the official narrative of medicine murder and to enlist its support in the struggle to end it. It was not an academic or an official document, and it made a point of demonstrating the Committee's responsiveness to the submissions sent in by members of the public, no matter how unhelpful or implausible, such as the proposals to send a Mosotho to a Moral Rearmament Conference, to make it unlawful to wear a charm, and to obtain from the South African police a machine which 'is able to photograph the retina of a murdered person's eyes, and to reproduce therefrom an image of the murderers, or at least of the last persons that the dead person saw before dying'. Although the Committee rejected these suggestions, and although it made many practical and sensible recommendations, it opened itself to ridicule in this way.[26]

In the High Commissioner's office J. A. Steward was contemptuous and dismissive, and suggested that it should now be made compulsory for every officer in Basutoland to go down to sea-level every year. He did not believe 'that the Basutoland Administration deliberately sets out to shroud its inactivity behind this smoke-screen of serio-comic surmise', but he was sure that some Basotho were deriving a lot of quiet amusement from it all.[27] The Attorney-General was 'exceedingly disappointed' with the report,[28] while Scrivenor, the Deputy High Commissioner, described it as 'a collection of trivialities and platitudes enlivened by a number of recommendations that could only bring the Administration into contempt and ridicule if they were published'. One of the recommendations that most provoked him was that 'the offer to admit a circumcised European official to a circumcision school to see and report on its conduct should be accepted'.[29] The High

Commissioner, le Rougetel, agreed that the report 'does nothing to eluci-
date and not a little to obscure the issue'.[30]

The High Commission was all the more contemptuous because it was
unimpressed by the anti-*liretlo* campaign. There were just as many murders
as before and, according to the Attorney-General, there was no real change
in public opinion and the police were finding it as hard as ever to get
evidence.[31] In public le Rougetel was guarded in his comments about the
government's efforts. When he spoke to the Basutoland National Council in
September 1954 he said that it was too soon to draw conclusions,[32] but two
months later his deputy, Tom Scrivenor, noted that the campaign was
having 'little or no effect' and that medicine murders were on the increase
again. 'I have never had much faith in the anti-*liretlo* campaign', Scrivenor
wrote. 'It is naive to believe that this sort of crime can be overcome by
education, Public Relations Officers, the establishment of secondary
industries and the licensing of initiation schools.'[33] At the same time he was
confirmed in his fears that Arrowsmith had made a bad mistake in holding
joint *pitsos* with 'Mantšebo, since this, he was told by a respected government officer, had 'made a laughing stock of the Basutoland Administration'.[34]
It was grimly ironic that a headman handed one of his followers the
government pamphlet on *liretlo* only a few days before enrolling him as an
accomplice in murder.[35]

The doubts of the High Commissioner and his officials had been
confirmed: Arrowsmith's strategy had failed. They now turned to their own
'short-term remedies', measures, they hoped, that were so tough that they
would shake the chiefs in the same way as the hangings of Bereng and
Gabashane. Because of the difficulties of judicial proof, Steward argued,
medicine murder should now be dealt with administratively, so that the
government could depose and banish offenders when it was satisfied
administratively of their guilt. 'The Law ...', he wrote, 'is designed for other
climates and other stages of civilization ...' This proposal was supported by
the Attorney-General, and although Scrivenor said that he did not like it he
himself was soon suggesting that chiefs in whose areas murders were
committed should be deposed and exiled. Le Rougetel also believed that
'immediate action' was required: 'Chiefs who are charged with or even
suspected of conniving at medicine murder ... should be automatically
suspended by administrative action and, if convicted, should, likewise, be
deprived once and for all of their administrative functions'.[36]

The chief most under threat was of course 'Mantšebo, and her deposition
would have shaken the whole country. She was alleged to have been
implicated in a series of cases, notably the murder of Stephen Thobeha at
Morija (1945/3, Case Study 1) and several murders in Mokhotlong (Case
Study 4). In another recent case (1952/6) a witness alleged that headman
Pheello Smith had spoken to him about taking pieces of flesh and human

blood to a mysterious personage at Matsieng, who was later identified as 'Mantšebo.[37] There were also anonymous letters accusing both her and her advisers of being responsible for medicine murder, and urging their removal.[38] But, as Arrowsmith noted, 'deposition of the Regent without there being grounds to use the ordinary processes of law would not only be contrary to our principles of justice, but would very probably lead to trouble with the Basuto'. These were powerful arguments, and it was no doubt for these reasons that nothing was done to implement the High Commission proposals either in 'Mantšebo's case or more generally. The only action that seems to have been taken was a directive from the High Commissioner that any chief found guilty of a crime should automatically be deposed, and even this does not seem to have been enforced, though it made the chiefs feel more under threat.[39]

There was also talk of 'Mantšebo's resigning, and of one of her advisers acting as Paramount Chief until the heir, Constantine Bereng Seeiso, came of age. Her health was poor and she was under enormous strain, not least because of the accusations of medicine murder, and at one meeting with Arrowsmith she 'broke down and wept', saying that she was 'sick and tired'. 'Our impression was that she is ready to throw her hand in', he wrote. But, as he warned the High Commissioner, she was 'unpredictable'.[40] She was grateful to the Resident Commissioner for ensuring that she would receive a pension, but in the end she stayed in office until 1960 and even then did everything to try to hold on to her position.

ATTACKS ON THE POLICE, 1956: THE COUNCIL AND THE CONFERENCE

The debate on the Liretlo Committee's report in the National Council was used as an opportunity to attack the police. The Special Session arranged to consider it in May 1956 could hardly have been held at a worse time. In the previous year the Council had rejected the Moore Report, and Arrowsmith had antagonised it by accusing it of acting irresponsibly. John Gunther's book, *Inside Africa*, had just been published, and councillors were infuriated by his concentration on medicine murder and his attack on 'Mantšebo. It made matters worse that, when in Basutoland, he had stayed with the Resident Commissioner and the Government Secretary. So, as Arrowsmith noted, the atmosphere was 'by no means easy, and was filled with suspicion and distrust'.[41]

As the Resident Commissioner looked around the Council Chamber he could not be sure of 'the exact number of acquitted medicine murderers in Council', but he noted two of the most prominent, Chiefs Theko Makhaola and Matlere Lerotholi. He might perhaps have derived some encouragement from the presence of two members of the Committee that had produced the report, Chiefs Leshoboro Majara and Kelebone Nkuebe, and from the presence of Nkuebe Mitchell, 'Mantšebo's representative, who had sat as an assessor in several medicine murder cases which had resulted in convictions.[42] If so he was to be sorely disappointed. His only good fortune was that Josiel Lefela was no longer a councillor. In the previous year he had been convicted of sedition for alleging that the police had tortured a Crown witness in the trial of Bereng and Gabashane in 1948 and that the government's doctors had murdered Paramount Chief Seeiso in 1940 for the purpose of obtaining medicine themselves.[43]

The debate lasted from 7 to 17 May. The Council went through the report recommendation by recommendation, but the driving force through-out the debate was a fierce hostility to the police. It was an unremitting onslaught, and there were very few councillors who did not go along with it. Leshoboro Majara complained of being falsely incriminated himself; Kelebone Nkuebe told the Council that it should forget that he had been a member of the Committee since he was now presenting the views of the Quthing District Council; Nkuebe Mitchell concentrated his fire on Gunther and was not at all satisfied with the official defence of the police.

As in previous debates, some councillors denied the existence of medicine murder, others were unsure, and others believed that, while murders were being committed, the wrong people – the chiefs – were being incriminated. But no matter what their starting point, they nearly all condemned the police on one count or another: for assuming that ordinary murders were medicine murders; for assuming that such murders were committed by chiefs, not commoners; for keeping witnesses in detention for long periods; for persuading innocent people to become Crown witnesses, or for torturing them and telling them what to say. Several chiefs gave vivid accounts of how they themselves had been falsely accused, and there were several stories of allegations of medicine murder being disproved when the alleged victims were found alive and well. Councillors found it particularly disgraceful that no action was taken against accomplice witnesses when the people they incriminated were found innocent. The Committee had recommended that accomplices should forfeit all civil privileges, irrespective of the result of the trial. After a long debate the Council resolved that they should be prose-cuted for contravening 'Mantšebo's order that no one should assist in a medicine murder and that, if the accused were found not guilty, they should be sued by the relatives of the deceased for compensation.

There can be no doubt, both from this debate and from other sources, that relations between the police and the chiefs had broken down. But criticisms of the police reflected wider discontents. Since the police were 'under the government', there were suspicions that they were acting on government orders. One speaker likened them to dogs which had been ordered by their owners to attack. There were suspicions that Gunther too had been primed by the government in his attacks on 'Mantšebo. It was symptomatic of the discussion in the Council that a more sympathetic view was taken of initiation schools and Basotho doctors,[44] and several speakers made a special point of denying that medicine murder was a Sesotho custom. In a report on a debate held a few months later the Council was described as closing ranks around the chieftainship.[45] It would have been a fitting description of this debate too.

A few speakers stood out against this wholesale assault. To deny the existence of medicine murder, said one of them, was to say that the sun had set when it could still be seen in the sky. They reported the widespread popular belief that the chiefs were heavily involved, and they opposed any action against accomplice witnesses. In reply they were accused of insulting the nation.

A shift in the centre of gravity of such public discussion over time was starkly evident. In the first debate in the Council on medicine murder, in 1946, speaker after speaker had acknowledged its horror and the shame it had brought on the Basotho nation. In this debate, ten years later, speaker after speaker had attacked the police. The official narrative had been overwhelmed. The counter-narrative now held the field.

Towards the end of the debate Paul Kitson, the newly appointed Commissioner of Police, was summoned to address the Council. He gave a long and spirited defence of the police but, as Arrowsmith reported, it was not well received. Far from winning over the councillors, Kitson's blunt words merely infuriated them more. They were mollified only when the Resident Commissioner acknowledged that some policemen might have made some mistakes and suggested that a conference should be called between the police, the people and the chiefs to explore ways of improving relations. This proposal was warmly welcomed.[46]

When the conference was held a few months later, in August 1956, Arrowsmith was on the point of leaving Basutoland, and it was chaired by the new Government Secretary, Gordon Hector. Twenty-four others were present. As well as the Director of Medical Services, there were several senior policemen, both white and Basotho; several chiefs and councillors; and 'four members of the public', including two leaders of the BAC – the President, Ntsu Mokhehle, and the Deputy Leader, Bennett Khaketla. It is significant that they had been invited with the express agreement of the regent.[47] In general she was deeply suspicious of the BAC.[48] On medicine murder, however, she felt that she could trust them, just as she had trusted Lefela before.

The conference lasted five days, from 27 to 31 August. Its centrepiece was, in effect, a confrontation between the two narratives of medicine murder and then, on Khaketla's prompting, an elaborate attempt to find common ground between them. Hector described it as having been conducted in an excellent spirit. Kitson, the Commissioner of Police, opened the meeting by pointing out that in the previous year, out of 10,626 investigations, only nine concerned medicine murder. But he then made what Hector called 'the innocent admission' that this type of death had been variously called witchcraft, ritual or medicine murder. This provoked a furious attack led by Chief Seepheephe Matete, until recently one of 'Mantšebo's advisers, 'volubly supported' by Ntsu Mokhehle, and finally directed by Bennett Khaketla. Senior representatives of the Basotho had previously objected to the term 'ritual murder' on the ground that it suggested that these murders were part of Sesotho custom and practice. Now they objected to the term 'medicine murder'. They accepted that mutilated bodies were being found and that murders were being committed, but they did not accept that these mutilations and murders were being carried out in order to obtain medicine. Khaketla, contrary to the evidence he had given in 1953 to the Round Table Conference, when he had suggested that the term 'medicine-horn murder' should be used, 'because at least it shows the purpose for which the murder is committed',[49] now argued that the correct term was *liretlo* murders. *Liretlo*, he said, referred to the cutting of flesh from animals or human beings, no more, no less. It did not mean the cutting of flesh to obtain medicine. *Liretlo* murder did not mean medicine murder, and Jones had been wrong in assuming that it did.

As Hector summed it up, the 'Basuto point of view' was that Jones 'had not proved scientifically beyond a peradventure the connection between these killings and medicine horns. Moreover, had not Gunther told the world in italics that no medicine horn had ever been found?' Jones had created a prejudice in the minds of the police: mutilated bodies implied medicine horns which implied the involvement of the chiefs. A more open approach was needed. 'Call it anything you like except medicine murder, and we will co-operate wholeheartedly.' In this 'illogical way', Hector reported, the Basotho thrashed out a reasonable system of closer integration between the chieftainship, the police and the government. It was agreed that the term *liretlo* murder should now be used instead of medicine murder; that a panel should be appointed in each district partly by recommendation from local chiefs to the Paramount Chief and partly by the District Council with the Paramount Chief's approval; that whenever a medicine murder was suspected, a member of this panel should accompany the police up to the time of the post-mortem examination; and that the conference should be reconvened to review progress from time to time. It was also agreed that ideally there should be a complete separation between the administration and the judiciary and, in particular, that District Commissioners should not sit as magistrates. The government noted that this would take some time to effect.[50]

Hector, new to the country, was struck by the sensitivity of the Basotho to the Jones report and more particularly to Gunther's chapter on Basutoland.

He was also impressed by how helpful and restrained Khaketla had been. Mokhehle's contribution, he said, was less valuable. He was not 'impervious to reasoned argument from the other side', but 'he allows his heart to run away with his head and loses the thread of his argument quite easily'.[51] Mokhehle might well have been sincere in his denial of medicine murder, but others were not. Nkherepe Molefe, one of the Basotho police officers present, remembered that after the conference he confronted Nkuebe Mitchell, one of the Paramount Chief's representatives, and others whom he described as 'Parliamentarians': 'I said, "Surely you don't seriously believe that there are no *liretlo*?" Nkuebe raised his hand and said, "Don't ask that question. You are a Mosotho". In other words, keep it quiet.'[52] It was a matter of national pride.

THE LATE 1950s AND THE EARLY 1960s: THE GOVERNMENT LOSES INTEREST

The conference of August 1956 was the last occasion on which the colonial authorities tried to mount any concerted initiative against medicine murder. Arrowsmith was replaced by Geoffrey Chaplin, and in November, after he had been in office for six weeks, the new Resident Commissioner wrote a long memorandum in which he set out his initial impressions of the country. Having grown up in East Griqualand, he had begun his service in Basutoland in the 1930s as a policeman and a junior administrative officer, and he spoke fluent Sesotho. After an absence of thirteen years what struck him most was the 'deterioration which appears to have taken place in the relations between the Central Government and the Native Administration'. The Basotho distrusted the government: they still feared incorporation into South Africa and they were reluctant to co-operate in any government scheme. He gave several reasons for this, including the Khubelu and Treasury reforms. He made no mention of medicine murder. This caused some surprise at the High Commission, but it was not regarded as a serious omission. Sir Percivale Liesching, who had succeeded le Rougetel as High Commissioner, was impressed by the memorandum, and merely noted that 'it could have been filled out by dealing with such matters as the incidence of medicine murder ...'[53]

A few months later, when Chaplin was interviewed by the *Basutoland News*, he played down the importance of medicine murders. 'None has been reported to us recently', he said, 'but these murders are not restricted to Basutoland. The position here has been dramatised. I am sure these things happen wherever there are primitive natives in southern Africa, even in the Union.'[54] It was typical of the government's slackening of concern that it was only in March 1958, at 'Mantšebo's request, that an interim report on the conference chaired by Gordon Hector was submitted to the Basutoland National Council, and that in spite of the Council's request the final report was never submitted for debate.[55] The most important outcome of the conference should have been the establishment of the district panels, but progress on this was so slow that it was not until November 1959, more than three years later, that the list was finally submitted to 'Mantšebo for approval, although the system had been operating informally.[56]

Apart from the recording of numbers, there was no longer any reference to medicine murder in the government's annual reports. One BAC official complained to the Secretary of State that 'Mr Chaplin, like most of your white officers here, treats this grave matter with no apparent seriousness'. Chief Leshoboro Majara accused the government of being 'just disinterested in this matter of *liretlo*'.[57] Murders also figured less prominently in the mission newspapers, *Leselinyana* and *Moeletsi*. There were still reports on individual cases, but there was much less editorial comment, and the debate in the correspondence columns was desultory and spasmodic.

At the end of 1959 the special conference on medicine murder was reconvened under Hector's chairmanship. The Basutoland Congress Party, the BCP (as the BAC had been renamed in 1958), had been pressing for an independent commission of enquiry into medicine murder, and one of the arguments used by government to resist this was that it was following up the recommendations made at the 1956 conference, in which Mokhehle and Khaketla had taken part so constructively.[58] It therefore had to show that some progress was being made on these recommendations.

The reconvened conference, however, was wrecked by Mokhehle. He had clearly lost any faith which he might have had in the process, and he was determined to get a new commission of enquiry. In the words of Hector's official report,

> The Anti-Liretlo Conference which was convened for a sitting on the 3rd November, ground to an ignominious halt on the third day, the 5th, entirely as a result of the obstructions and quite impossible behaviour of one of its members, Mr. Ntsu Mokhehle, who rendered the two days of the meeting at which he was present completely abortive.[59]

According to this account Mokhehle disputed the recorded outcome of the previous meeting and engaged in endless procedural wrangles. It made no mention, however, of the incident that made the greatest impression on the Basotho present, and that entered into the realm of a nationalist legend, vividly remembered many years later and recounted with much laughter. It was best described by Bennett Khaketla, who relates how 'Mokhehle's fiery temper often came to the fore when he had to deal with Europeans'. Among the police, he said, there was Captain Shott-Smith, Superintendent of Police. ('Shott-Smith' was Ken Shortt-Smith and, although Khaketla did not mention it, he too was renowned for his fiery temper.) As Khaketla described it,

In the course of discussion, Mokhehle warmed up to his subject. He castigated the administration violently for what he termed a 'trick'. He challenged the Police to prove that they did not use third-degree methods to extract 'so-called confessions' from the 'so-called accomplices'. As he spoke he kept pointing an accusing finger at Captain Sho[r]tt-Smith as a representative of the 'rotten Police' who represented 'an alien, rotten system'. Nobody could now stop him. Even I couldn't. Sho[r]tt-Smith became enraged, and said he would not allow a 'wearer of Her Majesty's uniform to be insulted in this manner'.

Both men promptly stood up. Mokhehle prepared to pull off his jacket and accept the challenge of Sho[r]tt-Smith who seemed ready to engage in a demonstration of his pugilistic skill. But Nkherepe Molefe intervened, and what might have developed into an ugly situation was averted.

'Needless to say', Khaketla concluded, 'no other conference was ever convened.'[60]

The government's loss of interest in medicine murders could not have been due to any decline in their numbers. Although only four were reported in 1956, in the following three years the numbers rose to twelve, thirteen and sixteen respectively, almost the same level as at the height of the crisis in 1948. Fewer cases were now reaching the courts, but this may be regarded as a result, not a cause, of the government's re-ordering of its priorities. Nor did the government lose interest because the senior chiefs were no longer involved. In the late 1950s there was again a struggle over the paramountcy, which resulted in 'Mantšebo's removal in 1960 to make way for her ward and successor, Constantine Bereng Seeiso. In 1959, in an apparent attempt to prevent this, there was another murder in Mokhotlong in which 'Mantšebo and Matlere Lerotholi were implicated (1959/1, Case Study 4).

No doubt Chaplin's personal views were partly responsible for the change in the government's attitude. He did not take a high moral line. Medicine murder was simply a fact of life, and not a very significant one at that. Previous Resident Commissioners had tolerated 'Mantšebo because they felt they had no alternative. There were constant reports of her involvement in medicine murder, but nothing that could prove her guilt. Chaplin however got on well with 'Mantšebo. He looked back with nostalgia to the time when Resident Commissioners enjoyed friendly relations with Paramount Chief Griffith and his successor, Seeiso, and he worked hard to establish the same kind of relationship with 'Mantšebo. His wife, a wealthy trader's daughter who also spoke fluent Sesotho, went shopping and to the races with her, and was even described as a 'great friend'. When the Sons of Moshoeshoe turned against 'Mantšebo and supported the installation of Constantine Bereng Seeiso, Chaplin accepted their decision, but very reluctantly.[61]

Chaplin's personal views were only a minor factor. He was not the first British official to think that the attention being given to medicine murders was out of proportion to their real significance. Tom Scrivenor, the Deputy High Commissioner, had made the same suggestion in 1954. He too suspected that medicine murders were just as common in the rest of southern Africa, but he observed that it was only in Basutoland that they were carried out almost exclusively for a small chiefly class.[62] In the late 1950s, as British and French colonies in sub-Saharan Africa began to achieve independence, it became clear that the future lay not with the chiefs, but with the newly emerging politicians. The authorities in Basutoland, especially Chaplin himself, might have been slow in learning that lesson, and they might even have claimed that things were different in Basutoland, but the men who now commanded the headlines were the leaders of the BCP. The pace of constitutional change was quickened, the National Council became a Legislative Council, the element of popular representation was increased, and in the first elections held in 1960 the BCP won thirty of the Council's forty elected seats. The forty non-elected seats were held by the twenty-two Principal and Ward Chiefs *ex officio*, fourteen nominees of the Paramount Chief, and four government officials headed by the Government Secretary. Independence was just over the horizon. In these circumstances a dozen or so medicine murders each year by chiefs and headmen whose national (though not local) importance was diminishing became a matter of peripheral concern.

For many Basotho, however, medicine murder continued to be a matter of deep shame and humiliation. The official narrative now commanded very little public support, however much it might have been privately accepted. In 1957 the BAC, as it still was, asked for a six-man commission of enquiry, and so too did 'Mantšebo, though she pretended that her request had nothing to do with the BAC's approach. Chaplin and Hector were persuaded of the BAC's sincerity and recommended that it be given a positive response, but in South Africa the High Commission was unimpressed: 'it is possible', Scrivenor wrote, 'to expend too much sympathy on the mental confusion of people who will not give government the support due from them as citizens until they have been satisfied by an independent enquiry that Government is not committing or rigging "liretlo" murders'.[63] In November 1959 Mokhehle, undeterred, used the reconvened conference on medicine murder to press again for a new commission, but no action was taken.

Murders continued in the early 1960s, though the numbers reported averaged fewer than five a year and even fewer reached the courts. The general impression was that they were a thing of the past. No-one in the administration was concerned: they were now a matter for the police and the judiciary. In March 1962, however, Chief Reentseng Griffith proposed in the National Council that the British government should appoint a commission to investigate the causes of medicine murder. In the course of the discussion this was amended, on a Congress initiative, to a proposal that the High Commissioner should ask the Paramount Chief to appoint a commission. There was not always a full house to debate the motion, but the most important councillors were there, including the Congress leadership.

The amended motion received support from every side of the house, except of course from the four government officials, who remained for the most part silent. They did not bother to mount any opposition, but merely pointed out the financial implications. In the fevered climate of pre-independence politics, when every effort was being made to remove the British, the attack on the colonial authorities was unrestrained and almost unanimous. As in previous debates there were some, like Reentseng Griffith himself, who thought that there might be medicine murders but that the wrong people were being convicted, while others denied the very existence of the crime. There were all the old accounts of false allegations, of supposed victims being found alive, and of police malpractice. The government's responsibility was roundly asserted and condemned by chiefs and Congress alike. According to Chief L. S. Griffith, who seconded the motion, 'Many people have been accused falsely by this very British Government'. The whole purpose of medicine murder trials, said Meshack Poola, a Congress representative, was to terrify the chiefs so that they toed the British line, and chiefs who would not comply would be 'liquidated'. 'These murders are staged and arranged by these British Government Officials', said Chief Jonathan Ntlama, who had recently been acquitted of medicine murder. 'Is there anyone amongst the Chiefs who does not suspect that we are being liquidated as a nation?', asked Philemon 'Mabathoana.

'We are fed up ... with this matter of "Liretlo"', said Chief Leshoboro Majara, the chief so trusted by the British administration. When the Commission was appointed he would not 'hesitate to expose the lies that are being planned against the lives of the Basotho'. Chief Sekhonyana 'Maseribane (later to become the first Prime Minister in an independent Lesotho) had sat as an assessor in at least one medicine murder trial, and yet he too accused the British government of coercing people 'to bring false accusations against others'. When old Chief Goliath Malebanye, a some-what eccentric character, asserted the existence of medicine murders, Ntsu Mokhehle accused him of having been taken in by the government's propaganda. Mokhehle also derided G. I. Jones and his report. He told the Council that when he enquired about Jones in London he was told 'he had been a colonial servant in several countries including Nigeria; he had a mentality of a civil servant and that was the only qualification that had him called in to Basutoland'.[64]

The motion was passed without a vote being needed, and on the advice of the Executive Council the High Commissioner asked the Resident Commissioner to invite the Paramount Chief to appoint a commission.[65] Constantine Bereng Seeiso had now been Paramount Chief for two years. He had been educated at Ampleforth, the Roman Catholic public school in England, and at Corpus Christi College, Oxford, where he had read Politics, Philosophy and Economics, though he had left before taking his degree in order to take up his chieftainship. He too was deeply disturbed by the debate about medicine murder, and soon after being placed he had angered the Resident Commissioner when he had alleged that false accusations were being made.[66] He was therefore particularly receptive to the proposal that a commission should be appointed.[67]

The British reaction was again dismissive. An official in London scribbled in the margin: 'Why is this subject being exhumed? Has there been a recent revival of such murders? Who is going to pay?' 'One can imagine Treasury reaction', wrote another, 'to a proposal that Basutoland grant-in-aid should be increased to cater for the cost of a Commission to enquire into medicine murders!'[68] That was the clinching argument. The British government at this time was becoming increasingly exasperated by the demands of the Basotho for more expenditure in one way or another, especially when they were coupled with the kind of attack that was exemplified in the debates about medicine murder. It saw no reason to spend more money on a commission to examine a subject which, as far as it was concerned, was now dead and buried.

INDEPENDENCE

In October 1966 the British Colony of Basutoland became the independent nation of Lesotho, and the Paramount Chief became King Moshoeshoe II. Contrary to many people's expectations, the pre-independence elections had been narrowly won not by the BCP, but by the Basutoland National Party (BNP), a chiefly, conservative organisation led by Leabua Jonathan and strongly supported by the Roman Catholic church. A third party, the Marema-Tlou Freedom Party, though backed by the Paramount Chief, had fared comparatively poorly. Although Leabua Jonathan himself was a minor chief, and although he derived much of his support from the chiefs, he made no attempt to revive the idea of an enquiry into the causes of medicine murder.

In 1967, the first full year of independence, eight medicine murders were reported, and in 1968 twenty more. It was the highest reported number in any year since 1948, the year in which Bereng and Gabashane were arrested. Nine more cases were reported in 1969, but after that the figures were subsumed under, and so lost in, the figures for murders generally. Medicine murder was no longer a matter of national concern or a subject of national debate.

How many medicine murders have taken place since then can only be a matter of speculation. According to one police source who did not want to be named, two to three mutilated bodies were being found each month during the late 1980s and early 1990s, an annual figure of twenty-four to thirty-six. Suspected cases have been reported in the police newspaper, *Leseli ka Sepolesa*. Anecdotes and rumours are commonplace. In recent times traders have been suspected as much as chiefs. Yet hardly any cases of medicine murder have come before the courts – as far as we know, there have been only eight since independence, three of them against traders, and of these only four after 1975. Nkherepe Molefe gave a simple explanation: 'After independence things were confused. We didn't know what to do'.[69]

Things were indeed confused. Leabua Jonathan's reaction to electoral defeat in January 1970 was to stage a coup to retain power.[70] This was bitterly resisted by the BCP under Mokhehle, which sought to instigate armed revolts in 1974 and in 1980. Leabua Jonathan was ousted by a military coup in 1986. The King's position, nominally that of a constitutional monarch, also proved highly volatile. He was exiled twice, and twice returned to Lesotho, but was later forced to abdicate by the Military Council. Mokhehle himself finally came to power through the restoration of a precarious parliamentary democracy in 1993, when the BCP won all sixty-five seats in the National Assembly. The King was reinstated, but he was killed in a car crash in 1996 and succeeded by his son Letsie III. The BCP split in 1997, with Mokhehle forming the break-away Lesotho Congress for Democracy (LCD). The LCD won a landslide election victory in May 1998, but a mutiny by a faction of the Lesotho Defence Force in September 1998 provoked a heavy-handed intervention by South Africa, which in turn provoked riots that devastated Maseru and other towns. The constitutional crisis remained unresolved. Meanwhile, the country has been ravaged by acute structural unemployment, yawning inequality, growing poverty and hunger, and the terrible scourge of HIV/AIDS. In these circumstances, medicine murder has barely raised a flicker on the screen of public consciousness.

INTERLUDE

MEDICINE MURDER AND
THE LITERARY IMAGINATION

> The Chief's eyes watered, and his voice grew thick. Turning to the Judge's Clerk, he asked: 'May I have water to drink?' The Judge leaned forward and instructed the Clerk to fetch from outside a glass of cool water. When the water had been handed to the Chief, and he had drunk of it, he said to the Judge: 'My Lord, you ordered your servant, the Clerk, to fetch me water to drink – he obeyed you! But had he refused to obey, would he not have been guilty of Contempt of Court? And would you not have punished him? ... So would these men here have been liable to severe punishment, had they disobeyed my orders! When I commanded them to find one of the Bafokeng Clan, and to kill him for the Medicine Horn, they carried out my orders because of their respect for me. And you, my Lord, and your Assessors, the Chiefs, should know that the respect of a Mosotho for his Chief, is greater even that that which he has for his father! ... Therefore, my Lord, do I ask that the punishment be mine! Whether or not *Liretlo* is right and lawful, still was it these men's duty to obey me, and I pray, my Lord, that you will allow them to go free!'
>
> And the Chief sat down and hid his eyes from all. Quiet as the dead of night was the Courtroom; then suddenly came a clapping of hands from some of the white men present, and then came the cheering of the Basotho people, whose admiration could not be restrained. Again the noble Judge made no motion with his hammer to end the noise – perhaps his secret feelings were the same as those openly displayed!
>
> Lanham and Mopeli-Paulus (1953: 303–4)

Medicine murder had striking resonances in Basotho folklore and history. At the height of the crisis in the late 1940s and early 1950s it was likened to Kholumolumo, the monster in the Sesotho folktale which devoured almost every living creature before being killed by the hero, the boy Senkatana. The murderers were compared to the cannibals who had terrorised the country during the times of the *lifaqane*. The great Moshoeshoe had put an end to cannibalism. Where were the leaders who could put an end to medicine murder?[1]

Novelists and playwrights were drawn to the subject. They read the lurid accounts in the press and one of them at least, Bennett Khaketla, attended the High Court and observed for himself the conduct of several cases.[2] They reproduced in their writings details of particular murders, and they also drew out, implicitly or explicitly, comments and arguments from contemporary debates.[3] Most of them were members of Christian churches, and some wrote in the strong tradition of the Christian novel in Sesotho. Yet the most prominent theme to emerge – not in every novel but in most – is the medicine murderer as tragic hero.

The most famous of all Sesotho novels is Thomas Mofolo's *Chaka*. Although this was first published in 1925, it is known to have been written by 1912.[4] The long delay before publication was due to the French missionaries' belief that it glorified 'pagan superstition'. Nhlanhla Maake argues that included in this was the glorification of *liretlo*.[5] In the novel, Chaka becomes a powerful chief because of the medicines given to him by Isanusi, a doctor from a far-off land. As he becomes more ambitious he needs stronger medicines, and he is persuaded by Isanusi to kill his own wife, Noliwe, and to make use of her blood for medicine. He does this when they are alone together by pushing a needle into her body under the arm. His empire is extended even further, and then he kills his mother Nandi 'in the same way that he had killed Noliwe'.[6] He enjoys no peace or happiness. The victims of his wars and his murders appear to him in dreams and visions, and in the end he is killed by his own brothers.

Maake believes that 'Mofolo wrote his text after the *diretlo* murders had become a source of concern'.[7] This is plainly wrong, but Mofolo was acutely aware of the belief in the power of human medicine. Several of the themes and devices of his novel – notably the murderer as a tragic hero led astray by an evil doctor, and later the reappearance of his victims in dreams – were to influence those who came after him. Behind Mofolo's Chaka we can surely detect the influence of Shakespeare's Macbeth, again a tragic hero who is led astray by witchcraft and whose victims reappear to trouble him in dreams and visions. Macbeth is also led astray by his wife, a theme which re-emerges in Khaketla's novel, *Mosali a Nkhola* ('The Woman Betrayed Me').

Of all the works which deal explicitly with medicine murder, the best-known is *Blanket Boy's Moon*. This was originally written by A. S. Mopeli-Paulus and then submitted to Peter Lanham, who had advertised himself as an agent for budding authors. Lanham revised the script – how much we do not know – and it was published in 1953 as a novel by Lanham 'based on an original story by A. S. Mopeli-Paulus, Chieftain of Basutoland'.[8] In fact, Mopeli-Paulus was not a chief in Basutoland, but a minor chief in the reserve of Witzieshoek, later Qwaqwa, which adjoined Basutoland to the north-east. During the last war between the Basotho and the Orange Free State in the 1860s Moshoeshoe's brother, Paulus Mopeli, had made a separate peace with the enemy, and he and his followers had been awarded this small mountainous enclave under Free State rule. Mopeli-Paulus, the author, was Paulus Mopeli's grandson. In his autobiography he explains how he 'hardly' believed in medicines, but was prepared to make use of them when he and others were brought to trial as a result of the disturbances in Witzieshoek in 1950. He emphasises, however, that, unlike some chiefs in Basutoland, they did not turn to medicine murder.[9]

One of the underlying themes in *Blanket Boy's Moon* is that Basutoland has been ruined by colonial rule and the consequent corruption of the chiefs, and this, of course, lies very close to the critique of Josiel Lefela and the Lekhotla la Bafo. The central character, Monare, is ordered by his chief's right-hand man to organise a medicine murder:

> You know that a new village is to be established. It is an important thing, this sending out of a Chief's son. You elders of the tribe should know just how important. According to our ancient custom, the witch doctors have decided that a medicine horn must be prepared to ward off bewitchment, and ensure prosperity and success to the new community. This medicine horn will require as one of its magic ingredients the blood and flesh of a man of the Bafokeng clan.[10]

The victim turns out to be Monare's own friend. 'I understand that it is against the law to commit murder', Monare says, 'but Ritual Murder is an old custom of Lesotho, and what the Chief orders, we must obey.'[11] The murderers are arrested and thrown into prison, and while they are there a Christian minister comes and gives an analysis of medicine murder that might have come straight from the early debates in the National Council. He explains that the trouble stems from the creation of the National Treasury, which has deprived the chiefs of their courts and turned them into salaried officials of the government.

> The Chiefs surrendered for a regular income, rights and privileges which have come down to them from their forefathers – they exchanged their birthright for a mess of pottage! ... How then shall their pride and dignity be protected, preserved, and upheld? Only through the remaining customs of Lesotho, chief among which is *Liretlo*!

And now Basutoland was ruled by a woman! How could she

> withstand the cunning of the white man? I say that the end of Lesotho is in sight and that it is the foolishness of the Chiefs that has brought the end so near ... I am afraid that in London they bargain with the Afrikaner over our dying homelands![12]

Throughout the novel Monare is treated sympathetically. He is a good man whose only fault is to obey his chief. And, as in the quotation at the head of this chapter, his chief also emerges as a leader of nobility, a man who insists on taking the blame himself and trying to exonerate his followers.

Blanket Boy's Moon forms part of the corpus of the counter-narrative of medicine murder. Mopeli-Paulus does not go so far as to say that medicine murder is a colonial invention, but he clearly implies that it is being exploited by the British to undermine the chieftainship and so to pave the way for Basutoland's incorporation in South Africa. Yet in two other novels on the same subject, *Liretlo*, published in Sesotho three years earlier in 1950, and *Turn to the Dark*, written in conjunction with Miriam Basner and published three years later in 1956,[13] no mention is made of the chieftainship reforms or of the role of the British.

Liretlo, in fact, is set in a Basutoland that has not yet come under colonial rule. Chris Dunton summarises its plot as follows:

> The village chief Lelume orders his Zulu *ngaka* Nkosikosi to carry out *liretlo* to ensure the succession of his son Ranne to the chieftaincy and to protect himself, Ranne, and Ranne's mother, Ngoajane, against political rivals. When, later, Nkosikosi suspects that this medicine lacks full strength, another victim is killed, and parts of his body are used to make a second medicine-horn. After his father's death, Ranne is elected chief. Nkosikosi and his colleague Qeko eventually die, leaving instructions to Ranne that no further murders should be committed since the medicine he took has proven sufficiently powerful. Ranne disobeys their instructions and has a third murder carried out. Growing increasingly corrupt, he takes to drink, as does gradually the whole village. The Principal Chief intervenes; details of the three murders are revealed, and Ranne is tried and sentenced.[14]

This plot fits much more easily into the official narrative. Medicine murder is presented as a common occurrence even before colonial rule: within the same village three murders are carried out in the space of two generations. And it is deeply rooted in Sesotho culture: although the doctors involved are Zulu, the initiative comes from the Basotho chiefs.

Turn to the Dark, which Mopeli-Paulus wrote with Miriam Basner, also makes no concessions to the counter-narrative. The central character, Lesiba, is the son of a Mosotho minister who returns to Lesotho from college in the Free State after leading his fellow students in a strike. He is welcomed back by the chief of his village, Johannes, and is overjoyed when he wins the chief's trust and becomes one of his advisers. But things are going badly in the village. There is a severe drought, land is scarce, and Johannes believes that he is being bewitched by a rival. Johannes is persuaded by his doctor, Mafa, and by another councillor, Khanya, that he must 'freshen' his medicine horn or else be overthrown. Lesiba is persuaded to become one of the accomplices, but in the event he takes no part in the actual killing. He is incriminated by two false witnesses, but the truth is revealed in court and Lesiba himself makes a full confession. While Johannes and others are convicted and hanged, Lesiba is convicted merely as an accessory and is given seven years' imprisonment with hard labour. Lesiba is treated sympathetically throughout the novel. Even more significantly, so is Johannes, so much so that towards the end he is commonly referred to as 'The Great One'. The villains of the piece are the doctor, Mafa, and to a lesser extent Johannes' councillor, Khanya.

Like Mopeli-Paulus, the playwright Sylvanus Matlosa was writing in the immediate aftermath of the Bereng and Gabashane case, but *Katiba*, published by the Catholic Centre at Mazenod in 1950 (though Matlosa was a member of the French Protestant Church), is set firmly within a Christian framework.[15] The chief, Katiba, believes in the power of Sesotho medicine. His wife, Nchoati, is a Christian and does not. There is a big meeting at Matsieng about the reorganisation of the chieftainship – an event which inevitably reminds the reader of the Khubelu and Treasury reforms. Katiba, whose representative attends the meeting with a medicated stick hidden under his blanket, is given more authority and is thereby confirmed in his belief in the power of medicine. This attracts the jealousy of other chiefs, who plot to kill him. He consults a Zulu doctor, Phothoma, who tells him that he needs fat from the kidneys of a Mokoena. The victim is attacked after a beer-drink, and the parts are delivered to Katiba. He becomes even more ambitious, praising the power of his Zulu medicines, but at this point he is demoted and his chieftainship is given to another man. One of his accomplices tells the police of the murder, and Katiba is imprisoned. After his victim appears to him in a dream he falls ill, and in the end he dies, saying, 'SEEK YE FIRST THE KINGDOM OF GOD AND HIS RIGHTEOUSNESS AND ALL THESE THINGS WILL BE ADDED UNTO YOU'.[16] Although a connection is drawn between the chieftainship reforms and medicine murder, there is no hint of any colonial conspiracy or police malpractice. There is a strong emphasis, however, on the part played by the Zulu doctor, Phothoma, and much praise of Zulu medicines.[17]

Bennett Khakhetla's novel, *Mosali a Nkhola* ('The Woman Betrayed Me'), is particularly interesting because, when giving evidence to the Round Table Conference in the early 1950s, Khaketla declared that these murders were being committed in order to obtain *liretlo* for medicine, whereas in the late 1950s, as Deputy Leader of the Basutoland African Congress, he had swung round to support Mokhehle's view that there was no firm evidence to connect the murders with medicine. His novel was published in 1960, but it was written, he tells us, in 1951. In his Introduction, written in 1959, he explains:

> In writing this novel I based it on much of what was said in cases of this sort, but that is not to say that it sets out my own thoughts about the

tragedy of *liretlo* … My object in this book was to rouse readers from their malaise, so that they could think carefully for themselves about *liretlo*, examine it on every side, and see how it could be brought to an end.[18]

One of the angles from which Khaketla might have invited his readers to consider medicine murder was the belief that it was being exploited by the colonial administration to undermine the chieftainship. There is, however, no reference to this. In some passages Khaketla is clearly speaking not through his characters, but in his own voice. He was writing as a committed Anglican, and *Mosali a Nkhola* is set very firmly in the Christian tradition. According to Khaketla, or at least Khaketla the novelist, medicine murder springs from Sesotho culture. The only hope is to turn to God.

The date is 1944, and the central character is a young chief, Mosito. He has been well educated, and when his father dies and he is placed as a chief he is told by the District Commissioner that, since he is educated, there is no need to warn him against medicine murders. But two elderly councillors advise him differently. One tells him that, in accordance with Sesotho custom, he should not continue living in his father's old village but should establish his own village nearby. Then he should

> strengthen it with a strong horn. In the olden days the horn was easily available because there were many wars, and the ingredients were not scarce; but nowadays there are no longer any wars and these ingredients are hard to come by.

The other says that he must get a human liver: 'That liver could be easily obtained by digging up a corpse, there at the graveyard, but it seems the medicine works well if the liver comes from a person who is killed deliberately'.[19] Mosito indignantly rejects their advice, but shortly afterwards the Treasury reforms are implemented and he is deprived of his right to hold a court. In their frustration the two councillors turn to Mosito's wife, 'Mathabo, and enlist her help in trying to persuade Mosito to accept their advice. 'Mathabo, who has not had the benefit of her husband's education, draws a clear distinction between Sekhooa and Sesotho, European and Sesotho ways of life and thinking. Mosito knows Sekhooa but not Sesotho, and because of this he lacks *seriti*, personal authority, and things are going badly for him. What he needs is a powerful medicine horn which would give him authority and success, make people fear and honour him, and make the senior chiefs and the District Commissioner respect his position.[20] The two councillors then introduce Mosito to an itinerant doctor, Selone, who gradually convinces him of his powers and finally persuades him to carry out a murder to obtain a man's liver for medicine. Several accomplices are enlisted, and after a feast on Christmas Day the victim is waylaid and killed. The murder comes to light, and Mosito and his accomplices are arrested.

We might have expected that, publishing a novel in 1960, Khaketla would have depicted the police as applying improper pressure and trying to bend the evidence to suit their case. In fact, they are shown as models of courtesy and propriety. When two of the accomplices want to give evidence for the Crown, the sergeant conducting the investigation makes them pause:

> I have already told you that you are not obliged to say anything. You should understand this well, because perhaps, when the case begins and Mosito's advocates are putting questions to you, you will say that the police forced you to speak ... Already on several occasions people like you have caused the police to fail in cases, because they tell lies, they say they were beaten when they said what they are reported to have said; or they say they have been bribed to tell lies implicating innocent people. This ... spoils the good name of the police, and we appear to the court to be wicked people, unable to investigate our case without coercing people by beating them. Do you still want to speak?[21]

Then, in words which might have been penned by a colonial official, Khaketla, clearly in his own voice, says that many people are amazed that some murderers are released after they have become Crown witnesses and believe that in this way the government is actually encouraging medicine murders.

> But if you think the matter through, you will find that this procedure is a great help, since it helps the police to obtain powerful evidence which is sufficient for the criminals to be convicted and which would not be obtained if the accomplice witnesses were to be killed as well.[22]

The trial scene is described in vivid and realistic detail. The accused are well defended by a white advocate known to the Basotho as Mokhaolaropo ('Rope-Cutter'), since he has often secured the acquittal of people who seemed destined for the gallows.[23] But the evidence against them is too strong and they are all condemned to death. Again, as in Matlosa's *Katiba*, the victim appears to Mosito in a dream, and he spends his last days with a minister of the church who prays for his soul. Mosito and his accomplices fall to the ground, recite the Lord's Prayer, and beg God to save their souls.

In Bennett Khaketla's novel, though not in Ntsu Mokhehle's critique, the government and the police are beyond reproach. Kemuel Edward Ntsane's novel, however, *Nna Sajene Kokobela CID*, which was published in 1963, reflects – overtly or by implication – several of Mokhehle's most powerful criticisms. It recounts the exploits of a policeman, Sergeant Kokobela, after the Second World War. A medicine murder has been committed in the Berea District, and the first question that Kokobela asks reveals his immediate assumption (a false assumption, according to Mokhehle, and, as it turns out, in this case as well) that chiefs are responsible for medicine murders: is there, he asks, any chief whose position is threatened? But in the absence of any helpful answer he discovers that a commoner, Mafethe, is responsible. The victim's wife had an affair with Mafethe, and connived with him and others to kill her husband. In this instance, therefore, the chiefs are absolved. Ntsane also portrays the police as beating an accomplice to extort an incriminating confession, though there is no suggestion that the confession is false.[24]

Over twenty years later, in 1986, Aaron Hlapisi's novel was published, entitled *Khooanyana oa ho hopoloa* ('Khooanyana, One to be Remembered').[25] In this the central character, Khooanyana, does well in his studies at a Bible College, arouses envy, and is killed in a medicine murder by a chief and ten accomplices. All eleven murderers are struck down by lightning. Once again we have a novel in the Christian tradition which makes no concessions to the critiques of Lekhotla la Bafo and the Basutoland African Congress.

Very different are the two powerfully moving poems of Makhokolotso Mokhomo, *Sello sa Basotho* ('Lament of the Basotho') and *Seoa sa Lesotho* ('The Calamity that has Befallen Lesotho').[26] Mokhomo was a pupil at the Basutoland High School in Maseru at the time when Khaketla was a teacher there, and went on to train and work as a nurse in South Africa. *Sello sa Basotho* is a lament for Bereng and Gabashane, and was written soon after they were hanged. It is shot through with the language of the praise poems, and the two chiefs are presented as great leaders who have been brought low by *liretlo*. The 'Calamity' of the second poem is medicine murder itself. The sombre mood of both poems is reminiscent of the speeches at Bereng's funeral at Matsieng. The whole country has been plunged into darkness, men and women alike are trembling and bewildered. Where can the Basotho turn for help?

Medicine murder has also attracted European writers. Leaving aside Mopeli-Paulus's two collaborators, Peter Lanham and Miriam Basner, the first off the mark was Nicholas Monsarrat (author of *The Cruel Sea*), who served as the Director of the UK Information Service in Johannesburg from 1946 to 1953. From this position he was well placed to observe events in the three High Commission Territories, and his long novel *The Tribe that Lost its Head*, published in 1956, draws heavily on the debates surrounding those events, in particular the marriage of Seretse Khama (the heir to the Bamangwato chieftainship in the Bechuanaland Protectorate) to a white woman, Ruth Williams. It also refers to oath-taking ceremonies that inevitably remind the reader of Mau Mau. It is set on a fictional island off the coast of South West Africa, Pharamaul, one of the Scheduled Territories. The people in the north of Pharamaul, the U-Maulas, have lived peacefully under British rule for many years, but are thrown into turmoil when their chief-to-be, Dinamaula, announces his intention of marrying a white woman. The refusal by the colonial authorities to allow him to become chief while the country is so unsettled provokes disturbances in which three whites – a District Officer, his wife and a local missionary – are killed in ways that differ from each other but are equally revolting. The wife is raped until she dies; the entrails are removed from the District Commissioner while he is still alive and then mixed with goat's blood to form a paste which is then drunk; and the missionary is crucified and his body cut up and eaten. The resonances with medicine murder are obvious. *The Tribe that Lost its Head* is, in effect, a particularly fierce and virulent expression of the official narrative. The ordinary U-Maulas are children, far behind the white man in civilisation; the imperial authorities, though not always wise, are benign; and there are whites, malicious or self-righteous or both – in particular a visiting journalist and an Anglican priest (clearly inspired by Michael Scott) – who are critical and contemptuous of the colonial administration and in their ignorance and presumption encourage the U-Maulas to rebel. The book was banned in South Africa.[27]

Other white authors kept more closely to the facts of medicine murder. Audrey Murray was the wife of a District Commissioner in Basutoland, and her novel *The Blanket*, published in 1957, is entirely consistent with the official narrative of medicine murder.[28] Lepotane, the central character, is the younger son of a chief in a remote village. His father, Phiri, is advised by his doctor that his horn needs replenishing, and he chooses one of his herdsmen, Maburu, as his victim. Maburu, however, gives his distinctive blanket to Phiri's eldest son, Simpi, and in the darkness of the night Simpi is killed by mistake. Lepotane, who was devoted to his brother Simpi, refuses to have anything more to do with lies and deceit and frankly confesses his part in the murder. He does not fully understand what he is doing, for he expects to be convicted and hanged, and instead, to his bewilderment, he is treated as a Crown witness and released. The judge, in a speech that is central to the novel, denounces the stupidity and cruelty of *liretlo* but believes it will continue 'because it is rooted in faith'. Lepotane is deeply ashamed when his father is hanged as a result of his evidence, and he is heavily criticised by his people when he returns as chief to his village. Instead of accepting their condemnation, however, he determines to root out medicine murder in his community.

Anthony Fulton, the author of *The Dark Side of Mercy*, published in 1968, served for ten years as a doctor in Basutoland after the Second World War, and then went into general practice in South Africa. According to the dust jacket of his book, in Basutoland he was 'appalled and intrigued' by the 'devastating effects of ancient beliefs upon the lives and actions of the Basuto people', and in South Africa 'by the shattering impact of ancient superstitions upon the lives of his patients'. There are three main characters in his novel: Michael Dugan, a Catholic doctor; Libe, a Mosotho Christian; and Abe Morris, a South African Jew. All face dilemmas which challenge their convictions of right and wrong, and for Libe this comes in the form of an order from his chief to take part in a medicine murder to obtain a good harvest. Although he is a Christian, he feels the power of his 'ancient' beliefs and his obligation to obey his chief. He is confident in the doctor's power to protect him, but he is betrayed by an accomplice witness and is convicted and sentenced to death. In gaol there is the inevitable meeting with the minister of religion, and in the end Libe is reconciled with his God and goes to his death calmly and confidently. Throughout the novel Sesotho belief in the power of medicine is set in a comparative context – Catholic beliefs about abortion, for example, and the beliefs of Jehovah's Witnesses about blood transfusions. And early on the old District Commissioner points out that, while civilisation cannot be imposed on a people from outside – 'it is something that has to develop inside each individual and that takes time' – even Europeans have "only the thinnest of veneers"'.[29]

Finally there is *Thaba Rau*, a novel by a South African journalist, Horace Flather, published in 1976.[30] This is focused on the white community in Basutoland, in particular in a mountain district which is obviously Mokhotlong, soon after the Second World War. Various characters are trundled out: a brusque and outspoken agricultural officer from Yorkshire, an old soak of a District Commissioner, a world-weary Resident Commissioner, a patrician judge, and at the centre a brutal doctor and his beautiful and ill-treated wife. The medicine murder is largely incidental to the working out of their relations. It is carried on the orders of a chieftainess to support the placing of her son, and the white doctor is killed by way of reprisal after the murderers are hanged. The novel serves largely as a vehicle for Flather's views about the British empire, South African history, African beliefs, and much else besides.

It is of course the Basotho writers who add most to our understanding of medicine murder. Without exception they see it as having its roots deep in the old Basotho way of life. Although the doctors involved are sometimes Zulu, there is no pretence that it is a practice taken over from the Zulu, and there is no suggestion that it is a colonial invention. Nor is it the concern of just a small minority of ruthlessly ambitious chiefs who impose their wishes on their reluctant subjects. The chief's councillors are heavily involved, and so too are the doctors. Several of their accomplices are afraid and act only out of obedience to their chief, but they all acknowledge the power of *liretlo* and understand why a murder is necessary.

Perhaps most revealing of all, in most of these works, as in Mofolo's *Chaka* and Shakespeare's *Macbeth*, the murderer is a tragic hero rather than a villain. He is a man of noble character brought low by the power of ancient belief, by ambition, loyalty or concern for his people. Several murderers, like the writers themselves, are well educated. They begin by resisting the whole notion of medicine murder, but are gradually forced to accept it by the blows of misfortune and, if they are commoners, by the orders of their chiefs or, if they are chiefs, by the importunities of their advisers and doctors. Unlike their counterparts in real life, they command respect and admiration by confessing what they have done. Even in the novels written or co-authored by whites the murderer emerges as a man worthy of our sympathy, perhaps reflecting the ambivalence in white attitudes to the crime which we discuss in the Conclusion to this book.

Murder is not condoned, but the murderers are understood and pitied as they are taken to meet their death.

> The last sun rose, and as the tired, despairing prisoners stretched themselves, all through the lands of Southern Africa did they live in the thoughts of many people. Basotho stood by the head-gear of mines in the City of Gold with sad faces; quietly, too, waited their home-boys far away on the docks in the City of Sugar; in the home-land, Basotho stood in the fields and in their homes, waiting for the hour to strike ... The signal passed, the trap-door opened, and down, down dropped the body of Monare of Lomontsa, the Mosotho ... And all Lesotho mourned, AS MONARE DIED.[31]

The last words of *Blanket Boy's Moon* might have been penned by Peter Lanham rather than by Mopeli-Paulus, but the pain and understanding that inspire and inform them reflect strong Sesotho sensibilities.

PART II

MEDICINE MURDER:
AN ANALYSIS OF PROCESS

6

MURDERERS AND THEIR MOTIVES

I am hated in my village and Chieftainess 'Makopoi hates me, she has cases against me because I refused to carry out her instructions ... As a result of Chieftainess 'Makopoi being placed, my subjects do not respect me as they should ... My remuneration from taxes stopped in 1940 ... I am aggrieved at this, and perhaps that is why they do not call me chief. Toko was one of my obedient subjects, and we are aggrieved at his death.

Statement of gazetted headman Seqhoe Noha,
24 January 1955

Chief Seqhoe told us that he wanted to make a medicine horn. He instructed us to get him a man ... The deceased's name was Toko.

Statement of Leqheka Mokhethi,
8 February 1955[1]

Who instigated medicine murders? What did they want to achieve, and why? Who were drawn in as accomplices? Were they driven by loyalty or fear? In considering these questions in this chapter we look at the evidence relating to individual cases in aggregate. This consists primarily of court records (where we have been able to find them), supported mainly by Jones' report and newspaper accounts. Our statistical analysis is confined to 129 cases in the colonial period in which legal proceedings were brought. Although, as we have pointed out before, the court was centrally concerned with establishing whether or not the accused were guilty of murder and rarely examined in any detail the social and political context, it is possible to analyse patterns of participation and varieties of motive through detailed scrutiny of the records as a whole.

INSTIGATORS

In most cases the identity of the instigator was clear. The court normally recorded the status or occupation of the instigator, and sometimes the age. Typically, a chief or headman who wanted *liretlo* enlisted the help of several accomplices and they carried out the murder together. In some cases there was more than one instigator, the best-known being those in which Chiefs Bereng and Gabashane were involved. In every case the court sought to establish, as far as possible, who among the accused had instigated the crime. This was not relevant to the question of guilt, since instigators and accomplices were guilty alike, nor did it determine the severity of the sentence, since until 1959 hanging was the sentence laid down by statute. But it helped the court to understand how the murder came to be committed, and it became relevant when pleas for mercy were considered by the High Commissioner, since instigators were less likely than accomplices to have their sentences commuted.

Sometimes the man or woman who seemed to be taking the lead might have been acting on behalf of someone else, perhaps a more senior chief who, unlike Bereng and Gabashane, kept well away from the scene of the crime and who, for lack of evidence, could not be brought to trial. Such absent principals were usually powerful figures, and their followers were afraid to testify against them. We refer to such people as shadow instigators, and where we encountered clear allegations of their involvement we include them in our analysis. The most notorious of the shadow instigators was the Paramount Chief regent, 'Mantšebo.

In some cases the evidence of shadow instigators' involvement was so strong that it is difficult to see why they were not brought to trial. In case 1953/1 Esthere Kabi, who had become headman of Pokane when her husband died, told her followers that she wanted a medicine horn because the affairs of her village were in a bad way. The victim was ambushed and killed, and when the murderers brought the body to Esthere's hut to be mutilated they were startled to find there Chief Tšepo Qefata, the son and heir of the Ward Chief of Quthing ('Mantšebo's brother, Qefata Sempe), together with several of his followers. Esthere's right-hand man, who was also one of Chief Tšepo's advisers, told them that they 'should not get frightened because it was in accordance with the plan that they were present'. After the various parts had been taken from the body, Chief Tšepo said that he was leaving. He did not want to take the *liretlo* with him that night because they were dripping with blood and might stain his followers' clothes, and so one of the accomplices took the *liretlo* in a billy-can to Tšepo's village the next day. Esthere told everyone who had taken part that they must never mention that Chief Tšepo and his followers had been present, and Chief Tšepo himself said that anyone who mentioned him even accidentally would be killed. Nevertheless at least seven witnesses gave evidence that Chief Tšepo and his men had been present. The Attorney-General decided that he was merely an 'inactive spectator' and for this reason did not charge him with a criminal offence, although he did recommend that strong administrative action should be taken against him for grave dereliction of duty.[2] Esthere Kabi and nine of her followers, by contrast, were convicted and hanged.

Another remarkable case was 1954/1, in which Chief Lepekola Joel and ten others were accused. Although there was evidence that at least two other gazetted chiefs were involved, as well as the Ward Chief of Butha-Buthe, none of them was brought to trial. In another case, 1957/1, one accomplice gave evidence that Chief Patso Tumo, Chief of Fobane, told him and others that he wanted human blood, and another accomplice gave evidence that he was asked to make medicine for Chief Patso's benefit. The appeal judges noted that there were 'doubtless good reasons why the Chief in question was not charged along with the accused, but the record does not specify what these reasons were; probably the evidence against the Chief was considered inadequate'.[3]

In other cases the evidence was largely circumstantial. In case 1943/1, in which a doctor was accused, the Attorney-General refused to prosecute because he believed that the real instigator was being protected. Because the murder took place in the village of Chief Matlere Lerotholi, Jones was convinced that Matlere must have been involved. Similarly he believed that Bereng Griffith was responsible for the murder in case 1944/2, since it took place in his village at Phamong. There must also have been cases where the involvement of shadow instigators was kept completely secret and where there was no apparent reason even for suspicion. On the other hand, the people arranging a murder might invoke the name of a senior chief in order to add to their persuasiveness when recruiting accomplices. Jones believed that this might have happened in case 1943/5, where it was said that the medicine was needed for 'the Chief Overseas', Ward Chief David Theko Makhaola of Ratšoleli's and Mashai, who was then leading the Basotho soldiers in the African Auxiliary Pioneer Corps in the Second World War.[4]

All these factors have to be taken into account in our analysis of alleged instigators and their motives. We have been able to identify 129 cases during the colonial period in which legal proceedings were brought. These cases threw up 139 alleged instigators,[5] of whom eleven were not identified by status or occupation. Of the 128 instigators whose status or occupation was identified, 117 were identified in one way, while eleven were each identified in two ways. Thus we have a total of 139 known designations of status or occupation. Of these designations, the great majority, 109 (78 per cent), relate to chiefs or headmen of one description or another: ten were Ward Chiefs, twenty were chiefs; seventy-nine were headmen. There were twenty-five shadow instigators identified, all of whom were chiefs or headmen, and each with one designation only: five were the Paramount Chief (the single person of 'Mantšebo); seven were Ward Chiefs; ten were chiefs; three were headmen.[6] Taking the social designations of instigators and shadow instigators together, we have a total of 164 designations, of which 134 (82 per cent) are of chiefs or headmen. The other thirty designations of instigators are as follows: four *matona* (councillors of one sort or another); seven doctors; three Basuto Court officials; four 'peasants' or 'commoners'; six traders (including owners of cafés and beerhalls); two shop assistants; a policeman; a herdboy acting on the instructions of two older men; a headman's mother wanting medicine for her son and her nephew; and a mother wanting to get her son back from the mines.

Of the 129 cases in which legal proceedings were brought, we have information on the status or occupation of the instigators in 118. Of these 118, chiefs or headmen were apparently involved in 104 (88 per cent). If we knew all the facts, this proportion would probably be higher. In some chiefs or headmen were allegedly joint instigators with others, such as 'peasants' or doctors; in some they were shadow instigators while 'peasants' or doctors carried out the murder; and in some they themselves were also traders or held some other position.

The overwhelming preponderance of chiefs and headmen as instigators or shadow instigators is one of the most important distinguishing features of medicine murder in colonial Basutoland as compared with other regions.[7] Towards the end of the colonial period, however, it seems to have been less marked and it appears to have fallen away since. In the 1960s, in the last years before independence in 1966, storekeepers and café-owners were the alleged instigators in at least three of the eleven cases that went to court,[8] and in the years after independence in four cases out of seven. The numbers are small, but they suggest a definite change. In popular fears traders now loom as large as chiefs.

Politicians were not involved, at least during the colonial period.[9] In 1972, after independence, Alphons [sic] Mphanya, the Assistant Secretary-General of the Basutoland Congress Party, was charged with medicine murder, along with fourteen other party members. It was alleged that in 1969 they had killed a member of the Basutoland National Party to make medicine to help them in the forthcoming election. This, however, was a crude attempt to frame them for political reasons, and they were all acquitted.[10]

In view of the importance attributed to them in public debate, it is interesting that doctors make up such a small proportion of those who allegedly instigated the crime. Of the seven who can be identified as possible instigators, one was also a headman, one was also a café-owner, and two at least were thought to be acting on behalf of chiefs or headmen. We discuss their role as accomplices later in this chapter.

Ashton suspected that, because of the insecurities surrounding their position, women were more likely to turn to medicine murder than men.[11] This is not borne out by the evidence. Of 109 persons identified as instigators who were also chiefs or headmen, and on whose sex we have information, only seven were women, a proportion which is much in line with the proportion of women among chiefs and headmen generally.[12] Women make up six of the twenty-five shadow instigators, but five of these are accounted for by the single person of 'Mantšebo.

At first it was thought that those responsible for the murders were likely to be drawn from the least educated and the most 'backward' sections of the community. In case 1942/3, in which a young herdboy was accused, some time was spent in court in establishing the state of 'civilisation' in the area and of the accused in particular. The main police witness said that the accused lived 'right up in the mountains ... The only civilization up there is churches and trading stations ...'[13] The herdboy himself said that he had been to school but because of his work he had not gone very often and he was not able to read. 'I never go to church', he said. 'The members of my family go to church, therefore I am not an uncivilised person or a barbarian.'[14] But it soon came to be realised that several of those responsible for the murders had been taught in white-run schools and even colleges. Gabashane Masupha was an outstanding example – he had been educated at Lovedale and Fort Hare – and Bereng Griffith was also described as well-educated and progressive. At a lower level Seshope Ramakoro, an ungazetted headman and the president of a Basuto Court, was described by the judge in case 1952/11 as a trusted servant of the government and a man far in advance of his fellows in literacy whose handwriting was better than the judge's own.

We do not have sufficient evidence to measure the involvement of professing Christians, and still less do we have evidence about their denominational loyalties. As the churches ruefully acknowledged, however, many of the alleged instigators and their accomplices were practising members of one church or another. Our case studies have already thrown up the examples of 'Mantšebo, Bereng, Gabashane, 'Mamakhabane, Matlere Lerotholi and Joseph Mabina Lerotholi. All of these were Catholics (though 'Mantšebo had been brought up in the Protestant faith), and Mabina Lerotholi, commonly known by his Christian name of Joseph, was renowned for his love of the rosary.[15] The story is still told today that at his trial (case 1948/24) he refused to be represented by defence counsel but said that he would rely on his rosary instead.[16] He made his religious beliefs an issue in the trial, implying that as a Christian he could never have been guilty of medicine murder. Conversely, in the second case against Matlere Lerotholi, the prosecution tried to show that, although he professed the Catholic faith, in practice he had often departed from Catholic teaching – in his polygyny, for example, and in being scarified.[17] David Theko Makhaola, Ward Chief of Ratšoleli's and Mashai, the alleged instigator in 1953/2, was also a leading Catholic. When he died in 1963, the Catholic paper, *Moeletsi*, declared that he had loved the Catholic Church with all his soul.[18]

Protestants were also involved, some of them men and women of considerable prominence. One of the earliest murders (1912/1) was carried out by an elderly member of the PEMS church at Thaba-Bosiu, and the French missionaries were particularly shocked that this murder, and another near Morija at roughly the same time (1912/2), were committed so close to the longest-established centres of Christian worship and teaching in the country.[19] In case 1927/2, several of the accomplices were members of the church at Morija, and as we have seen in Case Study 1, case 1945/3 involved a PEMS church leader, John Makume, and allegedly his headman, Mahao Matete, also. The case created a national sensation because of these two men's prominence in the Protestant religious establishment at Morija. And Esthere Kabi, a headman and the instigator in case 1953/1, was 'a member of the Anglican Church', 'very religious', 'an active churchwoman and a member of the Mothers' Union'.[20] It may have been true that Catholics were disproportionately represented but, as Jones pointed out, most of the leading chiefs were Catholics, and there is no doubt that men and women of all denominations were implicated as instigators or accomplices.

Though some of the chiefs who were accused or suspected of murder were incompetent drunkards, such as Jacottet Theko, Seeiso Maama and Solomon Api Ramabanta, others were among the most able and respected men in the country. We have already considered the examples of Bereng, Gabashane and Matlere Lerotholi. Two other leading chiefs indicted, David Theko Makhaola and Molapo Maama, were also widely admired. Theko Makhaola had won the gratitude of the government as the leader of the Basotho troops in the Second World War, and when he was appointed as one of 'Mantšebo's advisers in 1948, Baring and Forsyth-Thompson hoped that this would help in the battle against medicine murder.[21] In 1959 Gordon Hector, the Government Secretary, became aware of Molapo Maama's popularity, even after the murder for which he was convicted, when he had to attend Seeiso Maama's funeral at Thaba-Bosiu. He had agreed not only to release Molapo from prison for the day, but also to take him to the funeral in the government Jaguar. When they arrived at Thaba-Bosiu they were greeted with great warmth and enthusiasm, and Hector was profusely thanked for the respect and consideration he had shown.[22] Years later Rivers Thompson could not bring himself to believe that Molapo Maama was guilty of murder.[23]

The heavy involvement of junior chiefs and headmen has often been cited as an indication that the increase in murders was due to the Khubelu and Treasury reforms, and one of the arguments adduced in support is that of proportionality. It is simply put. It was the junior chiefs and headmen who suffered most through the reforms; it was the junior chiefs and headmen who carried out most of the medicine murders; therefore the junior chiefs and headmen turned to medicine murder because of the reforms.[24]

This argument is not convincing, however, in the light of our evidence on the respective proportions of senior chiefs and headmen involved. In 1939 twenty-seven chiefs, 245 sub-chiefs and 1,076 headmen were gazetted, a total of 1,348. In 1950, after the titles had been changed, twenty-three Principal and Ward Chiefs, 270 chiefs and 859 headmen were gazetted, a

total of 1,152. It is generally agreed that at least as many chiefs and
headmen were not gazetted as were, and nearly all of these would have been
headmen, since headmen were much more likely to be omitted than more
senior people. On this basis we can reasonably guess that headmen made up
about 90 per cent of the total number of chiefs and headmen. Of the alleged
instigators and shadow instigators whose social designations were given in
the court records, 134 designations were of chiefs or headmen. But headmen represent only eighty-three of this total of 134 (62 per cent). The
corresponding figures for the vital decade for the purpose of this argument,
the 1940s, are twenty-eight of a total of fifty-two (54 per cent). In propor-
tional rather than absolute terms, then, headmen were under-represented
rather than over-represented. Conversely, the Paramount Chief and the
Ward Chiefs made up less than 1 per cent of the total number of chiefs and
headmen but, together with the Paramount, twenty-two out of 134 (16 per
cent) of the social designations relating to chiefs and headmen together. For
the 1940s, the figures are fifteen out of fifty-two (29 per cent).

The alleged effect of the reforms, however, does not depend solely on the
argument of proportionality. It is possible that junior chiefs and headmen
turned to medicine murder because of the reforms at the same time as the
senior chiefs were turning to it for other reasons. If, however, the reforms
and the murders were connected, we might have expected that ungazetted
chiefs and headmen would have been more involved than those who were
gazetted. (Several speakers in the Basutoland National Council specifically
asserted that people committed murders because they had not been
gazetted.) Again, this is not supported by the figures we have. Our evidence
on gazetting is incomplete, but in the crucial period between 1940 and 1946
at least eight out of sixteen of the headmen who were instigators were
gazetted, and all of the chiefs, four out of four.

MOTIVES

The case records are not always helpful on motive. Judge Elyan summed up
the legal position:

> Proof of motive is not essential to the proof of *mens rea* [guilty mind]
> but undoubtedly proof that an accused had a motive for the commis-
> sion of the conduct charged is relevant to the question whether an
> accused was guilty of that conduct.[25]

Often the motive was expressed only in the most general terms: the *liretlo*
were needed to strengthen a man's chieftainship, to protect his village, or
simply for the purpose of replenishing his medicine horn, and the court saw
no need to look any further. But if it could be shown that the *liretlo* were
needed for a particular purpose, such as improving the chances of success in
a legal case, the court was prepared to take this into account.

In most cases the evidence of motive was provided by the accomplice witnesses.

> [Mahlomola Lerotholi] told me he was looking for a doctor who could give him medicine 'to prevent his being deposed from the chieftainship' and he ordered me ... to find for him a young girl who was a twin.[26]

> [Tumahole Bereng] told me he wanted this man Molumo to doctor his area as far as Phalo's, as it was being disputed. [He] then told me the doctor required human blood with which to concoct his medicines.[27]

> [Masiu Sephei] said he had a plan of killing a person by the name of Springkaan ... in order to confirm himself.[28]

In some cases the accomplices were not given the full story. They might have been given some general reason when in fact the instigator had a more specific purpose in mind. The accomplice witnesses in the Esthere Kabi case (1953/1) were not told beforehand about the involvement of Chief Tšepo Qefata Sempe. In case 1952/3 the headman involved confided to one accomplice that he was being worried by 'cases', and in particular by a move to depose him, but he told another only that he needed human blood to strengthen his medicine horn. In case 1948/1 (Case Study 2), Chieftainess 'Mamakhabane tried to mislead her followers into believing that she wanted medicine to support the placing of her son whereas in fact she wanted to prevent it.

In some cases there is no evidence of motive in the court record, but there may be indications from other sources. In case 1943/3, according to one accomplice, Seabatha Lerotholi 'did not say why' he wanted to kill the man he had chosen, and it appears that there was no reference to Chief Jacottet Theko's alleged motive in case 1945/10. In the first case, however, Jones recorded a report that Seabatha had been placed over another headman early in 1943 and that there was friction between them, and in the second he noted that Jacottet Theko had been deposed as Ward Chief a few years earlier and 'it was rumoured that he or his people wanted medicine to help him regain his position'.[29] The same instigator might have more than one motive. In case 1945/6 the mother of an acting headman wanted medicine to get her son confirmed in his position and also to strengthen her nephew, who had just been placed in another village. In case 1950/7 the instigator wanted medicine as a doctor for his practice and as a headman to strengthen his position.

In the 129 cases that went to court in the colonial period we have recorded 162 alleged motives. Doctors invariably wanted to get medicine, traders to improve their trade, and shop assistants and court officials to retain or to regain their positions. But it is the alleged motives of the chiefs and headmen that concern us here, and 145 of these have been recorded.

Ten of these relate to their activities in capacities other than as chiefs or headmen, for example as traders, doctors, court officials, or in one case a policeman. Leaving these aside, we have 135 recorded motives, of which

Forty-six were general. In case 1947/14 Motšeare Lerotholi needed a medicine horn 'to strengthen his village', and in case 1948/15 Lechesa Lehloenya needed protective medicine because, among other misfortunes, lightning had struck two of his followers' huts.

Thirteen were to support placings. In case 1954/1 Chief Lepekola Joel was said to have carried out a murder to support the placing of Joel Molapo Qhobela's son, and in case 1954/4 headman Sempe Theko was said to have told his followers that he wanted to 'peg' his village because it was not quite firm.

Eleven were to resist placings. The very first recorded murder, in case 1895/1, was carried out by the Makholokoe to resist the placing over them of Chief Qhobela Joel. In case 1952/4 headman Taoana Makhabane killed his own mother for medicine to resist the placing of headman Moshe.

Seventeen involved disputes over land. Seqhoe Noha, the gazetted headman quoted at the head of this chapter, told his followers that he wanted to recover two areas that had been taken away from him, although clearly he had other reasons as well. In case 1958/1 Makotoko Mosalla turned to medicine murder because he was involved in a dispute over certain lands with a neighbouring headman.

Thirty-six related to rivalries and disputes with other chiefs for reasons other than placings and land. The battle of medicine horns between 'Mantšebo and Bereng provides the best-known examples. In case 1950/4, Keneuoe Kennan Khethisa was acting for his elderly father, who was unwell, and turned to murder because he felt that his position was being threatened by his elder brother.

Six related to court cases other than cases about disputes with other chiefs about placings, land or other issues. One of the reasons given for the murder in case 1947/15 was to secure the acquittal of a chief who was in gaol awaiting trial for stock theft, and we have already noted cases 1948/18 and 1948/20, in which the murders were thought to have been carried out to secure Gabashane Masupha's release.

Three related to the chieftainship reforms.

Three related to other factors.

Only in a tiny minority of cases – just three in all – is there evidence of a direct and explicit connection with the reforms, and not even in all of these is the evidence strong. The first is case 1944/6, in which Lagden Majara, a gazetted chief, was the alleged instigator. This is one of two cases which Ashton suggested were 'possibly directly attributable' to the enquiries and discussions preceding the Treasury reforms.[30] We have not traced the court record on this case, but Jones, in his unpublished papers, recorded a rumour that Lagden Majara had had some headmen removed from his caretaking and wanted to get them back, while Ashton suggested the possibility that Lagden Majara resented a superior chief being placed over him.[31] The second case to which Ashton referred is 1944/7. The instigator here, Mahlomola Lerotholi, was a gazetted headman in the Mokhotlong District and a half-brother of Matlere Lerotholi. Mahlomola told one of his accomplices that 'the number of chiefs was to be reduced' and that he wanted a child for medicine to prevent his being deposed.[32]

In the third case, 1945/8 (which Ashton overlooked), the instigator was Tsotang Griffith, a headman at Motsitseng in the Mokhotlong District. Tsotang's account of his motives, which he gave to his accomplices in advance of the murder, was summed up by the judge as follows:

> No. 1 accused ... explained to [the people] that in addition to this Motsiteng area, Chief Griffith had promised to place him over the Mahesheleng area as well; that his name did not appear in the explanatory memorandum of the National Treasury as being one of the Chiefs endowed with administrative powers, and that in spite of certain dilatory promises made by his uncle Chief Matlere, he had acquired a date stamp but was not entitled to use it ...[33]

Although there is some confusion here, since, apart from the Ward Chiefs, the Explanatory Memorandum to the National Treasury did not list any chiefs at all, it is clear that the proposed reform was one of the factors which was weighing heavily on Tsotang Griffith's mind.

These are the only references to the reforms that we have been able to trace, and this indicates that very few murders were attributable to explicit and articulated worries about recognition and the right to hold a court. The alleged instigators were not reticent about expressing other specific concerns – about placings, conflicts with other chiefs, land disputes and court cases. If they were worried about not being gazetted or about losing their courts, there was no reason why they should not have said so.

Another argument that was advanced to link the apparent increase in medicine murder with the reforms was the alleged coincidence between wards where the reforms had a disproportionate impact and wards with a disproportionate number of murders. Jones drew attention to the confusion induced by the reforms in Chief Gabashane's ward of 'Mamathe's because of the disproportionately large reduction in the number of subordinate chiefs and headmen. Many years later Burns Machobane boldly identified as a 'corollary' to this reduction the fact that the ward 'sustained the highest number of ritual murders in the Territory'.[34] We discuss below the issue of clusters of murders in particular wards. Here it is sufficient to note that murders continued at a disproportionate rate in 'Mamathe's ward well into the 1960s, and that in at least one ward which was disproportionately affected by the reforms, Tlokoeng, there were comparatively very few murders.

We must stress that in this analysis we have concentrated on the reported motives for particular murders, as adduced in court or other evidence, rather than the underlying causes of insecurity which might have explained the increase in murders. Regardless of what instigators said or did not say, it can be argued that at this particular period it was the general insecurity induced by the reforms that made the chiefs and headmen turn to medicine murder. Whether they were gazetted or not, whether they had courts or not, they felt undermined because they were no longer chiefs and headmen by birth and they could no longer hold courts by virtue of this. These great rights and privileges now lay in the gift of the British High Commissioner or had been transferred to 'Native Courts'. Their people were aware of the change and so, it was argued, had less respect for them.

The chiefs had other reasons to feel insecure. Because of the excesses of the placing system there was a proliferation of petty chiefs and headmen who were no better-off than their subjects. *Matsema* rights were taken away, so that chiefs could no longer call on their subjects to work on their land, District Councils were set up, the National Council included more popular representation, and political parties critical of the chieftainship established new centres of loyalty and commitment. But after the period of *laissez-faire* it was the Khubelu and Treasury reforms that struck most directly at the status and functions of chiefs and headmen and administered the greatest shock to the chieftainship system as a whole. A pervasive sense of insecurity might have given rise to a disparate range of particular motives.

So far we have concentrated on the lesser chiefs and headmen. The argument that the murders were inspired by the reforms applies less to the more important chiefs. They too had to be gazetted and lost their right to hold courts, but their seniority ensured their recognition and they now had a fixed and settled income, less perhaps than they had enjoyed before, but one on which they could rely. Gabashane Masupha was a member of the committee that produced the Explanatory Memorandum on the Basuto National Treasury,[35] and Chieftainess 'Mamakhabane positively welcomed it. Now, she said, she would be paid '*real* money', not just 'tickeys' handed over by the people.[36]

When these senior chiefs became involved in medicine murder they nearly always had a particular reason for doing so which was unconnected with the reforms. The cases involving 'Mantšebo, Matlere Lerotholi, Bereng Griffith,

Gabashane Masupha and 'Mamakhabane have already been described. Similarly in Maama's ward Seeiso Maama and his brother Molapo were locked in a struggle for power that seems to have led to at least five murders (1941/3, 1942/1, 1944/4, 1948/22 and 1950/3), while it was rumoured that in the ward of Thaba-Bosiu Chief Jacottet Theko wanted to regain his position after being suspended for drunkenness and stock theft (1945/10).

It has also been argued, particularly by Ashton and Eldredge, that it was 'Mantšebo who was largely responsible for the increase in medicine murder because her apparent success and immunity from prosecution encouraged other chiefs to follow her example. This argument can be developed further. As more chiefs turned to medicine murder, so others were either readier to do so or else felt driven to it in self-defence. A competitive contagion developed, and in this way the whole country was affected. It seems almost inevitable that some chiefs turned to medicine murder because they saw and copied or else reacted to what was going on around them, and there is evidence of this happening in at least two cases. The chiefs involved did not refer specifically to 'Mantšebo's example: it would have been surprising if they had. In case 1949/5, when headman Shadrack Lebona consulted his followers, he was advised that '*these days* if a person wanted to be famous they should kill another person ... then, after this person has been killed, the body should be mutilated and the parts used as medicine' [our italics]. In case 1950/2, when headman Sera Motsie's doctor told him that he would make a horn with a bull, a black sheep, a ram, a tiger's claw and a lion's claw, Sera retorted that 'this was not the sort of horn to strengthen a village *in these days* and that to have the right horn a person should be looked for' [again, our italics].

Is it possible to go further and to argue that murders were most common in those wards where the Ward Chiefs themselves were allegedly involved in murder? The frequency distribution of medicine murders by ward is set out in Table 6.1, both for the whole period covered by the Appendix (1895–1966) and for the 1940s. The wards with the highest numbers, both overall and in the crucial decade of the 1940s, were 'Mamathe's, with twenty-three and thirteen respectively, Ratšoleli's and Mashai (Qacha's Nek), with twenty-two and eleven, and Mokhotlong, with seventeen and ten. If we take into account the distribution of the population between wards, taken from the 1956 census, and express the recorded figures for medicine murders as rates per standard unit of population, as shown in columns G and H in Table 6.1, we have a slightly different rank ordering of wards. For both the period as a whole and specifically for the 1940s, Mokhotlong (Matlere Lerotholi's ward) emerges as overwhelmingly the most 'susceptible' ward, followed by Maama's, 'Mamathe's (Gabashane Masupha's ward) and Ratšoleli's and Mashai (David Theko Makhaola's ward). At Maama's, through the 1940s, many of the murders were alleged to have been carried out by the Ward Chiefs themselves, such as the five murders said to be connected with the intense rivalry between Seeiso and Molapo Maama.

Thus the frequency distribution of murders by ward, whether considered in absolute numbers or in proportion to the respective ward populations, would appear to reflect, to a significant extent, the alleged involvement of particular Ward Chiefs themselves. Whether there was a significant contagious effect, in the sense of a 'spreading downwards' of murders from the level of those Ward Chiefs, is less clear.

In Chapter 2 we considered the evidence on whether or not there was a significant increase in the number of medicine murders in the 1940s. Although there was general agreement that there was, the extent of the increase was disputed. We then argued that, if it could be shown that a significant number of murders arose from causes specifically connected with the 1940s – the reforms, and 'Mantšebo's regency – the case for a real and substantial increase would be strengthened.

The evidence adduced in this chapter is inconclusive on this point. Our analysis of motives suggests that the Khubelu and Treasury reforms had little direct importance in themselves, in that chiefs and headmen did not commit murders because they had not been gazetted or had lost their courts. But they were central to the general insecurity that was besetting the chiefs at that time. Similarly we do not know that anyone turned to medicine murder in explicit imitation of 'Mantšebo. But her example was crucial in establishing a climate in which chiefs were more ready to commit themselves to murder.

ACCOMPLICES

No chief murdered alone. There was much to be done, including what the doctors described as their 'work'. The victim had to be selected, waylaid, overcome and mutilated. The blood drawn off and the parts cut out had to be collected in basins, billy-cans or bottles. The body had to be carried away, sometimes over long stretches of rough and mountainous country, and disposed of below a cliff or in a river. Later the medicine had to be prepared and administered. In addition to these practical considerations it seemed fitting and right that others should be involved, since a murder carried out for the chief could be seen as carried out for the whole community. Numbers also gave support and comfort in a grim and hazardous undertaking.

In the 129 cases in our records that came to court in the colonial period, we have been able to list (although not always identify by name) 1,325 alleged murderers: 138 instigators and 1,187 accomplices. Of the accomplices, we know of 273 who became accomplice witnesses, leaving 914 who were charged. Including the 138 instigators, our list therefore indicates a minimum of 1,052 people who were charged before the courts.[37]

Table 6.1 The distribution of suspected medicine murders by ward, for 1895–1966 and for the 1940s

No. Ward	A Pop. No.	B Pop. %	C MM No.	D MM %	E MM No. 1940s	F MM % 1940s	G Rate	H Rate 1940s
1 Butha-Buthe	31,798	4.0	12	5.7	4	4.7	3.8	1.26
2 Maama's	15,112	1.9	8	3.8	5	5.8	5.3	3.30
3 Majara's	9,847	1.2	2	1.0	1	1.2	2.0	1.02
4 'Mamathe's	55,026	6.9	23	11.0	13	15.1	4.2	2.36
5 Ratšoleli's & Mashai (Qacha's Nek)	53,984	6.8	22	10.5	11	12.8	4.1	2.04
6 Koeneng & Mapoteng	31,457	4.0	10	4.8	4	4.7	3.2	1.27
7 Kubake & Ramabanta's	7,196	0.9	2	1.0	0	0	2.8	0
8 Leribe	74,536	9.4	18	8.6	4	4.7	2.4	0.54
9 Likhoele	32,123	4.0	2	1.0	2	2.3	0.6	0.62
10 Makhoakhoeng	18,724	2.4	1	0.5	0	0	0.5	0
11 Tlokoeng	30,153	3.8	7	3.3	1	1.2	2.3	0.33
12 Matelile	16,548	2.1	3	1.4	3	3.5	1.8	1.81
13 Matsieng	78,245	9.9	13	7.1	3	3.5	2.0	0.38
14 Mokhotlong	19,278	2.4	17	8.1	10	11.6	8.8	5.19
15 Phamong	59,122	7.4	12	5.7	7	8.1	2.0	1.18
16 Quthing	63,565	8.0	8	3.8	1	1.2	1.3	0.16
17 Rothe etc. (incl. Kolo)	24,916	3.1	3	1.4	1	1.2	1.2	0.40
18 Tajane etc.	13,970	1.8	4	1.9	1	1.2	2.9	0.72
19 Taung	16,194	2.0	2	1.0	1	1.2	1.2	0.62
20 Tebang	17,947	2.3	0	0	0	0	0	0
21 Thaba-Bosiu	30,343	3.8	6	2.9	1	1.2	2.0	0.33
22 Tsikoane & Kolberg	51,996	6.6	10	4.8	5	5.8	1.9	0.96
Independent Chiefs	30,655	3.9	2	1.0	0	0	0.7	0
Other	10,904	1.4						
Not known			21	10.0	8	9.3		
Total	793,639	100	210	100.3	86	100.3		

Key
A. *De jure* population by ward, 1956 (census figures).
B. Percentage distribution of population by ward, 1956.
C. Number of medicine murders by ward, 1895–1966.
D. Percentage distribution of medicine murders by ward, 1895–1966.
E. Number of medicine murders by ward, 1940s.
F. Percentage distribution of medicine murders by ward, 1940s.
G. Rate of medicine murders, 1895–1966, per 10,000 of population 1956.
H. Rate of medicine murders, 1940s, per 10,000 of population 1956.

Notes to Table 6.1
1. This table includes all alleged or suspected medicine murders in the Appendix. The numbers of murders in the ward of 'Mamathe's may be overstated because in the 1960s the *Basutoland News* appears to have had a particularly active correspondent in that area. The numbers of murders in the wards of Quthing and Ratšoleli's and Mashai may be overstated because these wards are co-terminous with the districts of Quthing and Qacha's Nek, and so any murder that is attributed to the districts of Quthing and Qacha's Nek can be confidently attributed to the wards of Quthing and Ratšoleli's and Mashai respectively. (Other wards are not co-terminous with districts and corresponding attributions can not be made.)

In a few cases there were only one or two accomplices, and in several others just three or four. But in the first Bereng and Gabashane case more than sixty people took part. One headman, Pheello Smith, invited his whole village to help him, and more than fifty men and women appeared in court either as accused or as witnesses for the Crown (1952/6). In another case (1958/1), in which headman Makotoko Mosalla was the instigator, more than seventy men from seven villages were present when the murder was committed. These were the extremes. The median number of accomplices appearing before the court, including those who became Crown witnesses, was eight.

Ashton argued, and Jones agreed, that 'the more important the leader the more numerous the accomplices. Presumably their number is a measure of his importance and of his confidence that he will avoid detection'.[38] This is not borne out by the evidence. Bereng and Gabashane were Ward Chiefs, but Pheello Smith and Makotoko Mosalla were mere headmen. In the two murders which were allegedly carried out for David Theko Makhaola, the Ward Chief of Ratšoleli's and Mashai (1943/5 and 1953/2), there were only five and four accomplices respectively; and in the two murders (1952/12 and 1959/1) allegedly initiated by Matlere Lerotholi, 'Mantšebo's representative as Ward Chief of Mokhotlong, only seven and five. By contrast, in the last murder in the colonial period that went to court (1965/6), a trader was said to have enlisted twenty-seven acccomplices, and just two years earlier another trader had enlisted twenty-four (1963/1).

In the first Bereng and Gabashane case the Attorney-General thought it probable that 'everybody in that district was ordered to be present that night in order to get them implicated in the murder'.[39] In this way they would all be bound together in guilt, fear and complicity. If this was a stratagem to ensure their silence, it failed dramatically, since eight of the accomplices turned against the chiefs and gave evidence for the Crown. In case 1959/4, on the other hand, one of the accomplices objected to the enrolment of

---

2. The 1956 census included Tlokoeng with Mokhotlong, and so there are no separate official population figures for Tlokoeng in that year. According to Ashton, however (1952: 342–5), the numbers of taxpayers in 1949 were 6,603 (61 per cent) in Tlokoeng ward and 4,308 (39 per cent) in Mokhotlong ward. The Mokhotlong District figure given in the 1956 census, 49,431, has been divided accordingly into 30,153 for Tlokoeng ward and 19,278 for Mokhotlong ward.

3. The category 'Other' in the table refers to 'Residents at institutions, non-African premises, etc.'

4. The category 'Independent Chiefs' refers to certain holdings in the Mafeteng and Mohale's Hoek Districts that are listed in the 1950 Gazette as 'Wards of Independent Chiefs'. This category is explained in the Sources section.

5. One consequence of this complexity is that, particularly in respect of wards in Mafeteng and Mohale's Hoek Districts, it is very difficult to reconcile the population distribution shown in the 1956 census with the map showing wards and ward sections. For example, ward 17 (Rothe, etc.) is divided into several discrete sections (17a–17d) which obviously did not correspond cleanly with population enumeration areas.

more accomplices on the ground that this would jeopardise the under-taking. His advice was plausible: we might have expected that, the larger the number of accomplices, the larger the number of potential accomplice witnesses for the Crown and the greater the danger, for the accused, of being found guilty. In fact the number of accomplices did not significantly affect the chances of being convicted.

There were five main types of accomplice. First, and most important, any chief who was in trouble or involved in a dispute would naturally turn to his councillors, his *matona* (his right-hand men), and ask for their advice and help. They would be men whom he trusted – men of seniority and standing, some of them perhaps his relatives, whose interests were bound up with his own, who chaired his court, helped him to carry out his duties, and stood in for him when he was sick or away on other business. The qualities which were so admirable in other contexts – reliability, loyalty, clear thinking and a cool nerve – were also indispensable in the service of medicine murder.

Second, the chief might enlist the aid of other members of his family – people who were not councillors, perhaps his brothers or his sons, or even his female relatives, especially his wife or wives. Third, extra hands were nearly always drafted in, ordinary men, and occasionally women, of no great standing in the community, but people on whom the chief and his advisers felt they could rely. Some accomplices in their turn enrolled their relatives and lovers. Fourth, the chief might well consult a doctor. In some cases this would be a doctor living in the chief's own village, in others a travelling doctor who happened to be visiting the area. A few, especially in the earlier cases, were Zulu, like Khokong in case 1895/1, who was especially sum-moned from Natal, and Ngcobo in case 1945/8, a man who was visiting the area at the time and had a reputation for producing good results. But most were Basotho. Doctors are known to have been among the accomplices in forty-four of the 129 cases that came to court during the colonial period.

Fifth, it was often necessary to involve people who were relatives, lovers or friends of the proposed victim, or who stood in a certain relationship to the victim which gave them some measure of access and control. Ashton surmised that there might be some 'esoteric reason' for involving close relatives 'connected with the efficacy of the medicine to be made', but there is no evidence to support this. More plausibly he adduced the 'practical reason' that 'their participation will probably deter the victim's other kins-men from making too searching enquiries, for fear of making matters worse'.[40] But in many cases the main reason for approaching relatives, or for approaching lovers or friends, was that it was much easier for the murder to be carried out if they gave their help and consent. For example, Mohapi Mofo, whose elderly mother was being cared for by relatives, was able to inform the conspirators when these relatives left her to visit Maseru (1948/18); Kosenene invited his friend to smoke dagga with him in a remote spot where the murderers could attack him without being seen (1950/3); Molatoli Ramelefane gave medicine to his brother so that he became deranged and therefore easy to attack (1952/7); Lydia Dekezulu invited her lover to spend the night with her and held him fast from behind when the murderers rushed in and attacked him (1957/3). Ntsane Mofubelu might have been more willing to help because, according to one witness, his wife had been abusing him in front of his children and would not let him make advances to another woman (1948/15). 'Mankhopara, who sold her husband for £60, admitted that she was unhappy in her married life (1951/2); and Mokhele Nkolonyane was said to have had no objection to his mother's being killed because she was a great nuisance to him, always wandering around and sleeping at large so that he had to go and look for her repeatedly, and it would be better this time if he could find her dead (1949/3). For the most part, however, friends and relatives who agreed to take part seem to have been on good terms with the victim.

These, then, were the five main types of accomplice: the chief's councillors, other members of his family, ordinary subjects, doctors, and relatives or friends of the victim. Several accomplices fitted more than one type, such as a doctor who might be a councillor as well, but on many others we have no information to enable us to assign them to any type at all. There were also a few accomplices who were enlisted for other reasons. Koenehelo, a stock thief, approached a doctor and asked for medicine to protect him from arrest. The doctor replied he had run short of medicines: all he had was the rectum of a European, and he needed medicine prepared from an African. By a fortunate coincidence he had been called upon by a local headman to take part in a medicine murder, and he suggested that Koenehelo should join them (1944/4). In a few cases people who surprised the murderers at their work were forced to take part in the hope that this would stop them giving evidence. The most striking case was 1947/14, in which the brother-in-law of the victim happened to pass by while the mutilations were being carried out. He tried to run away, but the conspirators ran after him and caught him, and threatened to mutilate and kill him too if he did not take part. He was still reluctant to help, but then the victim, with what the judge described as 'cold-blooded gallantry', urged him to take part so that he would be allowed to live and could then look after the victim's children.

More men than women were called upon to help. Medicine murder was a matter of public as well as individual concern, and the chief's court was staffed entirely by men. Also the victim had to be physically overcome. There were certain roles, however, for which women were preferred. As lovers or wives they were able to entice the victims into their beds or into some out-of-the-way spot, and where little girls were the intended victims they could best lure them from their homes without suspicion (1944/7 and 1945/6). Later, in the actual mutilation and murder, women were often called upon to cauterise the wounds, to wash the body, and generally to clear up afterwards. Of the 1,025 accomplices and accomplice witnesses whose sex is known, while 894 (87 per cent) were men, a substantial minority, 131 (13 per cent), were women.

The ages of accomplices were not always given, and where they were given they were often approximations (twenty, thirty, forty and so on). The youngest of whom we have any record was a boy of seventeen (1942/4) and the oldest a doctor of ninety (1948/10). We were able to plot the frequency distribution in five-year cohorts of the ages of 340 accomplices and accomplice witnesses, based on their ages given at the time of trial and revised to take account of the lapse of time since the murder. The mean age of these was in the 40–44 cohort and the median age was 35–39. It was unusual for very young people to be involved, probably because they were not regarded as trustworthy enough. In case 1959/2 the enrolment of the notoriously unreliable Sesemane Kao, who was in his early thirties, was criticised by his uncle, Ntau Kali. 'He said I was too young', Sesemane told the court, 'and not fit to perform such a duty which requires strong men – men of age.' But in another case (1965/5) the alleged instigator was reported to have said that he would get two young men to help, presumably to add to the murderers' strength when the victim had to be overcome.

Many accomplices, like many instigators, were professing Christians. Going to church was no bar to being asked to take part. Two accused were evangelists, one a Catholic (1951/7) and the other from the Presbyterian Church of Africa (1948/24), and two others were employed at the Printing Works at Morija and stood out from the other accomplices by their European jackets (1927/2). John Makume in Case Study 1 (1945/3) was an elder of the French Protestant Church. We are told by the Catholic newspaper *Moeletsi* that, of the eleven who were hanged in case 1952/6, eight were Protestants and three were Catholics.[41] (*Moeletsi* was evidently trying to counter the allegation that only Catholics, or mainly Catholics, were guilty of medicine murder.) Several of Esthere Kabi's accomplices in case 1953/1 were strongly practising Anglicans.[42]

Sometimes information of this kind came out incidentally. For many Basotho Christian practice and belief were so embedded in their lives that they inevitably formed part of the background to their murderous activities. In case 1954/1 the murder took place after several of the alleged conspirators had attended a confirmation feast at the Anglican church at Sekubu; and in case 1957/1 the instigator and the victim's brother approached a doctor after attending a prayer meeting and asked him if he would prepare medicine with human blood for their chief. Several of those convicted, when asked if they had anything to say as to why they should not be condemned to death, called upon God, Christ or his angels to attest to their innocence. Taoana Makhabane, who had killed his own mother, likened himself to

Christ, destroyed by false witness (1952/4).

Sometimes the question of religious belief came directly under the spot-light. One man, who had helped to kill his own uncle on Christmas Day, told the court that he had been to the French Protestant church that morning. Under cross-examination he said that he had been a regular churchgoer for four years. He acknowledged that, according to the teaching of the church, 'witchcraft' was 'a heathen practice' and that it was wrong to kill, and said that he too believed this. 'I was unhappy about this brutal murder ...', he said, 'both from the church and the laws of the land.'[43] Another declared that he had joined the conspiracy to kill his cousin's wife 'as I see the Devil was with me'. He had contributed to the marriage cattle for the woman he had killed and he now had to look after her new-born child. The only possible explanation for such stupidity and wickedness was the agency of the Devil.[44]

On the other hand there were several accomplices who readily acknow-ledged their confidence in the power of human medicine, like one of those involved in case 1949/5, who told the court that he believed in 'the value of this sort of horn-freshening practice', and two others in case 1959/4, who said they had taken part in the murder because they believed that human medicine would stop the frosts blighting the crops. Some accomplices wanted medicines themselves, like the stock-thief Koenehelo who wanted medicine for protection against arrest (1942/1 and 1944/4), or the man who had a hard life because his crops were so poor and wanted medicine to improve his harvest (1957/4). One accomplice had been warned not to talk to the police, and believed that he had been struck dumb after a crow came and sat on his house (1945/4). The young herdsman who was nobly trying to convince the court that the murder for which he was being tried was not a medicine murder in which several of his family were involved, but an ordinary murder for which he alone was responsible, thought that he was adding to his persuasiveness when he claimed that the victim had bewitched him, and that after drinking her beer he had vomited three snakes (1942/3).

Several accomplices took part in more than one murder. The doctor Phoka Shea, for example, allegedly took part in 1942/1 and 1944/4, and so did the stock-thief Koenehelo Khau. Some of the men who helped Matlere Lerotholi in 1959/1 went on to help Edwin Hantsi Mathaba in 1959/2. One of them, Sesemane Kao, claimed to have taken part in eight murders (see Case Study 4).

One of the most difficult and important questions that we have to ask is why hundreds of accomplices agreed to take part in medicine murder, especially when so many of them were relatives and friends of the victim. What, in Jones' phrase, was the 'Basuto attitude to these murders'? The answers will have important implications for our understanding and per-ception of Sesotho belief and practice. If the accomplices regarded medicine murder as acceptable and willingly captured and mutilated the victim in order to help their chief and their community, the full horror extends far beyond the men and women who actually instigated the crime. If, on the other hand, they were appalled by the cruelty involved and took part only under fierce compulsion, they were clearly living under a terrible oppression and, to that extent at least, they bear less blame.

The first view is represented by the writer Joy Packer in the 1950s, who emphasised the community of interest between instigator and accomplice and their collective guilt:

> When a member of the ruling class has been advised by the witch-doctor to 'enhance his prestige' by taking human life, a whole district may find itself drawn into the ugly business. Moreover the district accepts the situation, because it believes that a chief so 'strengthened' will bring attendant blessings upon his people – better crops, fatter cattle and good rains.[45]

The second view is represented by the historian Elizabeth Eldredge, writing in the 1990s, who sought to draw a sharp distinction between the chiefs and those who helped them. Relying almost exclusively on the Bereng and Gabashane cases, she put forward one simple explanation – fear – for the accomplices' acquiescence. Accomplices, she said, were 'involuntary witnesses', 'unwilling participants', unlike the instigators who were 'specific ambitious individuals who represented neither their people nor their culture when they committed or ordered acts of murder'. The chiefs ruled by terror, and their accomplices were terrorised into taking part and into keeping quiet afterwards. The Basotho were as horrified by medicine murder as anyone else. Our revulsion should not be against the Basotho as a whole, but against particular individuals.[46]

Attitudes and behaviour were both more variable, and more subtle and complex, than expressed in these two extremes of interpretation. There were different types of accomplice, and the motivations of the chief's *matona* and relatives were unlikely to be the same as those of the ordinary commoners who were enlisted, or the doctors or the victim's relatives. We may roughly generalise that, the closer the accomplice to the chief, the stronger the identification with his interests and the greater the element of willing co-operation: the further away, the greater the element of coercion. The accomplice witnesses themselves had much to say about why they agreed to take part, but their testimony has to be interpreted with care. They had taken the risk – in relation to their fellow accomplices – of defecting to the Crown and they had to win the judge's confidence. It was inevitable that many of them should emphasise and perhaps exaggerate the factors of compulsion and fear in order to minimise their guilt.

We also have to bear in mind what Jones described as the 'Basuto attitude' to medicine murder. He acknowledged what he called the 'liberal view held

From 'parallel' to 'indirect' rule

1. Griffith Lerotholi (Paramount Chief 1913–39).
2. Seeiso Griffith (Paramount Chief 1939–40).
3. Charles Arden-Clarke (Resident Commissioner 1942–6).
4. A.D. Forsyth-Thompson (Resident Commissioner 1946–51).

1

2

3

4

The 1940s: key figures

5. 'Mantšebo Seeiso (Paramount Chief regent 1941–60).
6. Sir Evelyn Baring (High Commissioner 1944–51).
7. 'The Big Four' (from left to right, Chiefs Gabashane Masupha, Theko
   Makhaola, Bereng Griffith Lerotholi and Letsie Motšoene).

5

6

7

Two highly respected senior chiefs allegedly implicated in medicine murder

8. Molapo Maama, twice Acting Ward Chief of Maama's, who was convicted and gaoled (case 1950/3).
9. David Theko Makhaola, Ward Chief of Ratšoleli's and Mashai, who was acquitted (case 1953/2).

8

9

Primary sources of evidence

10. The High Court files in a cell below the magistrates' court, Maseru, 1998.
11. Police photograph of the upper body of a victim from Qacha's Nek who was extensively mutilated. She was identified by the bead necklace and the wrist bangle marked (B). Five men were hanged.

10

11

Investigators

12. Hugh Ashton, anthropologist, who wrote three 'secret' papers on medicine murder in 1949, relating especially to the Mokhotlong District.
13. G. I. Jones, sole Commissioner in the official enquiry of 1949.

12

13

The 1950s: British officials

14. Edwin Arrowsmith (Resident Commissioner 1952–6).
15. The arrival of Geoffrey Chaplin as Resident Commissioner in 1956, flanked on left by Gordon Hector (Government Secretary) and Paul Kitson (Commissioner of Police). Chaplin was RC from 1956 to 1962.

14

15

The 1950s: nationalist politicians and the regent with her advisers

16. Ntsu Mokhehle, leader of the Basutoland African Congress, who gave trenchant expression to the 'counter-narrative' in his long presidential address of December 1956.
17. Bennett Khaketla, deputy leader of the BAC and author of a novel about medicine murder published in 1960.
18. Paramount Chief regent 'Mantŝebo Seeiso with her advisers (from left, Patrick Mota, Nkuebe Mitchell, Leshoboro Majara and Leabua Jonathan).

16

17

18

The murder of Stephen Thobeha, May 1945 (case 1945/3)

Police enquiries: the starting point
19. The headless corpse, May 1945.
20. The Phahameng *krantz* where the body was found .
    A. 'Where body was first discovered.'
    B. 'Where headless body was found by police.'
    C. 'Where head was found by police.'
21. Sketch map of the site by Ken Shortt-Smith, January 1946.

19   **20**

21

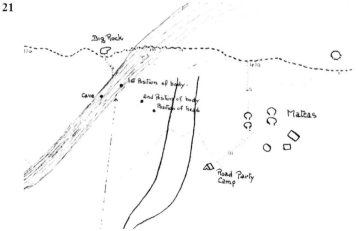

'A migratory body': a reconstruction of events

22. 'Maselloane's rocks, 'where witness Nkojoa alleges *riem* [strap] was put around deceased's neck'.
23. 'Maselloane's rocks, May 1999.
24. Rabele's forest, 'where witness Nkojoa alleges deceased's head was cut off'.

22

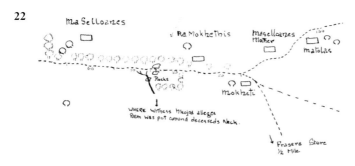

23

24

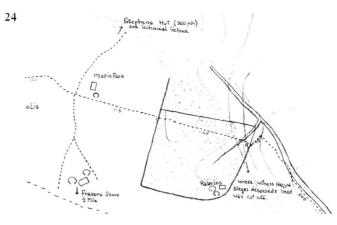

25. Rabele's forest, May 1999, looking north-west to Masite mountain.
26. Foreground: the foundations of Stephen Thobeha's rondavel, May 1999.

25

26

Morija: the context

27. The Lesotho Evangelical Church, which took ten years to build (1840s–1850s).
28. The *moreneng* (chief's place).

27

28

Dramatis personae

29. Mahao Matete (fourth from right) at his baptism in 1954.
30. Nkherepe Molefe, police officer, in retirement in May 1999. He gave a
    graphic account of his pursuit of Bernice Hlalele, known as Ntjahali, who had
    been asked to 'doctor' the head of Stephen Thobeha and whose evidence
    helped to convict John Makume.
31. Kelebone Nkuebe, whose evidence helped to acquit Mahao Matete.

29

30

31

The murder of Mocheseloa Khotso, January 1948 (case 1948/1)

32. Stimela Jason Jingoes, who took part in the search for the body and much later, in his published reminiscences (Jingoes 1975), analysed the political circumstances of the murder.

33. 'Mamakhabane Boshoane Peete, Ward Chieftainess regent of Koeneng and Mapoteng. Charged with the murder and suspended from her office, she looked on 'in mahogany impassivity' as Chief Gabashane Masupha was made responsible for her ward at the end of January 1948. She was hanged in June 1949.

34. 'Mamokhatsi Rachakane at Tsokung, December 1998. She was the eighteen-year-old bride, Ntsoaki Moloi, from whose marriage feast in the hamlet of Moqhotsa's Mocheseloa Khotso was abducted and murdered.

32

33

34

35. Josiel Lefela in 1948. His organisation, the Lekhotla la Bafo, made allegations of torture and coercion of witnesses against the police, and he was a consistent 'thorn in the side' of the colonial administration.
36. Rev. Michael Scott, another 'thorn in the side', who took up the allegations and brought them to the House of Commons in London in a 'drizzling mist' on Christmas Eve 1948.
37. Walter Harragin, the judge who presided at the trial, and who found it one of the strongest cases for the Crown that he had ever tried.
38. Nyalase Ntja Sebajoa at Koma-Koma in December 1998. He was brother to one accused and cousin to another.

35

36

37

38

The murder of 'Meleke Ntai, March 1948 (case 1948/6)

39. Bereng Griffith Lerotholi, Ward Chief of Phamong.
40. Gabashane Masupha, Ward Chief of 'Mamathe's.
41. Gideon Pott, District Commissioner of Berea, who recalled 'terrific tension' when he casually encountered the two chiefs in Teyateyaneng around the time of the murder.
42. Chieftainess 'Mamathe Gabashane Masupha.

39 **40**

41 **42**

43. Lebihan Masupha, junior half-brother to Gabashane. There was 'big trouble' between them over an incident of assault by Gabashane, and later dissension between Lebihan and Chieftainess 'Mamathe after her husband's death.
44. 'Maluke Rakokoli, widow of Fusi, the doctor, whose extravagant behaviour in court when the guilty verdicts were announced cast doubt on his mental stability and helped to reduce his prison sentence.
45. Ntsane Ntai, a distant cousin of the victim who rode with him on return from the funeral which they had both attended, who gave independent evidence for the Crown and who in 1999, as the only survivor amongst the witnesses involved, gave us the same clear account of events as he had given the court fifty years previously. Here, wearing a hat, he is standing with Khalaki Sello outside Fusi's homestead. In the background is the ravine where the corpse was discovered.

43

44

45

The murder of Tšoeunyane Rabolai, October 1952 (case 1952/12)

46. Police photograph of the corpse.
47. Sketch showing key sites immediately to the north of the confluence of the Orange (Senqu) and Moremoholo rivers.
   A. 'Where the victim is alleged to have been seized.'
   B. 'Spot where deceased is alleged to have been killed.'
   D. 'Spot where deceased's body is alleged to have been thrown into the Orange River.'
   E. 'Spot where deceased's body is alleged to have been found.'
   H. 'Two houses of deceased.'
   L. 'The village of Seane Klaas.'

46   47

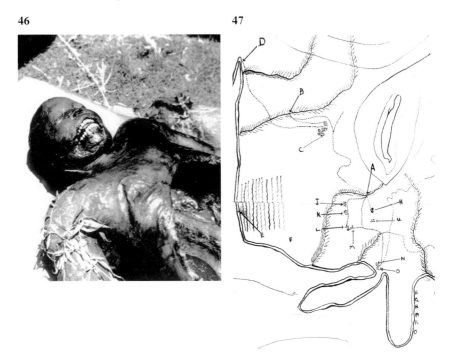

48. Matlere Lerotholi, 'Mantšebo's representative as Ward Chief of Mokhotlong. Having arrived in the district as 'Seeiso's herdboy', Matlere was widely resented as a 'usurper', alongside his brothers. Reputedly 'Mantšebo's lover, Matlere was also held in high regard as a strong chief by British officials. He was twice indicted for medicine murder and twice acquitted.
49. The homestead of Rabolai Tšoeunyane (behind the rectangular building), May 1999.

48

49

50. Spot where Rabolai was enticed, '219 paces from his huts'.
51. Seane Klaas, at home in May 1999, with Khalaki Sello on the left. Seane Klaas told the court that he had lured Tšoeunyane to his death by burning a powder on a fire and calling his name through the smoke. He was an accomplice witness for the Crown in 1953 but told us in 1999 that he had deliberately introduced to the court an inconsistency of evidence over the colour of a canvas bag, and thereby helped to secure acquittal of the accused.

50

51

by individual Christians and educated men whose moral values have become the same as those of Europeans' and who regarded medicine murders with horror. Against this, he wrote, was

> the more conservative view that the chief and his people are one and their interests identical, and that a medicine to further the political ambition of a chief is for his people's good. The killing of a victim to replenish his horn cannot therefore be regarded as a crime: at the worst it is a regrettable necessity, and in some cases it may become a public duty.[47]

Some Basotho held to the 'liberal view' and others to the 'more conservative view', but many, Jones said, were uncertain and confused, trying to reconcile them.

Finally there was the relationship between a chief and his subjects. We have already discussed this at some length, but in the particular context of medicine murder Bennett Khaketla, in his evidence to the Round Table Conference, was especially revealing and eloquent. 'The life of an ordinary Mosotho', he wrote,

> depends upon the goodwill and favour of his chief. It is from the chief that he gets lands to till and raise crops for the sustenance of his family. It is from the chief that he gets a site for his cattle-post. It is indeed from the chief that he looks for and gets protection and redress of his grievances ... Take away the goodwill and the subject is deprived of the site for his home, his lands, his cattle-post, his protection and fair redress of grievances. Such a person becomes a social outcast because he has lost the favour of the chief ... It is not surprising, therefore, that whenever a chief has had human flesh prescribed by his 'doctor' as an ingredient for his medicine to make him strong or regain his lost power, he should find no difficulty in obtaining the services of willing hearts ... for were people ordered to carry out this abominable task and they refused, the chief could and would make life so unbearable for them that they would be forced to leave his ward.[48]

As Khaketla makes clear, compulsion and fear often ran together with loyalty and duty. Accomplices who obeyed their chief's order to kill might well have wanted to stand well with him, but they were just as likely to be scared about the consequences of refusal. 'Men, if you wish to be loved by the Chiefs you must carry out their orders': the advice given to the accomplices in case 1948/24 was both a warning and a threat.[49] Obedience to the reasonable order of a chief was every Mosotho's duty. The chief was the civil authority: disobedience would render government impossible. For many witnesses who were asked why they had taken part, like the old threshing-floor cleaner in 1944/5 and the victim's grandmother in 1954/1, it was explanation enough that they had to obey their chief. In the second Bereng and Gabashane case (1948/6) one accomplice told the court that he had taken part simply because Gabashane had ordered him to do so, and when pressed he said he would have killed his wife or child if that had been Gabashane's order.

The inner conflict between what Jones described as the 'liberal' and 'conservative' views was perhaps most painfully revealed by Moketi Mokanohi in case 1951/9. He told the court that he was a Christian, but that he had taken part because he had to obey his chief. When cross-examined by the prosecutor he elaborated:

> Old established customs die slowly in Basutoland. Proper native custom is respected. [Maama Shoaepane] belongs to a very powerful family. As a Chief he is respected by me and obeyed by me ... Although I have embraced Christianity old customs and respect for the Chief are hard to overcome. So I obeyed my Chief and carried out his order against my better conscience.[50]

In another case (1949/5), Mphapha Lebona, a man about forty years old who had helped to kill his own mother-in-law, told the court, 'I would carry out my Chief's order be it right or wrong. I claim to be a Christian. If I am ordered by my Chief I would not refuse to contravene the law'. When it was pointed out to him that Paramount Chief regent 'Mantšebo had issued instructions that any conspiracy to murder should be reported to the police, he said that he had not obeyed this order because he feared his own chief.[51] Several chiefs scoffed at this. People repeatedly disobeyed their orders, they said, and one complained that some subjects would not even go to fetch a bar of soap.[52] Just as accomplices might exaggerate their duty to obey, so chiefs had an interest in playing it down.

Many accomplices seem to have taken part without any great qualms of conscience, and in some cases even with enthusiasm. In several cases it was the accomplices who first suggested that a murder should be carried out, and in at least two cases they chose the victim. The chief's councillors sometimes took the lead in making the practical arrangements for the murder, and the doctors of course were often prominent in prescribing the type of victim needed and the particular parts to be cut. Other accomplices needed little or no persuasion. Young Tseko Pitso, for example, was sitting on a hillside with his friend, and when he saw the conspirators, including his father, attack their victim he ran down and joined them without even being asked (1947/14). We have already given the example of the stock-thief Koenehelo who wanted medicine prepared from human flesh in order to avoid arrest (1944/4). In a similar case (1948/14) Lekhotla Setene persuaded his chief to employ his own doctor so that he and the doctor could get hold of some human parts (1948/14). Mphapha Lebona said that Shadrack

Lebona was his chief and the head of his village and he wanted to see him rich and powerful (1949/5). In another case (1962/2) the accomplice witness 'Matlhasinye Mahalika gave evidence of what happened when the instigator, Tšiu Lethola, summoned a meeting of his accomplices, told them of his land dispute with headman Mahlomola, and said he wanted 'to strengthen himself' with medicine prepared from one of Mahlomola's family. A man who seems to have been his chief councillor told Tšiu that he was right: 'we are now fed up with Headman Mahlomola who seems to regard this as his area ...' Then, said the witness, 'the whole pitso was unanimous that [Tšiu Lethola] should strengthen himself'. As the judge noted, all the accused were related to each other, and all had an interest in Tšiu's success.

There were many accomplices whose reluctance was overcome or whose obedience was strengthened by the promise of rewards. Normally they were offered money, ranging from £5 to £100. Some were offered land, and some were offered payment in kind, in the form of *liretlo* from the murder in which they were to help. Only rarely were they offered livestock, since this, it seems, would have been too conspicuous – giving cattle would 'cause noise', said one alleged instigator (1952/7). One man was offered chieftain-ship rights (1943/3). The accomplices who were most likely to be offered rewards were the relatives and friends of the victim, like the man who was offered £40 for his stepson (1948/8), the woman who was offered £60 if she gave up her husband (1951/2), and the man who sold his brother for the promise of £80, payable in two instalments, and who said that, if asked and if the price was right, he would have sold his wife (1952/7).[53]

These offers of rewards were clearly important for several accomplices. Some of them haggled over the price (1956/4), and one declared that but for the money he would never have agreed to take part (1954/1). Lekhaole Bakane, a poor man who was promised a brown cow and who had never owned a beast before, told the court that if you were in need a cow worth R50 (£25) was more valuable than a man's life (1962/1). Yet the rewards were rarely paid, and several witnesses declared in the box that they were still looking to the chief to fulfil his promise (for example, 1961/2).

Several accomplices were threatened with death if they refused to help, sometimes as victims of medicine murder themselves (for example, in cases 1945/4, 1947/13, 1948/6, 1954/1 and 1955/2). One man, less dramatically, was warned that if he did not help he would have a hard life in future (1952/6). A few were assailed on both fronts – by offers of rewards and threats of death (for example, in cases 1943/5, 1945/6 and 1952/5). Even when they were not explicitly threatened several witnesses spoke of being afraid of their chief (1954/9). Against this we know of at least two persons who refused to take part in murders and who appear to have suffered no adverse con-sequences (in cases 1953/2 and 1959/1), and of one woman who refused to give up her husband but who went on, it was said, to become an accomplice when another victim was chosen (1955/1).

For many accomplices the element of fear was very strong, and we shall see this again when we come to consider the mutilations and murders themselves. This fear was deeply rooted in the chiefs' power on the one hand and their subjects' dependence on the other, the relationship so well described by Bennett Khaketla. It is striking, however, that in the murders ascribed to traders and others almost exactly the same patterns of participation emerge. There were no accomplices in court who talked of fear or threats, but people were prepared to take part nonetheless. In fact, the average number of accomplices, nine, was even higher than the median of eight for chiefs and headmen, and in three murders allegedly instigated by traders in the 1960s the average was seventeen. Again, some of these accomplices were related to the instigators, some were dependents in the sense that they were employed, some were doctors, some were simply local people who were asked to help, and some were the victims' friends and relatives. Again, there were offers of rewards. In case 1961/2 the victim's father-in-law was promised five blankets, five pairs of riding breeches, a pair of boots, a shirt and £50. He was asked sarcastically if he was planning to open a wholesale shop, and replied very seriously that that was not his intention but he was 'going to be a rich man'.

The reasons for accomplices taking part varied widely from case to case and from one person to another. Some did so out of loyalty to the chief, or were attracted by the promised rewards. Others did so out of fear of the chief, or were terrified by the threats made against them. Those who were the closest to the chief, his councillors and relatives and perhaps his doctor, were more likely to be willing helpers and stood less in need of intimidation or inducement. Many of them, in fact, would have played some part in the decision to undertake the murder and in the choice of the victim. Ordinary commoners, especially the victims' friends and relatives, were more likely to need the kind of persuasion that was backed up by promises or threats.

The choice of accomplices, and the means taken to ensure their co-operation, were literally matters of life and death. If all went well from their point of view, the chief and his fellow conspirators formed a close and tight-knit band, many of them related to each other, all of them mutually familiar, and bound together, perhaps by trust and loyalty, perhaps by common interest, and if not by fear or hope of reward. In many cases this grim ideal was realised: the chiefs chose well, deployed their threats and promises wisely, and when the police came to investigate they were met by a wall of silence and in the end had to close their enquiries without any charges being made. But in all the cases that came to court there were individuals who broke ranks. Who they were and why they defected will be discussed in Chapter 8 below.

PLOTS, MURDERS, MUTILATIONS
AND MEDICINE

Villagers hearing the screams of 'Mapontso Tlotto [*sic*] ... were afraid
to go to her aid. Her badly mutilated body was found on the doorstep
of her hut. It would appear that some parts of her brain were also
removed. A chief has been arrested in connection with the murder.

Basutoland News, 7 September 1965 (1965/4)

INSTIGATING A MURDER

Our information about the instigation and planning of medicine murders
comes almost entirely from accomplice witnesses. Not all of them could be
very informative. Many were simply told, either by the chief or by one of his
councillors, that the chief had decided to kill a certain person for medicine
and that he wanted them to take part. But others were actually present when
the decision to carry out a murder was made or, if not present themselves,
were told later how the decision had been reached.

Some murders were planned months in advance, others just a few days,
but usually the meetings at which the murders were organised took place a
week or two beforehand. When a chief was thinking of murder he would first
sound out his closest advisers, and perhaps the doctor too if a doctor was
involved. In some cases meetings were then held to which all or most of the
accomplices were invited. Sometimes several meetings were held, and in
case 1965/6, in which nearly thirty accomplices were involved, it was
decided to form 'a committee'. In other cases, instead of holding meetings,
the chief or one of his advisers approached the accomplices individually.

Usually the idea of medicine murder seems to have come from the chief
himself. In at least half of the cases that came to court no doctor, it seems,
was involved, and even when a doctor was consulted the instigator often
knew what he wanted beforehand. In case 1950/4 headman Keneuoe
Kennan Khethisa told his doctor that he wanted medicine pegs to strengthen
his village, and when the doctor asked if a black sheep was available,
Keneuoe replied that as a chief he needed a human being, not a sheep.
When Setlotla Motlotla and Palinyane Mofammere consulted a doctor they
asked him specifically to mix human blood with medicine, which he agreed
to do if they paid him two head of cattle (1957/1).

In several cases, however, it was the doctor who advised that a murder was necessary. When headman Likhalile wanted to become rich in millet and livestock and to steal without being caught, he was advised by an itinerant Zulu doctor to carry out a medicine murder, to prepare a horn with the *liretlo*, and then to scarify himself and his family (1912/1); and when Chief Mojela Letsie consulted the doctor, 'Matumelo, she told him that for disputes over land she always needed human flesh (1927/2).[1]

In at least one case, 1949/5, the idea of murder was put forward by one of the chief's councillors. When Mphapha Lebona was asked for advice by his chief on how he could enhance his prestige, he suggested, in words that we have quoted before, 'that these days if a person wanted to be famous they should kill another person ... After this person has been killed, the body should be mutilated and parts used as medicine'.[2] In case 1945/11 headman Tumahole Bereng was advised by a doctor that if he was to succeed in a certain dispute over land he needed medicine prepared with human blood. He was not immediately persuaded, however, and asked one of his followers, Jan Gat, for his opinion. 'I said it would be a good thing', Jan said, 'as it would enable us to rule over the area in dispute without any further trouble.'[3]

All these discussions took place within the same shared framework of beliefs. No doubt several murders would not have taken place but for the doctors' advice, but in many cases no doctors were involved. The chiefs were not gullible innocents led astray by evil practitioners bent on increasing their power and influence and on being rewarded with cattle. They themselves believed that they stood to gain, often took the initiative and invariably assumed the responsibility.

CHOOSING A VICTIM

There were similar forces at work in the choice of the victim. Two questions had to be resolved: first, whether a particular type of victim was needed; and, second, which particular individual should be killed. Many instigators seem to have been confident in their own ability to make the right choice without turning to a doctor for advice. In one case (1943/3) the headman involved was said to have invited his accomplices to join him in killing an elderly Anglican clergyman. In another (1944/1) the instigators told one of their subjects to find a victim, and when he failed they chose the man himself.

When doctors were involved they no doubt gave advice about the victim to be chosen, even when this was not stated in the evidence. We can well imagine that in case 1954/4, in which the doctor said that a medicine murder was necessary, it was he who stipulated that a Mohlakoana victim was needed. But this was not always so. The doctor 'Matumelo said she needed human flesh but also that as far as she was concerned any person would do (1927/2). Sometimes the accomplices chose the victim. In one case (1943/5) there is evidence that the victim was chosen by the shadow instigator's court chairman. In another (1954/4) the chief said that he needed a Mohlakoana, and one of those present, himself a Mohlakoana, protested, but then thought of his nephew, and everyone agreed.

There were wide variations in the type of victim, for there was no consistency in respect of sex, age, physical condition or clan. In some cases we know why a particular victim was chosen – because he was a Motaung, for example, or because she was a *motsoetse*, a woman who had just given birth to a child – but we rarely know why it was that a victim of that type was needed. As Jones pointed out,

> Most people just do not know, and say that only the doctor who prescribed each particular medicine could answer this; while the doctors naturally say that they do not know anything about making such medicines, and cannot explain the professional secrets of those that do.[4]

In the days when medicines were prepared from the bodies of enemies who had fallen in battle, there was inevitably some degree of uniformity. The enemies were all adult men, and it is said that they had to be brave and strong, though this may not always have been observed in practice. It was also said that they had to belong to a clan other than the instigator's. So Moshoeshoe's horn, according to Jones, was said to contain no ingredients from Bakoena, but rather the flesh of Batlokoa, Matebele or other 'enemy tribesmen', so that Bakoena qualities could be reinforced by the qualities of other clans.[5] It appears, however, that this kind of factor was seldom considered in choosing the victims of medicine murder in the twentieth century.

We know the sex of 190 victims during the colonial period. Of these 124 (65 per cent) were male, and sixty-six (35 per cent) female. Precise ages are rarely given, but on a rough classification seventeen victims were children of sixteen years or younger and 169 were adults, of whom thirty-eight were elderly. The youngest was a new-born child (1953/5), the oldest a woman of ninety (1948/18).

Even among adult males strength and bravery were rarely sought. Several of them were described as healthy and vigorous, but the only victims who were said to have been chosen for these or comparable qualities were Liphapang Mpikinyane, who was 'a very strong man in public matters' (1952/9) and Mofolo Ramalumane, who was 'a hardy person and a brave man' (1958/1). Physical vigour was also considered, but in a different way, in the second Bereng and Gabashane case (1948/6). 'Meleke Ntai was known to be 'sickly'. That did not stop Gabashane and his men from choosing him as their victim, but when one of their accomplices cut off his lips, Bereng saw how little blood there was and rejected him. In several other cases the man chosen as a victim was known to be in poor health or even mad (for example, 1944/6, 1953/2 and 1962/1). Lejone Thakanyane, an elderly mason, had a crippled arm, but the headman said that he did not mind (1952/3).

According to Ashton, the stipulation that the victim should not belong to the same clan as the instigator was still observed, on the grounds that using a fellow-clansman would be close to cannibalism. Rivers Thompson agreed that, from the point of view of chiefs of the ruling clan, 'it mustn't have an ounce of Bakoena stuff in it' but added the 'theory' that the 'mixture' should be of different tribes.[6] No doubt these factors were present in the minds of at least some murderers. A young chief in the Leribe District, according to Hermann Dieterlen in 1912, had set out to make a medicine-horn containing the flesh of persons from seven clans. It was alleged that, when a potential victim was kidnapped and brought before 'Mantšebo and Matlere Lerotholi, the doctor said that since he was a Mokoena it was impossible to make any use of him (1945/2). On the other hand there is evidence in two cases that the victims were chosen because they were Bakoena (two victims in 1930/1 and one in 1943/5), and in eight others that the victim happened to be a Mokoena, though was not, it seems, specifically chosen for that reason (1927/1, 1945/2, 1945/11, 1947/15, 1948/6, 1951/5, 1952/12 and 1953/2). There were also two cases in which it was said that a victim from any clan would do (1944/1 and 1950/7).

Seventeen victims were said to have been chosen because they belonged to particular clans. As well as the three Bakoena, there were five Bahlakoana, three Bataung, two Basia, two Bafokeng, one Letebele and one Letsitsi. The two Basia victims were chosen, according to the court record, because the medicine made from them would *siama*, 'make right', the instigator's affairs (1948/18, 1951/7). In other cases the reasons for the choice were not made clear.[7]

In several cases the victims were related to the alleged instigators – as mother (1952/4), aunt (1947/4), daughter-in-law (1937/2), half-sister (1930/1), nephew (1930/1) and grand-daughter (1953/5). Headman Pheello Smith was asked how he could kill his own father-in-law, and he replied that if necessary he would kill his own mother (1952/6). There were many other cases in which the victim was related to one or more of the accomplices.

Nearly all the victims were local people, well known to the instigator and the accomplices and often on friendly terms with them. The Anglican priest who was killed in case 1943/3 was one of the alleged instigator's friends. Mokebisa Motloli was the friend of one accomplice and the secret lover of another (1945/8). Lepekola Mokhosi was the 'best friend' of one of the men who allegedly organised his murder (1953/2). In a few cases the victims were visitors or strangers – a sister or a brother visiting a relative (1944/2 and

1952/7), a stock-thief (1950/2), or a traveller passing through (1950/6) – but these were exceptions.

A few victims were chosen out of dislike or jealousy. Monnana Mokoloko was chosen because he selfishly refused to share his livestock with others (1950/4), and the reason for selecting old Tieho Matsora was that he had accused some of the accomplices of stock theft (1951/5). Tšoeunyane Rabolai had infuriated Matlere Lerotholi by interrupting him at a *pitso* and complaining about the treatment of one of his elderly relatives (1952/12, Case Study 4). When Tšoarelo Letsie told his people that he wanted to kill someone for medicine, they all said that they wanted Moralejoe Mphoso, because he was always troubling them and suing them in court (1954/7).

A few were chosen because, as Ashton puts it, their 'habits or state of health, for example, drunkenness or epilepsy, could corroborate the ostensible cause of death' – that they had strayed from the path and fallen over a cliff or into a river.[8] Katse Phatela, himself a heavy drinker, was chosen because his sister had fallen over a cliff while drunk (1945/11), while several victims were slightly mad (1944/2, 1944/6, 1947/7, 1952/3 and 1962/3, for example). One victim, Isaac Ramelefane, was sane and in perfectly good health, but was given some medicine which had the effect of making him like a person possessed by spirits, and he began walking about, dreaming and singing. After a few weeks he was secretly taken away from the place where he was staying and then, just as secretly, sent back. Mopeli Mohale, who was later accused of his murder, is alleged to have said that he did this 'so that when we take him for good it will be known that he usually disappears' (1952/7).[9]

Some victims were chosen for a particular quality – for being a twin, for example, or at least being thought to be a twin (1944/7 and 1948/10); for being a member of a family that had survived the 'flu epidemic of 1918 (1919/1); for being a bachelor (1951/9), an only child (1954/4), or an elderly person (1955/2); or, in the case of one little girl, for being a relative of the headman with whom the instigator was in dispute (1962/2). Several victims were women who had just given birth (1919/1, 1931/1, 1934/1, 1936/1 and 1943/4); others were pregnant (1937/1 and 1947/9). In one case (1952/11) the brains of an unborn child were wanted. No reasons were given for these particular requirements, except that in one case, where medicine was being sought to help Gabashane Masupha, the victim had to be blind so that the judge would be blind to the evidence against him in his trial (1948/18). The element of arbitrariness is often apparent, and Jones was probably right when he wrote that 'judging ... by the variation and lack of uniformity the choice is probably determined by inspiration, divination or in some other personal and unpredictable manner'.[10] In a few cases the witnesses stated explicitly that any person would do (1927/2, 1944/1, 1950/7 and 1956/4).

None of the victims was a person of any great standing in the community. As the common people pointed out to Jones, none of them came from 'the sons of Moshesh and other members of the ruling class of chiefs and headmen'.[11] Old Matingting Masalalla had been a leper and had spent some time in the Botšabelo hospital: she had only one eye and her feet were badly marked (1944/4). Lejone Thakanyane was a mason and a thatcher, but had recently become 'mentally deficient'. He lived with his sister-in-law, who had taken him to both white and Basotho doctors, but they had been unable to do anything for him. He was 'a very good man', a 'popular man' (1952/ 3). Kaizer Mofana, a young herdboy, was allegedly murdered to make medicine for Chief Matlere and Paramount Chief regent 'Mantšebo (1959/ 1, Case Study 4), and his headless body was hidden in the mountain snow. The judge thought he was between ten and twelve years old, while his father said he was fifteen. One of Matlere's sympathisers explained: 'He was small for his age. He was nobody. Nobody of importance. Who knew him? ... *But on his account great people have their names printed nastily in the newspapers*'.[12]

BEER-DRINKS AND AMBUSHES

If the intended victim was an adult, the most common plan was to invite them to a feast or ceremony of some kind, a *mokete*, to let them get drunk (or to make sure they got drunk), and then to attack them after they had left. This arrangement had three advantages. First, victims who were drunk were more easily overcome (they might also have felt less pain, but if this was a consideration it was never mentioned). Second, since feasts normally took place in the evening, the attack was carried out under cover of darkness. Third, when their bodies were found below cliffs or in rivers, it could be argued that they had been so drunk that they had wandered from their path and fallen over. The main drawback was that everyone at the feast could witness the movements of the conspirators and the victim immediately prior to the murder, and this could be particularly serious if they were seen going off together. There could also be complications if the conspirators themselves became drunk. One murder had to be postponed for two days after the alleged instigator became uncontrollably aggressive (1952/9). In another case the man who was supposed to be keeping guard while the mutilations were carried out fell fast asleep – with disastrous consequences when the victim's lover turned up and burst in on the scene (1948/10). Sometimes, however, what they had to do sobered the conspirators very quickly. 'We were all drunk', one said, but 'the events of this night produced an emotional strain on me. This had the effect of sobering me so that what I saw I saw clearly' (1951/9).

Feasts were common in Basotho villages. As well as important gatherings to celebrate weddings, initiation or various Christian festivals, a man might invite his friends and neighbours to a work-party and give them food and drink afterwards, and there were often small, private beer-drinks, 'usually over the week-end', as Ashton noted.[13] For the bigger feasts many gallons of beer were brewed, and the singing and the dancing often went on all night and well into the next day (1951/4). People flocked in for miles around. They did not have to be invited. As one alleged murderer told the court, 'whenever there is beer they congregate' (1945/11). Several of the victims were known to be drunkards, or at least fond of their drink, like Monnana Mokoloko, who 'lived on beer' according to his daughter (1950/4).

Whenever conspirators were planning a murder, there was usually some feast in the near future around which they could make their arrangements, and if not it was easy to arrange one. Murders were committed after feasts connected with marriage (1945/4 and 1957/2) and initiation (1952/2 and 1952/6), feasts after work-parties (1948/10 and 1957/4), and feasts for Easter (1942/1), confirmations (1954/1) and baptisms (1944/4 and 1954/ 6). Over a period of fourteen years no fewer than nine murders were planned for Christmas Day.[14] Moramang Letsie explained to his fellow conspirators that he had decided to kill his victim on Christmas Day because that was 'when people had taken much beer and it would be thought he had fallen over a cliff' (1943/5). It was also no coincidence that more murders were carried out on Saturdays than on any other day of the week.[15]

Normally, knowing their victim, the conspirators could be confident that he or she would turn up at the feast, but sometimes they made sure by issuing an invitation themselves. In one case (1943/5) Sekoati Mpheto, an old man, was met as he came from church on Christmas morning by a woman who had been especially smeared with fat to make her attractive, and throughout the day he followed her devotedly from one feast to another. Once at the feast the victims were sometimes plied with beer, or even brandy, to make sure they became drunk.

Some victims left the feast of their own accord and were attacked as they made their way home. Others left with one or more of the accomplices and were taken to the place where the murder would be carried out. In one case a wife who had agreed to betray her husband for £60 took him off and led him to a lonely spot where the other conspirators were waiting to kill him (1951/2). Some victims were killed out in the open. Others were taken to one of the murderers' huts. Not every plan went smoothly. Katse Phatela, who had been given brandy as well as beer, danced and sang war songs with his brother, and then fell fast asleep: he had to be carried outside (1945/11). One murder had to be put off because a policeman turned up at the feast (1954/5). Mpho Mothijoa was brought to a feast by one of the accomplices but, as the judge said, he had other ideas of his own and decided to leave before anything could be done (1957/3).

Another plan, though not quite as common, was to carry out the murder in some unfrequented place. Sometimes the victims went there of their own accord (in which case the conspirators might have been told about their movements by a friend or relative); sometimes at the suggestion or on the order of one of the conspirators. This scheme lacked the advantages associated with drunkenness: the victims were usually alert and, when their bodies were found at the foot of a cliff or in a river, it could not be argued that they had lost their way in a drunken stupor. Moreover they were attacked, as often as not, during the day: there were no guests at a feast to observe the movements of the conspirators, but there were sometimes herdboys and passers-by.

Sello Mashale set off early one Sunday morning to go fishing in the Orange River, and was attacked as he sat with his rods and lines at the spot known as the Witch's Pool (1947/14). Old Moqebelo Ramahlatsa was set upon as he was chopping wood in a valley, and afterwards the conspirators tried to make it appear that he had fallen into a stream as he worked (1957/ 7). Lesiamo Jane was ambushed as he rode back from a race meeting (1952/ 5), and Tšehlo Kabi was waylaid as he returned from a meeting in another village to make arrangements for his son's wedding – his wife had told the conspirators where he had gone (1953/1). Some victims were sent on errands (1954/8 and 1954/9); some went out to look for missing animals (1951/5 and 1958/2); some went out to meet their lovers (1944/1, 1946/2 and 1954/ 7).

Several victims were fetched or summoned from their homes before being taken off and killed. Isaac Ramelefane, the man who had been made mad, like a person possessed by spirits, was fetched from his brother's home one night and taken to the place where he was going to be killed (1952/7). 'Mapaki Naha, whose husband was away on the mines, was lying in bed with her lover when she was called outside by her brother-in-law. There was then some discussion of where she should be killed. One of the conspirators said the place they were in was 'too open', and so she was taken to the ruins of an abandoned village (1956/4).

Several victims were eventually taken to the home of one of the conspirators to be killed, but it was unusual for the instigator's home to be used. No doubt the chiefs were taking care not to endanger themselves, but there was also the practical reason that other people, not connected with the murder, were more likely to come to a chief's home. In one case (1945/8) this consideration was explicitly spelt out. A few victims, about five or six in all, were attacked and killed in their own huts.

The three herdboys who are known to have been murder victims spent most of their days in the open country and were therefore particularly vulnerable. In one case the boy's stepfather arranged for him to herd horses in a place where he could be easily caught (1948/8). In another the accomplice Sesemane Kao persuaded the boy to accompany him to a particular cattle-post on the ground that he needed someone to prepare his food (1959/1). These procedures were not without danger, since other herdboys witnessed what was happening. Similarly little girls could easily be lured away from their homes, but again there were usually people around who could later give evidence in court. In one case a girl of just two years of age was taken by one of the women accomplices when she was out picking blackberries with her friends (1962/2). In another case a little girl of four was taken from her home, and a passer-by saw tears streaming down her face as she walked along with one of the accomplices (1945/6). In several cases children were given sweets to keep them quiet.

Two murders were not initially planned as medicine murders. In the first case a headman shot a stock-thief and left him for dead, but when he found him still alive the next day he had him mutilated 'for a doctor to make him a *lenaka* [horn] which would be useful for court cases and make grain plentiful' (1928/1). In the second case two lovers were planning to kill the woman's husband, and a headman was said to have joined in to get *liretlo* (1957/5).[16]

In about a dozen cases the victim was not killed at once, but was held captive for several days or even weeks before being finally despatched. 'Mampolane Mofubelu, a strong, healthy, middle-aged woman, was apparently rendered insane by drugs and was kept in a wooded valley until she was weak and emaciated (1948/15). A little girl, 'Matšeliso Letsie, was kept in a drugged condition for two weeks in the home of one of the accomplices (1962/2). Lepekola Mokhosi was allegedly taken to a hut in a ruined village, gagged and tied up to a beam, and left with the door locked for three days (1953/2). About half of these cases involved children and in all of them, it seems, the victims were drugged.

It is difficult to know why this procedure was adopted. We have not found any explanation given by those who took part, and in practice it turned out to be very risky, especially when the victim was reported missing and a search was carried out. A woman who caught sight of 'Mampolane Mofubelu while collecting wood was told by the instigator to 'look after his eland', but later gave evidence in court against him. When a search was conducted for Lepekola Mokhosi, one of the alleged conspirators made himself suspect by refusing to unlock the door of the hut in which Lepekola was being imprisoned.

The use of drugs to quieten the victims, to 'tame' them or to take away their reason was only one of the uses to which medicines were put in the planning and preparation of medicine murders. In the very first recorded case the conspirators put medicine in their victim's beer which was said to have had the effect of making him follow them (1895/1). In four cases at least medicine was used to summon the victims to where the alleged murderers were waiting (1919/1, 1947/15, 1952/12, 1957/3). In one of these (1957/3) the victim had been particularly elusive, and so a cock was killed to call him when he was needed and a duck was killed to bring the rain which would wash his body away afterwards. In one case (1954/4) the alleged instigator was described as pouring yellow powder on the path and making the sign of a cross. This, he said, would make the victim weak when he passed along the path later in the day.

MUTILATING AND KILLING

As the victims were attacked – as the murderers burst in on them in a darkened hut, or loomed up before them in some remote valley, grabbing hold of their blankets or pulling them down from their horses – they screamed and shouted aloud for help, prayed to God, offered bribes, called for revenge, begged to be allowed to see their children, asked why they were being killed with such brutality, or pleaded for mercy, particularly from those who were their friends or kinsmen. It was all in vain. No-one came to help: no kinsman or friend showed any pity. But sometimes their screams and shouts were heard, and the evidence of those who heard them could help to convict their murderers. So they had to be silenced. Some were knocked unconscious with knobkerries, hammers, sticks or axes. Some were gagged with a woman's *doek* (headscarf). Some were throttled, but in such a way that they were still alive. In a few cases their cries were drowned by the conspirators' shouting and singing.

Before the murderers got down to work, there were other precautions to be taken. Blood-stains had to be avoided, and so if they were in a hut they usually placed the victim on an ox-hide or sacking. If they were out in the open they would move away from the path so that they were less likely to be seen and any blood-stains on the ground would not be immediately obvious (in 1943/5, for example). Sometimes they stripped the victims to avoid staining their clothes, and then after they were dead they dressed them again so that it might appear that they had met with some natural accident (in 1949/3, for example). Where they failed to do this, the victim's stained clothes might make it clear to the world that this was no accident but a murder. One victim was stabbed through his vest and blanket, and these items of clothing, with the gashes in them, were important exhibits in the court case that followed (1951/9). The murderers tried to avoid staining their own clothes as well, to the extent in one case of stripping themselves naked (1944/1), but they were not always successful. There were several trials in which blood-stained trousers and shirts were produced by the prosecution as evidence.

It was not always easy to control what was going on. Although several victims were drunk or drugged, and although many of them had been weakened by blows to the head, some of them went on kicking and struggling and had to be firmly held down. Some were tied up with leather straps or their own bootlaces. It was not unusual for about a score of people, several of them drunk, to be moving around in a hut less than five metres in diameter (as in 1957/3), lit only with a dim paraffin lamp or a sputtering candle. Those who murdered out in the open used lamps or torches, or in a few cases a fire. They were sometimes hindered by rain, and in one case by a strong wind that blew out their lamp (1954/7). One gang of murderers used matches and, in the trial that followed, the burnt-out matchsticks scattered on the grass helped to corroborate the Crown witnesses' story (1951/4).

There was almost invariably someone in charge – the instigator himself, a trusted councillor or a doctor – and that person, or perhaps some shadow instigator, had usually decided beforehand what parts they needed and who was to do the cutting. 'You already know what you have to do', Sankoela Mahlethole said to his kinsman Monnamoholo, who then took out his pen-knife and began cutting (1947/13). Tšoarelo Letsie, a shadow instigator, had given careful instructions about the parts that he needed, and so when two of his henchmen were carrying the victim's body away and one of them prepared to castrate him, the other checked him: 'No, you are doing something that you have not been ordered to do' (1953/4).

The instigator did not always take all the *liretlo*. In one case, according to the Crown, while one of the conspirators said he wanted the skull, another said he needed the arm and the heart (1945/3). In another a female doctor stepped in and said she wanted some flesh from near the breast (1954/3). One doctor, who was only taking part because he wanted to get *liretlo* for another client, caused some confusion when he asked for his 'share', but in the end he was allowed to take 'a small piece' (1948/15). In other cases, after the main parties had taken what they wanted, the rest of the conspirators were invited to help themselves (1944/7 and 1958/1).

There was a wide and apparently arbitrary variation in the *liretlo* taken. All that was found of Charlie Motona was his skull, backbone, pelvis, a few ribs and other bones and some flesh. His head had been severed and skinned, his eyes, tongue, ears and neck had been removed, and so too had some of the ribs, all his internal organs, his left arm, his right hand, and flesh from both his arms and his testicles (1941/1). In other cases only blood was taken, and it may be significant that this practice became increasingly common. Taking only those cases on which we have adequate information, in the 1940s 18 per cent involved blood only (nine out of forty-nine); in the 1950s this figure rose to 28 per cent (sixteen out of fifty-seven). The reason for this may have been given by Chief David Theko Makhaola: 'all he required', he allegedly told his accomplices, 'was blood – not cuts on the body, because doctors can detect cuts [in post-mortems]' (1953/2). In 1956 Dr Jacobson, the government's Director of Medical Services, said, with some exaggeration, that murderers were 'now experienced, and have become wiser ... At first a lot of parts of the body were taken, but now they are satisfied with a few drops of blood'. In this way they left 'no tell-tale wounds'.[17]

Almost any part of the body could be taken. As Jones pointed out, 'The parts most commonly taken were from the face and from the genitals'.[18] Ashton was more specific.

> For a *lenaka* [horn] required for general purposes ... no special part of the body is needed, although the best parts are blood (the vital fluid), the bowels and generative organs, as they are all the source of man's power and activity. For medicine required for specific purposes, such as to influence the courts, special parts may be an additional help, such as eyes and ears to help one see and hear the weak points of one's opponent's case, tongue and lips to help one speak well.[19]

Stimela Jingoes reinforces this, speaking of one of 'Mamakhabane's accomplices as taking the victim's lower lip so that he could speak to people with more authority and another as taking the victim's tongue to make him more eloquent.[20] There may well be some truth in these assertions, but we have not been able to find any correlation between the purpose for which the murder was committed and the type of *liretlo* taken.

For many murderers it was important that the *liretlo* should be taken before the victim was dead, and in several cases this was made explicit. As the accomplices held old Meriama Khokhoma at the end of a bridle-rein, the doctor, Phoka Shea, told them not to pull 'too tightly as they wanted to cut the flesh before she died' (1942/1). In another case directed by the same doctor he made it clear, according to one accomplice, that 'the intention was to cut a flesh while [the victim] was still alive' (1944/4). In a Mokhotlong case in 1945 the murderers were told to 'cut off the required portions because the man is now dying', and one of them told the court: 'It was not mentioned that he should be cut before he died but I have always heard that a man should be cut before he dies' (1945/8). This was the most common practice. There is even a Sesotho proverb, 'A person is cut while still alive', meaning 'One is useful to others while alive'.[21] Yet there were several cases in which no attempt was made to mutilate before murdering. In the first case recorded (1895/1), the conspirators killed their victim and took his body to the doctor, saying, 'Here is the game we have killed for you', and the doctor then cut the parts that he wanted. In another case a doctor and his assistant strangled their victim to death and then took her body on a donkey to a cave, where they kept it hidden for two days. Then they went back and the doctor cut the parts that he needed, put them on a stick and took them home (1931/1). There were many other cases in which the victim died while being mutilated, but the cutting went on regardless (for example, 1947/8). Not once, as far as we know, did the murderers observe that the victim had died and then stop for this reason. They noticed that the victim was still alive – that he (or she) was still breathing, that he groaned when being cut, that he was still kicking or moving his legs, that his eyes were wide open or fluttering, that his pulse was still beating. But the only case in which they hurried up their 'work' was the Mokhotlong case that we have quoted above. Some victims died very quickly. Others went on living for hours. The stock-thief Mahlomola had his mouth prised open and his tongue cut out and was then completely scalped. He was placed on a donkey, taken to a nearby village, and after he had been lifted down more flesh was cut from his buttocks. It was only then that he finally expired (1950/2).

A wide variety of instruments was used. Pen-knives were deployed to cut out eyes and ears, table-knives to hack out flesh or to sever heads, axes to split open skulls. Sticks were inserted through the anus and twisted to pull out bowels. Where blood was needed it was sometimes collected from wounds that had been made by knobkerries and other weapons when the victim had been overcome. Sometimes small punctures were made with umbrella stays, sailmakers' needles or pieces of sharp wire. In one case a thin spear was allegedly pushed hard up the victim's nostril and twisted, the sort of spear that was used for hunting rats (1954/4). The scalpels used by the government dispenser in the first Bereng and Gabashane case (1946/2) were atypical. The flesh was usually collected in bags, tins or billy-cans, the blood in basins, billy-cans, brandy bottles or vaseline bottles. The victims were often referred to as elands or other forms of game. It probably helped the murderers to dehumanise them in this way. When describing how he had stabbed one victim, his own uncle, an accomplice said that he had struck him behind the shoulder: 'it is a well-known spot to stab oxen', he explained (1951/9).

In some cases the mutilations were inflicted by one person alone, typically the instigator, a trusted councillor or the doctor. Taoana Makhabane, for example, cut his own mother (1952/4). But usually several of the accomplices were involved – nearly always men and rarely women – and in several cases we have accounts of the knife being passed around from one man to another. No doubt part of the reason for this was to implicate and enmesh them still more tightly in the murder so that they would be less likely to give information to the police. In one case (1963/1) all the women who were present were ordered to drink the victim's blood 'so as to keep their mouths shut'. The conspirators do not seem to have cut in any particular order, except that it was normal for the instigator to go first and the accomplices to follow. This, according to one accomplice witness, was a question of seniority: 'By your cutting first and then calling upon the others in turn, by custom shows the seniority by birth of a person' (1948/15). Similar arrangements apply in the placing of soil on the grave at funerals.

In a few cases where a woman was the victim the murderers had sexual intercourse with her before mutilating and murdering her. They even raped 'Mamohapi Mofo in this way, though she was ninety years old and blind (1948/18), but when a child was the victim they merely went through the motions (1944/7). Mojalefa Mapola had sex with 'Matlhoriso Malapa before taking the knife and cutting her, and he gave the explanation which probably lay behind all these cases: in this way, he told his accomplices, he would 'strengthen his medicine' (1954/3).

Where there were women accomplices they were generally given those tasks which were closest to their normal domestic duties. They were sometimes told to hold the bottles and billy-cans in which the blood was collected, and in one case they were told to wash and cook the *liretlo* as they were passed through to them in the kitchen (1953/1). But the responsibility most often assigned to them was to heat up water and wash the wounds, or to heat up flat irons or stones and cauterise them, in order to staunch the flow of blood. They were also told to clean up the place afterwards, to the extent in two cases of completely re-smearing the floor or the walls of the hut in which the murder was carried out (1955/1, 1962/2). There were moments of bizarre delicacy. When Mokhoele Leuta wanted to draw blood from 'Mapaki Naha's thighs he asked his female accomplices to take off her petticoat and to replace it after the blood had been taken (1956/4).

Most instigators and accomplices seem to have set about their task with a ruthless, cold-blooded efficiency. They were not motivated by hatred or hostility. They were not torturing their victims to punish them or make them talk. They were not sadists taking pleasure in the pain they inflicted – many victims were drugged or unconscious. But they were grimly deter-mined to get certain parts of their bodies, and to achieve this they inflicted appalling pain without, it seems, any hesitation, doubt or flickering of conscience. According to one witness, headman Nkemi Khoarai took an hour to cut out the private parts of his victim, and there was complete silence while he did so (1944/4). In another case, as fifty to sixty people looked on, Makotoko Mosalla took his knife and addressed his victim: 'Mofolo, may God receive your soul'. And then he began to cut (1958/1).

Some were sickened and terrified by what they saw. Several women could not bear to look but covered their faces or turned away (1942/4, 1947/13, 1951/2, 1954/3, 1962/2). 'Maletsema Mohapi, who was present when her brother was killed, was 'upset', 'screaming', and 'very afraid'. She tried to run out of the hut but was brought back and threatened with being killed herself (1947/13). Pheello Smith had involved his wife as an accomplice, but when she began crying she was warned to stop or else she too would be murdered (1952/6). Several men were equally affected. Mapeshoane Masupha, in the first Bereng and Gabashane case, was 'afraid and horrified at what was being done', but when he went outside he was ordered to go back in (1946/2). In another case an accomplice ran away but was caught, dragged back and forced to drink the victim's blood (1951/5). Others managed to get away. Two accomplices, who were supporting the victim while he was being cut, were so terrified and distressed that they fled (1944/1). In another case a doctor who had been pressed into service pretended that he had to fetch some medicines from his saddlebags, but when he got outside the house he mounted his horse and rode away (1950/4). Several witnesses confessed to being badly frightened, and there must have been many others who were deeply shaken by what they saw, but who, since they never confessed to the murder, did not give evidence about how they felt.

DISPOSING OF THE BODY

After the mutilations and the murder the body had to be disposed of. This was another critical and dangerous operation, and again it was important for the murderers to get it right and not to be observed. The plans for disposal were usually made beforehand, but in a surprising number of cases we find the conspirators standing over the mutilated corpse discussing what they should do (for example, 1944/1, 1945/4, 1951/9 and 1959/1). Ashton noted that, before being finally disposed of, the body was 'usually kept hidden for some time in a hut or cave or in the woods', and he speculated that 'a possible reason for this is that it may be necessary for the medicine to be prepared before the murder is discovered, lest its strength be impaired, and this delay gives the doctor time to do so'.[22]

In fact this was not the 'usual' practice: it was followed in fewer than a quarter of the cases on which we have relevant information (thirty-one out of 127). There is also no evidence in the court records to support Ashton's speculations about the reasons which lay behind it. The most probable explanation is that the murderers needed some respite before undertaking another major operation. By the time they had waylaid, mutilated and killed their victim they were exhausted emotionally, if not physically. They had often reached the early hours of the morning, and in several cases there was not time to dispose of the body as they wanted. It was therefore hidden until they could return, often on the following night, in order finally to get rid of it. In one case (1951/9) the accomplices hid the body close to the path, and their chief ordered them to go back and move it elsewhere. According to one of them, they left it in the first place 'because it was near morning'. In a similar case (1944/7) the murderers were planning to leave the body on the side of a mountain, but they knew they would not reach the place before dawn and so hid it for the night in a reed-bed. Sometimes murderers took the opportunity to cut out more *liretlo*.

The murderers no doubt had their reasons for this procedure, but it was fraught with danger. In at least six cases the body was seen by other people before it was finally disposed of. 'Mahali's body was kept in a stable, where it was seen by one of her children (1937/2); Petrose Makhele's body was hidden in the chief's hut, which was supposed to have been locked but was not, and a woman who went in to fetch some beer caught sight of it under the bed (1943/3). In one case the murderers hid the body in a hole in the ground, intending to go back the next day and to take it elsewhere. But when they returned the body had disappeared. Perhaps some opportunist had taken it in order to get *liretlo* for himself (1950/6).

The commonest way of disposing of the body was, as Ashton says, to leave it

> on an open hillside where death might be attributed to exposure, under a cliff or high bank over which the victim might be supposed to have fallen or in a river bed where the deceased might have drowned. Although this ruse is transparent enough in many cases, it has succeeded sufficiently often to be worth while, and it also gives the local chief or headman a reasonable excuse for attributing death to natural causes and having the body buried without delay.[23]

In 127 out of the 137 cases on which we have relevant information the body was left below cliffs (sixty-four), in a river, stream or donga (thirty-nine), or in a field or forest or on a mountainside (twenty-four). In one of these cases (1962/3) the body was buried but was dug up three months later and exposed. In three of the remaining ten cases the body was hidden in a cave; in four it was found in a hut; in two it was placed near a kraal for goats or pigs so that it would appear that the victim had been killed by thieves; and in one (1948/8) it was lightly covered with soil, but in such a way that it was sure to be discovered.

As well as the simulation of an accident, however, Ashton gave another reason for the practice of leaving the body out in the open:

> such public exposure of the body is said to be necessary to test the strength of the medicine and prove, through the non-detection of the crime, that it will be satisfactory and also to infuse it with additional power.

The fullest statement of this belief, linked with the belief that the body should be hidden for some time, was given in the newspaper *Mochochonono* in 1946. The corpse was left in a place where it would be found, and, just as people then gathered round it, so they would gather round the person who had used it and make him appear important.[24] Jones suggested that leaving the body exposed might be an attempt to simulate the older pattern and 'to treat the victim as an enemy warrior to be left on the field of battle'.[25]

The case in which this consideration was made most explicit was 1944/1 (and it was probably the evidence in this case which formed the basis for the article in *Mochochonono*). One of the instigators suggested that the victim's body should be buried, but the other refused on the ground that 'a warrior should not be buried but should be thrown away'. In the same case it was suggested that the reason for exposing the body would be to attract public attention, and 'as people are attracted and drawn to the body, so they will be drawn to and follow the person for whom the medicine has been made'. In another case the victim's body was dumped in a stream, but since it could not be seen from the nearby path the alleged instigator, a doctor, was said to have given orders that her skirts should be 'placed in the path as a clue', and the 'blankets were also left on the bank of the stream as a clue'. 'He said that that was how he worked' (1943/4). Chieftainess 'Mamakhabane told her accomplices to take the body to Setene's house, 'where it will remain until Tuesday, when those of you who live near will take it to a place where people will see it' (1948/1, Case Study 2).

For some murderers, however, it does not seem to have been a matter of any importance that the body should be exposed. In one case (1948/24) the chief is said to have suggested that the body should be buried, and the only reason given for rejecting this was that burial would take too long and so the body was dumped in a river instead. In another case (1959/2) a child's body was exposed only because the ground was too hard to dig a grave. Nor, it seems, was it always important that the body should be discovered. In many cases, as we shall see in the following chapter, it was found within a few days of the murder, but in others it was not found for months or even years, and there are several accounts of murderers 'helping' in the search for the victim and deliberately leading everyone else astray. We know of seven cases in which the body was never found. There must also have been many other victims whose bodies were not found and who were presumed not to have been killed, but to have disappeared. Such cases, of course, do not appear in the records. Finally we have to bear in mind that it was quite common for the dead victims of ordinary murders to be left at the foot of cliffs or out in the open.[26]

In short, the exposure and discovery of the body were not matters of fixed belief in every case, but the practice seems general enough to be significant. The need to simulate an accident also accounts for so many murders taking place after beer-drinks, when the victims were likely to be drunk. Even in the lowlands Lesotho is a rocky and dangerous country, full of ravines and sudden drops, and people going home drunk at night were liable to lose their way and to stumble in the open country, fall into a river, or tumble headlong over a cliff. If they were not killed at once they would soon die of exposure, particularly in the bitter cold of a winter's night.

The murderers often made elaborate arrangements to strengthen the impression of an accident. An accomplice wearing the victim's shoes would walk around on top of the cliff and the victim's body would be placed at its foot; the victim's walking stick would be left on top of the plateau while the body was placed below; articles of clothing would be left on bushes halfway down to make it appear that they had caught as the victim fell; bones in the legs and arms would be broken to simulate a fall. These ruses and deceits were not always carried through effectively. In one case (1914/1) it was impossible to reach the point on the cliffs from which the victim was supposed to have tumbled. In another (1947/1) not a single bone was broken in the body found at the foot of the 'Maletsunyane Falls, which are nearly 200 metres high. As Jones pointed out, 'bodies ... with frightful mutilations are exposed where they will be discovered almost immediately before putrefaction and the ravages of dogs and wild animals have destroyed the tell-tale wounds'. Jones believed that in cases like this

> the murderers appear to be conforming more to a set formula than genuinely trying to disguise the killing ... An incident may have happened, people may have seen it happen, but if the official version is that it has not happened, then it has not happened. People may talk about it privately among themselves, but that is off the record. In public there is only one correct version which may be given – the official one.[27]

It is possible that some murderers were not as careful as they might have been because they were confident of intimidating their followers into accepting their own version of what happened. Others were simply incompetent. The headman who made sure that his victim's body was swept away downstream gave himself away by placing his own belt round its waist (1950/2). The man who, according to one accomplice, boiled all the flesh off the bones in order to prevent identification left the victim's clothing and South African pass book, complete with photograph, by the skeleton (1957/10).

In at least seven cases the body was taken, or was alleged to have been taken, to another chief's area in order to divert suspicion from the murderers,[28] and many other precautions were taken. As the conspirators went back to their homes they were sometimes told to disperse so that they should not be seen travelling in a gang.[29] In one case blood-stains on the path were covered with manure (1927/2), and in two others the grass was burnt to remove any traces of blood (1941/1 and 1951/4). Sometimes accomplices were sent back to the scene of the crime to obliterate any tracks that had been left (1947/8, 1953/1). Almost invariably they were warned not to say a word about what they had done.

Many turned to the supposed power of medicine. In at least three cases, according to accomplice evidence, the place of the murder was sprinkled with medicine to prevent the crime ever coming to light (1942/1, 1948/10, 1962/1), and in one case the body of a female sheep, its face mutilated, was later placed at the spot where the victim's body had been found (1941/2). In two cases at least (1944/1 and 1944/5) the victim's body was doctored. The doctor in case 1944/5 shaved the victim's head and smeared his face with black medicine. He said this would ensure that the matter never came to light 'as this was the practice of his horn'. In some cases the murderers themselves were doctored. Otherwise, they were given medicines to make them brave and prevent their speaking about it (1952/11, 1957/3). In one case the young man who had betrayed his friend was so scared afterwards that he went to his own doctor and was given medicine to treat his fear. It evidently worked: 'I drank it', he told the court, 'and my fear departed' (1954/4).

Some turned to their Christianity for help and comfort. According to Stimela Jingoes, Chieftainess 'Mamakhabane was praying while Mocheseloa was being mutilated (1948/1), and headman Keneuoe Khethisa ordered his accomplices to kneel while one of them led prayers to God that their killing of old Monnana Mokoloko should not be discovered (1950/4). The most remarkable case was 1957/3, in which two headmen, Joel Malofo and Mokone Mathabela, instigated the murder of Mpho Mothijoa. After Mpho's death, the judge noted, two women prayed, an Anglican and a member of the Apostolic Church. The hymn 'Peace, perfect Peace' was then sung by all present. This was followed by two of the men performing war dances.[30] With Mpho's mutilated corpse lying on the ground, the blending of Christian and Sesotho beliefs could hardly have been demonstrated more dramatically.

In addition to all these precautions and defences, the murderers sometimes turned to their doctors again (or in some cases for the first time) in order to protect them against police enquiries, to secure their release from gaol, or to secure their acquittal in court proceedings. After several of his people had been taken into police custody Mopeli Mohale anxiously consulted Moleleki Khoanyane and asked for medicine to protect himself. 'I see the police here all the time', he said. 'They do not stop coming here. If you are able to stop it please stop this matter.' Moleleki gave him two medicines – a powder with which he was to wash himself 'so that they could not see him easily', and a stick which he was to chew 'so that they, the police, would go away from him and not come to him' (1952/7). In another case (1952/9) the doctor made elaborate use of an ox-switch, cow-dung, four eggs and some goat's milk, but it was all to no effect: two weeks later his client was arrested.

MAKING THE MEDICINE

The final stage in a medicine murder, the end for which the conspirators had inflicted such cruelty on their victims and run so many dangers themselves, was the preparation of medicine from the *liretlo* and then the use of that medicine. Even when the chief involved had organised the murder himself these tasks were nearly always carried out by a doctor.

There is very little evidence in the court records about the actual preparation of the medicine, but we know from other sources that the *liretlo* were normally burnt down and the ashes mixed with fat to form a black paste, *mohlabelo*. Some doctors prepared their medicine secretly and apart. One doctor told his client, Lekhotla Setoni, that 'he wanted to be alone'. He took the *liretlo*, 'a handful of flesh', into Lekhotla's kitchen hut, his *mokhoro*. 'I noticed some smoke coming out of the *mokhoro*', Lekhotla told the court. 'Later he came out with some medicine mixed in a tin which he handed to me' (1948/15). In another case (1962/3) there was a meeting at the instigator's home on the day after the murder, and after the flesh had been cut from the bones the doctor mixed it with some fatty medicine in an earthenware bowl. Although it was common to talk of a *lenaka*, a medicine horn, the medicine was just as likely to be kept in a tin, a bottle, or a jar for Vicks VapoRub or vaseline.

The two most common applications of this medicine were 'pegging' and scarification. We have several accounts of the medicine being smeared on sticks or pebbles which were then planted or buried around the chief's hut or his village to ward off witchcraft and evil spirits.[31] We also have several accounts of incisions being made on instigators and accomplices and of the medicine being rubbed into these.[32]

If a doctor had been involved in the earlier stages he or she was retained for these final tasks as well. Otherwise a new doctor had to be called in, which was a dangerous thing to do, since the new man or woman might refuse to help and later give evidence as an independent witness. In case 1945/3 (Case Study 1) Bernice Hlalele, 'Ntjahali', did precisely this. In another case (1957/7) a doctor, Makhabane Teisi, gave evidence that Jobere Motsie came to him 'saying that he wanted a medicine horn and had obtained human blood, the blood of Moqebelo'. Makhabane reminded him that Moqebelo was his grandfather, whereupon, it was alleged, Jobere apologised, saying that he had forgotten that, and offering the doctor five head of cattle to pardon him.

Until this point, in Chapters 6 and 7, we have considered medicine murders largely from the standpoint of the murderers themselves: who they were and why they embarked on such a hazardous undertaking; how they chose their victims and devised their plots; how they inflicted their mutilations and what steps they took to cover their tracks. Their task is complete. The murder has been committed and the body disposed of. Now the forces of law and order move in. In Chapters 8 and 9 we follow their response, from the disappearance of the victim through the police investigations and the court proceedings, either to the acquittal of the persons accused or to their being hanged at dawn in the Maseru gaol.

8

POLICE INVESTIGATIONS

During British rule murder was regarded as something very important. The British followed it up. But not any more. I was a policeman for thirty years and seven months. Comparing British rule with the government now, people aren't serious about their work.

PS interview, Mokhoele Mahao, former policeman,
1 June 1999

SEARCHING FOR THE BODY

If they were not in on the conspiracy themselves – and most of them were not – the victim's relatives first realised that something was wrong when he or she disappeared; a wife had gone off to a feast and not come back; a husband had not returned from a visit to a nearby village; a child had gone out to play and nothing had been seen of her since. Action had to be taken quickly. If the missing person was lying unconscious in the open country they would soon die of exposure, especially in the winter.

If the obvious and immediate enquiries failed, the next step was to raise the alarm at the chief's court, and it was the duty of the chief or his representative to send out a search party at once. In most cases this was done even when the chief himself was the murderer, and several of the accomplices might help in the search. But sometimes no action was taken. 'How can a drunkard be searched for?', the court chairman asked in one case (1951/7). In another the chief, one of the murderers, refused to help, arguing that the woman who had disappeared should never have come to live in his village (1954/3). One chief did nothing even though the victim's sister reported three times that her brother was missing (1952/9).

Some murderers deliberately misled the searchers. The most heartless was Molefi Senyotong, who had arranged for his own stepson, a young herdboy called Jakalasi, to be killed. When Jakalasi did not return home Molefi told his mother that he had gone to see his grandmother, and later he told her that he had seen him in Natal. Led on by Molefi, and by Chieftainess Lerato, who had allegedly instigated the murder, the distraught mother searched far and wide, even going to Natal herself. Search parties were eventually sent out in which several of the accomplices took part, but the body was not found until three months later (1948/8). In another case

(1948/15) the victim's husband, who had known about the killing, went through the pretence of consulting a diviner about his wife's disappearance and paying him £4 to throw his bones.

Occasionally the accomplices gave themselves away by revealing that they knew more than they should have done about the fate of the person who had disappeared or the whereabouts of the body. An employee at the printing works in Morija, the headquarters of the PEMS, who was alleged to have taken part in case 1927/2, actually upbraided the victim's mother, telling her that he might be dead and that she ought to search for him, especially as she was a member of the Mothers' Union. He then suggested that she should look in a certain direction where in fact the body was later found. In another case (1952/11) the chairman of the chief's court told the victim's relatives that they would find the body in a cave. Nevertheless most searches were organised and carried out in the normal way. In forty-one of the 108 cases (38 per cent) on which we have relevant information the body was found within one or two days, and (including these) in seventy-one (66 per cent) it was found within a week. In thirty cases (28 per cent) it was found after a week, usually by chance after the search had been abandoned, sometimes as long as several years afterwards. In seven cases (6 per cent) it was not found at all.

The sooner the body was found, the less likely it was that the wounds would have been obscured by putrefaction and the attentions of natural predators, and we might have expected that because of this it would have been easier to bring court proceedings and to obtain convictions. In fact this was only marginally so. Of the seventy-one cases where the body was found within a week, fifty-eight cases (82 per cent) went to court and thirty-eight (54 per cent) resulted in convictions. Of the thirty cases where the body was found after a week twenty-three (77 per cent) went to court and fourteen (47 per cent) resulted in convictions. Three of the seven cases where the body was not found at all went to court, and all three resulted in convictions.

As soon as the body was discovered, it was in the interests of the murderers to argue, if possible, that the deceased had met with an accident and to get the body buried at once. The chief of the area where the body was found could authorise the burial himself, though he usually reported to his senior chief, who in turn might report to the government, and they had to consult the victim's family.

In the earlier years, in the period of laissez-faire, there must have been many cases in which the body was buried and where, though murder was perhaps suspected, no formal allegation was made. According to Rivers Thompson, a District Officer:

> Of course it was kept quiet. The chiefs didn't report these things. Well they did, they'd say So-and-So fell over a krantz. We'd say, well bury him, why not? We didn't know it was a ritual murder.[1]

Paul Kitson, who was appointed as an Assistant Superintendent of Police in 1937, gave a similar account, and linked it with the practice of having to work through the chiefs:

> Before, when a body was found, the chief would send in a messenger. A junior policeman would then have to go out ... to the Principal Chief's, and the Principal Chief would give him a messenger. Then they would go to the scene of the crime, where they would have to report to the sub-chief or headman ... You had a very junior policeman with very senior messengers. Frequently he would arrive at the scene of the crime and the messenger would say that the person fell over a cliff while drunk. The young policeman would come back and report accordingly. I can remember occasions when a policeman would come back and say, 'Morena [Chief], we went with the chief and looked at the body. It was mutilated, but it was at the edge of a river and the mutilations were due to crabs'. The headman didn't report any suspicions and the policeman had no suspicions, and so that was how it ended.[2]

In the period up to the end of 1947, in at least thirteen out of the fifty-six cases that eventually came to light, and on which we have relevant information, the body had been buried and had to be exhumed. In November 1947, however, 'Mantšebo was prevailed upon to issue a circular ordering, or strengthening a previous order,[3] that if there was any doubt about the cause of death the body should not be moved and the police should be called in.[4] After this we know of only six cases (out of more than 100) in which the body was buried in advance of police investigation. This sharp decline in the number of burials was not due entirely to 'Mantšebo's circular – there was a greater awareness of medicine murder later – but in some cases it seems to have strengthened the victim's family in its resolve that the murder should be exposed and not concealed. Two cases, one before and one after the circular, best illustrate the change in local attitudes to burial without investigation.

On Boxing Day 1943 the mutilated body of old Sekoati Mpheto was discovered at the foot of a low cliff. Two of the men who examined the body said that it looked as if Sekoati had been struck by a battle-axe, but they told the court later that headman Moramang Letsie had said,

> 'No. You people should not mention things ... because if you do there might be suspicion'. He said 'if we go on talking about this body it will be said we should carry it to the Camp [i.e. report it to the district headquarters]' ... It was said we should say that deceased fell over a cliff.[5]

In the absence of any male relatives the body was buried (1943/5).

By 1952 the Paramount Chief's circular had been issued and was well known. So when Liphapang Mpikinyane's body was found at the bottom of a cliff, one of the men present insisted that no one should touch it: 'we had been given orders that bodies found in a mysterious way should not be touched. They are the Paramount Chief's and the Government's'. The body was guarded all night, but before it was taken to the district headquarters, one of the alleged accomplices told the dead man's cousin that 'she should allow the deceased to be buried'. She bluntly refused. Within a few days a post-mortem was held and a few months later the conspirators were arrested – though they were acquitted in the subsequent trial (1952/9).

THE POST-MORTEM EXAMINATION

As soon as a medicine murder was suspected, the local chief had a duty to report to the government, either to the district headquarters (the Camp) or to the nearest police station. If the body had been found, or if it had to be exhumed, a post-mortem examination had to be arranged as soon as possible. Post-mortems were usually carried out by government doctors, but a mission doctor might be called upon if the murder took place close to a mission station. The body was usually taken to the district headquarters, but in some cases it was examined on the spot. Paul Kitson, then a police superintendent, remembers going out in the early 1950s with an inexperienced young locum doctor.

> He had never been on a horse before. We had to go out and do a report on a body in a remote village beyond Marakabei. It was a four-hour ride from Marakabei. We arrived in the evening, about 5 pm, and we had to summon men to exhume the body. The doctor then carried out the post-mortem. I sat next to him with *sehalahala* [a strong-smelling plant] stuffed up my nose, writing down his notes. He punctured his finger on a sharp bone, and his dispenser, who had come with us, had not brought any disinfectant. He was terribly worried about septicaemia. I had brought a bottle of brandy with me, and we poured that over his finger. Anyhow, no harm was done ...[6]

Decomposition set in very quickly. Wounds immediately attracted flies, and within a few days a body could be swarming with maggots. Natural predators could move in at once – dogs and birds in the open veld, fish and crabs in the water. In several cases it was impossible to establish the cause of death because the body was so putrefied, or had been eaten by predators, or because so many parts had been removed at the time of the mutilation.[7] Usually, however, the doctor could identify the cause of death as haemorrhage or shock brought about by the injuries which he found on the body, or, less often, as a blow to the base of the skull, drowning or exposure. When, as was usual, he found such injuries, he had to say, if he could, what had caused them. This evidence would be of crucial importance in any subsequent trial. Judges were reluctant to rely on accomplice evidence alone, and if the doctor confirmed that the victim had been murdered, this would be vital corroboration.

If the body had been discovered at the foot of a cliff, the doctor needed to report whether death could have been caused by a fall. In a few cases he reported that it could, such as 1954/6, in which the evidence of 'a shattered skull, ruptured heart, broken arm and four fractured ribs' was held to be 'not irreconcilable with death from falling over a cliff'.[8] In rather more cases the doctor ruled out a fall. We have already noted the case in which a body was found at the foot of the 'Maletsunyane Falls without a single broken bone (1947/1), and there was a similar case in the Leribe District ten years later (1957/1). In one case (1952/6) death could not have been caused by a fall because of the absence of blood and bruises.

Similarly, if the body had been discovered in a stream, the doctor had to report if death was due to drowning. In one case (1953/2) he could assure the court that the victim had not drowned because of the absence of froth in the lungs.[9] Drowning, however, did not necessarily mean that the victim had not been murdered. 'Meleke Ntai, Bereng and Gabashane's victim, drowned after being dumped in a pool of water while still alive (1948/6, Case Study 3).[10]

In at least three cases (1951/2, 1952/10 and 1953/3) the doctor was able to say that, because of the clean edges of the cuts, they must have been caused by a sharp instrument and could not have been inflicted by predators. On the other hand, the doctor who examined 'Meleke Ntai found it impossible to say whether his lips had been cut away by a knife or nibbled away by crabs (1948/6). In another case (1953/1), although the body was infested by maggots, the doctor was able to suggest that a wound had been inflicted on the chest. 'Flies', he explained, 'do not lay their eggs on unbroken, unputrefied skin.' It was 'quite usual to find maggots in a body which has been lying for a week around the eyes, lips, nostrils, mouth and private parts as these parts usually have small invisible injuries'. But he was 'surprised to find so many maggots in the chest'. The post-mortem examination could throw up other information as well. For example, the absence of blood in the heart and the larger vessels might indicate that the wounds were inflicted before death, which would again argue against death by falling or drowning (1948/6).

As well as establishing, where possible, whether or not the victim had been murdered, the greatest evidential value of the post-mortem report lay in whether or not it was consistent with other details in the accounts given by the accomplice witnesses. If, for example, these witnesses testified that certain parts had been removed, did the report indicate that these parts were missing? In most cases the report was consistent with the witnesses' evidence, but sometimes there were significant, even startling, differences. In one case the witnesses said that a hole had been made in the victim's skull with a hammer and chisel, but the post-mortem revealed that the skull was intact (1954/1).[11]

Most post-mortem examinations were carried out quickly and efficiently, but in one case (1944/6) the judge complained about the delay; in another (1953/4) the body had to be exhumed and examined again, when further wounds were found; and in another (1957/3), because the victim was in such poor health, the doctor jumped to the conclusion that death was due to cerebral oedema with chronic tuberculosis as a contributing factor, and completely overlooked a wound in the armpit.

POLICE ENQUIRIES

While the arrangements were being made to conduct the post-mortem, one or two police officers, usually Basotho and sometimes accompanied by a white officer, would be sent to start making their enquiries. By the time they arrived in a village the whole community would be buzzing with talk about the murder. If the conspirators had been able to escape notice and keep silent, this talk would amount to nothing more than rumour and speculation. Often, however, there was much more to it than that. There might be people who had noticed the victim in the company of some of the murderers, or who had seen the body before it was disposed of. There might even be people who had witnessed the murder. In spite of their fears and anxieties these people could have told their relatives and friends what they had seen, and so the news would have spread. A graphic example of the rapid spread of such gossip, in this case through school children, is given in our account of the murder of Mocheseloa Khotso (1948/1, Case Study 2).

Just as important, the murderers themselves did not always keep silent. In spite of all the threats and injunctions not to say anything, there was an astonishing amount of loose talk, in some cases even before the murder was committed. In one case (1947/13) the judge concluded: 'There can be little doubt but that everyone in the village knew exactly what was going to happen to deceased days before'. In another case (1945/11) a man who was not one of the conspirators, but who evidently knew that a murder was being planned, warned his friend at a feast not to go home that night because there was 'a muddle-up ahead'. 'I did not ask what he meant', the friend said. 'I was frightened of what I heard.' In case 1944/7, according to the District Commissioner of Mokhotlong, everyone knew that Mahlomola Lerotholi was about to commit a murder: the District Commissioner's clerk even told him not to do it.[12] There were countless rumours and reports about intended murders, and in some cases the District Commissioners held warning *pitso*s in order to forestall the crime.[13]

After the killing many murderers were deeply troubled – troubled in their consciences about what they had done, and troubled in their minds at the prospect of being caught and hanged. To ease their tension many of them must have confided in their relatives and friends, who in turn might well have confided in others. Some seem to have blurted out their secret almost indiscriminately. Shortly after one murder the instigator, a doctor, met a distant relative, who was also the victim's grand-daughter, as she went to hoe in the lands. 'He said to me "I ask my God to forgive me. I have already done a terrible thing." I asked "What have you done?" He replied "I will tell you one day". Then he passed me.'[14]

Another murderer, a woman, told two men, one of them a distant relative who knew her well, that a person had been murdered at her home at Thotapeli. 'I do not think [she] was drunk', one of the men said, 'but she appeared to be very frightened' (1957/6). One murderer even boasted of what he had done. Shortly after the murder (1956/4), and before the body was found, Mokhoele Leuta met two women as they were coming home from the lands. 'He laughed', one of them testified later.

> He said that a team of oxen had gone apart. He said we would never see deceased 'Mapaki, and that deceased was on the slope of the mountains in the shrubs. We did not know at that time that deceased was dead ... On the Saturday we heard that the body of deceased had been found at the place stated by [Mokhoele].[15]

Another man, on the very night of a murder, went back and slept with his lover, the victim's wife, and in response to her anxious enquiries coolly assured her that her husband would not be coming home that night (1957/2). Others were simply careless, like the man who casually commented that the beer he was drinking was 'tasteful, like the beer we had before we killed the deceased' (1956/2). One woman gave the game away when, after the police had searched her house, she complained to the village head that she had not committed the murder, but named another accomplice (1956/4).

The very precautions taken by the murderers sometimes had the effect of spreading information still further. Some consulted doctors, either to remove their fear or to protect them against arrest, and these doctors might then have told others what they themselves had been told. Others tried to build up their alibis by asking others to give evidence on their behalf.[16] A headman is said to have instructed one of his councillors 'to tell all his subjects not to disclose this matter' (1952/9). In another case a woman told two of her friends that she had been threatened with death if she did not keep quiet (1957/2).

So in some cases many people in the village might suspect, or believe with good reason, or even know with certainty who the murderers were. Occasionally, but only very occasionally, a witness, perhaps even an accomplice, might come forward of his own volition and tell the police what he knew, but more often the investigating officers were met with what was commonly described as 'a wall of silence'. One reason, no doubt, was loyalty to the chief, but it was fear above all that closed people's mouths. Time and again in court proceedings accomplice and independent witnesses alike testified that they had been threatened with death if they spoke out of turn.[17] Nor was this threat to be disregarded. Several witnesses who went forward were killed or disappeared,[18] and there must have been many others whose lives were made wretched afterwards. Our case studies above, and the 'Aftermath' below, throw up several examples of accomplice witnesses who were unable to go back to their own villages after they had given evidence.

It was the job of the police to break down this wall of silence. Their methods varied over time. We have already noted that before 1947 they could carry out their investigations only with the co-operation of the chiefs, but that in November of that year 'Mantšebo was persuaded to allow them to operate more independently; that while this might possibly have added to their effectiveness, it embittered their relationship with the chiefs; and that because of this Resident Commissioner Arrowsmith, with 'Mantšebo's co-operation, set up a two-man Administrative Team to be present when statements were taken from accomplices.[19] Later it became common practice for the Paramount Chief (or a local chief, or both) to appoint a representative who would be present when arrests were made and statements taken. 'We have had a Chief's representative present', Paul Kitson said in 1956, 'at almost all recent medicine murder investigations.'[20] After the meeting held under Government Secretary Hector's chairmanship in August 1956 this procedure was made more formal, and in each district a panel of six persons was eventually established – three recommended by local chiefs to the Paramount Chief and three chosen by the District Council, with her approval, from which representatives were drawn to accompany the police during their investigations. Although there were criticisms of the way this system operated, these representatives sometimes appeared in court to give evidence that the police had conducted themselves properly.[21]

The second main change in procedures, touched on already in Chapter 3, concerned the detention of suspects and witnesses. Before 1949 the police would go to the village, make some preliminary enquiries, and then bring in the main suspects and potential witnesses to the district headquarters for interrogation. In many cases they kept them in custody for weeks or even months before charging them. This was unlawful, and the police knew it was unlawful. Under section 33(1) of the Criminal Procedure and Evidence Proclamation a person arrested without a warrant could be detained for only forty-eight hours, and they could be held for a longer period only if a warrant was obtained from a judicial officer (a term which included a District Officer and an Assistant District Officer). Under section 34(1), however, a suspect could be detained for longer than forty-eight hours only if the police had reasonable grounds of suspicion against him based on information taken on oath and if on this basis they had been able to persuade a judicial officer to issue a warrant of arrest. In practice, the police often ignored these provisions, and suspects were detained for long periods before being brought before a judicial officer on a charge.

When challenged on this in 1949 the Commissioner of Police, Lieutenant-Colonel A. F. Apthorp, explained that at the outset of an investigation it was not known whether people were suspects or witnesses: 'this information is gained after interrogating and checking which can last weeks'. The investigation could not take place where the murder had been committed, mainly because 'the persons concerned are under strong tribal influence of the Chief, Sub-Chief or Headman of the area, who in cases of Ritual Murder are almost invariably involved'. It was essential to remove them from the powerful constraints and pressures of their own community, and it was because of this that they were held in detention for so long. Also, he said, to conduct investigations on the spot would be too demanding on the police's limited resources.[22]

All this came to light when the Lekhotla la Bafo, with support from Michael Scott, challenged the procedures that had been used in the cases against 'Mamakhabane and Bereng and Gabashane. Resident Commissioner Forsyth-Thompson endorsed Apthorp's position, and suggested that the law should be changed to allow the practice to continue, especially since, in cases of medicine murder, chiefs' messengers could not be regarded as reliable. But Sir Evelyn Baring, the High Commissioner, recognised that the practice was indefensible, especially now that 'the spotlight has been turned on it', and told Forsyth-Thompson that he had to 'ensure that detention beyond the period permitted by law does not occur'. 'If we kept to the law', Forsyth-Thompson replied, 'I am afraid investigation of ritual murder would be brought almost to a standstill.'[23] He and Apthorp flew to Cape Town to try to persuade Baring to change his mind, but Baring told them that the Secretary of State would never agree to the grant of additional powers. The only course was to admit that they had done wrong and to promise to keep within the law in future, whatever the difficulties.[24] In the event Forsyth-Thompson's dire warnings were not borne out, and in terms of the number of cases brought to trial, and the proportion of those cases resulting in conviction, police operations were more successful in the early 1950s than they had been in the late 1940s.[25]

Later, when Colonel Paul Kitson became Deputy Commissioner of Police in the mid-1950s, a further change was introduced.

> If a medicine murder was committed in a remote village we set up an
> incident post, just a couple of tents or so, and the police investigating

went and lived there. So they were in constant contact with the local people and in that way they got far more information. That was more effective than bringing people in for questioning.[26]

There were other complaints against the police. Even after they had been charged, the accused were liable to be held for very long periods, and there appears to have been no improvement in this. The average interval between arrest and the preparatory examination was roughly three and a half months, and this remained constant throughout the 1940s and 1950s. Then there were often long delays between the preparatory examination and the High Court trial. In some cases it was more than a year before the accused finally appeared in the dock. This was not unlawful, but it was undesirable.

Witnesses, as well as the accused, were also detained for long periods, but in these cases the police were on stronger ground. After they had made their confessions and given their statements many witnesses were afraid to return home and asked instead for police protection. They were not imprisoned, but they stayed at the police barracks where they were given food and accommodation.[27] This inevitably raised the suspicion that they were being trained in what they should say. Most judges recognised, in the words of the Appeal Court in 1960, that 'to leave potential witnesses in the areas controlled by their chiefs and headmen might often render it virtually impossible for the Police to secure evidence in any case in which a Chief or headman was involved'.[28] But a few years later a High Court judge, Mr Justice Johnson, condemned the practice: there were 'no understandable reasons' for it, he said, and because in the case before him the witnesses might have been taught what to say, he gave the accused the benefit of the doubt (1965/5).

Regardless of the procedures used, there were some suspects who were more likely than others to give way to the various pressures being brought to bear on them – women were more likely than men,[29] younger people were more likely than old.[30] Those who were friends or relatives of the victim were more susceptible than those who were closely connected with the instigator, whether as friends, relatives, advisers or employees.[31] It is not clear whether the police were aware of this and brought pressure to bear accordingly. It is more likely that they relied on their instincts, sensing signs of weakness.

THE POLICE AGAINST THE CHIEFS?

The accusations about lengthy detention were merely part of the wider case against the police which we have already outlined in Case Studies 2 and 3. Whether it was articulated by the chiefs in the Basutoland National Council, by the Lekhotla la Bafo in its petitions to London and the United Nations, or by Ntsu Mokhehle in his articles in *Mohlabani*, the essential charge against the police was that they were engaged in a witch-hunt against the chiefs. If it was pointed out that the police responsible were themselves Basotho, it was replied that they were acting at the bidding of their British political masters or their South African senior officers; or that they had become dupes of an imperial lie; or that they were bent on gaining promotion.

As soon as a murder was reported, it was said, the investigating officers made up their mind that a chief was responsible, and they then detained people for weeks and even months, hammering away at them, threatening and cajoling them, trying to get them to incriminate the chief. There were also allegations of ill-treatment and torture. One man was alleged to have been handcuffed behind his back for three days, another was said to have been kicked about, and some were said to have been grabbed by their testicles.[32] More often there were complaints about conditions generally, about the cold and the alleged shortage of food.

In a typical statement Moloi Ntai, an accomplice in the Bereng and Gabashane case, whose particular complaints were outlined in Case Study 3, said that the police told him 'it was well known that I had not been acting on my own initiative but on the chief's [Gabashane's] instructions'. They suggested

> that I should say that the chief offered me money to kill the deceased. For four and a half months the police hammered this into me. By hammering I mean that repeated suggestions were made. I was also told that if I accepted this suggestion I should not be charged with murder. My feet suffered from the cold which was in the cell. I had only one blanket. I was also mentally tortured by being told that the chief had confiscated my lands and my cattle and ... that my wife had been assaulted with sticks and had many injuries and was in hospital but that I could not go and see her there.[33]

Drawing on evidence such as this Josiel Lefela was characteristically outspoken when, in September 1949, he told the Basutoland National Council:

> The Police do not make them cram the evidence into their brain, but they starve them, they expose them to cold, they torture them, all sorts of things. They do not even give them pails wherein to pass water, they have not even got buckets in their latrines, they starve for many days. And if they find that one of them passes water in a cell, he is kicked about, he is slapped in the face, and so on. And then those who persist in denying any knowledge are passed on to the other side and charged with the others.[34]

In articles in *Mohlabani* Ntsu Mokhehle quoted the statements of two women who were allegedly put under pressure to incriminate Chief Abisalome [Absalom] in 1949. One said:

> I was then asked to say that Abisalome had done it ... Sergeant
> 'Mannini said that ... he knows that Tsietsi was killed at Masaleng. He
> said it was at the time the Paramount Chief was passing through the
> Camp, scolding. Even then I denied ... They said they would send me
> to Maseru to be hanged ... I used to be locked in a room ...

The other woman alleged that she 'was once shown a picture of hell, and
told that I would go there if I did not say that Abisalome had killed this
person'.[35]

In the Basutoland National Council several chiefs recounted how the
police had tried to engineer accusations against them.[36] In some cases the
person who was supposed to have been killed was later found to be alive.
The most notorious example of this involved 'Mantšebo herself. We have
referred to this case briefly already, but more detail is appropriate here.
'Mantšebo had taken a man called Borane from Thabang, Matlere
Lerotholi's village in Mokhotlong, to Matsieng, where she employed him
as a herdboy. Towards the end of 1947 he disappeared from Matsieng, but
no report was made to the police. In August 1948 a headman in
Mokhotlong reported that Borane had disappeared, and there was a
suggestion that he had been killed. Enquiries were made at Matsieng.
'Mantšebo complained that she personally had been 'searched disgrace-
fully by the police ...' Her 'children', she said, had been arrested and asked
what she had done with a certain man called Borane, and they had been
advised 'that they should not sacrifice their lives for my sake, that they
should become crown witnesses and avoid death'.[37] According to the
police, they were careful to avoid any suggestion that 'Mantšebo was
responsible for Borane's disappearance. At that time, however, Bereng and
Gabashane were awaiting trial, and there were rumours that 'Mantšebo
was 'searching for a victim who was to be buried alive to hush up the
evidence' against the chiefs. Matsieng was said to be gripped by fear, and it
was in these highly charged circumstances that 'Mantšebo was asked to
help. On 6 September 1948 her messengers reported to police headquarters with Borane, whom they said they had found in the Mohale's
Hoek District. According to the police,

> He was found to be a complete imbecile, and unable to establish his
> own identity. He was practically incapable of speech, and it was
> impossible to obtain a statement from him. He was in a deplorable
> state physically, with sores on his face and body. It was remarkable
> that the Paramount Chief should have brought a person of this type
> from Mokhotlong for employment at Matsieng.[38]

Another case that was well known and frequently adduced was that against
Chieftainess 'Mamphe and her sons in or around 1947; again the case fell
away when the alleged victim was found alive and well.[39]

Jones did not believe that the police were in fact extorting false evidence against the chiefs, but the view that they were, he wrote,

> is not so unreasonable as it sounds. The majority of the prominent chiefs and headmen prosecuted for this crime were not enemies of society, but highly respectable members of it ... The evidence against them was necessarily mainly that of accomplices ... who had turned King's evidence to save their necks: the defence was a complete denial of having any knowledge of or connection with the crime. Relatives, friends and admirers of such chiefs would naturally find it easier to believe the evidence for the defence, in which case the evidence for the prosecution must be false. But it was equally hard to believe that these Crown witnesses would of their own volition have made up such charges against their chiefs; the only explanation which made sense was that they had been forced to do so, and some of these Crown witnesses, when they got home and were asked to explain why they had betrayed their chief or headman naturally found it easiest to say that they had been forced to do so ...[40]

Jones' account is convincing in part. We can readily believe that accomplices who had given evidence against their chiefs 'found it easiest to say that they had been forced to do so'. But it cannot explain those cases in which the people concerned did *not* give evidence against their chiefs, but said that the police had put pressure on them to do so; this is especially puzzling in cases, like that against 'Mantšebo, in which no accusations were brought.

Moreover, the allegations against the police are consistent, at least to some degree, with Jones' own account of how the police set about their interrogations, and in particular how they tried to break down the 'wall of silence'. 'The problem that faced the police', he wrote,

> was how to get a witness to tell what he knew about a crime when ... it was contrary to his accepted code of behaviour to betray the head of his community and ... it was very much against his own interests to do so. To break down this resistance the Basutoland police ... applied not third degree methods but sound psychological principles. They first detached the witness from his local community and kept him isolated from it; they examined him by himself as an individual, convinced him that the first statements he had given them were false and they knew what had actually happened; at the same time they sought to win his confidence and to convince him that he had more to gain than to lose if he told what he knew about the crime. By the time a witness had been confronted ... with proof of the inaccuracies in his original statement ... and at the same time had become convinced that someone else had already given the police the whole story, he had also begun to feel that the police could protect him if victimised by the

relatives and followers of the people concerned in the murder, and his
resistance gave way and he was prepared to speak without reserve.[41]

Paul Kitson, when asked what methods were used to get suspects to confess,
replied very simply: 'You always try to give suspects the idea that you know
far more than you do. That makes them afraid'.[42]

There are several points to note about this. It was against the interests of
accomplices to confess, partly because they would thereby be admitting that
they themselves were murderers, and partly because they were afraid of
incurring the hostility of their chiefs. By keeping them isolated the police
hoped to reduce their chiefs' influence. By pretending, as Jones said, that
they knew all about the murder, that 'someone else' had already given them
'the whole story', they hoped to induce in the accomplices a terror of being
convicted and hanged – a terror that would outweigh their fear of the chiefs.
If they suspected that a particular chief was responsible for the murder they
would no doubt pretend that they *knew* that he was responsible. This would
be an essential part of 'the whole story'. So they would ask knowing
questions, perhaps over and over again, or they would say, in effect: 'We
know that the chief did it. There's no point in keeping silent, in risking your
own neck to save your chief. If you tell us what you know, if you become a
Crown witness, we'll make sure you don't get hanged'. And this, of course,
was precisely what their critics were alleging. An accomplice who claimed
that he was innocent would say that he was being improperly threatened if
he was told that, if he did not confess, he was running the risk of prosecution
and hanging; and he would say that he was being offered an improper
inducement if he was told that, if he confessed, he would be immune from
prosecution.[43]

Very little of this surfaced in the courts. Most accomplices who had
become Crown witnesses tried to present themselves in the best possible
light. They admitted that at first they had denied all knowledge of the
murder, but then claimed to have been moved by their conscience or by
God to tell the truth.[44] Several, it is true, frankly acknowledged they had
confessed in order to save their own skins, or, more vaguely, because they
realised they would be in trouble if they did not.[45] Some said they saw that
their lies were not doing any good (1943/4, 1945/11). One stated that he
realised that the police knew everything, and so it was pointless keeping
silent (1957/4). Clearly the police had succeeded in persuading these people
that they had sufficient evidence to convict them if they did not confess. But
we have not found any evidence in their statements of any improper action
by the police.

There were some accomplice witnesses, however, who went back in the
preparatory examination on the statements they had given the police, and
others who went back in the High Court on the statements they had made in
the preparatory examination. Almost invariably they complained that they

had been placed under intolerable pressure by the police, but the usual official reaction was to believe they had backed down under pressure from their own communities and to consider whether or not they should be charged with perjury.[46] In one case (1947/13), however, a confession was disregarded on the ground that it might have been obtained under duress.

There were also several accomplices, not Crown witnesses, who complained in court about police misconduct, notably in the cases against 'Mamakhabane, Bereng and Gabashane, but on the whole they were not believed. When the defence in one case alleged a police 'frame-up', the judge commented that 'a suggestion of that kind may safely be ignored' (1945/6). Some accused said they were advised by their lawyers not to complain, or that their lawyers refused to advance their complaints.[47]

The case which most damaged the police's reputation did not arise from medicine murder at all, but was the arson case against members of the Lekhotla la Bafo which was being conducted at the same time as the cases against 'Mamakhabane and Bereng and Gabashane (Case Studies 2 and 3) and in which several of the same accused were involved. The prosecution was based partly on a confession obtained from Harold Velaphe, and the judge, Mr Justice F. E. T. Krause, was fiercely critical of the methods used by the police. First, Velaphe had been kept under arrest without being charged from May until September 1948. Second, both he and other accused 'had, from time to time, been ill-treated by ... the police'. Third, Sergeant

> Sebolai was not telling the truth when he said that he had not influenced Velaphi in any way before he made his statement. To question a prisoner repeatedly, and to continue to question him in the Police Office for a period from nine o'clock to twelve o'clock, especially after Velaphi had denied persistently knowledge of the alleged crime, I think requires a great deal of explanation ... There can be no doubt that improper methods were employed.[48]

As observed already in Case Study 2, if such methods were being used in the Velaphe case, at precisely the same time as the major crisis in medicine murder, and even involving some of the same people, there is all the more reason to believe that they were used in at least some medicine murder cases as well.

How widespread was such abuse? There is strong evidence that many allegations, if not wholly false, were certainly exaggerated (see Case Study 2). It was acknowledged by Major Donald and Chief Leshoboro Majara, the two-man Administrative Team, in 1953 that 'some policemen have undoubtedly used high-handed methods', but they added that 'with no offsetting friendly relationship between police and public, isolated, undesirable incidents are generally magnified and regarded as typical examples of a general tyrannical attitude on the part of the Police'.[49] The Committee set up by the Round Table Conference also acknowledged that 'there have been a few occasions on which individual policemen have used an improper degree of force against a prisoner', but emphasised that 'such isolated instances have been cited as examples of a general state of affairs'.[50] In 1956 the Resident Commissioner, Edwin Arrowsmith, told the National Council that 'in a force of 300 men it would be surprising if witnesses have not sometimes been roughed up', but he denied that this was police policy.[51]

Jones wrote that it was not 'seriously contended, even by the extremists, that the police have in any case employed what are usually termed "third degree" methods to extort incriminating statements from witnesses or accused, nor is there much reason to suspect it'.[52] In 1949, when Matlere Lerotholi complained to Ashton about the police, he made no mention of torture.[53] Even Ntsu Mokhehle, in the long series of articles in 1957, adduced only one example, that of the man who had been handcuffed for three days, and that went back to 1948.[54] One of the accused in case 1958/ 1, Sethabathaba Hatahata, told us that in this case the police did not beat people, but frightened them by telling them they would be hanged if they kept silent.[55]

The two white officers we have been able to consult, Paul Kitson and Gordon Blampied, both denied that any improper pressure was brought to bear on witnesses. 'I was always against anything illegal or underhand', Blampied wrote, 'and I always made this clear to the men serving under me'.[56] Nkherepe Molefe, however, who was involved at various levels, from Sergeant to Superintendent, in several cases from the 1940s to the 1960s, admitted that occasionally, when it was difficult to get a suspect to talk, 'we pinched him a bit [ra mo tsipatsipa]'. Handcuffs would be applied: 'I mean, you know, we twisted the balls. I never used it. Otherwise [we would use] a wet cloth around the neck. When it was difficult to crack the case, it was necessary to use these methods'. He was sure that the information obtained in this way would be the truth, since otherwise it would not 'tie up' with other evidence.[57] Did his senior officers know about the use of ho tsipatsipa? 'Of course they knew, Kitson, Shortt-Smith, Blampied. Otherwise we couldn't have done it. We never injured anyone.'[58] Other policemen have confirmed that, although they themselves did not use it, in tough cases the interrogators would resort to ho tsipatsipa, and that this was well known to their white officers.[59]

The overall impression is that the police, in their determination to gain convictions, and in their suspicion in some cases and their firm belief in others that particular chiefs were responsible for the murders, often put pressure on suspects to make a full confession and to incriminate the chiefs. In the period before 1949 they operated on a fairly free rein, and were prepared to ignore the law in detaining suspects for long periods without charging them. When, as Baring said, 'the spotlight' was turned on what they were doing, this practice was largely, if not entirely, discontinued. In some cases, however, prisoners continued to be ill-treated, sometimes severely. This pattern of investigation and these examples of misconduct both formed part of what we have described as the counter-narrative on medicine murder and, in respect of police misconduct, were generalised in order to strengthen it.

Two particular cases gave cause for concern. The first was the case in Butha-Buthe against Lepekola Joel and ten others (1954/1) in which several witnesses gave evidence that a hole was made in the victim's head and Lance Corporal Ncheke testified that there was such a hole, but when the body was exhumed the skull was found to be intact. Ncheke said he had been ordered by his senior officers, Inspector Sebolai and Corporal Mokhakhe, to give the evidence that he did. There was an enquiry into this case, but there was insufficient evidence to justify a prosecution for perjury.[60] In another case in Butha-Buthe Inspector Sebolai was strongly criticised for his dismissive and cavalier treatment of several difficulties in the prosecution case in the preparatory examination. The presiding officer, Peter Stutley, concluded that Sebolai was 'a very keen and conscientious officer', but it was 'clear during the course of this case that his own certainty of the guilt of the accused obscured his ability to view the evidence objectively ...'[61]

Although the police were keen to secure convictions, and although, since most murders were committed by chiefs, they might in some cases have assumed too readily that a chief was responsible for the murder, there was no systematic police 'witch-hunt' against the chiefs. In some cases they were complimented by the judges on their fairness in bringing forward evidence which tended to exonerate the accused.[62] In others there were suspicions, and even strong evidence, that they helped the chief to cover up the murder. According to one witness to the Round Table Conference, Mark Photane,

> One section of the police force consists of traitors ... When they have gone out to investigate a medicine murder case, they hold meetings with chiefs in the evenings and advise one another to have the crime completely concealed. A policeman says: 'Chief, although I am in the Government Service, that does not mean that I have forgotten the fact that I am a Mosuto ...' The police who do their work sincerely are threatened by Chiefs and their counsellors, by saying they are working as though they would never leave the Government service, and they are asked a question under whom, on retirement, they would seek residence since they no longer recognise the sons of Moshesh.[63]

We have already noted that in the earlier period of *laissez-faire*, before the Khubelu reforms, the junior policemen who were sent out when the discovery of a body was reported were easily persuaded by the chiefs and their councillors that there was no ground for suspicion. In some later cases also they appear to have fallen in too readily with the proposal that the body should be buried.[64] In two cases in 1947 (1947/6 and 1947/9) it was alleged, according to Jones, that the police were ineffective in their enquiries because they were related to the suspected murderers. There is also evidence in one case (1947/13) that a policeman was bribed (with £3 taken from the body of the victim) to agree that the victim had been eaten by crabs. A former policeman, Edwin Nohe Tšita, told us of Chief Selemo Lesalla Posholi trying to bribe him with a sheep in case 1944/5, and claimed that the same chief committed several murders which were not followed up because he was 'close' to the police. Bereng Griffith, he said, was also able to get away with murder because of his connections with various policemen.[65]

In 1959 the police objected to the nomination of ex-Sergeant Nchee to the district panel in Butha-Buthe on the basis of 'his extreme reluctance to investigate certain medicine murders in the Butha Buthe ward during his last years of service'. The District Commissioner, Waddington, explained:

> His personal position in those days was obviously very difficult. As a good chief's man about to retire and return to his home in Mopeli's Ward it would be most unfortunate for him if he were to antagonize the chieftainship.[66]

There were other reasons for police failure to take effective action. In the late 1950s a Mosotho inspector in the north was said not to believe in medicine murder,[67] while in Quthing the police were so incompetent that only one reported case out of twelve reached the High Court. Several dockets were wrongly closed and others 'mislaid', one later being found in a clutter of rubbish in the charge office. One corporal there was said to be the 'stool pigeon' of Chief Sekhonyana 'Maseribane.[68] It may be unlikely that blatant corruption was widespread, but the pressures on the police to take no action were clearly very strong.

There was the further complication that in some cases the police might have been misled by malicious witnesses who were trying to get rivals or enemies into trouble. This was certainly so in one case, when these witnesses deceived not only the police, but also the Administrative Team of Major Donald and Chief Leshoboro Majara, and they were accused and convicted of trying to defeat the course of justice.[69] But, at least in the cases that were taken to court, the police must clearly have had good reason for believing the accused had committed the crime. Prosecutions were brought only if the Attorney-General believed there was a strong *prima facie* case, and convictions were secured only if the judge was satisfied beyond all reasonable doubt that the accused were guilty. Even if the accused were found not guilty, that only meant that the Crown had been unable to satisfy the high standard of proof required. As for the cases that did not go to court,

Table 8.1. Rates of prosecution and conviction, 1895–1969, by five-year cohorts (1895–1939 aggregated)

Period	A	B	C	D	E	F	G D/B%	H D/A%	I F/D%
1895–1939		29	12	17	11	6	59		35
1940–4	17	24	7	17	9	8	71	100	47
1945–9	44	62	35	27	13	14	44	61	52
1950–4	48	45	9	36	12	24	80	75	67
1955–9	54	26	5	21	11	10	81	39	48
1960–4	27	14	5	9	6	3	64	33	33
1965–9	43	11	8	3	3	0	27	7	0
Totals		211	81	130	65	65	61		50

Key
A. Cases reported to the government (see Graph 2.2).
B. Cases recorded by Murray and Sanders (see Graph 2.2).
C. Cases which did not go to court.
D. Cases which did go to court (including cases that only went as far as the preparatory examination) (see Graph 2.2).
E. Cases which resulted in acquittal of all accused.
F. Cases which resulted in at least one conviction (see Graph 2.2).
G. Cases which went to court (D) as a percentage of suspected cases (B).
H. Cases which went to court (D) as a percentage of cases reported to the government (A).
I. Cases which resulted in at least one conviction (F) as a percentage of cases which went to court (D).

Note
Columns C and D are sub-sets of B, and E and F are sub-sets of D. The two columns G and H are intended to show the difference between the effectiveness of police investigations measured by reference to two different statistical bases: the cases recorded by Murray and Sanders (B) and the number of cases reported to the government (A). The significance of the difference and the uncertainty of interpretation which arises out of it are discussed in Chapter 2. The figure of 100 per cent under H for the period 1940–4 is a statistical anomaly which reflects the fact that we recorded more murders for the 1940s than were reported to the government. It should *not* be interpreted as an expression of a 'complete' record of prosecution.

again the police might well have been right in their suspicions but were unable to take action for lack of evidence.

Over the years the police improved in competence. In an early case (1919/1) we find a corporal going out to the scene of the crime, measuring the footprints near the body with a stick, and then measuring the feet of all the inhabitants of the village. In later cases we find bloodstains being sent to South Africa for medical analysis. In two cases heard in the mid-1940s one of the judges, Sir Walter Huggard, was severely critical of the police. The investigations had been carried out by junior and inexperienced policemen, and he had been told that senior officers 'had very important duties to perform in their offices, so that they were unable to go out'. He wondered what other duties they had that were more important than the investigation of murder.[70] By 1947, however, Huggard was complimenting the police on the excellence of their investigations (1944/7).

The improvement in police performance from the late 1940s through the 1950s is reflected firstly in the proportion of murders that were brought to trial, and secondly in the proportion of cases tried that resulted in convictions. The figures are set out in Table 8.1. Taking the cases recorded by us (column B) as the base, the percentage of cases brought to court (column G) was 71 per cent in the early 1940s and 44 per cent in the late 1940s, climbed to 80 per cent in the early 1950s and 81 per cent in the late 1950s, but then fell away to 64 per cent in the early 1960s and only 27 per cent in the late 1960s. For the later period, however, from the mid-1950s to the late 1960s, the number of cases recorded by us is only two-fifths of the number of murders reported to the government (column A). Taking the reported murders as an alternative base, the percentage of murders brought to trial (column H) rose significantly between the late 1940s (61 per cent) and the early 1950s (75 per cent), but thereafter dropped sharply to 39 per cent for the late 1950s and 33 per cent for the early 1960s, falling to only 7 per cent for the late 1960s.

The rate of conviction (column I), expressed as the percentage of cases brought to court in which at least one accused person was convicted, rose to 52 per cent in the late 1940s and 67 per cent in the early 1950s, but dropped to 48 per cent in the late 1950s and to 33 per cent in the early 1960s, and dramatically fell away to zero by the late 1960s (admittedly on very small numbers for the 1960s).

Once again the judges began to criticise the police. In one case (1962/3), the body was found in July 1962 and investigations were completed in December 1962, but the docket was forwarded to the Criminal Investigations Department only in June 1963, and it was February 1965, almost two years later, before the CID took action. The accused were arrested in May 1965, and proceedings began in August 1965. The Chief Justice found it deplorable that senior police officers refused to appear in court to explain these delays. In another case, 1963/1, the body of a woman was found two days after the murder. In spite of the mutilations the police officer allowed the body to be buried, and even accepted the lame explanation that the victim's bloomers were found a few yards from the body because she 'used to carry her bloomers when drunk'. The body was exhumed five months later, by which time it was so decomposed that there was no point in holding a post-mortem examination, and it was only in May 1965, more than two years after the murder, that the case finally came before the High Court. In a third case (1965/6) the police began their investigations promptly, at the beginning of November 1965, a week after the body was found, but three years passed before the accused were arrested towards the end of 1968, and the case only came before the High Court in December 1969. The Chief

Justice, H. R. Jacobs, commented drily that these delays had not helped the court, and the accused were acquitted. Such dilatory habits reflect the fact that by the mid-1960s, as discussed at the end of Chapter 5, the government and police had come to attach much less importance to medicine murder than before.

THE JUDICIAL PROCESS

After the Chief Justice, Sir Harold Willan, had settled in his chair, there was a dreadful silence as every person there composed his thoughts and pricked up his ears so as to hear clearly the terrible words which were about to be uttered by the Chief Justice ... Eyes were wide open, hearts throbbing; especially, we can guess, those of the accused ... From 2.15 p.m. until just after 3 p.m. the minds of those who were listening fluttered over the earth like the waves of the sea; the journalists could not hold their pens in their hands, because if they bent their heads they might miss what was being said. The learned Judge ... acquitted all the accused ... Shouts of joy burst out in the court, and arms were flung wide to congratulate Chief David Theko Makhaola – mine too, I say, and I took the lead. Ululations struck the heavens and joined the thunder and the lightning of the rain which began to patter down at that very moment. Out came the Chief of Ratšoleli's and Mashai, and we sang 'We People Rejoice'.

L. L. B. Monyako, article in *Moeletsi*, 13 February 1954
(case 1953/2) [translated from Sesotho]

THE PREPARATORY EXAMINATION

The judicial process began with the preparatory examination, which was usually held in the small courtroom attached to the District Commissioner's office in the headquarters of the district in which the murder was committed. There were a few exceptions, such as the case against Bereng and Gabashane and the two cases against Matlere Lerotholi, which were moved to Maseru to reduce the risk of local pressure on the witnesses. The case against Bereng and Gabashane was held in the Council Chamber of the Basutoland National Council to accommodate the crowds who wanted to be present.

The presiding officer was the District Officer, though towards the end of colonial rule – on the principle that it would be better to separate the judiciary from the administration – the government gradually introduced magistrates who took over most of the cases.[1] The prosecution, even in the biggest cases, was led by a police officer, and the accused were normally represented by lawyers. The purpose of the preparatory examination was to establish whether or not there was 'sufficient reason' for indicting the accused. If there was, the presiding officer would commit them for trial. If not, he would discharge them.

Although the preparatory examination enabled the Crown to try out its case in court, it conferred greater advantages on the accused. They could hear precisely what they were alleged to have done and what the evidence was against them. They could cross-examine the witnesses, and at the end of the Crown case they would be in a very good position to form some estimate of its strengths and weaknesses. They were not obliged to make any statement themselves, and most of them took advantage of this and reserved their defence for the trial in the High Court. While waiting for that trial and preparing their defence they were entitled to have a complete record of all the evidence taken in the preparatory examination.

In 1954 the Commissioner of Police, then D. R. Owens, wistfully noted that preparatory examinations had been abolished in Kenya for cases involving the Mau Mau. 'I wish we could have such an arrangement here!', he wrote. It was not the advantages to the accused that worried him, but the danger that the Crown's witnesses would vary their evidence between the preparatory examination and the trial.[2] Some of them, perhaps under pressure from the local community, went back on their statements and the Crown had to abandon them. Others, perhaps not too sure in their memory of what happened, gave a slightly or even substantially different account at the trial, and the defence was able to exploit these inconsistencies to cast doubt on their credibility in general. At one point, after the trial of Chief Theko Makhaola (1953/2), there were suspicions in the colonial administration that witnesses had devised a new technique, whereby they did not go back on their statements but deliberately varied them, and so, while undermining the case for the Crown, avoided the risk of being accused of perjury. We now have the evidence of Seane Klaas, an accomplice witness in the first Matlere Lerotholi trial, that this was precisely his course of action (1952/12, Case Study 4). The Attorney-General was not convinced at the time, however, that there was a change of strategy.[3]

The District Officer either discharged the accused or committed them for trial. If he committed them for trial, the papers were submitted to the Attorney-General who would then decide whether or not to prosecute. If there was not a strong enough case, he would enter a *nolle prosequi*. Otherwise there would be an indictment.

The Attorney-General was based in the office of the High Commissioner, and from January 1947 until 1955 or 1956, a period covering the most important years for our purposes, the post was held by A. C. Thompson. A South African, he had been wounded three times in France and won the Military Cross in 1917. He had practised as an advocate since 1922 in the Transvaal and Swaziland. In spite of his heavy drinking he was a man of considerable ability, and he was much respected by officers in Basutoland. Gideon Pott remarked of Thompson: 'Brilliant, hell of a boozer, but always dead sober in the morning'. He appeared regularly for the Crown in medicine murder cases and in 1954 he claimed to speak 'from over thirty years experience in which I have appeared in murder cases in every capacity (save that of accused)'.[4]

In total we know of 1,052 persons charged with medicine murder during the colonial period – a figure which includes ten in the first four cases before preparatory examinations were held. Of the 1,042 who appeared at preparatory examinations, two died, 112 were discharged and 928 were committed for trial at the High Court. Of these 928, the Attorney-General decided not to bring a prosecution against ninety-nine, and fifteen more accused died between the preparatory examination and the High Court trial. So finally, including the ten persons who went to trial without a preparatory examination, we know of 824 accused who appeared in the High Court.

THE COURTS AND THE JUDGES

Until 1939 cases of murder were tried in the Resident Commissioner's Court, though after 1928 the officer who presided was normally the Judicial Commissioner rather than the Resident Commissioner himself. In 1939 the Resident Commissioner's Court was replaced by the High Court of Basutoland.[5] At first there was no designated High Court building, and proceedings were held in the chamber of the Basutoland National Council. The judges found this inconvenient and objectionable. It was octagonal in shape, 'quite unsuitable for use as a Court', and 'bitterly cold' in winter. There were also fears that it might give the Basotho the impression that the judiciary was not independent of the government. It was only in 1956 that a new purpose-built High Court was opened.[6]

The High Court of Basutoland, together with the High Courts of Bechuanaland and Swaziland, was presided over by the Judge of the High Commission Territories, an officer whose title was changed in 1950 to the Chief Justice of the High Commission Territories. He was also legal adviser to the High Commissioner and acted as High Commissioner when the High Commissioner was away – an overlap between judicial and executive functions which was clearly objectionable. In 1952 the posts of legal adviser and judge were separated, and the Chief Justice of the three countries, instead of being stationed at the High Commission, was based in Maseru.[7]

The first Judge of the High Commission Territories was Sir Walter Huggard, who resigned owing to ill-health in 1948. When he was acting as High Commissioner, or when he was away through illness or on leave, his place was taken by a judge from South Africa, usually one who had recently retired. About half the medicine murder cases in the 1940s, including some of the most important, were heard by South African judges, such as Krause,

Pittman, de Beer, Grindley-Ferris and G. G. Sutton, who heard the Bereng and Gabashane case.

Where possible the High Commissioner appointed judges who had experience in other parts of the empire. Sir Walter Harragin, who replaced Huggard in 1948 and in 1950 became the first Chief Justice, had served as Chief Justice of the Gold Coast and President of the West African Court of Appeal,[8] and later Chief Justices included Sir Harold Willan, who had served in Malaya and Zanzibar, and Sir Herbert Cox, who had served in Northern Rhodesia and Tanganyika. In 1956 Victor Elyan was appointed as Puisne Judge of the High Court, but the pressure of work was such that the High Court sometimes had to be divided in two and other judges called in to help. One such judge in the late 1950s and 1960s, E. R. Roper, was formerly a judge of the Transvaal Division of the Supreme Court of South Africa, and had served when younger as Attorney-General of the High Commission Territories.

Until the mid-1950s appeals from the High Court lay direct to the Privy Council in London. Crawford described this arrangement as

> a serious defect in the judicial systems of the three territories, not only because appeal from the High Courts or their predecessors to the Privy Council was expensive and time-taking, but because the Privy Council is not a court of criminal appeal ... In the words of Viscount Simon ... 'broadly speaking, the Judicial Committee will only interfere where there has been an infringement of the essential principles of justice'.[9]

It was only in 1955 that the Court of Appeal for the High Commission Territories was established, with much wider powers in dealing with criminal appeals, and with a further right of appeal to the Privy Council. The Judges of Appeal, who included the Chief Justice and the Puisne Judge *ex officio*, were otherwise all retired judges from South Africa or other colonies.[10]

Inevitably some, if not all, of the judges shared the racial prejudices of the societies from which they came, and in the early years in particular several of them were very free with their comments about race. Sometimes they were patronising, even contemptuous. They were also free with their warnings about the wider implications of medicine murder. In 1946 (1945/3, Case Study 1) Mr Justice de Beer described a 'Bushman' witness as 'a member of a lowly uncivilized race and ... a poor member of a very poor race'. After giving judgement he 'addressed the Court and the Basuto Nation and said the Basuto people, who were the greatest Bantu race, were slowly destroying themselves by the practice of witchcraft'. In another case in the same year he mocked a witness for believing that Basotho doctors could foretell the future. 'A monkey which touches fire burns its paws and does not touch fire a second time. You who still believe in witchcraft have obviously no sense at all' (1945/8). In the following year Grindley-Ferris referred to the accused as 'ignorant natives' (1946/1), and although many individuals were described as bright and intelligent many others were dismissed as muddled and stupid.[11] 'In this case', said an appeal judge, Graham Paul, in 1955, 'as usual in such cases, the standard of intelligence of the witnesses is low' (1954/3).

Harragin was scornful of 'anthropologists and those who are interested in the advance of the peoples of this country and those who visit this country for a few weeks and imagine they know all about it', and suggested that the letter written by a chief telling his doctor that he needed the brain of a child for medicine 'should give [them] much food for thought' (1952/11). The Basotho, he told the Rand Women's Club in Johannesburg, 'are a virile, warlike, proud race, and boast that they have never been conquered ... Their recreations are beer drinks, cattle and sheep-stealing, and ritual murders.'[12] This statement, he said, might be disputed, but he made it 'in the same sense that I would say of the British working man that he lived for his football pools and horse-racing'.

Before the Jones report the judges' understanding of medicine murder was shaky and uncertain. De Beer thought he was dealing with 'a Satanic rite of the sacrifice of a human being' (1945/3). Krause in one case referred to the murderers being 'busy' for three days 'performing the usual ritual ceremony, namely tapping blood from the old woman by stabbing her with an awl in the leg and gathering the blood in a bottle' (1948/18). In a judgement given in 1948 Harragin declared that the purpose of 'ritual murder' was 'to procure from the heathen gods some particular medicine for a witchdoctor with which he will pretend to cure his patients or it may be to propitiate the gods so as to make the village "stronger" or something of that description'. As Ashton pointed out, no heathen gods were involved,[13] and after the Jones report the judges were at least better informed.

Several of them were not only old, but infirm. Krause, according to Rivers Thompson, was 'deaf as a doorpost, almost. He had a machine to help him but it didn't always work'.[14] In the course of 1959 and 1960 two out of the six appeal judges died, and one of the men who replaced them died as well. Nevertheless, measured in terms of objectivity in examining the evidence, legal expertise and independence of judgement, the overall standard of the judiciary, as in South Africa generally, was high. Only one judge fell short, it seems, and that was Grindley-Ferris, whom Baring found 'not ... entirely satisfactory' and who according to one official in London was 'a nice old thing but ... not highly thought of in the Union'.[15]

In spite of the overlap of functions in the early years between the Judge of the High Commission Territories and the High Commissioner, there was no hint of any collusion with the British authorities. On the contrary, officials were sometimes dismayed by unexpected acquittals, and Thompson, the

Attorney-General, complained about the judges' lack of consistency, especially in their treatment of accomplice evidence.[16] Insofar as there was any tendency to disregard or undervalue what Africans said as unreliable or untrue this was as likely to discredit the Crown witnesses as the accused. Judges were quick to reject the defence's alibis and denials, but they were just as quick to doubt the word of accomplice witnesses. Lourens Liebetrau, who appeared more frequently as attorney for the defence than any other lawyer, summed up his experience as follows:

> I did have the feeling that the judges were revolted by the thought of sentencing twenty or thirty people so they seized on any little discrepancy to get an acquittal. The judges were not what one could call hanging judges. They would acquit if there was the slightest ground of doubt.[17]

In the High Court the judge was assisted by African assessors and white advisers. The system varied over time, but for most of the period with which we are concerned there were two assessors and two advisers. They were all appointed by the Resident Commissioner. The advisers had to be administrative officers. The assessors were usually chiefs or civil servants in whom the government had confidence. The power of decision rested solely with the judge.[18]

While Thompson was Attorney-General he usually represented the Crown himself. Later there was an increasing tendency to appoint South African advocates to act on the Attorney-General's behalf – another indication of the declining importance which the government attached to medicine murder. The accused were nearly always represented by South African lawyers, sometimes, in the case of wealthy chiefs, by expensive counsel from Johannesburg, in other cases by advocates from the local Free State towns, notably Lourens Liebetrau from Ladybrand, who was appointed to act *pro deo* in some cases. Basutoland's judges had a high regard for Liebetrau, and in one case the Appeal Court commended his usual 'skill, painstaking thoroughness and meticulous fairness' (1957/1). Some accused chose to represent themselves, the best-known of these being Chief Mabina Lerotholi who put his trust in his rosary. Several accused who defended themselves got involved in serious difficulties, and in some cases the court had to disregard statements which had the effect of incriminating them.[19]

THE TRIAL

The High Court at first held two sessions a year, with special sessions being held as necessary, for example to deal with the case against Bereng and Gabashane. In 1958, because of the pressure of medicine murder cases, courts were held simultaneously by the Chief Justice and the Puisne Judge. By 1960, because of the pressure of business generally, four sessions were being held each year.[20]

The opening of a High Court Session was, by Basutoland's standards, a grand ceremonial occasion, when the police band, with a great following, marched down Kingsway, Maseru's main road. In January 1958 the *Basutoland News* waxed lyrical in its description of 'the hot sunshine' lighting up 'the contrasts of the scene – the brilliant scarlet of the judges' robes and the sombre black of the advocates' gowns, the dull khaki police uniforms lightened by shiny leather and the flash of sword or bayonet, the gorgeous band leader and the smart colourful band'. 'After the opening ceremony', it went on, 'His Honour the Resident Commissioner attended a sherry party in the Judge's Chambers. He then sat, by invitation, on the bench while Mr Justice Elyan heard the pleas in six murder cases', five of which were medicine murders.[21]

The horrors of the cases that followed provided a grim contrast to such sunlit scenes. When important chiefs were involved, the court room was often packed to overflowing, with people thronging the doorways and crowded on the verandah outside. In some cases the accused themselves were so numerous that they overspilled the dock, even in the new High Court, where a larger dock was provided. The proprieties, however, were carefully observed. In the Bereng and Gabashane case the two chiefs were accorded a place in the dock while most of their fellow accused had to sit outside.[22]

Each accused wore a large number plate, and careful arrangements were made to avoid any confusion between them. Witnesses referring to any of the accused had to go up and point out which one they meant, and that accused then had to stand to ensure that everyone knew that he or she was the person who had been identified.[23] The accused found another use for their number plates. When it was 'stifling hot', as in the Bereng and Gabashane case, they could use them for fanning themselves.[24] It was extremely rare for any of the accused to plead guilty, and when they did their pleas were changed to not guilty.[25]

The witnesses called by the Crown typically included the relatives who had last seen the victim alive, the persons who found the body, the policemen who were called to the scene and who submitted sketch-plans of the area and perhaps photographs of the body, the doctor who conducted the post-mortem examination, and then, most important, the accomplice witnesses and any independent witnesses who might corroborate the accomplices' evidence. Various articles would also be produced as exhibits – perhaps the weapons with which the victim had been killed, blood-stained articles of clothing, and medicines found at the homes of the accused. In the second case against Matlere Lerotholi (1959/1, see Case Study 4), for example, they were listed as Grey Blanket, Green Blanket, Grey Coat, Loin Cloth, Belt, Pair of Black Boots, Pair of Socks, Two Pins, Piece of Flesh, Flesh, Hair, Enamel Dish, Scissors, Bag, Horn, Blade, Bottle, Torch.

The typical defence was a denial of any involvement in the crime, strengthened in many cases by alibis and in some cases by allegations that the Crown's witnesses had reasons of their own for trying to incriminate the accused. A few admitted taking part but claimed that they had been acting under compulsion. In many cases the accused did not go into the witness box, in this way avoiding cross-examination.

Because of the numbers of accused, and because of the need for translation, cases commonly lasted for two or three weeks and the longest lasted nearly two months.[26] The judgements were correspondingly long, since the judge had to consider the evidence relating to every single one of the accused. Judge Elyan was particularly detailed and painstaking: his judgements were commonly thirty to forty pages long and took two to three hours to deliver. In one case, 1957/3, as *Moeletsi*'s court correspondent noted with querulous amazement, the Chief Justice, Sir Herbert Cox, began reading his judgement at 10.45 a.m. and did not stop until 4.05 p.m., without a break for lunch or even tea.[27]

ACCOMPLICE EVIDENCE

At the heart of almost every judgement was the question of the validity of accomplice evidence. An accomplice witness was defined, according to Harragin, as a person 'who might have been charged, with some prospect of success, with the crime with which the accused stand charged'.[28] Under section 228(1) of the Criminal Procedure and Evidence Proclamation an accomplice in an offence who agreed to give evidence on behalf of the Crown and who answered the questions put to him to the satisfaction of the Court was 'absolutely freed and discharged from all liability to prosecution for such offence'.

No-one was comfortable with this heavy reliance on accomplices. One judge described them as 'a species of human being who belongs really to the lowest type', another as a 'naturally depraved type of person', another as 'confessed murderers ... who are out to save their own skins'. 'Like everybody else concerned in the administration of justice', said Thompson as Attorney-General, 'I dislike the use we have to make of accomplices.'[29] Many speakers in the Basutoland National Council condemned them as liars and traitors for falsely incriminating their chiefs.[30] Most Basotho found it shocking that they were able to get off scot-free – as murderers if what they were saying was true, and as perjurors if not – and there was endless discussion about the possibility of creating at least some lesser offence, carrying a lesser punishment, which would not deter accomplices from giving evidence but would ensure that at least some measure of justice was done.[31] But, as Thompson pointed out, medicine murders were not like other murders. They were carried out in secret, usually at night, with no eye-witnesses to see what was happening, and they were surrounded by a wall of silence. In the end it all came down to this: 'Without [accomplice] evidence

we would never obtain a conviction: without a legal promise of full indem-
nity such evidence would be unobtainable'.[32]

There were serious dangers in relying on accomplice evidence. Accomplices could incriminate people who had not taken part or people against
whom they bore a grudge, and they could pass over in silence some of those
who had taken part, perhaps their relatives and friends. They were
murderers themselves and, in spite of all their protestations, they made their
confessions in order to save their own lives. The law therefore enjoined
extreme caution in the treatment of their evidence. But, as we have seen in
the cases against Bereng and Gabashane, the law was not the same
throughout our period and there were inconsistencies in its interpretation.
We need, briefly, to recapitulate the legal position.

For the most part Basutoland followed South African law. Its common
law, like South Africa's, was Roman-Dutch. In 1938, however, the law of
Basutoland on accomplice evidence was changed to the English rule of
practice, so that section 231 of the Basutoland Criminal and Procedure
Proclamation read as follows:

> Any court of law which is trying any person on a charge of any offence
> may convict him of any offence alleged against him in the indictment
> or summons on the single evidence of any accomplice:
> Provided that the testimony of the accomplice is corroborated by
> independent evidence which affects the accused by connecting or
> tending to connect him with the crime:
> Provided further that such evidence shall consist of evidence other
> than that of another accomplice or other accomplices.

In other words, to quote Sir Ralph Hone, who later advised the Commonwealth Relations Office, 'a Court could not, in any circumstances, find a
person guilty on the evidence of an accomplice unless that evidence was
corroborated and unless that corroboration was given by some person other
than another accomplice'.[33]

Until 1943 the courts in the High Commission Territories proceeded on
the assumption that an accessory after the fact was not an accomplice, and
so a court could convict on the evidence of an accomplice if it was
corroborated by that of an accessory after the fact. In a medicine murder
case an accessory after the fact was typically someone who had taken no part
in the murder itself but had helped to dispose of the body. In a Swaziland
case in that year, however, the Privy Council held that an accessory after the
fact had to be treated as an accomplice, and Walter Huggard, Basutoland's
High Court judge, protested that this would make it much more difficult to
secure convictions in medicine murder cases. Section 231 of the Basutoland
Criminal Procedure and Evidence Proclamation was therefore amended in
1944 to conform to South African law, so that it read as follows:

Any court which is trying any person on a charge of any offence may convict him of any offence alleged against him in the indictment or summons on the single evidence of any accomplice:
Provided that the offence has, by competent evidence, other than the single and unconfirmed evidence of the accomplice, been proved to the satisfaction of such court to have been actually committed.[34]

In other words, to quote Sir Ralph Hone again, 'a Court may convict on the uncorroborated evidence of one accomplice provided that the Court is satisfied by other reliable evidence that the offence charged was actually committed'.[35] In a medicine murder case such other evidence might typically be provided by another accomplice, by the post-mortem examination or by the evidence of the persons who found the body.

The statutory provision, however, was not the whole story, because it was buttressed by the South African rule of practice. This was best set out by Judge Schreiner in the case of *R* v. *Ncanana* in 1948. Under this the judge had to 'warn himself [and, in Basutoland, his assessors and advisers] of the special danger of convicting on the evidence of an accomplice'. This danger was not overcome simply by proof that an offence had been committed, or by evidence corroborating the accomplice 'in material respects not implicating the accused'. The risk would be reduced

in the most satisfactory way, if there is corroboration implicating the accused. But it will also be reduced if the accused shows himself to be a lying witness or if he does not give evidence to contradict or to explain that of the accomplice. And it will also be reduced, even in the absence of these features, if the trier of fact understands the peculiar danger inherent in accomplice evidence and appreciates that acceptance of the accomplice and rejection of the accused is, in such circumstances, only permissible where the merits of the former as a witness and the demerits of the latter are beyond question.

So we may sum up the position in the mid-1940s as follows. First, under statutory law – section 231 of the Basutoland Criminal Procedure and Evidence Proclamation – it was not possible to convict on the single evidence of an accomplice unless there was also evidence that a murder had actually been committed. Such evidence could be provided in various ways, for example by the evidence of another accomplice, or by the post-mortem examination. Second, under the South African rule of practice, even when there was evidence that a murder had been committed, a judge had to warn himself explicitly about the dangers of relying on accomplice evidence, and such dangers would be reduced 'in the most satisfactory way' if there was corroborative evidence implicating the accused. But even if such corroborative evidence were absent, it would also be reduced by the silence or falsehoods of the accused (in failing to rebut or explain the accomplice's evidence, for example, or in trying to set up a false alibi). And even if these features were absent, it would be reduced if the judge was completely satisfied of the merits of the accomplice witness and the demerits of the accused as witnesses.

In January 1949, however, the law was thrown into confusion by the Privy Council's judgement in the case of *R* v. *Tumahole Bereng and others* (1945/11). Judge Grindley-Ferris, with the unanimous agreement of his advisers and assessors, had convicted the accused on the evidence of two accomplice witnesses, and said that 'corroboration ... as to the commission of the crime, if such were necessary' was to be found in the post-mortem examination. In considering the appeals against this judgement the Privy Council placed a completely new construction on the statutory law. It held that under section 231 of the Basutoland Criminal Procedure and Evidence Proclamation 'the single evidence of any accomplice' meant not 'the evidence of a single accomplice', but 'the unsupported evidence of any accomplice or accomplices', and so the evidence of one accomplice witness could not be corroborated by the evidence of another. It also found, as a matter of fact in this particular case, that the evidence of the post-mortem examination could not bear the construction placed on it by the judge, and so there was no proof *aliunde* (that is, from sources other than the accomplices) that a murder had actually been committed. The appeals were therefore upheld.

Although it did not need to address this question, the Privy Council went on to decide that the rule of practice to be applied was not the South African rule, as the Crown argued, but the English rule, as the appellants argued. Under this the evidence of an accomplice had to be corroborated by some material evidence implicating the accused in the crime, and for this purpose it was not good enough to use another accomplice, or the failure of the accused to rebut or explain the accomplice's evidence, or false evidence given by the accused.[36]

This judgement was a setback for the colonial authority on two counts: first, the interpretation of the statutory law, and, second, the finding about the rule of practice. In future it would be more difficult to secure convictions for medicine murder. More immediately, and in the short term much more alarmingly, appeals were pending in the Bereng and Gabashane case, and there was now a serious danger – from the point of view of the colonial administration – that these appeals too would be upheld. We have already described in Case Study 3 how Thompson, the Attorney-General, drew up a powerful memorandum rebutting the Privy Council's reasoning, how he went to London himself to brief the counsel representing the Crown in the Bereng and Gabashane case, and how, in July 1949, only six months after the Tumahole judgement, the Privy Council dismissed all the appeals in that case.

The Council found that in the particular circumstances of the Bereng and Gabashane case there was in fact evidence *aliunde* that the victim had been murdered, and so it did not need to consider whether the Privy Council's previous interpretation of section 231 was correct; and that, contrary to the finding in the Tumahole case, it was perfectly in order for the judge to follow the South African rule of practice and not the English. This result, as an official in London observed, was 'a great personal triumph for the A-G', and in the following year this triumph was complete when the Privy Council, in a Swaziland case, *R* v. *Gideon Nkambule*, held that its previous interpretation of section 231 in the Tumahole case was also wrong.[37] So in future, for the purposes of this section, it would be possible to corroborate the evidence of one accomplice witness with that of another.

The Crown had now won both of the arguments which it had lost in the rogue judgement in the Tumahole case: the interpretation of the statutory law and the question of which rule of practice should be observed. We must now consider how the law was applied.

JUDGEMENTS: CONVICTIONS AND ACQUITTALS

We have been able to trace 112 cases of medicine murder which were heard in the High Court (before 1939 in the Resident Commissioner's Court) during the colonial period. Sixty-five of these cases (58 per cent), resulted in one or more convictions for murder. Of the 824 accused we have been able to record, 374 (45 per cent) were convicted of murder, twenty-one (3 per cent) were convicted as accessories before or after the fact, and 425 (52 per cent) were discharged or acquitted. Two of the accused died and two 'disappeared' after being committed for trial.

Of the 374 who were convicted of murder we know of 174 who appealed – before 1955 to the Privy Council and after that to the Court of Appeal. Twenty-three of them (13 per cent) had their appeals upheld, while 147 (84 per cent) had their appeals dismissed. Four died while their appeals were pending. None of those convicted of being an accessory before or after the fact is known to have appealed. One man who did not appeal was pardoned on the recommendation of the Court of Appeal. In respect of final outcomes, therefore, we know of 350 persons who were found guilty of murder, of whom fifty-seven were instigators and 293 were accomplices; twenty-one who were found guilty as accessories; and 449 who were found not guilty, a category which includes twenty-three whose appeals against conviction were upheld and one who was pardoned. In addition we know of 273 persons who gave evidence as accomplice witnesses, that is as persons who confessed to having taken part in the murders and were granted judicial immunity in return for giving evidence for the prosecution.

These overall figures conceal wide variations over time. As shown in Table 8.1, the proportion of cases resulting in one or more convictions rose from 47 per cent in 1940–4 through 52 per cent in 1945–9 to 67 per cent in 1950–4, and then fell through 48 per cent in 1955–9 and 33 per cent in 1960–4 to 0 per cent in 1965–9. We have already argued that the decline in the late 1950s and 1960s, especially when taken with the judges' criticisms of the police, is yet another indication of the diminishing importance attached by the authorities to medicine murder at that time.

We have identified only eleven cases[38] in which the judges were so convinced of the merits of the accomplice witnesses and the demerits of the accused that they were prepared to convict on the basis of accomplice evidence alone, and in three of these there was independent evidence as well which the judge did not need to take into account.[39] In one case (1952/6), Chief Justice Willan declared that 'even if there had been accomplice evidence alone I would have accepted it', but in fact there was 'ample corroboration' from three independent witnesses and the post-mortem examination. But relying on accomplices alone was dangerous, and in three cases of the eleven such convictions were overturned on appeal. In 1957/9 Judge Elyan had 'based his decision entirely on his view of the demeanour of the witnesses'. While he accepted the evidence of the accomplices, he rejected that of the accused 'on the ground that they gave their evidence "unimpressively"'. The appeal judges found that there were facts which 'should have raised a reasonable doubt in the mind of the learned judge as to the veracity of the accomplices', and the appeals were upheld.[40]

In the great majority of cases there was corroborative evidence of one sort or another to back up the accomplices. Among the most common types of corroboration was the post-mortem examination. In 1942/4, the accomplices told the court how an iron spike had been driven into the victim's brain through the top of the head, and the post-mortem examination, though carried out several months later, confirmed that there was a hole on the top of the skull which could have been made with the iron spike which was before the court as an exhibit. In 1952/3, the post-mortem examination confirmed the accomplices' account that a deep wound had been inflicted on the right side of the victim's neck. There were also several cases in which the findings of the post-mortem examination ruled out the ostensible cause of death, such as drowning or falling from a cliff.

In several cases there was corroborative evidence in the form of exhibits before the court. In 1950/2, the accomplices described how the headman responsible for the murder put his own belt on the victim, and this was still in place when the body was found after being washed down the Senqunyane river. In 1950/3, blood-stains were found on the blanket and saddlebags of the doctor, Phoka Shea, and on the blanket of one of the other accused. In 1951/9, there were gashes in the victim's vest and blanket, and this confirmed the accomplices' account that he had been wearing these clothes when he had been stabbed. One of the most striking exhibits was the letter written by Seshope Ramakoro instructing his henchman to get the brains of a child (1952/11).

Independent witnesses often provided vital corroboration. Many had observed the movements of the accused and the victim before the murder was carried out. In 1944/1, a woman was working in the fields when she saw some of the murderers ride by with the man they were going to kill. In 1951/4, a woman saw two of the murderers leaving a beer-party with their victim.[41] Some witnesses saw the victim while he or she was being detained by the murderers. In 1948/15, the victim was being kept in a forest before being killed, and a local woman came across her by chance when she was out collecting wood. One herdboy had the horrifying experience of finding the victim still alive and groaning after he had been mutilated but before he was finally killed (1945/4).

Others actually witnessed the murder itself: the women who were resting after their evening meal when the murderers came in with their victim (1942/4); the man who was walking along with the victim when the murderers attacked (1943/5); the man who witnessed the murder from a distance of about 90 metres and took care to keep out of the way (1947/8); the victim's brother-in-law who happened to be passing by, tried to run away, but was caught and forced to cut the victim himself (1947/14); the man who unexpectedly entered the hut where the murder was being carried out because the man keeping watch was so drunk that he had fallen asleep (1948/10); the little boy, the instigator's nephew, who saw what was happening because the door to the hut had not been completely closed (1950/4); the doctor who was unwillingly present at the killing and took the first opportunity to make his getaway (1950/4); the wife of one of the accomplices who arrived unexpectedly on the scene with three other women (1950/7); the man who had been passing by the hut where the murder was being carried out and had been compelled to join in (1957/3); and two young men, one of them the son of one of the accomplices, who looked through the door of the hut where the murder was being committed (1957/4).

Several of those who gave evidence had played some part in the arrangements for the murder, such as the woman who enticed the victim to a beer-party (1943/5), or the girl who took a message to the murderers to tell them that the man they wanted to kill had arrived (1950/6). Others were doctors who were called upon after the murder to make medicine from the *liretlo*. The most striking example, which we have quoted already, was that of Bernice Hlalele, who was presented with the victim's head and asked to make a medicine horn for the Paramount Chief (1945/3, Case Study 1).

We have already described how information about a murder might become known throughout a village, and as it spread outwards, sometimes from the murderers themselves, several witnesses were given incriminating information – such as the three women who worked for one of the accused and who were told that he had taken part in a murder the night before and were given his blood-stained trousers to wash (1951/2), or the lover of the man mentioned above who had unexpectedly burst in when the murder was being committed: in this case two of the accused told her about the murder in the mistaken belief that her lover had told her about it already (1948/10). There were other witnesses who heard the screams and last cries of the victims as they were attacked.[42] Their evidence was particularly damning when the words they reported were the same as those reported by the accomplices.

There were very few cases – only five that we have been able to find – in which there was corroboration in the form of a confession by one of the accused. This evidence could be taken into account, however, only insofar as it affected the person making the confession. In three of these cases (1945/8, 1947/15 and 1957/5), that person was the only accused to be convicted, while in another case, 1953/4, only two of the other six accused were found guilty, and that was on the basis of other evidence. In the fifth case, 1942/4, two women who confessed were the wives of the instigator, and they were acquitted since it was held that they had acted under compulsion.

As well as these positive forms of corroboration, judges also took into account the proven falsehoods told by the accused in their defence and, though rarely, the accused's decision not to go into the witness box (1953/4, for example).

In every case the judge was careful to spell out the corroborative evidence that he had taken into account against each of the accused, and in some judgements this was conveniently summarised. The examples that follow give some indication of the full range of evidence that might weigh with the judge in any particular case. In case 1943/5 the judge took into account the evidence of the woman who had enticed the victim to the beer-party; the evidence of the sister-in-law of one of the accomplices who had been told beforehand that a murder would be committed; the evidence of the man who had been with the victim when he was attacked; and the evidence of a little girl who had told her grandfather, one of the accused, that she had heard a person screaming, and who was told, 'I will kill you as I have killed that person', if she said anything about it. In case 1951/9 the judge was impressed by the evidence of a herdboy who saw some of the accused pushing the victim into the hut where the accomplices said he was killed and who later saw a bloodstain on the floor of that hut; the evidence of a doctor who was in prison with two of the accused (he was asked by one of them to tell his lover to hide his medicine, and by the other to help him, which he agreed to do if he was given some of the flesh of the murdered man); the medicine obtained after this doctor had reported to the police; the gashes in the blanket and vest of the deceased, which confirmed the evidence of the accomplices that he had been stabbed; the evidence of a woman who saw two of the accused holding a conversation as described by one of the accomplices; and the evidence of another woman who saw two other accused holding a conversation as described by one of the accomplices.

In case 1954/5 the Appeal Court summed up 'the items of independent corroboration' under seven heads:

> One, evidence that the deceased disappeared on the night of the alleged murder. Two, evidence that the appellants, the accomplice and the deceased were together on the evening of the alleged murder. Three, evidence that the appellants, the accomplice and the deceased were proceeding in the same direction on that evening. Four, evidence that the appellant no. 2 was walking with the deceased in the vicinity where the body was found and his omission to report that deceased had fallen over the cliff. Five, the finding of blood on the trousers of appellant no. 3. Six, the fact that the deceased's body when found appeared to have been placed in that position with his cap firmly on his head and his stick across his body and shoulder ... the position in which the body was found was consistent with the story of the accomplice. Seven, the absence of serious injury or injuries which might be expected had deceased fallen over the cliff.[43]

In one case, 1956/4, the judge listed fifteen items of corroboration, starting chronologically with the evidence of the victim's lover, who had been in bed with her when she had been called outside by one of the murderers, and ending with the angry remark made by one of the accused after her hut had been searched.

The reasons for acquittal can be regarded, for the most part, as the mirror images of the reasons for conviction. If the court had confidence in the accomplice witness or witnesses it convicted: if not, it acquitted. In some cases it found the accomplice witness or witnesses so unsatisfactory that it felt unable to rely on their evidence even when there was significant corroboration. In others, though impressed by what they said, the court decided it would be safer to acquit because there was no, or not enough corroboration.

Some accomplices were simply unreliable in themselves. Two at least had been so drunk that no reliance could be placed on what they said (1927/2 and 1959/4), and there were doubts about the sanity of another, who went distractedly from place to place because he thought he was being chased by people on horseback (1954/9). Two were regarded as men of 'bad character'. One of these was Sesemane, a witness in the second case against Matlere Lerotholi (1959/1, Case Study 4). Since doubts were cast on his character in that case, the Crown could not rely on him in another case (1959/2) that was due to be tried at roughly the same time.[44] In 1953/4 the Appeal Court overturned two convictions because the accomplice witnesses had appeared as such in a previous case, a fact of which the judge had been unaware. 'We trust', said the court, 'that the Crown legal advisers will take steps to ensure that in future such "professional" accomplices are not allowed to turn Queen's evidence and escape the consequences of their wickedness.'[45]

The dangers of relying on accomplice evidence were sharply exposed in at least seven cases in which the accomplices tried to deceive the court about who took part in the murder. In 1948/16 an accomplice witness had named two persons in his original statement but later admitted that he had only included them because they were his enemies. Sesemane, the witness in the second case against Matlere Lerotholi (1959/1), named several persons who had not taken part, apparently because Matlere had instructed him to try to confuse the police, and in the immediately following case (1959/2) he tried to incriminate six innocent people, including his own brother and Matlere himself, before giving the final version of his story. 'After the case involving Sesemane', we were told, 'accomplice evidence was totally discredited.'[46] In 1952/7, because there were suspicions that an accomplice witness had made a false accusation against the alleged instigator, the judge threw out the evidence of three other accomplices and acquitted all the accused.[47]

Several accomplices lost credibility because the evidence which they gave in the High Court was inconsistent either in itself or with the evidence they had given in the preparatory examination. We have already described the apparently deliberate inconsistencies of the accomplice witness Seane Klaas in the first case against Matlere Lerotholi (1952/12, Case Study 4). In an equally important case (1953/2), against Chief Theko Makhaola, an accomplice witness said in the preparatory examination that the chief had given certain instructions at a certain meeting, whereas in the High Court he denied it in spite of being questioned explicitly on this point.

More commonly, accomplice witnesses contradicted each other. Judges were prepared to accept minor inconsistencies – they were even suspicious of too much consistency – but the whole of the Crown's case could be invalidated by inconsistencies on matters of substance. In 1945/8, one accomplice witness said that he and his wife were present when the accused declared that they were going to kill their victim 'so as to get his eyelids, lip and lobe of the ear'. His wife, however, declared that 'she was present at the conspiracy and that the cutting up of the victim was never discussed there'. Since she was the victim's secret lover the judge found it impossible that she should have forgotten 'a conversation in which her lover ... was to be cut up, and his lips, which she had felt, his eyes which had looked at her, and his ears which had listened to her, that those three organs were to be removed'. In 1948/16 there was a disagreement between two of the accomplice witnesses on the crucial question of who had been present at the murder. The judge in 1965/6, though convinced that a medicine murder had been committed, was also convinced that the accomplice witnesses were lying. Their evidence, he said, 'bristles with inconsistencies and contradictions'. He dismissed the case without even calling on the defence.[48]

In at least nine cases accomplice evidence was rejected because it was inconsistent with the evidence of the post-mortem examination. In 1954/4 there were three accomplice witnesses and there was some independent evidence as well. The doctor who had conducted the post-mortem had found no wounds on the body, but because the case was so strong he was asked to conduct a second examination. Again he found no wounds, and the accused were all acquitted. There was only one case (1954/1), as far as we know, in which the judge preferred the evidence of the accomplices to that of the doctor who had conducted the post-mortem. Here the accomplices said that a hole had been made in the victim's head with a hammer and chisel, but the doctor made no mention of this in his report and the judge rashly assumed that he had overlooked it. This judgement, however, was over-turned on appeal after the body had been exhumed and no hole was found.[49]

Some accused were acquitted because, although there was evidence *aliunde* that a murder had been committed and therefore statutory law had been satisfied, there was nothing to corroborate the accomplice evidence in implicating them personally in the crime. Under the cautionary rule of practice such corroboration, though not always necessary, was generally held to be advisable. Sir Walter Harragin spelt out the law in the unusual case (1953/5) where a grandmother was accused of murdering her newly-born grandchild and cutting off its arm for medicine. The accomplice witness was the mother, and the main supporting evidence was that of some little boys whose dogs had found the body, and that of the doctor who conducted the post-mortem examination. There was no doubt that a crime had been committed, Harragin said, and if, for example, a witness had seen the woman accused carrying a bundle away from the hut on the night the baby was born, then the Crown's case would have been unanswerable.[50] As it was, there was nothing, apart from the accomplice's evidence, to connect the grandmother with the crime, and she was acquitted.

The judges were sometimes reluctant to acquit in cases where a cruel murder had clearly been committed. 'I wish I could have given another verdict', said Mr Justice Krause as he declared the accused not guilty (1948/18). Judge Roper told the accused that some of them were no doubt very lucky, and they would not be so fortunate if they murdered anyone else (1961/2).

The accused sometimes argued that, in giving evidence against them, the accomplices were motivated by malice. We know of only two cases, 1945/3 and 1952/11, in which this argument was clearly accepted. In 1945/3 (Case Study 1) Mpharane Mokoetla was acquitted because the only evidence against him was that of the accomplice witness Nkojoa Mokone, and they were known to have quarrelled. In 1952/11, in spite of some corroborative evidence, two of the accused were given the benefit of the doubt because they were able to prove that one of the acccomplices was on bad terms with them.

The most common defence was the alibi, and wives and friends were often called as witnesses to support it. It was rarely accepted, and the comments of Judge Elyan in case 1954/3 are typical of many:

> As I listened to the evidence of Accused 5, whose appearance and demeanour in the witness box I carefully observed, I formed the opinion that he was not a trustworthy witness. The Accused 6 gave her evidence in a most unconvincing manner. I have already indicated that I do not regard the witnesses called by the defence to give evidence in support of the evidence of Accuseds 5 and 6 as credible witnesses and I would only add the general remark that I formed the opinion, as I listened to the evidence of these witnesses ... that it was a tissue of deliberate falsehoods.

In the few cases where an alibi was accepted there were almost invariably exceptional factors which tilted the balance in favour of the accused. In three cases the accused were senior chiefs, or were supported by witnesses from Matsieng, or both. Theko Makhaola (1953/2) and Matlere Lerotholi (1959/1) were both acquitted on the basis at least in part of alibis, and so too was the alleged instigator in 1945/3 (Case Study 1), Mahao Matete, the head-man at Morija. Another accused whose alibi was accepted was an evangelist (1948/24), and another a highly successful trader (1961/2). In two other cases (1953/4 and 1956/3), in both of which the judgement was overturned on appeal, there was evidence supporting the alibi not just from the defence but from one of the Crown witnesses as well. Otherwise there was only one ordinary commoner, as far as we have been able to establish, whose alibi was accepted by the court (1954/1).[51]

Another defence that was sometimes put forward was that of compulsion, but to establish this the accused had to be able to prove

> that during the whole of the period of time covered by his alleged criminal conduct he was compelled to it by threats which produced a reasonable and substantial fear that immediate death or serious bodily harm to himself ... would follow upon his refusal.[52]

These criteria were difficult to meet. In 1942/4 two wives who had played only a minor part in the murder were able to prove that they had acted under the coercion of their husband, who had given them orders and threatened to kill them if they disobeyed. In a later case (1951/5), however, the Privy Council rejected the appeal of a man who had tried to run away when the murder was being committed but had been brought back and forced to drink blood.

Earlier in this chapter we gave the number of those who were initially accused of medicine murder before the courts: 1,052. In the course of the judicial process nineteen of these died and two disappeared,[53] leaving a total of 1,033. By the end of the judicial process 350 (34 per cent) of these 1,033

Graph 9.1 The outcomes of the judicial process, 1895–1966

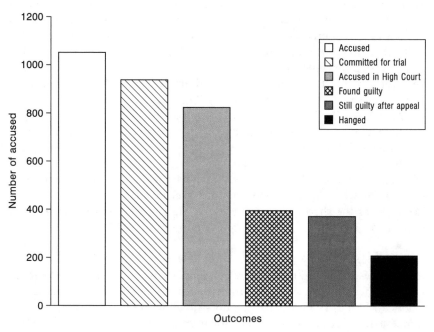

Accused
1,042 accused in PEs + 10 in first four cases who did not appear before PE (total 1,052).
Committed for trial
928 committed + 10 from first four cases (total 938).
Accused in High Court
824 accused in HC after Attorney-General decided not to prosecute 99 and 15 had died.
Found guilty
374 of murder, 21 as accessories (total 395).
Still guilty after appeal
350 of murder, 21 as accessories (total 371).
Hanged
206 for murder, 2 as accessories (total 208).

had been found guilty of murder, twenty-one (2 per cent) had been found guilty as accessories, and the rest, 660 (64 per cent), had been discharged, acquitted or pardoned.

Instigators were more likely to be convicted of murder than accomplices: fifty-seven out of 138 (41 per cent) compared with 293 out of 914 (32 per cent). If we also take into account the twenty-one accomplices who were found guilty as accessories, the rate of conviction for accomplices is 314 out of 914 (34 per cent). Taking instigators and accomplices together, of those whose sex we have been able to identify, women were slightly more likely to be found guilty, either as murderers or as accessories, than men: forty-three out of ninety-seven (44 per cent) compared with 325 out of 805 (40 per cent),[54] a surprising finding in view of their often marginal role. Those identified as doctors were more likely to be found guilty, either as accessories or as murderers, than others charged: twenty out of forty-seven (43 per cent), compared with 351 out of 1,005 (35 per cent) for the rest.

To this limited extent the judgements reflected the heavier responsibility of the instigators and the doctors. There were several individual cases, however, in which the verdict, though no doubt legally sound, was at variance with the social and political realities. The second case against Matlere Lerotholi (1959/1, Case Study 4), is an example: the alleged instigator escaped scot-free, while several of his accomplices were convicted. Then, on appeal, his right-hand man was acquitted, while the others had their appeals turned down. In 1945/3 (Case Study 1), it was the right-hand man, John Makume, who was convicted, whereas the headman who was alleged to have ordered the murder was acquitted. Paramount Chief regent 'Mantšebo, who was identified as the shadow instigator in the Matlere case and possibly in the Mahao Matete case as well, did not even appear in the dock.

THE DISCRETION OF THE HIGH COMMISSIONER

In some cases these injustices were softened when the question of clemency was considered by the High Commissioner (from 1960 by the Executive Council).[55] Until 1959, when discretion was allowed for extenuating circumstances, the statutory punishment for murder was hanging, but the High Commissioner could commute this to imprisonment.[56] There was always, however, a discretion for accessories before or after the fact.

The High Commissioner took into consideration reports from the judges (including the appeal judges where appropriate), the Attorney-General, and the Resident Commissioner and the District Commissioner, as well as pleas from the accused.[57] In deciding whether or not to commute the sentence, he was essentially considering whether or not there were any extenuating circumstances which might diminish the accused's responsibility for the murder. In the papers submitted to him recommendations for mercy were made for those accomplices who played only a minor part in the crime, for young people put under pressure by their elders, commoners put under pressure by their chiefs, and wives put under pressure by their husbands.[58] Although we have found no explicit statement to this effect, in some cases it seems that being a woman in itself was a reason for clemency. In 1945/6 the two women had their sentences commuted and the two men were hanged. One of the women was the instigator. In 1956/4 five accused had their sentences commuted, two men to twelve years' imprisonment and three women to eight years' imprisonment. 'Ignorance' or being 'steeped' in Sesotho custom were sometimes put forward. The three men condemned to death in the second Matlere Lerotholi case (1959/1) submitted their petitions in identical terms, evidently drafted by their legal representatives:

That your Petitioner is wholly illiterate, and a completely ignorant peasant steeped in the traditions of Basutho [*sic*] customs, so that he considered it his duty to carry out what he verily believed to be the orders of so powerful and influential a chief as the said MATLERE LEROTHOLI; which orders weighed more heavily with your Petitioner than would have been the case if he had been a more enlightened person.[59]

Our information about commutations of sentence is far from complete, but the outcome is reflected in the ultimate fate of those who were found guilty.[60] Of the 350 convicted of murder, 206 were hanged, 119 went to prison, four died, and we do not know the fate of twenty-one others. Instigators were more likely to be hanged than accomplices: forty-two out of fifty-seven (74 per cent), compared with 164 out of 293 (56 per cent). Men were more likely to be hanged than women: 194 out of 310 (63 per cent), compared with ten out of thirty-eight (26 per cent).[61] Doctors were more likely to be hanged than 'lay' persons: fourteen out of nineteen (74 per cent), compared with 192 out of 331 (58 per cent). Of the twenty-one accomplices convicted as accessories (fifteen men, five women and one of unknown sex), two were hanged and the remaining nineteen went to prison. Both of those who were hanged were men, and one of them was a doctor. The people who benefited most from the prerogative of mercy were therefore accomplices rather than instigators, women rather than men, and 'lay' persons rather than doctors.

EXECUTION

For those who were convicted and hanged the final records were the special warrant, edged in black, issued by the High Commissioner, authorising the carrying out of the sentence of death, and the certificate signed, among others, by the hangman confirming that this warrant had been duly executed.[62] The condemned men and women nearly all went to their deaths defiant and unrepentant. 'It is amazing', the Reverend Mphatšoe wrote in 1952, 'that all the accused, in every case, deny to the bitter end having taken part in the killing of the deceased. This is the reason why so many people think that the accused are innocent of these murders.' He held a prayer meeting with nine condemned persons on the day before they were due to be hanged, and when it was over

one of them stood up and said, 'Minister, you have been very kind to visit us, and to preach the Gospel since we have been condemned in these cells. I ask you to pray God to forgive my sins which I have committed since my childhood up to the present moment. As for the crime for which I am convicted, don't bother to pray for me. I am innocent. I am not guilty'. As he uttered the last sentence, all the others joined in with him, saying 'We are not guilty of this crime. We have no blood on our hands'.[63]

Not everyone was so firm and confident. Stephen Phakisi recalled:

> I used to go with *Moruti* [Minister] Mphatšoe to visit the prisoners in
> the condemned cell. They never confessed their guilt. But I remember
> one case. It was that of a chief from Mohale's Hoek District, and there
> were up to ten followers with him, all men. It was half an hour before
> they were due to be hanged. Mphatšoe said to them, 'Now is no time
> for the fear of man. Now is the time for the fear of God … If there is
> anything you have to say you must say it now'. One man put up his
> hand and said, *Joale he, joale he, ke tla bua 'nete* ['Now then, now then,
> I shall speak the truth'.] And he then started telling the story of what
> had happened. He was speaking for only three or four minutes, but he
> appeared to have something to say that was different from what he had
> said before. But then the chief became so much angry, he banged the
> table repeatedly: *Ha re bashanyana. Ha re lehlaka, lehlaka ha moea o
> hlaha koana le ea koana* ['We are not boys. We are not a reed, a reed
> blowing in the wind'.] The man became quiet and said no more. He
> had more respect for his chief than for God.[64]

Several convicts, while not confessing their guilt, were converted to Christianity
at this point. In 1947/14 two of the accused became Roman Catholics
shortly before they were hanged. In a case in 1951, a man repented and was
baptised in the condemned cell by the Anglican Bishop of Basutoland.[65]

Those who were acquitted, or who had their sentences commuted and
served terms of imprisonment, had to return sooner or later to their own
communities. Some accomplice witnesses, who had given evidence against
them, also returned home, while others fled to other parts of Basutoland or
to the Free State. Typically, there were two flows of anger: on the part of
those who had been accused against the accomplice witnesses and others
who had given evidence against them; and on the part of the victims' relatives against all those who were alleged to have taken part in the murder.
How did the people involved live together in the wake of such traumatic
events? How did communities recover? Sometimes resentments festered
quietly over the decades, sometimes they erupted into open and bitter
recrimination. In the Aftermath below we review some evidence of this kind.

AFTERMATH

It is very difficult to talk about this thing. It is always in my thoughts, never out of my mind.

> Chieftainess 'Mamathe Masupha,
> widow of Chief Gabashane Masupha[1]

I still feel the pain: every day I think of Mofolo. Our family and Mosalla's are still on bad terms. We live in the same place, but it is in our hearts.

> 'Mangoajane Mofolo, daughter-in-law of Mofolo Ramalumane,
> victim in case 1958/1[2]

This is very painful for me. I get angry when I remember.

> 'Mamoliehi Nyooko, grand-daughter of Meriama Khokhoma,
> victim in case 1942/1[3]

After half a century the wounds inflicted by medicine murder are still raw. There is still bitterness and hatred between the families of murderers, or alleged murderers, and the families of their victims. Most people are prepared to talk about what happened, but for many of them it is painful, even heartbreaking, to be reminded of such terrible events in which members of their own family were killed or hanged, or in which they themselves took part or were accused of taking part. Some are still frightened to speak. We here briefly review, in turn, some accounts from people connected with the alleged murderers, from people connected with the victims, and of mixed public reactions to the outcomes of trials.

Almost without exception, those who were connected with the murderers, or alleged murderers, protested their innocence, explained how it was that they came to be wrongly accused, and downplayed the subsequent bitterness and anger. The stories they told were constructions, sometimes very elaborate constructions, which helped them to live with a dreadful past and enabled them to save face in the world. In Case Study 3 we quoted Chieftainess 'Mamathe Masupha at length. She was convinced, she told us, that her husband Gabashane had been the victim of a British plot in which several of his rivals were pleased to take part. And in Case Study 4 we quoted Seane Klaas, the accomplice witness against Chief Matlere Lerotholi, who claimed to have been tortured into making his confession and then to have concocted conflicting evidence with a fellow accomplice witness in order to secure acquittals for the accused. Others whom we interviewed in different parts of the country – both survivors of such traumatic events, and descendants of people involved – likewise gave their own constructions of what had happened.

Chief Matita Makotoko is the grandson of Chief Makotoko Lechokha Mosalla, who was convicted of murder in case 1958/1 and hanged. We interviewed him at his home at Ha Mosalla, near Thaba-Bosiu, in 1999. He was a young man of about thirty. He told us that his grandfather was the last person to be hanged for medicine murder:

> Afterwards it was found he was innocent, and so no-one else was hanged after him. There was a boundary dispute between him and Chief Jeremiah Jobo of Thaba-Khupa, and it was Chief Jobo who got my grandfather into trouble. A certain person disappeared and was found dead. That was where it started. About seventeen other people were hanged. That was terrible. Chief Jobo got people to give false evidence against my grandfather.

He assured us that there was no bad feeling today arising out of the case, but at the end of our talk he asked nervously, 'Do these people [the victim's family] want compensation?'[4]

Sethabathaba Hatahata, who was acquitted in the same case, had another story drawn straight from the counter-narrative of medicine murder:

> [A certain accomplice witness] was called to give evidence against Chief Makotoko. He was called by the government. The English policemen had taught him what to say. But it wasn't like that at all. The British were killing the chieftainship. There was no medicine murder at all. The victim ... was killed ... by a man who was his rival in love ... The British exploited this ordinary murder in order to destroy the chiefs ... I heard that the police put pressure on people in custody. They tried to frighten them. They told them that if they kept silent they would be hanged. They did not beat them, but they frightened them ... I was acquitted because I had an alibi. I did not even know the dead man. My wife could prove that I was always here ... at home.[5]

Chief Joseph Molapo Maama, who was born in 1922, is the son of Chief Molapo Maama, who was suspected of several medicine murders and was convicted in case 1950/3. He was convinced, he said, of his father's innocence.

> He was sentenced to death. Then the case went on appeal to the Privy Council and his sentence was reduced to fifteen years. During that time Mr Rivers Thompson was DC at Mafeteng. He told me he was not satisfied with the judgement and that he had written to the Resident Commissioner about it. He knew that my father would never

have done such a thing. Around 1958 a reply was sent to Mr Thompson that my father was released on his recommendation ...

The accomplice witnesses were Kosenene Masaballa, Majorobela and Sesioana ... Very soon after the case they died because of their bad consciences. Sesioana fled to the Free State and died there. Kosenene and Majorobela died in Maseru, after they had given evidence against my father. They admitted that they had told lies against the chief. They did not claim that the police tortured them. It was just remorse: they had told lies.[6]

Old 'Mathuso Tšitang is the widow of Masimong Maketekete, who was acquitted on a charge of murder in case 1945/8. She admitted that many people believed that he had helped his chief, Tsotang Griffith, to carry out the murder, but she personally did not believe that they could have done it:

At the time my husband was at a cattle post, and some herdboys testified that he was there. The police came to measure the distance from here to the cattle post, and agreed that my husband could not have been present at the murder.

'Mathuso was unusual in admitting to bad relations with the family of the victim:

They didn't like us. They lived with my husband's brother, and he did not like us either. They believed my husband had killed Mokebisa. There was no violence, but hard words and hard thoughts.[7]

The fact that John Makume, a church elder at Morija, was the only one of the accused to be convicted and hanged in case 1945/3 raised questions for the church as well as for the family. The missionary Albert Brutsch explained that, being a Christian, Makume had to tell the truth; and that, while the rest of the accused denied their involvement, Makume freely admitted his guilt – an account that is at variance with the court record.[8] One of his descendants provided an explanation grounded in Sesotho belief rather than in Christianity. According to this view, the murder had been carried out by Chief Mahao Matete with the help of certain women who were witches. Mahao was a young man who worked at Matsieng, and he had appointed Makume to act for him as headman at Morija. He was now worried that Makume was getting too powerful and decided to pin the blame on him. To make sure that Makume was found guilty,

Mahao Matete used medicine against [Makume], so that when he was in court he could not speak. He became mute. That was why he alone was hanged. All the others could defend themselves. He couldn't.

The people who experienced the greatest difficulty were the accomplice witnesses. They were hated by the victim's family because they had killed the victim, and by the murderers' families because they had given evidence against them. Many fled to the Free State rather than return home. One of those who decided to stay away was Sesemane Kao, who gave evidence against Matlere Lerotholi in case 1959/1. Sesemane was no longer alive in 1999, but we were able to meet his half-brother, Molosi Kao, who told us that Matlere was 'very angry with him':

> Sesemane lived ... at Bafali ... After the ... case he went to Letšeng-la-Terae because he was scared. But eventually he went back home. It was a couple of years later at least ... Matlere was at Motsitseng and we were at Bafali, and so we were very much apart.[9]

Others gritted their teeth and went home without delay. Old 'Mathuso Tšitang was again direct and straightforward:

> The accomplice witnesses returned to the village after the trial, and we weren't happy with them at all. We weren't happy with them because they wanted to kill my husband and others. We didn't like them because they implicated my husband and others falsely.[10]

Unlike those connected with the murderers, or alleged murderers, people connected with the victims did not have to worry about warding off the disapproval and hostility of their neighbours and trying to defend their families' reputations. They had no hesitation in saying that medicine murders were committed and that they gave rise to bad relations.

'Mangoajane Mofolo, whom we quoted above, still felt angry about the death of her father-in-law, even though those connected with the murderers said that relations were good. But if the murderer was a chief, there was nothing to be done. Exinia Letsoela told us of a murder committed at Ha Mofoka in the late 1920s or early 1930s. There was, she said, 'great hatred between the families of the victim and the families of the murderers. They did not visit each other. Even now they don't, there is still that hatred'. But there was no open conflict. 'Because a chief had been involved people could do nothing. They respected him. They were afraid he might kill them if they showed their displeasure.'[11]

There were no such constraints on 'Mamoliehi Nyooko, whose grand-mother was killed in 1942 by a group of men led by Konstabole Mosi, a commoner (1942/1). Konstabole came back to live in the village, and, she said,

> relations were very bad between him and my parents. I remember being punished by my parents because I and one of my friends used to mock him. We shouted out, *Sebua-mala! Sebua-mala!* [literally, 'one who skins the intestines']. By that we meant he was a medicine murderer. He was like a witch. It was no use my parents punishing me. It served no purpose, because the following day we would do the same,

my friend Tiisetso and I. I was so angry about it. I even remember telling Konstabole, 'I know you're a murderer, so don't try to murder me'. We deliberately set out to put him to shame before other people.[12]

Among those who were not directly connected with the case opinion was often divided at the time, and it is still divided today. Important chiefs who were acquitted of medicine murder would always have followers who were prepared to support them, and there were cheers in court at the acquittals of Mabina Lerotholi (1948/24), not an important chief in his own right, but one of 'Mantšebo's closest allies; Chief Theko Makhaola (1953/2); Solomon Api Ramabanta (1955/1); Matlere Lerotholi (1959/1); and Dinizulu Nako (1959/4). Yet in Mabina's case, as Jones reported, it was locally expected that he would be convicted,[13] and in Dinizulu's case the reaction was divided.[14] In the late 1990s, at Molapo Maama's old village of Mokema, some regarded him as cruel and ambitious, an able man who ruined his reputation by resorting to medicine murder, and some revered him as 'a great chief, a real chief' who was innocent and wrongly convicted.

Even within one family, diversity of opinion and perspective may still be discerned long after the events concerned. The following three interviews illustrate this point. They all relate to one case, a murder that took place near Pitsi's Nek (Ha Motšoane), in the north of the Leribe District (1962/ 1).[15] The corpse of a local man, Moramosheshe Pholo, was found in January 1962, apparently murdered. Ten people were charged at a preparatory examination in November 1963. They included Ntitsoe Motlotla, a former village chairman; Malefane Thamahe (or Kobeli), the village headman; and three other local residents, one of whom was Tšabalira Bakane. Two accomplice witnesses emerged for the prosecution. Pakiso Ramphasa, a notorious 'doctor', attributed the plot to Ntitsoe Motlotla and Malefane Thamahe, explained his own involvement 'to use my charms so that what they were going to do should not come to light', said that he had been promised a piece of land for taking part in the conspiracy, and described the circumstances of the killing in a cave at the foot of a cliff, during which he had himself stabbed Moramosheshe with an iron bar. He did not receive the land he had been promised, and for that reason decided to divulge what had happened to the police.[16] Lekhaole Bakane, the second accomplice witness, corroborated much of what Pakiso Ramphasa said. All the accused were committed for trial at the High Court in March 1964, but the prosecution withdrew its case on the third day of the trial because the medical evidence from the post-mortem did not substantiate that a murder had taken place. All accused were discharged.

Lekhaole Bakane had been promised a dark brown cow if he helped with the murder: 'I am a man of straw and own nothing … The reward of the cow was commensurate with the risk'.[17] He was still a 'man of straw' – slight of build, sunken in features and nervous in manner – in January 1998. He initially denied any memory of the case. When pressed, however, he acknowledged that he had been a Crown witness against the accused but insisted, by way of explanation, that the police had forced him to support the incriminating evidence of Pakiso Ramphasa. 'The CID threw me to the ground very roughly' and beat him repeatedly, he said, until he agreed to the words that they gave him. He identified as responsible for this, in particular, Lance-Corporal Skundla who had carried out the police investigation. But he also claimed that Moramosheshe had not been killed, but had fallen to his death down a cliff.[18]

Lekhaole's elder brother, Basia Bakane, jovial and robust and completely different in character, had been sent by their father to Hlotse to listen to the preparatory examination in November 1963. 'Lekhaole was one of the supporters who changed [became a Crown witness] when they took this thing there [to court].' Basia expressed his view that 'the work' was led by Pakiso Ramphasa, the doctor who became principal accomplice witness and was therefore not amongst the accused before the court, but that it had been undertaken on behalf of the area chief, Jobo Motšoane, who wished to strengthen himself.[19] It was generally agreed, however, both in the record of the preparatory examination at the time and in local memories long thereafter, that part of the explanation for the murder was a land dispute between Moramosheshe, who had recently returned home from mine-work in South Africa, and Ntitsoe Motlotla, who had been wrongly in occupation of his land for several years. A court case over this matter, heard by the area chief in August 1961, was unresolved at the time of Moramosheshe's death.

'Mapuleng Bakane's husband Lehana had been an independent prosecution witness, and her husband's younger brother Tšabalira Bakane was one of those indicted. She said Lehana had given evidence on behalf of Tšabalira, to show that he could not have participated in the murder because they were together helping to supervise a circumcision school in the mountains at the time; whereas the record of the preparatory examination merely shows Lehana briefly giving evidence about the disappearance of the deceased and about the feast that took place beforehand. She was convinced that the 'owner' of the plot to kill Moramosheshe was Pakiso Ramphasa, the doctor. He was really hated, she said, when he returned home: 'People despised him and didn't want to see him when he went about'. Villagers had also closely questioned Lekhaole Bakane, for his part, on his return home. 'He said his heart was very sore. He shrivelled, to the size of this pen! Even now, when his wife insults him she says, "Get out! This thing killed Moramosheshe!"'[20]

From three different observers of these events at the time, one of whom had been directly involved as an accomplice witness, thus emerged three different accounts of what had happened and of who had been responsible. Lekhaole Bakane, the accomplice witness, strove both to deny that a medicine murder had taken place and specifically to explain his own part in the court case by reference to violent intimidation by the police. Basia Bakane, his brother, had no doubt that a murder had taken place, attributed responsibility to the doctor, the other accomplice witness, but identified the area chief, who was not indicted or apparently drawn into the investigation, as 'shadow' instigator of the murder. 'Mapuleng Bakane, who had married into the same extended family and whose husband gave independent evidence and whose brother-in-law was one of the accused, vigorously disclaimed her brother-in-law's involvement but had no doubt that Moramosheshe had been killed for medicine and attributed the plot primarily to the doctor.

CONCLUSION

Medicine murder evoked a particular horror. The perpetrators inflicted appalling suffering on their victims, who were usually their neighbours and often their friends or relatives. They did not kill in the heat of the moment, but made their plans well in advance. They operated in gangs, and they were inspired by a grotesquely misplaced belief in the power of human medicine.

In the late 1940s and early 1950s there was a widespread conviction among both Basotho and whites that medicine murder had increased dramatically. This conviction was strengthened by the detailed and widespread publicity given to the trials in Maseru. It gave rise to fear and terror, in that people were afraid to go about at night; to revulsion and contempt, in that many whites were confirmed in their prejudices about African backwardness and barbarity; to grief and shame, in that many Basotho were painfully aware of the damage done to their good name; to endless and anguished deliberations as ways were sought and efforts were made to put an end to these hideous crimes; and finally to anger and defiance, as many Basotho came to deny that there was any such thing as medicine murder or accused the British of exaggerating and exploiting it in order to undermine their chiefs.

All this we have described as a moral crisis. In the following sections of this concluding chapter, we identify and reject varieties of conspiracy theory; we summarise our view on the incidence of medicine murder and argue that a significant increase in the 1940s is most plausibly attributed to a form of competitive contagion, deriving mainly from the battle of the medicine horns between 'Mantšebo and Bereng, in a context of political insecurity, deriving mainly from the Khubelu and Treasury reforms; we seek to explain the moral crisis through the involvement of the highest chiefs in the land and the vigour of the British colonial response; we question a connection often loosely asserted between witchcraft and medicine murder; and, finally, we identify a pervasive ambivalence on the part of the Basotho and of the British and emphasise, despite widespread belief in the power of human medicine, the historical contingency of that belief.

CONSPIRACY THEORIES

Basotho nationalists, from Josiel Lefela to Ntsu Mokhehle, protested that there was no moral crisis at all, but only a colonial conspiracy, a big lie that gained acceptance through constant repetition. This view is still widely held. Such conspiracy theories have also received sympathetic consideration from white scholars. Dan Bosko suggested, in effect, that what happened might have been closer to a moral panic than a moral crisis. Relying mainly on fieldwork carried out over eighteen months in 1977–9, he argued that medicine murder was perhaps no more than a social construct, the outcome of either deception or self-delusion on the part of those who confessed to the crime and of a culturally conditioned credulity on the part of those to whom the confessions were made; and that it was then exploited by missionaries and others to discredit Sesotho culture.[1] David Coplan, in the context of a discussion of *lebollo* (initiation) and other controversial aspects of Sesotho culture including the alleged use of human medicine, disclaimed any outsider's capacity to form a reliable judgement. Invoking a post-colonial version of darkest Africa, impenetrable to European understanding, he concluded that no outsider was 'in any position to know. These things are *likoma*, secrets'.[2]

Marc Epprecht, while acknowledging the horror of medicine murder, believed that the British used the possibility of prosecution as a 'death threat' to check 'Mantšebo's 'growing arrogance', and at the same time staged a series of 'show trials' in order to get rid of 'anachronistic' chiefs. Whether they did this as 'a cynical, if not diabolical, plot' to destroy those chiefs who were opposed to their plans for 'modernization or incorporation in South Africa', Epprecht left open. But he condemned the 'insidious' use of accomplice witnesses, 'which effectively allowed anyone with a grievance to come forward with a story of how he had carried out a murder on the chief's command'. As for Jones, his report merely supported 'pre-existing assumptions' that the chiefs were responsible for medicine murders, and so, despite his 'worthy academic reputation ... it is hard not to [*sic*] escape the feeling that he was used by the colonial authorities to prove what they already suspected and hence to justify what they already wanted to do'.[3]

Many people, especially whites, were ready for their own reasons to see medicine murder under every stone. In some cases there were policemen who were over-zealous in pursuing their enquiries or accomplices who told lies to incriminate their enemies. But as explanations of the entire phenomenon of medicine murder, and as keys to understanding British policy at the time, both the nationalists' allegations and the academics' speculations are misdirected. They fail to account for the facts.

The first fact, of course, was the mutilated body. Because of the lapse of time it was sometimes impossible for the doctor conducting the post-mortem examination to be sure that the mutilations had been inflicted by human agency and had not been caused by natural predators. But in many cases the body was found very quickly and it was clear the mutilations could have been caused only by deliberate intent. Although the body was generally found in a river or at the foot of a cliff, the doctor was often able to establish that death had not been caused by drowning or by a fall, but by injuries inflicted by human hands. There were also many cases in which the wounds on the body were consistent with the accounts of the accomplice witnesses.

It was one of the weaknesses of the Basutoland African Congress (BAC) position that, while it accepted the fact of the mutilated bodies, it could not provide an explanation for them. Its annual conference in 1956, while denying the existence of medicine murder, confessed that it simply did not know 'just what brings about the occurance [*sic*] of dead mutilated bodies in Basutoland'.[4] Yet the evidence from the trials was overwhelming. The judges were reluctant to convict on accomplice evidence alone, and we have identified only eleven cases in which they did (and in three of these there was further evidence which they did not need to take into account). In most cases accomplice evidence was supported by independent evidence of varying kinds and varying strengths – by the post-mortem examination, by the exhibits produced before the court, and above all by independent witnesses – people, for example, who saw the victim being led away by the accused, or who heard the victim screaming. Bosko implied that their evidence could be discounted because, he claimed, none of them actually witnessed the murder itself. Even if his facts were right they would not support his conclusion. The evidence provided by independent witnesses was often powerfully corroborative of the accomplices' accounts. And in fact he was wrong: we know of ten cases in which an independent witness or witnesses actually saw the murder being carried out.[5] In view of the pre-cautions the murderers took to avoid being observed it is not surprising that there were not more.

On the whole the judges were extremely rigorous in applying the criminal standard of proof: that is, they only convicted if they were satisfied beyond all reasonable doubt that the accused were guilty. There were many cases in which, on the balance of probabilities, the accused appeared to have been guilty but in which they were given the benefit of the doubt.

There was also overwhelming evidence that the purpose for which the murders were committed was to obtain medicine made from human parts. The BAC again found itself in a dilemma. Bennett Khaketla, its deputy leader, admitted that bodily parts, *liretlo*, were cut away, but while he denied that they were used for medicine he could not provide any other explanation. Yet there was, and is, a widespread belief in the power of human medicine among the Basotho and many other African peoples of southern Africa. In the particular cases that came before the courts there was evidence not only about intention – for example that of chiefs and headmen who were said by witnesses to have stated plainly that they wanted to replenish their medicine horns – but also about the subsequent use of human medicine in pegging and scarification.

Thus the theory of a colonial conspiracy is not credible, whether in its fully developed form – that medicine murder was an 'invention' of the British authorities – or in its modified form – that, while medicine murder might have been practised by some unimportant headmen, it was exploited by the British to destroy the senior chiefs. Either way, those advancing this theory have to postulate the conscious involvement not only of the colonial officials, including the Attorney-General, the police and the prosecuting advocates, but of the accomplice witnesses and the independent witnesses as well, and perhaps also of the judges and their assessors (though they might have been the dupes rather than the perpetrators of the plot). Yet it is inconceivable that the colonial authorities could have suborned so many people in so many cases, especially when giving evidence against a chief was such a hazardous undertaking. In the 'Mamakhabane case (1948/1, Case Study 2), for instance, it would have to be argued that they enlisted the co-operation not just of four accomplices, but of a boy who saw the victim being captured and overheard him crying out and asking not to be killed, of a woman who also heard the victim cry out, of several people who observed the movements of the accused, and of two young boys who were woken by one of the accomplices and shown the victim's dead body. The judge said it was one of the strongest cases he had ever heard. And 'Mamakhabane's old adviser, Stimela Jingoes, had no doubt of her guilt.

The case against Bereng and Gabashane was not as strong as that against 'Mamakhabane, but it was strong enough to convince a respected South African judge and to survive an appeal to the Privy Council. Other senior chiefs, far from being wrongly convicted as the result of a colonial conspiracy, were probably lucky to get away with murder, especially Matlere Lerotholi who was acquitted twice, and to a lesser extent David Theko Makhaola. Others, notably 'Mantšebo herself, in the absence of strong enough evidence against them, were not brought before the courts at all. Once a case was started, especially when it involved men such as Bereng and Gabashane, the prosecution worked hard to secure convictions, but that does not mean that the whole case was inspired from the beginning by a colonial plot.

Such a conspiracy theory rests on false assumptions. So far from wanting to hand the country over to South Africa, the British authorities, Evelyn Baring above all, were determined to keep Basutoland under British rule, especially after the triumph of the National Party in 1948. And far from wanting to destroy the chieftainship, they had just made its development the lynch-pin of their administration by the belated introduction of indirect rule. They badly needed capable and co-operative men such as Bereng Griffith Lerotholi, Gabashane Masupha, Matlere Lerotholi and David Theko Makhaola. This conspiracy theory also fails to account both for the continuation of medicine murder as Basutoland began to move towards independence, when transfer to South Africa was no longer a live issue; and for its continuation after independence, when there was no longer a colonial presence.

Finally, if there had been such an extraordinary conspiracy we would surely have found at least some hint of it either in the public records or in officials' private papers and memoirs. Instead, what we find is bewilderment and anger that anyone could deny the fact of medicine murder and make such allegations, coupled with an earnest consideration of how such hideous crimes could be brought to an end. The adoption of the South African law on accomplice evidence was not, as Mokhehle argued, inspired by a determination to destroy the chiefs or to prepare the way for incorporation into South Africa, but by a resolve to secure convictions in cases where evidence was often hard to come by.

There was no reason for the British to invent medicine murder, and at first the Basotho saw no reason to deny it. The earliest debates in the National Council were marked by the councillors' unanimity that the crime was increasing and had to be stopped. But as more and more chiefs and their followers were convicted, and especially after the cases against Bereng and Gabashane, the chiefs themselves felt seriously threatened, and many Basotho, especially the nationalists, came to believe that their people and their culture were being held up as objects of horror and contempt. The denial of medicine murder became a matter of national pride and defiance.

Elizabeth Eldredge proposed another conspiracy, in some ways the opposite of the first – that the British created the crisis not by inventing medicine murder, nor by exploiting it to destroy the chiefs, but by condoning it and therefore encouraging its spread. This was done not by default but deliberately. The colonial authorities knew that 'Mantšebo was at the heart of this 'new wave of medicine murders', but they took no action against her. Instead they 'knowingly protected her' and 'kept her in place for twenty long and deadly years'. This was, first, because 'Mantšebo was their 'client' – they had appointed her, and not Bereng, because they had wanted a weak Paramount Chief – and, second, because, having centralised power in her hands, they were able to exploit the fear of her on the part of Basotho and in this way to consolidate their own authority. 'So we know why medicine murder reached epidemic proportions ...', Eldredge concluded: 'the government allowed 'Mantšebo and other major chiefs to commit murder with impunity, and the copycat effect continued'.[6] We have already dealt with the claim that the British authorities appointed 'Mantšebo because they wanted a weak Paramount Chief. The contemporary records make it clear that 'Mantšebo was the firm choice of the Sons of Moshoeshoe and that senior officials simply respected that choice.[7] The description of her as Britain's 'client' is tendentious and misleading.

The colonial authorities certainly believed that 'Mantšebo was guilty of medicine murder, but they could never bring a charge against her for the simple reason that they never had enough evidence. They did, however, take two of her closest supporters to court – Matlere Lerotholi (twice) and Mabina Lerotholi – but both men were able to escape conviction. The only case in which 'Mantšebo herself was directly implicated collapsed when the supposed victim, Borane, reappeared – a fiasco which was subsequently thrown up time and time again in officials' faces.

Eldredge also believed that the British protected 'Mantšebo by 'white-washing' the Jones report. As she rightly noted, Jones was convinced of 'Mantšebo's guilt (though the 'secret paper' which she quotes to prove this was written by Ashton, not Jones). But 'Jones was not allowed to include the evidence incriminating 'Mantšebo … and the report that was published was the product of a deliberate British colonial cover-up'.[8] In fact Jones' report was critical of 'Mantšebo: it referred to the popular belief that there was a 'battle of medicine horns between the Regent and Chief Bereng' and that many murders by lesser chiefs or headmen had been carried out on the orders of their superiors. The only evidence incriminating 'Mantšebo omitted by Jones was a paragraph in which, as distinct from reporting popular belief, he stated his own view that certain Mokhotlong murders could not have taken place without Matlere Lerotholi's knowledge, and that until the mystery surrounding these murders was cleared up people would continue to believe that Matlere and, through him, 'Mantšebo were involved in them. Forsyth-Thompson and Baring had suggested that he should amend this paragraph since it might expose him to a libel action by Matlere, and Baring was also worried that, unless the paragraph was amended, 'we could hardly continue with the present Regent in her office. Yet it might in present circumstances be unwise to depose her'. At a meeting held in London, at which both Jones and Baring were present, it was agreed that the paragraph should be deleted.[9] In short, the report was critical of 'Mantšebo, and but for the intervention of Baring and Forsyth-Thompson it would have been even more critical. Their main concern, however, was to avoid provoking a libel action and possibly a wider confrontation which would have damaging political consequences. To describe these senior officials' influence on the revision of the Jones report as a 'deliberate cover-up' is therefore, again, tendentious and misleading.

The colonial authorities had good reasons for not deposing 'Mantšebo. No paramount had ever been deposed before. 'Mantšebo had been chosen as regent by a large majority of the Sons of Moshoeshoe. There had never been any firm proof of her involvement in medicine murder: she had never been brought to court, let alone convicted. Though many Basotho were critical of the regent, the Basotho as a whole were fiercely protective of their chieftainship. When Gunther assailed 'Mantšebo in *Inside Africa*, the National Council was unanimous in denouncing him.[10] The authorities were well aware that if they deposed 'Mantšebo they would run into a storm of opposition: it would have been seen as an attack, not just on 'Mantšebo personally, but on the paramount chieftainship itself and so on the dignity and pride of the entire Basotho nation. There were even fears that it might provoke another outbreak of medicine murder, especially as throughout this period the heir, Constantine Bereng Seeiso, was a child or a student being educated in England and there was no obvious successor to 'Mantšebo as regent.[11] Jones was in favour of getting rid of 'Mantšebo but he recognised that this could only be done if the Basotho took action themselves.[12]

It is possible, though it seems unlikely, that Baring and his colleagues made an error of judgement, and that they could have got away with deposing 'Mantšebo without provoking a major crisis. But, whether they were right or wrong, they certainly did not keep her in position because they wanted to exploit the fear she inspired.

In a study of soil conservation in Mokhotlong Thackwray Driver went further and speculated that 'the Basutoland authorities were willing to be less harsh on Matlere [Lerotholi] and the Regent 'Mantšebo vis-à-vis their obvious involvement in medicine murders because they both embraced the concept of grazing control'. He acknowledged that he had 'no direct evidence' of this, but pointed to the importance that Baring attached to the role of the chiefs in soil conservation and to the praise heaped on Matlere by Baring and others for his work on grazing control. Such speculation, however, is out-weighed by the fact that Matlere was twice indicted for medicine murder.[13]

INSECURITY AND CONTAGION

Medicine murders were indeed the result of repeated conspiracy. The conspirators were, however, those who conceived and carried out the murder plots, not the colonial authorities. We have no doubt, then, as to the answer to the first key question identified in the Introduction to this book. Medicine murder was, and is, a hideous reality.

As regards the second key question, relating to the incidence of medicine murder, our information is incomplete and inconclusive. The common perception was that the number of murders increased dramatically in the 1940s, reaching a climax in 1948, but there are reasons for believing that this increase might have been less than was generally supposed. Our evidence leads us to conclude that there was a significant increase, though not as 'startling' as was commonly believed at the time. At the end of Chapter 4 we argued that the case for a significant increase would be strengthened if it could be shown that murders in the 1940s were motivated by certain factors that were specific to that period, namely the anxieties and uncertainties arising out of the Khubelu and Treasury reforms and the rivalries over the paramountcy.

Both factors are clearly relevant to an answer to the third key question, relating to the causes of the increase. Our analysis of declared or alleged motives in Chapter 6 revealed only three cases connected explicitly with the reforms. Nevertheless the lesser chiefs and headmen were suffering increasing pressure and insecurity, in part as a result of these reforms. Furthermore, because of the excesses of the placing system, there was an increasing number of minor chiefs and headmen who ruled no more than a few hundred people and who were little or no better off than their followers. They found it difficult to command the respect to which they felt entitled, and this anxiety and discontent might well have stirred their determination *ho tiisa borena*, 'to strengthen their chieftainship'.

The dispute over the regency, however, seems to us more important, not merely in explaining the murders to which it probably gave rise directly but also in creating a climate in which such murders came to be seen as an effective and even acceptable way of strengthening oneself at times of stress. 'Mantšebo's role was central. Like Ashton and Jones, we believe that she turned to medicine murder when she felt threatened by Bereng, and we also believe that she was heavily involved right up to the end of her regency. The incidence and timing of murders in the Mokhotlong District that we discussed in Case Study 4, although by no means conclusive, remain highly suggestive of this involvement. Whether or not we are right, what is important is that she was widely believed to be involved, that this involvement was widely believed to be successful, and that this became, in Ashton's words, a 'positive encouragement' to others to commit medicine murders.[14]

Bereng and Gabashane were among the first to follow her example, and others were no doubt influenced as well. It must have made a great impression on many chiefs and headmen that the most senior and respected chiefs in the land were now putting their trust in *liretlo*. It was only in 1960, when she was ousted against her will, that 'Mantšebo's run of success came to an end. She died in 1964, and it was no coincidence that, after her political demise, none of the senior chiefs, as far as we know, was caught up in medicine murders again.[15] The new paramount, Constantine Bereng Seeiso, seems to have been free from suspicion.

The marked increase in medicine murder in the 1940s occurred, we believe, partly because of the general insecurity at that time – to which the Khubelu and Treasury reforms contributed – but mainly because of the involvement of the senior chiefs and the influence they had throughout the country. The increase, then, was largely attributable to a form of competitive contagion in a particular context of insecurity.

EXPLAINING MORAL CRISIS

The increase in the number of murders does not simply or directly explain the intensity of the moral crisis we have identified. In seeking to answer our fourth key question, then – why the crisis arose and why it disappeared – we concentrate on the climate of acute political anxiety of the late 1940s and the early 1950s, to which the British colonial administration not only responded but also actively contributed, in many ways unwittingly; and on the later dissipation of that anxiety under changed political circumstances.

There were probably as many murders, overall, in the late 1950s and 1960s, but after about 1956 they attracted much less attention, and after about 1960 they were generally, but inaccurately, regarded as a thing of the past. A more important factor than the increase in numbers was the involvement, for the first time, of some of the most senior chiefs in the country and the horrified publicity which this attracted. The conviction and hanging of Bereng and Gabashane in particular were like a political thunderclap that stunned the whole country. The deaths of these two chiefs may have deterred other would-be murderers and in this way helped to keep the crisis within bounds.

In another sense, however, the crisis was heightened by the British response. Baring in particular was shocked by medicine murder and was determined to eliminate it. He saw the chiefs as the mainstay of British rule, and he was afraid that the chieftainship was going rotten. He shook the Basotho when he took the unusual step of coming personally in 1948 to address the opening of the National Council and to hold a special meeting with 'Mantšebo and her advisers, threatening the chiefs with deposition and the country with collective punishment. He wanted to reform and strengthen the chieftainship, but instead he was seen as threatening to end it. The administration's warnings, denunciations and exhortations were not simply a response to the crisis. They actively fuelled it. The attack on medicine murder was experienced as an attack on the chieftainship; and since the chieftainship was central to the strong sense of identity nurtured by most Basotho it was experienced as an attack on the Basotho nation. Hence the impassioned denial that the big chiefs were involved or even that there was any such thing as medicine murder.

The way in which the crisis disappeared tells us as much about its nature as the way in which it arose. It does not seem to have been due to any decline in the incidence of murders. The number reported in 1968, twenty, was as high as the number reported in 1948. It did, however, have something to do with the decline in the involvement of the senior chiefs. The murder allegedly carried out by Matlere Lerotholi for 'Mantšebo in 1959 (1959/1) seems to have been the last carried out for the chiefs at the very top of the hierarchy.

Just as important was the change in the official response. After Baring no High Commissioner took a strong interest in medicine murder, and after Arrowsmith no Resident Commissioner. Le Rougetel, Baring's successor, made suitable speeches when required, but devoted little energy or thought to the problem. Chaplin, Arrowsmith's successor, went out of his way to play down the importance of medicine murder. He simply accepted it as a fact of life and death in southern Africa. His predecessors, he implied, had got matters out of proportion.[16] It was also becoming clear, at the national level at least, that the chiefs were losing their power. The new paramount, Constantine Bereng Seeiso, would play an important role, but the future lay with the politicians, especially, or so it seemed at first, with Ntsu Mokhehle and the BAC.

In view of the debates in the Basutoland National Council it might have been expected that, after independence, the new government of Chief Leabua Jonathan would have established a commission of enquiry into medicine murder in order to remove what was commonly regarded as a stain on the character and culture of the Basotho. Instead there was total silence. After 1969 the numbers of medicine murders disappeared completely from the official record, and in the virtual absence of any trials they achieved little publicity. In 1970, when Chief Leabua's party lost the first post-independence election, he declared the results null and void and proclaimed a state of emergency. Lesotho was thrown into political turmoil. In the midst of recurring tremors of conflict and confusion no-one in power paid any attention to medicine murder. It is possible that during the independence period medicine murders were committed as frequently as in the 1940s, but there has been little evidence of involvement at high political levels, and the phenomenon is commonly regarded by officials as something that belongs to the past, above all to the colonial era. A recently retired police officer suggested that if we wanted to know more about medicine murder we would have to consult the archives.[17] Rumours of it and popular anxiety about it have persisted, however, in different parts of the country.

Perhaps there is a paradox here. The involvement of the most senior chiefs created the crisis in the 1940s, but it was heightened by the fierce response of Baring and Forsyth-Thompson. It is even possible, as was suggested at the time, that this colonial reaction confirmed many Basotho in their belief in the power of human medicine. For why otherwise should the British have reacted so strongly?[18]

Medicine murder did not significantly alter the path of Basutoland's political development. Many chiefs were incompetent and corrupt, and there was increasing demand from the educated élite for more popular representation and a system of justice that was free from the chiefs' vagaries and oppressions. There was also more pressure for economic development. Change was inevitable, and it came in the form of the Khubelu and Treasury reforms. The chiefs felt threatened and uneasy, and the government's fierce response to medicine murder, especially the hanging of Bereng and Gabashane, convinced them that the colonial administration had turned against them. The distancing of the administration from the chieftainship was bound to come. The crisis over medicine murder made it quicker and more bitter.

At first it seemed that medicine murder had weakened the paramountcy. But as the colonial response to medicine murder intensified, both chiefs and politicians closed ranks around the Paramount Chief, and in return many chiefs gave their support to Mokhehle's BAC. This alliance was merely temporary: the underlying conflict of interest between chiefs and politicians was much more important than their unanimity of reaction over medicine murder. But even as the BAC pulled away from the chiefs there was no general disaffection with 'Mantšebo, or indeed with the chiefs as a whole. It is significant that the Basutoland National Party, which narrowly won the pre-independence election and formed the first government of an independent Lesotho, was headed by several of 'Mantšebo's old advisers, notably Leabua Jonathan himself. This could not have happened if the old chieftainship had been completely discredited by *liretlo*.

WITCHCRAFT AND MEDICINE MURDER

Medicine murder was rooted in the beliefs held by many Basotho in the power of human medicine. This is largely shared amongst other African peoples in southern Africa. For this reason it seems unhelpful to argue whether the practice of *liretlo* murders was 'indigenous' to Basutoland or whether it was 'imported' from elsewhere in the region. Either way the moral responsibility for such crimes lies with those who committed them.

An analogy between medicine murder and witchcraft was drawn explicitly by the nationalist politician Ntsu Mokhehle.[19] Neither the belief in witchcraft nor the belief in the power of human medicine could be rationally justified, and just as the authorities in England wrongly killed suspected witches, so the authorities in Basutoland wrongly killed suspected medicine murderers. At the level of belief, such an analogy may be justified. At the level of practice, however, the analogy is misplaced. Witchcraft and medicine murder must be clearly distinguished. The 'evidence' in witchcraft accusations consisted in imputing malice to named individuals who were alleged through occult means to have caused a particular misfortune such as illness or death. To the extent that they were found guilty, they were found to have exerted powers which, in the rationalist view, they could not possibly have possessed. Medicine murderers, on the other hand, were found guilty of killing their victims in ways which were entirely consistent with the natural laws of cause and effect. The judges in Maseru did not have to believe in the power of human medicine in order to convict the accused. They merely had to believe that they were guilty of murder.

It is necessary, therefore, to question the connection (as opposed to the analogy) often asserted between witchcraft and medicine murder. Elsewhere in southern Africa, such a connection was taken for granted in the terms of reference of the Ralushai Commission, appointed in 1995 to investigate a wave of 'witchcraft violence and ritual murders' in the Northern

Province of South Africa, and by other investigators both official and unofficial.[20] In an influential article published in 1999, John and Jean Comaroff of the University of Chicago analysed both witchcraft and ritual murder, together with a variety of other phenomena such as trading in body parts, the production of 'zombies' and pyramid scams, as symbols of a dramatic rise in 'occult economies', by which they meant 'the deployment, real or imagined, of magical means for material ends'.[21] They discerned the roots of these allegedly resurgent phenomena in post-colonial societies, with particular reference to South Africa in the 1990s, in the perception on the one hand of some people's mysterious rise to prosperity, and in the experience on the other hand, particularly on the part of dispossessed youth, of permanent exclusion from the possibility of such prosperity. There is little justification, in our view, for the way in which they indiscriminately aggregated such disparate phenomena into 'occult economies', or indeed for the speculative flourishes with which they sought to explain them with reference to the contradiction between the consumerist propensities of 'late capitalism' and the realities of poverty, inequality and structural unemployment faced by the youth of modern South Africa.

The phrase 'witchcraft violence' itself needs to be carefully deconstructed. Insofar as it refers to the killing of suspected witches, it is a crime because it is murder. It took place because the self-appointed agents of 'community' vengeance, commonly the marginalised youth, sought to identify alleged witches and rid society of them by direct action. But medicine murder took place because a group of conspirators sought, without apparent malice against the individual victim – albeit with appalling cruelty in practice – to make use of bodily parts in medicines. Such conspiracies were usually initiated by men or women in positions of political authority. The challenge of explanation, in either case, lies in a thorough disentangling of the historical particulars of the circumstances in which these forms of murder, respectively, have flourished. Niehaus' book *Witchcraft, Power and Politics*, based on fieldwork in the 1990s, is an excellent example of such an effort, in relation to witchcraft in the eastern lowveld of South Africa.[22]

BELIEF, AMBIVALENCE AND CHANGE

In the case of mid-twentieth-century Basutoland, we have argued that an increase of medicine murders was attributable to a form of competitive contagion in a particular context of insecurity; and that the moral crisis that arose was partly stimulated by the British colonial response. Everywhere we turn, however, we find ambiguity and ambivalence of belief and of response. Most Basotho were repelled by the horrors of *liretlo*, and many were Christians who believed that God had given them a commandment not to kill. But they also believed in the efficacy of human medicine, the importance of the chief's horn, and their duty to obey the chief as the head of their community. Most chiefs pursued their interests and ambitions by other means than instigating a medicine murder. But a significant minority chose that route, and they seem to have experienced very little difficulty in recruiting men and women to help them. Some accomplices acted out of fear or compulsion, others out of loyalty and devotion, or perhaps hoping for some financial reward. Many were driven by a mixture of motives. One familiar device for disclaiming moral responsibility emerges from the judicial record in a number of cases. It was common, apparently, to dehumanise the victims who were selected: they were merely *liphofu*, elands, for example, there to be killed as game.

The ordinary people, as Jones reported, might have detested medicine murder, but they did not necessarily detest medicine murderers. Men and women who escaped conviction often returned to their communities as respected citizens, even if local people were still convinced of their guilt. Even some of those who were found guilty were still accorded respect. In Rivers Thompson's phrase, medicine murder was a crime without a stigma.[23] 'Mantšebo won general approval when she granted Bereng Griffith a funeral at Matsieng, which was attended by 5,000 people,[24] and two and a half years later thousands more attended the stone-laying ceremony at his grave when the Catholic Bishop of Basutoland declared that he had died in a state of grace.[25] Gladstone Phatela, who escaped the hangman's rope only because of a rogue judgement on appeal to the Privy Council, became a candidate for the Congress Party in the 1965 election and proudly included his appeal victory in his brief supporting *curriculum vitae*.[26] When Molapo Maama was released from prison for the day to attend his brother's funeral, the joy which greeted his unexpected appearance threatened to distract the mourners from the ceremony.[27] At David Theko Makhaola's funeral he was praised for the excellence of his administration and was said to have loved the Roman Catholic Church with all his heart.[28] There were similar eulogies for 'Mantšebo in 1964.[29] But perhaps the most telling statement was that which Jones recorded almost casually in a footnote to his report. In the Mafeteng District, he wrote, a man told him that when his chief was first placed he 'was very unpopular, people disliked him and intrigued against him, so that he had to have a killing to renew his *lenaka*. After that there was no further trouble and people liked and accepted him'.[30] A whole world of values is revealed in this laconic remark. In the more elevated field of Sesotho literature it is surely significant that the dominant representation of the medicine murderer, whether as instigator or accomplice, is that of the tragic hero.

Led at first by Josiel Lefela, and later by Ntsu Mokhehle, many Basotho went even further, reacting not with shame and revulsion, but with a wounded pride which found expression in denying the guilt of many of those convicted, or even in denying the very fact of medicine murder; and then in rounding on the British, their police collaborators and those accomplices who gave evidence for the Crown. They buttressed their arguments on medicine murder by defending initiation ceremonies and Sesotho medicine in general.[31] In effect, they closed ranks in defence of their chieftainship and their culture. So, in the later period at least, acquittals were sometimes greeted with cheers, and there was all the more reason for those who were acquitted to be welcomed back into the community.

The ambivalences of the Basotho were reflected in those of the British. Medicine murder was condemned and reviled as a throwback to the days of barbarism and savagery, but there was also a feeling that the murderers' guilt was to some extent mitigated because what they were doing was somehow explained and perhaps even sanctioned by Sesotho beliefs. This feeling was strengthened because several of the chiefs involved were men for whom the colonial administration had the highest regard. Gordon Hector, as Government Secretary, had to call in Matlere Lerotholi to tell him that he was about to be arrested for the murder of a young herdboy (1959/1).

> I didn't like calling him in. I had a very high regard for Matlere. I thought he was about the best of the chiefs we had to deal with. He was one of the old school ... We somehow had a rapport, Matlere and I. I liked the man. I told him: 'I'm sorry to have to tell you ...' And he just nodded and said, 'Thank you, sir, for telling me'. I still remember that interview – his bearing, his dignity, the sheer courtesy of the man. He just nodded, and 'Thank you, sir', he said.[32]

There was similar respect for men such as Bereng and Gabashane, David Theko Makhaola and Molapo Maama. It was held to be typical of their nobility of character that Bereng and Gabashane refused to escape from gaol when their fellow prisoners organised a break-out.[33] At the end even 'Mantšebo was on friendly terms with the Resident Commissioner, Geoffrey Chaplin, and his wife. One mission worker in the Catholic Church used to relish shocking her colleagues by telling them that some of her best friends were medicine murderers.[34]

We have already set out our view that 'Mantšebo's involvement was crucial, but we believe that Eldredge goes too far in her judgement that, because the 'epidemic' of the 1940s could be explained by the particular circumstances of 'Mantšebo's response to the pressures she faced, medicine murder was merely a temporary and tragic aberration that had no basis in Sesotho culture. It fails to account for those murders committed before and after 'Mantšebo's regency, and it is only a partial explanation of the crisis itself. It disregards the widespread belief in human medicine, the willing involvement of so many accomplices, and the widespread tolerance of medicine murderers. The instigators of these murders – the chiefs and headmen, and later the traders – believed that they stood to gain, and they were prepared to kill their fellow human beings in order to achieve their ends. Many were the most powerful and the wealthiest individuals in the community, and it was no doubt because of this that they were able to persuade so many others to carry out murders on their behalf.[35] A precondition of this complicity, however, was a shared belief in the efficacy of such medicine.

It is impossible to predict whether or not such belief will fall away, and if so over what period of time. Writing in the early 1950s, Lord Hailey was confident that what was needed in the long term was 'the improvement of the economic and social standards of the people'.[36] In the late twentieth century, facing inter-related crises of structural unemployment, extreme inequality and escalating poverty, many Basotho experienced an acute decline in their 'economic and social standards', so that Hailey's distinctively modernist confidence cannot (yet) be vindicated. The belief in the power of human medicine certainly persists.[37] Nevertheless, we would argue, beliefs and practices that have been described as integral to Sesotho culture are not immutable. They are not a 'heart of darkness' that will resist all change. Like many other beliefs and practices, such as the belief in witchcraft and the killing of witches in England, they are subject both to the short-term vicissitudes and to the long march of historical change.

ADDENDUM:
TOWARDS FRAMEWORKS OF
COMPARISON

At the end of the Introduction to this book we defined two possible frameworks for broader comparative study: first, ethnographically controlled
intra-regional comparison of medicine murder; second, chronologically
controlled inter-regional comparison of the circumstances of late colonial
rule in which various forms of murder, identified more loosely for this
purpose as 'ritual murder', took place and were investigated. Here we
illustrate some of the common features and some of the differences that
arise out of each approach in turn.

MEDICINE MURDER IN SOUTHERN AFRICA

Belief in the power of human medicine was, and is, widespread amongst the
African peoples of southern Africa. There were occasional reports of medicine
murder, going back to the 1860s, among the Ndebele, Pedi, Swazi, Tswana,
Venda and Zulu. Human medicine was used to strengthen chiefs and warriors,
to improve crops, to ward off evil, and to bring rain. In Bechuanaland (Botswana), for example, there were reports of human medicines being used to
increase the harvest (in 1871), in connection with initiation ceremonies (in
1924), and to bring rain (in 1935).[1]

Consistently with this widespread occurrence, Harriet Ngubane argued
that belief in the power of human medicine was deeply embedded in African
society. Drawing mainly on Zulu and Swazi material, she demonstrated
profound differences between western and African views of disease and how
it might be cured. Among Africans bodily illness was not sharply distinguished from other kinds of misfortune. People should live in harmony with
their surroundings, and this harmony was constantly under threat. Whereas
western medicine was confined to the disordered functioning of bodily parts
and organisms, African medicine was used to keep or restore harmony,
whether in the body or in the wider society. For this reason medicine
murder (or ritual homicide as she called it) could be prescribed by a healer
acting within the domain of his professional competence and obligations. So
an *inyanga* (doctor) who prescribed a medicine murder might be considering the best interests of his client 'within the framework of beliefs provided by the characteristic ... world-view of African traditional medicine'.
She believed that the increase in medicine murder in the late twentieth

century was an outcome of social change. Whereas in the past there was little call for such extreme measures, now there was a much greater need.[2]

Two examples of 'late twentieth-century' outbreaks in the southern African region are examined here: the crises in Swaziland in the 1970s and in Venda, in northern South Africa, in the late 1980s. Through the 1990s there were also frequent reports in the South African press and radio of medicine murders in various parts of the country, and of human medicine being on sale in the streets of Johannesburg. '*Muti* murder', as it is commonly called after the Zulu word for medicine, has become a familiar feature of South African media commentary. Similarly, one such murder in 1994 in Mochudi in south-eastern Botswana, of a fourteen–year-old school-girl, is reported to have triggered anxiety in that country about the allegedly increasing frequency of disappearances of this kind. According to rumour, they involved 'all those people who now go for riches, fame and power'.[3] As we will see, this theme recurs.

THE CRISIS IN SWAZILAND, 1970s

When Brian Marwick wrote his 'ethnographic account' of the Swazi in 1940 he was able to find thirteen cases of medicine murder in the court records, dating from 1908, and, as in Basutoland, there must have been many more which did not reach the courts. Four of these murders were carried out in order to strengthen the crops, three were 'for personal magnification', and there was no evidence about the motive for the other six.[4] In 1949 A. C. Thompson, the Attorney-General, noted that prosecutions for medicine murder in Swaziland averaged 'slightly over one per annum'. The chiefs, he believed, were not 'involved to any extent; the witchdoctors seem to be generally behind the crime'.[5]

There seems to have been an increase in the number of murders, at least in the early 1950s, and some suspicion began to fall on the leading chiefs. In 1952 a committee of enquiry into medicine murder reported that there had been thirty-four cases over the past twenty years, mainly to strengthen crops or to increase the power of a particular chief.[6] Cases continued to be heard in the courts and to be reported in the newspapers,[7] but not significantly more than before. Then, after Swaziland became independent in 1966, the number apparently began to rise, and some of those involved were of very high standing. In June 1974 King Sobhuza II called a special meeting of the Swazi nation to denounce the increase in murders.[8] As in Basutoland, the statistics are uncertain, and the causes of the increase are disputed.

In a biography of Sobhuza II, Hilda Kuper attributed the increase to the mounting political tensions which in 1973 led to the revocation of the Westminster constitution:

> There had been mysterious accidents, and strange rumours height-
> ened by a disturbing increase in murders practised by people, some in

responsible positions, who believed that by using human flesh they could get more respect and influence for themselves. Among the accused was a chief and member of Parliament who was married to one of the King's daughters, and among the victims was one of his close nephews. No one seemed safe and no one immune from suspicion. Strains were obvious on all fronts. There was a pathological increase in theft, in disputes over property, in family conflicts, and threats of industrial unrest.[9]

Alan Booth, writing in 1983, also believed that the rise in medicine murders was indicative of frustration arising from 'the king's actions in reversing the process of democratization'. He noted that 'it was among the working class and the petite bourgeoisie that the dashing of rising expectations was most acutely felt', and that a considerable number of the medicine murders were perpetrated by 'wage earners and school-leavers'. He wrote: 'During the post-1973 decade, ritual murders reached epidemic proportions'.[10]

Van Fossen, writing in 1985, agreed with Booth that there was a significant rise in medicine murder and that it arose out of the actions of the King. He attributed it, however, not to 'the working class and the petite bourgeoisie' but to the minor chiefs and headmen who were distant relatives of the King and adhered strongly to tradition. They were opposed to the King and his supporters, who centralised power at their expense, and to westernised intellectuals and the young, urban working class. They lost power because of the King's consolidation of power after independence, and it was the revocation of the Westminster constitution in 1973 and subsequent events that made them turn to medicine murder.[11]

Hilda Kuper returned to the subject of medicine murder in the revision of her standard work on the Swazi in 1986. Her analysis there was closer to van Fossen's than to Booth's. She drew the same distinction as Marwick between medicine murders to increase crops and medicine murders to magnify a person, but made a link between them by pointing out that the people involved were often important headmen and 'sometimes chiefs suffering economic or status insecurity'.[12]

The first person to measure these theories against the actual cases was Jeremy Evans.[13] The court records for the period before 1970 were unavailable, but he was able to trace fifty-eight trials between 1970 and 1988 relating to fifty-three murders. (A comparable figure for cases brought to trial in Basutoland between 1942 and 1960 is ninety-nine.) Of these murders he found that over half, twenty-eight, occurred between 1970 and 1975. After this, with the exception of 1981, in which there were seven murders,[14] the numbers declined. He concluded that 'there appears to have been only one fairly brief increase which faded after 1975, and indications are that this increase could well have started round about 1968'.

He agreed with Kuper, Booth and van Fossen that 'the killings ... occur in response to situations of social and economic pressure' (he might have added political pressure as well). But he argued that the factors adduced by Booth to account for the increase – 'industrialisation, urbanisation, and dispute over government to name but a few' – were continuing sources of stress in recent Swazi history. So if Booth was right the increase should have continued, and according to Evans this was not the case. Evans also argued that, if van Fossen was right, most murders should have been committed in the rural areas, whereas most of them occurred in those districts containing Swaziland's two major towns and industrial centres.

Evans did not provide a statistical breakdown of those responsible for the murders, but he demonstrated a wide variety in the people who carried them out and in their motives. In several cases high-ranking chiefs and civil servants were involved. In one notorious case 'the primary culprit ... was not only an *indvuna* but also in the employ of Prince Makhosini, then Prime Minister of Swaziland'. Makhosini was directly implicated by the accomplice witnesses, and although he was absolved of complicity by the High Court he died shortly afterwards and human parts were found in his refrigerator. Evans pointed out, however, that in some of these cases, and in 30 per cent of the cases overall, the motives of the perpetrators related to profit. The *indvuna* already referred to, for example, wanted to find money to pay for a car, to provide *lobolo* (bridewealth) for his third wife, and to supplement his income from selling vegetables. Evans also found that murders were 'often committed by people who occupy no formal political position in society', and 'out of desperation rather than a desire for self-advancement'. Some, as in Lesotho, were instigated by doctors.

He concluded that simple explanations of medicine murder 'mask much vital detail contained in the court cases', and recommended instead 'a combination of several different approaches'. 'A multi-faceted analysis of medicine murder', he believed, 'should prove a profitable method of situating fluctuating incidences of killings within their proper social and economic contexts.'[15] No such analysis has been carried out.

THE CRISIS IN VENDA, LATE 1980s

The other main crisis was concentrated in Venda in the northern Transvaal, South Africa (now part of Limpopo Province). There had been occasional reports of medicine murders among the Venda for many years. According to Minnaar, Offringa and Payze, 'Traditionally the chief (*khosi*) is allowed to sanction a medicine murder (*u via*) if it is for the benefit of or in the interests of the community. There is a traditional saying, *Makhosi a via* (chiefs commit ritual murder)'. Such murders were carried out, as among the Basotho, when a new chief was installed, or, as among the Swazi, to ensure the fertility of the harvest.[16] It was only in the late 1980s, however, that medicine murder became the subject of impassioned public debate, and as in

Lesotho it is far from clear how much this was due to an increase in its incidence.

In the past, according to witnesses to the Le Roux Commission, medicine murder was practised in secret by a chief in order to gain strength and prestige, 'and the ordinary citizen accepted it as an inevitable part of life'.[17] The Ralushai Commission agreed: 'chiefs ... have ritually killed a good number of people and no one in the beginning complained'.[18] Minnaar, Offringa and Payze pointed out that in the past a victim's disappearance was reported to his or her chief who was then responsible for taking action, whereas more recently the police investigated such cases, post-mortems were held and the perpetrators brought to justice.[19]

According to official sources, twelve medicine murder cases were heard in the Venda Supreme Court between 1979 (when Venda became formally independent) and 1988, an average of just over one a year. Then, between January and August 1988, twenty-one murders were reported to the police, of which four were medicine murders, all committed in a period of two and a half months, between 15 April and 30 June.[20] After that, between June 1989 and July 1991, only three other medicine murders were investigated by the Venda police. According to newspapaper reports, however, there was a 'spate' of fifteen medicine murders following the death of State President Mphephu in April 1988. As in Basutoland, the murders were always carried out by groups rather than individuals; the victims and the body organs to be taken were prescribed by doctors; the parts were cut out while the victim was still alive; and the victim's body was not buried, but was sometimes left in a river where the wounds could be confused with the damage done by crabs and fish.[21]

At the time of the crisis the Republic of Venda was formally an 'independent' state within South Africa. The government of President Mphephu was widely unpopular, and the opposition was led by groups associated with the African National Congress, the Pan-African Congress, the Azanian People's Organization (AZAPO) and the United Democratic Front. From 1984 onwards, like many other rural areas in South Africa, Venda was engulfed in political turmoil. According to the government, the opposition was exaggerating the incidence of medicine murders and falsely incriminating ministers as part of a political campaign. According to the forces opposed to the government, there were many more murders than those officially reported, and they were being covered up in order to protect certain people in high places.[22]

It was against this background that on 16 April 1988 the badly mutilated body of Fhatiwani Sharon Mashige was found. She was a victim of medicine murder – no-one disputed that – and six persons were arrested. Soon afterwards the accomplice on whose evidence the arrests had been made changed his statement, and five of the accused had to be released.[23] People knew that medicine murders were not carried out by one person alone and suspected that others were involved who were now being protected by the police.[24] On 17 April 1988, only a day after the discovery of Sharon Mashige's body, it was announced that State President Mphephu had died of unknown causes, and Chief Frank Ravele took over as Acting President. Many believed that Mphephu had been poisoned, and the press predicted not just a power struggle but possible civil war as well. In the subsequent in-fighting 'accusations that cabinet ministers and senior government officials were indulging in medicine murder to secure their positions soon surfaced'.[25] On 10 July 1988 the body of Mokhosi James Mavhina, the principal of Tshiemuemu High School, was found. It was given out that he had committed suicide, but the students at the school were convinced he was a victim of medicine murder and this belief rapidly gained ground.

There were three further medicine murders during this period, but there was no great outcry about these since those thought to be guilty were arrested.[26] 'However', according to le Roux, who later conducted an inquiry into these matters,

> the mere perpetration of a number of ritual murders within a short space of time gave rise to a feeling of fear in the minds of the people that this terrible crime was assuming proportions beyond the ordinary and that Venda was indeed going through extraordinary times. As such, these murders were simply added fuel to the fire which was already burning.[27]

On 24 July 1988 the local *City Press* reported that President Mphephu's death had sparked off a spate of ritual murders, and that 'at least fifteen' had been reported in a certain area since April, a figure that was later raised to seventeen. It also reported that 'highly placed' officials were implicated in the crimes.[28] Popular suspicion and anger centred on the Minister of Justice, A. A. Tshivhase. He was described to le Roux as a man of limitless ambition who would 'stop at nothing to reach the top of the ladder', and it was said his achievements could 'only be explained by very strong *muti* [medicine] derived from the vital organs of others'. It was widely believed that the police were protecting Tshivhase's friends and relatives.[29]

Disturbances broke out in July 1988. Schools were boycotted, shops were closed, telephone operators went on strike, and taxis and buses did not run. 'Most of the population' was said to be involved.[30] According to Minnaar, Offringa and Payze, 'the main reason for these actions was to protest against the involvement of certain cabinet ministers in "ritual" murders and the concealment of these actions'.[31] In response to popular demand a Commission of Inquiry was established and Tshivhase was dismissed as Minister of Justice.[32]

The sole commissioner was D. J. H. le Roux, the Chief Justice of the

Republic of Venda. His brief was to investigate and report on 'the causes of the present unrest, school boycotts and work stoppages in Venda, with reference *inter alia* to the circumstances surrounding the investigation of so-called ritual murders committed during 1988'. His report, submitted in the following year, supported the official narrative. He found that James Mavhina had committed suicide, that there was no evidence of cabinet ministers being implicated in the murder of Sharon Mashige, and that the opposition and its press had whipped up the crisis for political ends. He urged a campaign to promote pride amongst the youth in the nationhood of Venda and thereby to combat 'the evil plan formulated by the leaders of the ANC which sends its tentacles into every village, street and home to poison, activate and intimidate the people to accept the ANC and Communist principles'.[33] The winds of political change, however, were rapidly to overtake any initiative of this kind.

In 1992, Minnaar, Offringa and Payze published *To Live in Fear: Witch-burning and Medicine Murder in Venda*. They accepted le Roux's findings in the cases of James Mavhina and Sharon Mashige, and they agreed that the unrest in 1988 was apparently fomented by people with 'politically inspired motives'.[34] As the title of their book indicates, medicine murder was now linked with the dramatic outbreak of witch-burnings which began in 1989. Although there was no direct link between them, they have been analysed together as 'witchcraft-related violence'.[35] Witch-burnings were carried out openly and were apparently much more numerous, and the victims were nearly all old women. In March 1990 persons alleged to be witches were being burnt every night, and at one point about 400 refugees were seeking protection at police stations. The phenomenon is difficult to explain, and it lies outside the scope of our present discussion. Minnaar and his colleagues tentatively ascribed it – as well as medicine murder – to the political unrest at the time. They suggest that many of the witch-burnings were an attempt to oust an unpopular and unstable government, but they acknowledged that 'the exact nature of this link is unclear'.[36] At the same time there was further unrest arising from allegations of medicine murder and of the involvement of government ministers. The Commissioner of Police was forced to resign, and in April 1990 the Venda government was overthrown in a bloodless military coup.[37] The coup induced a sharp decline in violence and also helped to open the way to the re-incorporation of the homeland into a unitary South Africa.

According to le Roux, all the witnesses who gave evidence to him agreed that the numbers of medicine murders in 1988 'represent a drastic increase ... over the past nine years since independence'.[38] Though acknowledging the uncertainty of the statistics, Minnaar and his colleagues agreed, and they added that 'not all medicine killings are reported to the police'.[39] They felt obliged to account for this increase, and they took as their starting point the anthropologist Hammond-Tooke's statement that the incidence of medicine murders rises 'dramatically at times of political and social tension, insecurity and competition for economic resources'.[40] They concluded that there was

> good reason to believe that the occurrence and apparent increase in medicine murders which took place in Venda in 1988 was one of the consequences of social change that normally involves uncertainty and instability. Medicine murders may perhaps be seen as a traditional way of coping with problems which did not occur frequently within the traditional system ... Modern day rivalry in the business or political field has resulted in the utilisation of this type of killing for personal gain. In particular less-educated people associate medicine murders with the traditional *khosi* or chief system and business people and politicians in positions of power are easily suspected when someone disappears or when a mutilated body is found.[41]

Witch-burnings and the occasional medicine murder continued not only in Venda but in the neighbouring areas of Lebowa and Gazankulu. All three became part of the Northern (now Limpopo) Province of South Africa, and in 1995 the province's Executive Council appointed a Commission, chaired by Professor N. V. Ralushai, to enquire into 'the causes of witchcraft violence and ritual murders in the Northern Province' and to make recommendations to combat them. For our purposes this added very little to what le Roux, Minnaar, Offringa and Payze had already said. The Commission's proposals for ending medicine murder were reminiscent of similar proposals in Basutoland: educational programmes, for example, and a formal code of conduct for doctors.[42]

From our own reading of the evidence set out by le Roux, Minnaar, Offringa and Payze and the Ralushai Commission, we would suggest that there is not overwhelming evidence of a great increase in medicine murders in Venda in the late 1980s but that, rather, in the particular political circumstances of that time accusations of medicine murder assumed a new political significance. It is possible that in the prevailing tension and uncertainty people tried to shore up their position through the use of human medicine. It is certain that accusations of medicine murder found fertile ground in the Venda government's unpopularity and in the wider circumstances of popular struggle against the *apartheid* state. It was these circumstances, we suggest, more than a dramatic increase in the number of medicine murders, that created the crisis that commanded so much attention.

INTRA-REGIONAL COMPARISON: THE CASES OF SWAZILAND, VENDA AND BASUTOLAND

This brief summary of the crises in Swaziland and Venda throws up certain similarities to and differences from the crisis in Basutoland. There are the same doubts about the adequacy of the statistics. Was there really a significant increase in medicine murder, or was the attention it attracted due to other factors? In particular, was there a connection between the increased publicity and the alleged involvement of the leaders of society? Insofar as they believed that there was an increase, most scholars, like Jones in Basutoland, tended to look for explanations that were rooted in changes in society, and more specifically in circumstances of political and social tension and insecurity.

The most striking and obvious difference lies in the contrast of political circumstances relating to the counter-narrative. In Basutoland in the 1950s denial of the reality of medicine murder flourished amongst chiefs and nationalist politicians who identified white colonial rule as subversive of national integrity, Sesotho culture and the indigenous hierarchy of power. In independent Swaziland in the 1970s and in nominally independent Venda in the late 1980s, where there was significant integration of 'traditional' authority and the dominant political class, there was no widespread denial of the reality of medicine murder and no claim that it was an invention of whites. On the contrary, in August 1981 the Swazi Prime Minister, Prince Mabandla Dlamini, condemned medicine murders as 'a totally disgraceful and barbaric practice which left a stain on the Swazi nation',[43] and in February 1983 King Sobhuza II spoke in similar terms.[44] In Venda in the 1990s the Ralushai Commission, of which seven out of eight members were Africans, was forthright in its condemnation of medicine murder. Nevertheless, as in Basutoland in the 1940s and 1950s, accusations of instigation of, or complicity in, medicine murder touched individuals in high places. It is possible that some wealthy and powerful individuals were falsely implicated, through popular suspicion or the anger of the politicised youth. In Venda especially there were all the elements of a volatile brew in circumstances of rapid political change: an unpopular authoritarian regime; rampant unrest in the schools and tertiary institutions and the civil service; inflammatory allegations of 'ritual' murder and wild rumours of 'witches' and 'zombies'. Press reports of the time dramatise incompatible poles of interpretation that are familiar from our analysis of the Basutoland experience. On the one hand, it was said, 'Chiefs in Venda believed that in order to keep their positions of power they had to drink medicine made from human organs'. On the other hand, people were accused more or less randomly, it appeared, 'either of being witches or of being involved in ritual killings, and hacked or burnt to death'.[45]

INTER-REGIONAL COMPARISON: MURDER IN LATE COLONIAL AFRICA

Volatile brews of this kind – scandalous death, a local context of widespread public unease, and rippling rumours of the involvement of powerful individuals – were common to the murders we now briefly review in other parts of Africa in the time period with which we have been mainly concerned in this book.

In February 1944 in Kyebi, the capital of the Akan state of Akyem Abuakwa in the southern Gold Coast, a minor chief disappeared on the last day of the final obsequies for Nana Sir Ofori Atta, the ruler of the state. Bodily remains were eventually discovered, and eight members of the royal family were charged with murder. The motive remained mysterious, in the circumstances of grief and confusion that surrounded the funeral rites of a strong and deeply mourned ruler. Hints emerged, however, that human sacrifice or 'mortuary slaying' had taken place. The eight accused were tried in Accra in November 1944 and sentenced to death. Their appeal was rejected in West Africa in January 1945 but was taken to the Privy Council in London, and executions were stayed pending the outcome. Every legal twist and turn was exploited by lawyers both in the Gold Coast and in London to bring the verdict into question; ultimate resolution was repeatedly delayed by the vacillations of two different Secretaries of State for the Colonies in the Labour government who had to concede that the prerogative of mercy lay exclusively with the colonial governor, but who were themselves opposed in principle to the death penalty and who faced a vigorous campaign in parliament in London to commute the death sentences to life imprisonment. The colonial governor concerned, Sir Alan Burns, was brought to the brink of resignation in his exasperation over this protracted delay and its effect on public opinion in the Gold Coast. Eventually, in March 1947, three of the eight men convicted were hanged. The political repercussions of the case were significant. It exposed deep political cleavages at the heart of the complex machinery of the local state, and discredited, through the elaborately opportunistic manoeuvres of the defence lawyers, some prominent members of the local élite. Part of its aftermath was that the Akyem Abuakwa state and its representatives emerged 'on the losing side' in Ghanaian politics not only through the 1950s in the rancorous aftermath of the Kyebi murder but also through the years of the first post-independence Nkrumah government.[46]

On 19 March 1945 the body of a young girl was found on the beach near the town of Elmina, in the Cape Coast area. Parts of her body had been removed, leaving no doubt that she was the victim of a 'ritual murder'. The case became known as the Bridge House murder, for which five men were convicted and hanged. The murder was connected with bitter factional disputes over succession to the paramountcy of the local state, and once again it exposed the colonial judicial system to close scrutiny both in the Gold Coast and abroad. In an analysis of the case, Roger Gocking recognised that the use of protective medicine had a long history in the region but gave most emphasis to the ways in which indirect rule policies legitimised customary practices in general and opened up much scope for argument in apparently 'traditional' terms about conflicts and resources that were very much part of the modern world. Whereas an earlier generation of 'educated natives' would have condemned any participation in 'heathen and barbarous practices', 'during the 1930s and 1940s, it became essential for members of the "intelligentsia" with political ambitions to participate in customary religious rites to win support in the parochial politics of indirect rule'.[47]

In that same month of March 1945 an article in the *Nigerian Eastern Mail* triggered a three-year investigation into nearly 200 mysterious deaths between 1943 and 1948 in the dense oil-palm belt of southern Annang territory in the Calabar Province of south-eastern Nigeria. The people who died, it was alleged, were victims of 'man-leopard' murders in attacks from behind, typically at dusk and on isolated and deserted bush paths, that deliberately simulated killings by real leopards. The corpses were often mutilated. It was difficult forensically to distinguish between the one sort of attack and the other. As the investigation became what the British *Daily Mail* described as 'the strangest, biggest murder hunt in the world', the evidence shifted in favour of human agency, connected with secret 'leopard' societies; by the end of the official investigation early in 1948 ninety-six men had been convicted of murder, of whom seventy-seven were hanged. Confusion over motives and responsibility remained an 'enduring puzzle' throughout. Were they revenge attacks, connected with marriage disputes, land, money and debt – the small change of everyday life? Or were they related to performances at secret village shrines? 'Did the serial nature of the killings and the consistently precise pattern of mutilation not only conceal but reveal a ritual motive, the removal of human flesh and body parts for use in the performance of ceremonies to confer wealth or power on the killers and their confessors?'.[48] Two kinds of questions arose: those connected with the immediate motives of murderers and the social and political circumstances of particular murders; and those connected with understanding the incidence of such murders in a particular historical period. David Pratten identified a striking feature of the investigation into man-leopard murders: paradoxically, while the crimes themselves were by definition furtively executed and appeared to involve 'secret' societies, under the glare of official investigation, as he expressed it, 'all of the cast were present on stage at the same time. It was a cast of husbands and wives, chiefs and elites, church-goers and cult members, judges and litigants, and criminals and policemen'. 'The murders and the investigations revealed the social, economic and political fault-lines of Annang society during colonial rule.'

Pratten has argued that the outbreak was eventually brought to an end by a tour of the affected areas organised by the Ibibio Union in 1947, involving chiefs and 'important citizens', and the public administration of oaths used in the indigenous idiom both as lie-detector and deterrent. In this way he drew attention to an 'apparently unlikely alliance of the self-styled "intelligentsia" with the forces of rural conservatism ...'[49]

It is possible through this brief summary of cases of murder in other regions of Africa in the 1940s to identify five features of resonance, more or less strongly evident in each case, with our analysis of medicine murder in colonial Lesotho. First, the motives for murder, and the aetiology of cause and effect, could be understood only within local systems of belief that were difficult for outside observers to penetrate, and they remained mysterious and vexatious to colonial officials and police for this reason. Second, the murders and their investigations, within a context of indirect rule, threw into sharp relief the shifting relationships, the tensions and the conflicts between traditional authorities and colonial administrations. Third, through the competitive constructions of events that emerged from detailed court evidence or otherwise as a result of official investigations, they typically revealed some of the many layers and complexities of factional disputes, the intricacies and depths of local politics that would otherwise, probably, have remained obscure. Fourth, especially where doubts persisted as to motive, the validity of particular evidence or the behaviour of the police, the colonial context of the resolution of difficult capital cases placed remote villages or small towns in Africa firmly within the distant embrace of government departments, parliament and the Privy Council in London. As Rathbone expressed it, 'What had begun as a local and family tragedy was ... to engulf the colonial regime of the Gold Coast and ... the Colonial Office and British Parliament in its intricacies'.[50] Fifth, particularly evident in the Kyebi murder case and the Lesotho case, there were reverberations for nationalist politics through the 1950s and more generally for an understanding of strategic political alliances in the period before independence.[51]

APPENDIX

SUMMARY OF SUSPECTED MEDICINE MURDER CASES, 1895–1966

Note. The sources shown are the sources we have consulted. They are not necessarily exhaustive. The reference 'Jones, No. 5', for example, is to No. 5 in Appendix A ('List of murders believed to be medicine murders') of G. I. Jones' published report (1951). The reference 'Jones Papers, I' is to the file headed 'Correspondence re Diretlo Murder Report' in G. I. Jones' unpublished papers held in the Department of Social Anthropology at the University of Cambridge; while 'Jones Papers, V' is to the file headed 'Basutoland and Swaziland Schedule of Ritual Murders 1949 and Earlier'. The reference 'Ashton, Schedule' is to the schedule of cases attached to his 'secret' paper, 'Ritual Murder in Basutoland', and enclosed with Clark to Syers, 30 April 1949 (PRO, DO 35/4157).

1895/1

May 1895. Near Molope's, Butha-Buthe. Ward 1: Butha-Buthe.
R v. *Andries Molope and four others.*

The case for the Crown
The instigator of this murder was Molope, chief of the Makholokoe. According to Hermann Dieterlen, a French Protestant missionary, his motive was to secure the succession for one of his junior sons, and Dieterlen used this case to condemn polygamy and its attendant jealousies. Jones was more likely to be right when he ascribed the murder to Molope's determination to resist the placing of Chief Qhobela Joel in his area.

Molope summoned a Zulu doctor from Natal, Khokong, who told him that he needed a human bone. Molope and his sons chose their victim, a young man of their own clan called Daniel Makenyakenya. A few days later there was a beer-drink at a neighbouring village. The murderers put some medicine in Daniel's beer which had the effect of making him follow them when they left. As he went through a valley they attacked and killed him. They took the body to the doctor in an abandoned hut, and he cut off an ear, three or four fingers, three or four toes and perhaps some other parts. These parts were burnt, ground into a powder and mixed with other ingredients, and the resulting black medicine was then used in scarifying the murderers. The body was thrown into a field where it was found three days later.

The outcome
A Combined Court was held at Leribe presided over by the Acting Resident

Commissioner, Godfrey Lagden. He was assisted by two white officers and fourteen African assessors, among them several of the leading chiefs in the area. The accused were Andries Molope and four others, including Khokong. Although the court believed they were guilty of murder the evidence was not strong enough to sustain a conviction on that charge. However the accused and one other were convicted of conspiracy to obstruct the course of justice and sentenced to seven years' imprisonment each. A relative of the dead man was sentenced to one year's imprisonment for not bringing the murderers to justice. Molope was deposed and each of his men fined one beast.

Sources: Jones, No. 1; Ashton Papers, 'Copy of Proceedings of a Combined Court ...'; Basutoland Government, *Annual Report*, 1895/96, pp. 8–9; H. Dieterlen (1896: 263–6).

1899/1

March 1899. Salomane, near Phoofolo's, Berea. Ward 4: 'Mamathe's.
No criminal proceedings.
'Mamoyane, a widow, went to inspect her millet and did not return. The following day, after a long search by the people of Phoofolo's village, her blankets were found, then, about two kilometres away, her skin petticoats, and eventually her naked body on the Leribe side of the river. There were signs of a blow on her left eyebrow and a deep stab at the juncture of her shoulder and neck. Her neck had been twisted and broken. The body was buried. The Ward Chief, 'Mamathe (widow of Masupha I), told the Assistant Commissioner that a murder had been committed and that the body had been buried to hide it. The body was exhumed, but a post-mortem held in July, four months after the murder, could only confirm the broken neck.

An inquest was held and found: 'In absence of further evidence, case must at present be regarded as one of death by misadventure'.

Sources: Jones, No. 2 (Jones clearly had access to the inquest record); UCT, Ashton Papers, Report of Assistant Commissioner, Berea, 11 March 1899.

1907/1

October 1907. Hlakanelo's, Qacha's Nek. Ward 5: Ratšoleli's and Mashai.
R v. *'two persons'*. Criminal records not available.
'A death involved in mystery occurred of a middle-aged Mosuto, named Kose. His corpse was discovered near a small stream some distance beyond a little krantz, divested of all European clothing he possessed as it was found scattered near by. The deceased was returning home from a beer-drink. Two persons were arrested, tried for murder and acquitted.'

Source: Annual Report, Qacha's Nek District, 1907/8, quoted in Jones, No. 3.

1909/1

1909 or 1910. Lekhalo la Makhooa, Leribe. Ward 8: Leribe.
No criminal proceedings.
According to Jones, 'A native doctor saw the murder of two youths for medicine, by people of chief Tau. Was himself attacked by them, but managed to escape ... Insufficient evidence to bring accused before court'.

Source: Jones, No. 5.

1910/1

1910. Berea District.
No criminal proceedings, it seems.
'Another case occurred in 1910 in the Teyateyaneng [i.e. Berea] District.'
Source: Ashton, 'Ritual Murder in Basutoland', p. 10.

1911/1

October 1911. Mashili's, Leribe. Ward 8: Leribe.
No criminal proceedings.
According to Jones, the victim in this case was Lebitsa, an adult male. He was 'reported to have fallen over precipice in suspicious circumstances. There was no blood at the place where he had fallen and body appeared to have been placed there. Chief Motšoene accused a number of persons of this murder'.

An inquest was held in January 1912, but the records were not available when Jones conducted his enquiry.

Source: Jones, No. 6. Jones had access to 'Covering letter to Magistrate'.

1912/1

1912. Lekhalong, Thaba-Bosiu, Maseru. Ward 21: Thaba-Bosiu.
R v. *Likhalile and at least one other.*

The case for the Crown
Likhalile, an elderly headman at Lekhalong, in the pass between Thaba-Bosiu and Ntsane's, was worried that his medicine horn was almost finished and that he would have nothing to pass on to his son, Makope. He was advised by an itinerant Zulu doctor that, if he wanted to become rich in millet and livestock and to steal without being caught, he should kill someone in his village, taking beforehand certain pieces of flesh, and then prepare a medicine horn and scarify himself and his family with it. He and his accomplices took an elderly woman, 'Mampuo (or 'Malipuo), to a wood, where they drugged, mutilated and killed her.

'Mampuo's disappearance was reported to Khoabane Theko, the Ward Chief of Thaba-Bosiu, who reported it to the Paramount Chief, Letsie II. Letsie sent his doctor, who prepared a concoction which would make people speak. But no-one came forward. Some time later some herdboys smelt a rotting corpse and the body was found. In the course of police enquiries Makope produced some of the flesh.

The outcome
In the following trial Likhalile and Makope were found guilty and imprisoned. One of the accused – Likhalile it seems – was a member of the French Protestant Church.

Sources: H. Dieterlen (1912: 168–73); Jones, No. 4 (Jones was not aware of Dieterlen's article, and the date he gives, 1907–9, is wrong); PRO, DO 119/1382, M. B. Photane, 'Medicine Murders' (enclosure with Arrowsmith to Turnbull, 12 September 1953), pp. 21, 24; PS interview, Ford and Seabata Rafutho, 23 May 1999.

1912/2

According to Hermann Dieterlen, 'A few weeks after the death of 'Mampuo [1912/ 1 above] another woman was similarly killed, so that the son of a chief should outweigh his competitors' [translated from the French]. This murder took place not far from Morija. No further details are available.

Sources: H. Dieterlen (1912: 172); Baltzer (1912: 104).

1912/3

1912. Ha Mofoka, Maseru. Ward 13: Matsieng.
R v. *Pilietsane Mofoka and others.*

The case for the Crown
Pilietsane Mofoka, a headman, and others killed a widow for medicine. Jones reports: 'Alleged accused had been acting for persons of higher rank and that medicine was to aid Paramount Chief Letsie II who was very ill at the time ...'

The outcome
Pilietsane and his accomplices were brought to trial, convicted and imprisoned, but it was said that Paramount Chief Griffith, who succeeded Letsie II in 1913, interceded for them and secured a reduction of their sentence.

Source: Jones, No. 7. According to Jones, the court record was not available.

1914/1

1914. Leabina's, Leribe. Ward 22: Tsikoane?
No criminal proceedings.
The body of Jankola, an adult male, was found at the foot of a precipice. Jones reports: 'No evidence of foul play, but nothing to show how deceased could get to top of precipice from where he was alleged to have fallen. Relatives of deceased firmly convinced that he was murdered'.

Source: Jones, No. 8. Jones relied on correspondence relating to the inquest.

1919/1

1 April 1919. Ha Sechaba, Mafeteng. Ward 18: Tajane.
RCCR 365/19. *R* v. *Mahlatsi and four others.*

The case for the Crown
It is not clear who the instigator was in this case, but Mahlatsi was the first accused. According to Jones, a headman was involved, but he did not give his name and he cannot be relied on in this case – see below. There is also no evidence about the motive for this crime. The victim was a woman called Ralibuseng, who had just given birth to a child. According to Kotong, the single accomplice witness, Mahlatsi said that during the 1918 'flu epidemic no-one from her family had died. 'Hence they must have one of them killed.'

On the night of 1 April, Kotong called Ralibuseng 'by means of medicine', and when she came out the accused caught her and suffocated her with a blanket. They took her to Masemouse Spruit, where Mahlatsi broke her neck. They then cut out her genital organs and Mahlatsi took the parts away. They were 'to be roasted when dry and made into powder'. The body was carried to the bottom of a precipice, put on a ledge and then rolled off. Mahlatsi went to the top of the precipice and twisted some shrubs together to make it appear Ralibuseng had fallen.

When the body was found the police were summoned. By measuring with a stick the police found that the footprints at the top of the cliff fitted those of Mahlatsi. At a meeting summoned by the local chief, Sechaba, one of the accused claimed that the private parts were missing because Ralibuseng had syphilis. Others claimed she was suffering from hysteria, but her relatives denied this. It was only seven days since she had given birth. Chief Sechaba said that one of the accused had wanted to bury the body before the government messenger arrived. 'Maleqephola, later to be Accused No. 4, was a female doctor.

The police also found that some of the footprints were those of Kotong, the son of one of those to be accused, and he was taken aside to make a statement. In the ensuing trial he was the only accomplice witness.

The outcome

The preliminary examination was held at Mafeteng in May 1919 before the Assistant Commissioner. He found it difficult to understand some of the evidence about 'Maleqephola's activities. 'Description of witchcraft impossible to intelligently put into English.' The trial was held in October 1919 in the Resident Commissioner's Court at Mafeteng before the Deputy Resident Commissioner and the same Assistant Commissioner. The first four accused were found guilty of murder, with a recommendation of mercy for Nos. 3 and 4. No. 5 was found guilty as an accessory after the fact and sentenced to ten years' imprisonment with hard labour (IHL).

The final outcome is not known, but presumably Nos. 1 and 2 Accused were hanged.

Source: LNA, RCCR 365/19. Jones refers to two cases in this area, Nos. 9 and 10. For both he says that the criminal record was not available. With the benefit of the LNA record it is clear that the two cases were in fact the single case described above. According to Jones one of the accused, Raleqhapola, was said to be the father of Phoka Shea, also a doctor, who was accused in cases 1942/1 and 1944/4. There is probably some confusion here with 'Maleqephola, who may therefore have been the mother of Phoka Shea.

1923/1

22 September 1923. Koatake's, Mokhotlong. Ward 11: Tlokoeng.
No criminal proceedings.
According to Jones, the body of 'Moorosi, middle-aged adult' was 'found at foot of cliffs by Khubelu river. Neck broken, wound in left eye, wound over shoulder blade. Stabbing wound beneath left armpit. One boot was found on the far side of river, the other boot and his stick above the cliff, and the body at the bottom. Deceased was not drunk when last seen alive. Investigating officer was convinced he had been murdered and thrown over cliff and "case hushed up with help of influential people". It was rumoured that he was killed by headman Koatake and his anus removed for medicine for a court case'.

The police were unable to obtain sufficient evidence to support a prosecution against Koatake.

Source: Jones, No. 11. Jones used Mokhotlong Report 202/23 of 4 January.

1925/1

October 1925.

No criminal proceedings.

The instigator of this murder is not known. The victim, an unnamed man, became drunk at a beer party and was taken by his friends to a place near the site of an initiation school. He was surrounded and caught by a band of men, and a doctor came and mutilated him. He cut one foot off at the ankle with a knife, cut off the other leg with an axe, took out the marrow by banging the bone against a rock, and cut out the eyes and some pieces of flesh. The men sang the *mokorotlo*, the war-song, to drown the victim's cries, but his screams were heard by the boys in the initiation school, including two of his sons. Then he was killed and his body was thrown into some bushes.

According to the missionary, Georges Dieterlen, there was no reason for this crime other than 'paganism'. The doctor needed powerful medicines.

Source: G. Dieterlen (1926: 217–19). See also Ramseyer (1928: 69–70).

1927/1

23 April 1927. Thebe-ea-Khale, Qacha's Nek. Ward 5: Ratšoleli's and Mashai.
R v. *Mbutana, alias Mokone, and Mokhathala.*

The case for the Crown
The victim in this case was a man called Senyothi Bobere. According to Jones, the boys at an initiation school 'heard man singing praise songs suddenly stop and scream. They recognised his voice as father's brother's. When they returned from school, they found he was missing and reported to the A. C. [Assistant Commissioner]. Body was subsequently found at foot of a cliff near the Initiation school with head and other injuries'. The two men who were running the initiation school, Mbutana, a doctor, and Mokhathala, were suspected of the murder.

The outcome
It is not clear from Jones whether there was a court case. On the one hand he refers to '*Rex* v. *1. Mbutana …; 2. Mokhathala*'. On the other hand he says there was 'insufficient evidence to support a charge'. The headman of Thebe-ea-Khale was 'convicted and imprisoned for suppressing evidence'.

Source: Jones, No. 12. According to Jones, 'Records in this case have disappeared'. Although there are certain similarities between this case and 1925/1, there are enough differences, particularly on the date, to justify treating them as separate cases.

1927/2

15 October 1927. Phahameng, near Morija, Maseru. Ward 13: Matsieng.
RCCR 781/1928. *R* v. *Mojela Letsie and thirteen others.*

The case for the Crown
The instigator in this case, Mojela Letsie, had previously lived at Morija, but had moved away, and was later to be gazetted as a sub-chief living at Makhaleng Ha Lekhooa. He was involved in a case over land which was then being heard in the Paramount Chief's Court at Matsieng. He consulted a doctor, 'Matumelo, who said

that for disputes over land she always needed human flesh.

The victim, Motaoane Selematsela, was a compositor at the printing works at Morija, the headquarters of the Paris Evangelical Missionary Society. He was said to be on friendly terms with Mojela. Some of the accomplices came from Mojela's home in the Makhaleng valley, and some from Phahameng. Two were from Morija, including one of Motaoane's friends and fellow employees at the printing works. One of the accused, Mahau, was described in the court record as a peasant, but appears to have belonged to the Matete family who had chieftainship rights in the Morija area. It was said in evidence that he did not like Mojela returning to the area, and people were surprised to see him co-operating with Mojela.

One Saturday night, as Motaoane was making his way home after a beer-drink, he was attacked by the accused. He was struck on the head with a knobkerrie. As he lay on the ground his thighs were broken, and one of the accused cut out a testicle. Another cut some flesh between the thighs and beneath the armpit. Since it was late the body was hidden in a hole, and on the following night it was thrown over a cliff. Kraal manure was used to cover bloodstains on the path.

When the body was found it was assumed that Motaoane had fallen over the cliff when drunk and the body was buried. Later it was exhumed, but too late for any satisfactory medical evidence to be obtained.

In the meantime the doctor 'Matumelo prepared medicine from the parts given her, and Mojela and one other accused were scarified.

The outcome

After three weeks in detention one of the accomplices, Motebang, turned King's evidence and made a statement. At the preparatory examination he went back on it, but in the Resident Commissioner's Court he said the statement was true. His evidence was supported by an independent witness, an elderly woman who had seen the accused attacking Motaoane and heard him cry out. Both Motebang and the old woman had been drinking, and because of this, and because Motebang had gone back on his statement at the preparatory examination, the accused were all acquitted. The judge expressed his 'horror at the state of drunkenness' and said he 'would draw the attention of His Honour the Resident Commissioner and the Paramount Chief to this distressing state of [affairs]'.

More than twenty years later Mojela Letsie was suspected of instigating another medicine murder. (See 1948/14 below.) Other accused were involved in 1945/3 (Case Study 1).

Sources: Jones, No. 13; LNA, RCCR 781/1928; *Leselinyana*, 28.10.27 and 15.6.28; Perham (1974: 95).

1928/1

April 1928. Botapere, Mokhotlong. Ward 14: Mokhotlong.
RCCR 805/a/1929. *R* v. *four accused*. (The instigator, Thabanyane Shokupa, died while awaiting trial.)

The case for the Crown

This murder was not planned as a medicine murder, but the perpetrators took advantage of what was planned as an ordinary murder. The victim was Mankie, a notorious stock thief. According to Jones, 'Shokupa, a headman and five others (including one who turned King's evidence), enticed deceased ... into a trap where he was shot by 1st accused, stabbed in kidneys and hamstrung. 1st accused returned next day and finding him still alive, cut the tendons of his arms, then cut his throat and took the skin and ear from the right side of his face, his genitalia, and some fat from his kidneys for medicine for a doctor to make him a "lenaka" which would be useful for court cases and make grain plentiful. Following day accused returned again, removed body and lowered it over a cliff where it was found six weeks later'. Chief Matlere Lerotholi told Hugh Ashton that this murder was committed by a rich man and his sons to make them still richer.

The outcome
The Ward Chief of Mokhotlong, Seeiso Griffith, who later became Paramount Chief, rode into the mountains himself to help the police investigation, and it was because of his support that sufficient evidence was obtained to support a prosecution.

Shokupa died while awaiting trial; '4th accused was discharged, 1st and 2nd accused hanged and 3rd had his sentence reduced to 15 years'.

Sources: Jones, No. 14 and p. 34; Ashton, 'Analysis', p. 1; Morija Archives, How Papers, 'Basuto' to Marion Walsham How, 27 February 1954.

1929/1

1929? Mohale's Hoek District. Ward 19: Taung?
R v. Mohlomi and others.
A murder was allegedly committed by 'Mohlomi and others (Chief involved)' in the Mohale's Hoek District. No details are known. It is possible that Mohlomi was Mohlomi Monare, who was gazetted in 1939 as sub-chief at Linareng in the ward of Taung. The case was heard in 1929 and the accused were discharged.

Source: PRO, DO 119/1378, f. 65, Schedule A.

1930/1

3 August 1930. Mantšonyane, Mohale's Hoek. Ward 15: Phamong.
RCCR 186/35. *R* v. *'1. Maphoma Mohapi (headman) 2. Molumo Ramaron, (native doctor), Lepekola Mohapi, a sub-chief and one other'.*

The case for the Crown
The victims in this case were a widow called 'Mamotšeliso ['Matšeliso?], Tšeliso, her ten-year-old son, and Mohau, her infant son. Only the first two were used for medicine. According to Jones' notes, 'Maphoma, a headman, ... wanted promotion and to strengthen his position and to obtain the chief's favour'. His report however reads as follows: 'According to the evidence of another doctor who turned King's evidence, 1st accused was persuaded to arrange for the killing for protective medicine of his half-sister and her children who were in his care. 2nd accused said that part of the skull of a male and of the right arm of a female Kwena were needed, and that Tseliso would rank as a Kwena as his mother had no proper husband. Instead of his fee of five head of cattle he agreed to take such parts as he required for his medicines from the bodies of the two victims. On 3rd August, 1st, 2nd and 3rd accused and this witness entered 'Mamotselise's [*sic*] hut, having previously arranged for a youth who used to sleep there, and for most of the valuable property to be removed elsewhere and for roofing grass to be stacked against the walls. Her

throat was cut by 2nd accused who then sliced off the top of Tseliso's head with a knife and helped himself to those parts he required from both bodies. The hut was then set on fire, the infant perishing in the fire. The bodies were recovered and buried the next day, and no report was made. Later medical examination of the exhumed remains confirmed the absence of those bones said to have been taken by the accused'.

The outcome
In the subsequent trial all the accused were acquitted.

Sources: Jones, No. 15 and p. 16; Jones Papers, V; Mabille (1955: 138).

1931/1

8 July 1931. Ha Konstabole, Leribe. Ward 8: Leribe.
RCCR 919/31. *R* v. *Qhalasho (alias Qhanasa) Baholo.*

The case for the Crown
A local headman, Mopeli, who was not among the accused, approached Qhalasho, a doctor, and asked him to procure the flesh of a woman who had just given birth and who belonged to a particular clan. Qhalasho arranged with his assistant, who turned King's evidence, to murder Moliehi Letau. They were at a beer-drink where she was present, and as it was getting dark they all left. As they went along Qhalasho and his assistant caught hold of Moliehi, threw her to the ground and strangled her. They put the body on a donkey and took it to a cave, where they kept it hidden for two days. Then they went back and Qhalasho cut flesh from the right side of the face and head and from the right leg, and also the private parts. He put them on a stick and took them home. Two weeks later they removed the body to Paepae's village and threw it over a cliff so that suspicion would fall on Paepae's people.

The outcome
After the body was discovered the assistant made a full confession, and Qhalasho was convicted and hanged.

Sources: Jones, No. 16 and p. 16; LNA, RCCR 919/31.

1932/1

July/August 1932. Qenehelong, Qacha's Nek. Ward 5: Ratšoleli's and Mashai.
RCCR 1062/32. *R* v. *Kakene and Rafolatsane.* (A third accused was discharged at the preparatory examination.)

The case for the Crown
Poulo Malilimane, the son of a doctor, who collected roots and herbs for his father, was offered human fat by the two accused. They were 'full of beer', he said. They said they had killed a man, and they told him it would help him to get a good job with Europeans, which he believed. The price was £1. They threatened to kill him if he disclosed what they had told him: it would be the last of his seeing the sun.

About a week later the remains of Mokonya, an elderly doctor, were found beneath a cliff. The local sub-chief, Sekhonyana, should have reported this to the Ward Chief, but instead had the remains quietly buried. It was alleged that Mokonya's bag of medicines was found in Rafolatsane's hut.

The outcome
At the preparatory examination Sekhonyana was discharged, and at the trial in the Resident Commissioner's Court the remaining two accused, Kakene, a peasant, and Rafolatsane, a headman, were acquitted.

Sources: Jones, No. 17 and p. 16; LNA, RCCR 1062/32.

1932/2

Betweeen 1928 and 1936. Ha Mofoka, Maseru. Ward 13: Matsieng.
Criminal proceedings.

The case for the Crown
Our information about this case comes entirely from interviews in 1999 with 'Masempe Mofoka (born 1908) and Exinia Letsoela (born 1915). The murder took place after 'Masempe came to live at Mofoka's in 1928 and before Exinia's marriage in 1936. The instigator was Chief Peete Mofoka and several accomplices were involved. The reason for the murder is not known. The victim, a woman called Ralekhobola, was chosen because she had no children. She was betrayed by her boyfriend, Mashai, who came from the nearby village of Mokunutlung. He took her to an initiation feast, where the murderers seized her and took her to the fields where they killed her.

Mashai went to Johannesburg, but because of his bad conscience he came back and confessed. In the course of the enquiries Paramount Chief Griffith summoned all the villagers to Matsieng, and they had to take their stock with them too. 'There was the idea that if the truth wasn't told the animals wouldn't be returned.'

The outcome
In the ensuing trial Peete Mofoka and at least two of his accomplices were convicted and sentenced to imprisonment.

Sources: PS and MM interviews, 'Masempe Mofoka and Exinia Letsoela, 2 June 1999.

1934/1

1934. Matsoku Ha Khubetsoane, Mokhotlong. Ward 11: Tlokoeng.
Qacha's Nek PE 168/34. *R v. Hlolo Khubetsoane Ntsiki and seven others.*

The case for the Crown
Hlolo, a headman, wanted medicine for a land dispute, and with his accomplices ambushed the deceased, a woman who had recently given birth to a child, on her way back from a party. They murdered her, took the *liretlo* they wanted and left the body on the mountainside.

The outcome
After the preparatory examination the Attorney-General decided not to prosecute.

Sources: Jones, No. 18; Ashton, 'Analysis', p. 1, and 'Mokhotlong', p. 30.

1935/1

1935. Malingoaneng, Mokhotlong. Ward 11: Tlokoeng.
No criminal proceedings.
The administrative officer in Mokhotlong told Hugh Ashton in 1935 that he suspected a murder had been committed near Malingoaneng, possibly in connection

with the succession of Mosuoe to the chieftainship of the Batlokoa and with the disputes of the Batlokoa with the Ward Chief, Seeiso Griffith.

There was insufficient evidence to justify a prosecution.

Sources: Ashton, 'Mokhotlong', p. 30, and 'Analysis', p. 2.

1935/2

December 1935. Near Ntaote's, Qacha's Nek. Ward 5: Ratšoleli's and Mashai. Qacha's Nek PE 38/36. *R* v. *Maleme Sengoar* [*sic*], *Mankie Santi and two others.*

The case for the Crown
According to Jones' list of cases, the victim was 'Small coloured man, name unknown (probably a bushman)'. 'Murder came to light through the discovery, near Paray Mission, of a human forearm. The body, mainly a skeleton with many bones missing, was found in the valley below. It was said by one of the murderers who turned King's evidence, that 1st accused had wanted a man for medicine to doctor his village and had brought 2nd accused there to make it.' According to Jones' notes No. 1 Accused, presumably a headman, had heard that the chief's son was to be placed in his village and wanted to resist this. The deceased is said to have been strangled and his body wrapped in a blanket and placed in a cave.

The outcome
After the preparatory examination the Attorney-General decided not to prosecute.

Sources: Jones, No. 19; Jones Papers, V.

1936/1

1936. Motloaneng, Berea. Ward 6: Koeneng and Mapoteng.
No criminal proceedings.
This murder came to light only during the police investigation of case 1944/1. The victim was a woman who had recently given birth to a child. She was said to have been killed by headman Lejaha Puoane, the 15th accused in case 1944/1. Tabola Nkutu, the 1st accused in that case, was also involved.

No action was taken because Lejaha was hanged for his part in case 1944/1.

Source: Jones, No. 20. See also under 1944/1.

1936/2

1936. Motloaneng, Berea. Ward 6: Koeneng and Mapoteng.
No criminal proceedings.
A man named Lerata disappeared in the course of 1936. He was last seen in the company of headman Lejaha Puoane. This murder, like 1936/1, only came to light in the course of police enquiries in case 1944/1. It was said that Lerata was killed by Lejaha for the medicine horns of himself and Tabola Nkutu, respectively the 15th and 1st accused in that case.

No action was taken because Lejaha was hanged for his part in case 1944/1.

Sources: Jones, No. 21; Jones Papers, V. See also under 1944/1.

1937/1

12 September 1937. Api's, Maseru. Ward 7: Kubake and Ramabanta's.
HC 6/39. *R* v. *Molefi Qhofa and his mother.*

The case for the Crown
According to Jones, 'Makaji, son of 1st accused (a petty headman), abducted a girl whom he intended to marry ['Malika Tau] as he had made her pregnant. 1st accused asked him to give him the girl as he wanted her for medicines to protect his village. He paid him £3 for her, and with a man who died soon after is alleged to have strangled deceased, carried her body on a donkey to the mountain where he cut her body open and removed the parts he required. (These were not specified in the evidence, but the bowels and abdominal contents are said to have been missing when the body was found.) The body was hidden in a small rock shelter behind rocks where it was eventually found, by chance, six months later'.

The outcome
In the ensuing trial the accused were acquitted.

Sources: Jones, No. 22; Mabille (1955: 137).

1937/2

5 October 1937. Sehlabathebe, Qacha's Nek. Ward 5: Ratšoleli's and Mashai.
Qacha's Nek PE 69/37. *R* v. *Molekisane Mahasela and four others.*

The case for the Crown
According to Jones, the deceased, a woman called 'Mahali, was 'murdered by her father-in-law and others in a hut on a Tuesday. The neck was twisted and flesh taken from eyebrows, and according to those who found the body, from below the breasts and from her genitalia. Body was kept in a stable the following day, where it was seen by one of her children and finally placed in a pool in Linakeng river where it was found on Friday. The Medical Officer stated that advanced condition of putrefaction largely destroyed the value of medical evidence. He was of the opinion that death was due to exposure and ill health, and that the private parts had not been injured and marks below breasts and in back had been caused by ropes used in carrying body in to station'.

The outcome
After the preparatory examination the Attorney-General decided not to prosecute.

Source: Jones, No. 23.

1939/1

February 1939. Sehloho's, Butha-Buthe. Ward 1: Butha-Buthe.
No criminal proceedings.
The victim of this murder, Pade Nsolo, an old man, disappeared on 9 February. According to Jones, 'Pelvis and legs only were recovered on 14th under a cliff in a river bed. Alleged to have been killed for medicine in connection with a placing'.

This case, which was still under investigation when Jones carried out his enquiry ten years later, was eventually closed.

Sources: Jones, No. 14 and p. 63; Jones Papers, I.

1940/1

August 1940. Tsime, Butha-Buthe. Ward 1: Butha-Buthe.

No criminal proceedings.

According to Jones, the body of David Sholane Makanete [Makenete?], an old man, was 'found at the bottom of a cliff and buried. Police were told in 1940 that he had fallen over. No blood at the site but there was a wound on the head. Information that he was killed for medicine'. (According to PRO files the murder was first reported on 11 March 1948, i.e. more than seven years after it was committed.) 'The body was exhumed. The Post Mortem disclosed no bones broken but there were possible traces of wound on head which had not fractured skull but had discoloured the underlying bone.'

This case, which was still under investigation when Jones carried out his enquiry, was eventually closed.

Sources: Jones, No. 25 and p. 63; Jones Papers, I; PRO, DO 119/1378, f. 65, Schedule B.

1940/2

31 October 1940. Masaleng, Mokhotlong. Ward 14: Mokhotlong.

No criminal proceedings.

According to a Schedule of cases drawn up by Ashton in 1949, a medicine murder committed in the Mokhotlong District on 31 October 1940 was still under investigation in 1949. According to a Schedule of cases drawn up in the Secretariat in Maseru in 1949, a murder committed on 31 December 1940 and reported on 1 January 1941 at Matlere Lerotholi's village of Masaleng was still under investigation in 1949. It seems most likely that these two cases are the same.

Evidently no criminal proceedings were brought.

Sources: Ashton, Schedule; PRO, DO 119/1378, f. 65, Schedule B.

1940/3

Between 1940 and 1942. 'Mamosebetsi Qhobela's, Butha-Buthe. Ward 1: Butha-Buthe.

No criminal proceedings.

According to Jones, the body of Nthabisa Ngaka, an adult male, 'was found on veld suggesting death from exposure, but wounds are said to have been found on the body. It was buried though some of relatives objected and wanted an enquiry. It is now alleged he was murdered for medicine'.

This case, which was still under investigation when Jones carried out his enquiry in 1949, was eventually closed.

Sources: Jones, No. 26 and p. 63; Jones Papers, I.

1941/1

11 September 1941. Near Mohapeloa's village, Mohale's Hoek. Ward 18: Tajane.

HC 125/42. *R* v. *Mahanyapa Mahapali Molomo Mohale and six others.*

The case for the Crown

The instigator of this crime, Mahanyapa Molomo, gazetted in 1939 as sub-chief of Lifajaneng, had been placed there by Mohale 'Mako, the Ward Chief of Tajane.

According to information given to Jones, the village of Setlolela Mokhachane was also allocated to him, and this was resisted by Setlolela's people. It was suggested that Mahanyapa Molomo needed medicine to strengthen him in this situation.

The victim, Charlie Motona, was aged about sixty. He was the friend of most of the accused, a short man, strong and heavily built. One Thursday he left home and went from one beer-drink to another. He went on to spend the night at the home of his lover, 'Malejoe. One of the accused called him out, and he was attacked by a group of men. 'Malejoe, who had gone with him, was struck and ran away. Charlie's head was severed and skinned, his eyes, tongue, ears and neck removed, also some of the ribs, all the internal organs, the left arm, the right hand, flesh from both arms and the testicles. The body was then dragged away and left under a cliff, where it was found on the following Tuesday. It was identified as Charlie's by his trousers and boots.

The outcome

When the police began their enquiries the chief's messenger assigned to help them was one of the murderers. Within ten days of the murder the police had arrested all the accused. In the ensuing trial Accused No. 3 was discharged, but the other accused were convicted. They were hanged in October 1942.

Sources: Jones, No. 27; Jones Papers, V; LNA, HC 125/42; PRO, DO 119/1377, Forsyth-Thompson's discussions with 'Mantšebo and her advisers, enclosed with Forsyth-Thompson to Baring, 29 March 1949.

1941/2

13 June 1941. Lesala's, Mohale's Hoek. Ward 15: Phamong.
Preparatory examination. *R* v. *Kotjee Bafazini and two others*.

The case for the Crown

According to Jones, 'It was alleged that deceased [an old man called Rapitli Mahlahlama] had been detailed to watch the movements of a catechist who was the intended victim, but that he went and warned him; so deceased was killed in his place. A wound being made on his head with a sharp instrument, from which blood was collected in a tin, and he was then suffocated or strangled and thrown in a pool of water in a gorge, where his body was found. Two months after the crime the police found the body of a female sheep placed in the identical spot; its face had been mutilated, the left side of it including the ear and eye had been removed. It was rumoured that this murder was committed for medicine for Selemo Posholi'. (See case 1944/5 below.) According to information which Jones received but did not include in his report, Selemo Posholi needed medicine in his struggle with Chief Bereng Griffith.

The outcome

The accused were discharged at the preparatory examination.

Sources: Jones, No. 28; Jones Papers, V; PRO, DO 119/1378, f. 65, Schedule A. (We assume that Koki in this Schedule is the same as Kotjee in Jones.)

1941/3

1941. Mokema, Maseru. Ward 2: Maama's.
No criminal proceedings.

A woman was murdered at Mokema in 1941. No details are known, and the case was closed undetected. Mokema was the village of Molapo Maama, and it is possible that this murder was connected with the rivalry between him and his brother, Seeiso Maama. See 1942/1 below.

Source: PRO, DO 119/1378, f. 65, Schedule B.

1942/1

6 April 1942. Near Mokema, Maseru. Ward 2: Maama's.
HC 252/45. *R* v. *Constable Mosi and three others.*

The case for the Crown
The instigator of this murder, Constable Mosi, was a commoner living in Mokema, the village of Chief Molapo Maama. In 1936 Molapo Maama had been appointed as Acting Ward Chief in place of his brother Seeiso Maama, who had been suspended for drunkenness and incompetence. In 1941, however, Seeiso Maama had been reinstated. It was rumoured, and is still rumoured today, that this murder was carried out for Molapo Maama so that he could regain his position. There was no evidence to support this, but it would have been surprising if a murder was carried out in Molapo Maama's own village without his being aware of it. Whereas Seeiso Maama was 'just a drinker and a dagga smoker – an easy going man', Molapo Maama was able and ambitious.

Three of Constable Mosi's accomplices were doctors, among them Phoka Shea, who was also one of the accused in case 1944/4. The fourth accomplice, Koenehelo, wanted medicine to render him immune from arrest while he committed stock theft. Strengthened in this way, he began thieving again, but when he was arrested in 1944 he decided to report this murder to the authorities and turned King's evidence. The motive reported by Koenehelo was that he and Constable Mosi went to Phoka Shea to get doctored, but were told that he did not have enough medicine.

The victim, Meriama Khokhoma, lived in Molapo Maama's village. On Easter Monday she went to a mission feast at Makhahla's, and when she left she was caught and killed. The murderers tied a bridle rein round her neck, but were told not to pull too tightly so that she could be cut while she was still alive. Accused Nos. 3 and 4 began cutting flesh from her body, beginning with the legs, then the private parts, then the armpits and finally the tongue. Accused No. 3 cut her under the chin and pulled the tongue through the hole. No. 1 cut the armpits, and No. 4 from the buttocks. Meriama died when her tongue was pulled out. The body was hidden, but the murderers returned the next night and took some more fat.

The body was left in a donga where it was found about a week later. There was no flesh on the body at all from the head downwards, except the feet. It had been eaten by dogs. The accused were arrested in March and May 1945.

The outcome
The Crown's case rested entirely on the evidence of the accomplice, Koenehelo, and since the judge found this unreliable and inconsistent the accused were acquitted.

Other cases which were or might have been connected with the rivalry between Molapo Maama and Seeiso Maama are 1941/3, 1944/4, 1948/22 and 1950/3.

Sources: FCO, Box 1167, S197A, DC Maseru to GS 11 February 1942, and Box 1168, S 197E, confidential report on Molapo Maama, 1943; Jones, No. 29 and p.

16; Jones Papers, V; LNA, HC 252/45; *Basutoland News*, 11 December 1945; PS and MM interviews, Mokhoele Mahao and 'Mamoliehi Nyooko, 1 June 1999.

1942/2

October 1942. Molapo Qhobela's area, Butha-Buthe. Ward 1: Butha-Buthe.
No criminal proceedings.
The body of an old man, Lefaso Moneke, 'was found at bottom of krantz at Chaba's. Post-mortem disclosed death due to intercranial haemorrhage. Small wounds on forehead and vertex might have been caused by blunt instrument or falling on a stone. Victim alleged to have been murdered for medicine in donga in Molapo Qhobela's area'.

When Jones carried out his enquiry in 1949 this case was still under investigation, but it was eventually closed for lack of evidence.

Sources: Jones, No. 30 and p. 63; Jones Papers, I.

1942/3

9 October 1942. Near Mahlomola's village, Maseru. Ward 13: Matsieng.
HC 139/43. *R* v. *Mopeli Machakela*. Two other accused were discharged before the preparatory examination, one at the preparatory examination itself.

The case for the Crown
Mopeli Machakela, a young herdboy, was accused of murdering 'Matšitso Rasenekane, a middle-aged woman. At first he told the police that he had killed 'Matšitso with two other men, Molikeng and Mahlomola, who had wanted to make a medicine horn. Partly on this basis, Molikeng, Mahlomola, Mopeli and Mopeli's father, Seetsa, were all accused of murder at the preliminary examination. Mopeli went back on his original statement, however, and said that he alone had killed 'Matšitso. The other three accused were discharged, and Mopeli alone was accused of murder in the High Court.

He said that 'Matšitso had sworn at him because his cattle were damaging her crops and that she had threatened to bewitch him and his cattle. Later she gave him some beer and he felt some discomfort in the stomach. Convinced that he had been bewitched, he threw stones at 'Matšitso and killed her. On the morning after killing her he put the body in a donga. He then cut it on the ear and neck and threw away the flesh so that people would think that she had been murdered by 'savage people'. He was very frightened, and his grandfather, who was a doctor, scarified him on both sides of the nose to get rid of his fear. After being arrested he vomited up three snakes which must have been in the beer given him by 'Matšitso.

The outcome
The judge in the High Court, Walter Huggard, found Mopeli Machakela guilty, but he was convinced that he had been acting on the instructions of older and more senior men and he recommended that the High Commissioner, Lord Harlech, should commute the sentence to ten years' IHL. The Attorney-General agreed with this recommendation.

Presumably Lord Harlech accepted the judge's recommendation.

Sources: LNA, HC 139/43, including Huggard's letter to Lord Harlech, 6 April 1943. (This case is included in Ashton's Schedule of cases, but not in Jones' list.)

1942/4

25 December 1942. Theko Karabo's, Qacha's Nek. Ward 5: Ratšoleli's and Mashai. HC 160/43. *R* v. *'Molai Mooso and five others*. Two other accused were discharged at the preliminary examination because there was insufficient evidence against them.

The case for the Crown
The instigator in this case was a doctor who wanted human flesh for his medicines. Two of his accomplices were his brothers and two were his wives. The victim was an elderly widow, 'Mamosito Monyeso. She was related to all the accused and was on good terms with them. Late in the evening on Christmas Day, a Friday, Jela, a boy of seventeen who later turned King's evidence, conveyed a message to 'Mamosito inviting her to go to the hut of one of the accused. There she was set upon by two of the accused, her neck was twisted and broken, an iron spike was driven into her brain through the top of her head, boiling water was poured over her and into her mouth, a circular piece of the scalp was cut out with a knife, and she was disembowelled. Her body was taken back to her village and placed in an unoccupied hut, and later it was dumped over a cliff about seventy metres away.

When the body was found on the following Monday Accused No. 2, who was described as the chairman (presumably of the local chief's court), and the chief's messenger from Mashai's both said that 'Mamosito had died by falling over the cliff, and Accused Nos. 1 and 2 said that the missing parts had been taken by dogs. In spite of the suspicions of 'Mamosito's grand-daughter, the body was buried.

The grand-daughter's suspicions continued, fuelled by loose talk from 'Molai Mooso himself, and two months later the body was exhumed and a post-mortem held. In March and April the accused were arrested.

The outcome
At the preparatory examination evidence was given not only by Jela, the accomplice witness, but also by some women and children (aged four and five) who were resting in the hut after their evening meal when the murder was carried out. Two of the accused, the wives of 'Molai Mooso, made confessions. At the end of the preparatory examination two of the men accused were released for lack of evidence, and the remaining six accused were committed for trial.

At the end of the Crown case in the High Court two more of the accused were discharged, since the only evidence against them was that of the accomplice witness. The instigator, 'Molai Mooso, and one of his brothers were found guilty of murder. The two wives who were accused were acquitted since they were terrified and acting under the compulsion of their husband.

The first two accused were hanged.

Sources: Jones, No. 31 and p. 16; LNA, HC 160/43.

1943/1

January 1943. Masaleng, Mokhotlong. Ward 14: Mokhotlong.
R v. *Maqila Hlongwane and two others*.

The case for the Crown
The accused in this case were Zulu, one of whom was a doctor who was said to have been resident in Mokhotlong for a long time. There was also an accomplice who

turned King's evidence. He stated that the accused killed a woman called 'Mampo because they wanted fat from a woman's stomach. She was then dumped, still alive, in a pond, where her dead body was found later.

The outcome

After the preparatory examination the Attorney-General refused to prosecute because he thought that the accomplice was shielding the real murderers. In a paragraph in his report that was not published Jones made it clear that the person suspected was Chief Matlere Lerotholi, in whose village the murder took place. In the meantime Maqila had died in prison.

Sources: FCO, Box 1175, S 119, Clarke, Acting CP, to GS, 18 August 1949; Jones, No. 35; Ashton, 'Mokhotlong', pp. 30, 34–5, and 'Analysis', pp. 2–3; PRO, DO 35/ 4158, paragraph 106 of Jones' draft report.

1943/2

3 July 1943. Tebelo's, Mafeteng. Ward 12: Matelile.
HC 119/43. *R* v. *Robert Ramosoeu and six others.*

The case for the Crown

The instigator in this case was an ungazetted headman and had formerly been the chairman of Chieftainess 'Mabereng's court. The victim was a man called Sankoela, who was chosen because he was a Mohlakoana. In his report Jones gave the motive as Ramosoeu's wish to strengthen his chieftainship. In his unpublished papers there are handwritten notes, apparently by an administrative officer from Mafeteng, in which it is suggested that the murder might have been connected with Ramosoeu's disputes with 'Ma-Anna Ramosoeu, the widow of his elder brother, who had been appointed instead of him as acting headman when her husband died. It is also suggested that he might have wanted to be reinstated as chairman in 'Mabereng's court, a post from which he had been dismissed.

According to Jones, he was alleged 'to have conspired with the other accused and a Crown witness to murder deceased after a beer-drink. Deceased was hit on the head and body with sticks, was hidden that night and on the following day placed at the bottom of a kloof. A blanket and hat which had been thrown over a cliff were found the next day, the body not till three weeks later. No account of how *diretlo* was taken and the inquest disclosed no mutilation except a lacerated wound on the forehead'.

The outcome

According to Jones the Attorney-General decided not to prosecute. According to government sources the murderers were 'undetected' and the investigation was closed.

Sources: Jones, No. 32; Jones Papers, V; PRO, DO 119/1378, f. 65, Schedule B.

1943/3

3 July 1943. Seabatha's, Mokhotlong. Ward 14: Mokhotlong.
HC 303/46. *R* v. *Seabatha Lerotholi and three others.*

The case for the Crown

Seabatha Lerotholi, a half-brother of Matlere Lerotholi, was an ungazetted headman who had been placed in his area by Seeiso Griffith. Early in 1943 he was placed over another headman, Maraene Tšita, and there was friction between them. He believed that he needed medicine prepared from a Mohlakoana, and he chose his friend Petrose Makhele, an elderly man who was variously described as an Anglican priest or preacher.

He enlisted the help of five accomplices, two of whom later turned King's evidence. They stated that, after a beer party at which Petrose became very drunk, he was enticed into Seabatha's hut and given a chair. He was then seized, gagged and choked. A sailmaker's needle was stuck into his chest and a needle into his head and blood drawn off into a billy-can. Warm water was poured on the wounds to stop the flow of blood and he died. While this was happening a man tried to come into the hut but was chased off.

The body was wrapped in a blanket and placed under the bed, and on the following day, a Sunday, it was seen by another woman who was told not to say anything. That night it was taken to the Sehonghong river and so placed as to give the impression that he had fallen from a krantz into the water. It was found on the following Tuesday.

In October 1943 several people were arrested, including the four accused, but the investigations were inconclusive and they had to be released. In April 1946 they were rearrested. Two of the accomplices paid a doctor ten shillings to make them medicine which would secure their acquittal.

The outcome

In his judgement Mr Justice de Beer said that he found the case extremely difficult. His assessors were divided, and so the entire responsibility rested on him. He had grave doubts about the veracity of the two accomplice witnesses, he said, but it was the post-mortem examination that weighed most with him. This showed that Petrose had died from asphyxia. He had vomited and inhaled some of his vomit, and this was said to contain grit and sand which had no doubt come from the sandbank on which he had been deposited. This meant that he could not have died in Seabatha's hut as the two accomplice witnesses had described. The accused were therefore acquitted.

Sources: Jones, No. 33; Jones Papers, V; LNA, HC 303/46; *Basutoland News*, 3.12.46; *Moeletsi*, 26.10.43; PRO, DO 35/4155, Paramount Chief's petition, 16 September 1948; Ashton, 'Mokhotlong', p. 30, and 'Analysis', p. 3.

1943/4

4 September 1943. Thaba-Ntšo, Qacha's Nek. Ward 5: Ratšoleli's and Mashai. HC 185/44. *R* v. *Mabibini Mtandi and three others*.

The case for the Crown

The instigator in this case was a Zulu doctor who wanted human flesh for medicine, though some witnesses said that he and his five accomplices were acting on the orders of a higher chief. Two of the accomplices turned King's evidence. Their victim, 'Mapoone Matobe, was a woman who had just given birth to a child, and she was the sister-in-law of one of the accused.

It was arranged that 'Mapoone should be waylaid at a kloof after leaving a beer-drink. She was gagged and struck on the head with a knobkerrie. She was strangled, and after she had stopped breathing Mabibini cut her eyebrow and collected blood.

He also cut her private parts. The accused carried the body and threw it into a stream about 300 metres away. Her clothes were placed nearby as clues. That, Mabibini said, was how he worked.

The outcome

The accused were acquitted, but we have not been able to find a copy of the judgement and Jones does not give the reasons for the decision.

Sources: Jones, No. 34 and pp. 16, 17 (fn.); LNA, HC 185/44, PE only.

1943/5

25 December 1945. Matebeng, Qacha's Nek. Ward 5: Ratšoleli's and Mashai. HC 253/45. *R v. Pitso Ramatlali and four others.* (At the preparatory examination Accused No. 1 was Moramang Letsie, the gazetted headman of Patiseng Ha Moramang. He died in prison while awaiting trial in the High Court, and Pitso Ramatlali became Accused No. 1.)

The case for the Crown

Moramang told his accomplices that 'the Chief Overseas' needed some medicine from a Mokoena man. The Chief Overseas was the Ward Chief, David Theko Makhaola, who was leading the Basotho soldiers in the African Auxiliary Pioneer Corps 'up north' in the war. Chief Lelingoana Makhaola, the sub-chief of Matebeng, was also involved: his chairman played a part in choosing the victim, Moramang reported to him on the day following the murder, and he threatened people with death if they spoke about the murder. Theko himself later derided the allegation: why should he ask for medicine from Basutoland when there were so many dead bodies around where he was? Jones surmised that, while it was possible that Theko had given orders to obtain medicine, it was more likely that his followers decided to procure it to safeguard his local interests while he was away. It was also possible that *liretlo* were required for another purpose and that Theko's name was used to give greater justification to the killing. There was in fact evidence of conflict between Moramang and his elder brother Sefaha and of Moramang's frustrations in trying to exercise authority in his village.

The victim, an elderly man called Sekoati Mpheto, was chosen because he was a Mokoena and because he had made certain accusations against one of the accused. Moramang arranged that the murder 'would be done on Christmas Day when people had taken much beer so that it would be thought he had fallen over a cliff'. Sekoati went to church on Christmas morning, and when he came out he was met by a woman whose body and blankets had been smeared all over with medicinal fat to make her attractive to him. He went with her to various beer-drinks throughout the day, and late in the evening they left the last beer-drink together. The woman went into her home and Sekoati went on with another man, Nkherepe. He was then ambushed by the accused. Nkherepe was driven off, and Sekoati was beaten with a battle-axe, sticks and clubs and stabbed with a sword. He was carried a short distance away from the path to a spot where blood was collected from his head wound, his right eye was removed and small portions of flesh were taken from his side and leg. All the parts were put in a tin. A fire was obtained from the home of the woman who had been with Sekoati, and the wounds were cauterised. Sekoati was still breathing.

He was then carried to the edge of a cliff, and by this time he was dead. The body was rolled over, and the murderers were told to disperse and not to go home in a group. Sekoati's stick was placed at the top of the cliff.

The body was found the next day and buried. Sekoati's widow was dissatisfied and went repeatedly to Chief Lelingoana's to demand an enquiry. On the fourth time, several months after the murder, Lelingoana agreed to report the matter to government. The body was exhumed and an inconclusive post-mortem carried out.

The outcome

There had been a lot of loose talk about the murder, and the accused were arrested in April and May 1944. The case against them rested on the evidence, not just of the two accomplice witnesses, but of several independent witnesses, including the woman who had enticed Sekoati to the scene of the murder and Nkherepe, the man who had been with him when he was attacked. In October 1945 all five accused were found guilty, and in November they were all hanged.

Sources: Jones, No. 36 and pp. 16, 29–30; Jones Papers, V; LNA, HC 253/45; *Basutoland News*, 23.10.45; *Proc. (Special 1956) BNC, 7–17 May 1956*, p. 137, Theko Makhaola's speech, 14 May 1956.

1943/6

1943? Qacha's Nek District. Ward 5: Ratšoleli's and Mashai.
R v. *Malehi Ramakoae.*
All that is known about this case is that, according to a Schedule produced by the Basutoland Government in 1949, Malehi Ramakoae was convicted of a medicine murder in the Qacha's Nek District in 1943. It is surprising that the case was not included in the lists of cases drawn up by Ashton and Jones.

Source: PRO, DO 119/1378, f. 65, Schedule A.

1944/1

4 January 1944. Thebeng, Berea. Ward 6: Koeneng and Mapoteng.
HC 196/44. R v. *Tabola Nkutu and thirteen others.* (Four other accused were discharged at the preparatory examination.)

The case for the Crown

The two leading instigators in this case were Tabola Nkutu and Lejaha Puoane, who were both gazetted headmen under Chief Nkutu. According to the District Commissioner, Berea, Lejaha was much older than Tabola and exercised a strong influence over him. He had an 'extreme faith in the more savage aspects of witchcraft' and ruled his people by terror. The horns of the two men had previously been filled after the murder of Lerata in 1936 (1936/2 above), and they now needed replenishing. Tabola as the senior son of Nkutu should have succeeded his father, but was afraid that he would lose his rights because Nkutu favoured his younger son, Malibeng. Lejaha had lost status because Malibeng had been given some of his villages and he was now headman of one village only. They were joined by Manyonyoba Tsolo, a mine *induna* who had lost his job at the Nieuwkleinfontein Mine and who paid Tabola £50 for a horn which would secure his re-employment.

The two headmen asked Seleka Mosese to get a victim for them. He failed twice. They then decided to kill Seleka himself and enlisted the help of accomplices.

Tabola suggested that he and Seleka should go for a ride to see their lovers, and it was arranged that Tabola should go on ahead and Seleka would catch him up. Tabola and his accomplices waited for Seleka at Liotloaneng stream and when he came they seized him and tied him to a tree with his feet off the ground. They undressed him and stunned him. Lejaha directed operations. The murderers took off their clothes to avoid their being stained by blood. Tabola, as Nkutu's heir, cut first. Others followed. Flesh was cut from the armpit and blood collected in a billy-can. The biceps were cut and the right calf severed with a pen-knife; parts of the thumb and three fingers were cut off, and the whole of one small finger. The right eye was scooped out and the left leg was cut from the buttock to the heel. A circular piece of flesh was cut out, and a stick jabbed up the anus and pulled out with the male organs and anus. At this point Seleka died. Two of the accomplices, overcome by horror, ran away: they were the only two who had not removed their clothes. Another tried to run away, but came back because he was called a coward and because he was naked. The murderers washed themselves with water and the leaves of *mosikanokana* herb: in this way, they were told, the murder would flow away with the water and not come to light.

The body was washed. It was suggested that it should be buried, but Lejaha refused, saying that the deceased had died as a warrior and should be treated as such. It was hidden and later thrown away in a stream.

The body was found on 11 January. A policeman was called and, in spite of the mutilations, allowed it to be buried. Later, when Seleka's elder brother came home, he was told of the murder by one of the accused and told the police.

The outcome
Twenty-four men had taken part in the killing. Three of them turned King's evidence. One died and two disappeared. The other eighteen were accused at the preparatory examination. Four were discharged, and so there were fourteen accused in the High Court. Apart from the accomplice witnesses, there was corroborative evidence from a woman who saw some of the murderers ride by and who, with another woman, heard Seleka scream out, 'I am dying a cruel death; allow me to go and greet my children and friends first' – the words reported by the accomplice witnesses; and there was also evidence of statements made by some of the accused later admitting their guilt. All fourteen accused were found guilty and hanged.

One of the witnesses in this case, the victim's brother, was later murdered.

Sources: Jones, No. 37 and pp. 17, 30 and 67; Jones Papers, V; LNA, HC 196/44, PE report only; FCO, Box 1175, S 119, DC Berea to GS, 26 February 1945; FCO, Box 1177, S 262, Ashton, 'Ritual Murder in Berea', enclosed with Jones to Marwick, 4 August 1949; Ashton papers, which include the judgement in this case; Ashton, 'Ritual Murder in Basutoland', pp. 19–29; Ashton (1952: 311); van Straaten (1948b: 1161–2); Rivers Thompson, 'Reminiscences', p. 33 (Thompson was the magistrate who presided over the PE); Jingoes (1975: 188–90).

1944/2

11 May 1944. Phamong, Mohale's Hoek. Ward 15: Phamong.
R v. *Makhorole Putsane and two others.*

The case for the Crown
Our evidence on this case comes almost entirely from Jones. In his published report

he described the instigator as a 'minor village head' and says that he was obviously a subordinate acting for someone else. In an unpublished paragraph of his draft report he pointed out that the murder took place at Bereng's village at Phamong and said that it was very improbable that it could have taken place without Bereng's knowledge. If that was so, it is likely that it was related to the struggle between Bereng and 'Mantšebo, who were due to be involved in a court case only two weeks later.

The victim was 'Mamosia Kutlane, an old woman who was 'slightly mad'. According to Jones, 'Deceased came to visit her sister, and was last seen alive at 1st accused's village. Body was found in a donga nearby. Death was due to fracture of the skull by a blow on the head. A number of wounds were found on the forehead and the right side of the head and minor wounds on right fingers and toes, *diretlo* said to have been the latter. The deceased could not have received these wounds by falling into the donga'.

The outcome
It seems that a preparatory examination was held, after which the Attorney-General decided not to prosecute.

Sources: Jones, No. 38 and p. 16; Jones Papers, V; PRO, DO 35/4158, Jones' draft report; *Leselinyana*, 28.6.44.

1944/3

June 1944. Qacha's Nek District. Ward 5: Ratšoleli's and Mashai.
No criminal proceedings.
The details given above come from Ashton's Schedule. A list drawn up by the Basutoland Government in 1947 adds that the case was first reported to the police on 3 October 1945. The case was still under investigation when Ashton drew up his Schedule in 1949.

Sources: PRO, DO 35/4154, Forsyth-Thompson to Baring, 19 March 1948; Ashton, Schedule.

1944/4

11 September 1944. Khoarai's, Maseru. Ward 2: Maama's.
HC 250/45. *R* v. *Nkemi Khoarai and three others.* (One other accused was discharged at the end of the preparatory examination.)

The case for the Crown
This murder, like 1942/1, was rumoured to have been committed for Chief Molapo Maama, who had been appointed in May 1944 as Acting Ward Chief in place of his senior brother Seeiso and wanted to hold on to his position, but there was no evidence to confirm this. Phoka Shea, a doctor, was one of the accused in both cases, and Koenehelo Khau was an accomplice witness in both cases. The instigator, Nkemi Khoarai, was an ungazetted headman in Maama's ward. The victim, 'Matingting Masalalla, was an elderly widow who had only one eye and had formerly been a leper.

Koenehelo wanted some medicine for two reasons: that he should not be arrested for stock theft, and that he should not lose his work at Matsieng where he executed judgements for the Paramount Chief. Phoka Shea said he needed human medicine but he had run short: he only had the portion of the rectum of a European. He was going to take part in a murder for Khoarai, however, and it was arranged that

Koenehelo should join them. Phoka Shea assured Khoarai that Koenehelo was reliable and bold. It was arranged that 'Matingting should be killed after a baptismal feast at Khoarai's village when it was known there would be 'much drunkenness'. There was a lot of singing at the party, in which 'Matingting joined. She was very drunk and went out several times to pass water. On the last occasion she did not return.

Khoarai took her to the place where she was to be killed. She was gagged with her *doek* (headscarf) and according to Koenehelo 'the intention was to cut a flesh while she was still alive'. Her private parts were cut out, an operation that lasted about an hour and was conducted in complete silence. Pieces of flesh were cut from all over the body. All the flesh from her face was removed and a portion of the head. She died when her neck was cut. The body was dumped beneath a cliff where it was found some time afterwards, badly decomposed, the head being connected to the body by a small strip of flesh.

The police made investigations and arrested the accused. A bag taken from the home of one of the accused was sent for analysis and one item 'had appearance and characteristics of human fat'. By coincidence Koenehelo was arrested for stealing horses and found himself in the same gaol as the four accused. A medicated belt was supposed to help them, but when Koenehelo saw that it was useless he decided to make a full confession.

The outcome
In the ensuing trial the Crown relied heavily on Koenehelo's evidence, but since he had just been declared an unreliable witness in case 1942/1 the judge felt unable to depend on him in this case and all the accused were acquitted.

Sources: Jones, No. 39; Jones Papers, V (two references); LNA, HC 250/45; *Basutoland News*, 11.2.45; PS and MM interview, Mokhoele Mahao, 1 June 1999.

1944/5

18 September 1944. Maphutšeng, Mohale's Hoek. Ward 15: Phamong.
HC 217/45. *R* v. *Selemo Lesalla Posholi and ten others.*

The case for the Crown
The instigator, Selemo Lesalla Posholi, was the gazetted headman of Lehlohono-long and the acting sub-chief of Maphutšeng. He told his accomplices that he had a dispute with his Ward Chief, Bereng Griffith. He had appealed to the Paramount Chief about Bereng's intention to place one of his relatives in his area, and it seems that Selemo was also making plans to place his own son, Accused No. 2 in this case. He decided that he needed medicine prepared from a Motaung, and he chose an old man called Sefate Rasoeu, a builder who was then working at Maphutšeng.

One Sunday Sefate left Maphutšeng and said he was going to Nyake's. On the Monday evening he was attacked as he came away drunk from a beer-drink. He was strangled and killed and various parts were cut – the left arm, the palm of the right hand, flesh from the left armpit, the heart, a lung and the private parts. August Lemaha, later a Crown witness, was sure that he was dead when the cutting started.

One of the accomplices, a doctor called Butsane, shaved Sefate's body and covered his face with a black medicine. He said this would ensure that the matter never came to light 'as this was his practice of his horn'. Butsane also told the murderers to cut their hair since otherwise they would go mad.

The body was put in a cave and later dumped near Nyake Porota's village so as to cast suspicion on Nyake, with whom Selemo was on bad terms. About a fortnight later it was found in a ravine.

The outcome
In the ensuing preparatory examination there were three accomplice witnesses and also evidence relating to bloodstains on the clothing of the accused. We have not been able to find a copy of the judgement. The first eight accused were found guilty. Accused No. 10, who had been present at the disposal of the body but not at the murder, was given five years' IHL. The other two accused were acquitted. The eight found guilty were hanged.

Sources: Jones, No. 40; LNA, HC 217/45, PE record only; *Basutoland News*, 24.4.45; *Mochochonono*, 9.6.45; *Moeletsi*, 5.6.45; Ashton Papers, statement of August Lemaha, an accomplice witness; Ashton (1952: 311); PRO, DO 119/1377, f. 9b; PS and KS interview, Edwin Nohe Tšita, 4 June 1999.

1944/6

14 November 1944. Marabeng, Berea. Ward 3: Majara's.
HC 236/45. *R* v. *Lagden Majara and three others* (four others according to *Basutoland News*).

The case for the Crown
The instigator in this case, Lagden Majara, was a gazetted sub-chief, and one of his accomplices was his son, Dyke Majara. According to Jones, it was rumoured that Lagden had had some headmen removed from his caretaking and wanted to get them back. Ashton, in his 'Analysis', says that this case might be directly attributable to the National Treasury reforms, since preparations were being made to reduce the number of courts, but he adduces no evidence to support this. In his paper on 'Ritual Murder in Berea' he suggests another motive – that Lagden resented the placing of Leshoboro over him and was feeling insecure. The victim was an elderly Letebele, Bull Koatja, who was slightly mad and lived alone.

According to Jones, 'several witnesses heard [Koatja] calling for help one night and shouting that people were killing him and taking out his eye. The body was found dead next morning in his hut. The left eye was said to be missing, some flesh from right side of forehead and there was a wound on the right thumb. Medical evidence was unsatisfactory as the body was too decomposed before post-mortem held'.

The outcome
The case collapsed when Dyke Majara, who had turned King's evidence against his father, changed his statement in the High Court, alleging that his first statement was false and had been extracted under pressure by the police. He later disappeared from Basutoland. All the accused were acquitted. The judge, Walter Huggard, was very critical of the police's investigation (though not for the reasons given by Dyke Majara) and of the delays in conducting the post-mortem.

Sources: Jones, No. 41 and p. 62; Jones Papers, V; *Basutoland News*, 6.11.45; PRO, DO 35/4155, f. 11(f), 'Mantšebo's petition to RC, 16 September 1948; Ashton, 'Mokhotlong', p. 33, and 'Analysis', p. 11; FCO, Box 1177, S 262, Ashton, 'Ritual Murder in Berea', enclosed with Jones to Marwick, 4 August 1949.

1944/7

8 November 1944. Linotšing, Mokhotlong. Ward 14: Mokhotlong.
HC 335/47. *R* v. *Mahlomola Lerotholi and twelve others.* (One other accused was discharged at the end of the preparatory examination, and another, it seems, died before the trial in the High Court.)

The case for the Crown

The instigator in this case, Mahlomola Lerotholi, was a gazetted headman at Linotšing and was the half-brother of Matlere Lerotholi. In 1942 the Assistant District Commissioner of Mokhotlong described him as 'rotten – everything a chief should not be, corrupt, deceitful, not trustworthy, unreliable, rude and insolent at times'. Mahlomola believed that the number of chiefs was to be reduced and was afraid of being deposed. He wanted medicine prepared from a twin girl. The victim chosen was 'Malefu Guda (alternatively 'Mafukuthu), a girl of nine years old who was believed to be a twin but in fact was not. Among the accomplices were several women and a doctor. The child, who was living with her aunt, was kidnapped when she went out one evening to fetch some cattle. She was kept in a cattle post for several days and was moved around from one place to another while the search for her was being conducted. At various stages, on the instructions of the doctor, she had to be carried by a barren woman, her head was shaved and water was sprinkled over her, and the men pretended to have sexual intercourse with her. One of the accused cut off the tip of her nose and the lobe of her left ear before she was moved from his hut to Mahlomola's village, where she was taken to the huts of one of the accused. She was apparently drugged.

It was dark in the hut, but a paraffin lamp was alight. Blood was taken from a wound in 'Malefu's chest, and flesh from various parts of the trunk and abdomen, including the intestines, kidneys and fat and flesh from the arms, jaw, tongue, private parts, right arm and both legs. The child died when she was stabbed in the chest. The limbs and flesh were collected in a grain bag and Mahlomola took charge of them. The accused were told to cut a piece for themselves, whichever piece they liked, and the doctor would come later and make medicine for them. One witness said that people did not know what use they were going to make of these pieces. He himself took a piece of intestine and the doctor made medicine so that people would not kill him. Another hid a shoulder-blade under a roofing pole in his hut. Later the doctor was seen with some of the other accused, naked, and burying pebbles smeared with black medicine around the village.

The body was placed on a ledge below a perpendicular cliff where it was found by a herdboy about three months later.

The outcome

Mahlomola was arrested in March 1945, but he and his accomplices were not brought to trial until 1947. Although there were three accomplice witnesses there were several difficulties in the police investigation. One witness complained that he was being forced to make false allegations against Mahlomola, and Mahlomola's daughter retracted a statement that she had seen the dead body in a square hut. In the final judgement twelve of the thirteen accused were convicted, ten men and two women. Nine of the ten men were hanged, and the tenth man and the two women had their sentences commuted to various periods of imprisonment.

Sources: Jones, No. 42; Jones Papers, V; LNA, HC 335/47, PE record; *Basutoland News*, 6, 13 and 20.5.47, and 23.12.47; *Moeletsi*, 13, 20 and 27.5.47, 3 and 10.6.47; Ashton, 'Mokhotlong', p. 30, and 'Analysis', pp. 3, 11; Ambrose Archives, Mokhotlong Files, C2, Confidential Reports on Chiefs; FCO, Box 1176, S 119, f. 1284A; *Proc. (44) BNC*, Vol. I, p. 22, speech of Thabo Lerotholi, 21 September 1948; van Straaten (1948a: 146–7).

1944/8

24 December 1944. Kolo, Mafeteng, Ward 17: Rothe etc.
No criminal proceedings.
Apart from an entry in Ashton's Schedule of cases our only evidence on this case comes from Jones. The alleged instigator, Mitchell Bereng, was a gazetted headman and was involved in several chieftainship disputes. The victim was a Motaung boy, Rajane Mohanoe, who was two and a half years old.

According to Jones, no body was found, but the child 'was said to have been killed in a donga and most of the flesh to have been removed from its bones for medicine'.

Sources: Jones, No. 43; Jones Papers, I and V; Ashton, Schedule.

1945/1

10 February 1945. Tšepiso's, Mokhotlong. Ward 11: Tlokoeng.
No criminal proceedings.
The body of a man called Ramabanta Manakane was found at the foot of a cliff. Jones reports: 'Wounds on temple, bleeding from nose, wound behind right shoulderblade. A hat with glasses inside it was found about 30 yds. away. Horse grazing on top of cliff. The body was buried as his wife and mother were said to have agreed that death was due to falling over the cliff – it is now suspected to have been a murder case.'

The investigation was closed for lack of evidence.

Sources: Jones, No. 44; Jones Papers, I; Ashton, Schedule, 'Mokhotlong', p. 30, and 'Analysis', p. 3; PRO, DO 119/1378, f. 65, Schedule B.

1945/2

February 1945. Absalom's, Mokhotlong. Ward 14: Mokhotlong.
No criminal proceedings.
There are two main reports on this murder. Jones, whose report was published, says very little. Ashton, whose report was not published, is less cautious.
Jones simply says that the victim, a man called Tsietsi Mohapi, was reported missing, 'and his hat, blanket and part of his shirt were found in Sakeng stream. His horse was found near the stream. No body was found. There is a strong suspicion that he was murdered for medicine and his body buried near this village [Absalom's]'.

Ashton writes as follows: 'A man is said to have been kidnapped at this village [Absalom's] and taken to Matlere's village at Masaleng where both he and the Paramount Chief were present in person. The doctor there pointed out that the man belonged to the Bakoena clan and therefore could not be used. By that time he was dead so was taken back and buried near Absalom's village. It is also said that a man named Faralane who was changing his allegiance from Bereng ... and was going over to 'Mantšebo's side, was present and took an arm to use for medicine for his dispute with Bereng. It is said that 'Mantšebo needed medicine at this time in connection with the proposed placing of her daughter, Ntšebo, at Makhaleng. Ntšebo's husband, so it is rumoured, refused to allow her to accept this'.

In 1948 or 1949 two women claimed that the police had tried to get them to incriminate Absalom, the gazetted headman. One said that she was asked why she was afraid of Matlere, and that the police told her that when 'Mantšebo and Matlere came from Masaleng 'Mantšebo carried out human mutilations. These allegations later formed part of the case made out by Ntsu Mokhehle, leader of the Basutoland African Congress, about police malpractices.

Sources: Jones, No. 45; Jones Papers, I; Ashton, 'Analysis', p. 4, and 'Mokhotlong', p. 30; *Proc. (Special 1956) BNC, 7–17 May 1956*, pp. 123–4: speech of Mabina Lerotholi, 14 May 1956; Ntsu Mokhehle, article in *Mohlabani*, August 1957, pp. 9–10.

1945/3 (Case Study 1)

5 May 1945. Phahameng, Morija, Maseru. Ward 13: Matsieng.
HC 288/46. *R* v. *Toka Mafihlo and seven others.*

The case for the Crown

The instigator of this murder was allegedly Mahao Matete, the headman of Morija, where the French Protestant Mission had its headquarters in Basutoland. He was 'Mantšebo's private secretary and, although it was no part of the Crown's case, evidence was led that he was acting on her instructions. Her home at Matsieng was only a few kilometres from Morija. Because of his frequent absences at Matsieng, Mahao had appointed John Makume as acting headman of Morija. Like Mahao, Makume was a leading member of the Protestant Church. 'Mantšebo's alleged involvement was, it seems, kept secret from most of those who took part, and the motive given for the murder was that Mahao was planning to move his village and needed medicine to strengthen his new home.

The murder was organised by John Makume, who enlisted accomplices from both Morija and the nearby village of Phahameng. The victim was Stephen Thobeha, a local bootmaker. On Saturday, 5 May 1945, Stephen attended a feast at Phahameng. During the night he was lured away, a strap was thrown round his head and he was taken to a dense poplar plantation where he was flung to the ground. One of the accomplices severed his head from his trunk with a large table-knife. The body was hidden, but was later moved, and was eventually found on the cliff marking the boundary between Morija and Phahameng. Eleven men were accused of murder at the preparatory examination. Three were discharged and eight were committed for trial at the High Court.

The outcome

There was one accomplice witness, Nkojoa Mokone, and several independent witnesses who gave evidence about incriminating conversations and movements. The most important of these independent witnesses was a doctor, Bernice Hlalele, also known as Ntjahali, who stated that after the murder John Makume and another man, Liau Lekhula, had brought her Stephen Thobeha's head and told her, on the instructions of the Paramount Chief, to make medicine from it. She had refused. There were serious doubts about the evidence of the accomplice witness, Nkojoa Mokone, who was proved to have been lying at one point, and in view of this the only accused against whom there was a strong case were John Makume and Liau Lekhula. Liau was acquitted because it was Makume who had taken Thobeha's head in his saddlebags to Bernice Hlalele and there was some doubt as to whether Liau knew about the contents of the saddlebag. Makume therefore was the only one of the accused to be convicted, and he was hanged.

Sources: LNA, HC 288/46; Jones, No. 46 and p. 17; 'Ralitaba', 'Tsa kae le kae', *Moeletsi*, 16.10.45; Kekeletso Malakia Phakisi, 'Lenaka la Moshoeshoe', *Leselinyana*, 27.11.45, 12.10.68; *Basutoland News*, 26.3.46, 9.7.46, 13.8.46; *Mochochonono*, 27.7.46; FCO, Box 1175, S 119, CP to GS 24 June 1948; Mofokeng (n.d.); Ken Shortt-Smith, taped reminiscences c. late 1980s, in possession of Liz Shortt-Smith; PS interview, Albert Brutsch, 9 December 1996, 11 October 1997; PS interview, Stephen Gill, 7 October 1997; KS and CM interview, Nkherepe Molefe, 29 November 1998; KS and CM interview, Motsetsela Motsetsela, 17 May 1999; KS and PS interview, Nkherepe Molefe, 24 May 1999; KS and CM interviews, 'Mampoi Matete and 'Maiphepi 'Matli, 15 January 2000. See also references in endnotes to Case Study 1.

1945/4

31 August 1945. Mokete's, Qacha's Nek. Ward 5: Ratšoleli's and Mashai.
HC 336/47. *R* v. *Lehooe Letsikhoana and ten others.*

The case for the Crown

Lehooe Letsikhoana was a gazetted headman who was unpopular in his village and wanted to strengthen his chieftainship. He was on bad terms with the victim, a man called Lenkoe Motsotsoane. Lenkoe was attacked after he had left a marriage feast. He was carried to a donga where two stones were heated over a fire. He was stripped and his body was ironed with the stones. Lehooe cut round the socket of one eye and removed a portion of it. The knife was handed round to the other accused and portions of flesh were cut from the breast, right ear, right-hand side near the kidneys, and the other eye. The testicles were removed. Lenkoe was still alive and groaning. Hot stones were pressed on the wounds to prevent bleeding. Lenkoe was then dressed again, struck on the head with a knobkerrie, and left in the donga.

While he was still in the donga a herdboy saw him and heard him breathing and groaning. He was afraid to go near. He told one of the accused what he had seen and was threatened with death if he made a report. Later he saw Lehooe going to the donga with a *sjambok* and afterwards the body was no longer there. Lenkoe's dead body was finally discovered at the foot of the Vulture Cliff.

The outcome

In the ensuing trial there were two accomplice witnesses, and there was independent evidence from people who observed the movements of the accused and from the herdboy who had seen Lenkoe in the donga. All the accused were found guilty and hanged, except Accused No. 11 whose sentence was commuted to life imprisonment.

Sources: Jones No. 47; Jones Papers, V; LNA, HC 336/47; *Basutoland News*, 18.10.47; *Moeletsi*, 27.1.48; PRO, DO 119/1377, f. 9B; van Straaten (1948a: 148–9); FCO, Box 1176, S 119, f. 1284A; Hardegger (1987: 110–11).

1945/5

Reported 3 October 1945. Patlong, Qacha's Nek. Ward 5: Ratšoleli's and Mashai. No criminal proceedings.

All that is known about this case is an entry containing the details given above in a Schedule prepared by the Basutoland Government in 1949. Presumably the case was closed for lack of evidence.

Source: PRO, DO 119/1378, f. 65, Schedule B.

1945/6

5 October 1945. Koeneho's, Mokhotlong. Ward 14: Mokhotlong.
HC 272/46. *R* v. *'Mampho (or 'Manapo) Koeneho and three others.*

The case for the Crown
'Mampho Koeneho was the mother of Pikara Koeneho, who was her only son and who was acting as headman of Koeneho's village. The substantive headman, his elder half-brother, was away in Natal. 'Mampho's nephew, Tšiu Khoeli, had been placed as headman of the Libibing area three weeks before the murder. Neither man was gazetted. 'Mampho wanted a medicine horn to make her son superior to his step-brother and to strengthen her nephew in his new position. Both her son and her nephew were among her accomplices.

The victim was a four-year-old girl, Mookho, who was living at Koeneho's with her great-aunt Amelia. She was taken away from her home by 'Maneo, a young woman who was one of the accomplices. After various journeys, in the course of which the child was seen by one witness with tears streaming down her face, she was taken to 'Mampho's home. After being given medicine she was quiet and did not seem to notice anything, and for two or three days she was kept in a grain bag under the bed in the home of 'Mampho's son. Throughout this time a search was being conducted, and the door of the hut was kept locked.

On a Friday evening the child was taken to 'Maneo's home. There was no window, and a piece of sheet iron and a blanket were placed across the open entrance to stop people looking in. The child's arm was punctured with an umbrella rib and blood drawn off into a bottle. After this she appeared to be dead. Her body was then taken to a mountain where it was found by a herdboy the next day. She could not possibly have got there on her own.

The outcome
In the ensuing trial there were two accomplice witnesses, 'Maneo and another young woman, and there were two important independent witnesses as well. All four accused were found guilty. The two headmen – 'Mampho's son and nephew – were hanged. The sentences of 'Mampho and the other accused were commuted to life imprisonment.

Moeletsi paid particular attention to the case because several of the accused were practising Catholics – 'Mampho herself was a member of the Sisterhood of St Anne – and they were well-dressed and presentable. 'Maneo, the young accomplice witness, was described as a great beauty. Her husband had returned from the war only a few weeks before, but she had abandoned him for a local shop assistant.

Sources: Jones, No. 48 and p. 16; Jones Papers, V; LNA, HC 272/46; *Basutoland News*, 23.4.46; *Moeletsi*, 21.5.46; Ashton, 'Ritual Murder in Basutoland', p. 20, 'Mokhotlong', p. 30, and 'Analysis', pp. 4, 13 and 15; Ashton (1952: 311); PS interview, Elliot Teboho Morojele, 27 May 1999.

1945/7

30 October 1945. Mokhotlong District.

No criminal proceedings.

Our only evidence for this case is an entry with the details above in Ashton's Schedule.

Source: Ashton, Schedule.

1945/8

16 November 1945. Motsitseng, Mokhotlong. Ward 14: Mokhotlong.
HC 301/46. *R* v. *Tsotang Griffith and four others.*

The case for the Crown

Tsotang Griffith, a nephew of Matlere Lerotholi and a half-brother of the late Paramount Chief, Seeiso Griffith, was an ungazetted headman at Motsitseng. He told his accomplices that he had four reasons for complaint. First, Seeiso Griffith had promised him the area of Mahesheleng, but he had never received it. Second, his uncle Matlere would not let him use the date-stamp he had acquired for this area. Third, the Explanatory Memorandum to the Basuto National Treasury, which had recently been published, had said that only Ward Chiefs would have administrative powers (in fact he was mistaken in this). Lastly, some of the people of his village disobeyed his orders and did not give him sufficient respect. He decided to replenish his medicine horn with a Mosia, a man called Mokebisa Motloli, and he paid Ngcobo, a Zulu doctor, six to eight cattle to doctor him. Among the accomplices were Raboroko and his wife 'Mahlekehle, both of whom later turned King's evidence. 'Mahlekehle, unknown to Tsotang Griffith, was Mokebisa's lover. She did not warn him, she said, because she was afraid and her chief had given her orders.

Mokebisa was enticed to the home of Raboroko and 'Mahlekehle. Raboroko reported to Tsotang that he was there, and Tsotang and the other accused rushed into Raboroko's hut and struck Mokebisa with an axe. The eyelids of the left eye and the lobes of both ears were removed and blood was collected in a billy-can. Hot water was applied to the wounds to stop the flow of blood. The body was then dumped in the Moremoholo river below a cliff 600–700 metres away in the hope that the absence of the missing parts would be attributed to crabs.

The outcome

In the High Court the Crown case broke down because of discrepancies between the two accomplice witnesses. All the accused were acquitted except No. 2, who had made a full confession and was convicted and hanged.

One of the Crown witnesses was later tried for perjury and sentenced to three years' imprisonment. Tsotang Griffith was later sentenced to seven years' IHL for conspiring to murder a Crown witness.

Sources: Jones, No. 49; Jones Papers, V; LNA, copy of judgement attached to record of HC 348/47, the case of *R* v. *Simon Mokhoatle* on a charge of perjury; *Basutoland News*, 12 and 19.11.46, 10.12.46; *Mochochonono*, 16.11.46, 14.12.46, 17.5.47; *Mphatlalatsane*, 16.1.46, 21.12.46; Ashton, 'Ritual Murder in Basutoland', p. 20, 'Mokhotlong', p. 30, and 'Analysis', pp. 4–5, 13, 15; Ashton (1952: 311); PRO, DO 35/4155, f. 11(g), Sons and Daughters of Basutoland, memorandum of September 1948; PRO, DO 119/1377, 'Schedule A. Cases of Perjury' attached to CP to GS, 31/349; PS and KS interview, 'Mathuso Tšitang, 27 May 1999.

1945/9

21 November 1945. Ramoji's, Leribe. Ward 8: Leribe.
HC 34/48. *R* v. *Gabriel Thibeli and four others.*

The case for the Crown
The instigator in this case, Gabriel Thibeli, was an ungazetted headman, and the aim of the murderers was 'to support the chieftainship'. The victim, Nkola Mpeako, was a tall, thickset herdsman, aged 40–50, working in the mountains near the Matsoku river.

Nkola went missing on Wednesday, 21 November 1945, and on the following Tuesday his body was found floating in a pool in the river. It had been cut about the eyes, lips and ears, and there was a punctured wound on the neck. The police made enquiries, but nothing was discovered.

Two years later one of the women accomplices told the police that on the Wednesday night she and Accused No. 4 had taken Nkola to a spot on the river where the first three accused were waiting for him. They told her they were going to kill him. According to another woman accomplice Nkola was then brought into the kitchen of one of the accused and mutilated. On the Saturday this second woman entered the hut secretly and saw a body lying under an oilskin with the feet protruding.

The outcome
The Crown's case in the High Court in 1948 rested mainly on the evidence of these two women and a young herdboy who had helped to carry the body away. Although the judge was impressed by this evidence, he was also impressed by the alibis of the accused, and in view of the length of time that had elapsed he decided it would be safer to acquit.

Sources: Jones, No. 50; Jones Papers, V; LNA, HC 34/48.

1945/10

25 December 1945. Sekete's, Maseru. Ward 21: Thaba-Bosiu.
HC 300/46. *R* v. *Jacottet Theko and nine others.*

The case for the Crown
Jacottet Theko became Ward Chief of Thaba-Bosiu in 1942. Because he was a drunkard and a stock-thief he was suspended in 1944 and his uncle, Majara Theko, became acting chief. It was rumoured that he wanted medicine to help him regain his position. The victim was an old woman called 'Malipuo.

At the preparatory examination there was no evidence of the actual killing. Jones summarises the case as follows: 'A witness saw deceased being led away, another said 4th accused had said they had struck her with a knobkerrie and cut her with knives and cauterised the wounds with fire. The body was found next day beneath a cliff with alleged wounds on the face, insides of the arms and armpits. Medical evidence attributed death to a blow on the side of the head. The body had abrasions which might have been caused by dragging. No cuts could be distinguished. Injuries could not have been caused by a fall over the cliff'.

The outcome
Although the case was entered on the High Court roll the Attorney-General decided not to prosecute. 'Mantšebo complained later that Chief Jacottet had been arrested

without her knowledge, and Chief Jacottet himself claimed that his people had been kept for six months in prison being 'trained' by the police to incriminate him.

Sources: Jones, No. 51; PRO, DO 35/1177, Y837/7, Documents relating to Jacottet Theko's suspension; LNA, HC 300/46; *Basutoland News*, 12.11.46; *Mochochonono*, 8 and 15.6.46; *Moeletsi*, 3.12.46; PRO, DO 35/4155, f. 11(f), Paramount Chief's petition, 16 September 1948; *Proc. (Special 1956) BNC, 7–17 May 1956*, pp. 24–5, speech of Lerotholi K. Theko [Jacottet Theko], 7 May 1956.

1945/11

25 December 1945. Phatela's, Qacha's Nek. Ward 5: Ratšoleli's and Mashai.
HC 375/47. *R* v. *Tumahole Bereng, Gladstone Phatela and five others*. (Another accused died in prison before the preparatory examination.)

The case for the Crown
Tumahole Bereng and Gladstone Phatela were ungazetted headmen. Gladstone was also a corporal in the Basutoland Mounted Police (BMP). Tumahole wanted medicine to help him in a dispute over land. Gladstone wanted medicine, 'as he was often receiving accidents while working for Government'. The doctor whom Tumahole consulted said he needed human medicine. He said this was a small matter: he had killed many other people without getting punished. The man chosen to be the victim was Katse Phatela, a drunkard whose sister had fallen to her death while drunk and whose own death would therefore be attributed to drunkenness.

On Christmas Day there was dancing at Phatela's and beer was brought. Some policemen who were there were given beer too. Katse became very drunk and was given some brandy. He went on dancing and he and his brother sang war-songs. Then he fell asleep and the policemen left. Katse was carried to a spot where it had been arranged that he should be killed. He was hit on the back of the head with a pick-handle and throttled. The doctor pierced him at the back of the head with a long, sharp piece of iron and blood was collected in a tin.

A headscarf was tied round Katse's neck and a grain bag wrapped round his head. He was still alive and kicking as he was carried away. He was then thrown over a cliff into a stream, and two of the accused went down to make sure that he was dead. After the murder the doctor prepared and scattered medicine around the village and over the disputed land.

When the body was discovered everyone assumed that Katse had fallen over the cliff when drunk and drowned. The burial was held the next day. Gladstone Phatela, in his capacity as a corporal in the BMP, signed a report about Katse's disappearance. He claimed to be unaware of the Paramount Chief's instruction that a body found in these circumstances should be reported to the District Commissioner.

The police were not satisfied, however, and the post-mortem established that death was due not to drowning, but to a fractured skull and to a wound behind the ear. There were disagreements between Tumahole and one of his accomplices, Jan Gat, over stock-theft, and Gat and another accomplice turned King's evidence.

The outcome
In the ensuing trial all the accused were convicted, including a local Indian, but the doctor, Molumo Kaphe, had died in prison. The accused appealed to the Privy Council, and their appeal was upheld on the ground that the judge had misapplied the law

relating to accomplice evidence. This judgement is discussed in full in Chapter 9. It established a precedent, though only for a short time, and was particularly important because it came just before the appeal in the Bereng and Gabashane case.

Gladstone Phatela was still alive in 1997, a much respected member of the church and community at Tebellong. He said that Tumahole Bereng was a very strict chief, and that a man whom he beat for stock-theft decided falsely to incriminate him in a medicine murder case. The police told him to involve Gladstone as well. Tumahole was killed in 1953 when trying to impound some stock.

Sources: Jones, No. 52 and pp. 67–8; LNA, HC 375/47; *Basutoland News*, 21.10 and 4.11.47; Willan (1955a: 123–42); PRO, DO 35/4096 (a complete file on the case); PRO, DO 35/4102 (containing the reasons for the Privy Council's decision); van Straaten (1948a: 147–8); FCO, Box 1176, S 119, f. 1284A; PS interviews, Godfrey Kolisang, 3 October 1997, and Patrick Mohlalefi Bereng, 15 October 1997.

1946/1

9 November 1946. Phororong, Berea. Ward 6: Koeneng and Mapoteng.
HC 368/47. *R* v. *Lefa Mothebesoane, Molikuoa Majahobe Lejaha and two others.*

The case for the Crown
Lefa Mothebesoane, Accused No. 1, was in love with 'Mafebebane Maobane, the wife of a Mohlakoana man called Maobane Leboea. The story told by 'Mafebebane was that headman Molikuoa sent Lefa to tell her that he wanted to kill her husband for medicine. He offered to pay her £80. She agreed because she and her husband 'did not live in harmony'. On the following Sunday the four accused came to her home, accused Maobane of allowing his animals to trespass on headman Molikuoa's land, and attacked him. He ran outside but was caught, stabbed and struck with a hammer. Blood was drawn off into a bottle, and the dead body was placed in Maobane's goat kraal so that it should appear that he had been killed by thieves. In the subsequent trial 'Mafebebane turned King's evidence.

In his report Jones presents this as a straightforward medicine murder, but does not ascribe any reason for it. In his unpublished notes he writes: 'To my mind this appears as a murder by the first accused and this witness ['Mafebebane] who later tried to twist it into a ritual murder and to incriminate 2, 3 and 4'.

The outcome
The accused were acquitted, but the judge wanted them to know that it might well be the case that they did commit the murder, and if they did they were extremely lucky.

Sources: Jones, No. 53; Jones Papers, V; LNA, HC 368/47; *Basutoland* News, 14.10.47.

1946/2 (Case Study 3)

12 December 1946. 'Mamathe's, Berea. Ward 4: 'Mamathe's.
HC 15/49. *R* v. *Bereng Griffith, Gabashane Masupha and fourteen others.*

The case for the Crown
On 10 December Gabashane Masupha, Ward Chief of 'Mamathe's, and Bereng Griffith Lerotholi, Ward Chief of Phamong, held a meeting with some of their

followers at which Gabashane gave them instructions to waylay a man called Paramente Khothatso and to take him to Letsatsi Piiti's home in the nearby village of
Chaba's. That night the conspirators failed to catch him, but on the following night
they ambushed him as he returned from his lover's hut in the early dawn and took
him to Piiti's home as instructed. On the following night the accomplices gathered at
Piiti's home and one of them, Michael Tseki, who worked as the senior dispenser to
Dr Ogg, the medical officer at Teyateyaneng, skinned the deceased from the back of
his neck upwards, making use of the doctor's surgical instruments. At the end of the
mutilation the skull was attached to the trunk only by a piece of skin. The ears, eyes,
nose, lips and scalp were all removed. The body was carried away and left at
Malimong, where it was found about six days later.

It was widely believed that this murder was part of the 'battle of the medicine
horns' between Bereng and Gabashane on the one hand and 'Mantšebo on the
other. Over sixty people were involved.

The outcome
The murder of Paramente Khothatso did not come to light until the investigation of
the second case in which Gabashane and Bereng were implicated, 1948/6. Three of
the accomplice witnesses who gave evidence in that case also became accomplice
witnesses in this: Mapeshoane Masupha, Sepalami Mathibe and Sothi Chela. Five
other accomplices were also persuaded to testify for the Crown. Thirty-seven people
were charged at the preparatory examination, which was held in February 1949.
Five were discharged and the Attorney-General withdrew charges against eleven
others. Of the twenty-one who were indicted for trial in the High Court, five were
removed from the list: Bereng and Gabashane and the local headman, Makione
Mphiko – who had been hanged for the murder of 'Meleke Ntai a week before the trial
began – and two others who had each been sentenced to ten years' imprisonment for
the same murder. Of the sixteen remaining accused, four were convicted of murder.
Michael Tseki was sentenced to death but had his sentence commuted to life
imprisonment. Three others were convicted as accessories after the crime of murder
and also of the crime of assault. (Two of them were already in gaol for their part in
'Meleke Ntai's murder.) Another was convicted of assault only. They were
sentenced to various terms of imprisonment.

Sources: LNA, HC 15/49; Jones, No. 55, and pp. 16, 59, 61; *Basutoland News*,
22.2.49, 1.3.49, 17.5.49, 16 and 30.8.49; *Moeletsi*, 30.8.49, 6, 13 and 20.9.49;
PRO, DO 35/4158, Jones' draft report, para. 106; KS and CM interview, Nkherepe
Molefe, 29 November 1998; Eldredge (1997). See also references in case 1948/6
below and in endnotes to Case Study 3.

1947/1

4 January 1947. 'Maletsunyane Falls, Mafeteng. Ward 9: Likhoele.
No criminal proceedings.
In his report Jones records the victim as a young man called Mahlabakoana Moorosi.
'Body was found below falls, a 600 foot drop. Penis and fingers and toes were cut off.
Rest of body intact – no bones broken.' At the time of Jones' enquiry the case was
still under investigation.

In the notes provided for Jones by a government officer in Mafeteng it was said that headman Moahloli Makhetha and his son Paulus were suspected of the murder, and that they were resisting the placing of a man called Neo. Neo was said to be recognised by government because his name appeared in the tax register. There is no reference to Moahloli, Paulus or Neo in the 1939 or 1950 Gazettes. Jones also records that the case was closed for lack of evidence.

Sources: Ashton, Schedule; Jones, No. 55; Jones Papers, I and V; PRO, DO 119/1378, f. 65, Schedule B; PRO, DO 35/4154, Forsyth-Thompson to Baring, 19 March 1948.

1947/2

January 1947. Mafeteng District.
HC 419/48.
The information above, which is all that we have about this case, is taken from Ashton's Schedule.

Source: Ashton, Schedule.

1947/3

6 March 1947. Near Thupakubu Court, Senekal's, Berea. Ward 4: 'Mamathe's.
HC 417/48. *R* v. *Theko Kojane, Koloi Sebateli and four others.*

The case for the Crown
According to Jones' report, one of the accused, Koloi Sebateli, was a headman, and the victim was 'Majim Ranthara, an old Mofokeng woman. 'Body was found at the foot of a cliff with multiple injuries including two lacerated wounds on the back of the head behind the ear. Abrasions and scratches on right thigh. No evidence on actual killing. One witness heard her being led away screaming. Had she fallen over the cliff, injuries would have been more severe.' Ashton adds the details that Koloi was an ungazetted headman, and that the murder took place near Thupakubu Court.

The outcome
The accused were acquitted on 27 April 1948.

Sources: Jones, No. 56; Jones Papers, V; PRO, DO 119/1378, f. 65, Schedule A; FCO, Box 1177, S 262, Ashton, 'Ritual Murder in Berea', enclosed with Jones to Marwick, 4 August 1949.

1947/4

13 March 1947. Tumo Daniele's, Quthing. Ward 16: Quthing.
No criminal proceedings.
According to Jones' informant, R. A. P. H. Dutton, an officer based at Quthing, the victim in this case was 'Makhapolo, a Mophuthi woman of about fifty years of age who was the aunt of headman Tumo Daniele. She disappeared after a beer party, and her body was found three days later under a cliff. The left hand had been severed and was lying under the body. Tumo and his brother said there was no evidence of foul play and so the body was buried. Several influential villagers disagreed, however, and so the police came to hear of it. Tumo was arrested but had to be released for lack of evidence.

Dutton wrote: 'A native woman who at one time gave ample information to the point of garrulousness of a plot to murder the deceased which was carried out after the beer-drink by Tumo and his wife and others, later flatly denied such statements. She returned to her village, left there almost immediately and was traced as a domestic servant for Nohana's trading station in the Mohale's Hoek District. After a very short stay she again moved on to an unknown destination and has been untraced since. It is my considered opinion pressure was brought to bear on her and she had to get out'.

Sources: Jones, No. 57; Jones Papers, I, R. A. P. H. Dutton to Jones, 9 March 1950; PRO, DO 119/1378, f. 65, Schedule B.

1947/5

20 April 1947. Leribe District.
No criminal proceedings.
The only information that we have on this case is an entry in a list of cases drawn up by the Basutoland Government in 1948 (which gives the date as 20 April) and an entry in Ashton's Schedule drawn up in 1949 (which gives the date as 30 April).

Sources: PRO, DO 35/4154, Forsyth-Thompson to Baring, 19 March 1948; Ashton, Schedule.

1947/6

14 July 1947. Fobane, Leribe. Ward 22: Tsikoane.
No criminal proceedings.
Our only useful source of information for this case is Jones' report. The victim was a man called Mokoto. 'Alleged murder for chief's medicine horn. The right eye, top of the tongue and part of the genitalia removed. The body was hidden in a donga and removed thence to an unknown place. A witness handed over a piece of flesh and of fat which he said were given him before the murder, to make him afraid of nothing. Analysis confirmed they were human.' The investigation was closed for lack of evidence, allegedly because the police were related to the suspects.

Sources: Jones, No. 60; Jones Papers, I; FCO, Box 1175, S 119, CP to GS, 31 October 1949.

1947/7

21 July 1947. Moshe Karabo's, Mohale's Hoek. Ward 15: Phamong.
No criminal proceedings.
Jones' report is the only source for this case. The victim, an old woman called 'Maliboea Tšoeu, 'was said to have been slightly mad since December, suffering from obsession that she was going to be murdered for medicine. She disappeared from the village during a beer-drink and was found a week later in a donga. Blood found at top and bottom of it. Post-mortem disclosed death due to diffuse subdural haemorrhage from head injuries, lacerated wounds on forehead exposing bone and various other abrasions on the body. A small portion of the left lip had been excised'.

The case was under investigation when Jones wrote his report, and we have found no record of any court proceedings.

Source: Jones, No. 58.

1947/8

30 August 1947. Qhoasing river, Mohale's Hoek. Ward 15: Phamong.
HC 45/48. *R* v. *Molomo Kori and six others.*

The case for the Crown

The instigator in this case, Molomo Kori, was a gazetted headman at Matlapeng. Among his accomplices were several men associated with him in the administration of the village and an itinerant doctor, Tlali Maseholo, nicknamed 'Blackman', who happened to be visiting the area. The victim, a man called Mokhoabong, was about seventy-five years old. No motive for the murder was given except Molomo's wish to make a horn for his chieftainship.

Mokhoabong was ambushed near the Qhoasing river. He screamed and said, 'Are you really killing me? Kill me, God will see you; my head will claim itself'. His legs were tied, his eyes and his tongue were cut out, and he was strangled. Then he was carried along the Koti-Koti river, where he died. His armpits were then cut, and also the anus and the scrotum. The body was hidden in a cave and was found about a fortnight later. The post-mortem was conducted about a week after that, by which time all the cavities were infected by maggots and it was impossible to say if mutilation had occurred.

The outcome

Two of the accomplices turned King's evidence. There was also evidence from a man who had seen the murder from a distance of about 100 metres and had taken care to keep out of the way. The defence, as was common, was to put forward alibis and to claim that the Crown's witnesses were on bad terms with the accused. All the accused were found guilty, but in his report the judge recommended commutation of sentence for four of them. Three could be regarded as having been compelled by the first two accused, and one had played only a minor part in the killing. It also had to be borne in mind, he said, 'that the victim was a very old man, whose life must in any event have almost run its course'. The murder had not been committed out of malice, but whether that should be a mitigating factor was a matter of policy.

In the event three of the accused, including Molomo Kori and the doctor, Tlali Maseholo, were hanged, and the other four had their sentences commuted to terms varying between ten and fifteen years.

Sources: Jones, No. 59; Jones Papers, V; LNA, HC 45/48; *Basutoland News*, 14.12.48 and 22.11.49; *Moeletsi*, 15 and 22.2.49; FCO, Box 1176, S 119, f. 1284A; PS and KS interview, Edwin Nohe Tšita, 4 June 1999.

1947/9

1947. Fobane, Leribe. Ward 22: Tsikoane.
Preparatory examination. All accused discharged.

According to Jones, the victim was a pregnant woman, and no body was found. 'Alleged murder for a chief's medicine horn, of a pregnant woman to obtain the foetus. It was alleged that the reason no body was found in this case was that the police who were first sent to investigate them were related to the suspected murderers.' The case was apparently closed for lack of evidence.

In July 1951 investigations were re-opened when one Mphole Mokhosi wrote to the Resident Commissioner giving particulars of where the body was alleged to have been buried. However, the police found that the body had 'apparently been removed' from its original grave. In November the Commissioner of Police reported 'sufficient evidence' to justify the arrest of Chief Seetsa Tumo Jonathan Molapo of Fobane as principal suspect, but this was delayed while investigations continued. Meanwhile, on 5 November 1951 Chief Seetsa himself complained to the Resident Commissioner that he and several others had been wrongly arrested in connection with this murder in 1947 and gave the name of the victim as Sebabatso. He made a similar complaint in his speech to the National Council in 1956.

According to the Commissioner of Police, writing in 1958, Seetsa Tumo was accused of medicine murder in 1952 but was acquitted because two accomplice witnesses went back on their evidence. Both were convicted of perjury. Since we have no other evidence of such a case in 1952, and since Seetsa Tumo made no retrospective reference to a 1952 case in his speech in the National Council in 1956 but specifically repeated his complaint of 1951 (above) about the Sebabatso case, we have presumed the Commissioner of Police's reference was to this case. Seetsa Tumo in 1956 said that a preparatory examination had been held at Leribe, in which certain witnesses, who had been 'trained' by the police to incriminate him, 'proved themselves ignorant of the matter in which they were called as witness'.

Sources: Jones, No. 61; Jones Papers, I; Ashton, Schedule; FCO, Box 1175, S 119, CP to GS, 23 November 1951, and Chief Seetsa Tumo Jonathan Molapo to RC, 5 November 1951; Box 1176, S 119, CP to GS, 12 December 1958; *Proc. (Special 1956) BNC, 7–17 May 1956*, pp. 130–3, speech of Seetsa Tumo, 14 May 1956.

1947/10

September 1947. Tsikoane, Leribe. Ward 22: Tsikoane.
No criminal proceedings.
All that we know about this case comes from an entry in the Schedule of cases drawn up by the Basutoland authorities in 1949. This shows that the murder was both committed and reported in September 1947. It seems that the investigation was closed for lack of evidence.

Source: PRO, DO 119/1378, f. 65, Schedule B.

1947/11

6 September 1947. Mohale's Hoek District.
No criminal proceedings.
Our only information on this case is an entry in Ashton's Schedule.

Source: Ashton, Schedule.

1947/12

13 or 14 September 1947. Thabaneng, Qacha's Nek. Ward 5: Ratšoleli's and Mashai.
R v. *Mosiuoa Letsie and eighteen others.*

The case for the Crown
The instigator in this case, Mosiuoa Letsie, was a gazetted headman at Malibono. Among his accomplices was a doctor. Five of the accomplices were Bathepu (Thembu). Mosiuoa's aim, it seems, was to get more land. One of his accomplices said after the

murder that he would now get his father's ward, and the doctor said, 'I can now doctor you as I have got these parts'. The victim was a woman called 'Mangukulo Monayane [Monyane?].

According to Jones, 'It was stated that 1st accused with the rest of the accused and two Crown witnesses got one of their number to entice deceased into a river valley, where she was hit on the head with a knobkerrie. They cut out the left side of her vulva, drew milk from her breast into a bottle, and placed her naked body at the foot of a krantz and her clothes on the top'.

The outcome
After the preparatory examination the Attorney-General decided not to prosecute.

Sources: Jones, No. 62; Jones Papers, V; Ashton, Schedule.

1947/13

8 October 1947. Sankoela's, Butha-Buthe. Ward 1: Butha-Buthe.
HC 20/49. *R v. Sankoela Mahlethole and six others.*

The case for the Crown
Sankoela Mahlethole, the instigator in this case, was a headman, and his wife was among his six accomplices. His victim, a man called Lekoalanyane Mohapi, was chosen because he was a Letsitsi. No motive is given for the murder except that Sankoela needed medicine.

Sankoela held a baptismal feast for his wife. Lekoalanyane was given a billy-can of beer and became very drunk. For some reason he began to give his sister a thrashing. He was restrained and then decided to leave, but was persuaded by Sankoela's wife to stay. Others of the accused were summoned and came. One of them said, 'Is this the man who has been causing trouble?' They all attacked him and he was knocked unconscious. One of the accused took out a penknife and cut Lekoalanyane's upper eyelids and the ears. He cut his arm as well. Two of Lekoalanyane's sisters were there, and one was so terrified that she tried to run out of the hut but was stopped and brought back. Then Lekoalanyane was stabbed under the right breast. He was still alive and groaned when he was stabbed. Blood was collected. One of the accused then twisted Lekoalanyane's neck but could not do the job properly, and one of the others stepped in and finished him off. Sankoela's wife brought some hot water to stop the bleeding. The body was then thrown over a cliff into the stream below, where it was found the next day.

The accused made sure that everyone said that Lekoalanyane had fallen over the cliff when drunk. Wounds were noticed, but the policeman who was called declared that the body had been eaten by crabs, and it was alleged later that he had been bribed with money taken from Lekoalanyane's pockets.

The outcome
It was over a year later that the two sisters informed the police of their brother's murder, and they were the two main witnesses for the Crown in the ensuing trial. Although there were several discrepancies in their evidence, on the most important issues they were agreed. Two of the accused were discharged at the end of the Crown case: one of them had made a full confession, but had gone back on it in the trial and it was disregarded because it might have been extracted under duress. The other five accused were convicted.

We have no evidence on whether or not they were hanged.

Sources: Jones, No. 63; Jones Papers, V; LNA, HC 20/49; *Basutoland News*, 23.11.48, 9 and 16.8.49; *Moeletsi*, 23 and 30.8.49; *Manchester Guardian*, 5.8.48 (copy in PRO, DO 35/4099).

1947/14

19 October 1947. Patiseng, Qacha's Nek. Ward 5: Ratšoleli's and Mashai.
HC 415/48. *R* v. *Motšeare Lerotholi and seven others.*

The case for the Crown
The instigator, Motšeare Lerotholi, was a headman who wanted medicine in order to strengthen his village. The victim was a man called Sello Mashale.

One Sunday morning Sello set off from his home to fish in the Orange river at a place called the Witch's Pool. While he was there he was seized by the accused. Two young herdsmen saw what was happening from a slope overlooking the river. One, Sera, went away, but the other, Tseko Pitso, joined in, since one of the accomplices was his father and two of them his uncles. He later turned King's evidence. The accused took Sello to a less exposed spot where they could carry out their mutilation. As they began to cut, Sello's brother-in-law Khoali passed by. When Khoali saw what was happening he tried to run away but he was caught and ordered to cut Sello's buttocks. He was unwilling to do this, but Sello told him, 'Brother-in-law, agree to cut me so that they will let you live to look after my children'. The judge described this as an act of heroism: 'It is difficult to imagine more cold-blooded gallantry!' The parts that were cut included flesh from the tongue, eyelids, palate, armpits, testicles, buttocks, part of the intestines withdrawn through the anus, and blood drawn from a puncture made in the throat with an umbrella rib. The blood was kept in a bottle, the intestines in a dish.

The body was hidden for a few days and then thrown into the river, which at the time was very low. A search party was sent out, but one of the accused was in charge and made sure that it did not go near the body. When the rains came the body was washed downstream, and it was found about a fortnight later among some driftwood. It was implied that Sello must have fallen in the river while fishing, but against this it was argued that he was a good swimmer and the post-mortem established that he did not die of drowning.

The outcome
In the ensuing trial the three main witnesses for the Crown were Sera, Tseko and Khoali, of whom Tseko was treated as an accomplice witness. All the accused were convicted and hanged, two of them having been converted to the Roman Catholic faith.

Sources: Jones, No. 64; LNA, HC 415/48; *Basutoland News*, 11.5.48; *Moeletsi*, 29.6.48; van Straaten (1948b: 1162–3); FCO, Box 1176, S 119, f. 1284A.

1947/15

22 October 1947. Tšoloane's ruins, Maseru. Ward 2: Maama's.
HC 12/48. *R* v. *Masiu Sephei and eight others.*

The case for the Crown
The instigator in this case was a headman, Masiu Sephei. On a Tuesday evening he called a meeting of his proposed accomplices and said that he wanted to kill a man by the name of Springkaan Molibeli in order to strengthen himself. He asked all those

who agreed to raise their hands, and they all raised their hands. Later he made a statement in which he claimed to be acting for Chief Lekunutu Maama, who was in prison for stock-theft and had been displaced by Ntsane Maama. He subsequently withdrew this statement, saying that he had been terrified since he had been placed in a cell next to the execution chamber.

Springkaan's wife gave evidence that Springkaan got up early on the following Wednesday morning and that before he went out he said to her, ''Matšepo, what a cruel thing'. The judge later surmised that Springkaan had known that a murder was to be carried out, but had expected to be one of those taking part, not the victim. That Wednesday evening the accused gathered at a place called Tšoloane's ruins. Masiu made use of medicine and said, 'Go and bring Springkaan', and Springkaan duly appeared. As soon as he joined the group he was seized and taken towards a stream. After a struggle he was stabbed in the back of the head and scalped. As the scalp came off the right ear came with it, and the blood was caught in a dish. At first Springkaan was fully conscious and asked why he was being killed so cruelly, but he died while he was being cut. The body was hidden for a while and then dumped under a cliff.

After Springkaan had disappeared his wife went to one of the accused who was acting as a chief instead of his father, but he took no action. Ten days after the murder the body was found by a herdboy.

The outcome
Two of the murderers turned King's evidence, but there was no corroborative evidence relating to any of the accused except Masiu Sephei himself. He had made a statement confessing to the murder, and an old man was able to confirm the evidence of the two accomplice witnesses insofar as it related to him. While the eight other accused were all acquitted, Masiu was convicted and hanged.

Sources: Jones, No. 65; Jones Papers, V; LNA, HC 12/48; *Basutoland* News, 17.8.48, 7.9.48, 1.3.49; Ashton, 'Ritual Murder in Basutoland', p. 20; FCO, Box 1176, S 119, f. 1284A.

1947/16

29 December 1947. Berea District.
No criminal proceedings.
The only information about this case is an entry in Ashton's Schedule.

Source: Ashton, Schedule.

1947/17

1947. Near Hlotse Heights, Leribe. Ward 8: Leribe.
No criminal proceedings.
According to Jones, the victim was a man called Leronti Tsolo, and his pelvis and legs were found in the Caledon river close to the district headquarters. The investigation was closed for lack of evidence.

Sources: Jones, No. 66; Jones Papers, I.

1948/1 (Case Study 2)

17 January 1948. Moloi's, Berea. Ward 6: Koeneng and Mapoteng.
HC 14/48. *R* v. *'Mamakhabane Boshoane Peete and fourteen others.*

The case for the Crown

'Mamakhabane Boshoane Peete, Acting Ward Chief of Koeneng and Mapoteng, was due to hand over her chieftainship to her son, Makhabane, who was coming of age, but she wanted to retain it and to this end planned and carried out a medicine murder. She told her accomplices, however, that she wanted medicine for the opposite purpose – to strengthen Makhabane's placing. On Saturday, 17 January 1948, she went to a wedding feast in Moloi's village, where she ordered her accomplices to seize a man called Mocheseloa Khotso. They did so, and took him away from the village to a spot where they cut various pieces from his body by the light of an oil lamp. He died when his throat was cut. 'Mamakhabane thanked her followers and left. At her direction they took the body to the home of Setene Sebajoa, where it was kept for a few days before being taken at night to some cliffs near the village. It was found the following morning.

The outcome

Fifteen people, including 'Mamakhabane, were charged with murder, and after the preparatory examination in May 1948 they were all committed for trial at the High Court. As well as the testimony of three accomplice witnesses, there was a wealth of corroborative evidence – from people who observed the movements of the murderers and their victim and who heard the victim cry out; and, astonishingly, from Setene Sebajoa's son and his friend, who stated that Setene woke them up and showed them the body. Two of 'Mamakhabane's 'ladies-in-waiting' were discharged at the end of the Crown case as there was no evidence that they had played any active part in the murder. The other thirteen accused were found guilty. Two – 'Mamakhabane herself and her leading assistant, Dane Rachakane – were hanged. The rest served various periods of imprisonment.

Sources: LNA, HC 14/48; Jones, No. 67, and pp. 11–12, 17, 23–4; *Basutoland News*, 17, 24 and 31.8.48, 14.6.49; PRO, DO 35/4098, DO 35/4155 (enclosures with Byers to Gordon Walker, 20 January 1949), DO 119/1376 (record of case heard before DC Maseru on 4 February 1949 and following days), DO 119/1372 and DO 119/1377, f.1; FCO, Box 1177, S 245, ? to GS, 7 September 1948; *Proc. (44) BNC*, Vol. I, 1948, pp. 30–1, Josiel Lefela's speech, 21 September 1948; Ashton, 'Ritual Murder in Basutoland', p. 20; Ntsu Mokhehle, articles in *Mohlabani*, August 1957, p. 9, November 1947, p. 17, and December 1957, p. 15; Jingoes (1975: 152–70); Scott (1958: 194–8); Reed (1950: 230–1); Edgar (1987: 194–8); PS interview, Albert Brutsch, 7 October 1997; KS and CM interview, Nyalase Ntja Sebajoa, 3 December 1998. See also references in endnotes to Case Study 2.

1948/2

24 January 1948. Mphosong, Leribe. Ward 8: Leribe.

No criminal proceedings.

A man called Lehloka Senyenyana went missing on 24 January 1948. His remains were found on 11 February. According to Jones, 'The head was severed from the body. Left arm, right foot, neck and part of viscera were missing. The body was too decomposed to indicate cause of death'. The investigation was closed for lack of evidence.

Sources: Jones, No. 48; Jones Papers, I; Ashton, Schedule; PRO, DO 119/1378, f. 65, Schedule B.

1948/3

3 February 1948. Berea District.

No criminal proceedings.

Our only information on this case is an entry in Ashton's Schedule.

Source: Ashton, Schedule.

1948/4

19 February 1948. 'Mamathe's, Berea. Ward 4: 'Mamathe's.

No criminal proceedings.

Our only sure references to this case are entries in Ashton's Schedule and in the Schedule drawn up by the Basutoland Government in 1949. It is possible that it is the same case as that referred to in an article by the PEMS missionary Leenhardt. If so, the instigator was a chief, the victim was a boy aged between eight and twelve, and the object of the murder was to impart youth to the chief. According to Leenhardt, no arrests were made: fear closed people's mouths.

Sources: Ashton, Schedule; PRO, DO 119/1378, f. 65, Schedule B; Leenhardt (1948: 127–8).

1948/5

February 1948. Ratšelisetso's, Mohale's Hoek. Ward 19: Taung.

No criminal proceedings.

Apart from an entry in the schedule drawn up by the Basutoland Government, Jones is our only source of information for this murder. It was suspected that Ratšelisetso Raboroko, chief of Liphiring, was the instigator. The victim was a man called Molefi Ratutubale. According to Jones, 'The body was seen in a deep donga at nightfall. Before it could be recovered heavy rain had filled the donga and washed the body downstream and destroyed positive evidence of mutilation. When recovered, the head and two arms were found separate from the body, the trunk very decomposed and considerable portions missing, suggesting it had been cut about. Waist and legs were intact and relatively decomposed'. According to Jones' unpublished notes the body was buried, and when it was exhumed a year later it was not possible to determine the cause of death. 'Rumours of human meat being sold etc.' The investigation was closed for lack of evidence.

Sources: Jones, No. 69; Jones Papers, I and V; PRO, DO 119/1378, f. 65, Schedule B.

1948/6 (Case Study 3)

4 March 1948. Fusi's, 'Mamathe's, Berea. Ward 4: 'Mamathe's.

HC 19/48. *R* v. *Bereng Griffith, Gabashane Masupha and ten others.*

The case for the Crown

Gabashane Masupha, the Ward Chief of 'Mamathe's, prevailed on one of his subjects, Moloi Ntai, to 'sell' his relative 'Meleke Ntai to him for £100. The arrangements for capturing 'Meleke were made at a meeting on the evening of 3 March 1948 at which Gabashane was present, along with Bereng Griffith, the Ward Chief of Phamong, and several others. On the following day, with the connivance of Moloi Ntai and other relatives, 'Meleke was ambushed as he returned from a family funeral, and throttled and suffocated. One of the accomplices cut off his lips and handed them to

Bereng, who declared that he had no blood and was no good as a victim. His body was dumped in a ravine in a shallow pool of water where it was found early in the morning two days later. The post-mortem examination revealed death by drowning.

This murder was widely held to have been part of the 'battle of the medicine horns' between Bereng and Gabashane on the one hand and 'Mantšebo on the other.

The outcome

Thirteen men were arrested. One died in hospital while the case was pending, and the Attorney-General withdrew the charge against another, leaving eleven men in the dock. There were four accomplice witnesses, three of whom would also be accomplice witnesses in Case 1946/2 when that was brought to court, and there were several independent witnesses. Relying mainly on accomplice evidence, the judge found the eleven accused guilty.

Following the judgement in the Tumahole Bereng case (1945/11), the eleven convicted men appealed to the Privy Council on the grounds that the judge had relied on the evidence of accomplice witnesses alone, that one accomplice witness could not corroborate another, and that there was no evidence that the crime of murder had been committed. The Privy Council held that, as a matter of fact, a murder had been committed, since it could 'not be supposed that the deceased voluntarily dismounted, unsaddled his horse, walked in the direction of the donga and fell in', and that as a matter of law one accomplice witnesses could corroborate another. The appeal was therefore rejected. Four men were hanged, including Bereng and Gabashane. The other seven served various terms of imprisonment.

Sources: Jones, No. 70; LNA, HC 19/48, record of PE; PRO, DO 119/1372, HC judgement; PRO, DO 119/1373–4, Privy Council appeal. See also references in endnotes to Case Study 3.

1948/7

11 March 1948. Bela-Bela, Berea. Ward 6: Koeneng and Mapoteng.
No court proceedings.
The victim in this case was 'Mamataunyane Beleme, an old Letebele woman, who was crippled and half-blind. The local gossip was that this murder was committed to provide medicine as an antidote to the murder committed by 'Mamakhabane (1948/1). According to Jones, 'Mamatau[n]yane was removed from her hut at night. 'The body was found 500 yds. distant. Death was due to heart failure. There were no external signs of mutilation. Witnesses state that parts from the vagina were removed. The Medical Officer was unable to detect this on exhumed body. The investigation was closed through lack of medical evidence.'
Sources: Jones, No. 72 and pp. 17, 68; Jones Papers, I.

1948/8

12 March 1948. Molumong, Mokhotlong. Ward 14: Mokhotlong.
HC 41/48. *R* v. *Lerato Letsie and nine others.* (Another accused was discharged at the preparatory examination.)

The case for the Crown

The instigator in this case was Lerato Rafolatsane Letsie, acting chieftainess of Molumong. Rafolatsane Letsie had been placed in this mountain area in the 1890s, partly to keep a check on the Batlokoa of Chief Lelingoana. In 1925 Seeiso Griffith (later to be Paramount Chief) was placed over both Rafolatsane and Lelingoana. Seeiso was given land at Rafolatsane's expense. Seeiso's main adviser was Matlere Lerotholi, and when Seeiso became Paramount Chief, Matlere became his representative in the Mokhotlong District. In the meantime Rafolatsane had died, and in 1947, after several changes, the Rafolatsane chieftainship was entrusted to Lerato, the widow of one of the Rafolatsane chiefs. Ashton speculated that this murder might have been a move by the Rafolatsanes to counter the growing power of Matlere Lerotholi and his family. Among Lerato's accomplices were several chiefs and headmen and one doctor.

The victim was a herdboy, Jakalasie. According to his mother he was fourteen years old, but according to the judge he was nine. He was living with his mother and his step-father, Molefi Senyotong, who was one of the accomplices and who later turned King's evidence. Senyotong sold Jakalasie to Chieftainess Lerato for a promised £40 and arranged for him to herd his horses in a place where he could be easily seized by the accused.

As planned, Jakalasie was captured while herding horses on a mountainside. He was given a sweet which stopped him crying. Then he was stabbed with a needle on his chest and his blood was collected in a bottle. He was taken away, still alive, to another spot where he was killed by being suffocated with a handkerchief. His body was placed in a donga and covered with earth. Three days later some of the accused went back with the doctor and uncovered the body. They skinned the head and took the ears, the eyes, the nose and the lips, the testicles, both arms, the navel and, according to Jones, various other parts not mentioned in the evidence. These parts were taken away in a sack and the remainder of the body was covered with earth, but only lightly, so that it would be found.

When Jakalasie did not return home, Molefi told his mother that he had gone to see his grandmother. Then Chieftainess Lerato told Molefi to go to Natal and to pretend that he had seen Jakalasie there. The mother searched everywhere, even going to Natal. Molefi continued to mislead her, and several of the accused were involved in the searches. The body was discovered on 12 June, three months after the murder.

The outcome

At the ensuing trial the Crown's case rested heavily on the evidence of Jakalasie's step-father, Molefi. There were also three herdboys who had seen some of the accused carrying Jakalasie's body to the donga where it was buried, and two men who gave evidence about the second stage of the mutilation, after Jakalasie had died. Molefi was regarded as a man of 'bad character' and his evidence was regarded as unreliable. The other witnesses were not sure about several of the details which they reported. Because of this the judge decided, against the advice of his assessors, that although a murder had been committed there was not sufficient evidence to connect it with the accused and they were all acquitted.

Chieftainess Lerato was later accused of medicine murder in another case, 1961/1, and was acquitted.

Sources: Jones, No. 71; LNA, HC 41/48; Ashton, 'Ritual Murder in Basutoland', p. 21, 'Mokhotlong', p. 30, and 'Analysis', pp. 5, 13 and 15; *Moeletsi*, 1.2.49 and 31.5.49; Ambrose Archives, Mokhotlong files, C5, Rafolatsane Chieftainship; PS interview, Elliot Teboho Morojele, 27 May 1999.

1948/9

26 March 1948. Hloahloeng, Mafeteng. Ward 12: Matelile.

No criminal proceedings.

According to Jones' published report, 'four herd-boys say they saw the mutilated body of a woman in a donga. When the report reached the police they were unable to find the body. Nobody was reported missing in that area.'

According to notes supplied to Jones by the authorities in Mafeteng, headman Ntele Matete and three others were suspected of this murder. Ntele was acting as adviser to his chief, 'Mabereng Makoanyane, against the wishes of his Ward Chief, Joel Moholobela, and he wanted to retain this position. He also wanted to retain his position as assessor in the Basuto Court at Makhaleng. When the herdboys reported to Ntele and 'Mabereng that they had seen the body of a woman near Ntele's village with ears, tongue and eyes cut off they were laughed at and told they were telling lies. The suspects were detained for a long time at Mafeteng but eventually the investigation was closed for lack of evidence.

Sources: Jones No. 73; Jones Papers, I and V.

1948/10

5 April 1948. 'Mathabo's, Mokhotlong. Ward 14: Mokhotlong.

HC 36/48. *R* v. *Khethisa Molapo and five others*. (Two other accused were discharged at the preparatory examination.)

The case for the Crown

Khethisa Molapo, the instigator in this case, was a gazetted headman under the Ward Chief of Mokhotlong, Matlere Lerotholi. He was also Matlere's son-in-law. There was evidence that he committed the murder for Chief Matlere. Ashton speculates that Matlere wanted the medicine for 'Mantšebo to counter the second murder by Bereng and Gabashane (1948/6). Matlere wanted a Mosia or a Mofokeng, and the victim, a woman called 'Mafokotsa Tlhola, was in fact a Mofokeng. She was the lover of Accused No. 2, a headman, and she suspected Accused No. 5 of having an affair with him. Accused No. 3 was a doctor, ninety years old. Khethisa offered the accomplices £10 each if they would help him and gave them £2 in advance.

On 1 April there was a work-party, *letsema*, for cutting wheat, and afterwards there was beer and singing in the hut of 'Mafokotsa's rival, No. 5 Accused. 'Mafokotsa was said to have been enticed there in order to settle her dispute with No. 5 Accused. She was either drugged or became very drunk. The doctor, who had given the murderers medicine to make them unafraid, ordered the male accused to have sexual intercourse with 'Mafokotsa, but did not do so himself, saying that he was too tired. The details of the mutilation are uncertain, since the main accomplice witness in this case was told to go outside and keep guard. Later the body was found below some cliffs by a herdboy. The doctor conducting the post-mortem attributed death to shock and haemorrhage, and reported that flesh had been cut from the jaw, the left calf and the left foot. There was a hole in the top of the skull and numerous deep burns on various parts of the body. The wounds had been cauterised and the ribs fractured.

The outcome

In the ensuing trial there were two accomplice witnesses. One had arranged to bring

'Mafokotsa to the place where she was to be killed. The other had been present at the scene of the crime but had been sent outside to keep watch. He was so drunk that he had fallen asleep. While he was asleep a man looking for his lover had entered the hut and surprised the murderers, and he became an independent witness. Another independent witness was the man's lover, who was told of the murder by two of the accused on the mistaken assumption that he had already told her what he had seen. The defence consisted of alibis and allegations of bad relations between the Crown witnesses and the accused. All the accused were convicted, the first three were hanged, and the rest had their sentences commuted to fifteen years, seven years and five years.

Sources: Jones, No. 74, and pp. 16, 17; Jones Papers, V; LNA, HC 36/48; *Basutoland News*, 30.11.48 and 9.8.49; *Moeletsi*, 1.2.49; Ashton, 'Ritual Murder in Basutoland', p. 21, 'Mokhotlong', p. 21, and 'Analysis', pp. 5–6.

1948/11

28 May 1948. Tsikoane, Leribe. Ward 22: Tsikoane.
No criminal proceedings.
Apart from entries in Ashton's Schedule and a list drawn up by the Basutoland Government, all our information about this case comes from Jones. The victim was 'Mafagane Moleliki, an 'old mad woman'. She 'disappeared in May and a month later her remains were found by accident in the veld near Tsikoane. Parts had been eaten by dogs, and parts are said to have been taken for medicine. The door on which these parts had been placed gave positive reaction for human blood. Her stomach is said to have been taken to Johannesburg for sale'.

At the time of Jones' enquiry the case was still under investigation. Presumably it was subsequently closed.

Sources: Jones, No. 75 and p. 16; Ashton, Schedule; PRO, DO 119/1378, f. 65, Schedule B.

1948/12

9 June 1948. Malimong, Berea. Ward 4: 'Mamathe's.
No criminal proceedings.
Apart from an entry in Ashton's Schedule all our information about this case comes from Jones. The victim was a Mohlakoana woman, aged 45–50. 'Body was found at the foot of a krantz in suspicious circumstances. No apparent mutilations. Medical evidence negative.' The case was closed for lack of medical evidence.

Sources: Jones, No. 76; Jones Papers, I; Ashton, Schedule.

1948/13

c. July 1948. Maqabane's, Berea. Ward 4: 'Mamathe's.
No criminal proceedings.
Apart from an entry in a Schedule drawn up by the Basutoland Government, our only information on this case comes from Jones. The victim, a man called Ramakansi Molefi, was a Motaung. 'The remains of the skeleton were found accidentally in a cave below a krantz in December, 1948. It is alleged that the deceased was stabbed or struck at the back of the skull, and that blood was caught, the whole face removed, the belly opened and portions of liver and intestines removed, also the genitalia and

anus. Medical evidence confirms fracture of skull.' The investigation was closed through lack of medical evidence.

Sources: Jones, No. 77; Jones Papers, I; PRO, DO 119/1378, f. 65, Schedule B.

1948/14

July 1948. Mojela Letsie's, Maseru. Ward 13: Matsieng.
No criminal proceedings.
According to Jones' report the victim was a man called Motloheloa Motsieloa. 'Deceased was found dead on the veld after a beer-drink. Death was due to respiratory obstruction following aspiration of vomited gastric contents, possibly hastened by concussion and exposure. No injuries except a bruise on forehead and bleeding from nose. It was alleged that deceased was killed after a beer-drink and that blood was drawn from a small puncture in or behind the ear.'

His unpublished notes refer to the statement of a boy aged sixteen that he had heard that Mojela Letsie and others had killed Motloheloa after a beer-drink and drawn blood from a small puncture in or behind his ear. Jones commented that it 'doesn't sound like a ritual murder', but evidently changed his mind by the time he wrote his report. Mojela Letsie was the chief accused in case 1927/2.

Sources: Jones, No. 78; Jones Papers, V.

1948/15

c. 4 September 1948. Motsekuoa's, Mohale's Hoek. Ward 15: Phamong.
HC 40/50. *R* v. *Lechesa Lehloenya and ten others*. (Another accused died during the preparatory examination.)

The case for the Crown
Lechesa Lehloenya was a gazetted headman under Chief Ntoane Lerotholi, who was one of those originally accused with Bereng and Gabashane in case 1948/6. Lechesa was involved in a land dispute. He told one accomplice that he had troubles in his village: two of his villagers' huts had been struck by lightning. He also claimed that he and No. 2 Accused, Kopano Mphutlane, chairman of Ntoane's court and a headman in his own right, were acting on Ntoane's orders. Apart from Kopano there were two court chairmen among the accomplices and two doctors. One accomplice, who turned King's evidence, wanted medicine himself for a land dispute, and was told by one of the doctors that he needed human flesh. The victim, a woman called 'Mampalane Mofubelu, was a Motaung. One of the accomplices, Ntsane Mofubelu, was 'Mampalane's husband, who agreed to give up his wife. It was alleged that she had been hindering him in a love affair. She was made mad, apparently through the use of certain medicines, and was then kept in a forest in a kloof for some time. Although a stout woman with a strong physique, she became thin and emaciated. For two weeks a search was carried out, and the husband, Ntsane, even consulted a diviner and paid him £4 to throw his bones to find his wife. In fact a woman who was gathering wood saw 'Mampalane by chance, and Lechesa told her 'to herd his eland' and she kept quiet.

'Mampalane was taken to the home of one of the accused and mutilated. She was cut on the right side of her head, around her right breast and on the throat. She was then cut on the foot, and about this time she died. More flesh was cut from the thigh, the eye and the private parts. No. 2 Accused asked for a piece of flesh, and Lechesa cut him a piece. The body was found about a month after 'Mampalane had disappeared.

The outcome
In the ensuing trial there were two accomplice witnesses, as well as the woman who came across 'Mampalane by chance while collecting wood. Eight of the accused were convicted and three, including 'Mampalane's husband, acquitted. Four of those convicted were hanged, including Lechesa himself. The sentences on the other four were commuted.

Sources: Jones, No. 79; Jones Papers, I and V; LNA, HC 40/50; *Moeletsi*, 20 and 27.11.50; 4, 11, 18 and 25.12.50; 22.1.51; *Basutoland News*, 21.11.50; FCO, Box 1176, S 119, f. 1284A.

1948/16

6 August 1948. Tapole's, Mafeteng. Ward 12: Matelile.
HC 11/49. *R* v. *Sekhobe Moholobela and three others.* (Three other accused were discharged at the preparatory examination.)

The case for the Crown
Sekhobe Moholobela was a headman under his half-brother, Joel Moholobela, the Ward Chief of Matelile. Like two of his accomplices, he had served in the Second World War. He had been given a placing but the local headman appealed to the Paramount Chief who upheld the appeal. He felt that he had no place of his own, and he told one accomplice he wanted the blood of a Mohlakoana to make medicine as he was not comfortable in his position. The victim, a woman called Adelina Molomo, was a Mohlakoana.

A plan was made to waylay Adelina on her way home at night from a beer party. She was seized and stabbed in the back of the head, and her blood was collected in a billy-can. The body was hidden in a cave, and on the following day it was carried to the foot of a cliff near the home of another chief in the vain hope that the blame would be put on his people. The post-mortem established that death could not have been caused by a fall over the cliff.

The outcome
Three of the accomplices became Crown witnesses. The first was a very plausible witness, but on one crucial fact – the presence of one of the accused – he was contradicted by the second accomplice witness. The third, in his original statement, had included two persons as accessories to the murder but had then admitted that he had only included them because they were his enemies. This fact was brought to the Attorney-General's attention by the police, and he brought it to the court's attention – clear proof, said the judge, that the police were not bent on getting convictions at all costs. All the accused were acquitted.

Sources: Jones, No. 80 and pp. 2, 62 and 66; Jones Papers, V; LNA, HC 11/49; *Basutoland News*, 7 and 14.5.49, 5.7.49; *Moeletsi*, 31.5.49 and 7 and 14.6.49.

1948/17

2 September 1948. Maseru District.
No criminal proceedings, it seems.

The only information that we have about this case is an entry in Ashton's Schedule. The case was still under investigation when he prepared it.

Source: Ashton, Schedule.

1948/18

6 September 1948. Motloang's, Berea. Ward 4: 'Mamathe's.
HC 35/49. *R* v. *Rafariki Motloang and four others.*

The case for the Crown
Rafariki Motloang was a gazetted headman. He needed medicine 'to soften the hearts of the white men' and so to secure the release of his chief, Gabashane Masupha, who was about to be tried for medicine murder. His victim had to be a Mosia, male or female. This, according to Jones, was because the medicine would then *siama* the case (make it all right). And according to Jones the victim had to be blind since this would make the judge blind to the evidence against the chief. The victim was an old, blind Mosia woman, 'Mamohapi Mofo, from Ha Sofonia in the ward of Thaba-Bosiu, very close to the boundary of 'Mamathe's.

Mohapi, the victim's son, agreed to sell his mother for £60. He later turned King's evidence and complained in court that he had not received his reward but was still expecting it. The old woman was normally looked after by two female relatives, and when one Thursday they went to Maseru, Mohapi reported accordingly. 'Mamohapi was persuaded by another relative to go that night to a beer-drink. The accused met them, and 'Mamohapi was carried up over the escarpment of the Berea plateau. They struck her on the head with a knobkerrie and then took her to the hut of Accused No. 3. There they had sexual intercourse with her and one of them stabbed her on the legs with an awl and caught the blood in a Vaseline bottle. Some of the accused were then doctored. 'Mamohapi was kept in the hut until the Saturday, and then her body was dumped below the edge of the escarpment, where it was found the following Monday.

The outcome
There were three accomplice witnesses, including the man who had sold his mother. The only corroborative evidence was that of two herdboys who saw 'Mamohapi when she was being kept in the hut of Accused No. 3. Since there was no corroborative evidence relating to the rest of the accused, they were acquitted. No. 3 was convicted and hanged.

Sources: Jones, No. 81 and p. 68; Jones Papers, V; LNA, HC 35/49; *Moeletsi*, 20.11.49; Rivers Thompson, 'Reminiscences', p. 34; CM interview, Tsekelo Sofonia, 23 November 2001.

1948/19

7 September 1948. Mpiti, Qacha's Nek. Ward 5: Ratšoleli's and Mashai.
No criminal proceedings.
The only information that we have on this case is that given above. It seems that no charges were brought.

Sources: Ashton, Schedule; PRO, DO 119/1378, f. 65, Schedule B.

1948/20

8 October 1948. Leneha's, Berea. Ward 4: 'Mamathe's.
No criminal proceedings, it seems.

According to Jones, the victim in this case was a Mohlakoana woman called 'Maleang Matela. 'Deceased came on a visit. She left perfectly healthy and sober. Her body was found in a donga two miles from where she had been staying, in the exact spot where Meleke [the victim in case 1948/6] was found, and just before 1st *Rex* v. *Bereng etc.* trial ... [1948/6]. Medical reports stated there were no overt signs of mutilation or any damage to body and death was due to shock. No woman would wander about alone in this area, and she was bound to have hurt herself if she had fallen into the donga.'

Jones was clearly implying that the murder was committed to help Gabashane. Chief Lebihan Masupha, who described himself as 'running the administration then', made this explicit in a speech in the Basutoland National Council in 1956. The police, he said, were alleging that 'Maleang had been murdered to make medicine to help Gabashane to find his way out of gaol.

The investigation was closed through lack of medical evidence.

Sources: Jones, No. 82; Jones Papers, I; *Proc. (Special 1956) BNC, 7–17 May 1956*, pp. 99–101, speech of Lebihan Masupha, 11 May 1956.

1948/21

October 1948. On Mokhotlong border, Butha-Buthe District.
No criminal proceedings.

The victim was a three-year-old boy, Motsuelinyana Mafa. According to Jones, 'deceased disappeared on the 7th and found on the 11th – on the Mokhotlong border. Primary cause of death was not apparent, secondary cause was heart failure. Pressure marks on skin. Abrasion on forehead. Circular burn on body. Searchers for the child aided by dogs, found a bottle containing pieces of flesh and a pharynx, which the Medical Officer was satisfied were of human origin. These were not taken from Motsuelinyana's body'. The investigation was closed for lack of evidence.

Sources: Jones, No. 83 and p. 15; Jones Papers, I.

1948/22

2 December 1948. Seeiso Maama's, Maseru. Ward 2: Maama's.
No criminal proceedings.

The man suspected of this murder was Seeiso Maama, Ward Chief of Maama's. Although a strong chief, he had a bad reputation for stock-theft and intemperance. In 1936 he was suspended for maladministration but was reinstated in 1941. There was no improvement, and in 1944 he was suspended again and replaced by his younger brother, Molapo Maama. He was reinstated again in February 1948. The victim was an eight-year-old boy, Libono Moki.

According to Jones, Libono 'disappeared while herding cattle. The body was found that night in deserted hut, strangled, together with a stick that appeared to have been inserted in the anus and then withdrawn. Post-mortem confirmed strangulation and a wound in the large intestine, which could have been caused by this stick'. According to Jones' unpublished notes, some herdboys saw eight men from Seeiso Maama's village at or near the place of the murder, some of them going into the hut in which Libono was found.

Other cases which were or might have been connected with the dispute between Seeiso Maama and Molapo Maama are 1941/3, 1942/1, 1944/4 and 1950/2.

Sources: Jones, No. 84; Jones Papers, V; PRO, DO 119/1055, 1117, 1135, Confidential reports on chiefs for 1935, 1938 and 1940; PRO, DO 35/1177, Y837/7, Kennan to Administrative Secretary to the HC, 13 June 1944; *Leselinyana*, 13.10.58; *Moeletsi*, 21.3.59.

1948/23

25 December 1948. Qoati's, Leribe. Ward 8: Leribe.

No criminal proceedings.

According to Jones the victim in this case was a woman called Magadebe Sopeng. 'The body was found near Qoati's village. Post-mortem showed that she had died about two days before of shock. There was no blood in the heart or large vessels. There was an abrasion on the back of the neck. There was undue mobility of neck but without fracture or separation of the vertebrae. She had deserted her husband and was living apart from him.' The investigation was closed for lack of evidence.

Sources: Jones, No. 85; Jones Papers, I.

1948/24

25 December 1948. Maphiring, Mokhotlong. Ward 14: Mokhotlong.

HC 36/49. *R v. Joseph Mabina Lerotholi and five others.* (There was another, 7th, accused in the preparatory examination: it seems that he died before the trial in the High Court.)

The case for the Crown

Joseph Mabina Lerotholi, a half-brother of Matlere Lerotholi, was the gazetted headman of Maphiring. He was one of 'Mantšebo's advisers and a great favourite with her. Later he would act for her on at least one occasion when she was away. He was a devout Roman Catholic. In the trial in this case he dispensed with counsel, and it is said that he was relying on his rosary instead. He was at great pains to prove to the court that he did not drink beer and that he made no use of Sesotho medicine for warding off hail, doctoring his fields, etc. For some time he was political messenger for the Assistant District Commissioner in Mokhotlong – 'the worst type of Political messenger', wrote one, '... a pleasant fellow if things are to his liking, but unpleasant if pulled up'.

Two of the accomplice witnesses said that Mabina wanted medicine to protect himself against ambitious young chiefs who were 'already in front of him'. It was rumoured, however, that the medicine was wanted for 'Mantšebo whose daughter was to stand trial in January 1949 for murdering her husband. It was said, and thought to be significant, that the murder took place a day or two after Matlere had come to Mokhotlong from Matsieng. Among the accomplices were a chief from the house of Rafolatsane and an evangelist of the Presbyterian Church of Africa.

The first person chosen as a victim was rejected because he was disabled. The man chosen next, Mothibeli Nthontho, had served with Mabina in the army during the war.

Mothibeli was attacked at night after the Christmas festivities at Mabina's. There was some conflict of evidence about where he was attacked. One accomplice witness said that it was in Mabina's court, another that it was just outside the court, and another that it was in a stable. They were agreed, however, that he was struck on the head with a knobkerrie, and the mutilation took place in the stable by the light of a candle. The wound caused by the knobkerrie was opened up, blood was collected in a tin, and portions of skin were shaved off from the eyebrows and eyelids with a razor.

Mabina suggested that the body should be buried, but others pointed out that this would take too long. The body was put on a horse and taken about three kilometres away where it was dumped in the Sehonghong river, close to Mothibeli's own village. It was hoped that suspicion would be cast on 'his own people'. The body was discovered the next morning.

The outcome

Contrary to public expectations the accused were acquitted, mainly because the judge was unsettled by the conflicts between the accomplices' evidence. Moreover one of the accused, the evangelist, had a strong alibi. According to one press report, people 'cheered wildly' when the verdict was announced. When Jones carried out his enquiry he was told by one man that the acquittal was to be expected, since the judge, a South African national, wanted to encourage these crimes which were destroying Basutoland.

When 'Mantšebo's daughter was acquitted it was believed that the medicine obtained from this murder must have been very powerful.

Sources: Jones, No. 86 and pp. 58, 68; Ambrose Archives, Mokhotlong files, C4, Gideon Pott to DC Qacha's Nek, 12 May 1943; FCO, Box 1175, S 119, Gray, DC Mokhotlong, to Marwick, 19 June 1949, enclosing letter from Charles Garant OMI to Mabina Lerotholi; LNA, HC 36/49; *Basutoland News*, 15.11.49; *Moeletsi*, 22 and 29.11.49 and 13.12.49; Ashton, 'Ritual Murder in Basutoland', p. 21, 'Mokhotlong', p. 31, and 'Analysis', p. 6; PRO, DO 35/4158, unpublished para. 106, fn.8, of Jones' draft report; PRO, DO 35/4154, report from *Daily Herald*, 15.11.49; *Proc. (Special 1956) BNC, 7–17 May 1956*, pp. 60–1, 122–5, speeches of Mabina Lerotholi, 9 and 14 May 1956; PS interview, Patrick Mohlalefi Bereng, 15 October 1997.

1948/25

1948? Near Orange river, Mohale's Hoek. Ward 15: Phamong?

In 1948 the body of an unidentified young woman was discovered in the Orange river in the Mohale's Hoek District. According to the police she was the victim of medicine murder, and they believed that she was the daughter of 'Majonathane Lerotholi of Matsieng. Photographs of the body were taken, and 'Majonathane was asked to go to Maseru to identify it. 'Mantšebo refused to send her, and it was only after the Resident Commissioner had intervened that 'Majonathane was allowed to report to the police. No further details are known, except that 'Mantšebo was very angry and was critical of one of the Basotho policemen involved.

Source: FCO, Box 1178, S 161, Acting CP to GS, 28 July 1949.

1949/1

January 1949. Leqhutsung, Leribe. Ward 22: Tsikoane.
No criminal proceedings.
The victim in this case was 'Mahlopo Maletjane, a mad woman. According to Jones, she went missing on 7 January. 'The body was found in open veld on 9th. The cause

of death was not apparent. Contusions were found on the right shin and a circular punctured wound inside the left biceps above the elbow.' The investigation was closed for lack of evidence.

Sources: Jones, No. 87; Jones Papers, I.

1949/2

16 March 1949. Sefikeng, Berea. Ward 4: 'Mamathe's.
No criminal proceedings.
The victim was a man called Moraphira Mafereka. According to Jones, 'body was found in a stream on 18/3/49. Deceased was alleged to have been taken to a deserted hut, hit on the head, right eye, part of the upper eyebrow, and the right side of upper and lower lips are said to have been removed. Medical evidence attributed death to drowning and wounds possibly to crabs'. The investigation was closed for lack of medical evidence.

Sources: Jones, No. 88; Jones Papers, I.

1949/3

22 April 1949. Linokong, Berea. Ward 4: 'Mamathe's.
HC 45/49. *R* v. *Faku Sauer Masupha and seven others.*

The case for the Crown
Faku Sauer Masupha was the gazetted chief of Linokong. He said that he had run out of medicine for his horn and that he wanted a Motaung woman to replenish it. The victim was an elderly Motaung woman, 'Mamokhele Nkolonyane. Among the accomplices were the victim's son and his wife. The son complained that his mother was a great nuisance because she would wander off and he would have to look for her and it would be better this time if he could find her dead.

The son and his wife enticed 'Mamokhele to a spot where the other accused were waiting. She screamed when she was seized and was gagged and marched to a place below some cliffs. Her clothes were removed to avoid their becoming bloodstained. Her throat was cut, and her head was then skinned and taken from her body. Blood was collected in a billy-can. The body was reclothed and placed below a cliff in a small cave where it was found the next day. It was alleged that she had fallen over.

The outcome
In the ensuing trial the Crown's case rested on two accomplice witnesses. The judge felt that he could not rely on them: they were self-confessed murderers, he said, who admitted they were trying to save their own skins. A murder had been committed, but in the absence of any other incriminating evidence he acquitted all the accused.

Sources: Jones, No. 90 and p. 68; LNA, HC 45/49; *Basutoland News*, 29.11.49.

1949/4

Reported 31 May 1949. Thabana Morena, Mafeteng. Ward 9: Likhoele.
No criminal proceedings, it seems.
Our only information about this case comes from an article in *Moeletsi* complaining of the authorities' incompetence in tackling medicine murder. The victim was Turupu Leluma, and it seems that no criminal proceedings were brought.

Source: *Moeletsi*, 31.5.49 (copy in PRO, DO 119/1379, f. 8.1).

1949/5

1 June 1949. Thuathe, Berea. Ward 4: 'Mamathe's.
HC 44/49. *R* v. *Shadrack Lebona and two others.*

The case for the Crown

Shadrack Lebona was an ungazetted headman. The aim of the murder was to make him rich and famous, to replenish his horn for wealth in cattle. One of his accomplices told him, when consulted, that he had heard that these days if a person wanted to be famous they should kill another person. The victim was an old woman, 'Maseabatha Lijane. Another accomplice, who later turned King's evidence, was 'Maseabatha's son-in-law. He said, like many other such witnesses, that he would carry out his chief's orders, right or wrong. He knew of 'Mantšebo's instructions to warn the police if a murder was planned, but he feared his own chief more than 'Mantšebo.

There is no evidence about the actual killing, but the post-mortem revealed a severe wound and fracture on the left side of the face. The left eye and flesh from the left temporal area were missing. Evidence was led that the body had been wrapped in a blanket by night, placed on a sledge behind a span of oxen, and taken to a cliff where it was thrown over the edge. The police received a report on 2 June that 'Maseabatha was missing and the body was found on 5 June. When the deceased was found, according to Jones, she had 'a piece of putrified [*sic*] cows liver wrapped in a piece of newsprint ("Esquire") and tied round her waist with a piece of green cloth'.

The outcome

In the ensuing preparatory examination there were three accomplice witnesses. Another witness called by the Crown, Shadrack's son, began to give evidence which was different from that given in his statement to the police, and was declared a hostile witness.

At the time when Jones wrote his report the case was still pending in the High Court. The file in the LNA contains only the record of the preparatory examination. It is possible that the Attorney-General decided that the evidence was not strong enough for a prosecution.

Sources: Jones, No. 91; LNA, HC 44/49; PRO, DO 119/1378, f. 65, Schedule B; PRO, DO 119/1382, M.B. Photane, 'Medicine Murders' (enclosed with Arrowsmith to Turnbull, 12 September 1953), p. 24.

1949/6

16 September 1949. Mahleke's, Berea. Ward 4: 'Mamathe's.
No criminal proceedings, it seems.

The victim in this case was an elderly Letebele woman, 'Mamalioa Mbele. According to Jones, 'the body was found on 22nd. A post-mortem carried out at the spot on 24th reports that the right arm was removed, and all flesh from the right leg, the whole foot, flesh from the left leg, five left toes and the left breast. The body had been partly eaten by dogs. It is alleged that the nose and mouth and blood were taken for medicine. No blood was found in the body or at site. Mahliki's [*sic*] is the village of Ramabanta Mahliki [who was Accused No. 7 in the first Bereng and Gabashane case, 1946/2, and Accused No. 10 in the second Bereng and Gabashane case, 1948/6]'.

This case was under investigation when Jones wrote his report, and we have not found any evidence of subsequent legal proceedings.

Sources: Jones, No. 92 and pp. 66–7; Jones Papers, I; FCO, Box 1175, S 119, Acting CP to GS, 12 October 1949.

1949/7

14 November 1949. 'Mamathe's, Berea. Ward 4: 'Mamathe's.

No criminal proceedings, it seems.

The victim in this case was 'Mapapiso Molefi, an elderly Letebele woman. According to Jones, 'Deceased was seen alive and in good health on the evening of 14th. Her naked body was found next morning at the foot of high cliffs. Her blanket was found at the top. No bones were broken. There were no external signs of violence except a heavy bruise from a blow on the forehead and a cut on the forearm. There were small puncture wounds on front of left shoulder'.

The case was still under investigation when Jones wrote his report, but we have not been able to find any evidence of subsequent court proceedings. It would seem from a speech in 1956 by Chief Lebihan Masupha, who was temporarily in charge at 'Mamathe's, that no charges were brought.

Sources: Jones, No. 93 and p. 67; Jones Papers, I; *Proc. (Special 1956) BNC, 7–17 May 1956*, pp. 99–101, speech of Lebihan Masupha, 11 May 1956.

1950/1

Late 1949/early1950. Joppo's Drift, Mafeteng. Ward 13: Matsieng.

No criminal proceedings, it seems.

On 12 August 1950 the body of a man aged about twenty was found at Joppo's Drift. He had been dead between six months and a year. According to the Commissioner of Police, 'the body was in a good state of preservation, indicating that it had been kept in a dry place and only recently placed on the river bank where it was found … Some flesh is missing from the face, skull, hands and feet. A large clean wound on thigh. The testicles are missing and also a portion of the lower bowel. There is also a large wound in the anus region'.

Source: FCO, Box 1175, S 119, CP to GS, 15 August 1950.

1950/2

Autumn 1950. Putsoane's cattle post, Mafeteng. Ward of Independent Chiefs.

CRI/T/6/54. *R* v. *Sera Motsie and nine others.*

The case for the Crown

Sera Motsie was an ungazetted headman who wanted medicine to strengthen his village, which he said was shaky, and to help him to win his long-running dispute with his uncle, Masilo. He told one of his accomplices, a doctor, that the usual kind of horn – which might be prepared from a bull, a black sheep, a ram, a tiger's claw and a lion's claw – was not good enough 'in these days' and that 'to have the right horn a person should be looked for'. The victim was a stock-thief, Mahlomola.

Mahlomola was visiting the area for the purpose of obtaining stolen livestock. When he was at Putsoane's cattle posts he was attacked by the conspirators. They took off his clothes, prised open his mouth and cut out his tongue. He was then scalped and sacking was placed over his head. His clothes were divided out among the accused. He was placed on a donkey, on some bags stuffed with grass, and was taken to Au's village. He was unloaded from the donkey, still alive, and flesh was then cut from his rear. After this he died. The body was hidden in a cave on the banks of the Senqunyane river, which was then almost empty. When the rains came the river rose and the body was washed away. On 12 August it was discovered in the boughs of a tree overhanging the river about two kilometres downstream. No-one could identify it, and it was taken to the district headquarters of Qacha's Nek. Sera Motsie had put his own belt on the body, and it was still there. A post-mortem was held on 16 August, and the doctor said that death had occurred at least six weeks to two months earlier, perhaps even a year earlier. In the meantime Sera Motsie's village was 'pegged' (i.e. medicated pegs were put around the village).

The outcome

It was four years later that the accused were brought to trial. There were four accomplice witnesses, and there was corroborative evidence as well. In particular, Sera Motsie's belt had been found on the dead body, and his wife had worn Mahlomola's blanket when calling at the police station at Mafeteng. There was also evidence relating to the movements of the accused. The defence alleged a conspiracy against the accused, but the judge rejected this and found them all guilty. All ten were hanged in August 1954. Another man who had taken part in the murder could not be traced.

Sources: LNA, CRI/T/6/54; *Basutoland News*, 18.5.54; *Leselinyana*, 17.5.54; *Moeletsi*, 29.5.54 and 5.6.54; NUL, Leribe Files, Box 52, file 1199; Judicial Department, *Annual Report 1954*.

1950/3

10 August 1950. Mokema, Maseru. Ward 2: Maama's.
HC 53/50. *R* v. *Molapo Maama and five others*.

The case for the Crown

Molapo Maama, chief of Mokema, was regarded by the British as one of the finest chiefs in the country. He was a man of considerable ability, supported the government's development schemes, and had excellent relations with his people. For two periods when his elder brother Seeiso Maama was suspended as Ward Chief for maladministration, Molapo Maama took his place. Seeiso, however, was reinstated in 1948 and Molapo reverted to being chief of Mokema. He was made president of one of the Basuto Courts in the area, but at some time before the murder was committed he was deposed from that position too. He wanted medicine to restore him to prestige and power. Among his accomplices was the well-known doctor, Phoka Shea, who had taken part in medicine murders before, allegedly on behalf of Molapo Maama. (See 1942/1 and 1944/4 above.)

The victim was a man called Lithakong Rause. His friend Kosenene was one of Molapo Maama's accomplices. On Thursday, 10 August, Kosenene took him to the place where they usually smoked dagga together and the conspirators attacked him there. Molapo Maama took a table-knife and cut a large piece of flesh from the back of Lithakong's neck. According to the post-mortem report this probably caused Lithakong's death, but there is evidence that he went on struggling and kicking. Further cuts were made from the ear and the armpit, and the private parts were cut out. The *liretlo* were taken to Molapo Maama's home, but some were given to the doctor, Phoka Shea. The body was found the following day.

The outcome

In the trial that followed there were six accused: Molapo Maama and five others. Kosenene had died, and there were two accomplice witnesses. Bloodstains were found on the blanket and saddlebags of the doctor, Phoka Shea, and on the blanket of George Monyamane, Accused No. 3, and they were proved on analysis to be human blood. Because of this the judge had no hesitation in finding them guilty, though one of his white advisers thought that George Monyamane should have the benefit of the doubt. About the other four accused, especially Molapo Maama, there was more uncertainty.

Molapo claimed that he had been at home all day with bad feet, and he called to witness Nkuebe, who said he had brought Molapo a letter from his brother, Seeiso Maama, to the effect that he was required to appear at the court of the Paramount Chief at Matsieng on the following day. Nkuebe's evidence was supported by a man called Mohlaoli, who wrote a reply to Seeiso on Molapo's instructions. When Seeiso Maama was called to the witness box, however, he denied sending a message to Molapo through Nkuebe or receiving a reply written by Mohlaoli. The judge considered but rejected the possibility that Molapo had been framed by Seeiso. Instead he accepted Seeiso's evidence, rejected that of Nkuebe and Mohlaoli, and said that if Molapo really had been at home with bad feet that day there would have been many other witnesses of this.

The two white advisers thought that Molapo Maama and the remaining three accused should be given the benefit of the doubt. The two Basotho assessors thought that they were all guilty. The judge followed the advice of the Basotho assessors and all six accused were convicted.

There was an appeal to the Privy Council, followed by a supplementary petition when further evidence was forthcoming from the Paramount Chief's office about the correspondence referred to in Molapo Maama's defence. This showed that the judge should have believed Molapo, not Seeiso. The Privy Council referred the matter back for more enquiry. At a further hearing 'Mantšebo herself gave evidence, and the judge, Walter Harragin, submitted a further report to the Privy Council. Eventually the appeal was disallowed, but all the accused – except Phoka Shea, the doctor, who was hanged – had their sentences commuted to terms of imprisonment.

The suspicion that Molapo Maama was framed by Seeiso remained strong. Rivers Thompson believed that the murder was carried out by Seeiso and that instructions were given to the accomplices to tell the truth but to insert Molapo's name for Seeiso's. This seems unlikely: at least two of the accomplices appear to have been men from Molapo's own village, and probably the others were too. But Molapo Maama remained popular with many of his followers.

Sources: LNA, HC 53/50; *Basutoland News*, 22.8.50; *Moeletsi*, 27.11.50, 29.1.51, and 5, 12, 19 and 26.2.51. See also *Moeletsi*, 2.3.48, for animosity between Seeiso and Molapo; Rivers Thompson, 'Reminiscences', pp. 76–7; RHL, Hector Papers, Mss. Brit. Emp. S381/5, account of Seeiso Maama's funeral, 13 September 1959; PS and MM interviews, Chief Joseph Molapo Maama and Mokhoele Mahao, 1 June 1999.

1950/4

12 August 1950. Khethisa's, Leribe. Ward 8: Leribe.
HC 43/51. *R* v. *Keneuoe Kennan Khethisa and eleven others.*

The case for the Crown

Kennan Khethisa was the headman of Lower Bokong in the Maloti. He was acting for his father Kennan, the gazetted headman, who was old and unwell, and he wanted to strengthen his village. His position was threatened by his elder brother, Mensel. The victim, Monnana Mokoloko, was well known for his love of beer – his daughter gave evidence that he lived on beer – and was apparently chosen because of some disagreement over cattle.

A beer-drink was held, and after sunset Monnana was enticed into the hut of one of the conspirators. Four conspirators were placed on guard while the other conspirators entered the hut and struck Monnana to the ground with a bayonet, knobkerries and an axe. Three bottles of blood were collected from the wounds and from an armpit which was pierced with a pin. Kennan took the weapons away, and when he returned ordered a prayer to be said. The murderers all knelt, and Accused No. 3 led the prayer, asking God that the murder should not be discovered. They took the body to a precipice and threw it over, and then placed it in a stream. By that time it was cockcrow, but still dark. People were still asleep. When Monnana did not return home from the beer-drink the alarm was raised, and his body was found on the following Monday. Kennan, as the chief, led the search party.

The outcome

The Crown's case in the trial that followed rested on three main witnesses. The first was an accomplice. The second was a little boy, aged nine, who had witnessed the killing through the hut door, which had not been completely closed. The third was a Zulu doctor, Samuel Dambuza Nguni. Kennan had enlisted his help beforehand, insisting that, instead of using the usual black sheep, he should make use of human medicine instead. Kennan said he would do the business. Samuel was present at the killing, but went out on the pretence that he needed some medicine from his saddlebags, got on his horse and rode away. On this basis the judge found that there was sufficient evidence to convict five of the accused, including Kennan. The other seven were acquitted, although both the white advisers and the Basotho assessors thought that some of them should have been convicted. We have not found evidence on whether or not the five men who were convicted were hanged.

Sources: LNA, HC 43/51; *Basutoland News*, 5.6.51; *Leselinyana*, 11.6.51; *Moeletsi*, 27.8.51; FCO, Box 1176, S 119, f. 1284A.

1950/5

c. 19 September 1950. Tloharebue cattle post area 'in the Butha-Buthe District'. Ward 11: Tlokoeng.

No criminal proceedings, it seems.

On 1 November 1950 the Mokhotlong police received a report from Thabang that 'a body had been found in the cattle post area of Tloharebue in the Butha-Buthe District'. (Tloharebue is the political headquarters of Tlokoeng Ward, which presumably explains why the case was reported to the Mokhotlong police though the murder allegedly took place in the Butha-Buthe District.) A patrol was sent out and the body was brought to Mokhotlong on 4 November. It was identified as that of Sehloho Mpetsane, who was alleged to have disappeared from his home on 19 September.

The body was in an advanced state of decomposition. The post-mortem showed no apparent cause of death, but several parts were missing – 'a large area of skin and

subcutaneous tissues including the right side of the lower lip, the whole of the upper lips, the whole of the right cheek including the right side of the nose, the right eye and eyelids, the right eyebrows ... The left eye was also missing ... The greater part of the left side of the scrotum was absent. The glans penis and ... part of the foreskin were absent'.
The police suspected medicine murder.

Source: FCO, Box 1175, S 119, CP to GS, 24 November 1950.

1950/6

30 September 1950. Ketane, Mohale's Hoek. Ward 15: Phamong.
R v. Lejone Njamane, Fako and two others.

The case for the Crown
Lejone Njamane and Fako were two headmen who wanted medicine to counteract the placing of sub-chief Moiphepi Lerotholi over the area of the late sub-chief Masupha Choopho. They decided not to kill anyone who lived locally, and asked an old woman called 'Matšosane to let them know when she received a visitor. When a man called Litelu Moqa came to stay with her 'Matšosane sent a message to Lejone accordingly. Lejone and Fako came with their accomplices, caught Litelu, tied him up, and mutilated him 'in a shameful way'. They then took the body and threw it in a hole, intending to go back the next day and take it elsewhere. But when they returned it was no longer there, and in fact it was never found. It was therefore almost two years before the case was brought to court.

The outcome
There were two accomplice witnesses, as well as a girl who took the message from 'Matšosane to Lejone and who realised what was happening. Lejone, Fako and a third man were convicted and sentenced to death. The fourth accused was acquitted. We do not know whether the convicted men were hanged.

Sources: *Leselinyana*, 14.7.52; PRO, DO 119/1381, f. 48a, Annexure to Arrowsmith to Turnbull, 15 August 1952; FCO, Box 1176, S 119, f. 1284A.

1950/7

26 December 1950. Mahlekefane's, Butha-Buthe. Ward 1: Butha-Buthe.
HC 45/51. *R v. Thamae Kobeli and two others.*

The case for the Crown
Thamae Kobeli was an ungazetted headman and also a doctor. He wanted medicine to strengthen himself because his position as a headman was shaky. He decided that the murder should take place on Christmas Day 'as there would be many people who were drunk and there would be many strangers there'. There was no-one suitable on Christmas Day, but on Boxing Day a man called Teboho Sekoma Daniel came and was given lodging in the house of Lehlohonolo, one of Thamae's accomplices. While he was resting, Thamae and his four assistants seized him and took him outside the village. It was dark. They knocked him unconscious with the metal end of his belt and killed him by twisting his neck. Just as they were about to extract blood from him four women arrived on the scene, including Lehlohonolo's wife and mother. They were warned to say nothing, and nothing more was done. Lehlohonolo's wife wept aloud when she saw her visitor being killed.

Teboho's body was thrown off a cliff. The murderers put about the story that he had assaulted Lehlohonolo's wife (which was why she had cried out) and then run away, and this was their defence in the subsequent trial.

The outcome
The judge preferred to believe two of the accomplices, including Lehlohonolo, who had turned King's evidence, and the independent evidence of Lehlohonolo's wife and a boy who saw Teboho being struck with the belt and strangled. All three accused were convicted and hanged.

Sources: LNA, HC 45/51; *Leselinyana*, 18.6.51; *Moeletsi*, 3.9.51; PRO, DO 119/ 1381, Marwick to Chief Secretary, HC's Office, 18 October 1951; FCO, Box 1175, S 119, RC to Turnbull, 23 January 1951; Box 1176, S 119, f. 1284A.

1951/1

7 April 1951. Setumpa's, Mafeteng. Ward 9: Likhoele?
No criminal proceedings.
Pete Basi, a 'petty headman', and three others were suspected of killing a woman called Sarah Mathe. She was mutilated in a way which the mission newspaper, *Leselinyana*, thought unsuitable for publication. The discovery of the body was reported on 10 April, three days after the murder, and by 19 September the four suspects had been arrested. The charges were withdrawn because of insufficient evidence.

Sources: *Leselinyana*, 7.5.51; FCO, Box 1175, S 119, Acting CP to GS, 1 August 1952; PRO, DO 119/1381, ff. 33 and 48a, schedules of cases enclosed with Secretariat, Maseru, to Chief Secretary to HC, 19 September 1951, and with Arrowsmith to Turnbull, 15 August 1952.

1951/2

8 April 1951. Malemoha's, Berea. Ward 6: Koeneng and Mapoteng.
HC 5/52. *R* v. *Mokabo Molelle and four others.*

The case for the Crown
Mokabo Molelle was a gazetted headman and an acting sub-chief. It was said that he wanted to obtain medicine to consolidate his position as sub-chief. The victim was a man called Thulo Nkole. Among Mokabo's accomplices were Malemoha Ranyeoe, who ran a beer shop, and Thulo's wife, who was promised £60 if she made her husband available to be murdered.

One Sunday morning, as was his habit, Thulo left home and went to Malemoha's beer shop. His wife followed him, taking their grandchild with her, but later went back home. At the conspirators' request she went back to the beer shop to call Thulo, and that night as the two went back home they were waylaid. Thulo's wife did not witness the killing, since she was instructed to sit some way off with a blanket over her head. When the body was found in the Seteneng stream the next day five wounds were discovered. Skin and flesh from the right arm had been removed, half the eyelid from the right eye, the upper and lower lips and half of the left ear. There was a circular cut over the biceps.

On the morning after the murder Accused No. 2, Malemoha, told three women who worked for him that he had killed Thulo the night before and gave them his bloodstained trousers to wash.

The outcome
In the ensuing trial the only evidence against four of the accused, including Mokabo Molelle himself, was that of the accomplice witness, the victim's wife. Since there was no corroborative evidence they were acquitted. Against Malemoha there was also the evidence of the three women who worked for him, and he was convicted. We do not know if he was hanged.

Sources: LNA, HC 5/52; *Leselinyana*, 30.6.52 and 7.7.52; PRO, DO 119/1381, schedules of cases, ff. 33, 48a; FCO, Box 1176, S 119, f. 1284A.

1951/3

2 June 1951. Near Khabo's, Leribe. Ward 8: Leribe.
R v. *Lephethesang Majara and ten others.*
Lephethesang Majara, the son of Chief Majara, and ten others, including a headman, Nare(?) Ntsoakele, were charged with the murder of Bole Gauda. The murder was committed on 2 June and reported on 4 June, and ten arrests had been made by 19 September. After the preparatory examination the Attorney-General decided not to prosecute.

Sources: PRO, DO 119/1381, schedules of cases, ff. 33, 48a.

1951/4

2 August 1951. Nqosa's, Maseru. Ward 21: Thaba-Bosiu.
HC 113/51. *R* v. *Mokhethi Molepe and two others.* (Another accused was discharged at the preparatory examination.)

The case for the Crown
Mokhethi Molepe was a shop assistant who felt insecure because his white employer often dismissed his employees. By offering money he enlisted the help of several accomplices. The victim selected was a man called Molefe Libe. There was a beer party at Nqosa's one Wednesday, which went on to the Thursday. Molefe became very drunk. Just after dusk the conspirators went off with Molefe, and when they reached some rising ground above a cliff they moved away from the path and attacked him. Flesh was cut from the back of the head. Mokhethi told one of his accomplices to cut out the eye, but he failed, and Mokhethi himself took a knife, cut round the eye and lifted it out with his finger. Further cuts were made on the leg and the face. The parts cut out were given to Mokhethi. All the cutting was done by light from matches. The body was thrown over a small cliff and was then carried to a cave where it was found later. According to the post-mortem death was caused by the blow received from being thrown over the cliff.

The outcome
There were three accomplice witnesses at the trial, and the judge believed they were speaking the truth. There were two pieces of independent corroboration. First, there was a woman who saw two of the accomplices going off with Molefe on the Thursday evening. Second, there were burnt matchsticks at the scene of the crime. All three accused were convicted and sentenced to death. Mokhethi was hanged, but the sentences of the other two accused were commuted to ten years' IHL.

Sources: LNA, HC 113/51; *Basutoland News*, 10.6.52; *Leselinyana*, 9.6.52 and 25.8.52; PRO, DO 119/1381, schedule of cases, f. 33.

1951/5

20 August 1951. 'Red Pass', Berea. Ward 6: Koeneng and Mapoteng.
HC 5/53. *R* v. *Habofanoe Matsora and seven others.* (Another accused was discharged at the preparatory examination.)

The case for the Crown

Habofanoe Matsora, though described as a chief, was not gazetted in 1950. The only motive given for the murder was to replenish his horn. The victim, a man called Tieho Matsora, was presumably related to him in some way. He was chosen because he had alleged that some of Habofanoe's accomplices were stock-thieves.

Tieho had left home to look for some missing sheep, and on his way back he was waylaid and a strap was tied round his neck. He screamed out, but was struck on the head with an axe and fell to the ground. A further wound was inflicted with the axe, and blood was collected. The body was then carried to a hut. Four days later, at night, it was carried silently through the village and placed under a cliff twenty metres high. It was found almost immediately afterwards.

There was a delay of almost two years in bringing the case to court, partly because the police enquiries took so long, and partly because the doctor who conducted the post-mortem examination had gone to America and his evidence had to be taken on commission there.

The outcome

There were three accomplice witnesses at the preparatory examination, but it seems that one of these went back on his evidence at the High Court and was charged with perjury. There was independent evidence from witnesses who heard Tieho scream and from others who observed the movements of the accused. Habofanoe and six others were found guilty of murder, and one of the accused was acquitted.

One of the men convicted, Khotso, was given leave to appeal to the Privy Council. He claimed that he had been compelled to take part. He had tried to run away when the murder was being committed but had been brought back and forced to drink blood. His appeal was dismissed on the ground that he had failed to prove that there were 'threats inspiring in him, on reasonable grounds, fear of immediate death or serious bodily injury'.

Five of the seven convicted men were hanged, including Habofanoe, and two, including Khotso, had their sentences commuted.

Sources: LNA, HC 5/53; Willan (1955b: 60–4); *Basutoland News*, 14 and 21.7.53, 2.2.54; *Leselinyana*, 27.7.53; *Moeletsi*, 20 and 27.7, 3, 10, 17, 24 and 31.8.53; Judicial Department, *Annual Report 1953*, report on case 5/53; FCO, Box 1176, S 119, f. 1284A.

1951/6

25 September 1951. Tene's, Leribe. Ward 8: Leribe?
R v. *Tene Moholisa and five others.*

The case for the Crown

It was alleged that headman Tene Moholisa instigated this murder in order to get medicine for Chieftainess 'Makhethisa. The victim was a woman called 'Mamhlehle Vene.

The outcome

The charges were withdrawn at the preparatory examination.

Source: PRO, DO 119/1381, annexure to Arrowsmith to Turnbull, 15 August 1952.

1951/7

2 October 1951. Monyane Sealemetse's, Qacha's Nek. Ward 5: Ratšoleli's and Mashai.

HC 49/52. *R v. Monyane Sealemetse and seventeen others.* (Another accused was discharged at the preparatory examination.)

The case for the Crown

Monyane Sealemetse, the gazetted headman of Linakeng, wanted medicine to strengthen his village. 'It appears the *riems* [straps] are getting slack', he said, 'and they should be tightened again.' He said his chief should also get a medicine horn. He did not say who his chief was, but according to the 1950 Gazette he was under the chief of Sehonghong, Clarke Hlakanelo, who in turn was under the Ward Chief, David Theko Makhaola. Among his eighteen accomplices, one was the chairman of a chief's court, another was an evangelist in the Roman Catholic Church, and three were women, including Monyane's wife. At first he had wanted to take a woman, a *lethuela* (a person possessed), as his victim, but was persuaded against this. Instead he chose a doctor called Molato Moselenyane because he was a Mosia, and the medicine would *siama* (make right) his affairs. Monyane arranged a beer feast on the evening of Saturday, 30 September. As Molato came away drunk from the feast he was seized, tied and gagged. He was taken at some point to Monyane's hut, and on the Tuesday night, according to the accomplice witness, three wounds were inflicted on him with a table-knife – on top of the head, on the right temple and on the right forearm. Hot water was poured over the wounds, and as the accomplices ironed smoke shot up. Monyane washed himself in bloody water and said that his affairs must now come right. The body was then dumped at the foot of a cliff.

The relatives of the dead man reported his disappearance to one of the accused who was a court president for Chief Theko Bereng. He refused to help, asking, 'How can a drunkard be searched for?' The relatives conducted the search themselves and found the body at the foot of the cliff. The post-mortem revealed only one wound on the body, a punctured wound on the left temple.

After the murder Monyane consulted a doctor, admitting that he had murdered Molato and asking for medicine that would kill the case. The doctor refused, and said he would report to the police, which he did not. But he did tell the police when they started their investigations.

The outcome

The judge in the ensuing trial divided the Crown's case into three parts: the seizure of Molato on the Saturday; his detention in Monyane's huts until the Tuesday; and the murder on the Tuesday. For the first part there was an accomplice witness, but no satisfactory corroboration. For the second part there were three independent witnesses, two women and a small boy, who either observed or heard or were told about what was happening, but their versions were all different and the judge rejected them. For the third part there was an accomplice witness, whose account of the wounds inflicted was very different from what was found in the post-mortem examination. There was also an independent eye-witness, but according to the accomplice he was not there. The defence alibis were weak, but the judge decided that the Crown had failed to establish its case and all the accused were acquitted.

Monyane Sealemetse was also one of those accused, and acquitted, in case 1953/2.

Sources: LNA, HC 49/52; *Leselinyana*, 7.7.52; FCO, Box 1176, S 119, f. 1284A.

1951/8

14 December 1951. Likhetleng, Mafeteng. Ward 17: Rothe.
No criminal proceedings.
A woman called 'Malina Rategane was murdered and mutilated on 14 December, and the murder was reported on 16 December. The post-mortem examination could not establish whether the mutilations took place before or after death, and the case was closed for lack of evidence.

Source: PRO, DO 119/1381, annexure to Arrowsmith to Turnbull, 15 August 1952.

1951/9

25 December 1951. Shoaepane's, Maseru. Ward 13: Matsieng.
HC 53/52. *R* v. *Maama Shoaepane and eight others.*

The case for the Crown
Maama Shoaepane was the gazetted chief of Khubetsoana and Lesobeng. It is not known why he turned to medicine murder. The victim was Dolphy Mokanohi, an elderly man who was chosen because he was a bachelor. He had a dispute with Maama Shoaepane about his land, but this was not the reason why he was killed. The Commissioner of Police said that the motive was not known, but speculated that it might have been connected with the placing of a new chief in the area. Maama and his accomplices decided to kill Dolphy on Christmas Day, when a lot of beer would be drunk.

On Christmas morning Dolphy went to church in his church clothing. When he came home he changed into an old whitish blanket, a pair of corduroy trousers and an old blue felt hat and went to Maama's home to drink beer. About sunset he left the party with one of the accused and was waylaid and hit on the head with a knobkerrie. He was stabbed below the left shoulder-blade. According to the judge he died at once and the following parts were then cut off: 'private parts; skin of the face; left and right breasts; left arm; under the arm-pit; muscle of left leg; part of the back and a kidney. In addition the deceased's skull was prised off first by hacksaws and then by an axe and his brains removed'. All this was done by the light of two paraffin lamps. According to the accomplices he was alive throughout most of the mutilations and was struggling.

There was some argument about the disposal of the body. It was placed in a cave, but then one of the accused said it was too close to the path and it was later moved elsewhere. It was found on 3 January, nine days later, by which time it had been partly eaten by animals.

The outcome
In the subsequent trial there were four accomplice witnesses. (A fifth accomplice, the son of Accused No. 5, had been called at the preparatory examination but had gone back on his statement made to the police.) There was independent evidence

from a herdboy of ten who had observed the movements of some of the accused and Dolphy, and from two others who confirmed the account of the accomplice witnesses with regard to certain movements and conversations. Two other herdboys were called by the Crown but went back on their previous evidence. There was the evidence of Dolphy's blanket and vest, which were gashed where he had been stabbed. Most striking of all, there was the evidence of a doctor, Motlatsi Letuka, who had been serving a prison sentence in the same gaol as Accused Nos. 4 and 6. He was about to be released, and Accused No. 4 asked him to go to his lover and to tell her to hide the medicine which he had given her. Accused No. 6 asked him to help, which he promised to do if he was given medicine. Accused No. 6 told him to get the medicine from his mother. He reported this to the police, who waited in hiding while he was given a Vaseline bottle containing tissue and blood by No. 4's lover and a Nugget black shoe-polish tin containing flesh by No. 6's mother.

All nine accused were convicted and hanged.

Sources: LNA, HC 53/52; FCO, Box 1175, S 119, CP to GS, 26 February and 24 March 1952; *Basutoland News*, 24.6.52, 9.9.52; *Leselinyana*, 24.3.52, 25.8.52; FCO, Box 1176, S 119, f. 1284A.

1951/10

December 1951. Mohlapiso, Qacha's Nek. Ward 5: Ratšoleli's and Mashai.
R v. Sankoela Lisene and ten others.

The case for the Crown
Sankoela Lisene was an ungazetted headman. According to a newspaper account he wanted medicine to strengthen his café. According to the police he had no café, but wanted medicine for Chief Thaba Tsepa to strengthen his business as a trader on the Qacha's Nek reserve. Thaba Tsepa was the gazetted headman of Mosututsoana's.

According to the police his victim was an unnamed Mothepu (Thembu) man, and his body was discovered on 28 December 1951 on the banks of the Orange river opposite Mohlapiso's village. According to the newspaper account Sankoela asked an old woman to call some boys to her house for food, and when they did so his accomplices came in, strung up one of the boys, Rankisi, from a rafter, and mutilated him.

The outcome
In the ensuing trial there was a conflict of evidence between the two accomplice witnesses and the doctor, and in view of this and other discrepancies all the accused were acquitted.

Sources: FCO, Box 1175, CP to GS, 26 February and 9 May 1952; PRO, DO 119/ 1381, schedule of cases, f. 48a; *Leselinyana*, 21.6.52.

1952/1

14 January 1952. Malimong, Berea. Ward 4: 'Mamathe's.
No criminal proceedings.
The body of an 'African youngster', Sejake Pulu, or Sejake Paulus, was found wedged behind some small rocks about six metres from the base of a sheer cliff, about fifty metres high, near Malimong Court. It could not have fallen from the top of the cliff to this position. It was badly mutilated and in an advanced state of decomposition. The investigation was closed for lack of evidence.

Sources: FCO, Box 1175, S 119, CP to GS, 1 February 1952; PRO, DO 119/1381, f. 48a, Annexure to Arrowsmith to Turnbull, 15 August 1952.

1952/2

26 January 1952. Sekake, Qacha's Nek. Ward 5: Ratšoleli's and Mashai.
HC 54/52. *R* v. *'Mathabo Tautona and five others.*

The case for the Crown
'Mathabo Tautona had taken over the chieftainship of Patlong when her husband died. She had been suspected of medicine murder before. The floor of her house had been dug up by prisoners under police supervision – an event which her son still remembered in the mid-1990s – but nothing was found. The herdboy she was alleged to have murdered was said to have reappeared.

The only motive given for the murder in January 1952 was that 'Mathabo's medicine horn was finished. It is known, however, that there was tension between her and the relatives of her late husband, and that in carrying out her duties she relied much more on her own relatives. Among her accomplices there were three men who were later described by the judge as being in 'positions of authority'. The victim was a man called Ramajase Mokhele.

On 26 January Ramajase went to a feast in connection with an initiation ceremony. He left around dusk, going towards the initiation school. Some of the accomplices went with him, and at a certain spot they were joined by the other accomplices. Ramajase was twice hit on the back of the neck with a knobkerrie, and by the light of torches flesh was cut from his head, tongue and left armpit. The body was carried down a winding path to a place below a cliff and was placed in a donga. By the time it was found about a week later it was so decomposed that it was not possible for the doctor conducting the post-mortem to establish the cause of death.

The outcome
In the ensuing trial there were three accomplice witnesses. There were some discrepancies between their evidence, but they were not significant. Their accounts were supported by the independent evidence of three women, described as 'Mathabo's retainers, who had been woken up after they had gone to bed on the night of the murder and who had observed the movements of two of the accused. Another woman had witnessed the movements of a third accused. All the accused were found guilty. 'Mathabo and one other were hanged. The other four had their sentences commuted to ten years' IHL.

Sources: PRO, DO 35/4155, PC's petition, 16 September 1948, enclosed with Byers to Gordon Walker, 20 January 1949; FCO, Box 1168, S 197H, confidential report on 'Mathabo Tautona, 1943; Box 1175, S 119, CP to GS, 26 February and 9 May 1952; LNA, HC 54/52; *Leselinyana*, 25.8.52; *Moeletsi*, 14.7.52 and 15.9.52; FCO, Box 1176, S 119, f. 1284A;. PS interview, Patrick Mohlalefi Bereng, 15 October 1997. Hamnett (1975: 116–36) gives the background to the chieftainship in this area.

1952/3

31 January 1952. Lepoqo's, Leribe. Ward 22: Tsikoane.
HC 89/52. *R* v. *Qamaka Moiloa and four others.*

The case for the Crown
Qamaka Moiloa had been chosen to act as headman, and other members of the family thought they might have been chosen instead. He wanted to reinforce his medicine horn because people were bringing cases against him. One man wanted him deposed. The victim was Lejone Thakanyane, described as a good man and a popular man, who used to thatch huts, was now turning grey, had a crippled arm and had recently become mentally deranged.

Lejone was waylaid one night. A piece of flesh was cut from the right side of his neck and blood was collected in a billy-can. The body was left in a mealie field, on the spot where it had been mutilated, and it was found a few days later.

The outcome
There were three accomplice witnesses, and their evidence was supported by the post-mortem examination, which confirmed their account of the wound inflicted; the finding of Lejone's blanket near his body, which confirmed their statement that his blanket fell off during the struggle; and the fact that there was only a pair of trousers on the body, which again was consistent with what they had said.

All the accused were convicted, but only Qamaka Moiloa was hanged.

Sources: LNA, HC 89/52; *Basutoland News*, 2 and 9.12.52; *Moeletsi*, 15 and 22.12.52; PRO, DO 119/1382, Marwick to Chief Secretary to HC, 4 February 1953.

1952/4

25 February 1952. Morobong, Mohale's Hoek. Ward 15: Phamong.
R v. Taoana Makhabane and five others.

The case for the Crown
Taoana was acting as headman for his elder brother Mohale, and wanted medicine to resist Chief Moshe Lerotholi who had been placed as chief over the whole area. The victim was his own mother, 'Mantlama Makhabane, who was chosen because of her relationship with him. She was almost blind, and was unable to go outside without the aid of a stick.

After a beer-drink Taoana and his accomplices pushed and then carried 'Mantlama up a mountain. Taoana himself cut her with a knife on the back of the head, and her blood was collected in a billy-can. The body was placed below a cliff to make it appear as if she had fallen when drunk. It was found the next day. Taoana, as the headman and next of kin, ordered that it should be buried. When this was reported to the police the body was exhumed and the post-mortem examination established that death could not have been caused by a fall.

The outcome
There were three accomplice witnesses. It was clear that the old woman could not possibly have climbed the mountain from which she was alleged to have fallen, and her stick was still in her hut. Four of the six accused were found guilty, including Taoana, and the other two were acquitted. We do not know whether the convicted men were hanged.

Sources: PRO, DO 119/1381, Annexure to Arrowsmith to Turnbull, 15 August 1952; *Leselinyana*, 15.12.52; *Moeletsi*, 12 and 26.1.53; FCO, Box 1176, S 119, f. 1284a.

1952/5

1 March 1952. 'Moteng-'Malefiloane, Butha-Buthe. Ward 1: Butha-Buthe.
CRI/T/6/53. *R* v. *Joel Molapo Qhobela and seven others*. (Three other accused were
discharged at the preparatory examination.)

The case for the Crown
Joel Molapo Qhobela, the gazetted chief of 'Moteng, was at loggerheads with his
father, Molapo. Although the son of a chief, he had not yet been given chieftainship
rights, and he wanted medicine to doctor his village. The victim was a man called
Lesiamo Jane.

One Saturday Lesiamo went to a race meeting at Chaba's. On his way back he
was accompanied by a friend, one of the accused. They called at the home of another
accused, Bokvel, for some beer. As they went on in the dark the other accused
appeared, caught hold of Lesiamo and pulled him from his horse. As he was carried
away from the path he was kicking and praying out loud. He was stripped and, by the
light of a torch, his left ear, top lip, right breast and testicles were cut off. Joel then
caught him by the throat and he died.

The body was wrapped in a sack and carried on a stretcher to Joel's home in his
father's village. There is no evidence of what happened next, but some time later two
women at Sekhobe Mopeli's village found Lesiamo's corpse covered with peas on
the threshing floor. A man called Sekutlu came and saw it, and then went to report
the matter to Chief Sekhobe. While he was away some men came and, as the two
women hid themselves, took the body away. When Sekhobe arrived he said that this
matter should not be spoken about. The body was not found again.

The outcome
There were two accomplice witnesses at the preparatory examination. Bokvel was to have
been a third, but he went back on his statement and was included among the accused.

When, in advance of the High Court hearing, the Attorney-General went through
the case papers he found there was not a *prima facie* case against the accused. The
judge agreed and all the accused were discharged.

Joel Molapo Qhobela was also allegedly involved in case 1954/1.

Sources: LNA, CRI/T/6/53; *Leselinyana*, 27.7.53.

1952/6

16 May 1952. Kubung, Quthing. Ward 16: Quthing.
CRI/T/1/53. *R* v. *Pheello Smith and twenty others*. (Twenty-three other accused were
discharged at the preparatory examination.)

The case for the Crown
Pheello Smith was an ungazetted headman who wanted to strengthen himself. In
particular he wanted to build an impressive house and to improve his village in the
same way as one of his accomplices, Nkau Majara, a headman who, it was said, had
also killed a man for this purpose. According to one report the whole village was
invited to take part, and it became known in the British administration as the village
murder. There were six other headmen among the accomplices and three women,
including Pheello's mother and sister. The victim was Pheello's father-in-law, an
elderly Mothepu (Thembu) called Mthedwa Memane. When Pheello was asked

how he could kill his own father-in-law, he said that one might sometimes kill one's own mother for medicine. One witness stated that some of the *liretlo* would be taken to 'Mantšebo at Matsieng, but there was no further evidence to this effect.

At a feast at which girl initiates performed a dance, Mthedwa was brought into a certain hut. As he came the men sang the *mokorotlo*, the war-song, and the women ululated. He was given what was probably some kind of drug and was then undressed. He was stabbed in the side and Pheello's mother collected the blood in a bottle. Flesh was cut off the shoulders, thighs and soles of the feet. The head was then split open with an axe and the brain taken out. Mthedwa's daughter, Pheello's wife, cried out, but was told to stop or else she would be dealt with in the same way. The wounds were cauterized with an iron. The body was then wrapped in an ox-skin, put on a donkey, taken along a bridle-path and thrown over a cliff into a stream, where it was found later.

On the day following the murder a doctor placed medicated pegs round the village and Pheello and his men were scarified. As each man knelt, four assegais were driven into the ground around him, one to each of the points of the compass.

The outcome
There were no fewer than eight accomplice witnesses at the trial, six of them women, and three independent witnesses who saw some of the accused with the deceased. At the end of the Crown case, nine of the twenty-one accused were acquitted, and at the end of the trial eleven of the twelve remaining accused were convicted, including Pheello himself and his mother and sister. The twelfth, Nkau Majara, was the headman whose success Pheello was trying to emulate. He had not been present at the murder, but came in afterwards, and as a gazetted headman he had a duty to arrest the accused. He failed to do so and was convicted of being an accessory after the fact and given twelve years' IHL. His appeal against this was dismissed.

The eleven convicted accused were hanged – nine men and two women. The Catholic paper *Moeletsi* noted that three were Catholics and eight Protestants.

Sources: LNA, CRI/T/1/53; *Basutoland News*, 3 and 17.2.53; *Leselinyana*, 9 and 16.2.53; *Moeletsi*, 9 and 16.2.53, 2 and 9.3.53, 24.8.53; FCO, Box 1178, S 161, Arrowsmith to 'Mantšebo, 9 July 1953, and enclosure; Willan (1955b: 38–47); PRO, DO 119/1382, 'Report by Major A.H. Donald and Chief Leshoboro Majara on Medicine Murders and Proposals for Combating Them' (enclosed with Arrowsmith to Chief Secretary to HC, 31 July 1953), p. 2; PRO, DO 35/4503.

1952/7

1 June 1952. At or near Mokabi and Qekoaneng, Mohale's Hoek. Ward 18: Tajane. CRI/T/11/53. *R* v. *Mopeli Mohale and five others.*

The case for the Crown
Mopeli Mohale was a sub-chief under Ward Chief Nkhahle Mohale, and he was also the president of the Basuto Court at Pontšeng. He wanted medicine because his court was not firm, and because other chiefs were claiming his area. He wanted to rule all the area of Mohale along the Makhaleng. The victim, Isaac Ramelefane, was chosen because he was a Motaung.

Isaac normally lived with his wife at Zastron. In the spring of 1951 he went to Basutoland, to Koppie Alleen, where he stayed with his brother Molatoli. Mopeli persuaded Molatoli to let him have his brother Isaac for £80. In the subsequent court proceedings Molatoli said he liked his brother very much, but sold him because he was afraid of his chief. He would sell his wife for more or less than Isaac: it all depended on the buyer. As instructed by Mopeli, Molatoli gave some medicine to Isaac which had the effect of making him like a *lethuela*, a person possessed, singing, walking about, dreaming. One night he disappeared and then re-appeared the next morning without his blanket and shoes. In fact Molatoli had sent a man to take him away secretly and then to send him back. 'I do this,' he said, 'so that when we take him for good it will be known that he usually disappears.'

Some nights later another man came from Mopeli and Molatoli handed Isaac over to him. He was taken to some aloes, where the other accused seized hold of him. Isaac screamed out, but was choked. His clothes were removed and flesh was cut from his forehead, both eyebrows and one ear. His tongue was cut out, and he was stabbed in the throat, at which point he died. His lung and heart were pulled out through the throat. The parts were placed in a bag used to contain salt.

Mohale gave orders that the body should be taken to the area of a neighbouring chief, Phakiso. Those carrying it became tired, and left it on the way, and Mohale made them go back later and leave it at Manonyaneng, at the foot of a cliff. It was discovered later in the year by a man who hunted jackals in the mountains.

In the meantime stones smeared with black medicine were placed around Mohale's house, and Mohale and others were scarified. Mohale was also given medicines to protect him against police enquiries.

The outcome
At the subsequent trial there were four accomplice witnesses. In the course of the trial, however, a letter was produced from one of them in which he confessed that he had made a false accusation against Chief Mopeli. When the trial was resumed he denied that the letter was his, but it was proved that it was in his handwriting. Because of the uncertainty arising from this the accused were acquitted.

Sources: LNA, CRI/T/11/53; *Basutoland News*, 21 and 28.7.53; *Leselinyana*, 10.8.53 and 21.9.53; *Moeletsi*, 7, 14, 21 and 28.9.53, 5, 19 and 26.10.53, 2.11.53.

1952/8

June 1952. Butha-Buthe District. Ward 1: Butha-Buthe.
No criminal proceedings.
In 1954 the South African police, East London, informed the District Commissioner, Butha-Buthe, that 'Mpo Siyo', a prisoner in Fort Glamorgan gaol in East London, had confessed that in June 1952 he and Nkolo, on the orders of Chief de la Ray Qhobela, killed Gwayi of headman Hlatsa, and parts of the body were removed for medicine. There is no further record of this case.

Source: FCO, Box 1176, S 119, DC Butha-Buthe to GS, 14 August 1954.

1952/9

18 July 1952. Tšehlanyane, Leribe. Ward 8: Leribe.
CRI/T/11/53. *R* v. *Mohale Molapo and eight others.*

The case for the Crown
Mohale Molapo was the headman at Tšehlanyane. He had a dispute about boundaries

with the Ward Chief of Leribe. He had lost two cases, and an appeal (which he finally won) was pending. He engaged the services of a doctor who said he could manage the affair if he had parts from a man. The victim's blood should be poured out over the disputed land. Among the accomplices were three of Mohale's councillors and the chairman and the clerk of his court. The victim, Liphapang Mpikinyane, was chosen because he was a Motaung and 'a very strong man in public matters'.

It was arranged that the murder should be carried out at a party on a certain Tuesday, but there was a lot of rain, Mohale became drunk and started fighting, and so nothing was done. On the following Friday night Liphaphang was waylaid near the junction of two streams. He was stripped and scalped. Flesh was removed from the right side of his face, and his left hand and his anus were cut. He was still alive when these mutilations were carried out. The doctor said, 'We are working No. 1 Accused's area for him to strengthen him in his chieftainship and to help him win cases'. On the following Sunday night the body was loaded onto a horse and taken about five kilometres to Pela-Tšoeu, close to the village of Chief Majara Molapo, where it was left at the foot of a bank. This was done to divert suspicion from the murderers.

The body was found the following Wednesday at the Pela-Tšoeu stream. The relatives refused to allow it to be buried and it was taken to the district headquarters at Leribe (Hlotse). In the ensuing investigations Mohale told people to try to incriminate the people of Chief Majara Molapo. In the meantime the doctor in the case, Mphanya Linaka, used certain medicines to keep some of the accused out of trouble.

The outcome
There were three accomplice witnesses, but the judge had doubts about their reliability, especially as their evidence disagreed with that of the doctor who had conducted the post-mortem. All the accused were acquitted.

Sources: LNA, CRI/T/11/53; FCO, Box 1175, S 119, Acting CP to GS, 22 September 1952; *Basutoland News*, 7 and 14.4.53; *Leselinyana*, 20.4.53; *Moeletsi*, 4, 18 and 25.5.53.

1952/10

15 August 1952. Masupha Motšoene's, Leribe. Ward 8: Leribe.
No criminal proceedings, it seems.
In September 1952 the Acting Commissioner of Police reported the discovery of the body of Six Malepa at Nkisi's village near Lepaqoa's police post on 16 August 1952. Malepa was last seen alive at a feast at Masupha Motšoene's village on 15 August 1952. 'A post-mortem examination was conducted and revealed that death was due to cerebral haemorrhage and that certain wounds were found on the head. One of these had a clear cut edge and another behind the left ear showed that flesh was missing, the nature of which wounds supports the theory of medicine murder. The one arrest of Peete NTJETJANE has been made. An accomplice, NTLALEKOKO MOLEKO has imparted information to the Police implicating the accused ...' There is no further record of this case.

Source: FCO, Box 1175, S 119, Acting CP to GS, 22 September 1952.

1952/11

4 October 1952. Mapoteng, Teyateyaneng. Ward 6: Mapoteng.
CRI/T/1/54. *R* v. *Seshope Ramakoro and eight others.*

The case for the Crown

Seshope became chief of Khubetsoana in 1933, but was not gazetted. He was also the president of the Mapoteng Basuto Court. Judge Harragin described him as a trusted servant of the government, a man far in advance of his fellows in literacy, whose handwriting was better than the judge's own. He had held *pitso*s to discourage people from medicine murder. He needed medicine because he was involved in a boundary dispute with Chief Mahlomola Peete, and he decided that he needed the brains of a child. His victim was therefore a woman who was pregnant, 'Malieketso Thejane. Among Seshope's accomplices was 'Malieketso's husband.

She was fetched at night from her home, gagged, and taken to a cave where she was given some medicine to make her partly senseless. While her husband kept a look-out she was stripped and laid out on a flat rock near the cave. She was cut above the ear, blood was caught in a billy-can, and flesh was taken from below the abdomen. At that point she died. Two umbrella ribs were heated to make a puncture in her right ankle. Hot water was used to scald the wounds. The body was placed in a crevice between rocks and covered by branches. On their return to the village the doctor working with Seshope and his accomplices gave them some black medicine to 'make their hearts strong'. They were also told to wash with another medicine and to pour it away into holes so that the murder would never be discovered.

'Malieketso's husband reported that she had disappeared, and her parents and brother went out to look for her. Advised by Seshope's chairman, Accused No. 2, Mathankola Nkhahle, they found her where she had been hidden.

In April 1952, six months before the murder, Seshope had written a letter to Mathankola, instructing him to find for him the brains of a child. Judge Harragin said that its style was such that it 'might well be a letter written by the highest lady in the land to a tiresome butcher ...' This fell into the hands of the police who issued a public warning. Nevertheless, six months later, the murder was committed. At the time the police enquiries were fruitless, but about a year later one of the accomplices, Molefi, went of his own accord to the police. It seems that he had killed his grandmother and had been fined £40 by Seshope. Having been involved with Seshope in the murder of 'Malieketso a year before, he was so enraged that he decided to tell the full story.

The outcome

There was some delay in bringing the case to court because the doctor who had conducted the post-mortem had gone to America and evidence had to be obtained on commission. Molefi and one other accomplice gave evidence. There was corroborating evidence in the form of Seshope's letter, from people who had witnessed the movements of some of the accused, and from 'Malieketso's brother and mother, a 'poor, sad, old soul', who had been told by Mathankola where to look for her body. But two of the accused were able to prove that Molefi was on bad terms with them and therefore had to be given the benefit of the doubt. Since they were given the benefit of the doubt, so were the others. The only exceptions were Seshope and Mathankola, who were both found guilty and hanged.

Sources: PRO, DO 119/1175 (complete case record); *Basutoland News*, 17, 24 and 31.8.54; *Leselinyana*, 6.9.54, 7.3.55; *Moeletsi*, 11, 18 and 25.9.54, 2.10.55; FCO, Box 1176, S 368, DC Berea to GS, n.d.; Judicial Department, *Annual Report 1954*, case 1/54.

1952/12 (Case Study 4)

30 October 1952. Mohlaoli's, Mokhotlong. Ward 14: Mokhotlong.
CRI/T/4/53. *R* v. *Matlere Lerotholi and seven others*.

The case for the Crown
It was alleged that Chief Matlere Lerotholi instructed one of his headmen, Matjoa Tšita, to carry out a medicine murder and to recruit other accomplices. Matjoa enlisted Seane Klaas, and six other persons were drawn in. The intended victim was Tšoeunyane Rabolai, who had recently annoyed Matlere by protesting about the treatment of an elderly female relative. On the night of 30 October the accomplices burnt some medicine which Matlere had given them, and which, they said, induced Tšoeunyane to leave his home and come to them. They seized him, took him to a shallow stream, and cut out the parts which Matlere wanted. They placed the body in a hut for the night and on the following night it was thrown into the Orange river. Seane Klaas took the body parts to Matlere in the canvas bag which Matlere had given him for that purpose.

As well as four accomplice witnesses, including Matjoa Tšita and Seane Klaas, the prosecution was supported by a maidservant who said that she saw a man hand over the canvas bag to the chief, and that later the same day she saw this bag in a wardrobe and that it contained human parts. It was later wrapped in a roll of blanket belonging to Chief Mabina Lerotholi and taken on Chief Matlere's tractor to Mokhotlong airfield. It was then taken by Mabina to 'Mantšebo at Matsieng.

The outcome
The evidence of the maidservant was disregarded because of its inherent improbability: she said on the one hand that Matlere had warned her against looking in the wardrobe, on the other that he had told her to place two boxes of matches in the wardrobe. The evidence of the accomplice witnesses was also rejected because there was a conflict over the colour of the canvas bag and because of other discrepancies. (According to Seane Klaas many years later, the accomplices deliberately contradicted one another about the colour of the canvas bag so that their evidence would not be accepted.) The judge was satisfied that Tšoeunyane Rabolai had been cruelly murdered, but because of the inconsistencies of the accomplice evidence and the insufficiency of the corroboration he was unable to convict any of the accused.

Sources: LNA, CRI/T/4/53; *Basutoland News*, 20.1.53, 24.2.53; *Leselinyana*, 26.1.53, 9.2.53, 2 and 9.3.53; *Moeletsi*, 26.1.53, 16 and 23.2.53; PS interview, Paul Kitson, 5 October 1997; PS interview, Patrick Mohlalefi Bereng, 15 October 1997. See also references in endnotes to Case Study 4.

1952/13

Reported 24 November 1952. Maqhoka, Quthing. Ward 16: Quthing.
R v. *Mokhou Shapane and others*.

The case for the Crown

Our evidence for this case is a newspaper report that the body of Mtoyedwa, a Mothepu (Thembu), had been found at Maqhoka, a place belonging to Chief Nkuebe, in the caretaking of Chief Mashapha Letsie at headman Daniele Tseuoa's.

It seems likely that this is the same as the Quthing case in which the Commissioner of Police, in response to a request from the High Commissioner's Office about the clans of instigators and victims, identified the accused, Mokhou Shapane, as a Mohlakoana and the victim, Motetwa, as a Mothepu.

The outcome

According to the Commissioner the accused were found guilty.

Sources: *Moeletsi*, 24.11.52; FCO, Box 1176, S 119, f. 1284A.

1953/1

16 February 1953. Pokane area, Quthing. Ward 16: Quthing.
CRI/T/4/54. *R* v. *Esthere Kabi and eight others.*

The case for the Crown

Esthere Kabi had become the headman of Pokane when her husband died. She called a meeting at which she told her followers that the affairs of the village were in a bad way and she wanted a medicine horn. It became clear later that she was also acting on behalf of Chief Tšepo Sempe Qefata, the son and heir of the Ward Chief of Quthing, Qefata Sempe, who was a full brother of 'Mantšebo. In November 1952 Tšepo told the Resident Commissioner that he was afraid of being framed for medicine murder. His father was ineffective, and it was suspected that 'Mantšebo might want to take his place when Bereng Seeiso came of age and became Paramount Chief. Esthere's right-hand man, Europe Kabi, was one of Chief Tšepo's trusted followers. He was among Esthere's accomplices, and so too was Mafole Pitso, a traditional doctor who had been trained in Durban.

There were two theories about Tšepo's motives. The first, already alluded to, was suggested by the Resident Commissioner, Arrowsmith: that he wanted to strengthen himself as his father's heir against 'Mantšebo's plans to take his father's place. The second was put forward by the Acting District Commissioner, Quthing, Ray Cordery: 'There is bad feeling between the Paramount Chieftainess and her nephew [Tšepo]. It is probable that they first quarrelled when Chief Tšepo, who had been consorting with the Paramount Chieftainess' married daughter with the full approval of both these ladies, refused to sleep with her again. Since then there have been a number of family disputes in which Chief Tšepo has openly opposed his aunt. Some of the disputes were taken before the Courts. The political repercussion has been that the Paramount Chieftainess has strengthened her alliance with another brother, Chief Nkuebe Sempe, who is a subordinate chief in the Quthing district, whom she would like to re-appoint in the place of Chief Tšepo as Adviser to the district chief. It can be seen, therefore, that Chief Tšepo might well have been tempted to obtain medicine to strengthen his position against the Paramount Chieftainess and against Chief Nkuebe'.

The victim was a man called Tšehlo Kabi. Esthere and Europe persuaded and paid Tšehlo's wife to let them use her husband. He had to go to Qomoqomong to arrange his son's wedding, and on his return he was ambushed and throttled to death. His body was carried to Esthere's hut. As the conspirators were about to mutilate it they saw Chief Tšepo Qefata there, accompanied by several of his followers. On the doctor's instructions the left ear was cut off, the whole of the skin of the face and forehead, and the flesh from the chin down to the middle of the collar-bone. The heart, lungs and intestines were pulled out. Boiling water was poured on the wounds, and a woman accomplice then washed the bloodstains out of the sacks on which the body had been laid. As the parts were cut they were taken into the kitchen where they were washed and the intestines were cooked. The body was dressed and placed below a cliff. Footprints were made above the cliff, and Tšehlo's white bag was dropped so that it got caught in the branches of a tree above the body. When the body was found the following Saturday, five days later, everyone agreed to say that Tšehlo had fallen over the cliff. In the meantime a billy-can containing some of the *liretlo* had been taken to Chief Tšepo Qefata.

The outcome
At the subsequent trial the accused were Esthere Kabi and eight accomplices. Chief Tšepo was not accused, because, according to the Attorney-General, the evidence against him amounted to no more than establishing his presence as 'an inactive spectator'. As well as four accomplice witnesses (a fifth disappeared between the preparatory examination and the trial) there were three independent witnesses who confirmed what the accomplice witnesses had to say about Tšehlo's journey to and from Qomoqomong. There was also a boy of about seventeen who observed Tšehlo's body being carried into Esthere Kabi's home. He told others what he had seen, and he and another boy saw the body being carried out. The defence claimed a conspiracy against them by one of Esthere's relatives, but the judge was unimpressed.

    All nine accused were convicted and hanged. Two of them were accessories after the fact (the only two accessories in all these cases, as far as we know, who were hanged). According to a missionary report all the convicted murderers repented and went to the gallows 'singing hymns in which they stressed their hope of being saved from their sins by Jesus Christ'.

Sources: LNA, CRI/T/4/54; Willan (1955b: 27–37); PRO, DO 119/1381, Sofonia, Public Prosecutor, Quthing, to Officer Commanding CID, Maseru, 30 November 1953; FCO, Box 1168, S 197J, Deputy HC to RC, 28 March 1954; FCO, Box 1176, S 368, Report by Acting DC Quthing, submitted under cover of DC Quthing to GS, 10 March 1954; *Leselinyana*, 22.2.54; *Moeletsi*, 17.4.54; Mabille (1955: 153).

1953/2

24 April 1953. Matalatala's ruins, Qacha's Nek. Ward 5: Ratšoleli's and Mashai. CRI/T/3/54. *R v. David Theko Makhaola and four others.*

The case for the Crown
In fact the first accused in this case was Tlalinyane Letsilane, since Chief David Theko Makhaola, the Ward Chief of Ratšoleli's and Mashai, was added only later to the list of accused. But Chief Theko was said to be the instigator of the murder. Although he had been suspected before of medicine murder (case 1943/5) he had an excellent reputation with both the British authorities and his people. He had succeeded his father as Ward Chief in 1932 and had led the Basotho troops in the Second World War. He supported every government measure which he thought

would lead to progress, and was described as intelligent, progressive and well-respected. He was one of the outstanding speakers in the Basutoland National Council. He occasionally deputised for 'Mantšebo when she was absent but was no favourite of hers. He was a practising Catholic and had only one wife, but it was suspected that he also had two children by 'Mabereng, the mother of the future Paramount Chief. No reason was given for the murder except for Theko's alleged statement that his horn had become weak and that a Mokoena was needed to strengthen it. He said that he wanted only blood, and that the body should not be cut since cuts could be detected in post-mortem examinations. The victim, Lepekola Mokhosi, was a Mokoena, a great friend of Tlalinyane Letsilane.

Having made his plans, Theko went away on business. On Tuesday, 21 April, Lepekola was summoned to the ruins of Matalatala's old village, where the accused, except Theko himself, were lying in wait. They caught him and took him to a deserted hut where they gagged him and tied him to a beam in the roof. On the Friday they returned, struck him with stones, collected the blood in a basin, and then hit him with a hammer until he died. The injuries were meant to simulate those caused by a fall. The body was then reclothed and left in the hut. They came on the Saturday and took the body to the foot of a cliff by a stream. Lepekola's shoes were taken to make footprints on top of the cliff.

The body was found the following day, Sunday. Theko returned that day and said that in his opinion Lepekola had died of natural causes. He agreed, however, that the body should not be buried. The post-mortem established that Lepekola had not died through falling over the cliff.

The outcome

In the ensuing trial there were three accomplice witnesses. Lepekola's wife, an independent witness, gave evidence that one of the accused came and summoned her husband on the Tuesday night, and this was confirmed by her daughter-in-law. There was also evidence that later, when a search was being conducted for Lepekola, one of the accused refused to unlock the hut in which he was being kept. Another witness gave evidence that he had been asked to look for a victim for the chief. For various reasons all this evidence was found unsatisfactory. There were serious conflicts of evidence between the three accomplice witnesses, and one of them gave evidence which was at variance with the evidence which he had given at the preparatory examination. Lepekola's wife was found to have lied in another context and so was adjudged unreliable, and the witness who said he had been asked to find a victim also gave a different account at the preparatory examination. As for the refusal to allow the hut to be searched, it might have been connected with another medicine murder about which there were rumours at the time. Moreover, at the time when Theko was supposed to have been giving his instructions for the murder, he had an alibi supported by several witnesses.

The case was heard in a crowded courtoom, and when all five were acquitted the verdict was greeted with cheers and ululations.

One of the accomplices, Monyane Sealemetse, had been acquitted in another trial for medicine murder (case 1951/7).

Sources: LNA, CRI/T/3/54; PRO, DO 35/4361; FCO, Box 1178, S 161, vol. III, memo by P. Bridges, 20 July 1953; *Basutoland News*, 3.11.53 and 2.2.54;

Leselinyana, 8.2.54; *Moeletsi*, 25.1.54, 13, 20 and 27.2.54, 6, 13, 20 and 27.3.54, 3 and 10.4.54; *Moeletsi*, 21.9.63 (obituary of Theko Makhaola).

1953/3

4 May 1953. Near Kholong, Maseru. Ward 13: Matsieng.
CRI/T/17/53. *R* v. *Khopiso Lerotholi and five others.*

The case for the Crown
Khopiso was chief of Lesobeng, and it was alleged that he had been involved in previous medicine murders. No reason is known for this murder other than that he wanted to make a medicine horn. Two of his accomplices were officials in a Basuto Court. The victim was a local man called Mokotomane Mokale. It was arranged that one of the accomplices, Mokotomane's brother-in-law, Thabo Ralitau, who later gave evidence for the Crown, should take Mokotomane to a cliff to gather honey. As Mokotomane climbed towards the bees Ralitau pushed him down the cliff to where three of the accused were hiding in the grass. He was still alive, and flesh was cut from his face, forehead and left armpit. He was left there, still alive. That night some of the conspirators returned. By that time Mokotomane was dead. They cut the muscles from his legs and cut off the left leg below the knee. The body was left at the bottom of the cliff, where it was found a week later.

The outcome
In the ensuing trial Ralitau was the only accomplice witness. There was independent evidence from witnesses who observed the movements of Ralitau and some of the accused. The evidence against Accused No. 6 was so weak that the Attorney-General withdrew the charge against him. There was no independent evidence against Accused No. 4 and he was given the benefit of the doubt. The first two accused, including Khopiso Lerotholi, were found guilty of murder. Accused Nos. 3 and 5 were found guilty of being accessories after the fact, since they took part only in the mutilations that were carried out after Mokotomane was dead. They were each sentenced to seven years' IHL. On 16 June 1954 the first two accused were hanged.

Sources: LNA, CRI/T/17/53; Willan (1955a: 320–8); *Basutoland News*, 24.11.53 and 1.12.53; *Leselinyana*, 30.11.53; *Moeletsi*, 30.11.53 and 7, 21 and 28.12.53; Judicial Department, *Annual Report 1953*, case 17/53; PRO, DO 35/4505; PRO, DO 119/1383, Marwick to Scrivenor, 31 July 1954; FCO, Box 1176, S 119, f. 1284A.

1953/4

c. 30 July 1953. Methalaneng, Maseru. Ward 13: Matsieng.
CRI/T/14/55. *R* v. *Sekharume Lecheche and five others.* (Two other accused were discharged at the preparatory examination. Nine were committed for trial, but of these two were executed in connection with another medicine murder (1954/7) and a third was killed in a gaol riot. So only six appeared before the High Court.)

The case for the Crown
Although headman Sekharume Lecheche was the first accused, he was acting on behalf of Tšoarelo Letsie in his dispute with Molise Tsolo (see case 1954/7). Tšoarelo died before this case was heard. Sekharume had been one of his advisers.
    The victim was an elderly Letebele man called Tumesole (Dinizulu) Ramokhoabane. It was known that he would be travelling along a particular path at a

particular time and he was ambushed. He was struck on the head and blood was collected in a billy-can. He was carried to a pass, by which time he seemed to be dead. Sekharume then prepared to castrate him, but stopped when he was reminded by one of the accomplices that he had not been instructed to do this. Tumesole's body was left about two metres from the path, where it was found the next day.

The outcome

It was more than two years before the accused were brought to court, partly because the doctor who had conducted the post-mortem had gone to Hong Kong and evidence had to be obtained on commission. There were four accomplice witnesses at the preparatory examination, but one of them disappeared before the trial in the High Court. Sekharume made a full confession. There was some independent corroborative evidence, but regardless of this the judge felt sufficiently confident in the three accomplices to rest his judgement on them alone and to convict all six accused.

All six appealed. One appeal was upheld on the ground that the accused's alibi that he was with his sick wife had been corroborated by one of the Crown witnesses, a point that the judge had apparently overlooked. One of the appeal judges fortuitously remembered that two of the accomplice witnesses had been accomplice witnesses in another case (1954/7). The Appeal Court took the view that the judge might not have accepted their evidence against two of the accused who had put forward alibis had he been aware of this fact. The appeals of these two were therefore upheld. Three appeals, however, were dismissed: those of two accused who had not gone into the witness box, and that of Sekharume who had made a full confession. Their sentences were later commuted to ten years' IHL.

Sources: LNA, CRI/T/14/55; Elyan (1957: 12–15); *Basutoland News*, 26.6.56; NUL, Leribe files, Box 52, file 1199; Judicial Department, *Annual Report 1956*, 13/55 [sic]; FCO, Box 1176, S 119, f. 1284A.

1953/5

November 1953. Linotšing, Mokhotlong. Ward 14: Mokhotlong.
CRI/T/10/54. *R* v. *Makeletso Tšoeute*.

The case for the Crown

'Makeletso Tšoeute was accused of killing the newborn child of her daughter-in-law, 'Mamotšabi. Her object, it was said, was to make medicine to bring her son back from the mines, where he had been for the last ten years. Although the crime was carried out in the village of Mahlomola Lerotholi, Chief Matlere's half-brother, who had been involved in a previous medicine murder case (1944/7), there was no evidence to connect him with this murder.

'Mamotšabi and 'Makeletso lived together and were on good terms together. 'Mamotšabi said that when she became pregnant 'Makeletso told her to keep it a secret, and that when the child, a girl, was born 'Makeletso took her away. The child's arm was cut off while she was still alive. The body was discovered later by some little boys with dogs.

The outcome

The authorities in the village summoned all the young women in the village and examined their breasts for milk, and in this way discovered that 'Mamotšabi was the mother. She then told the story given above. In the ensuing trial 'Makeletso denied

'Mamotšabi's account, and since there was no corroborative evidence to link her with the murder she was acquitted.

Sources: LNA, CRI/T/10/54; *Moeletsi*, 26.6.54.

1953/6

26 November 1953. Near Mpiti's, Qacha's Nek. Ward 5: Ratšoleli's and Mashai.
No criminal proceedings, it seems.
The only information that we have on this case is a report by the District Commissioner, Qacha's Nek, followed by a report from the Commissioner of Police. According to these reports the Ward Chief, Theko Makhaola, recommended that Sejanamane Mpiti should succeed to the Pheelong chieftainship when his elder brother, Seisa, died. The Paramount Chief's office rejected this recommendation and a medicine murder was the result. The victim was a man called Befole Akhosi, and the alleged murderers were Sejanamane Mpiti, Nkiani Mpiti, Nkhilane Motšoane, Tsietsi Tholo and Pheelo Peta. It was alleged that the victim's eye was removed, a piece of the tongue and a portion of the private parts, but because the body was so decomposed the Medical Officer was unable to ascertain if any parts were missing.

Sources: FCO, Box 1176, S 119, DC Qacha's Nek to GS, 16 December 1953, and CP to GS, 29 December 1953.

1954/1

24 January 1954. Sekubu?, Butha-Buthe. Ward 1: Butha-Buthe.
CRI/T/2/58. R v. *Lepekola Joel and ten others.*

The case for the Crown
Lepekola Joel was the gazetted chief of Sekubu. It was said that he needed medicine which he would take to 'Malefiloane to support the placing there of the son of Joel Molapo Qhobela, chief of 'Moteng. Several chiefs appear to have known what was happening, including the Ward Chief, Kuini Mopeli. The victim was 'Masebokoane Pule. Among Lepekola's accomplices were her sister, grandmother, lover and friend.

One Sunday there was a confirmation service at the Anglican church at Sekubu, and afterwards there was a lot of eating and drinking. Lepekola bought 'Masebokoane beer to the value of 1s. 6d., but it seems she did not become drunk. She was lured to a deep and narrow donga by a message supposedly from her lover. She was caught and gagged, and all the men had sexual intercourse with her. Afterwards she was carried to a hut and according to the accomplice witnesses at the trial a hole was made in the top of her head with a hammer and a chisel. Before she died blood was collected and flesh was cut from the private parts. At this point the owner of the hut, who was not one of the conspirators, came in unexpectedly. She was distressed and was told to say nothing. The body was thrown over a cliff.

Afterwards the *liretlo* were taken to 'Malefiloane to be used in the placing of Chief Joel Molapo Qhobela's son. On their way there Lepekola and his companions received a message from Kuini Mopeli, the Ward Chief, that he was ill and unable to come. Four chiefs were present – Joel Molapo Qhobela, Jameson Qhobela (chief of 'Muela) and two of Joel Molapo's sons – and Joel Molapo gave thanks to Lepekola Joel and those who had brought the *liretlo*.

The outcome

It was four years before the accused were brought to trial. By then four of those who had taken part in the murder were dead. There were seven accomplice witnesses, of whom five were women. The judge noted that the doctor conducting the post-mortem had not recorded the hole in the head, but presumed that he must have overlooked it since there was 'abundant evidence' that there was such a hole when the body was discovered. This evidence came not just from the accomplice witnesses, but from a policeman who had examined the body. There were several discrepancies in the evidence of the accomplice witnesses, but the judge decided that they were not such as to destroy their credibility. There was also the independent evidence of the owner of the hut, who had entered unexpectedly when the murder was being carried out, though she was very old and unreliable. The defence relied on alibis.

Six of the accused were convicted, including Lepekola Joel. The other five were acquitted. One of these had proved his alibi and the other four were given the benefit of the doubt.

It was apparently at the instigation of the police that 'Masebokoane's body was exhumed, and it was found that, contrary to evidence of the accomplice witnesses, there was no hole on the top of the head. As a result of this applications were made to the Court of Appeal. By this time two of the six persons convicted had died. The convictions and sentences of the other four were set aside.

The policeman who gave evidence that he had seen the hole in the victim's skull said that he had been ordered to give this evidence by his senior officers, but there was not a strong enough case to support a prosecution for perjury.

Sources: LNA, CRI/T/2/58; PRO, DO 119/1189; *Basutoland News*, 29.7.58 and 27.1.59; *Moeletsi*, 8.2.58 and 26.7.58; Judicial Department, *Report 1957–60*, 38/58 [*sic*]; FCO, Box 1175, S 488.

1954/2

Reported 1 March 1954. 'Maletsunyane, Mafeteng.
No criminal proceedings.
Our only information about this case is a newspaper report that on 1 March enquiries were still being made into a medicine murder case involving the people of 'Maletsunyane and some petty headmen.

Source: *Leselinyana*, 1.3.54.

1954/3

19 March 1954. Makoabating, Qacha's Nek. Ward 5: Ratšoleli and Mashai.
CRI/T/4/55. *R* v. *Mojalefa Mapola and five others*.

The case for the Crown

Mojalefa Mapola was the gazetted headman of Letsatseng, and had been an accomplice witness in case 1945/4. It was said that he needed medicine because his horn was empty. Major Donald, a member of the administrative team which checked on the investigation of medicine murders, suspected that he was working for the Ward Chief, Theko Makhaola. Mojalefa spent some time with Theko after the disappearance of the victim, and a certain General Mapola, who according to some witnesses was present after the killing but before the body was removed, was said to have been closely associated with Theko since Theko was a boy. But no further evidence was forthcoming.

Among Mojalefa's accomplices were a woman doctor, between seventy-five and eighty years old, and two people who were training to be doctors. The victim, a woman called 'Matlhoriso Malapa, had come to train as a doctor with the wife of a man called Matjoba. At first Mojalefa had wanted to kill Matjoba, since he was always taking him to court, but he had failed and decided on 'Matlhoriso instead. One of his accomplices was 'Matlhoriso's brother, another her aunt, and another her grandfather.

One Sunday night 'Matlhoriso's brother called her and she came out of Matjoba's huts. She was seized, gagged, and taken to a place called Senokonokong where she was kept for five days. On the Friday night she was brought to the doctor's hut. Mojalefa had sexual intercourse with her, explaining to his accomplices that this would strengthen the medicine, and flesh was cut from her private parts, thigh and armpit. Then she was scalped, and her tongue and left eye were removed. The body was taken to a small donga and covered with earth, and on the following night it was taken and thrown into the Orange river.

Matjoba asked Mojalefa to conduct a search, but he refused. The body was found on 15 April, almost a month later, 20–25 kilometres from the spot where it was thrown in. 'Matlhoriso was identified by means of her necklace and a bangle on her arm.

The outcome

In the ensuing trial there were four accomplice witnesses, including 'Matlhoriso's grandfather. There was also independent evidence in the form of the report of the doctor who conducted the post-mortem and the skins on which 'Matlhoriso had been placed when she was mutilated and which were later found in the doctor's hut. All six accused were found guilty.

One died in prison. The other five appealed, but their appeals were dismissed, and they were all hanged on 24 January 1956.

Sources: LNA, CRI/T/4/55; FCO, Box 1168, S 197H, Donald's report on 'Mojalefa Mapola & Others', 1 June 1954; *Basutoland News*, 12.7.55, 31.1.56; *Leselinyana*, 25.7.55; *Moeletsi*, 31.12.55; NUL, Leribe Files, Box 52, file 1199; PRO, DO 119/ 1383, Marwick to Scrivenor, 31 July 1954; Judicial Department, *Annual Report 1956*, case 4/55; PS and KS interview, Edwin Nohe Tšita, 28 May 1999.

1954/4

9 April 1954. Ha Sempe Theko, Maseru. Ward 21: Thaba-Bosiu.
CRI/T/3/55. *R v. Sempe Theko and three others.*

The case for the Crown

Sempe Theko was an ungazetted headman at Lirahalibonoe. He had established his village without the authority of his elder brother, who had complained to the Ward Chief of Thaba-Bosiu. Sempe wanted medicine to 'peg' his village with *lithakhisa*, since he had not done this since establishing it. His victim was Matota Ranoto Metsing, a young man of about sixteen, who was chosen because he was an only child and a Mohlakoana.

It was arranged that when Matota left his home to go to a shop at Ha Khotso one of his friends, Mongateng, should so arrange matters that he could be ambushed on the way either going or coming back. This arrangement was carried out. On their way back, as it was getting dark, Matota's companions went on ahead while he and Mongateng lingered behind. Matota was attacked and thrown to the ground by Sempe and his accomplices. He was stabbed with a *tsenene*, a spear for hunting rats, in the region of the kidneys and the nose, and blood was collected in a bottle. By this time he was dead. A stranger appeared unexpectedly on the scene. The conspirators chased and caught him, but he struggled free and escaped.

The body was carried below a cliff and thrown onto some bushes. It was found there three days later. A post-mortem was conducted, but no incriminating wounds were found and so the body was buried. Later it was exhumed and another post-mortem conducted, but still no incriminating wounds were found.

The medicine prepared from Matota was smeared on pegs which were planted around Sempe's house and around the village. Mongateng, Matota's friend, was so frightened after the murder that he had to be treated with medicine to make his fear depart.

The outcome

Thabo Motiea, the man who had appeared at the scene of the crime and run away, was later convicted of stock-theft and sentenced to three months in prison. While there he saw and recognised Sempe Theko. In spite of Sempe's threats he reported the murder to the police, and he gave evidence in the subsequent preparatory examination.

By the time of the trial, however, he had disappeared. There were three accomplice witnesses, including Mongateng, but because the main independent witness was no longer available, and because of the conflict of evidence between the accomplice witnesses and the post-mortem report, all the accused were acquitted.

Sources: LNA, CRI/T/3/55; Willan (1956: 10–12); PRO, DO 119/1383, Marwick to Scrivenor, 31 July 1954; *Leselinyana*, 7.3.55; *Moeletsi*, 26.2.55.

1954/5

24 July 1954. Makoetje's, Maseru. Ward 13: Matsieng.
CRI/T/10/55. *R* v. *Samuel Motsoete Makoetje and four others*.

The case for the Crown

Makoetje was the gazetted headman of Makoetje's and was the clerk in a Basuto Court. He felt that he was failing in his court duties and wanted medicine to strengthen himself. The victim was a man called Ntona Ngoane.

One of Makoetje's accomplices took Ntona to a party, but a policeman was there and so nothing could be done. He then took him to another party. As Ntona went away befuddled with drink he was struck on the head with sticks and the blood flowing from his nose was collected in a bottle. After he died his body was thrown over a cliff. It was found a month later.

The outcome

In the ensuing trial there were two accomplice witnesses, and there was independent evidence too, including a pair of bloodstained trousers which belonged to Accused No. 3 and which he was unable to explain to the satisfaction of the court. One of the accomplices claimed that he had accompanied Ntona on his way home, that Ntona had fallen over a cliff, and that he had been too frightened to report the accident. He had previously told the police that Ntona had been strangled by something in his presence, but he could not say what it was. The court rejected this story. All the accused were found guilty, and when they appealed their appeals were dismissed. Two of those convicted were hanged, including Samuel Makoetje himself, and the sentences of the other three were commuted to life imprisonment.

Sources: LNA, CRI/T/10/55; *Basutoland News*, 6.9.55, 13.9.55 and 31.1.56; NUL, Leribe Files, Box 52, file 1199; Willan (1956: 64–9); Judicial Department, *Annual Report 1955* and *Annual Report 1956*, case 10/55; FCO, Box 1176, S 119, f. 1284A..

1954/6

19 August 1954. Molomo's Hoek, Mafeteng. Ward 18: Tajane etc.
CRI/T/9/55. *R* v. *Peete Lesaoana and four others.*

The case for the Crown

Peete Lesaoana, the gazetted headman of Tsoaing, wanted to make a medicine horn in order to strengthen his beer hall. The beer, it was said, was not fetching a good price. He chose as his victim a man called Liau Monnamoholo Makhata. One of Lesaoana's accomplices was Liau's cousin.

On Thursday, 19 August a baptismal feast was held at Lesaoana's. At dusk Liau left the feast and was lured to a donga where he was waylaid by Lesaoana and his accomplices. They beat Liau with their sticks so that he was bleeding from his mouth, his nose and his ears. The blood was collected in a basin, and the body was then placed in a cave in such a way that it would appear to have fallen from the cliff above. It was found on the Sunday.

The outcome

The Crown's case rested mainly on the evidence of four accomplice witnesses. The judge found two of them unreliable, though not dishonest, but he accepted the evidence of the other two. Although there was evidence which tended to support what they said the judge did not regard it as satisfactory independent corroboration. Nevertheless, relying on the two accomplices, he found all five accused guilty of murder.

Their appeals against this decision, the first to be heard in the new Court of Appeal, were dismissed and they were hanged on 30 August 1955.

Sources: LNA, CRI/T/9/55; Willan (1956: 28–36); *Basutoland News*, 10.5.55, 12.7.55, 6.9.55; *Leselinyana*, 16.5.55; *Moeletsi*, 21.5.55, 4.6.55 and 30.7.55; NUL Leribe Files, Box 52, file 1199; Judicial Department, *Annual Report 1955*; FCO, Box 1176, S 119, f. 1284A.

1954/7

29 August 1954. Methalaneng, Maseru. Ward 13: Matsieng.
CRI/T/8/55. *R* v. *Tšoarelo Letsie and eight others.*

The case for the Crown

Tšoarelo Letsie, an ungazetted headman, wanted medicine because he 'was having constant trouble about his area' and wanted 'to settle down comfortably'. He had been involved in a boundary dispute with a neighbouring headman, Molise Tsolo. (See also case 1953/4.) The victim, Moralejoe Mphoso, was chosen because he had been involved in disputes both with Tšoarelo and with the men Tšoarelo involved as his accomplices.

On Sunday, 29 August, the conspirators made use of 'Malekoekoe, Moralejoe's lover, to entice him to a certain spot where he was waylaid just after sunset. He was gagged, his legs were tied together with his bootlaces, and he was carried to a donga about 200 metres way. His eye was removed with a short spear, and he was stabbed on top of his head and on the chin in order to get blood. A strap was tied round his neck to stop the bleeding and he died. His body was then carried on an ox-skin to a hut in which prayer-meetings were normally held. Two women were now involved: one owned the hut, and the other washed the body. The body was kept in the prayer hut until the following night, when it was carried away and rolled over the edge of a cliff. Moralejoe's blanket, hat and stick were thrown over the cliff as well. The body was found on the Wednesday. The post-mortem, which was held on the Saturday, established that the injuries on the body were not consistent with falling from the cliff.

The outcome

In the subsequent trial there were three accomplice witnesses. The judge dismissed one as unreliable, but he accepted the evidence of the other two. (Two of them subsequently appeared as accomplice witnesses in case 1953/4.) Although there was evidence supporting their accounts, the judge did not find that it amounted to satisfactory independent corroboration, but he was content to rely on their evidence alone. He convicted seven of the accused of murder and sentenced them to death; and he convicted two, both women, of being accessories after the fact and sentenced them to seven years' IHL.

All the accused appealed. Their appeals were dismissed, but the sentences on the two women convicted of being accessories after the fact were reduced to two years' IHL. The High Commissioner subsequently commuted the sentences of two of the convicted men to ten years' IHL. The other five convicted men, including Tšoarelo Letsie, were hanged on 30 August 1955.

In a subsequent case (CRI/T/11/55) Tšoarelo's son, Leboto Letsie, was accused of trying to defeat the ends of justice by suggesting to some of the witnesses that they should change their statements. He pointed out that in an earlier case some of the accused had been discharged because the witnesses had changed their statements. The Attorney-General decided not to press this charge.

Sources: LNA, CRI/T/8/55 and CRI/T/11/55; Willan (1956: 22–7); *Basutoland News*, 10, 17 and 24.5.55, 6.9.55; *Leselinyana*, 6.6.55; *Moeletsi*, 28.5.55, 11, 18 and 25.6.55, 2.7.55; NUL, Leribe Files, Box 52, file 1199; FCO, Box 1176, S 119, f. 1284A..

1954/8

31 August 1954. Mokhoabong, Mohale's Hoek. Ward 15: Phamong.
CRI/T/13/55. *R* v. *Lehloenya Lethena Lehloenya and four others.*

The case for the Crown

In 1950 Lehloenya was gazetted as headman of Qaqatu. In 1951 a man named Kheleli, who had been working in the Union, returned to Basutoland and claimed the headmanship. His claim was upheld in court, and Lehloenya turned to medicine murder. The victim was a man called Raletšolo Moseli.

Raletšolo was waylaid as he went to Maphutseng to collect an animal. On the instructions of one of the accomplices who was a doctor, he was scalped from the base of the neck upwards, and the tip of the tongue and the flesh of one leg from the calf down were cut off. The flesh was put into a canvas bag. The body was placed at the foot of a cliff where it was found several weeks later.

The outcome
In the ensuing trial there were three accomplice witnesses. The judge felt he could not rely on one, not because he was lying, but because his memory was so poor. He accepted the evidence of the other two. There was independent evidence in the form of the post-mortem report and a bag of medicines found in the home of the doctor. The defence put forward alibis, but the judge rejected these. All the accused were convicted.

They appealed on the ground that the decision was against the weight of the evidence. All the appeals were dismissed. The sentences of all five were commuted to life imprisonment.

Sources: LNA, CRI/T/13/55; NUL, Leribe Files, Box 52, file 1199; *Basutoland News*, 23.8.55; *Leselinyana*, 5.9.55; *Moeletsi*, 3 and 19.9.55, 1, 8, 15, 22 and 29.10.55; Judicial Department, *Annual Report 1955* and *Annual Report 1956*; FCO, Box 1176, S 119, f. 1284A.

1954/9

13 November 1954. Senqunyane, Maseru. Ward 13: Matsieng.
CRI/T/4/56. *R* v. *Seqhoe Noha and ten others.*

The case for the Crown
Seqhoe Noha had been the headman of Senqunyane Ha Noha since 1927. He had suffered difficulties since Chieftainess 'Makopoi was placed over him in 1943. He had lost some of his land and his subjects to her and to another chief, and his people no longer respected and obeyed him. He needed medicine to recover his land and his people. The victim was a man called Thoko Molaoli. Seqhoe said that he was one of his most obedient subjects and claimed that he grieved over his death.

Thoko was sent on an errand and was ambushed on his return. He was throttled with a *doek* (headscarf) so that he could not cry out. Wounds were made on the head and blood collected in a billy-can. A fire was lit, and a heated iron was used to cauterize the wounds. The body was taken and thrown over a cliff near the lands of one of Seqhoe's rivals.

The outcome
Although five accomplice witnesses gave evidence at the preparatory examination, in the course of the High Court trial the Attorney-General decided not to proceed because their evidence was not satisfactory. This may well have been connected with the evidence of one accomplice witness that he had been ill in 1954, going distractedly from place to place because he was being chased by people on horses. A doctor told him he was being pursued by a *thokolosi* (an evil spirit).

Sources: LNA, CRI/T/4/56; *Basutoland News*, 22.5.56.

1955/1

16 May 1955. Ramabanta's, Maseru. Ward 7: Kubake and Ramabanta's.
CRI/T/1/56. *R* v. *Solomon Api Ramabanta and thirteen others.*

The case for the Crown

Solomon Api Ramabanta was the Ward Chief of Ramabanta's – a drunkard, 'hopeless' and 'beyond redemption', according to the District Commissioner, Maseru. For about two years he had been looking for an opportunity to fill his medicine horn. He asked 'Mankopo Lerotholi if she would give him her husband, but she refused. He then asked 'Masikeme Motale for her husband, Motale Sefamo. She refused at first, saying that she would have no-one to look after her. Solomon said, 'You are my people, and I can do with you what I like'. She should not worry about being looked after, since he had given her husband a piece of land. Solomon's accomplices included several of his own relatives.

A feast was held in the hut of Solomon's aunt on the evening of 16 May. Motale was not there, but in a hut nearby. A small boy was sent to call him, but without success. Then Solomon and two others went to fetch him, but he was not there since he had gone to feed his pigs. Eventually he came. He was struck on the head with a knife and gagged. The little boy who had been sent to fetch him before began crying and was taken outside. Motale's ear was cut off and blood collected. He was still showing signs of life. He was thrown over a cliff near the pigsty, and some pig's food was placed in a dish nearby to make it appear as if he had fallen with it. Two of the women accomplices then cleaned the house to remove traces of blood.

Motale's body was found three days later and the post-mortem examination established that he did not die through a fall.

The outcome

In the ensuing case two of the women accomplices surprised the judge by pleading guilty, but pleas of not guilty were entered. There were six accomplice witnesses, and independent evidence from the little boy who had been sent to fetch Motale and others who had observed the movements of the accused. The judge found however that the post-mortem examination did not establish that a crime had been committed, since the wounds could have been inflicted after death, and that in general there was too much uncertainty to sustain a conviction. He therefore acquitted all the accused. He was going on to say that his assessors and advisers agreed with him, but the crowd burst out cheering and the court was emptied. When the judge continued his address there were only a few whites and newspaper reporters in the court.

'Mamathealira Api, Solomon's wife, who was one of those accused in this case, and who succeeded Solomon when he died in 1981, was accused and acquitted in another medicine murder trial in 1991.

Sources: FCO, Box 1168, S 197E, DC Maseru to GS, 5 May 1954; Box 1176, S 119, CP to GS, 16 August 1955, and report by Administrative Team, 25 August 1955; *Leselinyana*, 2.4.56; *Moeletsi*, 7.4.56, 12 and 26.5.56, 30.6.56, 7, 14, 21 and 28.7.56; NUL, Leribe Files, Box 52, file 1199.

1955/2

c. 14 July 1955. Ponoane's, Maseru. Ward 21: Thaba-Bosiu.
CRI/T/3/59. *R* v. *Tjoetso Pholo and four others.*

The case for the Crown

Headman Tjoetso Pholo felt undermined because his Ward Chief, Jacottet Theko, had instructed him not to cut thatching grass in his area. He decided to strengthen his village by killing one of his own people, a man called Tebello.

Tebello was seized after a beer-drink. His hands were tied behind his back and he was gagged, and then he was pushed along into a kloof where he was struck twice with a knobkerrie and stabbed behind the shoulder-blade with a knife. Blood was collected in a billy-can. It seems that Tebello was then cut on the buttocks. The body was placed in a donga where it was found about a week later.

The outcome
There were five accused in the trial that followed, but two of them disappeared in the course of the trial. There were also two accomplice witnesses, one of them being Tebello's brother-in-law. At the end of the Crown case the judge declared that he was not satisfied that the Crown had established a case against the remaining three accused, and they were acquitted.

Sources: LNA, CRI/T/3/59; *Moeletsi*, 7.2.59, 11 and 25.4.59.

1955/3

July 1955? Near Phamong, Mohale's Hoek. Ward 15: Phamong.
No criminal proceedings.
In October 1955 the Commissioner of Police reported that in July that year the body of Ntoa Mohanoe was found on the Mohale's Hoek side of the Orange river near Phamong. There was bruising and dried blood around the nose and the upper lip. Death was due to asphyxia. Information was received that Chief Sekhonyana 'Maseribane and Lepipi Makara had arranged for the killing to obtain medicine in order to strengthen their businesses, a café and a butcher's shop respectively. Ntoa was allegedly lured to a beer-drink and was waylaid on his return home by Chief Sekhonyana and five others. The nose was pierced with a sharp instrument and blood was collected. There is no further record of this case.

Sources: FCO, Box 1176, S 119, CP to GS, 13 and 27 October 1955.

1956/1

April/May 1956. Pitseng, Leribe. Ward 8: Leribe.
No criminal proceedings, it seems.
Our only information on this case is a newspaper article under the heading 'Liretlo Pitseng' ('Medicine Murder at Pitseng'). The remnants of a man's body were discovered by two women coming out of church. The man had disappeared ten days before.

Source: *Moeletsi*, 21.7.56.

1956/2

1 November 1956. Tsiloane's, Maseru. Ward 13: Matsieng.
CRI/T/1/58. *R* v. *'Matsilo Tsilo and three others*.

The case for the Crown
'Matsilo Tsilo was governing Tsiloane's village in place of her son, Tsilo. The victim was a distant relative, an old man called Mathibela Teele, who always used a walking stick when he went out. No particular motive for the murder is known.

On Thursday, 1 November, the conspirators entered Mathibela's hut where he lay asleep. They gagged him, tied him up, and took him to some huts which belonged to the mother of one of the accused. They took flesh from the head, the ear and the feet, and collected blood in the lid of a billy-can. They then left, locking the door with a padlock. They came back the next day and moved the body to a donga about a kilometre away. The body was found on the Sunday, but the stick which Mathibela always used was found in his hut beside the bed.

The outcome

It proved difficult to obtain any evidence about the case, and it was August 1957 before any arrests were made. In the ensuing trial the judge accepted the evidence of the two accomplice witnesses, and there was independent corroborative evidence in the form of the post-mortem report. All four accused were found guilty. They all appealed, and their appeals were dismissed. The first three accused, including 'Matsilo Tsilo, were hanged on 24 June 1958. The fourth accused, a woman who was acting under pressure from her husband, who became an accomplice witness, had her sentence commuted to five years' IHL.

Sources: LNA, CRI/T/1/58; Elyan (1959: 15–18); *Basutoland News*, 21 and 28.1.58, 4 and 11.2.58, 1.4.58, 17.6.58; *Leselinyana*, 17.2.58 and 7.4.58; *Moeletsi*, 8 and 22.2.58, 19.7.58; Judicial Department, *Report 1957–60*, 20/58.

1956/3

10 December 1956. Ha Khabo (?), Leribe. Ward 8: Leribe.
CRI/T/16/57. *R* v. *Lehloka Khabo Molapo and five others.*

The case for the Crown

Lehloka Khabo Molapo, a headman, wanted human blood to make medicine to keep hail away from his crops and to bring good luck. The victim, who had to be a Khabo man, was Pekane Pekane.

Pekane was attacked after he left a beer party. Three of the accomplices held him down while the others hit him over the head and drew blood. The body was placed in a river where it was found the following day. The alarm was raised and people gathered at the scene, but Lehloka did not come, saying it was the territory of Chief Khabo, who was hostile to him, and that on the occasion of a previous killing he had been accused of having been the murderer.

The outcome

The case for the Crown rested mainly on two accomplice witnesses. For some of the accused there was independent evidence from witnesses who had observed them with Pekane. For others there was no independent evidence. The judge accepted the evidence of the accomplices and convicted all six accused.

All six appealed. Two appeals were upheld, the first on the ground that the judge had overlooked the evidence of a Crown witness in supporting the appellant's alibi, the second on the ground that the judge had misdirected himself in saying that the appellant's alibi was not supported by his witnesses whereas in fact it was. The other four appeals were dismissed. Three of those found guilty were hanged, including Lehloka. The fourth evidently had his sentence commuted.

It was alleged that Lehloka had committed another medicine murder, but the details are not known.

Sources: LNA, CRI/T/16/57; *Basutoland News*, 1.4.56, 25.3.58, 1.4.58; *Moeletsi*, 19.10.57, 9 and 16.11.57, 14.12.57.

1956/4

25 December 1956. Mauteng Ha Sanaha, Maseru. Ward 13: Matsieng.
CRI/T/29/58. *R v. Mokhoele Leuta and six others.*

The case for the Crown
Mokhoele Leuta was an ungazetted headman who said that he wanted medicine, not only to strengthen himself, but also for 'our chief'. The witness who gave this evidence said she did not ask which chief he meant, but 'Chief Semako' was responsible for allocating lands. 'Chief Semako' was probably a transcriber's error for Chief Semapo Sanaha of Mauteng. It seems, however, that the chief who was immediately senior to Mokhoele was 'Mantenako, who was under Semapo Sanaha. The victim was a woman called 'Mapaki Naha. Mokhoele, who said 'Any person would do', also believed that she was bewitching his son.

On Christmas night, a Tuesday, 'Mapaki was in bed with her lover. (Her husband was away on the mines.) She was very drunk. Her brother-in-law, one of Mokhoele's accomplices, came in and took her away to a ruined hut. She was throttled and gagged. She was hit with a stone on the forehead and stabbed on the thigh, and blood was collected in a tin. The body was then hidden under some thatching grass by the wall, and two nights later it was moved and placed near the bottom of a nearby cliff. It was discovered two days after that, on a Saturday.

The outcome
There was a lot of loose talk about the murder, and it was clear that many people, including the chieftainess, 'Mantenako, knew who was responsible. There were three accomplice witnesses in the preparatory examination, but only two in the High Court, since one of them had disappeared in the interim. The judge accepted the evidence of these two witnesses, and listed fifteen items of independent evidence, such as the statement by 'Mapaki's lover that she was called out of the hut by her brother-in-law, various details in the post-mortem report, the knife used by Mokhoele, and the statement by a doctor who was asked to supply Mokhoele with medicine because the police were troubling him. All six accused were convicted, and their appeals were all dismissed. Mokhoele Leuta was hanged, and the other five had their sentences commuted by the High Commissioner. Three, all women, were given eight years' IHL, and two, both men, were given twelve years' IHL.

Sources: LNA, CRI/T/29/58; Elyan (1960: 28–31); *Basutoland News*, 18.8.59, 19.7.60; *Moeletsi*, 15 and 29.11.58, 14, 21 and 28.3.58, and 23.7.60; Judicial Department, *Report 1957–60*, 18/58.

1957/1

9 January 1957. Fobane Ha Mafata, Leribe. Ward 22: Tsikoane.
CRI/T/3/58. *R v. Setlotla Motlotla and nine others.*

The case for the Crown
Setlotla Motlotla was a 'bugle' – the chief's spokesman – at Chief Patso's village, but not gazetted. He was said to be acting on Patso's instructions in carrying out this murder. The appeal judges noted that there were no doubt good reasons for not charging Patso but they were not aware of them. It was alleged that Patso needed medicine because he was not respected by his paternal uncle, Chief Seetsa, but in

court Patso and Seetsa said they enjoyed a good relationship. The victim was a man called Tumane Mofammere. Among Setlotla's accomplices were his brother, his mother and his wife.

After a prayer meeting Setlotla and Palinyane Mofammere (Tumane's elder brother) approached a doctor and asked him if he would prepare medicine with human blood for Chief Patso. He agreed to do so if he was paid two head of cattle. Later he was called to Palinyane's hut where he heard a noise as of a person being struck and went in. He found Setlotla and his accomplices there, and Tumane lying on the floor with blood coming from his mouth. There was a wound at the back of his head. Blood was collected in a basin from his mouth and nose. He was then pierced in the right ampit with a thin pin like an umbrella rib and more blood was collected. The blood was poured into two brandy bottles. The doctor placed medicines in the bottles, one to be used for conferring dignity on a person and the other for pegging and for bathing. The body was placed in a disused hut, and the following night, Thursday, it was placed on an ox-hide and eight men carried it to the foot of a cliff. Palinyane later told the police that his brother might have been thrown over the cliff by his own *thokolosi* (evil spirit). The post-mortem established that no bones were broken and so Tumane could not have met his death by falling over the cliff. Later Setlotla was seen going towards Fobane, Chief Patso's village, with bottles containing medicine.

Before the ensuing trial was held Patso was believed to have instigated another medicine murder in order to secure the acquittal of Setlotla and his accomplices (see 1957/9). If this was so, he was only partly successful.

The outcome
In this case there were two accomplice witnesses, including the doctor. The judge decided that he could rely on their evidence. He convicted Setlotla Motlotla and Palinyane Mofammere of murder and sentenced them to death. He convicted the other eight of being accessories after the fact and sentenced them to terms of imprisonment that varied from seven years' IHL for an ungazetted headman to one year in prison without hard labour for Tumane's elderly mother. Five of those convicted appealed, and all these appeals were dismissed. Setlotla and Palinyane were hanged on 27 September 1958.

Sources: LNA, CRI/T/3/58; *Basutoland News*, 4, 11 and 18.3.58, 29.7.58, 2.9.58; *Moeletsi*, 8.2.58, 26.7.58; Judicial Department, *Report 1957–60*, 25/58.

1957/2

1 March 1957. Nqechane, Leribe. Ward 8: Leribe.
CRI/T/15/58. *R* v. *Leketekete Ketso and six others.*

The case for the Crown
Lekeketekete Ketso was an ungazetted headman who wanted blood for medicine to strengthen himself, as he was not firm in his position. He said he wanted to be senior to another chief. The victim was a man called Tlhoriso Potjo.

On 1 March there was a feast at which a future daughter-in-law was welcomed by her husband's family. There was singing and dancing and Tlhoriso, like many others, had a lot to drink, though according to one witness he was not staggering. After he left the feast he was attacked by Leketekete and his accomplices. He was pierced at the back of the neck with a sharp pin and then his neck was broken and he was thrown to the ground and struck on the side with a stick. His nose was pierced and blood was collected. He died, it seems, as he was carried away. His naked body was thrown into a deep donga and his clothes were thrown down after him. The body was discovered the following day, and was recovered with great difficulty and taken to the district headquarters at Leribe (Hlotse).

The outcome

In the ensuing trial there were two accomplice witnesses, and a lot of evidence about statements alleged to have been made by the accused. There was also evidence from Tlhoriso's wife to the effect that one of the accused, who was her lover, slept with her on the night of the murder and assured her that her husband would not be coming home. The two assessors were divided in their opinions. The judge, however, attached no weight to the evidence about all these alleged conversations and felt that he could not rely on the two accomplice witnesses. All the accused were acquitted.

Sources: LNA, CRI/T/15/58; *Basutoland News*, 5.8.58.

1957/3

26 April 1957. Tša-le-Moleka, Butha-Buthe. Ward 1: Butha-Buthe.
CRI/T/17/57. *R* v. *Joel Malofo, Mokone Mathabela and sixteen others.* (Another accused died before the High Court trial.)

The case for the Crown

Joel Malofo and Mokone Mathabela were gazetted headmen and planned the murder together. The judge believed that Joel's motive might have been connected with a land dispute with a senior chief which had gone against him. Mokone wanted medicine to make himself more dignified. Their victim was one of Mokone's subjects called Mpho Mothijoa, who was chosen because he was a Mohlakoana.

Mokone approached one of Mpho's friends and eventually persuaded him to bring Mpho to a feast at Joel's village and then to take him to the hut of Joel's father's youngest wife. Mpho went to the feast but then went off elsewhere. Joel, Malofo and their accomplices were all gathered together, and a doctor called Sekoatle went through certain rites with a cock and duck, saying that the cock would summon Mpho on the correct day and the duck would bring rain which would wash away Mpho's body so that it would be thought he had drowned.

Arrangements were then made for Mpho to be killed when he visited his lover, Lydia Dekezulu. After he had entered Lydia's house Joel went in, waved his arms in some kind of ritual, and then called in one of his accomplices, Sepatlapatla, to seize Mpho. Mpho, however, threw Sepatlapatla across the floor. Another accomplice came in, Lietso, and Mpho knocked him down with a grinding stone. Lydia then seized him round the waist from behind and he became docile, perhaps thinking she was trying to restrain him. Joel, Mokone and the other accomplices rushed in and overwhelmed him. Two of them cut flesh from the left eyebrow and stabbed him in the armpit. Mpho was crying out and screaming, and so they gagged him, and three women collected the blood from his armpit in a clay pot. Mpho then died. One of the women, an Anglican, said a prayer and made the sign of the Cross. Another woman, a member of the Apostolic Church, said another prayer, and all those present sang 'Peace, perfect peace'. ('I do not imagine', the judge said, 'that the hymn was sung out loud and lustily.') Then, at the bidding of Joel and the doctor, the two men who had actually inflicted the wounds on Mpho performed a war-dance. The body was placed on a ladder and all the men took it to the Qalo river, where they slid it down the bank.

After the body was found, a post-mortem examination was conducted. Mpho, it transpired, had been suffering from chronic tuberculosis, and the doctor believed that this was a contributing cause. He also failed to observe the wound in the armpit. The body was therefore buried.

On the day after the burial the police were told by a man called Gabriel Sekutu that Mpho had been murdered for medicine. Gabriel had not been one of the original conspirators but had been passing by Lydia's home when the murder was being committed and was forced to join in. He escaped as soon as he could and reported to the police.

The outcome

There were four accomplice witnesses, including Gabriel and Lydia, Mpho's lover. The defence consisted of alibis and, in some cases, allegations of bad relations between the accused and the Crown witnesses. There was an element of doubt in the case against four of the accused, and they were acquitted. The other fourteen were all convicted, including Joel and Mokone. They appealed and their appeals were dismissed. Five of them were hanged, included Joel Malofo and Mokone Mathabela, and the other nine had their sentences commuted to various terms of imprisonment.

Sources: LNA, CRI/T/17/57; *Basutoland News*, 1.4.58; *Moeletsi*, 9 and 16.11.57; Judicial Department, *Report 1957–60*, p. 62, 17/57.

1957/4

2 August 1957. Maoa-Mafubelu Ha Matsoso, Leribe. Ward 8: Leribe.
CRI/T/5/58. *R* v. *Ramokoteli Setlaba Shepiri and sixteen others*. (Another accused was discharged at the preparatory examination.)

The case for the Crown

Ramokoteli Setlaba Shepiri was acting as headman for Ramafikeng, his nephew. He needed blood for medicine partly because he wanted to improve his crops, and partly because he was disputing the right of chieftainship with Ramafikeng. The victim was his aunt, Makote Ramonyokolane.

On Friday, 2 August a work-party was held for cutting grass and afterwards beer was drunk. Makote staggered home long after sunset. She left an empty billy-can in her hut and went out again without saying anything. She evidently went to a hut in Matsoso's village. About twenty people were in the hut, which was lit by a lamp made from a Vaseline bottle. Makote was attacked by Ramokoteli and his accomplices. She was gagged and held in a kneeling position while she was cut across the forehead so severely as almost to be scalped. Blood was collected in a billy-can. The wound was washed and then dressed. The body was taken and thrown into a stream face downwards. It was found there the following day.

Because of the large number of defendants, the case lasted nearly two months and the judgement took over five hours to deliver. There were two accomplice witnesses, and there was crucial independent evidence from a boy aged sixteen, the son of one of the accomplices, and another young man who looked through the door of the hut and saw the murder being carried out. Six of the accused were found guilty – Ramokoteli himself, his wife, another woman and three men. The rest were acquitted. The appeals from the six who were convicted were dismissed, but the sentences of the two women were commuted to seven years' IHL. Ramokoteli and three of his accomplices were hanged on 30 June 1959.

Sources: LNA, CRI/T/5/58; *Basutoland News*, 8.7.58, 7.7.59; *Leselinyana*, 14.7.58; *Moeletsi*, 8.2.58, 24 and 31.5.58, 7, 14 and 21.6.58, 26.7.58.

1957/5

21 August 1957. Phoqoane, Mafeteng. Ward of Independent Chiefs.
CRI/T/4/58. *R* v. *'Masebina Tekane and three others*.

The case for the Crown
This is an unusual case, in that it was planned as an ordinary murder by a woman and her lover to get rid of her husband, and another took the opportunity to join in and obtain medicine.

The woman was 'Masebina Tekane and her husband was Mosito Tekane. 'Masebina had originally been the wife of Mosito's elder brother, but when he died Mosito became her husband by the custom of *ho kenela*. The other man, Ramohope Mochekoane, claimed that he ought to have been the headman of Mochekoane's instead of 'Nete. There was litigation because he had refused to obey 'Nete's orders.

One night, after a beer party, Mosito went out to look for a horse. When he came back without it 'Masebina told him to go out again, and when he went out she followed him. He was then ambushed by Ramohope and his accomplices. He was stabbed in the thigh and blood was caught in a billy-can, and he was killed by being struck with a stick on the back of the head. His body was dropped over a small cliff about half a kilometre away, and it was found the following day.

The outcome
In the ensuing trial there were two accomplice witnesses, whose evidence the judge found unreliable without corroborative evidence. The woman, 'Masebina, however, made a confession, and there was also the evidence of 'Masebina's daughter that her mother had told her that she had killed Mosito. The judge convicted 'Masebina of murder, but gave the benefit of the doubt to the other three. We do not know if 'Masebina was hanged.

Sources: LNA, CRI/T/4/58; *Leselinyana*, 18.11.57; *Basutoland News*, 11, 18 and 25.2.58; *Moeletsi*, 8.2.58.

1957/6

21 August 1957. Pitsaneng, Berea. Ward 4: 'Mamathe's.
CRI/T/18/58. *R* v. *Pule Matololi and fourteen others*.

The case for the Crown
Pule Matololi was a commoner, and no evidence is available about his motive for committing this murder. The victim was a man called Kau Rachere.

Kau was attacked after he had been to a feast. He was put on a blanket and carried to a stream. He was then stabbed on the forehead and on the back of the head, and blood was collected in a billy-can. After he died flesh and blood were taken from his left calf. The body was placed in the stream below some poplar trees. When it was found it was said that Kau must have fallen over, but the post-mortem established that he had been murdered.

In her fright one of the accused, a woman, let it be known that Kau had been murdered.

The outcome

In the ensuing trial there were two accomplice witnesses. Although the judge was impressed by one of them, the other was hesitant and inconsistent, and in the absence of any corroborative evidence all the accused were acquitted, even the woman who had said that Kau had been murdered.

Sources: LNA, CRI/T/18/58; FCO, Box 1176, S 119, Assistant Superintendent of Police, Teyateyaneng, to CP, 31 August 1957; *Basutoland News*, 19.8.58.

1957/7

30 August 1957. Fikaleaoa stream, Maseru. Ward 2: Maama's.
CRI/T/25/58. *R* v. *Jobere Motsie and at least seven others.*

The case for the Crown

Jobere Motsie was a gazetted headman and had long presided over the administrative court of Chieftainess 'Malekunutu. He needed medicine because he was about to move his court from Auplaas to Khumamela, and also because he wanted to get another piece of land. It was Chieftainess 'Malekunutu who decided that the court should be moved. All, except one, of Jobere's accomplices were her subjects: one was her brother-in-law and another her pound-master. Jobere needed an elderly person for his victim, and he chose a man called Moqebelo Ramahlatsa.

Moqebelo was attacked in a valley where he had been chopping wood. As he was held down cuts were made on the back of his head and his forehead, flesh was cut from his upper lip and the blood was collected in a billy-can. The body was carried to a donga and Jobere knocked the head against a stone to make it appear that Moqebelo had struck a stone when falling accidentally into the donga. Some bushes on the edge of the donga were cut with Moqebelo's axe so that people would think he had fallen over the edge while working. The body was found the following day.

The outcome

In the ensuing trial there were two accomplice witnesses, both of whom the judge found 'worthy of credence'. There was also independent evidence from the doctor who conducted the post-mortem examination and a witness who observed the movements of Jobere and one of the accomplice witnesses. There was evidence too from a doctor who said that he was asked by Jobere after the murder to prepare medicine from the parts taken from Moqebelo. He said that he pointed out to Jobere that Moqebelo was his grandfather, whereupon Jobere apologised. The judge dismissed this particular account as unlikely. Even so he found there was sufficient evidence to convict all the accused of murder. Their appeals were dismissed, but the High Commissioner commuted the sentence of one of them to seven years' IHL.

Jobere and six accomplices were hanged on 30 June 1959.

Sources: LNA, CRI/T/25/58; Elyan (1960: 3–7); *Basutoland News*, 28.9.58, 27.1.59, 7.7.59; *Moeletsi*, 4.10.58; Judicial Department, *Report 1957–60*, 51/58.

1957/8

1957? Butha-Buthe District. Ward 1: Butha-Buthe.

R v. *Kopano Selomo and nine others.*

The only information that we have about this case is that the preparatory examination was concluded on 13 December 1957 and that all the accused were discharged. The police officer in charge of the prosecution, Inspector Sebolai, was severely criticised for his conduct of the case. His manner was 'high-handed' and he failed to identify a photograph correctly.

Sources: FCO, Box 1176, S 119, note by CP, 13 August 1959; Stutley to Gillett, 18 November 1959, enclosing Stutley to Attorney-General, 16 November 1959.

1957/9

17 October 1957. Molumong plateau, Leribe. Ward 22: Tsikoane.

CRI/T/23/58. *R* v. *Maopelo 'Moko and six others.*

The case for the Crown

Maopelo 'Moko, an ungazetted headman, carried out this murder for Chief Patso, who wanted medicine in order to secure the release of Setlotla Motlotla and his accomplices in another medicine murder case. (See 1957/1.) He was looking for a Mofokeng boy who had not yet had sexual intercourse with a woman. He enlisted the help of several accomplices, including four instructors at an initiation school at Molumong. They brought a boy called Nkuebe to the school's playing area, and then brought out some sticks to frighten him away so that they could chase after him and catch him at some distance from the school. He did run away, but they could not catch him. They tried the same plan with a boy called Shadrack, but he too, it was said, escaped. On the Thursday evening they brought a boy called Molahlehi Mohapi to visit his brother in the school. He too ran away but they ran after him and caught him.

Maopelo 'Moko was not there himself, but by the light of a torch his accomplices pierced Molahlehi in the nostril with a pointed wire, cut his gum, jabbed his penis, and collected the blood. Molahlehi died after being mutilated. His body was washed, soil was smeared on his head to make it appear he had fallen over, and the body was placed under a cliff where it was discovered a day or two later.

The outcome

There were two accomplice witnesses. There was very little independent evidence, but the judge felt confident enough in the evidence of the two accomplices to convict all the accused of murder.

Six of the seven convicted men appealed. The appeal judges observed that the trial judge had relied entirely on the evidence of the two accomplice witnesses and had rejected the defences put forward by the accused. There were two issues, however, on which the accomplices' evidence was open to question unless the evidence for the defence was rebutted. First, the accomplices had said that a Mofokeng victim was required, but neither Nkuebe nor Shadrack was a Mofokeng. Second, the accomplices had said that Shadrack had escaped, whereas both Shadrack and several of the accused had said that he had been caught and brought back to the school. Nkuebe had not been called as a witness, nor had several others whose evidence might have supported the Crown. The Court of Appeal held that these facts should have raised a reasonable doubt in the judge's mind and upheld all six appeals. It recommended that the seventh man convicted, who had not appealed, should be granted a pardon. This, it seems, was done.

Sources: LNA, CRI/T/23/58; *Basutoland News*, 2.9.58 and 17.1.59; Judicial Department, *Report 1957–60*, 44/58.

1957/10

28 December 1957. Ralehlatsa's, Peka, Leribe. Ward 22: Tsikoane.
CRI/T/26/58. *R* v. *Mashophoro Joseph Pholosi and three others*. (Another accused, Mashophoro's sister-in-law, died before the trial began.)

The case for the Crown
Mashophoro Joseph Pholosi was the brother of a headman who had died in 1953. The headman's son and heir, Mohloai Pholosi, was a young man working in Germiston, and another brother was acting as headman for Mohloai. According to Mohloai, who became a witness for the Crown, Mashophoro and his five accomplices committed this murder with his accomplices 'in order that they should become people'. They wanted to be like chiefs, police and Europeans in that people should be afraid when they appeared before them. The victim was a man called Hlalele Mothahaseli.

Hlalele was seized in the evening after a baptismal feast for Mohloai's wife. He was strangled and cut over the head, and his blood was collected in a billy-can by Mashophoro's wife. To prevent identification all the flesh was stripped from the bones and placed in a bag or bags for sugar. At first these bags were kept in a hut, but they gave off such a terrible smell that they were weighted and sunk in a river. Even then the hut gave off a strong smell and so all the roofing was pulled down and removed. The bones were boiled in a three-legged pot and left at the foot of a cliff where they were found about twelve days later. Though all these efforts were made to prevent identification, it was still possible to identify Hlalele through his blankets, hat, shirt, shoes and stick, and even his pass book from the Union with his photograph and his mine badge with the number of the compound where he worked.

The outcome
In the ensuing trial the only accomplice witness was Mashophoro's nephew, Mohloai Pholosi. The judge had certain reservations about Mohloai as a witness, and in the absence of any strong supporting evidence he acquitted the accused.

Sources: LNA, CRI/T/26/58; *Basutoland News*, 7.10.58; *Moeletsi*, 4 and 11.10.58.

1958/1

23 March 1958. Ntlo-Kholo, Maseru. Ward 21: Thaba-Bosiu.
CRI/T/19/59. *R* v. *Makotoko Lechokha Mosalla and twenty-three others*. (Four other accused were discharged at the preparatory examination.)

The case for the Crown
Makotoko Lechokha Mosalla, a gazetted headman, had won several court cases with the help of medicine prepared from human flesh. He was now engaged in a dispute with a neighbouring headman over a certain area of land and he wanted to replenish his horn. He enlisted the help of about eighty accomplices, drawn from seven

different villages, including men from the village of his rival who joined him because they believed he would win his case.

The victim, Mofolo Ramalumane, was chosen because he was 'a hardy person and a brave man'. One of the accomplices, a close friend of Mofolo, was given medicine by Makotoko to rub on him some months in advance in order to make him 'tame'. One Sunday Mofolo visited a 'concubine' at Ntlo-Kholo and was ambushed as he was returning home. About eighty people were there, and they formed a circle around Mofolo. After he had been stripped, and after Makotoko had commended his soul to God, he was cut across the throat, his tongue was pulled out, and his blood was collected in a billy-can. More flesh was cut from the chest and shoulders, the testicles and penis were removed, the intestines were taken out, the waist severed, and the neck cut from the shoulders. Those who were present were invited to help themselves. One accomplice who cut himself a piece of flesh did not know how it was to be used, but was told that if a person was scarified with the medicine prepared from it he would become 'more dignified'. The remains of the body were placed at the foot of a cliff where they were found the following month.

The outcome
Several witnesses were kept in detention for several months, a practice which the defence counsel criticised, but which the Court of Appeal regarded as necessary since they could not be left in the areas controlled by their chiefs and headmen.

Because of the large number of accused the ensuing case lasted twenty-seven days. There were five accomplice witnesses, but two of them defected. There was very little independent evidence, but the judge believed that he could rely on the accomplices and rejected the alibis put forward by the accused and their witnesses. (Crown counsel had been particularly critical of one woman who fingered her rosary in the witness box in order to help her to tell the truth.) Fourteen of the accused were convicted, thirteen of murder and one of being an accessory after the fact. They appealed, but their appeals were dismissed.

Because of constitutional changes, pleas for clemency were now considered by the new Executive Council, not the High Commissioner, and because of this the thirteen who had been convicted of murder spent almost six months in the condemned cell. Their pleas were rejected and they were all hanged. The man convicted as an accessory after the fact was given eight years' IHL.

Sources: LNA, CRI/T/19/59; Elyan (1961: 1–6); *Basutoland News*, 11, 18 and 25.8.59; 1 and 15.9.59, 26.1.60, and 28.6.60; *Leselinyana*, 8.8.59, 19.9.59, 3.10.59; *Moeletsi*, 23.5.59, 1, 8, 22 and 29.8.59; 19 and 26.9.59, 10, 17, 24 and 31.10.59; 7, 14, 21 and 28.11.59; 5.12.59; Ford Rafutho and PS interview, 'Mangoajane Mofolo, 23 May 1999; PS and MM interviews, Matita Makotoko, 3 June 1999, and Sethabathaba Hatahata, 3 June 1999.

1958/2

December 1958. Mokema (?), Maseru. Ward 2: Maama's (?).
R v. 'an adviser to the Headman's Chairman' and six others.

The case for the Crown
Our only information on this case comes from press reports. The victim, Rathuso Kojoane, described as a peasant from Mokema, left home one Monday to look for

sheep and was not seen again. His body was found the following Thursday in a deep donga, lying in shallow water. The instigator of this murder was said to be an 'adviser to the Headman's Chairman' who needed medicine to strengthen himself.

The outcome
The Crown's case failed because the evidence of the single accomplice witness, that Rathuso's skull had been pierced with an awl, was contradicted by the evidence of the post-mortem examination, which discovered no such wound. All the accused were acquitted.

Source: *Basutoland News*, 16 and 23.6.59.

1958/3

1958?
R v. *Mohlaoli Mosebo and six others.*
Our only information on this case is a note by the Commissioner of Police that all the accused were found not guilty by the High Court on 15 June 1959. The police denied allegations of misconduct but acknowledged that one or two of the accused had been detained for long periods before their arrest.

Source: FCO, Box 1176, S 119, note by CP, 13 August 1959.

1959/1 (Case Study 4)

29 May 1959. Tumo's cattle post, Mokhotlong. Ward 14: Mokhotlong. CRI/T/34/60. *R* v. *Matlere Lerotholi and five others.*

The case for the Crown
On Matlere Lerotholi's instructions the alleged murderers induced a young herdboy, Kaiser Mofana, to join them at a disused cattle post on a ridge between the Moremoholo and Bafali streams. They cut his throat and collected the blood in a billy-can, and then cut off his head and some flesh from various parts of his body. The body was deposited beneath some cliffs near Nkuebe's cattle post. Two of the accomplices took the *liretlo* to Matlere's home in Motsitseng. Matlere called in a Zulu doctor, Maqhomisa, who prepared some of the parts for medicine and then scarified Matlere. The head and the blood were taken to Matsieng, where 'Mantšebo needed them for medicine in her conflict with Constantine Bereng Seeiso. Kaiser's body was discovered in the snow four months later.

The outcome
The judge relied mainly on the evidence of Sesemane Kao, who, although not an impressive witness, was supported in part by two other accomplice witnesses. The fourth accomplice witness was the Zulu doctor, but because of the difficulties of mutual understanding it was not possible to rely on what he said. The defence relied on alibis, and Matlere was able to show that on the date named (perhaps wrongly) by one of the accomplice witnesses he was in Maseru. Because of this Matlere was acquitted, but the other five accused were convicted.

The five all appealed. One died while the appeal was pending. The appeal judges upheld the appeal of Makhahlela Lerotholi, since he had been convicted on the basis of Sesemane Kao's evidence and they took the view that the trial judge had given Sesemane too much credence. The remaining three convictions stood, but since the ringleaders had now escaped conviction the sentences were commuted to twelve years each.

Sources: PRO, DO 119/1386, 1387, 1388 (complete court record and official correspondence); Judicial Department, *Report 1957–60*, 34/60; *Moeletsi*, 17 and 24.9.60, 1.10.60, 19.11.60, 3, 10, 17 and 24.12.60; *Leselinyana*, 14.11.59, 1.10.60; *Basutoland News*, 2.8.60, 30.9.60, 1, 8, 15 and 22.11.60, 20.6.61. See also references in endnotes to Case Study 4.

1959/2 (Case Study 4)

5 June 1959. Between Tololi and Tolotsane mountains, Mokhotlong. Ward 14: Mokhotlong.
CRI/T/41/60. *R* v. *Edwin Hantsi Mathaba and two others.*

The case for the Crown
At a preparatory examination in February 1960, three people were accused of murder: Edwin Hantsi Mathaba, a fairly well-educated senior assistant at Storm's store, Mokhotlong, and a close friend of Matlere Lerotholi; Morabaraba Motjama, a doctor; and Ntau Kali. The victim was a three-year-old boy, Motheea Ntjanyana. The motive for the killing was Mathaba's wish to strengthen himself and his stock, and the doctor, Morabaraba, wanted medicine for himself. It was alleged that Morabaraba enticed the boy to Mathaba's hut, where incisions were made and blood collected. The child was then taken up a mountain and left there overnight. On the following day he was still alive and so he was taken further away, to a pass between Tololi and Tolotsane mountains, and left to die there. The body was found by two herdboys on Sunday, 7 June.

The outcome
Morabaraba Motjama and Ntau Kali were convicted in case 1959/1, and so their names were withdrawn and Mathaba remained as the only accused. Sesemane Kao, who was the victim's uncle, was again an accomplice witness, as in 1959/1. Three other accomplice witnesses defected because they had been convicted of murder in that same case. The judge was not prepared to convict on the basis of Sesemane's evidence alone, and so Mathaba was acquitted.

Sources: LNA, CRI/T/41/60; PRO, DO 119/1388, f. 44, Lichtenberg's (prosecuting counsel) opening address to the court; PRO, DO 119/1386, Lichtenberg to Attorney-General, 4 August 1961; *Leselinyana*, 25.7.59, 14.11.59; *Basutoland News*, 10, 17 and 31.1.61. See also references in endnotes to Case Study 4.

1959/3

15 June 1959. Mokae's, Quthing. Ward 16: Quthing.
No criminal proceedings.
A man called Valelo Mbuvusa, aged twenty-eight, disappeared near Mokae's on 15 June 1959: he had been to a feast and a beer-drink. His body was found near Mokae's stream on 18 June 1959. Flesh had been removed from the whole of the face, neck and upper part of the chest. Dr Germond, who carried out the post-mortem, said the injuries to the body could have been caused by animals. The deceased had left a beer-drink late at night, very drunk. He could not be persuaded to stay, saying he was going home. At the inquest held on 30 and 31 July 1959 the District Commissioner recorded a verdict of accidental death. Proceedings were reviewed by the

Legal Secretary, and on 10 September 1959 he directed that no further action was required.

On 17 September, however, information was received that Valelo had been murdered. On 21 September a statement was taken from a herdsman, Motsamai Rakotola, aged twenty-one, who said that he was an accomplice to the murder. He named four other men who had taken part. He believed that the murder had been committed on the orders of headman Mohlori, but he could not substantiate this. Two of the suspected murderers were questioned, but neither admitted to the crime. Further statements showed that the suspects were near the scene of the crime on the night in question. One woman said that on the day following Valelo's disappearance one of the suspects came to their jointly held lands and took some medicine from a bottle, some of which he rubbed on his heart and head and some of which he sprinkled on the wheat.

On 28 October 1959 the man in whose house the feast and beer-drink had been held, 'Mofa Molete, said that when Valelo left he was surrounded and carried by six men to a hut some distance away. He named three of the four mentioned by Motsamai. He said that he followed the group to the hut and saw them remove the flesh. Valelo died there. One of the murderers used an ordinary table-fork to make scratches on the body and 'Mofa heard him say, 'Now the police will think he has been eaten by dogs'. The same man said: 'Now Tšepo will have the flesh of a man, as well as the flesh of a woman and his village will be strong'.

Tšepo was Tšepo Qefata, the deposed adviser of the Ward Chief of Quthing, who was his father. He had previously been involved in case 1953/1.

The woman's flesh referred to was thought to be that of 'Mamofana Tjotja, who had allegedly been the victim of another medicine murder. The case file was found in a clutter of rubbish in the charge office on 10 October 1959. In this second case flesh had been removed from around both eyes of the deceased. The file contained a confession by the deceased's husband, in which he claimed that he alone killed his wife and removed the flesh for medicine. This story, however, was contradicted by a female eyewitness who named five men as murderers. According to her another woman, the 'concubine' of the deceased's husband, was also an eyewitness. This latter woman denied being present, but knew that 'Mamofana had been murdered.

The Quthing police reported that there were other indications pointing to Tšepo Qefata's involvement, but no firm evidence. According to the District Commissioner, Tšepo had been 'behaving very strangely lately – almost like a person in the wilderness seeking "friends" and support for himself and trying to unseat Chief Nkuebe'.

'Mofa's statement was not formally recorded, and in several respects it contradicted that of Motsamai. It was no doubt partly for these reasons that no criminal proceedings were brought.

Sources: FCO, Box 1176, S 119, DC Quthing to GS, 29 and 31 October 1959.

1959/4

c. 23 September 1959. Makhalaneng, Maseru. Ward 17: Rothe etc.
CRI/T/33/60. *R v. Dinizulu Nako and five others.*

The case for the Crown

Dinizulu Nako was chief of Serooeng. He needed medicine because the country had been devastated the previous year by frosts and he wanted to stop that happening again. He also wanted human flesh because he believed that by placing it in the bed of his ailing daughter-in-law he would be able to cure her. The victim, 'Mamoqeneheloa Lekhooa, was chosen because she was elderly.

'Mamoqeneheloa asked one of the accomplices to obtain a *bewys* for her – a certificate to show that she had authority to move the stock shown in it from one place to another. Dinizulu made a deliberate mistake on the *bewys*, and because of this 'Mamoqeneheloa had to come back. As she returned at night, singing, she was ambushed at the Makhalaneng river by Dinizulu's accomplices but not by the chief himself. She was cut around her eyes, and her upper and lower lips were removed. Further cuts were made on the windpipe, an arm, the calves and above the breast. The cutting lasted about twenty minutes. The parts taken were placed in a mug. The body was then placed on the other side of the river.

The outcome

In the subsequent trial there were three accomplice witnesses, whose evidence was supported to a certain extent by an independent witness who observed the presence of the accused at or near the scene of the murder on the day in question. One of the accomplice witnesses, however, was drunk, and his evidence therefore fell away, and there were significant conflicts of evidence between the other two. The judge felt obliged to find the accused not guilty.

According to one newspaper report the verdict was greeted with cheering and shouting. According to another it met with a divided reception, with some clapping and others crying out in astonishment.

Sources: LNA, CRI/T/33/60; *Basutoland News*, 13.12.60; *Moeletsi*, 19.11.60 and 24.12.60.

1959/5

26 September 1959? Phomolong, Butha-Buthe. Ward 10: Makhoakhoeng
No criminal proceedings, it seems.
In October 1959 the District Commissioner, Butha-Buthe, reported a suspected medicine murder in the area of headman Hlakametsa Ntlobo under Chief Tumane Matela in the area of Makhoakhoeng. The deceased, Motšoane Raposholi, was called from his home at Mabothile in Leribe District, ostensibly to arrange bridewealth between himself and a woman called 'Malenka. He was last seen alive on 26 September 1959 at 'Malenka's home. His body was discovered by some herdboys in a poplar plantation. The bare skull was lying about four paces from the trunk. The flesh of the neck, right shoulder, chest and back was missing, also a large portion of the bowels. The lower part of the body, covered by trousers, was intact apart from decomposition. According to the Medical Officer who carried out the post-mortem, the body was so decomposed that he could not say with certainty whether the injuries had been inflicted before or after death. Most of the skeleton was missing and the remaining ribs had suffered fractures. The District Commissioner reported that from preliminary reports it would seem this murder was connected with forthcoming elections. He had already been informed that

headman Hlakametsa Ntlobo had been stopping his people from attending election meetings and he had reported him to his Ward Chief.

It would appear that no criminal proceedings were brought.

Source: FCO, Box 1176, S 119, DC Butha-Buthe to GS, 17 October 1959.

1959/6

Reported 28 November 1959. Molumong, Mokhotlong. Ward 14: Mokhotlong. No criminal proceedings, it seems.

Our only information about this case comes from a newspaper report. A ten-year-old girl, a descendant of Mapheleba Ntho Mokeke, disappeared from Molumong. Three days later her body was found near the Senqu (Orange) river, on the Tlokoeng side, at Koatake's, with all the flesh below the waist removed, and with the marrow removed from the bones.

Source: *Leselinyana*, 28.11.59.

1960/1

May 1960. Sefikeng?, Berea. Ward 4: 'Mamathe's. No criminal proceedings, it seems.

Our only information about this case comes from a newspaper report. This reads as follows:

> The deceased, Jone Kharafunyane of Mahleke's village at Masoeling, had been asked by Mr Thomas Lillane to drive his livestock to be slaughtered at the St Michael RC Mission parish in Maseru district, for a matrimonial feast in May this year. Unfortunately he gave in on the journey on account of being pressed by close-fitting boots which he wore off [*sic*] and carried, while his mate went on to avoid the animals trespassing into the lands which closely border on one another. His mate who outpaced him spent the night at the appointed village; when the women going with them who were coming after, did not see him at all even on the same footpath they began to suspect. This month, his head was found on the footpath early in the morning by the female churchgoers. Sub-Chieftainess Mampoi Moeketsi Masupha of Sefikeng then reported the incident to the police. On the same day, found also at different places, were his legs from the knees downwards, and reported also to the police officers, whose members are not yet successful in tracing the body. The local community take it for granted that the finding of the man's parts in different places is the undoubtful fact [*sic*] that the missing parts are hidden for replenishing the medicine.

Source: *Basutoland News*, 12.7.60.

1961/1

Reported 4 August 1961. Popa, Mokhotlong. Ward 11: Tlokoeng.
R v. *Mohlabakobo Sekonyela, Lerato Rafolatsane and fourteen others.*
In March 1961 the District Commissioner, Mokhotlong, reported on a preparatory examination in a medicine murder case in which Chief Mohlabakobo, Chieftainess Lerato Rafolatsane and fourteen others had to be discharged when five accomplice witnesses defected. There was fairly reliable information, he wrote, that these witnesses had been 'got at' by Chief Matlere Lerotholi with the assistance of the Paramount

Chief's representative who was purportedly working with the police. In August, E. K. W. Lichtenberg, who had acted as Crown counsel, gave a similar report, adding: 'This type of thing goes on all the time in Mokhotlong, the district with, I think, the highest frequency of ritual murders in Basutoland'. The alleged victim was a boy called Ntho from Molumong. The motive for the alleged murder is not known.

Chieftainess Lerato had been acquitted in another medicine murder case (1948/8).

The outcome
All the accused were discharged.

Sources: FCO, Box 1168, S 197G, DC Mokhotlong to GS, 30 March 1961; PRO, DO 119/1386, Lichtenberg to Attorney-General, 4 August 1961; PS and KS interview, Nkherepe Molefe, 24 May 1999; PS interview, Elliot Teboho Morojele, 27 May 1999.

1961/2

6 August 1961. Moses' Nek, Mokhotlong. Ward 11: Tlokoeng.
CRI/T/8/63. *R* v. *Vincent Mothibe Rakaibe and eight others.* (Another accused died before the trial in the High Court.)

The case for the Crown
Vincent Rakaibe was a trader. He had begun life as a hawker and gone on to own two shops, one at Likhameng in the Mokhotlong District, and one at Seetsa's in the Leribe District. It was said that he needed medicine to improve his business. The victim was a man called Sebaka 'Moloki. Among Rakaibe's accomplices were Sebaka's brother, his father-in-law and his brother-in-law.

Sebaka's father-in-law, Mofana Lehlehla, agreed to give him up for five blankets, five pairs of riding breeches, a pair of boots, a shirt and £50. At the time of the trial he was still expecting payment. Sebaka was away in Johannesburg at the time, but when he returned Mofana informed Rakaibe and the plans for the murder were made. Mofana sent Sebaka to fetch his wife from Tsime in the Butha-Buthe District, and arranged for him to be ambushed on the way at Moses' Nek. When he was attacked Sebaka ran away. One of the accomplices hit him with a stone and knocked him down. He was then hit with a stick on the head and taken to some ruined huts. He was unconscious and breathing feebly. He was undressed. Rakaibe stabbed him under the chin and took out his tongue. He cut flesh from the shoulders and chest and took out the lungs, the left eye, the left ear and the left cheek. He cut the bridge of the nose and part of the mouth. All these pieces were placed in a white bucket, and blood was collected in a billy-can.

That night the body was taken to Rakaibe's house. It was then wrapped up and put on a horse, and three men travelled with it for several days before disposing of it near 'Moteng in the Butha-Buthe District. It was found on 15 August.

The outcome
It was almost two years before the accused were brought to trial. There were five accomplice witnesses, but the main feature of the trial was Rakaibe's elaborate alibi, for he claimed that he was on a trading journey from 5 to 15 August and was able to produce receipts and other written documentation to prove it. He was therefore acquitted. The judge was sure that some of the other eight accused had taken part in

the murder, but it was difficult to distinguish who was guilty and who was not. All the accused were therefore acquitted, with the judge warning them that some of them were very lucky and that they would not be so lucky if they murdered anyone else.

Sources: LNA, CRI/T/8/63; *Moeletsi*, 11, 18 and 25.5.63.

1961/3

c. 29 August 1961. Ha Ntšebele, Mokhotlong. Ward 14: Mokhotlong.
CRI/T/65/62. *R v. Mothoasebaka Letsie, Rammone and four others.*

The case for the Crown

Mothoasebaka Letsie was a gazetted headman and Rammone seems to have been an ungazetted headman. One of the accomplices testified later that Mothoasebaka wanted to kill a person in order to strengthen Rammone. The victim was a woman called 'Mamojabeng Selikane.

'Mamojabeng went to a marriage feast at Chief Mafana Morojele's. She left very late, after sunset, and she was then seized by the accused. She was gagged and stabbed in the head with a tethering iron. Blood was collected and flesh cut from the mouth. The body was left in a stream, where it was discovered a day or two later.

The outcome

In the trial that followed there were two accomplice witnesses, but, in spite of strong independent evidence, there were such serious discrepancies between them that the judge concluded that it would be dangerous to convict. All the accused were acquitted.

Sources: LNA, CRI/T/65/62; LNA, loose file of High Court rolls; *Moeletsi*, 16 and 23.3.63.

1961/4

1961. 'Mamathe's, Berea. Ward 4: 'Mamathe's.
R v. Jonathan Ntlama and fifteen others.

The case for the Crown

Jonathan Ntlama was the gazetted chief of Raletšoane's. He had formerly been a clerk in a Basuto Court, and was an assistant adviser to the Ward Chief, 'Mamathe, Gabashane Masupha's widow. In 1960 he was nominated to the Basutoland National Council by the Paramount Chief. The victim was one of his subjects, a man called Fono Rampo. No motive for the murder is known.

The outcome

Our main source of information about this case is a press report in January 1962 that a preparatory examination was held, attended by a crowd of more than 700 people. It would seem that the Attorney-General decided not to proceed with the prosecution, since two months later Jonathan Ntlama was contributing to a debate on medicine murder in the Basutoland National Council and alleging that the police had applied pressure on people to incriminate him.

According to Chief Lebihan Masupha, interviewed in 1999, it was believed that Fono Rampo had shot himself accidentally, that there was no firm evidence of medicine murder, and that Jonathan Ntlama was suspected only because of his association with 'Mamathe.

Sources: *Basutoland News*, 2.1.62; *Proc. BNC, Legislative Council Debates*, pp. 188–92, speech of Jonathan Ntlama, 16 March 1962; CM and KS interview, Lebihan Masupha, 21 May 1999.

1962/1

5 January 1962. Ha Motšoane, Leribe. Ward 8: Leribe.
CRI/T/2/64. *R* v. *Ntitsoe Motlotla, Malefane Thamahe and at least eight others.*

The case for the Crown
Ntitsoe Motlotla was the chairman of Jobo Motšoane, the chief of Pitsi's Nek. He was involved in a dispute over land with Moramosheshe Pholo, who had been working in South Africa for a long time but had now returned and was claiming the land which Ntitsoe was tilling. Ntitsoe decided to kill him for medicine. Malefane Thamahe, the headman of Chief Jobo's village, had always said that he wanted a medicine horn, and so he was persuaded to join in and to provide the accomplices.

Moramosheshe was waylaid as he was returning home in the dark after a feast. He was struck on the head, gagged, and had his hands tied with his own belt. He was then taken on horseback up a mountainside to a cave. He was stabbed in the armpit and blood was collected. He was still alive, and so he was stabbed on the head. The body was taken some distance below the cave, and blood was smeared on a rock by the cave to give the impression that he had fallen from the cave down the cliff. His hat was left between the cave and the body.

One of the accomplices, a doctor, had been asked to prepare charms so that the crime would not come to light. He went to the scene of the murder carrying a bowl of medicine and an ox-tail. After the body had been taken away, he sprinkled the medicine over the accused. For this service Ntitsoe and Malefane promised him that a piece of land which had been taken away would be restored to him.

The body was found three days after the murder. A post-mortem was conducted on the spot. The body was decomposed, and full of worms and maggots. The ribs were broken, and this would have been consistent with a fall from the cliff.

The doctor who had been promised the restoration of his land, and a poor man who had been promised a cow, both became Crown witnesses because the promises had not been fulfilled. The police carried out searches, and various medicines, horns and weapons were found in the homes of several of the accused.

The outcome
In the trial that followed there were two accomplice witnesses, the doctor and the poor man who had not been given his cow, but there was no independent evidence, and so the Crown withdrew its prosecution on the third day. The judge agreed with this decision, and pointed out that the medical evidence had not established that a murder had been committed, and insofar as the doctor conducting the post-mortem had not found any wound on the head it was inconsistent with the evidence of the accomplice witnesses. All the accused were acquitted.

Sources: LNA, CRI/T/2/64; Scobie (1965: 48); CM interviews, Basia Bakane, Lekhaole Bakane and 'Mapuleng Bakane, 19 January 1998.

1962/2

9 February 1962. Masenkane, Quthing. Ward 16: Quthing.
CRI/T/69/62. *R* v. *Tšiu Lethola and eight others.*

The case for the Crown

Tšiu Lethola was the ungazetted headman of Masenkane. He was engaged in a dispute over land with Mahlomola, the headman of the neighbouring village of Mphaki. Mahlomola had twice been successful in the Basuto Courts, and Tšiu was granted what was perhaps an invalid order in an administrative court annulling the judgement against him. He wanted a child of Mahlomola's family so that he could bury the flesh on the disputed land. He held a meeting of his followers, and everyone agreed that that was the right course to take. Seven of his accomplices lived in his own village. Two lived in Mahlomola's village: one, however, had been the main witness for Tšiu in the dispute over the land, and the other, a woman, was on bad terms with Mahlomola because he had objected to her love affair with his grandson.

The victim was a little girl aged two, 'Matšeliso Letsie, Mahlomola's granddaughter. With the help of the woman who lived in Mahlomola's village, the girl was kidnapped when she went blackberrying with other children. She was then kept in the home of another accomplice, a woman called 'Malefu. On 9 February Tšiu and his accomplices gathered at 'Malefu's, and there were only two adult inhabitants of the village who were not there. The child was held on the ground on a sack. Her private parts were cut off and the blood was collected. The mouth was cut down to the neck so that the tongue could be cut out, and it was at this point that the child died. The right eye was cut out, then flesh from the forehead, then the left eye, and then flesh from the buttocks. The wounds were cauterized with a hot iron. After the murder the women smeared the hut and cleaned the village, which consisted of about fifteen huts.

The body was taken to the junction of two streams, and later to a mountainside. The child's disappearance had been reported to the local chief at once, but he had taken no action. As the judge pointed out, if he had sent out a search party at once the child might still have been alive. The body was discovered by a herdsman's dog three days after the murder. It was five kilometres away from the child's home at Mahlomola's, and the mountain was too steep for her to have climbed it by herself.

The outcome

In the trial that followed there were six accomplice witnesses. One of them, 'Malefu, claimed that she had been forced to make her statement by the police and by Setho Letsie, Mahlomola's son (who would later be the Minister for Public Works, Posts and Telegraphs in the first Basotho administration under self-governmment). But the others, it seems, were credible witnesses. Although there was some independent evidence, relating, for example, to the presence of the child in the village of the accused before she was murdered, and to the smearing and cleaning of the village after the murder, the judge treated the case as one which rested entirely on the evidence of the accomplice witnesses. Since he regarded them as trustworthy, he convicted eight of the accused, four men and four women, acquitting only the woman who lived in Mahlomola's village on the ground that when she abducted the child she might not have known that a murder was intended.

All eight appealed on the grounds that the convictions were against the weight of the evidence and that the judge had not properly applied the principles governing accomplice evidence. The appeals were dismissed. The four men were hanged. The four women had their sentences commuted to twelve years' IHL.

Sources: LNA, CRI/T/69/62; *Basutoland News*, 5.3.63 and 17.12.63; *Moeletsi*, 16 and 23.2.63.

1962/3

May 1962. Tlhaku's, Quthing. Ward 16: Quthing.
CRI/T/42/65. *R* v. *Motloang Monoane and seven others*. (Another accused was discharged at the preparatory examination.)

The case for the Crown
The instigator of this murder was Makhakhe, a café-owner, but he died before the preparatory examination was held. He wanted medicine to strengthen himself and his business. The victim was a woman called Lisetse Monoane. She was mentally unwell and was being treated by Makhakhe's wife, who was a doctor. Motloang Monoane, Accused No. 1, was Lisetse's husband, and it was suggested that he might have thought, in view of her illness, that her death would be for the good of the community. There was, however, no evidence for this.

Lisetse was led out by her husband from the hut where she was sleeping, and she was taken to a stream. She was knocked down, and then extensively mutilated: her thighs, the lower part of her abdomen, one of her breasts, her left arm, her liver and tongue were all cut out. The body was buried by the side of the Qhoali river, but two or three months later it was dug up and put in a field on the other side of the river in order to cast suspicion on the chief there, Soko Tlhaku.

In the meantime Makhakhe prepared some medicine from the flesh that had been taken, and the bones were ground and thrown into the foundations of the wall of the kraal, which was then rebuilt.

The body was found in July, but because of delays in the investigation it was May 1965 before the accused were arrested and August 1965 before legal proceedings were started.

The outcome
There were four accomplice witnesses. As the judge pointed out, it was difficult to see why one was treated as an accomplice, since she merely observed Lisetse being taken away from her hut. One of the other accomplices was unreliable, but the remaining two were in broad agreement with each other. Two of the accused were acquitted and six convicted. All six appealed, but their appeals were dismissed. The judge recommended that the sentences of five of the accused should be commuted to fifteen years' IHL. Presumably this recommendation was accepted and the sixth person, the victim's husband, was hanged.

Sources: LNA, CRI/T/42/65; *Basutoland News*, 7.12.65; *Moeletsi*, 1.1.66.

1963/1

March 1963. Makoae's, Quthing. Ward 16: Quthing.
R v. *'Mathabang Molapo and sixteen others*. (Two other accused, it seems, were discharged at the preparatory examination, and two more died while awaiting trial.)

The case for the Crown

'Mathabang Molapo appears to have been a headman. The victim was a young woman called 'Makikine Masike. Her husband had been among those accused, but he was one of the two who had died while awaiting trial. Various reasons were given for the murder: that medicine was needed for a certain Chief Soko, who wanted to strengthen his position; that it was needed to strengthen the crops; and that 'Mathabang Molapo wanted to strengthen a shop which she had just bought.

'Makikine was lured away by a group of women, who handed her over to the male accomplices. She was stabbed to death and then mutilated, and the women who were still present were ordered to drink her blood 'so as to keep their mouths shut'. Her body was placed at the bottom of a cliff, with the legs broken, so as to give the impression of accidental death. Her bloomers were placed a few metres away.

The body was found two days later, and the investigating police officer was told by 'Makikine's relatives that she used to carry her bloomers around when she was drunk. Since both the police officer and the local chief were both satisfied that death was due to natural causes, the body was buried without a post-mortem examination being held. Five months later it was exhumed, but still no examination was held, presumably because it was at such an advanced stage of decomposition.

There were further delays, and in the end it was two years after the murder that the case was brought to court.

The outcome

In spite of the lack of corroborative evidence, the judge was impressed by the four accomplice witnesses and fifteen of the accused were convicted. Eight (seven men and one woman) were sentenced to death, and seven (four men and three women) were given various sentences of IHL. All fifteen appealed unsuccessfully. Five of the eight sentenced to death had their sentences commuted.

Sources: LNA, High Court and Appeal Court judgements; *Basutoland News*, 23.11.65; *Lesotho Times*, 4.6.65; *Moeletsi*, 12.6.65 and 11.12.65.

1963/2

15 July 1963. About eight kilometres from Maseru, Maseru District (?). Ward 3: Majara's.
No criminal proceedings, it seems.
Our only information about this case is the following newspaper report:

> A man from Majara's Ward, five miles from Maseru, was reported missing at the Maseru police office on 15th July. It is believed that he was invited to conduct the music and dancing at a circumcision school near the Berea/Maseru boundary. A search was instigated and his mutilated body was found in a donga near the school.

Source: *Basutoland News*, 6.8.63.

1963/3

October? 1963. 'Mamathe's, Berea. Ward 4: 'Mamathe's.
No criminal proceedings, it seems.
Our only information about this case comes from the following newspaper report:

> Ritual Murder. The body of an old woman with an eye removed and flesh cut from the calf of her leg was found in Chieftainess 'Mamathe's village. The woman

was identified as 'Matsietso Mahlabe, the victim of a ritual murder. The police are investigating.

Source: *Basutoland News*, 5.11.63.

1963/4

October/November? 1963. Lebese Masopha's village or Qopo, Berea?
No criminal proceedings, it seems.
Our only information about this case is the following newspaper report:

> Another Ritual Murder? The badly mutilated body of Daniel Lekeli (48) from Chief Lebese Masopha's village was found at the foot of a cliff. Both his feet, his right arm, part of his brain and flesh cut from various parts of his body were missing. There was no trace of any blood anywhere. It is understood that the deceased and his wife had visited his wife's parents at Qopo.

Source: *Basutoland News*, 12.11.63.

1964/1

c. 18 January 1964. Nqtho's [*sic*], Berea (?).
No criminal proceedings, it seems.
Our only information about this case is the following newspaper report:

> Another Ritual Murder? Jeremiah Oetsi (69) of Nqtho's village about one and a half miles from the principal village was found dead in his bed on the night of 19th January. The deceased's eyelids had some cuts, possibly made with a sharp instrument, and some parts of his body were missing. The body was taken to the TY [Teyateyaneng] mortuary for post mortem. The police are investigating.

Source: *Basutoland News*, 28.1.64.

1964/2

4 April 1964. Near border with Berea District, Maseru. Ward 4: 'Mamathe's.
R v. *ten men from Thupa-Kubu.*
Our information about this case comes from two articles in the *Basutoland News*. Ten men from the Thupa-Kubu sub-ward in the Basutoland mountains, 'three chiefs, two teachers, a manager of a big trading station, a trader and three others', were arrested in June 1966 as suspects for the 'ritual murder' of Liau Taleng, a sixty-two-year-old night watchman at a trading store. He disappeared on 4 April 1964 and his body was later found in a forest. 'Evidence of a ritual murder was discovered.' One of the accused, Thulo Nketjane, who was employed by Hertig Mpeta, the Principal of the Thupa-Kubu Lower Primary School, died in prison.

Thirteen Crown witnesses gave evidence at the preparatory examination, which was adjourned to 15 August 1966.

Source: *Basutoland News*, 28.6.66 and 9.8.66.

1965/1

March 1965? Kepi Motiane's, Berea. Ward 4: 'Mamathe's.
No criminal proceedings, it seems.
There are two reports in the *Basutoland News* which appear to refer to the same case.
On 16 March 1965 it was reported that the body of an unknown woman had been

found at the foot of a twenty metre-high cliff near Teyateyaneng. 'The body, which was naked except for a skirt twisted round her neck, was minus the right arm and flesh was cut from the left arm. Bloodstained stones were found about 150 yards from the body. The body was found by Headman Kepi Motiane whose village adjoins Teyateyaneng. The police are investigating.'

In a later report the victim was identified as 'Mantšo Peane Moshoeshoe, a woman of twenty-five from the village of Chieftainess 'Mamathe Gabashane Masupha who had been working in Teyateyaneng.

Sources: *Basutoland News*, 16.3.65 and 11.5.65.

1965/2

Reported 1965. A few kilometres from Teyateyaneng, Berea. Ward 4: 'Mamathe's. No criminal proceedings, it seems.

The body of 'a poor old blind woman', the skull shattered, was found at the bottom of a cliff, close to a village a few kilometres away from Teyateyaneng. A headman was in trouble and needed medicine. He and 'some tribesmen' were arrested. It is not known whether or not they were brought to trial.

Source: Swanson (1965: 55–6).

1965/3

Reported 1965.

The victim in this case was a young girl. Donald Swanson claimed to have seen those arrested for the murder, among whom was 'a good-looking young Basuto ... in his middle twenties. His European shirt and trousers, though grubby, were expensive and in good taste. Slung about his shoulders was a particularly gaudy British-made Basuto blanket, bedecked, of all things, with a pattern of aeroplanes against a background of azure blue'. He was said to be the son of a wealthy chief who had been educated at one of the best Mission schools in Basutoland and then at Fort Hare. He was 'very bright' and had been studying medicine, but after three years he had got bored and had returned to Basutoland. When cutting up the girl he wore the surgical mask and gown which he had worn at university and used the scalpels and tools which he had used in the dissecting room. He told Swanson that it was necessary to kill the girl. If Swanson's account is correct, this is almost the only case in which a person confessed to having carried out a medicine murder.

Source: Swanson (1965: 56–7).

1965/4

August 1965? Near Pilot Project, Berea. Ward 4: 'Mamathe's. No criminal proceedings, it seems.

Our only information about this case is the following report in the *Basutoland News*:

> Ritual Murder. Villagers hearing the screams of 'Mapontso Tlotto [*sic*], a middle-aged woman, near the Pilot Project, were afraid to go to her aid. Her badly mutilated body was found on the doorstep of her hut. It would appear that some parts of her brain were also removed. A chief has been arrested in connection with the murder.

Source: *Basutoland News*, 7.9.65.

1965/5

15 August 1965. Area of Lejone's, Leribe. Ward 8: Leribe
R v. *Thabang Moloi and four others.*

The case for the Crown
Thabang Moloi does not appear to have been a headman, and all five accused were subjects of Chief Lejone. The reason for the murder is not known. The victim, a man called Pakane Mohale, was chosen because he was a Letebele.

Between 12 and 15 August Pakane attended several beer parties in and around his village. On the evening of 15 August he was in the company of Thabang Moloi and his accomplices at the home of one of the accused. They put a rope round his neck and threw him to the ground. They cut him on the forehead and collected blood in a basin. Then they broke his neck, and the wound on his forehead was washed with hot water. The body was taken some distance away to the cliffs of Sekoko.

The doctor who conducted the post-mortem noted the wound on the forehead but said that it was impossible to determine the cause of death.

The outcome
In the ensuing trial there were two accomplice witnesses, but they had been kept at police quarters over a long period and this raised a serious doubt in the judge's mind about their reliability. There were also several discrepancies in their evidence. All the accused were acquitted.

Source: *Moeletsi*, 10 and 17.9.66.

1965/6

c. 25 October 1965. Makhoroane's village, Berea. Ward 6: Koeneng and Mapoteng. CRI/T/51/69. *R* v. *Sabilone Nalana and twenty-four others.* (Another accused was discharged at the preparatory examination. Another accomplice, who played a leading part in the murder, died before the preparatory examination was held.)

The case for the Crown
Sabilone Nalana wanted a person for medicine because his business was not doing well. He held several meetings with his accomplices beforehand and a 'committee' was formed to arrange the murder. The victim, Setholane Lekhoele, was a man in his late thirties.

One evening, when Setholane was drinking in a beer hall at Masakeng, Sabilone and his accomplices went in and seized him. Some boys who were there were chased off. Setholane was tied up, placed on an ox-skin and gagged. He was then scalped and his private parts were removed. His chest was opened and his lungs, heart and liver were taken out. His right eye was removed, then his upper arms, and then flesh from his thighs. His head was cut off, and the body was cut in half at the waist. A woman came in for some beer, and was given some and sent out. The flesh cut off was collected in two sacks, and the body was removed to a cave. The women who were there squeezed the contents out of the intestines. Some of the accused were told to put the bones into sacks, and they had to approach the bones 'in a stooping manner'. By that time it was early in the morning, and the accomplices were told to disperse. They returned in the evening and took the sacks, went towards Setholane's villgage, and emptied the sacks of bones near some flat rocks. Once again they had to stoop as they went.

The body was found within a week of the murder, and the witnesses made statements within two to three months. But it was 1969 before the accused were brought to trial.

The outcome

There were two accomplice witnesses, but their evidence 'bristled' with inconsistencies and all the accused were acquitted. They might have been lucky, the judge said. If so, they should not ascribe this to powerful medicine, but to the fact that they lived in a country with a civilised system of law. 'Lesotho is an independent state and I am proud to serve as its Chief Justice. There is however no place in this country for misguided people who think that by killing a person they can reach anything. My advice to you citizens of Lesotho is that if anyone approaches you to take part in this sort of thing ... go to the police immediately. Then ... you will be able to hold your heads high and talk about independence and voting rights.'

Source: LNA, CRI/T/51/69.

1966/1

Early 1966? Leribe District.

Our only evidence on this case is an entry in the diary of Dr Bertha Hardegger under 21 May 1966. She rode with a white policeman to a remote place where a ritual murder had taken place. The white postmaster had been suspected and was detained for several weeks, and his wife suffered under false accusations.

Source: Hardegger (1987: 215).

1966/2

Reported 31 May 1966. Berea District.

No criminal proceedings, it seems.

According to a press report in May 1966 the victim in this case was a man called Tšepo Poloki, whose body was found with an eye and ear missing. One person gave himself up to the police and another suspect was being detained at Teyateyaneng.

Source: *Basutoland News*, 31.5.66.

1966/3

July 1966? Leribe District.

All that is known of this case is an entry in the diary of Dr Bertha Hardegger under 21 July 1966. She read through the evidence of 'our new medicine murder', apparently at the police station at Leribe. According to the evidence it was a clear case of murder. Blood had been collected in a basin, and many people were involved.

Source: Hardegger (1987: 219).

1966/4

Reported 2 September 1966. Maseru District?

No criminal proceedings, it seems.

Our only information on this case is a short newspaper report on 2 September 1966 headed 'Maseru'. A woman's foot had been found by herdboys, and the police had found further limbs and clothing in the same vicinity. 'Ritual murder is suspected.'

Source: *The World*, 2.9.66.

NOTES

INTRODUCTION

1. Jones (1951: 15–18, 64–5).
2. Jones (1951: 2–3, 15, 40).
3. PRO, DO 119/1380, Baring to Gordon Walker, 28 November 1950; *CAR 1949*, p. 55; *CAR 1950*, p. 61.
4. Gunther (1957: 555–6); Packer (1953: 99–103, 108). See also Interlude.
5. H. Dieterlen (1896: 263–6).
6. The views of some protagonists in this debate are explored in the Conclusion.
7. Jones (1951, Appendix A: 79–103).
8. We have also recorded numerous cases of suspected medicine murder in the period since independence, but very few of these were brought to court, as indicated above, and largely for this reason the evidence for the period since 1966 is much more sparse. Accordingly, we have not attempted to summarise these cases here nor to analyse their incidence nor significance.

CHAPTER 1

1. PRO, DO 35/1172, Y701/1/10.
2. PRO, DO 119/1380, Baring's interim comments on the Jones report, drafted by W. A. W. Clark, addressed to Patrick Gordon Walker, Secretary of State for Commonwealth Relations, and forwarded to London 10 June 1950.
3. These statements are cited in Machobane (1990: 72).
4. Lagden (1901: 261).
5. For later expressions of this view see, for example, Ntsu Mokhehle's articles in *Mochochonono*, 5 April and 14 June 1947; articles and letters in *Moeletsi*, 21 January 1947, 2 September 1947, 9 December 1947, 24 and 31 January 1950; and *Proc. (44) BNC*, vol. II, pp. 411–23, debate on 5 October 1948.
6. Pim (1935: 11, 77).
7. PRO, DO 119/1382, Mark Photane, 'Medicine Murders', enclosure with Arrowsmith to Turnbull, 12 September 1953, p. 18.
8. Bryce (1900: 357).
9. Quoted in E. Smith (1926: 167).
10. Headlam (1931, vol. I: 163, 169).
11. E. Smith (1926: 167). For the attitude of 'philanthropists' generally, see Spence (1968: 14).
12. Lagden (1909, vol. II: 642).
13. Pim (1935: 191–2); see also Murray (1981: 14).
14. Pim (1935: 34).
15. *CAR 1898–9*, cited in Murray (1981: 14); Lagden (1909, vol. II: 642); see also Pim (1935: 193).
16. Pim (1935: 55). This was the position in 1932–3.

17. Hodgson and Ballinger (1931: 9); Perham (1935: 124); Murray (1981: 24).
18. Pim (1935: 45); *Basutoland Census 1946* (Basutoland Government 1951: 22).
19. Weisfelder (1974: 140).
20. Bardill and Cobbe (1985: 30).
21. Weisfelder (1974: 137).
22. The Fund was set up in 1927: see Pim (1935: 103). Before this a system of grants was in operation.
23. Perham (1974: 129).
24. Gamble (1935: 55).
25. Lagden (1909, vol. II: 620, also 626–7 and 628–9).
26. Cited in Machobane (1990: 115).
27. Paramount Chief Letsie II's metaphor, quoted in Machobane (1990: 121).
28. For example the petition of Paramount Chief Letsie II and others to King Edward VII in 1909, quoted in Lagden (1909, vol. II: 621); the address by Paramount Chief Griffith and his chiefs to the High Commissioner, Lord Buxton, in 1919, referred to in *Pitso of Basuto Nation at Maseru, May 23, 1919: speech of His Excellency the High Commissioner Viscount Buxton* (n.d.: 6); and *Basutoland News*, 25 December 1951.
29. *Royal Colonial Institute: Report of Proceedings XXXII*, 1900–01, pp. 254–84, Proceedings of the Seventh Ordinary Meeting, 14 May 1901, which was addressed by Sir Godfrey Lagden; Perham (1935: 119).
30. Milner to Chamberlain, 17 August 1897, in Headlam (1931, vol. I: 158); Fincher (1918: 811–16).
31. E. Smith (1926: 167).
32. Pim (1935: 5–7).
33. For a discussion of these factors, see Bardill and Cobbe (1985: 24–7).
34. Hailey (1953, part V: 67); Spence (1968: 18); Murray (1981: 18).
35. Machobane (1990: 122).
36. Brookes (1927: 106); see also Gocking (1997: 72).
37. Burman (1981: 75–90).
38. Ashton (1952: 221); Edgar (1987: 12–14).
39. For example, LNA, S3/22/2/1, Clifford to Sturrock, 8 October 1928, cited in Edgar (1987: 3); Weisfelder (1974: 98).
40. For example, the difficulties of the Baphuthi under Mocheko in 1899 and following years: see Machobane (1990: 97–9).
41. Ashton (1952: 217, 221); Hamnett (1975: 88).
42. Ashton (1952: 217); Jones (1951: 41); Hailey (1953, part V: 97, 135).
43. Hailey (1953, part V: 73); Machobane (1990: 82).
44. Edgar (1987: 7). For the Lekhotla la Bafo generally, see Edgar's book. There are also detailed records in FCO, Box 1178, S 34.
45. Weisfelder (1974: 152).
46. Edgar (1987: 26).
47. See, for example, Weisfelder (1969: 397–409); Edgar (1987: 25–6); and an article by Edwin Leanya of the BPA in *Leselinyana*, 8 March 1954.
48. Hailey (1953, part V: 73); Machobane (1990: 130); Edgar (1987: 7).
49. Pim (1935: 47); Jones (1951: 41); Hailey (1953, part V: 81); Ashton (1952: 212–3). The chiefs' huge American cars attracted much attention in the 1930s and the 1940s and are still well remembered.
50. Jones (1951: 39, 41–2); Ashton (1952: 207); Bardill and Cobbe (1985: 21).
51. RHL, MSS Afr. S1002, Pim Papers, African Papers, 1930–53, pp. 447–51, Louis Mabille to HC, undated, enclosed with Mabille to Armstrong, 18 October 1934; Pim (1935: 42, 50–2); Jones (1951: 41); Hailey (1953, part V: 81);

Weisfelder (1974: 96–7); Machobane (1990: 160–2); Edgar (1987: 10–11).

52. Ashton (1952: 220).
53. Jones (1951: 35–6); Sanders (1975: 58, 72).
54. Cited in Pim (1935: 48).
55. The exact number of Ward Chiefs was not always certain and varied over time. Machobane (1990: 82) reckoned that there were about twenty in 1910; Hailey (1953, part V: 74–5) said there were thirty-two wards, some of them very small, in 1938. Ashton (1952: 186) said that in 1939 the country was divided into eighteen districts (his term for wards), varying in size from 30,000 to 130,000 inhabitants. The *Explanatory Memorandum to the Basuto National Treasury* (1944, p. 48) listed twenty-four persons to be recognised as Ward Chiefs for the purpose of assessing salaries. In 1948 ten Ward Chiefs were picked out for the honour of being Principal Chiefs (Ashton 1952: 188). The *Basutoland Census 1956* (Basutoland Government 1958: 75, 80) listed twenty-five wards. The 1960 Constitution recognised twenty-two Principal and Ward Chiefs. The 1993 Constitution recognised all twenty-two as Principal Chiefs (and *ex officio* members of Senate).
56. See, for example, Pim (1935: 48, 177–8, 182); Ashton (1952: 203); Machobane (1990: 97, 99).
57. Casalis (1861: 214); Ashton (1952: 220).
58. Cited in Machobane (1990: 164–5).
59. *Proc. (44) BNC*, vol. I, p. 62, speech of I. Moqakasa, 22 September 1948; see also Hamnett (1975: 87).
60. Jingoes (1975: 170).
61. PRO, DO 119/1380, Baring to Gordon Walker, 28 November 1950; PRO, DO 35/4025, 'Basutoland Notes' attached to C. G. L. S. [Cecil Syers] to Patrick Gordon Walker, 6 January 1949, p. 1; Edwards (1955); Weisfelder (1974: 99, 109).
62. LNA, S3/22/2/1, Clifford to Sturrock, 8 October 1928, cited in Edgar (1987: 3).
63. Hailey (1953, part V: 66); Machobane (1990: 168–71).
64. HC to Secretary of State for the Colonies, 6 October 1924, cited in Machobane (1990: 172).
65. Amery (1953: 415).
66. LNA, S3/16A/5/2, memorandum by Sturrock, 8 February 1928, cited in Machobane (1990: 178).
67. Pim (1935: 26–8); Hailey (1953, part V: 68).
68. Proclamation No. 20 of 1930: see Crawford (1969–70: 478).
69. The most damning criticism was that of Hodgson and Ballinger (1931); see also Barnes (1932) and M. B. Smith (c. 1937).
70. Pim (1935: 48–9, 180–1).
71. Hailey (1953, part V: 81); Machobane (1990: 184).
72. Machobane (1990: 184–5).
73. The English version has a blue cover: *The Basutoland Native Administration Proclamation (No. 61 of 1938) and The Basutoland Native Courts Proclamation (No. 62 of 1938). An Explanatory Memorandum*. No place or date of publication is given, but the memorandum is dated July 1939.
74. *An Explanatory Memorandum*, p. 6.
75. *An Explanatory Memorandum*, p. 16.
76. *Official Gazette of the High Commissioner for Basutoland, the Bechuanaland Protectorate, and Swaziland*, High Commissioner's Notice no. 171 of 1939.
77. The figure usually given is 1,340, but the number of posts listed is 1,348.
78. Jones Papers, Box S1, file on 'Correspondence re Diretlo Murder Report', 'Comments on Mr G. I. Jones' Report', enclosed with Baring to Jones, 6 June 1950.

79. RHL, MSS Brit. Emp. S381, Hector Papers, file 3/2, Kennan, 'A Sketch', p. 6; also Hailey (1953, part V: 75); Machobane (1990: 185); Ashton (1952: 211); Hamnett (1975: 36); Jones (1951: 43–5).

80. Duncan (1960: 50).

81. Jingoes (1975: 180–1, 185). Even Armstrong admitted that this happened in some instances. See also PRO, DO 119/1384, 'Report of the Committee Appointed by the Round Table Conference on Medicine Murder' (enclosed with Acting RC to Deputy HC, 22 October 1954), p. 9; and Hamnett (1975: 36).

82. Jones (1951: 43).

83. *An Explanatory Memorandum*, p. 16.

84. Jingoes (1975: 185–6).

85. Hailey (1953, part V: 82).

86. See Armstrong's comments in Jones Papers (note 78 above), and Hailey (1953, part V: 136), quoting *CAR 1938*, p. 88.

87. According to Armstrong, in his comments in Jones Papers (note 78 above), about half of the placings during the war went through without any control. See also PRO, DO 119/1377, Ashton, 'Analysis of ritual murders and their relation to various administrative events', p. 14, sent under cover of Forsyth-Thompson to Baring, 21 April 1949; Hailey (1953, part V: 88–9). Forsyth-Thompson, writing in 1950, commented that it was only in the last three or four years that 'the brake [had] been applied to placings': see Jones Papers, Box S1, file on 'Correspondence re Diretlo Murder Report', 'Comments on Mr G. I. Jones' Report', enclosed with Baring to Jones, 6 June 1950.

88. Hailey (1953, part V: 82, 88–9).

89. Hailey (1953, part V: 136).

90. NUL, Rivers Thompson, 'Reminiscences', p. 32. See also PRO, DO 35/912/1, Harding to Eden, 18 and 29 February 1940.

91. Rooney (1982: 57–61). Arden-Clarke later went on to achieve distinction as the last Governor of the Gold Coast, when he won Kwame Nkrumah's confidence and presided over that colony's transition to independence as Ghana.

92. PRO, DO 35/1172, Y701/1/10, Sir Evelyn Baring to Lord Cranborne, 21 December 1944; PRO, DO 119/1377, Baring, 'Memorandum on Certain Aspects of Ritual Murder in Basutoland', sent under cover of Baring to Forsyth-Thompson, 31 March 1949; Jones (1951: 42).

93. 'Resident Commissioner's Statement to the Basutoland National Council', November 1942, in *Explanatory Memorandum: Basuto National Treasury*, p. 5.

94. *Explanatory Memorandum: Basuto National Treasury*. For a summary of the Committee's proposals, see pp. 8–10.

95. PRO, DO 35/1176, Y793/4, Arden-Clarke to Harlech, 16 April, 6 May and 2 November 1943, and Kennan to Clarke, 15 June 1943; PRO, DO 35/1172, Y701/1/14, Baring to Viscount Addison, 16 February 1946; Jingoes (1975: 191, 193–4).

96. For the Treasury reforms generally, see Hailey (1953, part V: 93–4); Machobane (1990: 220–7); Jingoes (1975: 191–2).

97. PRO, DO 35/4010, Baring to Liesching, 20 July 1951. Baring says the average payment was £20 a year.

98. Machobane (1990: 227). Hailey (1953, part V: 105) says that in practice only those headmen with more than 100 taxpayers received payment, and UCT, Ashton Papers, 'Mokhotlong District', p. 21, supports this.

99. Hailey (1953, part V: 109); Hamnett (1975: 94–6).

100. *CAR 1947*, p. 10; Jones (1951: 43, 52); Hailey (1953, part V: 108–9); Jingoes (1975: 200).

101. Hailey (1953, part V: 95).
102. PRO, DO 35/4007, Baring to Machtig, 24 June 1947; Ashton, 'Mokhotlong District', p. 26; Jones (1951: 53); Hailey (1953, part V: 109–10); Hamnett (1975: 96).
103. Ashton, 'Mokhotlong District', p. 23; Jones (1951: 52–3); Weisfelder (1974: 166, 168).
104. Ashton (2nd edn 1967: xxiv); see also Hailey (1953, part V: 143).
105. For example, *Proc. (42) BNC*, vol. I, p. 182, speech of Goliath Malebanye, 18 October 1946; *Proc. (47) BNC, 10th September 1951*, vol. I, p. 7, motion from Mafeteng District Council; *Proc. (Special 1955) BNC*, pp. 166–8, speech of Chief Leabua Jonathan.
106. Rivers Thompson, 'Reminiscences', p. 63.
107. Jones (1951: 54–6); Hailey (1953, part V: 99 and, for conclusions, 130–47).
108. PRO, DO 119/1380, Baring's interim comments on the Jones report, forwarded to London, 10 June 1950.
109. Jones Papers, Box S1, file on 'Correspondence re Diretlo Murder Report', Baring to Jones, 6 June 1950. See also PRO, DO 1172, Y701/1/14, Baring to Viscount Addison, 16 February 1946.
110. Hailey (1953, part V: 83).
111. Machobane (1990: 107).
112. LNA, S3/5/14/2.
113. Damane and Sanders (1974: 242–3); Machobane (1990: 188–96).
114. Josiel Lefela's letter to G. I. Jones in *Inkululeko*, 19 November 1949; Thabo Rust to CM, 13 October 1971.
115. The choice of Seeiso as Paramount Chief is outlined in PRO, DO 35/911/20, and FCO, Box 1164, S 18. A vivid account of Seeiso's popularity is in FCO, Box 1176, S 119, Marion Walsham-How to Chaplin, 20 April 1957.
116. A. G. Brightmore, 'Looking back', *Basutoland News*, 18 July 1961; Rivers Thompson, 'Reminiscences', p. 71. An account of Bereng's encroachments is in FCO, Box 1177, S 85, Thompson to Elliot, 6 November 1946, and enclosures.
117. PRO, DO 119/1135, 'Confidential reports on native chiefs (1940)'.
118. Hailey (1953, part V: 128).
119. Brightmore, 'Looking back'.
120. Rivers Thompson, 'Reminiscences', p. 70. See also PRO, DO 35/1181, Y981/2, letter from E. G. Dutton, 2 January 1941.
121. Rivers Thompson, 'Reminiscences', p. 70.
122. PRO, DO 119/1135, 'Confidential reports on native chiefs (1940)'. See also PRO, DO 119/1117, 'Confidential reports on native chiefs for the year 1938'.
123. Rivers Thompson, 'Reminiscences', p. 70.
124. Machobane (1990: 195); Rivers Thompson, 'Reminiscences', pp. 70–1.
125. Tylden (1950: 221); see also Edgar (1987: 37); Rivers Thompson, 'Reminiscences', p. 70. According to official accounts, Seeiso was taken into hospital with severe abdominal pains: it was found he had a seriously enlarged gallbladder and that the duct leading from it was blocked. He was operated on and seemed to be recovering, but then died of acute cardiac failure: see PRO, DO 35/192/2. There were rumours, unsubstantiated, that he had been poisoned by Bereng: see Eldredge (1997: 8). Josiel Lefela of the Lekhotla la Bafo later alleged that the government had poisoned Seeiso, and even that he had been the victim of a medicine murder by the government. He was charged with and convicted of sedition. See *Basutoland News*, 12 July 1955; Edgar (1987: 37). (Edgar's account is different from that given in *Basutoland News*, and is no doubt based on the court record shown to him by Rivers Thompson.)

126. RHL, MSS Brit. Emp. S381, Hector Papers, file 3/1.
127. The choice of 'Mantšebo is outlined in PRO, DO 35/912/2, and the Lesotho Evangelical Church, Morija Archives, How Papers, Marion Walsham How to Arden-Clarke, 27 August 1942. For a detailed account of the dispute, see Machobane (1990: 196–200).
128. Eldredge (1997: 9); see also Gocking (1997); Coplan and Quinlan (1997: 38); Damane (1973–4: 49–50); Epprecht (2000: 110) asserts, however, though without citing his evidence, that the British wanted Bereng to become regent.
129. PRO, DO 35/912/2, RC to HC, 15 January 1941. In the country as a whole opinion seems to have been divided: FCO, Box 1177, S 85, District Officers' reports, April 1943.
130. Machobane (1990: 198–200). For the judgement, see Willan (1955a: 50–84).
131. The best source on Bereng's disputes with 'Mantšebo is FCO, Box 1177, S 85. Two cases which give the background on the boundary dispute between Phamong and Matsieng are LNA, CIV/APN/143/87 and Court of Appeal (Civil) no. 17 of 1987. See also PRO, DO 35/1172, Y701/1/14, Baring to Viscount Addison, 16 February 1946; *Proc. (42) BNC*, vols I and II, debates on 17 and 18 October 1946; *Mochochonono*, 17 November 1945, 25 May 1946 and 15 February 1947; *Moeletsi*, 30 October 1945, 13 and 20 November 1945, 11 December 1945.
132. FCO, Box 1167, S 197A, Kennan to Administrative Secretary to HC, 27 February 1943.
133. Douglas-Home (1978: 197); FCO, Box 1177, S 85, Arden-Clarke to Harlech, 23 October 1942.
134. PRO, DO 35/1172, Y701/1/10, Baring to Lord Cranborne, 21 December 1944. Another example is the article by J. A. Gray in *South Africa*, stamped 27 November 1949, in PRO, DO 35/4154.
135. PRO, DO 35/1177, Arden-Clarke to Sir Walter Huggard, 13 October 1944, and enclosures, and comment by H. B. Lawrence of the HC's Office, 14 November 1944. For Baring's comment, see PRO, DO 35/1172, Y701/1/14, Baring to Viscount Addison, 16 February 1946. There are confidential reports on 'Mantšebo in FCO, Box 1167, S 197A, and Box 1168, S 197E. For a sympathetic assessment of 'Mantšebo, see Epprecht (2000: 110–20).
136. Comment by Lawrence, note 135 above.
137. PRO, DO 35/4154, 'Secretary of State's Visit to Southern Africa. Basutoland: Ritual Murders', November 1950, p. 2.

CASE STUDY 1

1. LNA, HC 288/46, PE March 1946, evidence of Nkojoa Mokone, pp. 11–18, and Bernice Hlalele, pp. 42–6.
2. The modern village of Phahameng lies below the terrace. The ruins of 'old' Phahameng may still be discerned in the long grass. The village was moved c. 1950 from the old site to the new as part of a scheme of administrative consolidation and environmental conservation.
3. LNA, HC 288/46, HC trial record, pp. 936–7.
4. LNA, HC 288/46, PE March 1946, evidence of Sergeant Thabiso Mohloboli, pp. 39–42.
5. LNA, HC 288/46, HC trial record, judgement, p. 966.
6. LNA, HC 288/46, HC trial record, judgement, p. 960.
7. Toka Mafihlo (No. 2), Mojalefa Moholi (No. 3), Seleke Marabe (No. 7), Mahao Matete (No. 8), John Makume (No. 9), Liau Lekhula (No. 10), Josiel Thoso (No. 13), Mpharane Mokoetla (No. 15).

8. *Basutoland News*, 9 July 1946; Kekeletso Malakia Phakisi, 'Lenaka la Moshoeshoe', *Leselinyana*, 27 November 1945.
9. LNA, HC 288/46, PE March 1946, evidence of Bernice Hlalele; KS and PS interview, Nkherepe Molefe, 24 May 1999.
10. PS interview, Albert Brutsch, 11 October 1997.
11. KS and PS interview, Nkherepe Molefe, 24 May 1999.
12. Nor was it a stranger to 'ordinary' murder of a sensational kind. In December 1920 Rev. Edouard Jacottet. Director of the Theological School at the Morija mission, was poisoned. In the context of the history of the mission from 1833, the story is told in detail in Couzens (2003).
13. Ken Shortt-Smith, taped reminiscences c. late 1980s, Tape 7, in possession of Liz Shortt-Smith.
14. The political context of this observation is explained in Case Study 4, as part of the background to a series of cases of medicine murder in the Mokhotlong District.
15. KS and CM interview, Nkherepe Molefe, 29 November 1998. Molefe spoke partly in English and partly in Sesotho, and CM's fieldnotes retain a 'mixed' quality accordingly.
16. KS and PS interview, Nkherepe Molefe, 24 May 1999.
17. Article by 'Ralitaba', 'Tsa kae le kae', *Moeletsi*, 16 October 1945.
18. LNA, HC 288/46, judgement, pp. 972–3.
19. LNA, HC 288/46, PE March 1946, evidence of Nkojoa Mokone.
20. LNA, HC 288/46, PE March 1946, evidence of Kuili Rammotseng, pp. 2–10.
21. LNA, HC 288/46, PE March 1946, evidence of Tšeliso Shata, pp. 50–2.
22. LNA, HC 288/46, PE March 1946, evidence of Napo Khashole, pp. 49–50.
23. LNA, HC 288/46, PE March 1946, evidence of Bernice Hlalele. Her statement also appears in UCT, BC 859, Ashton Papers, B5.
24. LNA, HC 288/46, HC trial record, cross-examination of John Makume, pp. 902–33.
25. LNA, HC 288/46, HC trial record, cross-examination of Josiel Thoso, pp. 934–52.
26. LNA, HC 288/46, HC trial record, judgement, pp. 978–9, 981–2. Nkojoa Mokone told the High Court that the meeting took place on Friday, 4 May, whereas he had asserted at the PE that it took place on the Friday of the previous week. The judge explicitly referred to this discrepancy (judgement, pp. 959, 971) as one of the unsatisfactory aspects of Nkojoa Mokone's evidence.
27. LNA, HC 288/46, HC trial record, judgement, p. 964.
28. LNA, HC 288/46, HC trial record, judgement, p. 966.
29. LNA, HC 288/46, HC trial record, judgement, p. 977.
30. LNA, HC 288/46, HC trial record, judgement, p. 1001.
31. *Basutoland News*, 9 July 1946.
32. *Mochochonono*, 27 July 1946.
33. LNA, HC 288/46, PE March 1946, evidence of Bernice Hlalele (the italics are ours); FCO, Box 1178, S 161, vol. III, ff. 71, 98, evidence of Bernice Hlalele in the HC.
34. FCO, Box 1178, S 161 vol. III, 'Mantšebo to Acting PC, 27 April 1953.
35. 'Mamakhabane was a case in point: see Case Study 2 below.
36. Jones (1951: 17).
37. Three years after the murder of Stephen Thobeha there were rumours that Mahao's mother and Josiel Thoso were conspiring to commit another murder, and a warning *pitso* was held by Chief Theko Makhaola, who was then acting as PC. FCO, Box 1175, S 119, CP to GS, 24 June 1948.
38. Mofokeng (n.d.).
39. KS and CM interview, Motsetsela Motsetsela, 17 May 1999.

40. KS and CM interview, 'Mampoi Matete, 15 January 2000.
41. *Leselinyana*, 12 October 1968.
42. KS and CM interview, 'Maiphepi 'Matli, 15 January 2000.
43. Mofokeng (n.d.: 12).
44. KS reminiscences, Maseru, 29 November 1998.
45. KS and CM interview, Nkherepe Molefe, 29 November 1998.

CHAPTER 2

1. Ellenberger (1912: 106–7).
2. Ashton (1952: 282, 312).
3. Casalis (1861: 256–7).
4. See, for example, *Proc. (Special 1956) BNC*, p. 91, 11 May 1956, speech of Chief Moeketsi Mokhele; Damane (1973–4: 48–50).
5. For example, *Proc. (42) BNC*, vol. II, speech of Acting RC, 18 October 1946, p. 181; PRO, DO 119/1382, 'Report by Major A. H. Donald and Chief Leshoboro Majara on Medicine Murders and Proposals for Combating Them' (enclosure with Arrowsmith to Chief Secretary to HC, 31 July 1953) p. 14; *Proc. (Special 1956) BNC*, 11 May 1956, speeches of Arrowsmith, the President, pp. 79, 87.
6. See, for example, Griffith (1878: 89); H. Dieterlen (1930 : 21–2); Ashton (1952: 282); Jones (1951: 22).
7. Casalis (1861: 257).
8. For medicine generally, see Casalis (1861: 256–61); H. Dieterlen (1930); Motlamelle (1950); Jones (1951: 12–14); Ashton (1952: 282–316); Damane (1973–4: 48–59); Laydevant (1939: 128).
9. Casalis (1861: 257–8).
10. Lye (1975: 95).
11. A. M. Sekese, articles in *Leselinyana*, 1 July 1892 and 15 April 1906; Ellenberger (1912: 170); Msebenzi (1938: 44–5).
12. McKay (1871: 262); Theal (1883, vol. I: lxvi); Orpen (1857: 102).
13. Anonymous letter, 30 April 1858, in *The Friend*, 7 May 1858; J. M. Howell, letter in *The Friend*, 28 May 1858; J. A. Roosema, Secretary of the Krygsraad, to the Landdrost of Smithfield, 30 April 1858, in Theal (1883, vol. II: 354); Arbousset's letter of 22 June 1858, reprinted in *Cape Argus*, 3 August 1858.
14. Theal (1883: 76, 96–7); the praises of Letsika Matela and Mokhalinyane Ramakau in Mangoaela (1957: 149, 155).
15. Wepener (1934: 67). F. D. J. Wepener was Louw Wepener's son. See also Perham (1974: 122); RHL, MSS Brit. Emp. S381, Hector Papers, file 2/6, 'Minutes of Conference on Diretlo ... commencing on the 27th of August, 1956', p. 29, statement by B. M. Khaketla.
16. Widdicombe (1895: 176); Woon (1909: 124, 128, 168).
17. RHL, MSS Afr. S969, Kennan Papers, Miles Kennan's account of his father's involvement in the Moorosi War, p. 12; Tylden (1950: 164); Burman (1981: 149).
18. Barkly (1893: 43–4).
19. Laydevant (1951: 227).
20. For example, Laydevant (1937: 214–15; 1950: 138–9).
21. See Chapter 7; also G. Dieterlen (1926: 218); Ramseyer (1928: 69).
22. Woon (1909: 124).
23. The only exception, it seems, was Ntsu Mokhehle, President of the BAC: RHL, MSS Brit. Emp. S381, Hector Papers, file 2/6, 'Minutes of Conference on Diretlo', p. 4.
24. In 1963 the Roman Catholic Mission in Basutoland published a booklet by an anonymous Mosotho on *Lebollo* (initiation). This gave rise to a debate in the

National Council and the booklet had to be withdrawn. The debate is reported in *Ba re'ng batho ka buka ea 'Lebollo'?* (What are people saying about the book 'Lebollo'?) (Mazenod, n.d.).

25. Damane and Sanders (1974: 65). For other evidence of human flesh being used in initiation medicines, see, for example, the definition of *sehoere* in Mabille and Dieterlen (1904); Laydevant (1951: 224); Jones (1951: 26); PRO, DO 119/1382, M. B. Photane, 'Medicine Murders' (enclosure with Arrowsmith to Turnbull, 12 September 1953), p. 26; PRO, DO 119/1384, 'Report of the Committee appointed by the the Round Table Conference on Medicine Murder' (enclosed with Acting RC to Deputy HC, 22 October 1954), p. 4, where it is stated that 'a large number of people' believed that human flesh was used; editorial in *Moeletsi*, 24 August 1953; *Ba re'ng batho ka buka ea 'Lebollo'?*

26. UCT, Ashton Papers, 'Mokhotlong District', p. 35.

27. Casalis (1861: 297); H. Dieterlen (1930: 29ff.); Sanders (1975: 123).

28. Ashton (1952: 316); Jones (1951: 23).

29. Barkly (1893: 133).

30. Sekese, 'Tsekhela 'Mele le Moea', *Leselinyana*, 30 March 1932.

31. *Proc. (42) BNC*, vol. II, record of the debate on 18 and 21 October 1946. The quotations from Joel Mataboe, William Lethunya, Edwin Ntsasa and B. K. Taoana are on pp. 187, 189, 190–1 and 191–2 respectively. Ashton ('Analysis', p. 9) noted that 'Mantšebo had surrounded her village at Matsieng with *lithakhisa*, medicine pegs.

32. *Leselinyana*, 22 March 1954. Apparently many Christians used medicine pegs to protect their houses: PRO, DO 119/1382, M. B. Photane, 'Medicine Murders' (enclosure with Arrowsmith to Turnbull, 12 September 1953), p. 16. For the ban on *mohlabelo*, see Ashton, 'Analysis', p. 8.

33. J. K. M., article in *Leselinyana*, 8 March 1954. The word *seriti*, which we have translated as 'authority', has no exact counterpart in English. The dictionary definition (Mabille and Dieterlen, revised by Paroz) is 'shadow, ghost; respectability, authority; *motho ea nang le seriti*, important, influential person'.

34. PRO, DO 119/1382, 'What is meant by "Liretlo"?' (enclosed with Arrowsmith to Turnbull, 12 September 1953), p. 5. Khaketla was soon to become Deputy Leader of the Basutoland African Congress, and subsequently founded the Freedom Party.

35. Ashton (1952: 313–14, 316).

36. H. Dieterlen (1896: 265; 1912: 170, 173; 1930: 17–18).

37. Jones (1951: 13); *Proc. (42) BNC*, vol. II, p. 181, speech of Chief Goliath Malebanye, 18 October 1946; PRO, DO 119/1382, 'Report by Major A. H. Donald and Chief Leshoboro Majara' (enclosed with Arrowsmith to Chief Secretary to HC, 31 July 1953), p. 2; enclosures with Arrowsmith to Turnbull, 12 September 1953, B. M. Khaketla, 'Memorandum on "Liretlo"', pp. 2–3, and M. B. Photane, 'Medicine Murders', p. 27; PRO, DO 119/1384, 'Report of the Committee Appointed by the Round Table Conference on Medicine Murder' (enclosed with Acting RC to Deputy HC, 22 October 1954), p. 3; Khaketla (1972: 26).

38. Jones (1951: 16); PRO, DO 119/1382, Khaketla, 'Memorandum on "Liretlo"' (enclosed with Acting RC to Deputy HC, 22 October 1954), p. 26.

39. The use of persons who had died of natural causes was not entirely unknown: Sachot (1946: 110); H. Dieterlen (1930: 25). According to the *Basutoland News*, 9 March 1965, even Josiel Lefela of Lekhotla La Bafo, afraid that his body might be exhumed from a public cemetery, requested that on his death he be buried very close to his own front door.

40. Ashton (1952: 310) and Jones (1951: 14). Jones drew a sharp distinction between

litlo, the parts cut from the body of a dead enemy, and *liretlo*, the parts cut from a living victim, and in his conversations with Rivers Thompson Chief Ntsekhe Molapo drew the same distinction: Rivers Thompson, 'Reminiscences', p. 33. There is, however, no dictionary authority for this.

41. See Chapter 7.

42. H. Dieterlen (1912: 172); Thorpe (1950: 63); Jones (1951: 13); Ashton (1952: 307); evidence of Chiefs Matlere Lerotholi and Mosuoe Lelingoana given in Ashton, 'Mokhotlong District', p. 34; Mabille (1955: 134, 136); Maake (1998: 95).

43. G. Dieterlen (1926: 218), referring to 'other tribes'; Ramseyer (1928: 70), referring to 'les Cafres'; Scott (1958: 199), where the Hlubi and the Ngwane are mentioned; Laydevant (1939: 136).

44. H. Dieterlen (1912: 169–70); Jones (1951: 13); Maake (1998: 95).

45. H. Dieterlen (1896: 264; 1912: 169–70).

46. 1919/1, 1925/1 and 1927/2.

47. LNA, RCCR 781/1928 (R v. Letsie Mojela and 13 others, case 1927/2), statement of 'Matumelo.

48. A summary of each of these cases may be found in the Appendix.

49. The cut-off date of 1969, instead of 1966, is selected here to facilitate comparison over the period for which official figures for murders of this kind are available. We have therefore included one case from 1968 in this total.

50. Jones (1951: 1, 15).

51. Ralitaba, 'Tsa kae le kae', *Moeletsi*, 1 May 1945; Amicus Patriae, 'Murder wave in Basutoland', *Moeletsi*, 15 May 1945; Mathias Thakabatso, letter in *Moeletsi*, 4 December 1945; David Gaboutloeloe, 'Murder cases in Basutoland', *Mochochonono*, 24 November 1945; Observer, 'We are made to understand', *Mochochonono*, 15 December 1945; Kekeletso Malakia Phakisi, 'Lenaka la Moshoeshoe', *Leselinyana*, 27 November 1945.

52. *Mochochonono*, 27 July 1946.

53. NUL Archives, Leribe Files, Box 54, file 754. See also Chapter 3.

54. *Proc. (42) BNC*, vol. II, proceedings for 18 and 21 October 1946, speeches of Talimo Joel, Dinizulu Maime, Goliath Malebanye and Josiel Lefela on pp. 195, 198, 182 and 186 respectively.

55. *Basutoland News*, 7 September 1948.

56. Ashton, 'Mokhotlong District', p. 34; 'Ritual murder in Basutoland', p. 11.

57. Quoted by Ntsu Mokhehle in *Mohlabani*, June 1957, p. 13, 'President speaks on "Liretlo" murders'.

58. Jones (1951: 57).

59. PRO, DO 119/1382, enclosures with Arrowsmith to Turnbull, 12 September 1953, Khaketla, 'Memorandum on "Liretlo"', p. 3, and Photane, 'Medicine Murders', pp. 1 and 10.

60. Gaboutloeloe, 'Murder cases in Basutoland', *Mochochonono*, 24 November 1945. See also Amicus Patriae, 'Murder wave in Basutoland', *Moeletsi*, 15 May 1945.

61. NUL Archives, Leribe Files, Box 54, file 754. See also Gaboutloeloe, 'Murder cases in Basutoland', *Mochochonono*, 24 November 1945; and *Basutoland News*, 13 August 1946.

62. *Proc. (42) BNC*, vol. II, p. 191, 18 October 1946; NUL Archives, Leribe Files, Box 54, L. Dupuis to DC Leribe, 31 May 1947.

63. Ashton (1952: 312) (Ashton's Introduction to the book was written in 1949). See also PRO, DO 119/1382, note by le Rougetel on visit to Basutoland, 18 March 1953.

64. FCO, Box 1178, S 161, vol. III, evidence of Bernice Hlalele in the High Court, f. 99.

65. LNA, HC 375/1947 (case 1945/11), PE, evidence of Jan Gat; LNA, CRI/T/19/

59 (case 1958/1), judgement; *Basutoland News,* 17 January 1961. See also Jones (1951: 18, fn. 10), for a murder allegedly committed in the Mafeteng District. In case 1948/21 human parts were found, but had not been taken from the victim. In case 1952/6 the instigator said that his rival had improved his village by killing a man. There is also a reference to a previous (unidentified) murder in case 1956/3.

66. Dutton (1923).
67. Ashton (1943). It seems that the first draft of his book *The Basuto* had little or nothing on medicine murder: DO 119/1377, Forsyth-Thompson to Baring, 1 April 1949.
68. LNA, RCCR 781/1928 (case 1927/2), evidence of 'Matumelo.
69. H. Dieterlen (1912: 172–3).
70. G. Dieterlen (1926: 218).
71. PRO, DO 119/1382, Khaketla, 'Memorandum on "Liretlo"' (enclosed with Arrowsmith to Turnbull, 12 September 1953), p. 3.
72. Ashton, 'Ritual Murder in Basutoland', pp. 10–12.
73. PRO, DO 119/1377, Forsyth-Thompson to Baring, 1 April 1949.
74. Ashton, 'Ritual Murder in Basutoland', p. 12.
75. The seven districts were Leribe, Berea (or Teyateyaneng), Maseru, Mafeteng, Mohale's Hoek, Quthing and Qacha's Nek. Butha-Buthe was a sub-district of Leribe and Mokhotlong a sub-district of Qacha's Nek.
76. Pim (1935: 5, 51, 77–80, 84).
77. M. B. Smith (n.d.: 9).
78. *CAR 1946,* p. 51, and *CAR 1950,* p. 57.
79. *CAR 1946,* pp. 51–3. By 1948 it was only marginally larger, with fifteen white staff on the establishment and 300 African staff. See *CAR 1948,* p. 85.
80. *The Basutoland Native Administration Proclamation (No. 61 of 1938) and The Basutoland Native Courts Proclamation (No. 62 of 1938): An Explanatory Memorandum,* pp. 9–10.
81. PRO, DO 119/1377, Extract from a note of a discussion between the RC and the PC and her advisers, enclosed with Forsyth-Thompson to Baring, 29 March 1949.
82. FCO, Box 1177, S 245, PC's circulars no. 22 of 1946, 20 June 1946, and no. 42 of 1947, 4 November 1947.
83. Ashton, 'Ritual Murder in Basutoland', p. 13.
84. *CAR 1948,* p. 87.
85. FCO, Box 1175, S 119, minute by JC, 6 March 1947, quoted in Forsyth-Thompson to Baring, 22 April 1947; see also Becker (1956: 36).
86. PRO, DO 119/1376, Forsyth-Thompson to Baring, 9 March 1946; PRO, DO 119/1381, Arrowsmith (reporting the views of District Officers) to Turnbull, 15 August 1952; PRO, DO 35/4154, GS to Administrative Secretary to HC, 21 May 1947; *Basutoland News,* 17 August 1948, quoted at the head of this chapter; PRO, DO 119/1384, 'Report of the Committee appointed by the Round Table Conference on Medicine Murder' (enclosed with Acting RC to Deputy HC, 22 October 1954), p. 8; PRO, DO 119/1383, Scrivenor to A. E. M. Jansen, Secretary for Justice, Cape Town, 5 March 1954; and PRO, DO 119/1384, Scrivenor's note of 16 April 1956, reporting the view of a DC, Jack Elliot.
87. Ashton, 'Ritual Murder in Basutoland', pp. 13–14.

CASE STUDY 2

1. Speech of Chief Theko Makhaola before Makhabane Peete's installation as Ward Chief of Koeneng and Mapoteng, 1948, recorded in Jingoes (1975: 166).
2. Jingoes (1975), Chapter 6.
3. Jingoes (1975: 164).
4. LNA, HC 14/48, HC trial record, judgement, p. 618. There are some discrepancies over names. See text below.
5. Jingoes (1975: 164).
6. Jones (1951: 11–12).
7. Jingoes (1975: 169, 161).
8. Jones (1951: 17); FCO, Box 1177, S 262, Ashton, 'Ritual Murder in Berea', enclosed with Jones to Marwick, 4 August 1949.
9. Jingoes (1975: 161–3).
10. KS and CM interview, Nyalase Ntja Sebajoa, 3 December 1998.
11. KS and CM interview, 'Mamokhatsi Rachakane, 3 December 1998.
12. Jingoes (1975: 164–5).
13. LNA, HC 14/48, vol. 8, PE record, Annexure 'A', p. 727.
14. LNA, HC 14/48, HC trial record, judgement, p. 617.
15. LNA, HC 14/48, vol. 8, PE record, p. 69.
16. LNA, HC 14/48, HC trial record, judgement, pp. 624–5.
17. LNA, HC 14/48, HC trial record, judgement, p. 633.
18. PRO, DO 35/4098, Y3200/11, Harragin to HC, 28 August 1948.
19. This area lay between the lands of Molapo and Masupha, sons in Moshoeshoe's first house. There were many boundary battles between the three chiefdoms.
20. Rivers Thompson, 'Reminiscences', pp. 35, 81.
21. PRO, DO 119/1135, 884, 'Confidential reports on native chiefs (1940)'.
22. KS and CM interview, Mohale Peete, 3 December 1998. Jingoes (1975: 152) gives December 1940.
23. Jingoes (1975: 153).
24. Jingoes (1975: 152–61).
25. Jones (1951: 17).
26. Jingoes (1975: 168).
27. PRO, DO 119/1376, Record of case heard in DC's Court, Maseru, before E. C. Butler on 4 February 1949 and following days, evidence of Mashapha Pokonyane, Raletsukana Posholi and Molato Rachakane; FCO, Box 1177, S 245, ? to GS, 7 September 1948.
28. LNA, HC 14/48, HC trial record, judgement, pp. 620, 631–4.
29. *Proc. (44) BNC*, vol. I, 1948, pp. 30–1, Josiel Lefela's speech, 21 September 1948.
30. Edgar (1987).
31. Scott (1958: 194).
32. Scott (1958); a profile of Scott was published in *The Observer*, 4 December 1949.
33. PRO, DO 119/1377, 9916, CP to GS, 31 March 1949, Appendix B attached to RC's circular, 25 April 1949. Thomas Mofolo's best-known work is *Chaka*, published in 1925, in which belief in the power of human medicine is a dominant theme. See 'Interlude' below.
34. Scott (1958: 202).
35. *Inkululeko*, August 1948.
36. Edgar (1987: 36, 194–8); PRO, DO 119/1377, 9916, CP to GS, 31 March 1949, Appendix B attached to RC's circular, 25 April 1949.
37. Scott (1958: 198).
38. Scott (1958: 195–6).

39. PRO, CO 35/4155, Y3515/3, enclosures with Frank Byers to Patrick Gordon Walker, 20 January 1949.
40. PRO, DO 119/1376, Record of case heard in DC's Court, Maseru, before E. C. Butler on 4 February 1949 and following days.
41. Edgar (1987: 50).
42. PRO, DO 119/1377, 9916, CP to GS, 22 March 1949; Note of Meeting with RC, GS and CP, 12 April 1949; Appendix B to RC's circular to all DCs on 'ritual murder' 25 April 1949, CP to GS, 31/349.
43. Cited by Ntsu Mokhehle in *Mohlabani*, November 1957, p. 17. See also *Mohlabani*, December 1957, p. 15.
44. Scott (1958: 204–5).
45. PRO, DO 35/4098, Y3200/11, F. C. Byers to Gordon Walker, 31 December 1948; Gordon Walker to Byers, 3 January 1949; minute H. N. Tait to A. McNulty, 1 January 1949; minutes of meeting 11 January 1949.
46. PRO, DO 35/4098, Y3200/11, 'Mamakhabane Peete and others to Secretary of the Judicial Committee of the Privy Council, London, 17 November 1948.
47. LNA, HC 14/48, Lefela to Registrar of Judicial Committee of the Privy Council, 2 January 1949, p. 5.
48. PRO, DO 35/4098, Y3200/11, minute by Tait, 24 January 1949; CRO telegram to HC, 28 January 1949.
49. PRO, DO 35/4098, Y3200/1, Petition for leave to appeal; telegram HC to CRO, 28 May 1949; Burchell to McNulty, 30 May 1949; *The Times*, 31 May 1949.
50. KS and CM interviews, Nyalase Sebajoa, Nkapo Sebajoa, 3 December 1998.

CHAPTER 3

1. *Proc. (44) BNC*, vol. I, 1948, p. 29.
2. *Proc. (44) BNC*, vol. I, 1948, p. 21.
3. PRO, DO 35/1172, Y701/1/10, Baring to Lord Cranborne, 21 December 1944, and Y701/1/14, Baring to Viscount Addison, 16 February 1946.
4. PRO, DO 35/1172, Y708/19.
5. NUL Archives, Leribe Files, Box 54, file 754, Kennan to DCs etc., Circular Minute no. 20 of 1946. The PC's circular is quoted in this Circular Minute. According to Eldredge (1997: 27, fn. 4), it was Circular no. 1 of 1946, dated 10 January 1946.
6. Ambrose Archives, Mokhotlong Papers, C2, Henderson, DC Mokhotlong, to GS, 21 September 1946. The suspicions in Henderson's report must have been held for some time.
7. See Case Study 4, and Table CS4.1.
8. This circular, no. 28 of 31 July 1946, is cited in Eldredge (1997: 14–16). See also PRO, DO 119/1376, Apthorp to GS, 30 May 1947.
9. *Basutoland News*, 13 August 1946.
10. Cited in *Basutoland News*, 13 August 1946.
11. Seven cases were reported in 1946, and there were several trials in that year of earlier cases.
12. Mokhotlong Papers, C2, Henderson to GS, 21 September 1946. See also PRO, DO 119/1376, Apthorp to GS, 30 May 1947.
13. *Proc. (42) BNC*, vol. I, 18 and 21 October 1946, pp. 178, 182–3, 186–7, 194, 196–7, 200. See also speeches of William Lethunya, p. 189, and Leshoboro Majara, p. 199.
14. *Proc. (42) BNC*, vol. I, 18 and 21 October 1946, pp. 179, 190, 197.
15. Eldredge (1997: 16).
16. Kneen and Juta (1950, vol. I, cap. 62: 611–13); see also Maake (1998: 93).

17. FCO, Box 1177, S 245, PC's Circulars no. 22 of 1946, 20 June 1946, and no. 42 of 1947, 4 November 1947. The background correspondence is in PRO, DO 119/1376, Forsyth-Thompson to Baring, 9 March 1949; and PRO, DO 35/ 4154, Forsyth-Thompson to 'Mantšebo, 25 June 1947, and 'Mantšebo to Forsyth-Thompson, 3 July 1947, both enclosed with Baring to Machtig, 9 August 1947.

18. PRO, DO 119/1382, 'Report by Major A.H. Donald and Chief Leshoboro Majara', c. July 1953, p. 19.

19. The name given is Lerotholi Theko, who appears elsewhere as Jacottet Lerotholi Khoabane Theko. FCO, Box 1168, S 197E, confidential report, 1948.

20. PRO, DO 35/4155, 'Mantšebo's petition to RC, 16 September 1948, enclosed with Byers to Gordon Walker, 20 January 1949.

21. PRO, DO 35/4157, 'Memorandum on Certain Aspects of Ritual Murder in Basutoland', enclosed with Baring to Secretary of State, 28 April 1949.

22. 'Britain is trying to enslave us. Basuto people complain to UNO': *The Guardian*, 13 January 1949, cited in Edgar (1987: 199–201); Hailey (1963: 89–90); Douglas-Home (1978: 169).

23. PRO, DO 119/1377, original statements recorded by Michael Scott and sent to W. F. Mackenzie from the Secretariat, Maseru.

24. Scott (1958: 203).

25. Douglas-Home (1978: 161).

26. Foreword by E. Baring in Gray (1953).

27. Baring (1952), and Douglas-Home (1978: 162–71).

28. *Basutoland News*, 13 December 1949, quoting from an article by Sir William Clark in *The Spectator*.

29. University of Durham Library, GRE/1/9/3, Lord Cranborne to Baring, 15 September 1945, and Douglas-Home (1978: 162).

30. On the whole question of incorporation, see Hailey (1963).

31. PRO, DO 35/4154, 'Meeting at which His Excellency addressed the Paramount Chief and Principal Chiefs', 20 September 1948, enclosed with Baring to Machtig, 3 November 1948; PRO, DO 119/1380, Baring's interim comments on the Jones report, drafted by Clark and forwarded to London 10 June 1950; PRO, DO 119/1376, W. A. W. Clark, memorandum, c. January 1949; PRO, DO 35/ 4158, Gibson's minute of 22 November 1950; and Douglas-Home (1978: 184).

32. PRO, DO 35/4154, Baring to Machtig, Dominions Office, 12 June 1947.

33. PRO, DO 35/4157, 'Memorandum on Certain Aspects of Ritual Murder in Basutoland'.

34. Examples are in PRO, DO 35/4154, Kennan to Baring, 21 May 1947; PRO, DO 119/1376, Forsyth-Thompson to Baring, 9 March 1949 and enclosures; and editorial on 'Ritual Murders', *Mochochonono*, 7 June 1947.

35. Baring (1952).

36. PRO, DO 35/4154, Baring to Machtig, 23 July 1947.

37. PRO, DO 35/4157, 'Memorandum on Certain Aspects of Ritual Murder in Basutoland'; University of Durham Library, GRE/1/15/4, Baring's speech to Royal Empire Society on 28 February 1952.

38. Douglas-Home (1978: 199).

39. PRO, DO 35/4007, HC's address at opening of 48th Session of BNC, 18 September 1948, enclosed with Baring to Noel-Baker, 12 November 1948.

40. Douglas-Home (1978: 199).

41. PRO, DO 35/4007, Baring to Noel-Baker, 12 November 1948.

42. Douglas-Home (1978: 199).

43. PRO, DO 35/4007, Baring to Noel-Baker, 12 November 1948. See also Douglas-

Home (1978: 199). The official account of this meeting is given in PRO, DO 35/ 4154, enclosure with Baring to Machtig, 3 November 1948.

44. *Proc. (44) BNC*, vol. I, 21 September 1948, pp. 25, 33. See also *Proc. (Special 1956) BNC*, 12 May 1956, p. 108, Councillor Bolokoe Malebanye.

45. *Proc. (44) BNC*, vol. I, 21 September 1948, pp. 14, 20, 22, 40; 22 September, p. 64.

46. See also Malei Peshoane of the Lekhotla la Bafo to Trygve Lie, United Nations Organisation, 25 July 1948, quoted in Edgar (1987: 198).

47. *Proc. (44) BNC*, vol. I, 21 September 1948, pp. 32–4, 59.

48. *Moeletsi*, 31 May 1949. A translation of this is in PRO, DO 119/1379.

49. Jingoes (1975: 166–7). See also Interlude.

50. Ashton, 'Ritual Murder in Basutoland', p. 24. For their ineffectiveness, see also editorial, 'Paramount Chief on her feet', *Mochochonono*, 28 May 1949.

51. PRO, DO 119/1378, Notes of meeting held on 17 March 1949 between RC and PC to consider the recommendations of the Basutoland Council on ritual murder.

52. PRO, DO 119/1383, Summary of evidence submitted to the Committee (set up by the Round Table Conference), prepared by Major Donald, Chief Leshoboro Majara and B. K. Taoana, 1953.

53. Editorial, 'Paramount Chief on her feet', *Mochochonono*, 28 May 1949.

54. PRO, DO 119/1376, GS to Chief Secretary to HC, 8 February 1949, enclosing minutes of 'Meeting of the Paramount Chief's Messengers with … the Resident Commissioner in the afternoon of the 26th January 1949'; Forsyth-Thompson to HC, 9 March 1949; PRO, DO 119/1377, Note on discussion between RC and PC and her advisers, enclosed with Forsyth-Thompson to Baring, 29 March 1949.

55. PRO, DO 119/1377, Note on discussion between RC and PC and her advisers, enclosed with Forsyth-Thompson to Baring, 29 March 1949; PRO, DO 35/ 4157, 'Memorandum on Certain Aspects of Ritual Murder in Basutoland'.

56. PRO, DO 119/1378, Note on a meeting held on 17 March 1949 between RC and PC and her advisers. Baring's proclamation was strongly opposed by the BPA: *Mochochonono*, 5 March 1949.

57. PRO, DO 35/4155, Maphutseng Lefela to Trygve Lie, 21 November 1948.

58. PRO, DO 35/4155, Minute on item 13: Syers to Gordon Walker, 1 February 1949.

59. PRO, DO 35/4097; see Chapter 9 on the judicial process.

60. PRO, DO 119/1377; for a full discussion of the issue, see Chapter 8 on police investigations.

61. This new initiative is outlined in PRO, DO 119/1377, Baring to Forsyth-Thompson, 16 April 1949, and enclosures; Forsyth-Thompson to Baring, 21 April 1949; and Baring to Secretary of State, 28 April 1949, and enclosures. We were told by officers serving in Basutoland at the time that Baring had a poor opinion of Forsyth-Thompson himself, but this is not reflected in the surviving correspondence.

62. PRO, DO 119/1373, Acting RC to Baring, 29 July 1949.

CASE STUDY 3

1. KS and CM interview, Nkherepe Molefe, 29 November 1998.

2. LNA, Box 58, Criminal Records High Court 1947, incomplete papers relating to this case, wrongly filed in a 1947 box. The case reference is given by Jones as HC 15/49. The description of Michael Tseki is drawn from Monks (1955: 305).

3. LNA, Box 58, Criminal Records High Court 1947, HC 15/49, HC trial, opening address of Attorney-General.

4. LNA, HC 19/48, PE record, evidence of Mapeshoane Masupha; PRO, DO 119/1372, 9657I, HC record, judgement, pp. 792–804; Jones (1951: 97).
5. PRO, DO 119/1372, 9657I, Judge Sutton to HC, 28 December 1948, p. 2.
6. PRO, DO 35/4099, Y3200/13, comments of Forsyth-Thompson, 19 March 1949.
7. LNA, Box 58, Criminal Records High Court 1947, HC 15/49, evidence of Lieutenant Castle.
8. These disputes are outlined in FCO, Box 1177, S 85.
9. FCO, Box 1177, S 85, Rivers Thompson, DC Mafeteng, to Elliot, 6 November 1946 and enclosures, and RC to PC, 31 December 1946; Brightmore, 'Looking Back'; *Proc. (42) BNC*, vol. I, 17 and 18 October 1946; and copy of judgements (in possession of David Ambrose) in CIV/APN/143/87, which refers to the recommendations of the Boundary Commission being confirmed by the RC on 24 February 1948, and Court of Appeal (Civil) no. 17 of 1987, which refers to the boundary being determined by the HC and the PC on 24 March 1948.
10. *Basutoland News*, 30 August 1949.
11. PRO, DO 35/4154, Y3515/1, note by T. W. Fraser, a Basutoland official seconded to the Colonial Office in London.
12. PRO, DO 35/4158, Jones' draft report, para. 106 (which was omitted from the published report).
13. PRO, DO 119/1135, 884, 'Confidential reports on native chiefs, 1940'.
14. Rivers Thompson, 'Reminiscences', p. 41.
15. LNA, HC 19/48, PE record, evidence of Mapeshoane Masupha.
16. FCO, Box 1167, S 197A, confidential reports, 1943–6.
17. *Basutoland News*, 23 August 1949; Reed (1950: 233).
18. FCO, Box 1167, S 197A, confidential report, 1946.
19. Letsie Motšoene was Ward Chief of Leribe, Theko Makhaola Ward Chief of Ratšoleli's and Mashai.
20. FCO, Box 1178, S 161: see, for example, Kennan to Priestman, 16 September 1946; Balfe to Kennan, n.d.; note on meeting between RC and Bereng, 20 January 1947; DC Teyateyaneng [Berea] to GS, 28 January 1947; DC Quthing to Elliot, n.d.; DC Mohale's Hoek (Wilson) to Elliot, 13 February 1947.
21. PRO, DO 119/1372, 9657I, Jack Lempepe, Cape Town, to HC, 18 November 1948; KS and CM interview, Lebihan Masupha, 19 May 1999; Patrick Mohlalefi Bereng and PS interview, 'Mamathe Gabashane Masupha, 3 June 1999.
22. Rivers Thompson, 'Reminiscences', p. 35.
23. PRO, DO 35/4160, Y3535/1, Forsyth-Thompson to Sir Walter Huggard, 24 December 1946. The incident and court proceedings were reported in *Moeletsi*, 18 December 1945, 5 March 1946, 30 April 1946.
24. KS and CM interview, Lebihan Masupha, 19 May 1999. The timing suggested by Lebihan is broadly supported by Ashton, who states that Gabashane was said to have turned against 'Mantšebo and joined forces with Bereng by the end of 1946: PRO, DO 119/1377, 9916, Ashton, 'Ritual Murder', p. 14. In 1949 an official identified 'the beginning of the fall-out between 'Mantšebo and Gabashane' as a series of incidents on a train to Johannesburg in late 1945, in which Gabashane, travelling with the regent, behaved in a 'most insulting and disgusting manner' and was severely reprimanded by her: FCO, Box 1177, S 262, DC Quthing to GS, 26 August 1949. It is also possible that Gabashane found that his influence at Matsieng had been waning for some time before these incidents. The question of the timing of Gabashane's shift of alliance is interesting for another reason also. Gabashane had a close friendship with Solomon Lion, leader of the Zion Apostolic Faith Mission, based at Maboloka, north-west of Pretoria. They had attended Fort Hare together, and Lion visited Basutoland frequently

through the 1940s. Their friendship was cemented in the next generation, after Gabashane's death, through the marriage of Lion's son and heir to Gabashane's eldest daughter. According to Ashton, Solomon Lion was also rumoured to have demonstrated a medicine murder before 'Mantšebo at Matsieng 'in order to regain the position his father [Edward Lion] had lost in Basutoland', though there is no specific date attached to this suggestion. Yet it seems improbable, during the late 1940s at least, that Lion should both have sustained an active friendship with Gabashane and assisted the regent to plot medicine murder. For sources on this intriguing conjunction, see Murray (1999: 359 and fns 53–6). See also FCO, Box 1177, S 262, office of CP Maseru to Commissioner of South African Police, Pretoria, 31 August 1949, when Solomon Lion was being tried for murder. Lion was also reported to be a close friend of Josiel Lefela.

25. *Explanatory Memorandum: Basuto National Treasury* (1944), pp. 48–9.
26. Reed (1950: 230).
27. FCO, Box 1167, S 197A, Peko to Gillett, 11 October 1960.
28. KS and CM interview, Lebihan Masupha, 19 May 1999.
29. The formal position after Gabashane's death was that 'Mamathe was appointed as acting Ward Chief, a figurehead only, with Lebihan as her official adviser, an arrangement required by the administration and resented by 'Mamathe. Their relationship broke down in 1955, with Lebihan reported to be suffering from stress and acute alcoholism. He was also susceptible, officials noted, to the influence of the BAC. 'Mamathe and Lebihan each alleged that the other was trying to organise a medicine murder. These difficulties are outlined in detail in FCO, Box 1167, S 197A, Notes, Berea District, January 1954; and S 52, Rivers Thompson to Arrowsmith, 1 May 1956.
30. PRO, DO 119/1383, 9657II, Petition of Bishop C. J. Ferguson-Davie and others on behalf of Chief Gabashane and others to HC, 30 July 1949.
31. PRO, DO 119/1372, 9657I, Judge Sutton to HC, 28 December 1948, pp. 3–4.
32. KS and CM interview, Lebihan Masupha, 19 May 1999.
33. Gideon Pott to CM, 9 August 1983. Years later, in a debate on the merits of Basotho doctors, Ntsu Mokhehle pointed to Fusi's successes as proof that white doctors had no monopoly of wisdom: *Proc. (Special 1957) BNC*, May 1957, vol. II, p. 243.
34. PRO, DO 119/1372, 9657I, HC trial record, judgement, pp. 789–91.
35. Reed (1950: 235, 227).
36. KS and CM interview, 'Maluke Rakokoli, 20 May 1999. 'Maluke was a daughter in the third house of Moorosana, a son of Chief Masupha.
37. LNA, HC 19/48, PE record, evidence of Mapeshoane Masupha; PRO, DO 119/1372, 9657I, evidence of 'Masiele Ntai, 'Meleke Ntai's wife, cited in judgement, pp. 789–90; KS and CM interview, Nkherepe Molefe, 29 November 1998.
38. PS interview, Albert Brutsch, 11 October 1997.
39. KS and CM interview, Ntsane Ntai, 19 May 1999.
40. PRO, DO 35/4154, Y3515, J. A. Gray, 'The Land of Moshesh ...', *South Africa*, November 1948.
41. PRO, DO 119/1372, 9657I, Jack Lempepe to HC, 18 November 1948.
42. PRO, DO 119/1372, 9657I, Judge Sutton to HC, 28 December 1948, p. 4.
43. PRO, DO 119/1372, 9657I, Judge Sutton to HC, 28 December 1948; HC's response, 2 March 1949.
44. Xavier [Safere] Ntsoso's and Moloi Ntai's statements to Scott, at Maseru gaol on 10 August 1948, are in PRO, DO 119/1377, 9916.
45. PRO, DO 119/1372, 9657I, HC 19/48, judgement, pp. 818–26. Fusi Rakokoli's and Moloi Ntai's allegations are also found in PRO, DO 119/1376, Record of case heard in DC's Court, Maseru, before E. C. Butler on 4 February 1949 and following days.

46. PRO, DO 119/1377, 9916, statement of Anacleta Masupha, Maseru, 11 August 1948. TY is Teyateyaneng.
47. PRO, DO 119/1377, 9916, statement of Anacleta Masupha enclosed with Appendix B (CP report to GS, 31 March 1949) to RC's circular to all DCs on ritual murder, 25 April 1949.
48. Miriam Basner to CM, 6 October 1995.
49. Thabo Rust (son of Ludwig Charles Rust) to CM, 13 October 1971.
50. Gideon Pott to CM, 9 August 1983; CM interview, Gideon Pott, 7 August 1998.
51. PRO, DO 4099, Y3200/13, A. A. Golds, minute, 18 January 1949. Cooper assured Golds that 'he was no lover of melodrama' and not a 'crank or a fusspot' but 'a solid, sober South African man of business (which he appeared indeed to be) ...' See also PRO, DO 119/1372, 9657I, Cooper to Golds, 22 January 1949.
52. PRO, DO 119/1373, 9657II, Petition of Bishop C. J. Ferguson-Davie and others on behalf of Chief Gabashane Masupha and others to HC, 30 July 1949.
53. PRO, DO 119/1373, 9657II, Z. K. Matthews to Bishop Ferguson-Davie, 28 February 1949.
54. FCO, Box 1175, S 119, Duncan to Forsyth-Thompson, 2 April 1948. See also PRO, DO 119/1372, 9657I, Jack Lempepe to HC, 18 November 1948.
55. PRO, DO 35/4096, Y3200/8, Privy Council Appeal no. 32 and correspondence relating thereto.
56. PRO, DO 119/1373, 9657II, A. C. Thompson, 'Memorandum on Ritual Murders in the High Commission Territories'.
57. PRO, DO 119/1373, 9657II, Privy Council Appeal no. 6 of 1949, Case for the Appellants and Case for the Respondent.
58. Willan (1955a), Privy Council Appeal no. 6 of 1949, Judgement, pp. 149–59.
59. Jones (1951: 59).
60. PRO, DO 35/7332, 222/11/5, Nking Monokoa, Secretary-General of the BAC, to Secretary of State for Commonwealth Relations, 29 January 1957; RHL, MSS Brit. Emp. S381, Hector Papers, 'Confidential Minutes of Conference on Diretlo ... commencing 27 August 1956', remarks of B. M. Khaketla, 27 August, p. 13.
61. Jones (1951: 59).
62. PRO, DO 119/1373, 9657II, RC to HC, 29 July 1949; DO 119/1374, 9657III, L. W. Clark, Acting Lieutenant-Colonel and CP, to GS, Maseru, 16 August 1949.
63. PRO, DO 119/1373, 9675II, GS, Maseru, to Chief Secretary, Pretoria, 29 July 1949.
64. Bereng to Baring, 2 August 1949, quoted in *Inkululeko*, 19 November 1949.
65. PRO, DO 119/1373, 9657II, Acting RC to HC, 19 July 1949; Bishop Ferguson-Davie, Pietermaritzburg, to HC, 28 July 1948, and letters attached; Chief Secretary, Pretoria, to GS, Maseru, 2 August 1949; *Mochochonono*, 13 August 1949.
66. PRO, DO 119/1373, 9657II, *Pretoria News*, 3 August 1949; DO 35/4099, Y3200/13, *The Scotsman*, 4 August 1949.
67. *Mochochonono*, 13 August 1949. See Jones (1951: 20) for his summary of the reaction.
68. Reed (1950: 233).
69. John Perry to CM, 19 May 1998.
70. Patrick Mohlalefi Bereng and PS interview, 'Mamathe Gabashane Masupha, 3 June 1999.

CHAPTER 4

1. *Inkululeko*, 19 November 1949.
2. PRO, DO 119/1373, GS to Chief Secretary to HC, 19 July 1949; RC to Baring, 29 July 1949.
3. See Pratten (forthcoming b). While his professional experience had been in another part of Africa, Jones was familiar both with problems of colonial administrative reform and with phenomena comparable to that of medicine murder in Basutoland.
4. The correspondence about Jones' appointment is in PRO, DO 35/4154, 4155, 4156 and 4157, and DO 119/1376, 1377 and 1378.
5. Jones (1951: 1). The analysis below is based on a detailed scrutiny of Jones' report.
6. All this press comment is in PRO, DO 35/4158.
7. PRO, DO 119/1378, testimonial from Bishop Ferguson-Davie of Pietermaritzburg, 26 August 1949.
8. Jones (1951: 1).
8. Jones (1951: 2).
10. 'Ritual Murder in Basutoland', p. 1. Full references to all three of Ashton's 'secret' papers are given in section A of the Sources, under 'Jagger Library, University of Cape Town'.
11. *Proc. (45) BNC*, vol. II, 12 September 1949, p. 2; for the full debate, see pp. 26–36. 'Ritual' was translated as *moetlo*, which is defined in the dictionary as 'manner, custom'.
12. Jones Papers, Box S1, file on 'Correspondence re Diretlo Murder Report', W. A. W. Clark to Jones, 8 January 1951; PRO, DO 35/4154, Gordon Walker's handwritten note, 6 November 1950, on the briefing for his visit to Southern Africa, 'Basutoland: Ritual Murders', dated November 1950.
13. In fact, there appear to have been two cases of this type (1925/1 and 1927/1).
14. One of the most virulent denunciations of Roman Catholicism was expressed by Gideon Pott, DC of Berea, in an undated 'Memorandum on Ritual Murders in Basutoland': University of the Witwatersrand Library, Rheinallt Jones Papers, A394/G7/8.
15. Ashton, 'Ritual Murder in Basutoland', pp. 13, 20, and 'Analysis', p. 11. The two cases were 1944/6 (*R* v. *Lagden Majara and three others*) and 1944/7 (*R* v. *Mahlomola Lerotholi and fourteen others*).
16. Ashton, 'Ritual Murder in Basutoland', p. 14; 'Mokhotlong District', pp. 33–4; 'Analysis', pp. 8–10.
17. Jones (1951: 65).
18. PRO, DO 35/7332, Hector to Scrivenor, 11 February 1958; Scott (1958: 206).
19. PRO, DO 119/1378, *The Friend*, 14 April 1950, quoting *Moeletsi*.
20. Jones (1951: v); PRO, DO 119/1380, Baring's interim comments on the Jones report, drafted by Clark and forwarded to London 10 June 1950.
21. Jones Papers, Box S1, file on 'Correspondence re Diretlo Murder Report', Baring to Jones, 6 June 1950, enclosing Forsyth-Thompson's comments.
22. Rivers Thompson, 'Reminiscences', p. 31.
23. Jones Papers, Box S1, file on 'Correspondence re Diretlo Murder Report', Armstrong's comments quoted in Forsyth-Thompson, 'Comments on Mr G. I. Jones' Report', sent to Jones under cover of Baring's letter of 6 June 1950.
24. PRO, DO 35/4158, Minute by W. A. W. Clark, 17 January 1951; PRO, DO 119/1380, Minute by Clark, 5 June 1950, and Baring's interim comments on the Jones report, drafted by Clark and forwarded to London 10 June 1950.
25. *CAR 1952*, p. 75.
26. FCO, Box 1177, S 262, Sheddick to GS, 21 June 1950.

27. Hailey (1953, part V: 131–2).
28. PRO, DO 119/1382, Minute by official with illegible signature, 13 January 1953.
29. Jones (1951: 35).
30. PRO, DO 35/4158, Y3515/11, Jones' draft report, para. 106.
31. PRO, DO 35/4154, Note prepared in November 1950 in the CRO for the Secretary of State's visit to Southern Africa, entitled 'Basutoland: Ritual Murders'; PRO, DO 35/4158, Baring's memorandum of December 1949 ('Left by Sir E. Baring for our file').
32. PRO, DO 119/1380, Forsyth-Thompson to Baring, 14 April 1950.
33. PRO, DO 35/4158, Baring to Jones, 6 June 1950.
34. PRO, DO 35/4158, 'Note of a meeting in Mr Baxter's room on Friday, 30th June [1950]'.
35. Jones Papers, Box S1, file on 'Correspondence re Diretlo Murder Report', marginal note on Baring to Jones, 6 June 1950; PRO, DO 35/4158, Jones to Baring, 13 June 1950.
36. PRO, DO 35/4158, telegram Turnbull to Baxter, 25 January 1951; Baring to Jones, 6 June 1950.
37. This correspondence is in PRO, DO 119/1380, ff. 26–47.
38. PRO, DO 119/1380, Baring to Gordon Walker, 18 November 1950.
39. Jones (1951: v); PRO, DO 35/4010, Baring to Gordon Walker, 22 September 1950.
40. Jones (1951: 2–3); CAR 1950, p. 61; Laydevant (1950: 141).
41. PRO, DO 35/4010, Baring to Gordon Walker, 22 September 1950.
42. Basutoland News, 13 February 1951.
43. This visit is described in FCO, Box 1178, S 161, vol. II, secret report by Fraser enclosed with ? to Dashwood, 8 January 1951; PRO, DO 35/4175, 4176 and 4177; and in Sekoai (1961).
44. See Case Study 4 (1952/12); PRO, DO 119/1382, Acting GS, Maseru, to HC, 28 January 1953.
45. The meanings of the phrase 'heart of darkness' have been much dissected in many different ways over the course of the century since publication of Conrad's famous short novel. Our use of it here in one particular sense reflects the predominant tone of comment on medicine murder in Basutoland by officials and outsiders in the later 1940s and early 1950s.
46. Ashton (1952: 313).
47. PRO, DO 119/1382, 'Report by Major A. H. Donald and Chief Leshoboro Majara', enclosure with Arrowsmith to Chief Secretary to HC, 31 July 1953, p. 3.
48. In 1949 the Church of England, for example, used it to raise funds to establish a new diocese in Basutoland: PRO, DO 119/1378, Forsyth-Thompson's speech reported in The Star, 31 May 1949; Basutoland News, 23 August 1949; Forsyth-Thompson (1949).
49. H. Dieterlen (1896: 263).
50. G. Dieterlen (1950: 46).
51. Quoted in The Friend, 6 March 1950: see PRO, DO 119/1378.
52. Laydevant (1937: 214–5; 1950: 138–9); PS interview, Albert Brutsch, 9 December 1996. (Brutsch and Laydevant were both members of the Committee set up by the Round Table Conference.)
53. Daily Despatch, 6 October 1949, quoted by Ntsu Mokhehle in Mohlabani, June 1957, p. 14.
54. Church Times, 25 May 1949, and The Outspan, 24 June 1949, quoted by Ntsu Mokhehle in Mohlabani, June 1957, p. 11. Cyprian Thorpe's views are fully elaborated in PRO, DO 35/4155, memorandum on 'Ritual Murder in Basuto-

land', enclosed with Byers to Gordon Walker, 20 January 1949.

55. *The Star*, 12 November 1949, quoted in *Basutoland News*, 20 December 1949; see van Straaten's articles (1948a; 1948b; 1949) in *The Nongqai*, a South African police journal.

56. PRO, DO 119/1380, Baring's interim comments on the Jones report, drafted by Clark and forwarded to London 10 June 1950.

57. PRO, DO 119/1384, Minute, 30 October 1954.

58. Cited in *Basutoland News*, 20 December 1949.

59. Editorial, 'Lipolao tsa Manaka Li Felisoe', *Mochochonono*, 27 July 1946; E. P. Mopeli, 'Lingaka', *Mochochonono*, 5 February 1949; E. J. Makhotla, article in *Leselinyana*, 24–31 December 1951; Philip Kazhila, article in *Leselinyana*, 14 January 1952; 'Khomo-e-tšehla', article in *Leselinyana*, 19 May 1952; Mathias Matjeleka, article in *Moeletsi*, 15 September 1952; Matšaba (1953: 26–7).

60. *Cape Argus*, 28 April 1951 (copy in PRO, DO 119/1381). On the whole, though, the South African press was restrained, and the *Argus* pointed out that there 'were plenty of white people whose own civilization is hardly more than a veneer'; see PRO, DO 119/1381, ff. 12–15.

61. Packer (1953: 97–107).

62. Gunther (1957). He had published an article in *Reader's Digest* (Gunther 1954: 6–8), but this provoked less comment.

63. Gunther (1957: 555–62).

64. Jones (1951: 21).

65. Philip L. Mokhatla, 'Mr Josiel Lefela ka tsa Liretlo Mafeteng', *Moeletsi*, 24 January 1950. Lefela's reply is in *Inkululeko*, 18 February and 4 March 1950; FCO, Box 1178, S 34, CP to GS, 1 May 1952.

66. PRO, DO 119/1382, note by le Rougetel, 18 March 1953; le Rougetel to Secretary of State, 23 April 1953.

67. PRO, DO 119/1383, Arrowsmith to Deputy HC, 16 March 1954; Weisfelder (1999: 7–8).

68. Mokhehle (2nd edn 1990: ix); the first edition, which was less developed in argument, was published in 1976.

69. Khaketla (1971: 50).

70. Machobane (1990: 253–6).

71. *Basutoland News*, 16 June 1953; Moleleki (1994: 49).

72. Khaketla (1971: 50).

73. PRO, DO 35/7332, Presidential Address to the Annual Conference of the BAC, 29–31 December 1956. Except for the last five pages, it was reprinted in five issues of the BAC's newspaper, *Mohlabani*, from May 1957 to December 1957. Except where otherwise indicated, quotations are from *Mohlabani*.

74. Mokhehle's analysis of the law was not completely accurate; see Chapter 9.

75. PRO, DO 35/7332, Presidential Address, p. 20.

76. PRO, DO 35/7332, Resolutions attached to Presidential Address.

77. Khaketla (1971: 50); Moleleki (1994: 49).

78. This development is analysed in Weisfelder (1999: 9–11). 'Mantšebo's fears are referred to in PRO, DO 35/4361, Tergos, no. 11, November 1955.

79. PRO, DO 119/1384, Arrowsmith to Scrivenor, 10 February 1956.

80. PRO, DO 35/7332, Tergos, June 1958.

81. *Leselinyana*, 8 March and 1 November 1954; Kaizer Mohlakola, 'Liretlo Lesotho', *Leselinyana*, 10 January 1955; B. M. H. Masilo, 'Ba re Liretlo ha li eo Lesotho', *Leselinyana*, 4 February 1957.

82. *Moeletsi*, 6 April 1957, 5 December 1959.

83. Jones (1951: 21).

84. See, for example, PRO, DO 119/1382, Note by le Rougetel on visit to Basutoland, 18 March 1953; PRO, DO 119/1382, Arrowsmith to Turnbull, 12 September 1953; PRO, DO 119/1383, RC's address to Anti-Liretlo Pitsos, enclosed with Arrowsmith to Deputy HC, 4 March 1954; PRO, DO 119/1384, Arrowsmith to Scrivenor, 10 February 1956; PRO, DO 119/1384, Arrowsmith, minute of 26 June 1956.
85. Kaizer Mohlakola, 'Liretlo Lesotho', *Leselinyana*, 10 January 1955.

CASE STUDY 4

1. Alexander (1992: 29–30).
2. Cordery (1993: 36).
3. KS and PS interview, Molosi Kao, 27 May 1999.
4. Alexander (1992: 28).
5. The political structure of the Mokhotlong District in 1936 and 1939 is shown diagrammatically in Ashton (1952: 189, 191). The 1950 Gazette shows 'the Chief of Malingoaneng' as subordinate to the Principal [or Ward] Chief of Mokhotlong. See HC's Notice no. 176 of 1950.
6. An additional case, 1950/5, is anomalous in the sense that it is listed in the Appendix as belonging to Tlokoeng Ward and Butha-Buthe District. For consistency, we have omitted this case from the present analysis, relating to Mokhotlong District, but included it in Table 6.1 in the total for Tlokoeng Ward.
7. Ashton, in 'Mokhotlong District', p. 11, indicates that 'Mantšebo's area had 2,723 taxpayers out of 10,599 in the district as a whole. Other relevant population figures are given in Ashton (1952: 189–192, and Appendix V: 342–5).
8. Ambrose Archives, Mokhotlong files, C2, Henderson, DC Mokhotlong, to GS, Maseru, 21 September 1946.
9. Mokhotlong files, C2, Confidential Reports on Chiefs, Gray on Matlere 29 April 1948; PRO, DO 119/1382, S/117I, Arrowsmith to Wray, 26 November 1952; Driver (1996); PS interviews, Desmond Taylor, 27 September 1995, and Ray Cordery, 23 January 1998.
10. Ashton, 'Mokhotlong District', p. 31.
11. Mokhotlong files; Ashton, 'Ritual Murder in Basutoland', 'Mokhotlong District' and 'Analysis'; PRO, DO 35/914/10, Affairs of the Batlokoa Tribe, Basutoland [1937–43].
12. 'Mokhotlong District' and 'Analysis'. Both were marked 'secret', and Ashton is not explicitly identified as the author of them. Full references are given in section A of the Sources, under 'Jagger Library, University of Cape Town'.
13. Ashton, 'Mokhotlong District', p. 2.
14. Rivers Thompson, 'Reminiscences', p. 31; *Basutoland News*, 19 December 1933, reprinted in *Basutoland News*, 16 December 1958.
15. Ashton (1952: 201–3); 'Mokhotlong District', p. 6.
16. Ashton, 'Mokhotlong District', p. 8; UCT, BC859, Ashton Papers, records of JC 31/46, judgement.
17. Ashton, 'Mokhotlong District', pp. 2–3.
18. Rivers Thompson, 'Reminiscences', p. 70.
19. Mokhotlong files, C2, Confidential Reports on Chiefs, 1936; Ashton, 'Mokhotlong District', pp. 3–4; 'Analysis', p. 2; Ashton (1952: 201).
20. Mokhotlong files, C5, Rafolatsane Chieftainship, notes by G. B. Gray, 13 November 1950; DC Mokhotlong to GS, Maseru, 16 May 1954; J. P. I. Hennessy to GS, Maseru, 31 July 1954.
21. Ashton (1952: 82 fn. 1). Lerotholi had over sixty wives: Ashton, 'Mokhotlong District', p. 5.

22. Ashton, 'Mokhotlong District', pp. 13–14.
23. Ashton, 'Mokhotlong District', pp. 13–14; Ashton (1952, Appendix V: 342–5).
24. LNA, HC 303/46, PE record [case 1943/3], evidence of Maraene Tšita; Ashton (1952: 342).
25. Ashton, 'Analysis', p. 2. This opinion was clearly based on that expressed by D. M. Wilson, the Assistant DC, to his superior officer in Qacha's Nek, 28 February 1941: Mokhotlong files, C4, Thabang Chieftainship and Court.
26. Mokhotlong files, C4, Thabang Chieftainship and Court, Gideon Pott to DC Qacha's Nek, 20 August 1941, 29 October 1942.
27. Ashton, 'Mokhotlong District', pp. 5–6, 11–13, 32; Ashton, 'Analysis', p. 5.
28. Ashton, 'Mokhotlong District', pp. 10, 12.
29. Ashton, 'Mokhotlong District', pp. 20–1, 34.
30. Ashton, 'Analysis', p. 3.
31. Ashton, 'Analysis', p. 3; *Basutoland News* 6, 13, 20 May 1947, 23 December 1947; Jones Papers, Box S1, file on 'Basutoland and Swaziland, Schedule of Ritual Murders 1949 and Earlier', notes on 'Case no. 29: *R* v. *Mahlomola Lerotholi and others*' [no. 42 in Jones' published Appendix A].
32. Ashton, 'Analysis', p. 4.
33. Ashton, 'Analysis', p. 6.
34. FCO, Box 1175, S 119, Mokhotlong telegram to CP, 8 February 1950; Thompson to Arrowsmith, 12 November 1952; also FCO, Box 1176, S 119, Stenton to GS, 4 December 1958, and Stenton to Gillett, 7 December 1959.
35. LNA, CRI/T/4/53, PE record, evidence of Dr P. A. N. Dale Lace; HC trial record, judgement, pp. 1–2; *Basutoland News*, 17 February 1953.
36. LNA, CRI/T/4/53, PE record, evidence of Matjoa Tšita.
37. *Basutoland News*, 20 January 1953.
38. LNA, CRI/T/4/53, HC trial record, judgement, pp. 2–4; *Basutoland News*, 17 February 1953.
39. FCO, Box 1175, S 119, Arrowsmith to Turnbull, 23 March 1953; PS telephone interview, Paul Kitson, 21 October 1997.
40. *Basutoland News*, 24 February 1953; PRO, DO 119/1382, Acting GS to Chief Secretary to HC, 28 January 1953, enclosing CP to GS, 19 January 1953; Arrowsmith to Turnbull, 23 March 1953.
41. PRO, DO 119/1382, S/117I, Arrowsmith to Wray, 26 November 1952. A year and a half later Arrowsmith acknowledged that, since Constantine Bereng would only be sixteen in May 1954, there was 'no possibility of an early accession': PRO, DO 119/1383, Arrowsmith to Deputy HC, 4 March 1954.
42. See discussion of this issue in Chapter 9.
43. This might have been Lieutenant van Straaten, who led the prosecution case at the preparatory examination.
44. KS and PS interview, Seane Klaas, 26 May 1999.
45. KS and PS interview, Seane Klaas, 26 May 1999.
46. KS and PS interview, Motleri Clement Rabolai, 27 May 1999.
47. FCO, Box 1175, S 119, Arrowsmith to Wray, 26 November 1952, Inglis (DC Mokhotlong) to GS, 6 March 1953, Attorney-General to CP, 23 March 1953, etc.
48. KS and PS interview, Seane Klaas, 26 May 1999.
49. KS and PS interview, Elliot Teboho Morojele, 27 May 1999.
50. PRO, DO 119/1388, judgement, p. 412 (the judgement is also in LNA, CRI/T/ 34/60).
51. PRO, DO 119/1386, f. 3, undated memo from ? CID Maseru.
52. PRO, DO 119/1388, judgement, p. 413.

53. PRO, DO 119/1388, judgement, pp. 418–19.
54. PRO, DO 119/1388, judgement, pp. 420–1.
55. PRO, DO 119/1388, HC record, pp. 214–29.
56. PRO, DO 119/1386, J. A. Steward for HC to Secretary for External Affairs, Pretoria, 19 September 1960, and note dated 31 October.
57. PRO, DO 119/1388, judgement, p. 423.
58. PRO, DO 119/1388, HC record, pp. 212–13, evidence of June Margaret Nicholas.
59. PRO, DO 119/1388, judgement, p. 428.
60. PRO, DO 119/1386, Roper to HC, 25 November 1960.
61. LNA, CRI/T/34/60, judgement in the appeal of Makhahlela Lerotholi and others.
62. PRO, DO 119/1388, Minutes of Executive Council, 5 September 1961.
63. PRO, DO 119/1386, Chief Justice Herbert Cox to HC, 12 June 1961.
64. PRO, DO 119/1386, Lichtenberg to Attorney-General, C. B. O'Beirne, 4 August 1961.
65. PRO, DO 119/1386, Chief Justice Herbert Cox to HC, 12 June 1961.
66. KS and PS interview, Molosi Kao, 27 May 1999.
67. *Basutoland News*, 17 January 1961.

CHAPTER 5

1. RHL, MSS Brit. Emp. S381, Hector Papers, file 3/4.
2. *Basutoland News*, 29 September 1953; *Leselinyana*, 12 October 1953.
3. PS interviews, Ray Cordery, 23 January 1998; Sir James Hennessy, 16 October 1995; and Desmond Taylor, 27 September 1995; CM interview, Gideon Pott, 7 August 1998; and Rivers Thompson, 'Reminiscences', pp. 64–6.
4. Epprecht (2000: 115).
5. *Basutoland: Report of the Administrative Reforms Committee* (1954), p. 5.
6. Hailey (1953, part V: 136–42).
7. PRO, DO 119/1384, M1, J. A. S[teward] to Deputy HC, 30 October 1954; J. A. S[teward], 'Note on the Recording of Hereditary Rights in Basutoland', 11 December 1954; M10, T. V. S[crivenor], 28 January 1955.
8. *Basutoland: Report of the Administrative Reforms Committee* (1954), and *Proc. (Special 1955) BNC*, 22 March to 30 March 1955. See also Patrick Duncan's article in *The Friend*, reproduced in *Basutoland News*, 18 January 1955; *Mohlabani*, March 1955, pp. 12–15, and April–May 1955, pp. 3–5; and *Basutoland News*, 5 April 1955.
9. FCO, Box 1175, S 119, Deputy CP to CP, 26 April 1952; 'Bara ba Moshoeshoe Matsieng', *Mochochonono*, 3 and 10 May 1952.
10. There are many editorials, articles and letters in *Leselinyana*, *Moeletsi* and elsewhere.
11. Hailey (1953, part V: 132).
12. FCO, Box 1175, S 119, Wray, HC's Office, to ? in London, 5 January 1953.
13. FCO, Box 1175, S 119, 'Summary of suggestions discussed by District Commissioners on the subject of means to prevent medicine murders'; PRO, DO 119/1382, Marwick to Chief Secretary to HC, 4 February 1953.
14. FCO, Box 1175, S 119, Arrowsmith to Turnbull, 15 August 1952; Arrowsmith to Wray, 26 November 1952.
15. FCO, Box 1178, S 161, vol. III, transcript of telephone conversation, Arrowsmith and Acting Chief Secretary to HC, 29 January 1953; FCO, Box 1176, S 119, Arrowsmith's undated minute on a meeting held on 11 March 1954.
16. PRO, DO 119/1382, Arrowsmith to Turnbull, 12 September 1953; PRO, DO

119/1383, draft annual report of CP for 1953, quoted in Arrowsmith to Deputy HC, 4 March 1953; and *Proc. (49) BNC*, vol. II, 26 September 1953, p. 4.

17. PRO, DO 119/1382, enclosure with Arrowsmith to Chief Secretary to HC, 31 July 1953.

18. PRO, DO 119/1382, Arrowsmith to Turnbull, 12 September 1953, with enclosure.

19. *Basutoland News*, 11 September 1953.

20. PRO, DO 119/1383, Summary of evidence submitted to the Conference prepared by Major Donald, Chief Leshoboro Majara and B. K. Taoana.

21. PRO, DO 119/1383, Arrowsmith to Deputy HC, 16 March 1954.

22. PRO, DO 119/1382, enclosure with Arrowsmith to Turnbull, 12 September 1953.

23. Official reports on the anti-*liretlo* campaign are in PRO, DO 119/1383, Arrowsmith to Deputy HC, 4 March 1954, and Marwick to Scrivenor, 31 July 1954. 'Resident Commissioner's Address' and 'Address of the Honourable Paramount Chief' are in RHL, MSS Brit. Emp. S511/3/3, Arrowsmith Papers. The pamphlet *Liretlo, Liretlo, Liretlo?* (1953) was published by the government with a Foreword from 'Mantšebo. It was written originally by a trader, K. Nolan (PRO, DO 119/1382, Marwick to Chief Secretary to HC, 4 February 1953). Press reports on the campaign are in *Leselinyana*, 28 September 1953, 22 March 1954, 30 August 1954; *Moeletsi*, 6 February 1954; *Basutoland News*, 13 October 1953, 26 January 1954, 9 February 1954, 23 February 1954, 2 March 1954.

24. PRO, DO 119/1383, Arrowsmith to Deputy HC, 4 March 1954.

25. PRO, DO 119/1382, evidence of Mark Photane, enclosure with Arrowsmith to Turnbull, 12 September 1953.

26. PRO, DO 119/1384, 'Report of the Committee appointed by the Round Table Conference on Medicine Murder', enclosed with Acting RC to Deputy HC, 22 October 1954.

27. PRO, DO 119/1384, M1, J. A. S[teward] to Deputy HC, 30 October 1954.

28. PRO, DO 119/1384, M4, Attorney-General, 12 November 1954.

29. PRO, DO 119/1384, M7, Scrivenor to HC, 23 November 1954.

30. PRO, DO 119/1384, M8, le Rougetel to Scrivenor, 6 December 1954.

31. PRO, DO 119/1383, Minute to Deputy HC, 24 February 1954.

32. *Basutoland News*, 28 September 1954; *Leselinyana*, 4 October 1954.

33. PRO, DO 119/1384, M6, Scrivenor to le Rougetel, 23 November 1954.

34. PRO, DO 119/1384, M7, Scrivenor to le Rougetel, 30 November 1954; PRO, DO 119/1382, minutes at front of file.

35. PRO, DO 119/1383, Marwick to Scrivenor, 31 July 1954.

36. PRO, DO 119/1384, M1, J. A. S[teward] to Deputy HC, 30 October 1954; M4, Minute by Attorney-General, 12 November 1954; M6, Scrivenor to le Rougetel, 23 November 1954, and M7, Scrivenor to le Rougetel, 30 November 1954; M8, le Rougetel to Scrivenor, 6 December 1954.

37. FCO, Box 1178, S 161, vol. III, f. 22, transcript of part of HC record in CRI/T/ 1/53, *R v Pheello Smith and others*.

38. FCO, Box 1176, S 119, 'Pro Bono Publico' (an anonymous writer, apparently from Mapoteng), 14 August 1954; PRO, DO 119/1383, letter from 'Basuto' to Marion Walsham-How, 27 February 1954, enclosed with Marion Walsham How to le Rougetel, 11 March 1954.

39. FCO, Box 1175, Box 119, Arrowsmith to Wray, 8 April 1954; PRO, DO 119/ 1383, Marwick to Scrivenor, 31 July 1954; *Proc. (52) BNC*, 1956, vol. II, p. 253.

40. FCO, Box 1178, S 161, Arrowsmith to Scrivenor, 12 June 1954.

41. PRO, DO 119/1384, Arrowsmith to Deputy HC, 30 May 1956.

42. 1945/4, 1945/6, 1945/8 and 1945/11.
43. *Basutoland News*, 12 July 1955; Edgar (1987: 37).
44. For another debate in which Sesotho medicine was strongly supported, see *Proc. (Special 1957) BNC*, May 1957, vol. II, pp. 240–6.
45. PRO, DO 35/4489, Liesching to Laithwaite, 7 December 1956.
46. *Proc. (Special 1956) BNC*, 7–17 May 1956; PRO, DO 119/1384, Arrowsmith to Scrivenor, 30 May 1956.
47. RHL, MSS Brit. Emp. S381, Hector Papers, file 2/6, draft 'Report of Meetings held between Representatives of the Resident Commissioner, Paramount Chief, Basutoland Mounted Police, District Councils and the General Public between 27–31 August, 1956', p. 1. This is the draft of the report that was subsequently submitted to the BNC. The fullest account of the meeting, also in file 2/6, is the 'Minutes of Conference on Diretlo held in the Education Department Board Room, Maseru, Commencing on the 27th of August, 1956'. See also PRO, DO 119/1384, Hector's report, 1 September 1956, enclosed with Arrowsmith to Marwick, 4 September 1956; and RHL, MSS Brit. Emp. S381, Hector Papers, file 3/4, Hector to his parents, 2 September 1956, quoted at the head of this chapter.
48. PRO, DO 35/4361, Tergos (an intelligence report), September 1955.
49. PRO, DO 119/1382, Khaketla, 'Memorandum on "Liretlo"' (enclosed with Arrowsmith to Turnbull, 12 September 1953), p. 1.
50. PRO, DO 35/7332, telegram HC to CRO, 13 March 1957, and attachment to Hector to HC, 11 February 1958.
51. All quotations, except where otherwise indicated, are from PRO, DO 119/1384, Hector's report, 1 September 1956, enclosed with Arrowsmith to Marwick, 4 September 1956. See also RHL, MSS Brit. Emp. S381, Hector Papers, file 2/6, 'Minutes of Conference on Diretlo held in the Education Department Board Room, Maseru, Commencing on the 27th of August, 1956', and draft 'Report on Meetings held between Representatives of the Resident Commissioner, Paramount Chief, Basutoland Mounted Police, District Councils and the General Public between 27–31 August, 1956'.
52. KS and PS interview, Nkherepe Molefe, 24 May 1999.
53. PRO, DO 35/4462, Liesching to Laithwaite, 21 November 1956, and enclosure.
54. *Basutoland News*, 26 March 1957.
55. *Proc. (52) BNC*, 1956, vol. I, p. 32, minutes of proceedings on 11 October 1956; *Proc. (53) BNC*, vol. II (1959), pp. 444–62, proceedings of 20 March 1958; PRO, DO 35/7332, HC to CRO, 1 April 1958.
56. FCO, Box 1176, S 119, RC to PC, 16 November 1959.
57. PRO, DO 35/7332, Stephen Motlamelle to Lord Home, Secretary of State for Commonwealth Relations, 6 January 1958; *Proc. (53) BNC*, vol. II (1959), proceedings of 20 March 1958, p. 446.
58. FCO, Box 1176, S 119, Hector to Nking Monokoa, 25 May 1957; HC to Secretary of State, 9 April 1958.
59. FCO, Box 1176, f. 1344B, memorandum by Hector, 18 November 1959.
60. Khaketla (1971: 50–1). Khaketla's account was confirmed by Nkherepe Molefe: KS and PS interview, 24 May 1999.
61. RHL, MSS Afr. S1773, Lady Jean Redcliffe-Maud, Diaries, 1959–63, Box II, account of a visit to Basutoland, 22 June 1959; PS telephone interview, Gordon Hector (GS throughout Chaplin's period of office), August 1997.
62. In 1954 Scrivenor asked A. E. M. Jansen, the South African Secretary for Justice, if he had any evidence about medicine murders in southern Africa generally. Jansen replied that there had been very few. This correspondence is in PRO, DO 119/1383, Scrivenor to Jansen, 5 March 1954, Jansen to Scrivenor, 24 May 1954,

Steward to Scrivenor, 23 June 1954, and Scrivenor's minute of 23 June 1954.
63. PRO, DO 35/7332, Scrivenor to Hunt, 5 March 1958.
64. *BNC, Legislative Council Debates*, 23 March 1962 and following. The quotations are taken from the following pages: L. S. Griffith, p. 249; Meshack Poola, pp. 166–7; Jonathan Ntlama, p. 188; Philemon 'Mabathoana, p. 294; Leshoboro Majara, p. 251; Sekhonyana 'Maseribane, pp. 286–7; Goliath Malebanye, p. 254; Ntsu Mokhehle, pp. 259, 260, 265.
65. This correspondence is in PRO, CO 1048/260.
66. PC's speech at the formal opening of the Legislative Council on 26 January 1962; PS, personal recollection.
67. PRO, CO 1048/260, PC to RC, 20 November 1962.
68. PRO, CO 1048/260, marginal note dated 31 December 1962; Jenkins, minute dated 7 January 1963.
69. PS and KS interview, Nkherepe Molefe, 24 May 1999.
70. Khaketla (1971).

INTERLUDE

1. For Kholumolumo, *Leselinyana*, 25 May 1953 and 19 June 1953, and *Moeletsi*, 22 June 1953. For the cannibals, the *lifaqane* and Moshoeshoe, *Leselinyana*, 14 April 1952, 7 December 1953 and 13 October 1958. 'Mantšebo also sought inspiration from history, or at least made an appearance of doing so, in her message to the Basotho people in the anti-*liretlo* campaign (*Liretlo, Liretlo, Liretlo*, p. 3).
2. PS interview, Bennett Khaketla, 10 December 1996.
3. For an analysis of this 'intertextuality' between 'fictional texts and historical discourse', see Maake (1998).
4. Willet and Ambrose (1980: entry no. 2151). All references to *Chaka* in the footnotes are to the English translation, *Chaka the Zulu* (1949).
5. Maake (1998: 92).
6. Mofolo, *Chaka the Zulu*, p. 108.
7. Maake (1998: 101).
8. Lanham and Mopeli-Paulus (1953); see Dunton (1990).
9. Morija Archives, manuscript of Autobiography of A. S. Mopeli-Paulus, 218–24.
10. Lanham and Mopeli-Paulus (1953: 98).
11. Lanham and Mopeli-Paulus (1953: 108).
12. Lanham and Mopeli-Paulus (1953: 293–4).
13. Mopeli-Paulus (1950); Mopeli-Paulus and Basner (1956).
14. Dunton (1990: 106).
15. Personal communication from David Ambrose, 1 January 1999; Matlosa (1994).
16. Matlosa (1994: 104). Capital letters in the original Sesotho.
17. Maake (1998: 92–5).
18. Khaketla (1972), Introduction dated 22 September 1959. This and other quotations are translated from Sesotho.
19. Khaketla (1972: 22, 26).
20. Khaketla (1972: 81–2).
21. Khaketla (1972: 152–3).
22. Khaketla (1972: 154).
23. Khaketla (1972: 161).
24. Ntsane (1963). This analysis is based on Maake (1998: 99–100). Ntsane (1920–83) was educated at Morija and won a scholarship to Britain in 1946. He worked variously as a teacher, a clerk in the gold mines, an editor of *Hansard*, and Press Secretary to Prime Minister Leabua Jonathan (information provided by David Ambrose).

25. Hlapisi (1986).
26. Mokhomo (1954). We are grateful to David Ambrose for bringing this to our attention.
27. Monsarrat (1956); FCO, Box 1176, S 119, photocopy of article in *The Manchester Guardian*, 20 September 1956.
28. A. A. Murray (1957).
29. Fulton (1968: 57).
30. Flather (1976).
31. Lanham and Mopeli-Paulus (1953: 317–18).

CHAPTER 6

1. LNA, CRI/T/4/56, Exhibits G and D (case 1954/9).
2. FCO, Box 1168, S 197J, Deputy HC to RC, 28 March 1954.
3. LNA, CRI/A/25–28/58, Court of Appeal, judgement, p. 2.
4. See also Tlale (1949: 12).
5. These include the instigator in case 1962/3, Makhakhe, who died before legal proceedings began.
6. Where a person was an acting Ward Chief or chief or headman, he or she was classified respectively as a Ward Chief, chief or headman. A person who was both an acting chief and a headman was classified as a chief.
7. For some comparative evidence, see the Addendum.
8. In two cases, 1964/2 and 1965/5, we have no evidence about status or occupation.
9. According to A. M. Mafelesi of the Basutoland African Herbalists Association, however, medicine murders were 'caused by elections' in 1959: FCO, Box 1176, S 119, Mafelesi's address to the Association in Mokhotlong, 21 November 1959.
10. Maqutu (1995: 1–2).
11. 'Ritual Murder in Basutoland', p. 23. See also Epprecht (2000: 118, 241).
12. An examination of the gazetted names in 1950 suggests that the proportion was about 7–8 per cent. Many of these women were acting until their children came of age.
13. LNA, HC 139/43, HC record, p. 2, evidence of Sergeant Philemon, 1 April 1943.
14. LNA, HC 139/43, HC record, p. 20, evidence of Mopeli Machakela, 2 April 1943.
15. *Proc. (Special 1956) BNC*, p. 124, 14 May 1956, speech of Mabina Lerotholi.
16. PS interview, Patrick Mohlalefi Bereng, 15 October 1997.
17. 1959/1; the full court record is in PRO, DO 119/1387 and 1388.
18. *Moeletsi*, 21 September 1963.
19. Baltzer (1912: 104).
20. FCO, Box 1176, S 368, Acting DC Quthing to GS, 10 March 1954, and enclosed report.
21. PRO, DO 35/4007, Baring to Noel-Baker, 12 November 1948.
22. RHL, MSS Brit. Emp. S381, Hector Papers, file 5, account of funeral, 13 September 1959.
23. Rivers Thompson, 'Reminiscences', pp. 76–7.
24. Jones (1951: 65); Weisfelder (1974: 166–7); Machobane (1990: 229–30); Gocking (1997: 77).
25. 1957/5: LNA, CRI/T/4/58, judgement, p. 289.
26. LNA, HC 335/47, PE record, evidence of Mofela Khobotle (1944/7).
27. LNA, HC 375/47, PE record, evidence of Jan Gat, 16 April 1947 (1945/11).
28. LNA, HC 12/48, evidence of Makhoahela Raboko (1947/15).
29. Jones (1951: 93).

30. Ashton, 'Analysis', p. 11.
31. Jones Papers, Box S1, file on 'Basutoland and Swaziland, Schedule of Ritual Murders 1949 and earlier', notes on '*Rex* vs. *Lagden Majara and others*' [no. 41 in Jones' published Appendix A]; FCO, Box 1177, S 262, Ashton, 'Ritual Murder in Berea', enclosed with Jones to Marwick, 4 August 1949.
32. LNA, HC 355/47, PE record, evidence of Mofela Khobotle.
33. This judgement is attached to LNA, HC 348/47, a perjury case arising out of the case against Tsotang Griffith. The quotation is from p. 376.
34. Jones (1951: 43–5, 104); Machobane (1990: 29).
35. *Basuto National Treasury: Explanatory Memorandum*, p. 7.
36. Jingoes (1975: 191–2). A tickey was a threepenny bit.
37. There must have been many accomplices who were never brought to court. In eleven cases either the number of accomplices or the number of accomplice witnesses is not known, or both. The figures given in this paragraph relating to accomplices and accomplice witnesses cannot therefore be definitive. They are the minimum figures justified by our evidence. The figure of 138 instigators who came before the court differs from the figure of 139 previously given because of the death of the instigator in case 1962/3 before the preparatory examination.
38. Ashton, 'Ritual Murder in Basutoland', p. 16; Jones (1951: 16); see also Ashton (1952: 309).
39. LNA, HC 15/49 (case 1946/2, Case Study 3).
40. Ashton, 'Ritual Murder in Basutoland', p. 16; Ashton (1952: 309).
41. *Moeletsi*, 24 August 1953.
42. FCO, Box 1176, S 368, Acting DC Quthing to GS, 10 March 1954, and enclosed report.
43. LNA, HC 53/52, PE record, evidence of Moketi Mokanohi (1951/9).
44. LNA, HC 185/44, PE record, evidence of Moeketsane Molefe (1943/4).
45. Packer (1953: 101).
46. Eldredge (1997: 4–6).
47. Jones (1951: 18).
48. PRO, DO 119/1382, Khaketla, 'Memorandum on "Liretlo"' (enclosed with Arrowsmith to Turnbull, 12 September 1953), pp. 7–8.
49. LNA, HC 36/49, PE record, evidence of Sejakhosi Rafolatsane.
50. LNA, HC 53/52, PE record, evidence of Moketi Mokhanohi.
51. LNA, HC 44/49, PE record, evidence of Mphapha Lebona.
52. *Proc. (Special 1956) BNC*, 8 May 1956, p. 51, speech of Chief Sekhonyana 'Maseribane; *Proc. (42) BNC*, vol. I, 18 October 1946, p. 179, speech of Chief Leloko Lerotholi.
53. Other examples are cases 1948/6, 1948/10, 1948/18, 1953/3, 1954/4, 1954/6, 1958/1, 1959/2 and 1961/2. In our analysis of cases in the Appendix we recorded sixty-eight accomplices who had been offered rewards. Of these fourteen were friends or relatives of the victim, compared with six who were closely connected with the instigator.

CHAPTER 7

1. Other cases in which doctors are said to have advised that *liretlo* were needed are 1895/1, 1912/1, 1930/1, 1944/4, 1952/9, 1952/11, 1954/4.
2. LNA, HC 44/49, PE record, evidence of Mphapha Lebona.
3. LNA, HC 375/47, PE record, evidence of Jan Gat.
4. Jones (1951: 17).
5. Jones (1951: 14).
6. Ashton (1952: 309); Rivers Thompson, 'Reminiscences', p. 33.

454   NOTES TO CHAPTER 8

7. In all the clans of sixty-three victims are known – twelve Bahlakoana, ten Bakoena, nine Matebele, nine Bataung, five Bathepu (Thembu), three Basia, two Makho-lokoe, two Makhoakhoa, one Mokubung, one Letsitsi. Many of these clan affilia-tions are taken from FCO, Box 1176, S 119, list attached to CP to GS, 7 January 1958.

8. Ashton (1952: 310).

9. LNA, CRI/T/7/53, PE record, evidence of Letsatsi Lekoeneha, 24 February 1953.

10. Jones (1951: 17).

11. Jones (1951: 16).

12. Scobie (1965: 34).

13. Ashton (1952: 95).

14. They were 1942/4, 1943/5, 1945/10, 1945/11, 1948/23, 1948/24, 1950/7, 1951/ 9 and 1956/4. In 1950/7 the murder was committed on Boxing Day as no suitable victim could be found on Christmas Day.

15. The days of the week are known in 138 cases. The breakdown is Saturday thirty-two; Friday twenty-seven; Tuesday and Thursday nineteen, Monday eighteen, Sunday twelve and Wednesday eleven.

16. 1946/1 might also have been a case of this type.

17. Ntsu Mokhehle, 'President speaks on "Liretlo" murders', *Mohlabani*, May 1957, p. 14, and November 1957, p. 18.

18. Jones (1951: 16)

19. 'Ritual Murder', pp. 7–8.

20. Jingoes (1975: 162).

21. Mokitimi (1997: 23).

22. Ashton (1952: 310–11).

23. Ashton (1952: 311).

24. *Mochochonono*, 27 July 1946.

25. Jones (1951: 17).

26. LNA, CRI/T/2/53; *Moeletsi*, 30 March 1953; PRO, DO 119/1382, Photane, 'Medicine Murders' (enclosure with Arrowsmith to Turnbull, 12 September 1953), pp. 21–2; *Basutoland News*, 31 March 1953, 11 November 1958.

27. Jones (1951: 17).

28. 1931/1, 1944/5, 1948/16, 1948/24, 1952/7, 1962/2, 1962/3.

29. For example, 1919/1 and 1943/5.

30. LNA, CRI/T/17/57, judgement, pp. 483–4.

31. 1944/7, 1948/15, 1950/2, 1950/4, 1952/6, 1952/7 and 1954/4.

32. 1948/18, 1952/6, 1952/7, 1959/1.

CHAPTER 8

1. Rivers Thompson, 'Reminiscences', p. 66.

2. PS telephone interview, Paul Kitson, 5 October 1997.

3. In case 1945/11 reference was made to an order from 'Mantšebo that bodies found in suspicious circumstances should be reported to the DC.

4. See Chapter 3.

5. LNA, HC 253/45, PE record, evidence of Moronti Masilo.

6. PS telephone interview, Paul Kitson, 5 October 1997.

7. 1927/2, 1937/2, 1944/7, 1947/8, 1948/2, 1954/3, 1958/1 and 1965/5.

8. Other examples are 1952/7 and 1958/2.

9. See also 1957/4.

10. Another case in which death was due to drowning was 1949/2.

11. Other cases in which the post-mortem examination was inconsistent with

witnesses' evidence were 1943/3, 1951/7, 1951/10, 1952/9, 1952/11, 1954/4, 1958/2 and 1962/1.

12. FCO, Box 1175, S 119, Gray to Collins, 4 November 1948.

13. Examples are in FCO, Boxes 1175 and 1176, S 119, DC Qacha's Nek to GS, 30 December 1955; DC Mokhotlong to GS, 4 December 1958 and 7 December 1959; DC Butha-Buthe to First Assistant Secretary (Administration), 22 August 1959.

14. LNA, HC 160/43, PE record, evidence of Francina Sibonaki (1942/4).

15. LNA, CRI/T/29/58, PE record, p. 29, evidence of Anna Nkaotana,13 May 1958.

16. For example 1947/15, a case in which two people asked to give evidence in this way reported to the police.

17. For example, 1942/4, 1944/1, 1945/3, 1945/4, 1945/11, 1948/1, 1948/8, 1953/ 1, 1954/1.

18. 1944/1, 1945/8, 1947/4, 1953/4, 1954/4, 1956/4.

19. Chapters 3 and 5.

20. *Proc. (Special 1956) BNC*, p. 145, 11 May 1956, speech of CP. See also p. 146.

21. For example in cases 1961/2, 1962/2, 1962/3.

22. PRO, DO 119/1377, Apthorp to GS, 22 March 1949, enclosed with Forsyth-Thompson to Baring, 29 March 1949.

23. PRO, DO 119/1376, Forsyth-Thompson to Baring, 9 March 1949, and enclosures; PRO, DO 119/1377, Forsyth-Thompson to Baring, 29 March 1949; Forsyth-Thompson to Baring, 6 April 1949, quoting Baring's changes to draft Memorandum prepared by CP; Baring to Forsyth-Thompson, 5 April 1949, and Notes (undated but evidently prepared in April 1949) for discussion with RC, GS and CP on ritual murders; PRO, DO 119/1377, Forsyth-Thompson to Baring, 6 April 1949.

24. These discussions are in PRO, DO 119/1377; RHL, Brit. Emp. S381, Hector Papers, file 2/6, 'Minutes of Conference on Diretlo held in the Education Department Board Room, Maseru, Commencing on the 27th of August, 1956', pp. 23–4, statement of CP Paul Kitson.

25. See Table 8.1 and discussion below.

26. PS telephone interview, Paul Kitson, 5 October 1997.

27. For example, 1951/2, 1954/1, 1954/9, 1958/1.

28. LNA, CRI/T/19/59, Criminal Appeal no. 20 of 1959, judgement of the Court of Appeal, p. 9 (1958/1).

29. Of the 243 accomplice witnesses whose sex is known, 201 (83 per cent) were men and forty-two (17 per cent) women. The figures for accomplices as a whole (including accomplice witnesses) are 896 men (87 per cent) and 130 women (13 per cent). So 22 per cent of accomplices identified as male became Crown witnesses and 32 per cent of accomplices identified as female.

30. The mean age of accomplices generally, including accomplice witnesses, was 40–44 and the median age 35–39. For accomplice witnesses the mean age was 35–39 and the median age 30–34.

31. It is impossible to give reliable comparative statistics, since so many accomplices must have been friends, relatives, advisers or employees of the instigator, without this being stated in the court record. It is striking, however, that of the sixty-five accomplices we have identified as friends or relatives of the victim no fewer than twenty-seven became Crown witnesses.

32. *Proc. (Special 1956) BNC*, 14 May 1956, p. 122, speech of Chief Mabina Lerotholi; 8 May 1956, p. 50, speech of Chief Sekhonyana 'Maseribane; 14 May 1956, p. 132, speech of Chief Seetsa Tumo; Ntsu Mokhehle, *Mohlabani*, August 1957, p. 11.

33. PRO, DO 119/1377, 9916, statement of Moloi Ntai, Maseru gaol, 10 August 1948; Scott (1958: 200–1).

34. *Proc. (45) BNC*, vol. II, 12 September 1949, p. 31.
35. *Mohlabani*, August 1957, pp. 9–10. In January 1956 Mokhehle also confronted Arrowsmith with two women from the Berea District who complained of police pressure to incriminate an alleged murderer. The case was investigated and, according to the government, was found to be groundless: FCO, Box 1176, S 119, note by Arrowsmith, 5 January 1956; Shearer (Acting GS) to Mokhehle, 13 March 1956.
36. *Proc. (Special 1956) BNC*, 11 and 14 May 1956, p. 113, speech of Ntsoeleng Tšepo Nkuebe; p. 123, speech of Mabina Lerotholi; and pp. 131–3, speech of Seetsa Tumo.
37. PRO, DO 35/4155, 'Mantšebo's petition of 16 September 1948, enclosed with Byers to Gordon Walker, 20 January 1949: see also Ntsu Mokhehle, *Mohlabani*, May 1957, p. 15; and statement of Patrick Lehloenya, cited in Epprecht (2000: 114).
38. FCO, Box 1178, S 161, CP to GS, 18 May 1953.
39. PRO, DO 35/4155, 'Mantšebo's petition of 16 September 1948.
40. Jones (1951: 60).
41. Jones (1951: 61–2).
42. PS telephone interview, Paul Kitson, 5 October 1997.
43. PRO, DO 119/1384, 'Report of the Committee Appointed by the Round Table Conference on Medicine Murder' (enclosed with Acting RC to Deputy HC, 22 October 1954), p. 32.
44. For example 1952/9, 1953/3, 1957/4, 1957/6, 1957/9.
45. For example 1944/4, 1948/15, 1949/3, 1958/1.
46. For example 1927/2, 1944/6, 1948/6, 1949/5, 1951/5, 1951/9, 1952/5, 1952/7, 1958/1, 1959/1 and 1965/5. In case 1947/15 an instigator claimed that he had made a statement under duress. Several witnesses were charged with perjury and convicted: PRO, DO 119/1376, Forsyth-Thompson to Baring, 9 March 1949 and enclosures. See also *Proc. (48) BNC, 13 September 1952*, vol. I, p. 7, 10 October 1952, answer to question by Stirling Makakane; RHL, MSS Brit. Emp. S381, Hector Papers, file 2, 'Minutes of Conference on Diretlo held in the Education Department Board Room, Maseru, commencing on the 27th of August, 1956', pp. 10–11.
47. PRO, DO 119/1376, Record of case heard in DC's Court, Maseru, before E. C. Butler on 4 February 1948 and following days, *R v. Maphutseng Lefela*, evidence of Mashapha Pokonyane and Raletsukana Posholi.
48. Quoted by Ntsu Mokhehle in *Mohlabani*, November 1957, p. 17; *Mohlabani*, December 1957, p. 15. See also FCO, Box 1178, S 34, Harragin to Forsyth-Thompson, 10 December 1949.
49. PRO, DO 119/1382, 'Report by Major A. H. Donald and Chief Leshoboro Majara', enclosed with Arrowsmith to Chief Secretary to HC, 31 July 1953, p. 20; *Proc. (Special 1956) BNC*, 9 May 1956, speech of President (RC), p. 61.
50. PRO, DO 119/1384, 'Report of the Committee Appointed by the Round Table Conference on Medicine Murder', enclosed with Acting RC to Deputy HC, 22 October 1954, p. 32.
51. *Proc. (Special 1956) BNC*, 15 May 1956, pp. 148–9.
52. Jones (1951: 61).
53. Ashton, 'Mokhotlong District', pp. 32–3.
54. *Mohlabani*, August 1957, p. 11.
55. MM and PS interview, Sethabathaba Hatahata, 3 June 1999.
56. Gordon Blampied to PS, 23 September 1998.
57. KS and CM interview, Nkherepe Molefe, 29 November 1998.

58. KS and PS interview, Nkherepe Molefe, 28 May 1999.
59. KS and PS interview, Edwin Nohe Tšita, 28 May 1999; MM and PS interviews, Chief Joseph Molapo Maama and Mokhoele Mahao, 1 June 1999.
60. FCO, Box 1175, S 488.
61. FCO, Box 1176, S 119, Stutley to Attorney-General, 16 November 1959.
62. 1948/16, 1954/1.
63. PRO, DO 119/1382, Photane, 'Medicine Murders', enclosed with Arrowsmith to Turnbull, 12 September 1953, p. 20.
64. For example 1944/1 and 1963/1.
65. KS and PS interview, Edwin Nohe Tšita, 28 May 1999.
66. FCO, Box 1176, S 119, Waddington to Hughes, 18 February 1959.
67. FCO, Box 1176, S 119, Scrivenor, minute of 18 April 1958. It is possible that this officer, though an 'inspector', was in fact Sergeant Nchee.
68. FCO, Box 1176, S 119, DC Quthing to GS, 31 October 1959, and attached report.
69. *Moeletsi*, 9 July 1955: *R* v. *Lefeela Khakahali and 'Mamatsela Moorosi*.
70. 1944/6. According to the report in *Basutoland News*, 6 November 1945, Huggard had voiced these criticisms once before.

CHAPTER 9

1. 1959/4 seems to have been the first preparatory examination in a medicine murder case that was heard by a magistrate.
2. PRO, DO 119/1383, Owens to Attorney-General, 1 April 1954.
3. PRO, DO 119/1383, Arrowsmith to Scrivenor, 13 February 1954; Attorney-General, minute to Scrivenor, 24 February 1954.
4. PRO, DO 35/1181, Y981/15, Thompson's letter of application, 19 March 1946; CM interview, Gideon Pott, 7 August 1998; PS interview, Sir James Hennessy, 16 December 1998; PRO, DO 119/1384, minute 4, Attorney-General, 12 November 1954.
5. Kneen and Juta (1950, vol. I), Cap. 3, High Court Proclamation; Gocking (1997: 75). A detailed account of the judicial system is given in Crawford (1969, 1970).
6. *Annual Report of the Judicial Department*, 1955, p. 19; *Basutoland News*, 3 April 1956.
7. Crawford (1970: 77); correspondence in PRO, DO 35/4094.
8. Harragin had been prosecuting counsel in the Erroll murder ('White Mischief') case in Kenya in 1941, and in the Gold Coast in January 1945 he had heard the appeal of the convicted men in the 'Kibi murder' of February 1944 (Rathbone, 1993: 104). He was described by the journalist Noel Monks (1955: 301) as 'tall, impressive and amiable (except when pronouncing the death sentence)'.
9. Crawford (1970: 80).
10. For the personnel of the Court of Appeal, see the Annual Reports of the Judicial Department.
11. For example, Harragin's comments in 1947/14 and 1947/15, and Elyan's comments in 1958/1.
12. *Foundation*, April 1953, p. 5.
13. 'Ritual Murder', pp. 1–2.
14. Rivers Thompson, 'Reminiscences', p. 34.
15. PRO, DO 35/4096, minute by Tait, 15 January 1949, and note (illegible signature) to Gordon Walker, 17 January 1949.
16. PRO, DO 119/1384, minute 4, Attorney-General, 12 November 1954; Jones (1951: 67–8).
17. CM interview, Lourens Liebetrau, 27 November 1998.

18. Kneen and Juta (1950, vol. I), Cap. 3, High Court Proclamation, Sections 7 and 8. Harragin said that in his experience 'Basuto assessors ... are prone to accept the Crown evidence rather than that for the defence' (PRO, DO 119/1384, M4, minute by Attorney-General, 12 November 1954). The judges were supposed to record the advice given to them by their assessors and advisers, but they did not always do so and they did not always distinguish between them. In most cases they merely recorded that the assessors agreed with their verdict. In some cases the assessors would have convicted some or all of the accused who were acquitted (for example 1948/8, 1950/4, 1952/11 and 1957/2), but in others they would have acquitted some or all of those who were convicted (for example 1956/3, 1959/1, and 1962/3). It may be that as the counter-narrative gained strength assessors became slightly less likely to convict, but the pattern is not strong enough for any conclusions to be drawn.
19. For example, 1944/1 and 1951/2.
20. *Basutoland News*, 17 August 1948, 19 April 1958, 1 November 1960.
21. *Basutoland News*, 21 January 1958.
22. PRO, DO 35/4154, press cutting, 27 November 1948: J. A. Gray, 'The Land of Moshesh – Burial of a Beloved Chief – A Talk with the Paramount Chief – Menace of Ritual Murder', *South Africa*.
23. For example 1957/3 (LNA, CRI/T/17/57, judgement, p. 475) and 1957/4 (LNA, CRI/T/4/58, judgement, p. 897).
24. Gray, 'The Land of Moshesh ...'
25. For example 1945/8 and 1955/1.
26. 1957/4 and 1958/1.
27. *Moeletsi*, 16 November 1957.
28. 1947/14, judgement, p. 284; see also Lansdown (1960: 369).
29. 1944/1, judgement, p. 11; 1945/8, de Beer, judgement, p. 385; 1949/3, Krause, judgement; PRO, DO 119/1384, note by Attorney-General, enclosed with Scrivenor to Arrowsmith, 29 December 1955.
30. *Proc. (Special 1956) BNC*, debate on Round Table Conference Report, 7, 8 and 9 May 1956, and in particular 16 and 17 May 1956, when the recommendation on accomplice witnesses was discussed.
31. PRO, DO 119/1382, 'Report by Major A. R. Donald and Chief Leshoboro Majara', enclosed with Arrowsmith to Chief Secretary to HC, 31 July 1953, pp. 17–18; 'Report of the Committee appointed by the Round Table Conference on Medicine Murder', enclosed with Acting RC to Deputy HC, 22 October 1954, p. 32; and the discussion on the Committee's proposals in PRO, DO 119/1384.
32. PRO, DO 119/1384, Attorney-General's memorandum enclosed with Scrivenor to Arrowsmith, 29 December 1955; PRO, DO 119/1373, Attorney-General's 'Memorandum on Ritual Murders in the High Commission Territories', March 1949.
33. PRO, DO 35/7332, note by Sir Ralph Hone, 21 March 1957.
34. For the correspondence which led to this change, see PRO, DO 35/1181, Y991/3.
35. PRO, DO 35/7332, note by Sir Ralph Hone, 21 March 1957.
36. Willan (1955a: 123–41).
37. Willan (1955a: 181–99).
38. The cases in question are 1950/3, 1952/6, 1953/4, 1956/3, 1957/1, 1957/3, 1957/9, 1958/1, 1962/2, 1962/3 (where, as the judges in both the High Court and the Appeal Court observed, one of the accomplice witnesses should have been regarded as an independent witness) and 1963/1.
39. 1952/6, 1953/4 and 1962/2.
40. The other two cases were 1953/4 and 1956/3.

41. Similar cases were 1945/4, 1945/6, 1948/1, 1948/6, 1950/2, 1951/5, 1951/9, 1952/2, 1952/6, 1952/11, 1953/1, 1953/3, 1956/3, 1957/7.
42. For example 1944/1, 1948/1, 1949/3, 1965/4.
43. LNA, CRI/T/10/55, judgement of Court of Appeal, 25 November 1955.
44. The other was Molefi Senyotong in 1948/8.
45. The quotation is from Elyan (1957: 14)
46. PS interview, Mr Justice Maqutu, 15 October 1997.
47. Other such cases were 1945/3 (Case Study 1) and 1952/11.
48. Other cases of this sort were 1948/24, 1953/2, 1959/4, 1961/3 and 1965/5.
49. Other cases in which accomplice evidence was undermined by the post-mortem examination were 1943/3, 1951/7, 1951/10, 1952/9, 1954/4, 1958/2 and 1962/1.
50. LNA, CRI/T/10/54, judgement given orally by Acting Chief Justice, 8 June 1954.
51. In 1945/9 the Crown case failed mainly because of the length of time that had elapsed. The judge noted, however, the alibis set up by three of the accused 'were supported by evidence it is impossible to reject as worthless'.
52. Lansdown (1960: 60).
53. There were also four men who were found guilty of murder who died while waiting for their appeals to be heard.
54. There were three accomplices whose sex we do not know who were found guilty – two of murder, one as an accessory.
55. Our evidence about pleas for clemency is not comprehensive. It seldom appears in the High Court files or in the High Commissioner's files. The local newspapers often reported hangings, which would only have taken place if pleas for clemency had been rejected, and the High Commissioner's decisions were recorded in the Annual Reports of the Judicial Department in Basutoland, which cover only 1953–60. For the period up to 1949 the Jones report provides us with the decisions, though not with the reasons for them.
56. Criminal Procedure and Evidence Proclamation, s. 286(1), 313, 314. It seems that hanging was not the statutory punishment for accessories before or after the fact.
57. PRO, DO 35/7332, Scrivenor to Hunt, 17 April 1958.
58. For example, LNA, HC 139/43, Huggard to Lord Harlech, 6 April 1943 (1942/3); PRO, DO 35/4098, Harragin to HC, 28 August 1948 (1948/1); PRO, DO 119/1372, Sutton to HC, 28 December 1948 (1948/6); FCO, Box 1176, S 368, Report by Acting DC, Quthing, enclosed with Acting DC Quthing to GS, 10 March 1954 (1953/1), and Report by DC Berea to GS (1952/11); PRO, DO 119/1386, Roper to HC, 25 November 1960 (1959/1); LNA, CRI/T/42/65, Benson to British Government Representative, 7 January 1966 (1962/3). Two reports from DCs, on the other hand, convey strong local feeling that the accused should be hanged: PRO, DO 119/1386, DC Mokhotlong to GS, 19 July 1961 (1959/2); and LNA, CRI/T/42/65, DC Mohale's Hoek to Permanent Secretary for Home Affairs, Maseru, 31 May 1966 (1962/3).
59. PRO, DO 119/1386, petitions of Tumo Khajoane, Ntau Kali and Khoaele Lekhoba, all dated 31 July 1961, forwarded under cover of Registrar of the High Court, Maseru, to Deputy HC, 10 August 1961. See also LNA, HC 45/48, Pittman's report (1947/8).
60. Even after discretion was allowed, and hanging was no longer a statutory requirement, there was only one case, 1963/1, in which this discretion was exercised. In that case eight were condemned to hang (of whom five had their sentences commuted subsequently) and seven were sentenced to terms of imprisonment.
61. Two persons whose sex we do not know were found guilty and hanged.

62. Criminal Procedure and Evidence Proclamation, s. 289.
63. Mphatšoe (1952: 83–4).
64. KS and PS interview, Stephen Phakisi, 25 May 1999. Phakisi was unable to recognise any of the names of the Mohale's Hoek chiefs who were hanged for murder.
65. *Moeletsi*, 29 June 1948; PRO, DO 119/1381, copy of 'E. V. L.', 'Albert was hanged for the Medicine Horn murder', *The Star* (Johannesburg), 6 October 1951.

AFTERMATH

1. Patrick Mohlalefi Bereng and PS interview, 3 June 1999.
2. Ford Rafutho and PS interview, 23 May 1999.
3. MM and PS interview, 1 June 1999.
4. MM and PS interview, Chief Matita Makotoko, 3 June 1999. In fact, thirteen people were hanged for this murder, and they were not the last to be hanged for medicine murder.
5. MM and PS interview, Sethabathaba Hatahata, 3 June 1999.
6. MM and PS interview, Chief Joseph Molapo Maama, 1 June 1999. Kosenene died in the early stages of the investigation and did not actually give evidence at the High Court trial.
7. KS and PS interview, 'Mathuso Tšitang, 27 May 1999.
8. PS interview, Albert Brutsch, 7 October 1997.
9. KS and PS interview, Molosi Kao, 27 May 1999.
10. KS and PS interview, 'Mathuso Tšitang, 27 May 1999.
11. MM and PS interview, Exinia Letsoela, 2 June 1999.
12. MM and PS interview, 'Mamoliehi Nyooko, 1 June 1999.
13. Jones (1951: 58).
14. *Moeletsi*, 24 December 1960.
15. All three interviewees, and some of the principals involved in the case, had been known to CM since 1972–4, when he carried out fieldwork in the village. He had not at that time, however, known of the murder.
16. LNA, CRI/T/2/64, *R* v. *Ntitsoe Motlotla and nine others*, PE record, 20 November 1963, evidence of Pakiso Ramphasa, pp. 10–18.
17. LNA, CRI/T/2/64, *R* v. *Ntitsoe Motlotla and nine others*, 20 November 1963, evidence of Lekhaole Bakane, p. 23.
18. CM interview, Lekhaole Bakane, 19 January 1998.
19. CM interview, Basia Bakane, 19 January 1998.
20. CM interview, 'Mapuleng Bakane, 19 January 1998.

CONCLUSION

1. Bosko (1983), in particular Chapter IV, 'The Uses of the Concept of Ritual Murder'.
2. Coplan (1994: 110).
3. Epprecht (2000: 113, 118–19, 241 n. 100).
4. PRO, DO 35/7332, Resolutions attached to Ntsu Mokhehle's Presidential Address at the 4th Annual Conference of the BAC, Maseru, 29–31 December 1956; for full discussion see Chapter 4.
5. See Chapter 9.
6. Eldredge (1997: 22–3).
7. See Chapter 1.
8. Eldredge (1997: 25).
9. See Chapter 4.
10. *Proc. (52) BNC*, 1956, vol. II, pp. 40–1.

11. PRO, DO 119/1383, Arrowsmith to Deputy HC, 4 March 1954; DO 35/4361, minute by P. Liesching, 24 May 1955; Gunther (1957: 562).
12. PRO, DO 35/4154, 'Secretary of State's visit to Southern Africa. Basutoland: Ritual Murders', November 1950.
13. Driver (1996: 11–12). In this context, see RHL, MSS Brit. Emp. S511/3, Arrowsmith Papers, Arrowsmith to Armstrong, 2 May 1953: 'I expect you heard all about Matlere getting off on a charge of medicine murder [case 1952/12], much to the disgust of the Police, but greatly to the relief of the Agricultural Department'.
14. 'Analysis', p. 9. See also 'Mokhotlong District', p. 33.
15. In 1990 Ward Chief 'Mamathealira Api was accused with others of medicine murder, but was acquitted: the case was CRI/T/24/90.
16. *Basutoland News*, 26 March 1957; see Chapter 5.
17. David Ambrose interview, Major Refiloe Motaung, reported to PS 5 October 1997.
18. PRO, DO 119/1381, Arrowsmith to Turnbull, 15 August 1952; DO 119/1384, 'Report of the Committee appointed by the Round Table Conference on Medicine Murder', enclosed with Acting RC to Deputy HC, 22 October 1954, p. 10.
19. For Mokhehle's views, see Chapter 4.
20. See the Addendum for an account of the crisis in Venda, the Ralushai Commission's view and various preceding analyses; see also Gulbrandsen (2002: 215–33).
21. Comaroff and Comaroff (1999: 279–303).
22. Niehaus, with Mohlala and Shokane (2001); another example is the historian Peter Delius' sensitive analysis, in Chapter 6 of his book *A Lion Amongst the Cattle*, of the issue of witchcraft in relation to the politics of youth revolt in mid-1980s Sekhukhuneland, where 'the eradication of witches was seen as a fundamental part of the creation of a new community freed of the oppression, iniquity and misfortune which had dogged village life under apartheid' (1996: 198).
23. Rivers Thompson, 'Reminiscences', p. 73.
24. *Mochochonono*, 13 August 1949.
25. *Mochochonono*, 5 April 1952.
26. *Baemeli ba Mahatammoho* [Congress candidates] *1965*, p. 55.
27. See Chapter 6.
28. *Moeletsi*, 21 September 1963.
29. *Moeletsi*, 4, 11 and 25 April 1964.
30. Jones (1951: 18).
31. See, for example, the debate on the proposed Witchcraft Proclamation in *Proc. (Special 1957) BNC*, May 1957, vol. II, pp. 240–6.
32. PS telephone interview, Gordon Hector, 25 November 1996.
33. Cordery (1993: 35); Rivers Thompson, 'Reminiscences', pp. 34–5.
34. Arthur Jenkins (formerly of the Pius XII College, Roma), personal communication to PS, October 1998.
35. Bosko (1983: 101) argues that they attracted suspicion because of their 'liminal status'. This was perhaps true in some cases, but the main reason for their attracting suspicion was their actual involvement.
36. Hailey (1953, Part V: 132).
37. In 1984 a Roman Catholic priest, Augustinus Lekhotla Pula, in the only relevant survey of which we are aware, found that, among people living near Catholic missions, 79 per cent still believed in the effectiveness of medicine murder; see Pula (1988: 74, 76).

ADDENDUM

1. See entries in van Warmelo (1977), under 'ritual murder' and 'human flesh'.
2. Ngubane (1986: 189–204).
3. Gulbrandsen (2002: 217).
4. Marwick (1940: 196–217).
5. PRO, DO 119/1373, A. C. Thompson, 'Memorandum on Ritual Murders in the High Commission Territories', March 1949.
6. PRO, DO 119/1406; see also Butler (1952) and Packer (1953: 161).
7. Including one extraordinary case in which two men were convicted and hanged for a murder in 1950, but many years later, in 1959, the alleged victim turned up alive. The Commission of Enquiry which followed, uncovering, apparently, a mass of perjured evidence, is reported in detail in PRO, DO 35/7333–5.
8. Grotpeter (1975), entry under 'ritual murder'.
9. Kuper (1978: 333).
10. Booth (1983: 75–6).
11. Van Fossen (1985). We derive this account of van Fossen's work from Evans (1990).
12. Kuper (1986: 69).
13. Evans (1990).
14. According to Swazi police sources, there were nine; see *The Star* (Johannesburg), 15 February 1983.
15. Evans (1990).
16. Minnaar, Offringa and Payze (1992: 20).
17. Le Roux (1989: 76–7).
18. Ralushai and others (1996: 272).
19. Minnaar, Offringa and Payze (1992: 22).
20. Le Roux (1989: 80).
21. Minnaar, Offringa and Payze (1992: 21–2).
22. Le Roux (1989); Minnaar, Offringa and Payze (1992: xii).
23. Le Roux (1989: 53–4).
24. Le Roux (1989: 56, 176).
25. Minnaar, Offringa and Payze (1992: 33).
26. Le Roux (1989: 58); Minnaar, Offringa and Payze (1992: 35–6).
27. Le Roux (1989: 58).
28. Le Roux (1989: 37–8, 100). Later, in October 1988, the magazine *Drum* reported that Sharon Mashige's murder had marked the beginning of a spate of murders. See also Minnaar, Offringa and Payze (1992: 44).
29. Le Roux (1989: 183, 101).
30. Le Roux (1989: 49). Detailed summaries of the unrest in Venda during 1988–90 are also given in the annual *Surveys* of the South African Institute of Race Relations (SAIRR, 1989: 95–7; 1990: 532–9).
31. Minnaar, Offringa and Payze (1992: 34).
32. Le Roux (1989: 184); Minnaar, Offringa and Payze (1992: 34).
33. The findings of the report are summarised in SAIRR (1990: 532–3).
34. Minnaar, Offringa and Payze (1992: 36).
35. Minnaar, Offringa and Payze (1992: ix, 23).
36. Minnaar, Offringa and Payze (1992: 29).
37. Minnaar, Offringa and Payze (1992: 38–9); SAIRR (1990: 538–9).
38. Le Roux (1989: 80).
39. Minnaar, Offringa and Payze (1992: 45).
40. Minnaar, Offringa and Payze (1992: 31).

41. Minnaar, Offringa and Payze (1992: 46).
42. Ralushai and others (1996: 60–86).
43. *Rand Daily Mail*, 18 August 1981.
44. *Star*, 15 February 1983.
45. SAIRR (1990: 534–5).
46. Rathbone (1993).
47. Gocking (2000: 217).
48. Pratten (forthcoming b: 13). Pratten also analysed, as part of the comparative framework for his own work, outbreaks of 'leopard' murders in Sierra Leone at the end of the nineteenth century and Congo in the 1920s, and of 'lion' murders in Tanganyika in the 1940s. Of the last, he observed that the outbreak followed political reforms which 'sought to empower decentralized traditional political structures', and reflected in part the impact of a colonial judicial system which could not recognise witchcraft accusations in court. See Pratten (forthcoming b: 23).
49. Pratten (forthcoming b: 14; forthcoming a: 18).
50. Rathbone (1993: 104).
51. While the Mau Mau experience in Kenya in the 1950s is perhaps not directly comparable, there is also resonance through secret oath-taking, the political construction of 'barbarism' and the very controversial question, recently explored at length by David Anderson (2004), of the extent to which and the ways in which, partly as a result of intense settler political pressure, officials of the colonial administration were induced to initiate and to participate in systematic abuses of proper judicial procedure.

SOURCES

A ARCHIVAL SOURCES
1 Official

a Public Record Office [PRO], Kew, London (now National Archives)
DO 35 series. Dominions Office/Commonwealth Relations Office.
DO 119 series. High Commission, South Africa.
CO 1048 series. Colonial Office.

b Foreign and Commonwealth Office, Hanslope Park [FCO]
Box 1164, File S 18, Succession to the Paramount Chief.
  File S 60, Paramount Chief Designate.
  File S 300, Appeals to His Majesty by the Paramount Chief.
Box 1167, Files S 197A, B and C, Confidential reports on chiefs.
  File S 388, Criminous chiefs.
Box 1168, Files S 197D–J, Confidential reports on chiefs.
Box 1175, File S 119, Basutoland Medicine Murders, Witchcraft (1947–62), vols 1–8.
  File S 488, Medicine Murder: Lepekola Joel and others (1959–60).
  File S 151, Basutoland Criminal Procedure (1943–62), vols 1–2.
Box 1176, File S 119, Basutoland Medicine Murders, Witchcraft, vols 9–15.
  File S 368, District Commissioners' Reports on Medicine Murders (1954).
  File S 377, Action against Witch Doctors.
Box 1177, File S 85, Bereng Griffith Lerotholi.
  File S 245, Ritual Murder, Communal Punishment Legislation, vols 1–3.
  File S 258, Advisers to the Paramount Chief, 1948–57.
  File S 262, Ritual Murder: Commission of Inquiry and Documents.
  File S 262A, G. I. Jones' Report: Ritual Murder.
Box 1178, File S 34, Lekhotla la Bafo and Native Unrest in the Orange Free State, vols 1–8.
  File S 161, Regent PC 'Mantšebo (1939–64), Personal, vols 1–3.

c Lesotho National Archives [LNA]
These archives, which were once kept at the National University of Lesotho, Roma, were divided and moved in October 1997.

The High Court and Court of Appeal files were taken to a cell beneath the Magistrates' Court and then to a basement in the Palace of Justice in Maseru. They could be examined there, but with great difficulty, since we found them in complete disarray. We were able to find most of what we needed while the files were still at Roma.

The rest of the files were locked in a government-owned house in Maseru, where they have remained inaccessible and unusable since October 1997. We examined only one file while they were still kept at Roma: S3/5/14/2, 'Claim to Paramount Chieftainship. Seeiso and Bereng Griffith'.

d National University of Lesotho, Roma [NUL]

Files relating to the Leribe District recovered from Major Bell's fort at Hlotse: Box 52, file 1199; Box 54, file 754.

e Ambrose Archives

Files relating to the Mokhotlong District collected by Rivers Thompson [Mokhotlong files].

Judgements relating to Matsieng/Phamong boundary.

2 Unofficial

a Missionary Archives

Lesotho Evangelical Church Archives, Morija
  Marion Walsham How, Papers.
  A. S. Mopeli-Paulus, Autobiography.

b University Libraries

i Department of Social Anthropology, University of Cambridge

G. I. Jones, Papers. S1, 'Central Africa' [sic]. This box contains five unnumbered files. We adopted the following classification, in relation to the two files of particular relevance to our research:
  I. 'Correspondence re Diretlo Murder Report';
  V. 'Basutoland and Swaziland. Schedule of Ritual Murders 1949 and Earlier'.

ii Jagger Library, University of Cape Town [UCT]

E. H. Ashton, Papers. BC859. Ashton wrote three 'secret' and unattributed papers on medicine murder in 1949. The first, 'Ritual Murder in Basutoland', is in PRO, DO 119/1377, enclosed with Forsyth-Thompson to Baring, 21 April 1949 (a copy was also in the Jones Papers at Cambridge University, above). The second and third, prepared in August 1949 and relating specifically to Mokhotlong District, were 'Mokhotlong District' and 'Analysis of Ritual Murders and their Relation to Various Administrative Events'. These are held in the Ashton Papers in the Jagger Library and also in FCO, Box 1177, S 245.

iii University Library, University of Durham

E. Baring, Papers. GRE/1/9, 10, 11, 13, 15, 120.

iv University Library, National University of Lesotho [NUL]

Rivers Fendall Thompson, 'Reminiscences: as transcribed from tapes made at the National University of Lesotho in May 1980', Roma: limited edition produced by David Ambrose, March 1984.

v Rhodes House Library, University of Oxford [RHL]

Africa Bureau, MSS Afr. S1681, Box 219, files 1, 5.

Arrowsmith Papers, MSS Brit. Emp. S511.

Hector Papers, MSS Brit. Emp. S381.

Kennan Papers, MSS Afr. S969.

Lagden Papers, MSS Afr. S142–208.

Sir R. Latimer, Transcript of tape recorded by Sir R. Latimer, MSS Afr. S1444.

Pim Papers, MSS Afr. S1002.

Redcliffe-Maud, Lady Jean, Diaries, MSS Afr. S1773.

Wilson, Douglas, Correspondence and Papers, 1958–9, relating to 'Mantšebo's visit
    to the United Kingdom, MSS Afr. S965.

vi University Library, University of the Witwatersrand

Rheinallt Jones, Papers. A394/G7/8: G. E. Pott, 'A Memorandum on Ritual Murders
    in Basutoland', n.d.

vii Borthwick Institute, University of York

Patrick Duncan, Papers. DU, Southern African Archives.

B NEWSPAPERS

The six most important newspaper sources on medicine murder are: *Basutoland
News*; *Inkululeko*; *Leselinyana la Lesotho*; *Mochochonono*; *Moeletsi oa Basotho*; and
Mphatlalatsane. *Mohlabani* (May–December 1957) contains an important series of
articles by Ntsu Mokhehle. Other articles on medicine murder are to be found in a
wide variety of Basutoland/Lesotho, South African and British newspapers. In
recent years the main source of information is the police newspaper, *Leseli ka
Sepolesa*.

C ILLUSTRATIONS

1 Maps, figure and tables

The District Map was drawn from the 1978 edition of the *Atlas for Lesotho* (Johannesburg: Collins, and Cape Town: Longman), supplemented by Christine Prince's
map of 1976 printed in the second edition of David Ambrose's *Guide to Lesotho*
(Johannesburg: Winchester Press) and qualified in some respects by reference to the
1978 and 1994 editions of the 1:250,000 Map of Lesotho. It proved extremely
difficult to reconstruct accurately certain district boundaries for the 1950s, notably
those for the eastern (Senqunyane) section of the Mafeteng District. The Ward Map
was drawn from the 2001 edition of the *Primary Atlas for Lesotho* (Longman Lesotho),
with further advice from David Ambrose. The boundaries in both maps should be
understood as approximate only.

  The 'selective genealogy' in Figure 2.1 was composed largely from information in
Jones (1966). It shows the key patrilineal relationships between senior members of
the ruling Bakoena family, the 'Sons of Moshoeshoe'. Nineteen of the ward
chieftainships are held by descendants of Moshoeshoe himself, his full-brother
Makhabane and his half-brother Mohale. These individuals were also related in
many other ways. Some of the complexities of inter-marriage, dynastic politics, the
effects of the 'placing' system and conflicts over succession are outlined in Jones

(1966), Hamnett (1975) and Machobane (1990). The arrangements made by Moshoeshoe himself are explained in detail in Sanders (1975).

The category 'Independent Chiefs' that appears in Table 6.1 refers to individuals and/or their descendants who were able to hold out against the logic of being 'downgraded' that was implied by successive super-imposed placings, and who were thereby able to retain direct subordination to the Paramount Chief rather than have to accept subordination to some other Principal or Ward Chief. In the 1950 Gazette the districts of Mafeteng and Mohale's Hoek both contain 'Wards of Independent Chiefs', with ward sections variously distributed through the two districts. These sections were mainly, but not entirely, ruled by descendants of Mohale, Moshoeshoe's junior half-brother (see Figure 1.2). For example, the area of Senqunyane, under Chief Solomon Mohale, a descendant of the third house of Mohale, appears in 1950 in Mafeteng District (eastern section); the areas of Thaba-Tšoeu, under Nkhahle Lebona, a descendant of the second house of Mohale, and Likoeneng, under Goliath Malebanye, a descendant of the third house of Mohale, appear in Mohale's Hoek District. Later, some of these 'independent' ward sections were, in effect, absorbed into the ward of Matsieng. The areas of Likoeneng and Thaba-Tšoeu survived this process of absorption, which is why they are shown separately in the Ward Map, marked respectively as A and C. See also Jones (1966). The fact that some of these ward sections did not survive as 'independent' explains both why they do not appear on the Ward Map and why, in two cases of medicine murder, 1950/2 and 1957/5, it was difficult to reconcile the district and ward attributions we have made with the district and ward boundaries as they appear in the maps. Similarly, case 1947/1, which is shown on the Ward Map on the southern boundary of Matsieng Ward, appears anomalous there in the sense that, on the evidence available, we have attributed it to a separate small section of Likhoele Ward which is not marked on the Ward Map.

2 Photographs

1. Postcard, Morija Archives.
2. Postcard, Morija Archives.
3. Foreign and Commonwealth Office Library, London.
4. *Basutoland Lesotho* (Royal Visit to Basutoland 1947), p. 60.
5. *CAR 1946*, p. 44, with permission of HMSO.
6. *Basutoland Lesotho* (Royal Visit to Basutoland 1947), p. 58.
7. *Basutoland Lesotho* (Royal Visit to Basutoland 1947), p. 48.
8. *Basutoland Lesotho* (Royal Visit to Basutoland 1947), p. 109.
9. *Leselinyana*, 14 May 1960.
11. High Court file CRI/T/4/55.
12. Original in possession of Hugo Ashton, with permission.
13. Original in possession of Ursula Jones, with permission.
14. Foreign and Commonwealth Office Library, London.
15. Foreign and Commonwealth Office Library, London.
16. Khaketla (1971), p. 35, with permission of C. Hurst & Co.
17. Khaketla (1971), back cover, with permission of C. Hurst & Co.
18. Foreign and Commonwealth Office Library, London.
19. High Court file 288/46 [case 1945/3].

20.   High Court file 288/46 [case 1945/3].
21.   High Court file 288/46 [case 1945/3].
22.   High Court file 288/46 [case 1945/3].
24.   High Court file 288/46 [case 1945/3].
27.   Original by David Ambrose, with permission.
29.   Original in possession of Ranthomeng Matete, with permission.
31.   *CAR 1958*, p. 6, with permission of HMSO.
32.   Jingoes (1975), p. 169, with permission of Oxford University Press.
33.   *Basutoland Lesotho* (Royal Visit to Basutoland 1947), p. 103.
35.   Original in possession of Robert Edgar, with permission.
36.   *The Observer* (London), 4 December 1949, with permission.
37.   Errol Trzebinski (2000), *The Life and Death of Lord Erroll: The Truth Behind the Happy Valley Murder* (London: Fourth Estate), No. 53.
39.   Patrick Mohlalefi Bereng and Patrick Lehloenya Lehloenya (1991), *Haboo* (Roma: National University of Lesotho Publishing House), p. 64.
40.   *Haboo*, p. 108.
41.   *Basutoland Lesotho* (Royal Visit to Basutoland 1947), p. 70.
42.   *Leselinyana*, 17 October 1959.
46.   High Court file CRI/T/4/53 [case 1952/12].
47.   High Court file CRI/T/4/53 [case 1952/12].
48.   *Leselinyana*, 17 September 1960.
Other photographs were taken by the authors.

D PRINTED BOOKS, ARTICLES, ETC.
1 Official

Basutoland (Colonial Annual Reports) [*CARs*]
The Basutoland Native Administration Proclamation (No. 61 of 1938) and The Basutoland Native Courts Proclamation (No. 62 of 1938): An Explanatory Memorandum (1939), n.p.
Explanatory Memorandum: Basuto National Treasury (1944), n.p.
Basutoland: Report of the Administrative Reforms Committee (April–July 1954).
Basutoland: Annual Report of the Commissioner of Police (1961, 1966, 1968, 1969, 1970).
Basutoland: Annual Report of the Judicial Department (1953, 1954, 1955, 1956, 1957–60).
Basutoland Census 1936 (Pretoria, 1937); *1946* (Morija, 1951); *1956* (Maseru, 1958); *1966* (Maseru, n.d.).
Liretlo, Liretlo, Liretlo? (1953), Matsieng.
Official Gazette of the High Commissioner for Basutoland, the Bechuanaland Protectorate and Swaziland.
Proceedings of the Basutoland National Council, various years. The full titles of the *Proceedings* differ between years, and an approximately common form of short reference has been adopted here. Thus, for example, *Proc. (44) BNC* refers to the *Proceedings of the 44th Session (1948) of the Basutoland National Council*; *Proc. (Special 1956) BNC* refers to the *Proceedings of the Special (1956) Session of the Basutoland Council 7th to 23rd May 1956.*

2 Unofficial

Alexander, David (c. 1992) , *Sani Pass: Riding the Dragon*, Durban: privately published.

Ambrose, D. P. (1993), review of L. B. B. J. Machobane, *Government and Change in Lesotho 1800–1966, Journal of Southern African Studies*, 19(2), 349–52.

Amery, L. S. (1953), *My Political Life; 'War and Peace' 1914–1929*, London: Hutchinson.

Anderson, David M. (2004), *Histories of the Hanged: Britain's Dirty War in Kenya and the End of Empire*, London: Weidenfeld & Nicolson, and New York: W.W. Norton.

Ashton, E. H. (1943), 'Medicine, magic, and sorcery among the Southern Sotho', *Communications from the School of African Studies, University of Cape Town*, New Series no. 10, December.

Ashton, Hugh [1952] (1967), *The Basuto*, London: Oxford University Press for the International African Institute.

Ba re'ng batho ka buka ea Lebollo? ['What do people say about the book *Lebollo?*'] (c. 1974), Mazenod: Social Centre.

Baemeli ba Mahatammoho, 1965 ['Congress Candidates, 1965'] (1965), Maseru: Basutoland Congress Party.

Baltzer, G. (1912), 'Rapport Annuel de la Conference du Lessouto. Année 1911', *JME*, 1912.

Bardill, John E., and James H. Cobbe (1985), *Lesotho: Dilemmas of Dependence in Southern Africa*, Boulder, Colorado: Westview Press, and London: Gower.

Baring, Sir Evelyn (1952), 'Problems of the High Commission Territories', *International Affairs*, 28(2), April.

Barkly, Fanny (1893), *Among Boers and Basutos*, London: Remington.

Barnes, Leonard (1932), *The New Boer War*, London: Hogarth Press.

Becker, Peter (1956a), *Sandy Tracks to the Kraals*, Johannesburg: Dagbreek Bookstore.

Becker, Peter (1956b), 'Reflections on Basutoland', *Lantern*, February, 264–6.

Booth, Alan R. (1983), *Swaziland: Tradition and Change in a Southern African Kingdom*, Boulder, Colorado: Westview.

Brookes, Edgar H. [1924] (1927), *The History of Native Policy in South Africa from 1830 to the Present Day*, Pretoria: J. L. van Schaik.

Bryce, Lord James [1897] (1900), *Impressions of South Africa*, London: Macmillan.

Burman, Sandra (1981), *Chiefdom Politics and Alien Law*, London and Basingstoke: Macmillan Press.

Butler, R. (1952), 'Ritual murder, grim offspring of witchcraft is increasing in Swaziland', *Outspan*, v. 51.

Casalis, E. (1861), *The Basutos; or Twenty-Three Years in South Africa*, London: James Nisbet.

Coates, Austin (1966), *Basutoland*, London: HMSO.

Comaroff, Jean, and John L. Comaroff (1999), 'Occult economies and the violence of abstraction: notes from the South African postcolony', *American Ethnologist* 26(4), 279–309.

Coplan, David B. (1994), *In the Time of Cannibals: the Word Music of South Africa's Basotho Migrants*, Chicago: University of Chicago Press.

Coplan, David B., and Tim Quinlan (1997), 'A chief by the people: nation versus state in Lesotho', *Africa* 67(1), 27–59.

Cordery, Ray (1993), *Reflections of Mokhotlong and the Sani Pass*, Studland: privately published.

Couzens, Tim (2003), *Murder at Morija*, Johannesburg: Random House.

Crawford, J. R. (1969–70), 'The history and nature of the judicial system of Botswana, Lesotho and Swaziland – introduction and the superior courts', *The South African Law Journal*, 86(4), November 1969, 476–9, and 87(1), February 1970, 76–86.

Damane, Mosebi (1953), 'A challenge to the Christian church in Basutoland', *Basutoland Witness*, 7(2), April–June, 18–21.

Damane, Mosebi (1973–4), 'Sotho medicine', *Lesotho: Notes and Records*, 10, 1973–4, 48–59.

Damane, Mosebi, and Peter Sanders (1974), *Lithoko: Sotho Praise-Poems*, Oxford: Clarendon Press.

Davidson, Basil (1952), *Report on Southern Africa*, London: Jonathan Cape.

Davis, Gordon (1964), *The High Commission Territories Law Reports 1961 & 1962*, Maseru: High Court.

Davis, Gordon (1976), *The Lesotho Law Reports 1967–70*, Maseru: High Court.

Delius, Peter (1996), *A Lion Amongst the Cattle: Reconstruction and Resistance in the Northern Transvaal*, Portsmouth, NH: Heinemann, and Johannesburg: Ravan Press, and Oxford: James Currey.

Dieterlen, Georges (1926), 'Le paganisme toujours vivant', *JME*, 217–9.

Dieterlen, Georges (1950), 'Some manifestations of modern heathenism in Basutoland', *The Basutoland Witness*, 4(4), July–Aug. 46–9.

Dieterlen, Hermann (1896), 'Où le pagnisme peut aboutir', *JME*, 263–6.

Dieterlen, Hermann (1912), 'Paganisme concentré', *JME*, 168–73.

Dieterlen, Hermann (1930), *La Médecine et les Médecins au Lessouto*, Paris: Société des Missions Evangéliques.

Douglas-Home, Charles (1978), *Evelyn Baring: The Last Proconsul*, London: Collins.

Driver, Thackwray (1996), 'Soil conservation policies in Mokhotlong District, Lesotho – 1947–55: successful non-implementation', draft paper, SOAS African History Seminar, 1 May.

Duncan, Patrick (1960), *Sotho Laws and Customs*, Cape Town: Oxford University Press.

Dunton, Chris (1990), 'Mopeli-Paulus and Blanket Boy's Moon', *Research in African Literature*, 21(4), Winter, 105–20.

Dutton, E. A. T. (1923), *The Basuto of Basutoland*, London: Jonathan Cape.

Edgar, Robert (1987), *Prophets with Honour: A Documentary History of Lekhotla la Bafo*, Johannesburg: Ravan Press.

Edwards, Isobel (1955), *Basutoland Enquiry*, London: Africa Bureau.

Edwards, Isobel (1956), *Protectorates or Native Reserves?*, London: Africa Bureau.

Eldredge, Elizabeth (1997), 'Medicine murder and power: the consolidation of colonial control in British Basutoland in the 1940s', paper presented to the South African Historical Society 16th Biennial Conference, Pretoria, 6–9 July.

Ellenberger, D. F. (1912), *History of the Basuto Ancient and Modern*, written in English by J. C. Macgregor, London: Caxton Publishing Company.

Elyan, Isadore Victor (1957), *The High Commission Territories Law Reports 1956*, Maseru: High Court.

Elyan, Isadore Victor (1959), *The High Commission Territories Law Reports 1958*, Maseru: High Court.

Elyan, Isadore Victor (1960), *The High Commission Territories Law Reports 1959*, Maseru: High Court.

Elyan, Isadore Victor (1961), *The High Commission Territories Law Reports 1960*, Maseru: High Court.

Epprecht, Marc (2000), *'This Matter of Women is Getting Very Bad': Gender, Development and Politics in Colonial Lesotho*, Pietermaritzburg: University of Natal Press.

Evans, Jeremy (1990), '"How can we get a beast without hair?". Suggestions towards the nature of medicine murder in Swaziland from 1970 to 1988', paper for the annual conference of the Association for Anthropology in Southern Africa, 5–8 September.

Fincher, Nellie (1918), 'Basutoland. A modern utopia', *South African Railways and Harbours Magazine*, December, 811–6.

Flather, Horace (1976), *Thaba Rau*, Cape Town: Purnell.

Forsyth-Thompson, A. D. (1949), 'Basutoland – a new Diocese?', *The East and West Review. An Anglican Missionary Quarterly*, 15(4), October, 100–3.

Fulton, Anthony (1968), *The Dark Side of Mercy*, Cape Town: Purnell.

Gamble, David (1935), 'Basutoland the Golden', *African Observer*, 3(2), 52–60.

Gocking, Roger (1997), 'Colonial rule and the "legal factor" in Ghana and Lesotho', *Africa* 67(1), 61–85.

Gocking, Roger (2000), 'A chieftaincy dispute and ritual murder in Elmina, Ghana, 1945–6', *Journal of African History*, 41(2), 197–219.

Gray, Brian (1953), *Basuto Soldiers in Hitler's War*, Maseru: Basutoland Government.

Griffith, Charles (1878), 'Some observations on witchcraft in Basutoland', *The Transactions of the South African Philosophical Society*, 1(2), 87–92.

Grotpeter, John P. (1975), *Historical Dictionary of Swaziland*, Metuchen, New Jersey: The Scarecrow Press.

Gulbrandsen, Ø. (2002), 'The discourse of "ritual murder": popular reaction to political leaders in Botswana', in B. Kapferer (ed.), *Beyond Rationalism: Rethinking Magic, Witchcraft and Sorcery*, New York: Berghahn Books.

Gunther, John (1954), 'Murder most foul in Basutoland', *Reader's Digest*, March, 6–8.

Gunther, John [1955] (1957), *Inside Africa*, London: Reprint Society.

Hailey, Lord William (1953), *Native Administration in the British African Territories. Part V. The High Commission Territories: Basutoland, the Bechuanaland Protectorate and Swaziland*, London: HMSO.

Hailey, Lord William (1963), *The Republic of South Africa and the High Commission Territories*, London: Oxford University Press.

Haliburton, Gordon (1977), *Historical Dictionary of Lesotho*, Metuchen, New Jersey: The Scarecrow Press.

Hamnett, Ian (1975), *Chieftainship and Legitimacy. An Anthropological Study of Executive Law in Lesotho*, London and Boston: Routledge and Kegan Paul.

Hardegger, Bertha (1985), *Bertha Hardegger, M.D.: Mother of the Basotho*, trans. and ed, Felix Baerlocher, Saxville, New Brunswick: Felix Baerlocher.

Hardegger, Bertha (1987), *Bertha Hardegger, Mutter der Basuto*, ed. Josef P. Specker, Walter-Verlag Olten und Freiburg im Breisgau.

Harragin, Sir Walter (1953), 'The High Commission Territories', *Foundation*, April, 4–9.

Headlam, Cecil (1931), *The Milner Papers: South Africa. 1897–1899*, vol. 1, London: Cassell.

Hlapisi, Aaron (1986), *Khooanyana oa ho hopoloa*, Morija, Sesuto Book Depot.

Hodgson, Margaret, and W. G. Ballinger (1931), *Indirect Rule in Southern Africa: Basutoland*, Lovedale: Lovedale Press.

Jingoes, Stimela Jason (1975), *A Chief is a Chief by the People: The Autobiography of Stimela Jason Jingoes*, ed. John and Cassandra Perry, London: Oxford University Press.

Jones, G. I. (1951), *Basutoland Medicine Murder: A Report on the Recent Outbreak of 'Diretlo' Murders in Basutoland*, London: HMSO, Cmd. 8209.

Jones, G. I. (1966), 'Chiefly succession in Basutoland', in J. Goody (ed.), *Succession to High Office*, London: Cambridge University Press, pp. 57–81.

Khaketla, B. M. (1971), *Lesotho 1970: An African Coup under the Microscope*, London: C. Hurst.

Khaketla, B. M. [1960] (1972), *Mosali a Nkhola*, Morija: Sesuto Book Depot.

Kimble, Judith M. (1999), *Migrant Labour and Colonial Rule in Basutoland, 1890–1930*, Grahamstown: Institute of Social and Economic Research, Rhodes University.

Kneen, J. G., and H. C. Juta (1950), *Revised Edition of the Laws of Basutoland in force on the 1st Day of January, 1948*, 3 vols, Maseru: Basutoland Government.

Kruger, Etienne (1951), 'Les "Meutres Rituels" au Basutoland', *Le Monde nonChrétien*, 18, Avril–Juin, 237–43.

Kuper, Hilda (1978), *Sobhuza II: Ngwenyama and King of Swaziland. The Story of an Hereditary Ruler and his Country*, New York: Africana Publishing Company.

Kuper, Hilda [1963] (1986), *The Swazi: A South African Kingdom*, New York: Holt, Rinehart and Winston.

Lagden, Sir Godfrey (1901), 'Basutoland and the Basutos', *Royal Colonial Institute: Report of Proceedings*, 32, 254–84.

Lagden, Sir Godfrey (1909), *The Basutos: The Mountaineers and their Country*, 2 vols, London: Hutchinson.

Lanham, Peter, and A. S. Mopeli-Paulus (1953), *Blanket Boy's Moon*, London: Collins.

Lansdown, Alfred V. (1960), *Outlines of South African Criminal Law and Procedure* (2nd edn), Cape Town: Wynberg, and Johannesburg: Juta.

Laydevant, François (1937), 'La sorcellerie en Basutoland', *Etudes Missionaires* (Paris), 7, 209–17.

Laydevant, François (1939), 'Initiation du Médecin-Sorcier en Basutoland', *Annali Lateranensi*, 3, 99–139.

Laydevant, François (1950), 'Remèdes magiques ou meutres rituels', *Bulletin des Missions* (Belgium), 24(2), 134–41.

Laydevant, François (1951), 'Les rites de l'initiation au Basutoland', *Anthropos: International Review of Ethnology and Linguistics*, 46, 221–55.

Le Roux, D. H. J. (1989), *Report of the Commission of Inquiry into the causes of the unrest and ritual murders in Venda during 1988*. The report carries an ISBN (0–86959–253–X), but was not formally published.

Lebollo ['Circumcision'] (1963?), Mazenod.

Leenhardt, Roland (1948), 'Meutres rituels', *JME*, 127.

Lye, William F. (ed.) (1975), *Andrew Smith's Journal of his expedition into the interior of South Africa, 1834–36*, Cape Town: Balkema.

Maake, Nhlanhla (1998), '"Murder they cried": revisiting *diretlo* – medicine murders in literature', *South African Journal of African Languages*, 18(4), November, 91–101.

Mabille, Adolphe, and Hermann Dieterlen (1904), *Sesuto-English Dictionary*, Morija: Sesuto Book Depot.

Mabille, G. (1955), 'Crimes rituels ou médicinaux au Basutoland', *Le Monde nonChrétien*, 34, April–June, 127–53.

Machobane, L. B. B. J. (1986), 'The political dilemma of chieftaincy in colonial Lesotho with reference to the Administration and Courts Reforms of 1938', ISAS Occasional Paper no. 1, National University of Lesotho.

Machobane, L. B. B. J. (1990), *Government and Change in Lesotho, 1800–1966*, Basingstoke and London: Macmillan.

Mangoaela, Z. D. (1957), *Lithoko tsa Marena a Basotho* (Morija, 6th edn).

Maqutu, W. C. M. (1995), *The Lesotho Law Reports. Decisions of the Court of Appeal and the High Court of Maseru 1982–1984*, Maseru: High Court.

Marena a Lesotho 1984 (Mazenod: Mazenod Book Centre).

Martin, Minnie (1903), *Basutoland: Its Legends and Customs*, London: Nichols.

Marwick, Brian Allan (1940), *The Swazi: An Ethnographic Account of the Natives of the Swaziland Protectorate*, Cambridge: Cambridge University Press.

Matlosa, S. [1950] (1994), *Katiba*, Mazenod: The Catholic Centre.

Matšaba, J. K. (1953), 'Power-Possessions. Happiness', *Basutoland Witness*, 2(3), April–June, 26–7.

McKay, James (1871), *Reminiscences of the Last Kafir War, Illustrated with Numerous Anecdotes*, Grahamstown: Richards, Glanville.

Minnaar, A. de V., D. Offringa and C. Payze (1992), *To live in fear. Witchburning and Medicine Murder in Venda*, Pretoria: Human Sciences Research Council.

Minnaar, Anthony (1997), 'Witchpurging in the Northern Province of South Africa: a victim profile and an assessment of initiatives to deal with witchcraft', paper presented to the 9th International World Symposium on Victimology, Amsterdam, August.

Mofokeng, Jeremiah H. (n.d.), *Seqhebolla*, Johannesburg: n.p.

Mofolo, Thomas [1925] (1949), *Chaka the Zulu*, London: Oxford University Press for the International African Institute. Original (1925) edition published in Sesotho as *Chaka*, Morija: Sesuto Book Depot.

Mokhehle, Ntsu [1976] (1990), *Moshoeshoe I: Profile: Se-Moshoeshoe*, Maseru: Mmoho Publications.

Mokhomo, Makhokolotso A. (1954), *Sebabatso* ['A wonderful thing'], Johannesburg: Afrikaanse Pers and the Booksellers.

Mokitimi, 'Makali Isabella (1997), *Proverbs of the Basotho*, Ibadan, Nigeria: Daystar Press and Sefer Books.

Moleleki, Monyane (1994), *Pale ea Bophelo ba Ntsu*, Morija: Monyane Moleleki.

Monks, Noel (1955), *Eyewitness*, London: Frederick Muller.

Monsarrat, Nicholas (1956), *The Tribe that Lost its Head*, London: Cassell.

Mopeli-Paulus, A. S. (1950), *Liretlo*, Bloemfontein: Via Afrika-Boekwinkel.

Mopeli-Paulus, A. S., and Miriam Basner (1956), *Turn to the Dark*, London: Jonathan Cape.

Motlamelle, M. P. [1937] (1950), *Ngaka ea Mosotho*, Morija: Morija Sesuto Book Depot.

Mphatšoe, Ed (1952), 'Ritual murders in Basutoland', *Basutoland Witness*, 6(4), October–December, 82–5.

Msebenzi (1938), *History of Matiwane and the Amangwane Tribe as told by Msebenzi to his Kinsman Albert Hlongwane*, ed. N. J. van Warmelo, Pretoria: Department of Native Affairs, Union of South Africa.

Murray, A. A. (1957), *The Blanket*, London: Deutsch.

Murray, Colin (1981), *Families Divided: The Impact of Migrant Labour in Lesotho*, Cambridge: Cambridge University Press, and Johannesburg: Ravan Press.

Murray, Colin (1999), 'The Father, the Son and the Holy Spirit: resistance and abuse in the life of Solomon Lion (1908–1987)', *Journal of Religion in Africa*, 29(3), 341–86.

Murray, Colin, and Peter Sanders (2000), 'Medicine murder in Basutoland: colonial rule and moral crisis', *Africa*, 70(1), 49–78.

Ngubane, Harriet (1986), 'The predicament of the sinister healer', in Murray Last and G. L. Chavunduka (eds), *The Professionalisation of African Medicine*, Manchester: Manchester University Press for the International African Institute.

Niehaus, Isak, with Eliazaar Mohlala and Kally Shokane (2001), *Witchcraft, Power and Politics: Exploring the Occult in the South African Lowveld*, London: Pluto Press, and Cape Town: David Philip.

Ntsane, Kemuel Edward (1963), *Nna Sajene Kokobela, CID* ['I, Sergeant Kokobela, CID'], Pretoria: Afrikaanse Pers-Boekhandel.

Orpen, J. M. (1857), *History of the Basutus of South Africa*, Cape Town: Saul Solomon.

Packer, Joy (1953), *Apes and Ivory*, London: Eyre & Spottiswoode.

Perham, Margery (1935), 'The Basuto and their country', *The Geographical Magazine*, 1(2) June, 117–25.

Perham, Margery (1974), *African Apprenticeship: An Autobiographical Journey in Southern Africa, 1929*, London: Faber & Faber.

Perham, Margery, and Lionel Curtis (1935), *The Protectorates of South Africa: The Question of their Transfer to the Union*, London: Oxford University Press.

Pim, A. W. (1935), *Financial and Economic Position of Basutoland. Report of the Commission appointed by the Secretary of State for Dominion Affairs*, London: HMSO.

Pitso of Basuto Nation at Maseru, May 23 1919. Speech of His Excellency the High Commissioner Viscount Buxton (1919), Morija: Sesuto Book Depot.

Poulter, Jane Anne Marie (n.d.), *The Lesotho Law Reports. 1971–73*, Maseru: High Court.

Poulter, Jane Anne Marie (1980), *The Lesotho Law Reports. 1974–75*, Maseru: High Court.

Pratten, David T. (forthcoming a), 'The district clerk and the "Man-Leopard Murders": mediating law and authority in colonial Nigeria', in B. N. Lawrance, E. L. Osborn and R. L. Roberts (eds), *Intermediaries, Interpreters and Clerks: African Employees and the Making of Colonial Africa*, Madison: University of Wisconsin Press.

Pratten, David T. (forthcoming b), *The Man-Leopard Murder Mysteries: History and Society in Colonial Nigeria.*

Pula, Augustinus Lekhotla (1988), *Maemo a litaba tšabo ea balimo le boloi har'a Basotho 'a shejoa ke Mosotho oa Mokriste'* ['The situation regarding fear of the ancestors and of witchcraft among the Basotho "as it appears to a Mosotho Christian"'], Mazenod Printing Works.

Ralushai , N. V., M. G. Masingi, D. M. M. Madiba, J. A. van den Heever, T. J. Mathiba, M. E. Mphapuli, M. W. Mokwena, P. N. Vele Ndou, D. Matabane (1996), *Report of the Commission of Inquiry into Witchcraft Violence and Ritual Murders in the Northern Province of the Republic of South Africa* (the Ralushai Commission report), mimeo, n.p.

Ramseyer, Paul (1914), 'Le Solaboea', *JME*, 130–4.

Ramseyer, Paul (1928), 'La Circoncision chez les Bassoutos', *Revue d'Ethnologie et des Traditions Populaires*, 9, 40–70.

Rathbone, Richard (1993), *Murder and Politics in Colonial Ghana*, New Haven, CT, and London: Yale University Press.

Redcliffe-Maud, Jean (1989), *From the Cape to Cairo 1932*, Poulton: Englang Publishing.

Redcliffe-Maud, Jean (1990), *High Commission to Embassy: South Africa 1959–1963*, Poulton: Englang Publishing.

Reed, Douglas (1950), *Somewhere South of Suez*, London: Jonathan Cape.

Roche, Aimé (1949), 'Vaines Immolations!', *Voix du Basutoland*, Avril–Juin, 11(41) 5–8, 32.

Rooney, David (1982), *Sir Charles Arden-Clarke*, London: Rex Collings.

Sachot, Joseph, OMI (1946), *Chez les Apollons de Bronze*, n.p.: Editions Spes.

SAIRR, *Race Relations Survey 1988/89* (1989); *1989/90* (1990), Johannesburg: South African Institute of Race Relations.

Sanders, Peter (1975), *Moshoeshoe, Chief of the Sotho*, London: Heinemann.

Sanders, Peter (2000), *The Last of the Queen's Men: A Lesotho Experience*, Johannesburg: Witwatersrand University Press, and Morija: Morija Museum and Archives.

Scobie, Alastair (1965), *Murder for Magic: Witchcraft in Africa*, London: Cassell.

Scott, Michael (1958), *A Time to Speak*, London: Faber.

Sekoai, S. Nkoto (1961), *Ntho di Bonwa ho Tsamailwe*, Morija, 1955; first edition in South African orthography, Morija, 1961.

Sheddick, V. G. J. (1953), *The Southern Sotho*, London: International African Institute.

Smith, Edwin W. (1926), *The Golden Stool*, London: Holborn Publishing House.

Smith, Mervyn Bosworth (n.d.), *Basutoland from Within. Some Views by Mervyn Bosworth Smith ('Basutolander') 1935 and 1937*, printed at Wepener.

Snyman, C. R. (1967), *The High Commission Territories Law Reports 1963–66*, Maseru: High Court.

Spence, J. E. (1968), *Lesotho: The Politics of Dependence*, London: Oxford University Press.

Stevens, Richard P. (1967), *Lesotho, Botswana, and Swaziland: The Former High Commission Territories in Southern Africa*, London: Pall Mall Press.

Swanson, Donald (1965), *Assignment Africa*, Cape Town: Simondium Publishers.

Theal, G. M. (ed.) (1883), *Basutoland Records*, 3 vols, Cape Town: W. A. Richards.

Theal, G. M. (1886), *A Fragment of Basuto History: 1854 to 1871*, Cape Town: Saul Solomon.

Thompson, Kenneth (1998), *Moral Panics*, London and New York: Routledge.

Thorpe, Cyprian (1950), *The Great Queen's Blanket*, London: SPG.

Tlale, N. M. (1949), 'Ritual murders in Basutoland. Superstitious beliefs responsible for recent crime wave', *African World*, February, 11–12.

Tracey, Hugh (1940), 'Basutoland and its new Paramount Chief', *Journal of the Royal African Society*, 39, 306–15.

Tylden, G. (1950), *The Rise of the Basuto*, Cape Town: Juta.

Van Fossen, A. B. (1985), 'Ritual murder, polity and identity in Swaziland', paper presented to 80th Congress of the International Association for the History of Religions, Sydney.

Van Straaten, M. C. (1948a), '"Muti" made from human flesh', *The Nongqai*, 39, February, 146–9.

Van Straaten, M. C. (1948b), 'Shades of Moshesh', *The Nongqai*, 39, September, 1160–3.

Van Straaten, M. C. (1949), 'Basutoland ritual murders', *The Nongqai*, 40, September, 1122–6.

Van Warmelo, N. J. (ed.) (1977), *Anthropology of Southern Africa in Periodicals to 1950*, Johannesburg: Witwatersrand University Press.

Villaret, François (1953), 'Au Basutoland sauvage', *Revue: Litterature, Histoire, Arts et Sciences des Deux Mondes*, 15 November, 335–46.

Weisfelder, Richard F. (1969), 'Early voices of protest in Basutoland: the Progressive Association and Lekhotla la Bafo', *African Studies Review*, 17(2), 397–409.

Weisfelder, Richard F. (1999), *Political Contention in Lesotho 1952–1965*, Roma, Lesotho: Institute of Southern African Studies.

Wepener, F. D. J. (1934), *Louw Wepener: Die Oorloë van die Oranje Vrystaat met Basoetoeland*, Pretoria: De Bussy.

Widdicombe, Canon J. (1895), *In the Lesuto: A Sketch of African Mission Life*, London: SPCK.

Willan, Sir Harold (1955a), *The High Commission Territories Law Reports 1926–1953*, Maseru: High Court.

Willan, Sir Harold (1955b), *The High Commission Territories Law Reports 1954*, Maseru: High Court.

Willan, Sir Harold (1956), *The High Commission Territories Law Reports 1955*, Maseru: High Court.

Willet, Shelagh M., and David P. Ambrose (1980), *Lesotho: A Comprehensive Bibliography*, Clio Press, Oxford and Santa Barbara.

Woon, H. V. ('A Colonial Officer') (1909), *Twenty-five Years Soldiering in South Africa: A Personal Narrative*, London: Andrew Melrose.

E UNPUBLISHED THESES

Bosko, Dan (1983), 'Social organisational aspects of religious change among Basotho', DPhil. thesis, New York University.

Driver, Thackwray (1998), 'The theory and politics of mountain rangeland conservation and pastoral development in Lesotho', PhD thesis, University of London.

Stallmach, Ingrid (1988), 'Der gerichts ärztliche Dienst im Entwicklungsland Lesotho' ['The forensic medical service in the developing country of Lesotho'], thesis for the degree of Doctor of Medicine, Johannes Gutenberg Universität Mainz.

Weisfelder, R. F. (1974), 'Defining national purpose: the roots of factionalism in Lesotho', PhD thesis, Harvard University.

F INTERVIEWS AND PERSONAL COMMUNICATIONS

Key: KS: Khalaki Sello. CM: Colin Murray. MM: Monaheng Maichu. PS: Peter Sanders.

Ambrose, David P. PS interviews, Roma, Maseru District, 7–19 December 1996, and 5 and 19 October 1997.

Ashton, Hugh. CM interview, Johannesburg, 19 March 1996; and letter to CM, 9 August 1996.

Bakane, Basia. CM interview, Pitsi's Nek, Leribe District, 19 January 1998.

Bakane, Lekhaole. CM interview, Pitsi's Nek, Leribe District, 19 January 1998.

Bakane, 'Mapuleng. CM interview, Pitsi's Nek, Leribe District, 19 January 1998.

Basner, Miriam. Letter to CM, 6 October 1995.

Bereng, Patrick Mohlalefi. PS interviews, Morija, Maseru District, 15 October 1997, and 2 and 3 June 1999.

Blampied, Gordon. Letter to PS, 23 September 1998.

Brutsch, Albert. PS interviews, Morija, Maseru District, 9 December 1996, and 7 October 1997; and communication to PS, 18 December 1996.

Clarke, Anna. CM interview, Ladybrand (Free State), 28 November 1998.

Cordery, Ray. PS interview, Studland (England), 23 January 1998.

Gill, Stephen. PS interviews, Morija, Maseru District, 7 October 1997, and 29 May 1999.

Hatahata, Sethabathaba. MM and PS interview, Ha Majoro, Maseru District, 3 June 1999.

Hector, Gordon. PS telephone conversations, 25 November 1996, and August 1997.

Hennessy, Sir James. PS interview, Cambridge (England), 16 October 1995.

Jenkins, Arthur. Personal communication to PS, October 1998.

Jones, Ursula. CM interview, Cambridge (England), 24 September 1996.

Kao, Molosi (Mlozi). KS and PS interview, Senqu river valley, Mokhotlong District, 27 May 1999.

Khaketla, Bennett. PS interview, Maseru, 10 December 1996.

Kitson, Paul. CM interview, Somerset West (Western Cape), 14 July 1996; and PS telephone interviews, 5 and 21 October 1997.

Klaas, Seane. KS and PS interviews, Senqu river valley, Mokhotlong District, 26 and 27 May 1999.

Kolisang, Godfrey M. PS interviews, Roma, Maseru District, 8 December 1996, and 3 October 1997.

Leanya, Thabo. KS and CM interview, Morija, Maseru District, 16 May 1999.

Letsoela, Exinia. MM and PS interview, Ha Mofoka, Maseru District, 2 June 1999.

Liebetrau, Lourens. CM interview, Maseru, 27 November 1998.

Maama, Chief Joseph Molapo. PS interview, Mokema, Maseru District, 1 June 1999.

'Mabathoana, 'Mabatho. David Ambrose and PS interview, Mokhokhong, Maseru District, 30 May 1999.

Mahao, Mokhoele. MM and PS interview, Mokema, Maseru District, 1 June 1999.

Makotoko, Chief Matita. MM and PS interview, Ha Mosalla, Maseru District, 3 June 1999.

Malahleha, Gwen. PS interview, Roma, Maseru District, 9 October 1997.

Maqutu, W. C. M. PS interview, Maseru, 15 October 1997.

Masupha, Chief Lebihan. KS and CM interview, Ha Bose, Berea District, 19 and 21 May 1999.

Masupha, Chieftainess 'Mamathe. Patrick Mohlalefi Bereng and PS interview, 'Mamathe's, Berea District, 3 June 1999.

Matete, 'Mampoi. KS and CM interview, Morija, Maseru District, 15 January 2000.

Matete, Chief Ranthomeng. PS interview, Morija, Maseru District, 5 June 1999.

'Matli, 'Maiphepi. KS and CM interview, Maseru, 15 January 2000.

Mofoka, 'Masempe. MM and PS interview, Ha Mofoka, Maseru District, 2 June 1999.

Mofolo, 'Mangoajane. Ford Rafutho and PS interview, Ha Mosalla, Maseru District, 23 May 1999.

Molefe, Nkherepe. KS and CM interview, Maseru, 29 November 1998; KS and PS interviews, Hlotse, Leribe District, 24 and 28 May 1999.

Morojele, Elliot Teboho. PS interviews, Mokhotlong, 27 and 28 May 1999.

Motsetsela, Motsetsela. KS and CM interview, Morija, Maseru District, 17 May 1999.

Ntai, Ntsane. KS and CM interview, 'Mamathe's, Berea District, 19 May 1999.

Nyooko, 'Mamoliehi. MM and PS interview, Mokema, Maseru District, 1 June 1999.

Peete, Mohale. KS and CM interview, Koma-Koma, Berea District, 3 December 1998.

Perry, John. Letter to CM, 19 May 1998.

Phakisi, Stephen. KS and PS interview, Mokhotlong, 25 May 1999.

Polaki, 'Mapolaki. MM and PS interview, Mokema, Maseru District, 1 June 1999.

Pott, Gideon. Letter to CM, 9 August 1983; and CM interview, Moffat (Scotland), 7 August 1998.

Rabolai, Motleri Clement. KS and PS interview, Senqu river valley, Mokhotlong District, 27 May 1999.

Rachane, 'Mamokhatsi. KS and CM interview, Tsokung, Berea District, 3 December 1998.

Rafutho, Ford, and Rafutho, Seabatha. PS interview, Thaba-Bosiu, Maseru District, 23 May 1998.

Rakokoli, 'Maluke. KS and CM interview, Ha Molapo (near 'Mamathe's), Berea District, 20 May 1999.

Rust, E. A. (Thabo). Letters to CM, 13 October 1971, and 24 April 1996; and CM interview, Johannesburg, 8 May 1999.

Sebajoa, Nyalase Ntja. KS and CM interview, Koma-Koma, Berea District, 3 December 1998.

Sebajoa, Nkapo. KS and CM interview, Koma-Koma, Berea District, 3 December 1998.

Shortt-Smith, Liz. CM interview, near George (Western Cape), 27 January 2000.

Sofonia, Tsekelo. CM interview, Ha Sofonia, Maseru District, 23 November 2001.

Taylor, Desmond. PS interview, Petersfield (England), 27 September 1995.

Thorpe, Cyprian. Letter to PS, 13 November 1997; and PS telephone interview, 29 November 1997.

Thoso, Tšepiso Jameson. KS and CM interview, Morija, Maseru District, 16 May 1999.

Tšita, Edwin Nohe. KS and PS interviews, Teyateyaneng, Berea District, 28 May 1999; and Maseru, 4 June 1999.

Tšitang, 'Mathuso. KS and PS interview, Moremoholo valley, Mokhotlong District, 27 May 1999.

INDEX

In the mid-nineteenth century the Basotho did not use surnames. Moshoeshoe, for example, was known simply as Moshoeshoe and his son Letsie as Letsie. Later, the father's name was sometimes used as a second name, which meant that the second name changed from one generation to the next. So Maama might be known as Maama Letsie, and his sons were known as Seeiso Maama and Molapo Maama. In some families, especially those most influenced by the missions, one of these names became established as the 'surname'. Among such families in particular the use of English Christian names was common, often alongside a Sesotho name. Women were known by the name they were given at birth or the name they assumed when they gave birth to a child. Later they were given their husband's name as a surname. In this index we classify Basotho by their first names except where, as for example in the case of the very large extended Lerotholi family, the habitual use of a common 'surname' has been clearly established. Complete consistency on the question of surnames is impossible. The practice we have adopted here, inevitably arbitrary to some degree, reflects our understanding of common usage in the mid-twentieth century and our judgement of what is appropriate for this book.

References to names and subjects in the Appendix, shown here in italics, have been included only where there are references to these names and subjects in the main text. Examples are 'accomplice evidence, law on', and 'Absalom Letsie'. References to subjects which appear throughout the Appendix have not been individually included in the index. An example is 'alibis'.

Where there is a photograph of the subject, a reference is given in bold to a number in the series of photographs that appears between pages 208 and 209, as for example in 'Makhaola, David Theko, **ph7**, **ph9**'.

Names beginning 'Ma… are listed alphabetically under double M.